GREAT FRONT PAGES

D-DAY TO VICTORY

1944-1945

INTRODUCED BY
Wynford Vaughan-Thomas

Newspapers reproduced from the John Frost Historic Newspaper Service

COLLINS
8, GRAFTON STREET,
LONDON, W1
1984

Great front pages.
1. World War, 1939-1945
940.53 D743
ISBN 0 00 217343 3

Produced by Nutshell Ltd
for William Collins Sons and Co Ltd
London • Glasgow • Sydney • Auckland
Toronto • Johannesburg

Printed in Great Britain
by William Collins, Sons & Co Ltd
Compiled and designed by Stanley Glazer
Typesetting by H&J Graphics

INTRODUCTION

Wynford Vaughan-Thomas

HISTORY IN HEADLINES! Surely the most exciting way to relive the most momentous year in the story of modern Britain — from D-Day in June, 1944 to VE-Day in May, 1945. How vividly it all comes back as you turn over these historic front pages. It was through them that the average man and woman learned all about the shocks, disasters and triumphs of the world at war. Consciously or unconsciously, the newspapers became one of the main buttresses of national morale. As you look at these pages — from both British and American papers — you realise that the editors were in the war too. In Britain newsprint was severely restricted, for it was brought to the beleaguered island through the constant threat of U-boat action, and the crowded front pages reflect the need for maximum information in minimum space. The Americans were luckier, as their front page style shows. News was censored —you cannot fight a successful war if you publish your plans in advance — but still the public bought newspapers avidly. They mirror the spirit with which the country 'saw it through'. As well as the traditional press, service papers were printed to boost morale. Often produced in the actual theatres of war, these brought the news back from the front line. Three examples appear here, although there were many, many more.

In those first summer days of June, 1944, southern Britain was an extraordinary place. Nothing like it had been seen before, nor has been seen since. In London the people in the street would look hurriedly up to the sky. The drone of a 'buzz-bomb' would suddenly stop. Then came the few seconds of sinister silence, followed by the dull thud of the explosion. The city paused — and then went bravely back to business. The British had become hardened by four years of war.

Yet, now, there was a new excitement in the air. You could not disguise the huge columns of lorries, tanks and guns moving down towards south coast ports. These too were busy, crowded with an astonishing variety of shipping, including landing-craft with bows that could open up like the jaws of a giant whale and vomit out strange weapons of war — tanks that could swim and tanks with whirling flails that would thrash their way through minefields. Day and night the skies throbbed with the huge air fleets setting out to drop their bombloads on the bridges, rail junctions and war factories of Hitler's 'Fortress Europe'. The country pubs were empty of their usual boisterous service customers. The locals sipped their watery wartime beer under the warning notices 'Careless Talk Costs Lives' and 'Walls Have Ears' and gave their considered opinion: 'Well, it won't be long now'. *It* was D-Day!

There was no secret about it. From the moment the British army had been pushed off the soil of Europe at Dunkirk in the dark days of 1940, it was clear that one day it would have to return if the war was ever to be won. But over this major operation hung three stark, simple questions — when, how and where. The first question almost answered itself. Nothing could be done until Britain had acquired an ally with enough strength and will to join her in the hazardous business of landing an army on a heavily defended coast. The Russians, as a great land power, never understood the sea problem. Stalin clamoured for action as soon as Hitler turned on him. The walls of Britain were covered with demands for the 'Second Front Now'. To Stalin, it was simply a matter of flinging as many men ashore as soon as possible. Russia had enormous reserves of man power. So what did one repulse matter? After the briefing for the Anzio landing in Italy in January, 1944, the army spokesman explained that the first assault wave would consist of two divisions. 'Ah, I see,' said the Tass news agency man, 'an affair of outposts.'

The Americans were also for an assault across the Channel as soon as possible. General Marshall had even proposed that it should be launched in the spring of 1943. The Russians may have been prodigal with manpower, but the Americans were equally prodigal with material. They were the biggest industrial nation in the world. With their overwhelming strength in arms, they could surely smash their way through Hitler's Atlantic Wall. When one American general was asked how he was going to solve the problems of landing, he replied, 'Sir, in the American army we don't solve our problems, we overwhelm them.'

On their side, the British were only too aware of the difficulties. Bitter experience — from Gallipoli in the First World War to Dieppe in the Second — had taught them the dangers of landing without overwhelming strength at the decisive point, and of not driving boldly ahead once you had landed. When the Anzio landing simply fortified itself around the beaches to await a German counter-attack, Churchill sent off one of

The British had become hardened by four years of war. Yet, now, there was a new excitement in the air.

his celebrated reprimands. 'I thought I was flinging a wild-cat ashore, and all I have got is a stranded whale!' This time, the planners were determined to give him a wild-cat. The planning for the Normandy landing — code name Overlord — was a marvel of ingenuity and daring. The planners seemed to have thought of everything. A port might not be secured quickly enough after landing. Very well — the armies would take their port with them. So the Mulberry harbours were constructed out of huge concrete caissons that could be sunk offshore. Oil would be a problem. The Overlord planners solved this by supplying a pipeline (Pluto) that simply ran under the sea.

All through the winter of 1943 and the spring of 1944 the work went busily on. More and more American troops were ferried across the Atlantic to that overcrowded aircraft-carrier permanently anchored off the shores of Europe which still called itself Great Britain. There were enormous problems to be overcome in training for the assault and in maintaining morale. It wasn't easy for the American troops in a strange land, and their hosts had problems, too. Wry little jokes circulated about the Americans being 'over sexed, over paid and over here'.

The marvel remains, that in spite of all difficulties, the British and Americans worked together as a brilliantly succesful team. The troops of both armies were being led by men of established reputations and strong views. At the head of the British 21st Army Group was General Bernard Montgomery, now at the height of his fame and 'Monty' to all his men. His brisk figure, complete with black beret covered with regimental badges, had impressed itself on the imagination of the British public and seemed to them almost a guarantee of victory. He would be in command of the actual assault and, for that operation, he would also have temporary control of the US First Army of Lieutenant-General Omar Bradley. An American unit under British control! It would have been a situation fraught with possible trouble but for the fact that in overall charge was General Dwight D Eisenhower. 'Ike' made no claims to be a great general in the field. His strengths lay elsewhere. He was the man of tact, the coordinator. If he was not a great tactician, he was certainly a great emollient. He could soothe and charm men who had stubbornly-held views. He made the whole machine work. And, after all, it would be Eisenhower who would have to take the great decisions. He would have to give the vital order, 'Go'.

The questions of 'when' and 'how' had been settled. There remained the question of 'where'. It is intriguing, now that so many years have passed and we can read all the memoirs, to look back across the Channel from the German side on those first, fateful days of June, 1944. Of course, it was obvious to the Germans that an invasion was bound to be launched once reasonably calm weather could be expected in the Channel in early summer. Hitler even welcomed it. He was confident that the Allies would not solve their invasion problems. 'The assault,' he proclaimed, 'will be broken on the Atlantic Wall.' Once the attack from the west had been broken, he would be free to bring his troops back to the east and deal finally with the Russians. The unhappy Allies would be penned back in their island base of Britain, under constant attack by his new and formidable weapons of flying bombs and V-2s while the new electro-U-boat starved them out. They would be glad to agree to a negotiated peace. So Hitler reasoned, isolated in his war HQ far away on the eastern front and with no-one around him who dared to question his judgement or puncture his illusions.

His commander in the west was von Rundstedt, a professional soldier of the old school who had won enormous prestige in the early years of the war in the Polish and Russian campaigns. He had wanted to retire but Hitler needed him as an imposing figurehead in the west. Von Rundstedt was now 69 and needed the comfort and soporific of alcohol before he could sleep at night. Hitler imported the dynamic Rommel over his head. Von Rundstedt lamented, 'As C-in-C West my sole prerogative was to change the guard in front of my gate.' He was also orthodox in his ideas as to how the invasion should be countered. He wanted to hold back his armour until he was certain exactly where the Allied drive was going. Rommel would have none of this. He declared: 'The enemy must be met with all strength on the beaches themselves... The high-water line must be the main fighting line.'

But where exactly would that fighting line be? Rommel thought that it would be westwards from Pas de Calais to the Seine, with Le Havre as the port to be seized. The Allies had chosen Normandy with Cherbourg as the port.

The marvel remains, that in spite of all difficulties, the British and Americans worked together as a brilliantly successful team.

So the two sides stood poised, separated by the waters of the Channel; the British and American troops tense and trained to the limit, the Germans divided in their strategy but confident in the strength of the Atlantic Wall. The time had come, as Churchill said, 'to put these great matters to the test.'

The exact moment of invasion depended on the state of the tides and a late-rising full moon and the weather. The troops were packed into their ships, the aircraft were ready for take-off, the parachute troops were making a last check on their equipment, the fleet was moving to position. There was not much margin of time to play with. Soldiers get seasick if they are kept too long rocking at anchor. In the first days of June, Eisenhower was with his top commanders at Southwick House outside Portsmouth, anxiously awaiting the forecast of his Met expert, Dr Stagg. Stagg could not be confident. As Admiral Creasey remarked, 'Six foot two of Stagg and six foot one of gloom.' Tension increased — how could this vast invasion machine be kept idling without disaster? The Channel was still stormy and so were tempers at Southwick House. Stagg, at last, gave some faint hope. There would be an unexpected break in the weather, which might last for a short time before more gales arrived. Was this tiny gap enough, when the fate of this great enterprise was at risk? Around the conference table at HQ, everyone looked towards Eisenhower. This would be the C-in-C's decision and his alone. For this, a man is made Supreme Commander. Eisenhower paused for a moment and then said crisply, 'OK. We'll go.'

June 6, 1944. D-Day. The Longest Day in the memory of every one of the half-a-million men who took part in it on the Allied side. Every minute of it would remain etched in the minds of the D-Day veterans, but the day was longer than most of them imagined, for it had begun long before dawn. Around 3am a strange, ghost army floated down from the skies on the still sleeping countryside. At each end of a 35 mile section of the heavily defended Normandy coast, paratroopers and gliders were dropping miles behind Hitler's impregnable Atlantic Wall. There were losses. Parachutists fell into the sea and gliders crashed. But the British, on the right, rallied and did the daring task they had risked so much to achieve. They seized and blew up the bridges along the river Orne. Away to the west, the Americans also dropped down from the sky. They were not so lucky. The drop went astray and the men were scattered over the countryside — 'like pepper from a pot', as one parachutist described it. Yet the scattered bands also rallied. They, too, did the job demanded in Monty's plan. They held the western boundary of the landing area. The prelude was over. The dawn curtain could now rise on the main drama. And drama it certainly turned out to be — desperate, bloody, with success hanging in the balance, a nightmare of bombs, burning vehicles, bursting shells and nerve-shattering noise until the tired, battle-weary survivors looked around them as darkness fell and realised, with a feeling of triumph, that they had done the impossible. They had broken through the Atlantic Wall.

They had done it through their guts and skill, but also through the brilliance of the planning that lay behind the greatest amphibious operation ever mounted in the whole history of warfare. Monty had carefully studied the accounts of the disastrous raid on Dieppe. It had failed, he argued, because the infantry had no armour to protect them. He decided that he would not fling his men against a strongly entrenched enemy unless he had tanks out in front in the first wave. But how were the tanks to land through the minefields, the soft sands and all those underwater obstacles known to the troops as 'Rommel's asparagus'? The problem was solved by the ingenuity of the remarkable General Sir Percy Hobart, who created the 7th Armoured Division of specialised tanks — 'Crabs' that could flail down minefields, tanks that could lay down a track over soft sand and, above all, tanks that could swim ashore under their own power. They were the aces up the sleeves of the invaders. On Omaha Beach, where the specialised tanks were not used and the DD (duplex drive) tanks were launched too far off the shore, the landing nearly failed. The infantry, without armour, were pinned for hours on a beach which became a bloody chaos. Only the dauntless courage of the individual GIs got the Americans their toe-hold as darkness fell.

Ike and Monty could now breathe a sigh of relief. They had got their men in strength onto the continent of Europe. It was safe to announce the news to the world. As the public rushed to snatch the papers from the news-vendors, the whole free world felt a lift of the heart.

Eisenhower - the Supreme Commander - paused for a moment and then said crisply, 'OK. We'll go.'

Only the day before, the headlines had announced the capture of Rome, the first European capital to be liberated. Paris would be next on the list — then Brussels, the Hague and on towards Berlin and the long-awaited end!

Not yet! There would be hard days ahead in which the beachhead had to be enlarged and made safe against the German counter-attack. The Germans had been surprised. Using their overwhelming air superiority, the Allies had been able to isolate the landing zones and confuse the German radar. Intelligence in the enemy High Command had been outsmarted. Rommel and von Rundstedt still thought that the Normandy landing was a feint and that the main attack would eventually come in at Pas de Calais. They were determined to keep their main reserves east of the Seine, so they used all their troops on the spot to build up a containing screen in the beautiful and tangled country south of the landing zones known as the Bocage. Tourists, before the war, called it the Normandy Switzerland — an area of hedgerows, steep little wooded valleys and farms rich in Calvados and Camembert. Great country for a holiday, but hell for tanks. The Allies had also just missed capturing Caen on D-Day. The Germans fought stubbornly. The Battle of the Beaches slowly turned into the Battle of the Build-Up.

The dour, grim, dogged fight went on through the hot summer months. The Germans now realised that their fate in the west depended on Normandy. They threw in everything they had; Hitler from his eyrie in Berchtesgaden bombarding Rommel with orders to hold every hedgerow. But it was Monty who won. By August he had enough strength on the beachhead to break out. He had deliberately drawn the main strength of the German army onto the British and Canadians fighting around Caen. Caen was the hinge on which the whole front would turn. At the end of July, the moment had arrived for the Americans to kick open the door. In Operation Cobra, they broke out and sent the venomous snakes of Patton's armoured columns swarming across Brittany and then turning east to encircle the Germans held by the British in the crucible of Caen.

Suddenly, the whole German front started to crumble. The High Command must have thought that the Gods of War were cruelly deserting them. Rommel, the arch fox, was severely wounded when his car was shot up by a British fighter outside a village ironically named St Foylde Montgomery. On July 20, Hitler had nearly been assassinated in his eastern HQ. Now the Army of the West was scrambling back across the Seine, leaving a huge haul of prisoners and equipment behind it in the Falaise Gap. As the battle-worn British, Canadian and American soldiers chased their broken enemies eastwards, they savoured, for the first time, the excitements and delights of liberation. In every little town and village they were cheered, garlanded with flowers and plied with wine. Paris fell amid scenes of enthusiastic delirium.

On August 15, a force from Italy landed in the South of France in Operation Anvil. Military critics maintained that these troops might have been better employed forestalling the Russians in the Balkans. The soldiers had other things on their minds. They were liberating a succession of towns, from Châteauneuf-du-Pape to Tavel, with names like a succession of popping corks. On the outskirts of Burgundy, the Free French army paused. France would never forgive them if they fought over the sacred soil. The problem was solved when a young *sous-lieutenant* burst into the command post. 'Courage, my generals,' he shouted, 'I have found the weak spots of the German defences. Every one is in a vineyard of inferior quality!'

But where was now the main German defensive line in the west? Could they even establish one at all? If the Allies acted with speed and boldness, they might even sweep over the last barrier of the Rhine. And always, to help them on their way, were the Russians, keeping up their remorseless pressure in the east. Could the war be ended in 1944? While the happy warriors swept forward towards Brussels, Lorraine and the Vosges, the debate raged over their heads in the Allied High Command. Should the armies advance on a broad front to the Rhine or should they put everything into a narrow thrust up from Brussels straight to the Ruhr? Once the Ruhr had been reached, Germany's industrial production would be hopelessly dislocated. The war would be over. Montgomery argued strongly for the single thrust but Eisenhower opted for the broad front. To give Monty his narrow thrust, he would have to stop Patton's advance on the southern flank and give his petrol to the northern armies. Patton roared, 'My men can eat

As the battle-worn British, Canadian and American soldiers chased their broken enemies eastwards, they savoured, for the first time, the excitements and delights of liberation.

their belts, but my tanks gotta have gasoline!' He got it, and to all Monty's arguments Ike 'said no, continued saying no... and ended by saying no in every form known to the English language.'

The British seized Brussels and raced into Antwerp but the great opportunity was passing. Monty decided to try one more plan to catch the Germans off-balance before they recovered. The Allied Airborne Army was still available in England. He would use it to seize the two vital bridges at Nijmegen over the Waal and at Arnhem over the Rhine, and link them by driving General Horrocks's corps boldly up through Eindhoven. On September 17, 1944, the vast air fleet of gliders, protected by over a thousand fighters, appeared in the afternoon sky. The Dutch looked up in hope, and cheered as the freedom squadrons roared overhead. The drop at Nijmegen was successful, but that at Arnhem failed. The plan had been put into effect just a few days too late, for the Germans had managed to get troops into the area. The link-up force reached Nijmegen, but Germans held Arnhem bridge. The gallant paratroopers fought desperately with heavy losses, then the survivors retired across the river. Arnhem had been 'A Bridge Too Far.'

There was now no help for it — the Allies would have to wait for the spring before delivering the knockout blow to Hitler's Thousand Year Reich. The fateful year of 1944 drew towards its end with the coldest weather for 50 years. The soldiers shivered in their forward positions among the bare trees of the Reichwald and the bleak slopes of the Ardennes. Snow and ice were the unpleasant heralds of Christmas. On December 16, Montgomery wrote a friendly letter to Eisenhower reminding him of his bet that the war would be over by Christmas. Ike replied with a smile that there were still nine days to go before he need pay up. Who knows what could happen in that time? At that moment, German tanks were moving into position in the snow of the Ardennes. Suddenly, under the cover of clouds that blanketed the Allied air force, a torrent of armour poured down on the unsuspecting American 106th Division. Within minutes the front was broken in the 'Battle of the Bulge'. A 20-mile gap opened up in the American line and the Germans poured through. The Panzer raced westwards and the Allies faced their greatest military disaster since 1940.

The German recovery had been remarkable. They had raked new units together and equipped them with new tanks, guns and ammunition. They were swirling out of the Ardennes and it seemed that nothing would stop them before they captured Antwerp. Control had to be established at all costs, and Eisenhower took the bold step of appointing Montgomery to command all American and British units north of the Bulge. American feelings were ruffled, for they resented what they felt was Monty's superior manner. When he assured an American colonel that the troops 'had their tails well up', the colonel growled, 'Excuse me, General, up what?'

But Monty's arrival did the trick. The German offensive came to a halt, as he prophesied, because they had no petrol. When they failed to capture the American fuel dumps, they came to a standstill. Hitler's last gamble had failed and as soon as the new year dawned, the Allies resumed their task of pushing their way to the Rhine. The Germans fought hard in those rainy months of January and February, but as March drew to its damp end, the advance to the great river was completed. There was One More River To Cross! It would be the toughest of the lot!

The Rhine was Hitler's last defensive moat. If it was crossed it would be the end of Nazi Germany — Götterdämmerung — the twilight of the gods. Montgomery orchestrated the crossing with Wagnerian power. He prepared the greatest artillery barrage of the war to be followed, after the crossing, by the greatest air drop. True, an American unit had seized the Remagen bridge over the Rhine further south, but it led nowhere. Monty would still have to get his army across in the face of the last, desperate German defence.

As a BBC correspondent, I was 'lucky' enough to be in the leading Buffalo — an armoured, amphibious troop-carrier, packed with Scottish soldiers. I asked a private from Glasgow, 'Do you think you will be the first across?' 'Not if I can help it,' came the cheerful reply. But he was, all the same. The earsplitting barrage crashed overhead and the column of Buffaloes chugged towards the river. They climbed the great dyke and then breasted the swollen stream, running red with the glare of burning farms and flecked with the dropping mortar shells. As the amphibion touched the ground on

Should the armies advance on a broad front to the Rhine or should they put everything into a narrow thrust up from Brussels straight to the Ruhr?

the other side, a piper stood up to fulfil a long tradition. He would pipe the bra' lads into battle. I cautiously raised my microphone as the piper blew. Only a hollow groan. A bullet had gone right through the bagpipes!

But not even the absence of pipe music could stop the British army, or the American armies further south, as they now drove eastwards, outflanking the ruined Ruhr as they went. There was some scattered resistance from fanatics making a last, desperate gesture, but total collapse was now in the air. White flags hung from the windows of every country farmhouse. The devastating effects of the Allied air-raids became only too obvious, and the tanks entered town after town that had been reduced to rubble and gaunt ruins. The few inhabitants who watched the conquering columns go by seemed cowed and silent. Grim evidence now started to appear about what had been happening inside Nazi Germany.

A message reached a British unit that typhus had broken out in the camp up ahead. Would they send help? I went with a medical team to the camp, located in the centre of a dark pine wood. The guard saluted and opened the gates — to a scene of festering horror that no-one who saw it will ever be able to cleanse from his mind. This was Belsen. The whole world was soon to know about the atrocities in this and other camps in all their gruesome detail, from the shaven heads of the pitifully emaciated prisoners to the heaped corpses in the death pits. But this evil belongs not to the new, reborn Germany which is playing a vital part in Europe, but to the old Germany, perverted by the Nazis, which was now being wiped from the map by the advancing Allied armies in the momentous days that followed the Rhine crossing.

The great cities lay broken and helpless. Hamburg was a ghost, reduced to ruins by the bombing. In the radio station I saw the desk used by 'Lord Haw-Haw' — the traitor William Joyce, whose rasping voice had harrassed the listeners of Britain throughout the war. His last script lay on his writing pad. It ended, 'Germany will never be conquered. *Heil Hitler!* ' An empty gin bottle rattled dismally in the top drawer. But where was the Führer, the extraordinary, sinister figure who had personally created all this chaos? Would he fall into British hands? And where were Himmler, Goering and the rest of them? In an advancing British column I was with, excitement ran high when a message reached us that, in a farmhouse ahead, a Field Marshal wished to surrender. It was bound to be Goering. A strong squadron was immediately organised and tanks surrounded the house. I watched as a young lieutenant, covered by guards with rifles at the ready, carefully approached the door. It was opened by an elderly female servant who bowed and said, 'The Field Marshal will receive you in the library.' To his astonishment, the lieutenant was ushered into the presence of the oldest soldier he had ever seen. The aged figure was covered with medals and wore the faded uniform of Kaiser Wilhelm's Death's Head Hussars. It was none other than the 90-year-old Von Mackensen, who had conquered Rumania in the First World War. Somehow he seemed a symbol of the ruin that had overtaken the old Germany. That evening the radio announced that Hitler had committed suicide in his bunker in Berlin.

In the north, British troops had already crossed the Elbe and entered Lübeck. I drove with them along the coast towards Wismar through the German army, without a single eyebrow being raised. These soldiers had packed it all in.

They sat along the road in their thousands, with the paper from the regimental records emptied into the ditches and, all around, their lorries, and horses and carts. Some waved bottles as the British passed. Others shouted 'Russkies, Russkies,' and pointed to the east. For them the war was over. Let the Allies get on with it now. Just beyond Wismar the roads became deserted again. The scout cars slowed down and stopped. Coming towards them were cars packed with soldiers in unfamiliar uniforms.

At last, the Russians! An impromptu party started in the middle of the road. Whisky and vodka were exchanged, with happy back-slapping. A second party arrived, still polite, but the first party withdrew. The newcomers exchanged cigarettes and showed photographs of their families, until a third party arrived in a lorry carrying posts and poles. Before nightfall there was a barrier across the road.

The Iron Curtain had fallen.

The Rhine was Hitler's last defensive moat. If it was crossed it would be the end of Nazi Germany...

POSTSCRIPT

John Frost

D-DAY WAS THE MOST GUARDED SECRET OF THE WAR — and yet to Londoners it was the most open secret.

Where else could all those military vehicles be going, day and night? For weeks, long convoys of troops, tank carriers and lorries moved along London's arterial roads, all heading in one direction — London docks.

As an army driver, I recall that first week in June 1944 so well. There were flags and bunting all the way along the North Circular Road, with cheering crowds yelling 'Good luck boys!' and giving us cups of tea to help us along.

Once at the docks we were sealed off from the outside world. No letters, no phoning, for we had now been told officially our destination was France.

Work consisted of water-proofing vehicles and checking equipment and guns. Once aboard, we rendezvoused with a naval escort and put our vomiting bags to good use. I wrote to my mother: 'Here I am, en route to Normandy, by courtesy of the Royal Navy — not a Jerry plane in sight, the RAF rules the skies.' It was to be four weeks before I could post the letter.

Luckily, our landing was dry. I clearly remember driving across the beach between white ribbons — the sign that it had been cleared of landmines.

The few houses were just ruins. British bombers had gone in before us, the Germans had retreated and the fighting was going on ahead of us. But British troops and tanks were everywhere.

We headed a little inland to a deserted farmhouse. Our first task was to unload the camouflage nets and remove sticky water-proofing from our hot engines, and then dig in. What a noisy and bombing night that was!

The first memorable thing about that first day in France was the smell: the stench of death. Not human flesh but cattle — scores of them lying on their sides pot-bellied and dead. The sun didn't help much.

It wasn't until we advanced to Bayeux several days later that we actually saw some French people. As far as the fighting went on our front reaching towards Caen, there was a stalemate for some weeks while the Americans battled for Cherbourg. We made up for it later when we covered 400 miles in six days in August to be the first troops in Antwerp.

The organisation and planning of the D-Day operation was brilliant — absolutely nothing was forgotten. Aboard ship, every man received a printed message from the Supreme Commander, General Eisenhower, wishing 'Good luck on the great crusade.'

On landing, each man was given a preprinted field postcard on which to write home. It consisted of preprinted sentences such as 'I am well' or 'I have been wounded,' which one could strike out.

We all had tin rations plus a portable 'Tommy Cooker' with tiny solid fuel tablets.

I can still recall the delicious steak and kidney puddings.

It was many weeks, though, before we had bread and so biscuits were the order of the day, supplemented by the compulsory daily vitamin pill.

Special praise, too, for the army laundry ablution units. Dirty shirts and underwear were just exchanged for clean ones and if they fitted you were lucky!

Every day was an uncertain one, but comradeship and spirit have never been equalled. We were the British Liberation Army and we knew we were going to win.

We were the British Liberation Army and we knew we were going to win.

COMPLETE NEWS—MAGAZINE SECTION—COMIC FEATURES

New York Post

FOUNDED 1801. VOLUME 143, NO. 169. COPYRIGHT, 1944, NEW YORK POST.

TWO SECTIONS NEW YORK, TUESDAY, JUNE 6, 1944 40 PAGES

INVASION

SMASHING AHEAD!

Nazis Say We're 10 Miles In; Sky Troops Far Beyond Lines

TUESDAY, JUNE 6, 1944

FINAL NIGHT

Evening Standard

37,357 BLACK-OUT 10.57 pm to 5.0 am. MOON Rises 9.50 pm; Sets 6.29 am. ONE PENNY

Churchill Announces Successful Massed Air Landings Behind Enemy in France

4000 SHIPS, THOUSANDS OF SMALLER VESSELS

"So Far All Goes to Plan"—11,000 First Line Airplanes

An immense armada of more than 4000 ships, with several thousand smaller craft, have crossed the Channel, said Mr. Churchill to-day, announcing the invasion.

"MASSED AIRBORNE LANDINGS HAVE BEEN SUCCESSFULLY EFFECTED BEHIND THE ENEMY'S LINES," HE SAID.

MR. CHURCHILL DESCRIBED THE LANDINGS AS THE "FIRST OF A SERIES IN FORCE ON THE EUROPEAN CONTINENT."

The landings on the beaches are proceeding at various points at the present time. The fire of the shore batteries has been largely quelled, said Mr. Churchill.

The obstacles which were constructed in the sea have not proved so difficult as was apprehended.

The Anglo-American Allies are sustained by about 11,000 first line aircraft, which can be drawn upon as may be needed for the purposes of the battle.

There are already hopes that actual tactical surprise has been attained, said the Premier, and we hope to furnish the enemy with a succession of surprises during the course of the fighting.

"The battle which is now beginning will grow constantly in scale and in intensity for many weeks to come, and I shall not attempt to speculate upon its course.

COMPLETE UNITY

"Complete unity prevails throughout the Allied Armies. (Cheers.)

"There is a brotherhood in arms between us and our friends in the United States.

"There is complete confidence in the Supreme Commander, General Eisenhower, and in his lieutenants, and also in the Commander of the Expeditionary Force, General Montgomery.

"The ardour and spirit of the troops as I saw them myself embarking in these last few days was splendid.

"Nothing that equipment, science and forethought can do has been neglected, and the whole process of opening this great new front will be pursued with the utmost resolution both by the commanders and by the U.S. and British Governments whom they serve.

Replying to Mr. Greenwood, Mr. Churchill said that certainly in the early part of the battle he would endeavour to keep the House fully informed.

"It may be," he added, "that I shall ask their indulgence to press myself upon them before we rise to-night.

"So far the commanders who are engaged report that everything is proceeding according to plan," he said—"and what a plan!"

This vast operation is undoubtedly the most complicated and difficult which has ever occurred.

Mr. Greenwood said Mr. Churchill's statement ranks second only to the declaration of war of September 3. 1939.

THE KING ON RADIO TO-NIGHT

It was officially announced from Buckingham Palace to-day that the King will broadcast at 9 o'clock to-night.

No. 1

At 9.30 a.m. to-day the following communiqué was issued from General Eisenhower's Supreme Headquarters:

"Under the command of General Eisenhower, Allied naval forces, supported by strong air forces, began landing Allied armies this morning on the Northern coast of France."

The statement was marked "Communiqué No. 1." At the same time it was revealed that General Montgomery is in command of the Army Group carrying out the assault. This Army Group includes British, Canadian and U.S. forces.

TEN MILES INLAND—*Berlin*

THE ALLIED TROOPS LANDED ON THE COAST OF NORMANDY BETWEEN 6 A.M. AND 8.15. THEY CAME FROM THE SEA, UNDER COVER OF NAVAL BOMBARDMENT, AND WERE DROPPED FROM THE AIR AS WELL.

According to the Germans, the entire coast was involved between Le Havre and Cherbourg—two of France's most important ports—with the main attackk 30 miles from Havre.

It was officially stated at Allied Headquarters this morning that so far this was the naval phase of the operations. The naval bombardment went "in the manner planned," so that first reports are therefore good.

HITLER IN COMMAND

Hitler is taking personal command of all the anti-invasion operations, according to news reaching London from underground sources.

His four marshals are Rundstedt. titular commander-in-chief: Rommel. Inspector-General: Sperrle. in charge of air forces; and Blaskowitz, acting deputy to Rommel.

The Germans mentioned particularly the stretch of coast between the estuaries of the Orne and the Vire—two rivers running northwards to the coast and running into Seine Bay between 40 and 50 miles apart.

"FOCAL POINT"

Caen—a few miles inland up the Orne—was described as "the first focal point" where sharp fighting was taking place.

Soon afterwards the enemy reported that Allied troops were fighting ten miles inland.

Later the Germans reported that while strong American airborne forces jumped near Barfleur, on the tip of the Cherbourg Peninsula, a mass landing, supported by considerable naval forces, was carried out at St. Vaast la Houge.

The Germans claimed to have sunk during this action one cruiser and one large landing craft laden with troops.

More amphibious operations were directed against the Vire Estuary and the Orne.

The centre of gravity of the air operations was, beside Barfleur, at Carentan on the Orne Estuary, north-east of Caen and between the Seine and Orne Estuary.

The great convoys were preceeded by minesweepers which had to cover many miles of minefields before the naval vessels—both British and American and including battleships—got into position to bombard the enemy's shore batteries and defences, writes James Stuart, Evening Standard reporter at Supreme H.Q.

Special ships had to be used to go in under the enemy's nose to clear the underwater obstacles around the landing area.

All this was covered by a great air bombardment carefully timed.

AIR ASSAULT

I understand that almost every type of Allied aircraft took part in the assault.

Meanwhile the troop carriers of Air Transport Command swept in over the enemy coastline to drop and land the airborne troops in the enemy's rear. When the troop-carrying airplanes returned the pilots reported that the men had been landed with few casualties.

The German broadcasts were constantly emphasising the size of the operations. "The Anglo-American attack is an operation of great scope in its territorial extension, as well as in the number of troops taking part.

"It's extent goes far beyond that of a Commando action, and must be considered undoubtedly a first stage of invasion."

The airborne landings were described as being "in great depth" in the whole area of Normandy.

At least four Allied, airborne divisions were observed between

(Continued on Back Page, Col. Two)

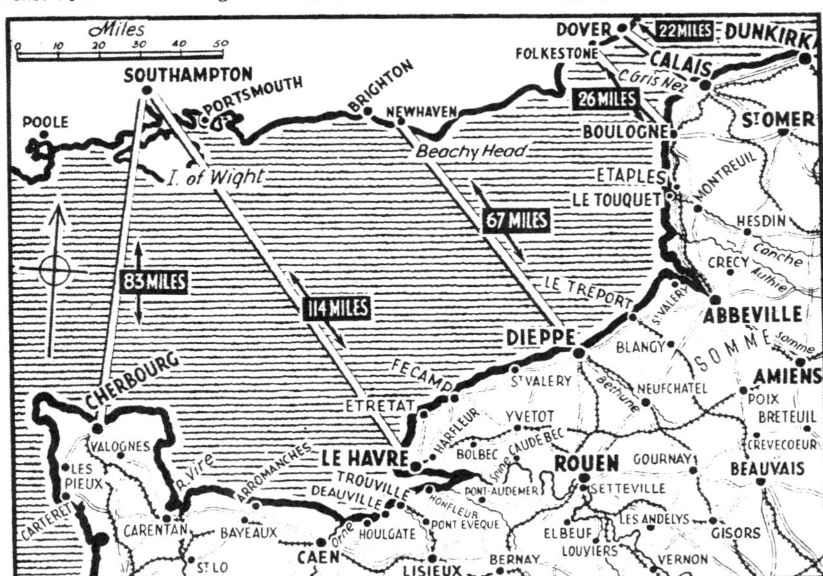

Saw First Troops Wade Ashore

Allied infantry scrambled ashore at 7 a.m. this morning in two areas of the French coast, apparently without heavy opposition, according to fighter pilots returning from over the landing areas, says Robert Richards, British United Press war correspondent at a U.S. Fighter Base.

One of the pilots, an American Colonel. William Curry, told me:

"I saw the first troops wading ashore about 7 a.m., from light landing craft. From the height at which I was flying they did not appear to be meeting heavy opposition and were covered by extensive and heavy naval bombardment from our warships.

"Flying Fortresses were also bombing the beach which appeared to be marshy instead of sandy.

Major John Locke, of Texas, who led a squadron of Thunderbolts, said:

"I have never seen so many ships in all my life. Flying over the harbour at one port I counted great numbers of cruisers, destroyers, corvettes and other craft. The constant flashes from their guns indicated that the beach was getting a heavy pounding.

"Behind this advance brigade, stretching in a never-ending stream across the Channel, came line after line of L.C.T.s (landing craft, tanks) escorted by corvettes and P.T. boats.

"We were never attacked by enemy airplanes although the flak was terrific."

Second Lieut. Benson, from Iowa, said: "The Channel waters were fairly calm and the boats bounced along smoothly. They were constantly patrolled by warships and many were towing barrage balloons."

Colonel William Schwartz added: "When I arrived over the beach our battleships brought all their fire to bear on the shore."

Eisenhower Sees Paratroops Off

General Eisenhower spent last night from early evening until after dusk paying informal visits to U.S. paratroop units due to make early morning landings in France.

He chatted with pararoops as, with charcoal-blackened faces, and loaded with equipment, they marched to their aircraft.

He later watched the take-off of he first C.47s loaded with paratroops, as they set out in the fading light to open the Second Front.

Earlier he had paid an informal visit to a British infantry battalion and wished the men good luck as tyhe boarded their landing craft.

DAILY MIRROR, Wednesday, June 7, 1944.

Daily Mirror

JUNE 7

No. 12,627
ONE PENNY
Registered at the G.P.O. as a Newspaper.

Midnight news: Landings are successful

Naval losses "regarded as very light"

INVADERS THRUSTING INLAND

What the Germans are saying

GERMAN radio last night reported new Allied landings at Calais and Boulogne.

Powerful paratroop formations dropped behind Boulogne and north of Rouen were said to be engaged in "vicious" fighting. Other paratroops had a firm grip on a nineteen mile stretch of the Cherbourg-Caen road.

Sertorius, military commentator, said the offensive had extended to the entire Normandy peninsula.

Paris claimed a German counter-attack in the Cherbourg region was "still developing" late last night.

Our bridgehead, said to be fifteen miles long and several miles deep, was first reported to be between Villers-sur-Mer and Trouville.

Later broadcasts corrected this to further west on both sides of the River Orne and north-west of Bayeux, between Caen and Isigny.

A British-American group, with light tanks and tank reconnaissance cars, was operating on dunes north-east of Bayeux "trying to link up with the larger bridgehead," said Berlin.

Other enemy radio reports were:

Allied reinforcements "pouring in."

Except for the beachhead at Caen, all invasion troops landed from the sea thrown back. This beachhead narrowed down in some places.

"Navy Off Dunkirk"

Strong Allied naval forces seen off Dunkirk and Calais.

Fifteen cruisers with fifty to sixty destroyers operating off Le Havre last night, with landing craft, apparently waiting to attack.

Allied airborne troops on the Cherbourg peninsula "wiped out to a man" at Barfleur and La Pernelle, but more airborne troops pressing against Caen.

Allied landings on Channel Islands. Troops from 280 ships attacking Arromanches and Ouistrehem between Cherbourg and Le Havre. Cliffs scaled by ladder and tanks landed.

Allied landing craft penetrated Orne and Vire Estuaries; main centres of the big landing between St. Vaast de la Hogue and the Cherbourg peninsula tip.

In heavy artillery duel with coastal batteries off St. Vaast, a cruiser and troop-carrying landing craft were sunk.

Paratroops made twelve landings in all from Cherbourg to Boulogne. First and Sixth British and 28th and 101st American airborne divisions engaged.

Allied troops tried to break into Carentan, west of Isigny.

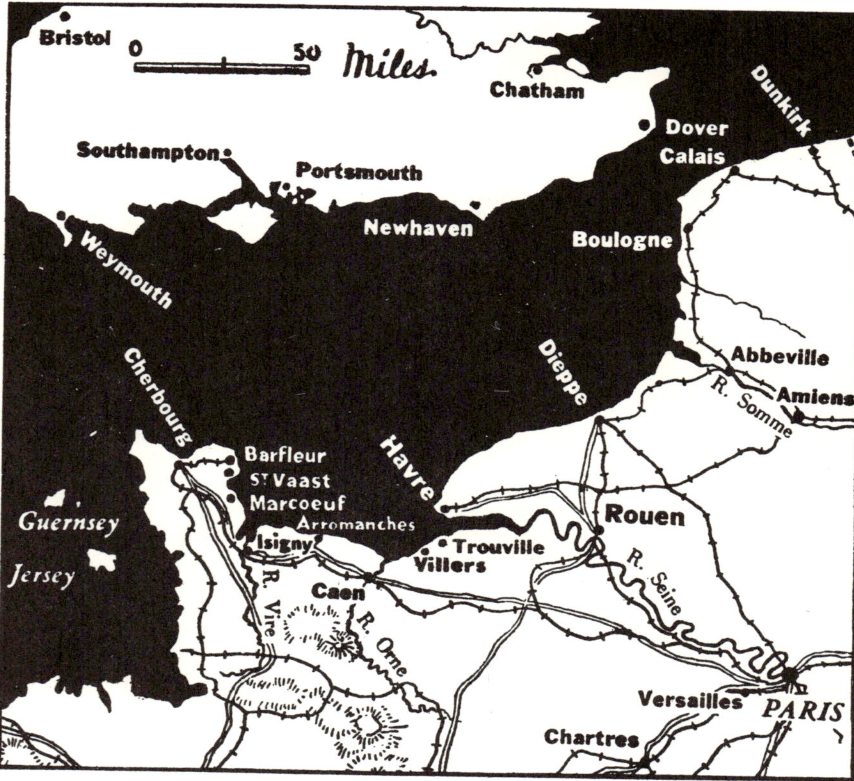

The invasion coast, showing the chief centres of activity between Cherbourg and Havre. Latest German radio reports suggest new Allied landings further north near Boulogne and Calais

MIDNIGHT COMMUNIQUE FROM SUPREME ALLIED H.Q. ANNOUNCED: "REPORTS OF OPERATIONS SO FAR SHOW THAT OUR FORCES SUCCEEDED IN THEIR INITIAL LANDINGS. FIGHTING CONTINUES.

"Our aircraft met with little enemy fighter opposition or AA gunfire. Naval casualties are regarded as being very light, especially when the magnitude of the operation is taken into account."

In Washington, Mr. Henry Stimson, U.S. War Secretary, said the invasion was "going very nicely." President Roosevelt said it was "running to schedule." Up to noon, U.S. naval losses were two destroyers and a landing vessel. Air losses were about one per cent.

Allied airmen returning from attacks on North France last evening reported that our troops were moving inland. There was no longer any opposition on the beaches now guarded by balloons. One pilot saw the Stars and Stripes flying over a French town.

According to earlier reports, British, Canadian and American spearhead troops of the Allied Armies have gained footholds along the Normandy coast, and in some places have thrust several miles inland.

Fighting is going on inside the town of Caen, seven miles from the coast, and several intact bridges have been captured.

BATTLING STILL FURTHER INLAND, AND WELL ESTABLISHED, IS THE GREATEST AIRBORNE ARMY EVER FLOWN INTO ACTION. THESE TROOPS WERE LANDED WITH GREAT ACCURACY AND VERY LITTLE LOSS.

The airborne fleet consisted of 1,000 troop-carrying planes, including gliders.

But though several vital obstacles have been overcome with much less loss than expected, the Germans will concentrate their reserves. Heavy battles are looming.

This was the situation outlined in the Commons last night by Mr. Churchill.

(Continued on Back Page)

I saw them leap to beach

ABOARD A BRITISH DESTROYER, OFF NORTH FRANCE, Tuesday.

GUNS are belching flame from more than 600 Allied warships. Thousands of bombers are roaring overhead, and fighters are weaving in and out of the clouds.

The invasion of Western Europe has begun.

Rolling clouds of dense black and grey smoke cover the beaches south-west of Le Havre, writes Desmond Tighe, of Reuter.

We are standing some 8,000 yards off the beaches of Berniere-sur-Mer, seven miles east of Arromanches, and from the bridge of this destroyer I can see vast numbers of naval craft.

In ten minutes more than 2,000 tons of H.E. shells have gone down on the beach-head.

It is now exactly 7.25 a.m., and through my glasses I can see the first wave of assault troops touching down on the water's edge and fan up the beach.

Under the supreme command of Admiral Sir Bertram Ramsay, Allied Naval Commander, Expeditionary Force, two great forces are taking part.

An eastern task force, mostly British and Canadian warships, is led by Rear-Admiral Sir Phillip Vian, of Cossack fame.

A western task force, mainly of American warships, is commanded by U.S Rear-Admiral Alan G. Kirk.

The weather for the landings was not perfect, but despite high running seas and a strong north-westerly wind a bold decision was taken to go ahead.

The plans allowed for four phases:

1. —*Landings by airborne paratroops in the rear.*
2. —*A tremendous night bombing by the RAF on the landing beaches themselves.*
3. —*A bombardment by more than 600 Allied warships from battleships, cruisers, monitors and destroyers.*
4. —*A daybreak bombing attack by the full force of the U.S. Air Force just after dawn and before the first troops went in.*

Events moved rapidly after 4 a.m., and I will put on record the diary kept on the bridge:

5.7 a.m.—Lying eight miles from the lowering position for invasion craft.

5.20.—Dawn. Innumerable assault ships appear smudgily.

5.27.—Night bombing has ceased, and the great naval bombardment begins.

5.33.—We move in slowly.

5.36.—Cruisers open fire. We

Continued on Back Page

FIRST WOUNDED ARE BACK IN ENGLAND

The first Allied wounded were landed back in England yesterday. Some were taken to an East Anglian hospital.

Despite their wounds, many were smiling cheerfully.

Officially recorded next-of-kin of a wounded soldier on the danger list in a hospital at home will be sent a telegram, production of which at a police station will secure travel warrants for two persons.

MONDAY D-DAY HELD UP BY WEATHER

The invasion was delayed twenty-four hours, it was revealed at S.H.A.E.F. last night.

With his D-Day fixed for Monday morning, General Eisenhower was told by weather experts that conditions would be too bad.

But they forecast that by Tuesday there would be an improvement.

Eisenhower had to make a decision knowing that, once launched, the invasion could not be called off.

He took the decision to go in on Tuesday—and though the weather was not kind, the experts' forecast was largely fulfilled.

The landing craft, except for four, were able to battle on to the other side.

Rain fell in the Straits last night and the outlook was unsettled. The sea was smooth.

THURSDAY, JUNE 8, 1944

Latest Prices

BLACK OUT 10.59 to 4.59 | Moon Rises 11.59 p.m. Sets 8.16 a.m. | New Moon, June 20 | Radio Page 7

LATE NIGHT

THE STAR

No. 17,461 ONE PENNY

Monty: 'All Is Going Excellently'

DRIVING AHEAD FROM BAYEUX

Fierce Tank Battles

First Prisoners

These were among the first German prisoners to be captured by the Allied invasion forces on French territory.

(More invasion pictures on Pages 4 and 5.)

AS OUR ARMIES PUSHED ON INTO NORMANDY TODAY FROM NEWLY CAPTURED BAYEUX, GENERAL MONTGOMERY WAS QUOTED BY A COMBINED PRESS CORRESPONDENT AS SAYING, IN AN INTERVIEW AT SEA OFF THE INVASION BEACHES: "EVERYTHING IS GOING EXCELLENTLY."

Fierce tank and infantry fighting is now going on, but it was stated at Allied Supreme Headquarters this afternoon that the capture of Bayeux may open up an Allied advance from that point.

General Eisenhower's Invasion Communique No. 5 today said: "Bayeux has fallen to our troops, who have also crossed the Bayeux-Caen road at several points. Progress continues despite determined enemy resistance.

"Fierce armoured and infantry fighting his taken place. Contact has been established between our seaborne and airborne troops. The steady build-up of our force has continued.

"During the night forces of E-boats made unsuccessful attempts to interfere with the continual arrival of supplies.

"Support fire from Allied warships continued throughout yesterday. Our air forces have given invaluable support to the ground troops on all sectors of the front.

"Advantage was taken of favourable weather over Northern France yesterday afternoon and evening to attack enemy rail and road centres, concentrations of men and material, and to bomb airfields and other targets up to 100 miles in advance of our troops. More than 9,000 sorties were flown in tactical support of land and naval forces.

"Out for the second time yesterday, heavy bombers, with fighter escort, in the late afternoon attacked airfields north-west of Lorient and railroad bridges and focal points in the area from the Bay of Biscay to the Seine. The bombers encountered no enemy fighter opposition, but our fighters reported shooting down 64 enemy aircraft in combat and they destroyed more than a score on the ground.

"After bombing rail and road objectives in the immediate zone of operations, medium and light bombers, flying as low as 1,000 feet just behind the enemy lines, strafed gun emplacements and crews, staff cars and trains. Allied fighter bombers and fighters were also extremely active, flying armed reconnaissance over the assault area, covering naval operations, and carrying out low-level attacks on bridges north

CONTINUED ON BACK PAGE, Col. TWO

PREMIER WARNS

WE MUST NOT BE OVER OPTIMISTIC

MR. CHURCHILL, after replying to questions put to him in Parliament today, said: "May I for the convenience of the House mention that I do not propose to make any statement about the battles this morning, and I shall not do so unless something exceptional turns up.

"As a matter of fact, I think all the points which had occurred to me are very fully met in the excellent reports furnished by our able and upright Press.

"I would say that if this is the last time I speak to the House before the week-end, I earnestly hope that when Members go to their constituencies they will not only maintain morale as far as that is necessary, but also give strong warnings against over-optimism and against the idea that these things are going to be settled in a rush.

"Remember, although great dangers lie behind, enormous exertions lie before us."

Mr. Granville (Ind., Eye) Will he give an assurance that the reason he is not going to make a statement in the immediate future is not that he is going to make a visit to the coast of France?

There was no further reply.

Station Death

A man who was killed when he fell from a platform at Knightsbridge Underground station was identified today as Mr. Thomas M. Leary, aged 74, of Hammersmith-road, W.

"It Was The Sand Of France"

A Frenchman who landed with the Invasion Army writes:

"I jumped on to the beach yesterday and seized a handful of sand—the sand of France—and thanked God for permitting me to return to my native land after four years.

"When I met the first Frenchman on French soil since 1940, I hailed him and he smiled—a magnificent smile. He had lost his wireless and had not heard Eisenhower's appeal, but naturally he guided the Allied soldiers.

"An Allied officer has just told me that the mayor of the village offered his services spontaneously, although his daughter and sons had been killed by a shell."

Invasion Man On Leave

A young RASC soldier was said by Mr. C. G. du Cann, barrister, at Old-street, today, to have been "brought back from the invasion" to give evidence in a case.

"He has been given special leave," he added.

De Gaulle's Report

The French Committee of National Liberation are holding an extraordinary meeting to hear an important report from General de Gaulle, says Reuter from Algiers.

Luftwaffe Gets A Beating

114 NAZI PLANES WIPED OUT

GOERING has at last sent up some of his planes to challenge the Allied landings. And the Luftwaffe has suffered a smashing defeat.

Between dawn yesterday and midnight, 114 German aircraft were destroyed in the invasion zone, 94 in the air and 20 on the ground.

Many of them were bombers trying to attack Allied shipping and landing operations.

Spitfires patrolling the landing beaches shot down 30 German machines, while Mustangs accounted for ten out of a formation of thirty M.E. 109's which tried to break through the giant Allied air umbrella.

Under cover of darkness German planes last night approached the main assault area. Allied night fighters were on the spot, and there were many combats

Night fighters of Air Defence of Great Britain over Continental bases by the light of the "intruders' moon" shot down five enemy aircraft, as well as another three destroyed in the Channel near Cherbourg.

One plane which had just taken off at Dreux was sent crashing in flames by F./O. F. E. Pringle, of Croydon, who was making his first

CONTINUED ON BACK PAGE, Col. FIVE

SUNDAY SPECIAL

NEWS OF THE WORLD

No. 5,250 [Estab. 1843] Registered at the General Post Office as a Newspaper — Telephones: Central 3030 — SUNDAY, JUNE 11, 1944 — Telegrams: Worldly, Fleet, London — PRICE TWOPENCE

*Certified Net Sale Exceeds **4,000,000** Copies Per Issue*

40 MILES OF SOLID FRONT

Americans Capture Isigny: Eve of the Battle for Cherbourg

BRITISH PARATROOPS ARE HOLDING FAST OUTSIDE OF CAEN

THE most momentous news from Normandy this morning is the capture by the Allies of the little town of Isigny, three miles inland on the road from Caen to Carentan, and a Berlin report, for what it may be worth, that "the battle for Cherbourg has begun."

German troops are known to have pulled out north-west towards the port in face of renewed attacks by the Americans in the Carentan—St. Mere Eglise sector.

British paratroops continue firmly to hold their hard-won ground east of Caen, which town, like the equally important one of Carentan, is now directly threatened by new Allied advances.

Correspondents in the battle area report a solid front for 40 miles across Normandy, from the British sector just north of Caen to the American at Isigny.

Already 2,000 German prisoners have been landed in this country; thousands more are behind the wire on the other side.

BUILD-UP GOES ON IN SPITE OF THE WEATHER

ON this the morning of "D Plus Five," it is possible to give some clearer view of the situation as it stands to-day and of developments during the hard and bitter fighting since the Allies landed on the beaches.

In the first place, however, the official news that Isigny has been captured by the Americans is important, for the town lies on the lateral road between Carentan and Bayeux. Naturally, too, it takes us much nearer to Carentan.

Here is the latest communique from Supreme Headquarters, Advanced Command Post:

"American troops have captured Isigny.

"Despite unfavourable weather conditions the disembarkation of further men and material was uninterrupted.

"Withstanding heavy enemy attacks by infantry and armour, British and Canadian troops stood firm in the Caen area and our forces have made contact with strong enemy forces near Conde sur Seulles.

"There is continuous fighting in other sectors.

"Adverse weather during daylight confined our air activity to limited patrols over the immediate battle area and to coastal aircraft operations.

"An enemy destroyer, driven ashore off Batz, in the Brest Peninsula, earlier in the day by naval surface forces, was attacked and left a smouldering hulk.

"At night a strong force of heavy bombers, eight of which are missing, attacked enemy airfields at Flers, Rennes, Laval, and Le Mans in north-western France, and the railway centre at Etampes. Light bombers pounded enemy communications in the rear of the battle zone.

"Night fighters and intruder aircraft shot down four enemy planes over the beachhead."

"Coastal aircraft are co-operating with naval surface forces in a vigorous offensive against U-boats which are threatening to attack our lines of communication to the assault area."

PANZERS AT CAEN

As we move our forces in and up to the battle zone the enemy, too, is straining every nerve to reinforce.

There are now three panzer divisions in the area of Caen and to the west of that town in the neighbourhood of which fierce fighting continues.

It is significant that there are many foreigners among the thousands of German prisoners. The enemy, indeed, are understood to have elements of almost all the occupied countries in each of their divisions, and certainly in the coastal defence areas.

It is not easy to assess their morale, but, generally speaking, it may be said that their attitude is "If we don't shoot the Allies then probably we shall be shot by the Germans."

It is now quite evident that before our attack was made the Germans had so to dispose their forces in the West as to meet a general threat. They did not know the point of our assault, and for that reason were unable to concentrate the bulk of their forces—other than coastal infantry—in any one place.

The immediate and natural reaction to the Normandy landing was to try to deal with the immediate situation and to cope with it somehow with the forces on the spot.

FOILING VON RUNDSTEDT

There is now no doubt that the Allies forced the beaches with unexpected rapidity from the enemy's point of view.

The obvious German preoccupation thereafter was to seal off, if he could, our landing, and prevent rapid exploitation of the situation towards the north.

With this object, the Germans made very determined efforts in the Orne area, and simultaneously endeavoured to drive north with such reserves as they had available and split up our individual landings.

The immediate strategy for the enemy was, in fact, to keep the landings separate.

Thus, Von Rundstedt attempted to achieve quick results on the beaches—but, as the world knows to-day, he failed.

Allied air and naval superiority had given us a firm beach-hold, from which we were unlikely to be turned off.

Von Rundstedt recognised this fact, and thereupon the next phase developed.

This has led to heavy and continuous fighting in the Caen area, with the Germans attempting to drive a wedge between our forces which he might have expected to find to the north-west and north-east of the town.

Simultaneously they are fighting hard to maintain a hold on Carentan, for the Germans are presumably manoeuvring to keep separate our forces north of the town.

ENEMY ARMOUR HELD

The enemy's main effort, however, is still in the Caen area, and it is here that German armour, which has arrived in the battle area, is for the most part being used.

In their two preliminary, but important objectives, the Germans have been unsuccessful.

They have failed to drive towards the beaches and failed to cross the Caen-Bayeux road.

There is no doubt that the enemy will continue to fight very hard to defend Caen, for clearly it is of the utmost importance both to them and to us.

They are still attempting to advance north-west from the town, but without any success; indeed the fighting to-day is much nearer to Caen, because it is the Allies who have advanced.

Similarly the enemy's main armoured attacks between Caen and Bayeux are also being held. Rundstedt appears to be moving up his reserves both by day and by night, and it is possible that a spell of bad flying weather was very useful for him in this respect.

One of his principal difficulties must have been to balance his reserves against immediate use and future possibilities.

He does not appear to have made any attempt to reinforce the Cherbourg Peninsula by means of sea or airborne landings.

Allied bombing of the rear areas is affecting, and will continue to affect, the movement of German reserves, and there will therefore be a considerable period during which the enemy must be forced to attempt to hold up with what he has got at the moment, which may be of the order of ten divisions, for elements of that number have been identified so far.

BEACH OF "HELL"

THE PRICE THEY PAID IN ITS WINNING

"Those Americans who assaulted one of the beaches and lived said it was hell—just plain, unadulterated hell."

Thus Reuter's correspondent, William Stringer, in a delayed cable from Normandy yesterday. The first 24 hours on this beach, says Stringer, were a vivid nightmare of torn bodies, exploding mines, sinking barges, bursting shells—of blood and filth and death.

Whole bodies were blasted through the air by the ferocious German artillery fire.

Many men, hurled out of their assault boats by artillery bursts, died in the water. Some reached the beach and crawled a few yards over the egg-shaped rocks before they were hit.

I watched more than half of that inch by inch struggle up the beach from a landing craft a mile offshore and unable to discharge its gun cargo until positions had been secured.

For about 36 hours the American assault forces fought one of the war's bloodiest beach-head struggles against a bit of the best defended coast in the world.

There is plenty of evidence of the intensity of the fight.

They still fish an American boy out of the water every now and then. There are already a few of them on the beach, lying on stretchers and covered with blankets. We haven't had time to bury them yet.

Looking down the beach you can see masses and masses of junk—stamped envelopes in which some boy hoped to send letters home, the dress uniform a second-lieutenant hoped to wear in Paris, binoculars, shoes, leggings, blankets, cigarettes.

Dozens of lifebelts are piled on the rocks and sand, suitcases have been blasted open, and shoe polish, tooth-brushes, and towels scattered over a beach pocked with shell holes, fox holes, and trenches.

A SERGEANT'S PRAYER

Once in a while you see a little mound of sand with a bayonet stuck at the head and a helmet hanging on the bayonet.

The only way you can tell whether it is a German or an American grave is by that helmet.

At one end of the beach they are loading casualties for the trip back to England. There's a sergeant, an engineer, who was hit lightly by shrapnel. It is broad daylight, and he is on his knees praying.

"I don't know how to pray," he said. "I've never prayed. But I'm starting now."

He told me he didn't know how he got off the beach alive. He and seven other men started up together.

"Suddenly there was a crash, and I fell on my face, blinded by an orange flame," he said. "When I got up I saw the others were dead. All I got was a bit of shrapnel in the back."

Though the battle for the beach has been over many hours, the beach still is not quiet.

There is a steady stream of men and vehicles pouring ashore, rolling over the stained sands and up the hill, past the fire-blackened German pillboxes towards the front.

There are German prisoners on the beach, too. They are helping to evacuate their own and the American casualties.

These Germans look a little bewildered, but so do a lot of Americans just landing and getting their first look at one of the beaches of Normandy.

"STAND TO THE LAST"

RUTHLESS ROMMEL'S ORDER TO THE GERMANS

Stand to the last orders have been issued to the Germans opposing the Americans in the St. Mere Eglise sector.

Henry Gorrell, of the B.U.P., said yesterday:—

We have captured placards issued to Rommel's men which say: "Delay the Americans to all possible length. Stand fast to the last man."

There are signs, adds Gorrell, that the Germans are preparing a counter-attack in an effort to regain their lost positions here, but warships and large bomber formations are helping the artillery to lay down a heavy general barrage

We are now at artillery strength and the impact of the combined assault seems to have dampened the spirits of the German gunners, who up to a few hours ago were making it tough for the U.S. infantry.

During the night, airborne and infantry slogged it out with German suicide units at St. Mere Eglise.

Under cover of darkness, a U.S. corps some miles on our left is reported to have moved up against the 21st Panzer Division—the division which once was with Rommel in Libya.

GERMANS CLAIM 1,500 PRISONERS

The German Overseas News Agency claimed yesterday afternoon that in the first three days of the invasion fighting they took 1,500 prisoners and destroyed 175 Allied tanks.

They also claimed to have sunk two cruisers, three destroyers, six transports, five armoured landing craft, and seven armoured landing boats.

PROUD FOREFATHERS.

Hidden German Tanks Blown Sky-High

OUR BOMBERS SET FOREST ON FIRE

MARAUDER Base, Saturday. — I saw German tanks blown sky-high to-day out of their place of concealment in a forest south-east of Caen during a low-level attack by Marauders, says Collie Small, B.U.P. war correspondent.

From the Marauder in which I flew I could see Caen burning fiercely, as well as the rubble of three devastated villages. Tons of high explosive were rained down on the German panzers.

I saw hundreds of Allied ships ranged like a summer regatta in a crescent-shaped bay north of the Cherbourg peninsula, with the sun glinting on their barrage balloons.

It was a great contrast to D-Day, when the whole shoreline seemed to be erupting in great gouts of smoke and flame.

Except for a few men in lorries and barges it was quiet to-day. The German shore batteries were silent, but for miles behind the beaches the flat, green farmland is pocked with huge craters from the terrific naval bombardment on D-Day.

I saw farm buildings flattened where the battle had rolled over them. Near one village I could see Allied lorries shuttling along the roads with their white stars plainly visible.

SMOKE AND FLAMES

Caen was wreathed in smoke, and I could see the flames making ugly red patches in the grey blanket stretched over the doomed town.

Bayeux was quiet, and, although it appeared to have been heavily shelled, there was no smoke or fire visible. A junction on the main line to Cherbourg was burning.

As we swept in over a forest we saw one patch of woods burst into flame, and clouds of black smoke rolled up as if a fuel dump had been hit. The bomb-bay doors opened, and I looked down and saw camouflaged tanks rustling in the forest.

Flight after flight of Marauders sent their bombs hurtling into the forest, and the entire wooded area burst into flames.

The panzer unit was apparently caught by surprise, and not a single tank turned its turret on us as the Marauders weaved through the light flak barrage thrown up by mobile guns.

The bombers flew so low that the concussion from our bombs made the plane leap with every explosion. As we swung north after leaving the target I saw black smoke and clouds rolling up from the green woods, as blotches of fire melted into each other like pools of treacle.

ROADS CLOGGED

All the roads leading to Caen are clogged with supply columns stretching back as far as 15 miles from the town.

Pilots, flying Thunderbolts, left a ten-mile trail of blasted, wrecked and blazing German lorries laden with ammunition or petrol, bombing and strafing the convoy lines without opposition either from the air or the ground.

BIG BOMB ATTACKS

GUNS, TANKS, TROOPS WERE TARGETS

In a day of great air activity medium-sized forces of Flying Fortresses and Liberators yesterday attacked enemy aerodromes in several parts of Brittany and Normandy, as well as gun positions and defended areas near the north coast.

Medium-sized forces of Mustangs, Lightnings, and Thunderbolts escorted the heavy bombers and engaged in strafing sweeps before they returned.

Marauders and Havocs, flying in strength, resumed their close support of ground forces in Normandy with attacks on many enemy targets close behind the fighting lines.

Objectives were railway yards and tracks, highways, and a heavy gun position, and a concentration of troops and tanks. These targets were spread out from one to 15 miles behind the battle lines.

Good bomb-hits were scored on an important highway attacked by the Marauders. Crews reported that the road for a mile and a half was made useless, and that tanks dispersed along the edge of it were blocked off.

The day activity followed a night in which more than 30 4,000-lb. block-busters were dropped on Berlin in a three-minute lightning attack by Mosquitoes.

How a strong force of Lancasters and Halifaxes attacked four airfields in Northern France, to make them useless to the enemy, was told by Air Ministry News Service last night.

The object of the attacks was to "crater" the airfields with high-explosive bombs, prevent aircraft already there from taking off, and deprive the enemy of the most convenient bases for aircraft intervening in the battle. The airfields were at Flers, Rennes, Laval, Le Mans.

The bombers had to fly through thick cloud and extremely heavy rain, but the crews report that results seemed good.

Almost at the same time as these attacks on the airfields, Lancasters were making a heavy raid on the railway centre at Etampes, about 30 miles south of Paris. Three important lines meet at this junction, and damage to it would block German military traffic moving from south to north, and east to west.

Pilots of Air Defence of Great Britain, continuing their defensive patrols over the battle areas in Northern France, added another five enemy aircraft to their beach-head bag.

Three Junkers and a Dornier were shot out of the air, and another Junkers was blown to pieces on an airfield as it was about to take off.

TUNNEL BLOCKED

Photographs taken of the tunnel at Saumur, just south of the River Loire, bombed by the R.A.F. on Thursday night, show that there is a hole 100 feet long in the roof of the tunnel, which completely blocks the south entrance, and that there are two other craters in the deep cutting leading to the tunnel.

LATEST NEWS

"ALLIED PROGRESS CONTINUES"

Allied aircraft now operating from bases in beachhead.

New York Radio said at midnight that Ninth U.S. Army Air Force had established H.Q. on French territory.

Trevieres, five miles from coast, and halfway between Isigny and Bayeux, captured.

Allied progress continues along whole front.

Large number aircraft continued offensive action over battle area.

DUNKIRK LANDING COMING

—SAYS BERLIN

THE Germans expect a new large-scale Allied invasion on the Channel coast, possibly in the Dunkirk-Ostend area during the next few days.

Special Canadian formations, airborne troops and tank divisions are ready for the new landings, said the Official German News Agency.

New Allied landings in Europe are imminent, according to Mr. Carlton Hayes, the U.S. Ambassador to Spain.

In a speech in Madrid he said: "The Herculean struggle is now rapidly nearing its climax."

Plans to meet a possible Allied invasion of Norway have been discussed at a meeting between General Falkenhorst, the Nazi commander in Norway, and many high German officers in Oslo, according to Norwegian underground reports reaching Stockholm.

At least 21 German generals are reported to have attended this invasion conference.—B.U.P.

Panic Flight by Nazis in Italy

Allies Sweeping on Towards Florence

From GEORGE HARRISON,
"News of the World" War Correspondent in Italy

DRIVING relentlessly north after Kesselring's fleeing forces, the Eighth and Fifth Armies are now more than halfway between beflagged Rome and Italy's second greatest pride—the lovely city of Florence.

Leaving only skeleton batches of snipers and demolition men to cover their retreat, the Germans are withdrawing in panic-stricken haste.

The speed of our chase after them is now governed largely by the rapidity with which we can overcome the widespread trail of demolished roads and bridges left by the Nazis.

In a 40-mile advance in one area British troops were unable even to contact the enemy, so quickly is he withdrawing.

It is just a month since we launched our offensive against the Gustav Line at Cassino. In this brief space of time a great deal of water has flowed under the gaps where bridges used to be, and men of the mighty Eighth and Fifth Armies have inexorably marched a third of the way to the Brenner Pass, gateway to Germany itself.

Bitter fighting lies ahead, but Kesselring has already lost the greater part of his army and much of his first-class material, and despite the fact that he is able to choose his own places to stand and fight in terrain most suitable, his defence position is becoming critical.

Distances on maps, great though they may be, are beginning to mean nothing out here to the confident Allies, to whom the news from France is a spur to even more terrific endeavours.

NEWS ON TREES

Flashes from radio bulletins about the progress of Allied forces in the West are being written in big letters on sheets of cardboard and nailed on trees and telegraph poles along the route of our advance, so that the troops can read them while sweeping fast on Kesselring's heels.

Allied air forces are plastering German traffic and communication lines as they withdraw.

Roaring low over roads yesterday, fighter-bombers wiped out 250 vehicles, damaged another 150, and destroyed 300 railway trucks, many packed with material the enemy was trying to get away.

Among prisoners taken are 14-year-old cooks, butchers, and bakers, who have been brought in to help fill the enormous gaps in Nazi strength.

Mackensen's 14th Army, fleeing north-west, has been thrown out of contact with the Tenth Army, which is consequently having to provide its own flank protection.

The Tenth Army losses have been very heavy, and the Hermann Goering Division, which was one of its mainstays, has been reduced to shredded batches.

"PURSUIT CONTINUES"

ALLIES CAPTURE MORE IMPORTANT TOWNS

Capture of several more important towns by both the Fifth and Eighth Armies is reported in the latest Allied communique from Italy, which says:

"**Army**: The pursuit of the German 14th Army by the Fifth Army continues. Viterbo, Tuscania and Tarquinia have been occupied (Viterbo is 45 miles north of Rome).

"Troops of the Eighth Army are still engaged with enemy rearguards east of the Tiber. Moricone and Arsoli have been taken.

"Our troops in the Adriatic sector are now on the move and have crossed the River Foro at some places, and have occupied Giuliano, Guardiagrele, and Orsogna.

"**Air**.—Strong forces of heavy bombers attacked objectives in the Munich area and oil storage installations at Porto Marghera.

"Medium bombers struck at numerous bridges throughout Central Italy.

"Light bombers and fighter bombers were active against roads, bridges, gun positions, motor transport, and horse-drawn vehicles in the battle area, railway lines and rolling stock, and the harbour at Porto Ferraia.

"In these operations 34 enemy aircraft were destroyed. Twenty-three of ours, including 18 heavy bombers, are missing."

Von Mackensen's 14th Army is officially described as withdrawing from the area north of Rome "in a complete disorganised fashion." Stragglers and deserters are coming in hourly.

The Allied Command, for the first time, officially declared yesterday that a "catastrophe" had befallen Kesselring's forces in Italy.

Vichy Radio put out this excuse for the German retreat: "It appears that Marshal Kesselring's withdrawals in Italy are part of a vast strategic plan."—Reuter and A.P.

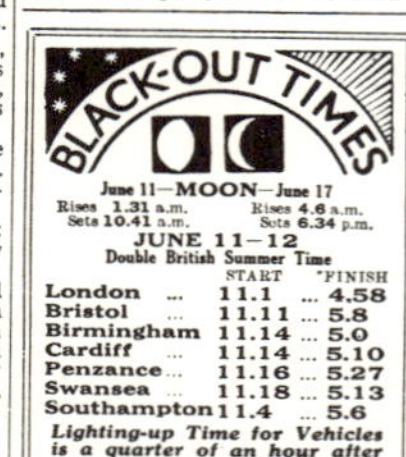

BLACK-OUT TIMES

June 11—MOON—June 17
Rises 1.31 a.m. Sets 10.41 a.m. — Rises 4.6 a.m. Sets 6.34 p.m.

JUNE 11–12
Double British Summer Time

	START	FINISH
London	11.1	4.58
Bristol	11.11	5.8
Birmingham	11.14	5.0
Cardiff	11.14	5.10
Penzance	11.16	5.27
Swansea	11.18	5.13
Southampton	11.4	5.6

Lighting-up Time for Vehicles is a quarter of an hour after Black-out Time.

Radio Programmes on Page 7

Armed Enemy Trawlers Sunk Off Holland

WHILE on offensive patrol off the coast of Holland early yesterday morning, light coastal forces of the Royal Navy, under the command of Lieut.-Comdr. K. Gemmell, D.S.C., R.N.V.R., engaged four heavily-armed enemy trawlers south-west of Imuiden.

Three of the enemy ships were sunk by torpedo, while many hits with gunfire were obtained on the fourth, which was last seen making for the enemy coast in a damaged condition, says an Admiralty communique.

Later three other armed trawlers were sighted, apparently searching for survivors from the vessels which had been sunk.

Our ships again attacked, and, after being hit with a torpedo, one of the trawlers was seen to sink.

In the course of this engagement one of our motor torpedo boats was sunk.

There were only two casualties. The remainder of the ship's company were rescued by other ships of the force.

The next-of-kin of casualties are being informed as soon as possible.

The remainder of our ships all returned safely to harbour, having suffered no casualties.

Lieut.-Comdr. Gemmell, who comes from Bridlington, Yorks, was awarded the D.S.C. 12 months ago for bravery in the Channel.

One hundred and forty survivors from the German destroyer, sunk on Friday night, when a force of German destroyers were intercepted off Ushant, were picked up by a British destroyer of the Tribal class, H.M.S. Ashanti.

In the action in company were H.M.S. Ashanti, H.M.S. Tartar, H.M. Canadian ships Haida and Huron, and H.M.S. Eskimo.

A second enemy destroyer was driven ashore in flames, while two others escaped after receiving damage by gunfire.

STRAITS: IMPROVEMENT

There was a slight improvement in the weather in the Straits of Dover yesterday, although it was threatening and changeable in the afternoon

For some time heavy black storm-clouds hung over the sea, but later it was brighter again.

The wind, which went round from south-west to north-west, was still light and the sea smooth, with good visibility, though earlier it had been lumpy. At times the French coast could be distantly seen from this side. The barometer had advanced a little since early morning.

NIGHT EDITION ★★★★★ MARKET OPENING SCHOOL NEWS ON PAGE 28

The Sun

Copyright, 1944, by The New York Sun, Inc.

LATE NEWS SCHOOLS — PICTURES

Today partly cloudy with scattered showers this afternoon and evening; rather humid. Temperatures—Minimum, 62; Maximum, 71. Sun rises 5:24 A. M. Sun sets 8:29 P. M. (Detailed weather report on page 38.)

VOL. 111—NO. 240. Entered as Second Class Matter Post Office, New York, N. Y. NEW YORK, WEDNESDAY, JUNE 14, 1944. FIVE CENTS EVERYWHERE

BRITISH PLUNGE DEEP BEHIND FOE

New York Boys in Normandy Battle

Brooklyn Lad, 17, Was Less Scared Under Fire Than He Had Expected to Be.

By GAULT MacGOWAN.

Special to The New York Sun.

With the United States Navy, June 13 (Delayed).—A lad who once sailed paper boats on the Bronx River and dreamed that he was John Paul Jones, a 17-year-old kid from Brooklyn who was not so scared as he had thought he'd be, and one of the Grand street boys—these were among the New Yorkers who saw and participated in the hell that was D day on the coast of Normandy.

The youthful John Paul Jones who was sailing paper boats just a few years ago was Seaman Joseph Gasparro of 3011 Schley avenue, the Bronx. He was aboard the third ship that hit the beach with the first division. He saw a small ship next to his own blown up by a mine, saw men killed, saw others drop into the sea and swim for their lives.

"I never saw a fight like that before," said the Grand street boy, Nathan Levine, whose home is still at 420 Grand street. He's a ship's cook out here on the English Channel, cooking the meals that feed the boys on the way to Normandy.

"Mines were exploding on the beaches, shells were shrieking overhead and bombs dropped from the skies, one ahead and one astern," he said.

Reinforcements by the Carload.

They are going over by the carload — reinforcements to widen and deepen our beachheads. The German General Staff would dearly love to pick up their morning papers and read the figures of carloadings from English ports, but for the present they, like you, can only guess at the figures. Until the Army has secured the beachhead, the building up of the beaches now won depends upon the Navy's success in keeping the Channel open.

Into the beaches on D day went Pharmacist's Mate Arthur Krener of 1471 West Ninth street, Brooklyn, to deliver urgently needed medical supplies.

"I didn't know it when I landed," he said, "but a colonel told me, 'Get out quick; you are in the line of fire.' So we pulled out, leaving our stuff with the beach battalion.

"The beach battalions did a helluva job rescuing the wounded. We picked up lots of them to take back—Canadians, Commandos, Army men and one French civilian 70 years old, who was was wounded in the attack but who was determined to be the first to greet us. He had two boys with the Underground."

Brooklyn Boy Is 17.

The Navy's coolest seaman was Vincent Jafuri, 329 37th street, Brooklyn, who is only 17 years

Continued on Page 7.

ARMY FLYER GETS 30 YEARS IN PRISON

Santa Ana, Cal., June 14 (A. P.).—Convicted by Army general court-martial on specifications alleging statutory rape, three other morals offenses, bigamy and larceny, Capt. Morrison J. Wilkinson Jr. today had this to say to reporters of his sentence to thirty years' imprisonment at hard labor:

"Pretty severe, I think, for a slight indiscretion."

Wilkinson also was ordered dismissed from the service. He was acquitted on four other morals counts by the court panel of ten superior officers, which reached its verdict last night after deliberating an hour and thirty-five minutes.

The 28-year-old former China war theater flyer is confined to a jail at this air base pending review of the seven-day trial's evidence by regional and Washington military authorities and by the President, expected to require several weeks.

With stony calm, his shoulders back, Wilkinson heard the verdict and, a moment later, the click of handcuffs on his wrists. But he appeared morose after he had been led from the court room.

Two Hurt When Cab And Jeep Collide

A taxicab driver and his passenger were both injured today in a collision with a Navy jeep at Madison avenue and 48th street. The taxicab was overturned. The driver, David Siskind of 840 Stebbins avenue, the Bronx, suffering a leg injury, and the passenger, Arnold Rittenberg of Albany, suffering a head injury, were taken to City Hospital for treatment and observation.

The jeep was operated by Seaman David Trader, who was accompanied by a Navy lieutenant.

CHURCHILL DELAYS COMMONS DEBATE ON DE GAULLE ISSUE

Hints U. S.-British Stand May Be Clarified at Later Date.

London, June 14 (A. P.). — Prime Minister Winston Churchill won today a postponement of a full-dress debate in the House of Commons on the controversial issue of Anglo-American relations with the French Committee of National Liberation, parrying a demand for a showdown with the assertion that "it would do more harm than good now." In his first appearance before the House since his daring trip to the beachhead in Normandy on Monday, Mr. Churchill made only scant reference to the progress of the war, declaring that any anxiety over the De Gaulle Committee question "should properly be directed to our gallant soldiers and to the great operations which are in progress, which give hope, as well as anxiety."

The Prime Minister contended that full discussion of the subject should be held off until negotiations among the French Committee, the United States and Britain can be completed. The House of Commons turned to other subjects after Mr. Churchill said that he would not be seeking to delay the debate "if I had no hopes of a better solution than I can announce at the present time."

"The Government has taken great trouble over the conduct of this business and, on the whole, it may be said that it has been conducted with success," the Prime Minister declared, amid cheers. "When you look at the advance in Italy and the extraordinary advance across the channel, a fair-minded man would consider that the administration has a right to the confidence of the House when they state that they do not want this particular subject to be discussed."

Several Questions Posed.

Mr. Churchill, just back from a daring visit to the Normandy beachhead, took the floor in response to several questions pending before the House on subjects relating to Gen. de Gaulle. There has been a persistent editorial demand in the British press—a demand which has been intensified since the French leader's recent arrival in London—for a clearer understanding between

Continued on Page 2.

In The Sun Today

School News Appears in the Night Edition.

Dave Boone Says:

My idea of a complete "phony" is the feller who takes off his hat when the flag passes, stands when they play the national anthem, says the boys on the battlefronts are doing a great job and sounds off on what we are going to do to the world, and then takes a "let George do it" attitude in the buying of War Bonds.

Why, a person who even has to be urged to come across in a War Bond drive ain't fit to be mentioned in the same breath with America and its fighting men. He's like a fellow who, if he were drowning, would resent a slight charge for the rope thrown to him.

Of course, the man who buys them and then goes out and sells them pretty quickly instead of holding them ain't much better. He's just playing a trick on his country and on its soldiers and sailors.

But he's playing the biggest trick on himself, because he can't see that War Bonds are the best investment he can make, that they're a protection for the future and that a chump who would rush to sell 'em is like a fellow who would hock a life preserver in a hurricane at sea.

I hope Hitler's getting reports on how successful this Fifth War Bond drive is. Anything to increase his state of nerves.

A PLANE, AND NOT A FRIENDLY ONE

Associated Press Wirephoto, from United States Signal Corps Radiophoto.

Prime Minister Churchill (see the cigar) and other Allied leaders watch an enemy plane zoom overhead as they stand somewhere on a beachhead in France. With the Prime Minister, left to right, are: Jan C. Smuts, South African Premier; Gen. Sir Bernard L. Montgomery, Allied ground commander, and Sir Alan Brooke, chief of the British Imperial Staff.

FIFTH TROOPS FLANK ORTEBELLO IN DRIVE NORTH

Road Junction Beyond City Captured—Eighth Gaining Too.

Rome, June 14 (A. P.).—Fifth Army elements have swung around the heavily defended strong point of Orbetello, seventy-one miles northwest of Rome, and captured the important junction of Highways No. 1 and 74, some four and a half miles beyond the town, Allied Headquarters announced today.

Reconnaissance elements pushed still further north.

"In the coastal sector our troops, having encountered increased resistance south of Orbetello, developed their strength in the mountains and late June 12 cut the road junction of Highways No. 1 and 74. Reconnaissance elements are moving farther north," said a headquarters communique.

[This movement presumably blocked the retreat route of the Germans defending Orbetello.]

To the east the Eighth Army advanced 60 miles north of Rome. Gains also were made both east and west of Lake Bolsena and Allied troops were closing in on Narni, seven and a half miles below Terni and 43 miles due north of Rome.

Latera Gathered In.

The town of Latera, four miles northeast of Valentano, was gathered in by Fifth Army units and the advance moved on toward Gradioli, less than two miles farther northeast.

Other Fifth Army forces were closing in on Bolsena, on the eastern shore of the lake.

Meanwhile the Eighth Army

Continued on Page 7.

French Undermine Nazi Plans

Rising Resistance Forces Germans to Clamp Rigid Military Rule on Central Zone.

Madrid, June 14 (A. P.).—Reports out of underground France asserted today that a methodic, persistent rising by the greater part of the French nation is undermining the Germans' best laid plans to hold the Allied invasion.

These advices, filtering through many points on the Franco-Spanish frontier and through diplomatic channels, said that guerrillas and the organized underground were actively leading the French in making trouble and yet more trouble for the Germans.

That the Germans recognized the danger was demonstrated by an order placing eleven departments in central France and parts of four others under the same military rules as those prevailing in the Atlantic wall zone.

Tarbes Firmly Held.

From Irun came a report that Maquis still firmly held the city of Tarbes, in the foothills of the Pyrenees, thereby cutting off a large section of southern France from the Mediterranean road and rail route so important to the Germans. Travelers said the German occupation command was too busy with other troubles at present to send forces needed to recapture Tarbes.

It was reported that Limoges also was held by these Maquis fighters, while northeast of Bordeaux, Angouleme and Periguex were out of communication with the rest of France. In the Limousin Mountains and the plateau Millevaches in Vienne and Correze departments a powerful guerrilla army was reported organizing with arms and munitions supplied by plane.

From the Mediterranean frontier at Portbou it was reported guerrillas and Maquis of Savoy

Continued on Page 6.

CLARK IS TRAILING IN IDAHO PRIMARY

Boise, Idaho, June 14 (A. P.).—Glen H. Taylor, onetime Idaho cowpuncher and later a radio entertainer, jumped ahead today in the race for the Democratic senatorial nomination in the Idaho primary as Senator D. Worth Clark trailed in third place.

Taylor, 40-year-old Pocatello resident, moved into the lead after James H. Hawley, Boise attorney, had held the lead for the first four hours of counting. During the campaign Hawley accused Clark of voting against national preparedness measures.

Totals for 207 of Idaho's 845 precincts give Taylor 3,002, Hawley 2,872, Clark 2,679, John Cornell 578.

The Republican senatorial nomination contest saw Gov. C. A. Bottolfsen pile up a formidable lead over Ben Johnson, 37-year-old Preston attorney, a political unknown. Bottolfsen polled 7,872 votes in 207 precincts to Johnson's 4,363.

No opposition was furnished for the State's two representatives, Compton I. White of Clark Fork, Democrat, and Henry C. Dworshak, Burley newspaper publisher, Republican.

MONTGOMERY'S MEN 23 MILES INLAND

Americans Force Nazis Back Several Miles West of Carentan—Enemy Concedes Loss of Towns—Counter-blows Continue.

Supreme Headquarters, Allied Expeditionary Force, June 14 (A. P.).—American and British armored attacks have cut through German defenses in Normandy at two points, it was announced today, the British tanks outflanking Caen in a drive that carried twenty-three miles inland and the Americans smashing the Germans back several miles west of Carentan.

Germans defending Cherbourg against the American drive on the port, counter-attacked at Montebourg, fourteen miles to the southeast, and the Americans and Germans were fighting in that city's streets.

Striking as he often did against Field Marshal Erwin Rommel in the African desert, Gen. Sir Bernard L. Montgomery, Allied ground commander, sent tanks rumbling south of Bayeux along the central sector of the front. They smashed through Caumont and Villers-Bocage, then turned east and north to drive into the German flank protecting Caen on the west. They struck with great effect, Supreme Headquarters said.

Caen itself was under heavy naval bombardment from Allied warships. A flyer who flew over the city said it seemed "scarcely possible for life to exist there."

Villers-Bocage stands athwart a main highway to Caen, sixteen miles to the southwest. Caumont, seven miles west and slightly north of Villers-Bocage, commands a secondary route, also leading to Caen. The sudden Allied drive apparently by-passed Tilly-sur-Deulles.

Nazis Counter British Thrust.

A fierce German counter-attack was made on British forces in newly captured Troarn in an attempt to blunt or cut off a column threatening to flank Caen on the east. This Allied thrust is in the Montgomery tradition of attacking on the flanks to cut off a large force of Germans and take them prisoner or destroy them rather than push them back.

On the western end of the Allied beachhead, now enlarged to a 100-mile fighting front, Americans used armored forces to break a deadlock at Carentan, six miles from the sea. The German radio acknowledged a Nazi withdrawal west and north of Carentan to spare German lives. This several-mile withdrawal

Continued on Page 3.

WEATHER IDEAL IN THE CHANNEL

London, June 14 (A. P.).—Weather conditions in the Dover Strait area were excellent today, with a warm sun shining from a cloudless sky and visibility excellent.

A light southwesterly breeze rippled the sea and the barometer was rising steadily. The night was unusually cool, but by 8 A. M. the temperature had risen to 70 degrees.

BMT Seat Grabbers Fined $10 Each

Three men charged with climbing through the windows of subway cars in the Queens Plaza station of the BMT in order to get seats were fined $10 each in Brooklyn-Queens Night Court last night.

They were Henry Rice, 24 years old, of 40-37 Lawrence street, Flushing; Peter De Marco, 20, 235 East Fifth street, Manhattan, and William Berndt, 50, of 32-42 33d street, Astoria.

1000 U. S. Planes Pound Nazis

Fortresses and Liberators Attack Behind Lines in France and Belgium.

Supreme Headquarters, Allied Expeditionary Force, June 14 (A. P.).—A force of around 1,000 Flying Fortresses and Liberators spilt up today and attacked the oil refinery at Emmerich, Germany, and enemy air bases and bridges in France and Belgium. The assaults extended the simultaneous bombing of the battle area and the German homeland around the clock.

The American force, aggregating upward of 1,500 bombers and fighters, attacked, among other targets, the Le Bourget and Creil airfields at Paris, Etampes-Mondesir and Chateaudun, in France; Brussels-Melsbroeck and Eindhoven, in Belgium. Meanwhile another American heavy bomber force, the German radio said, surged up from Italy for an attack on Adolf Hitler's Europe, which had undergone heavy attacks from the south in the Munich area both yesterday and last night.

Weather Helps Airmen.

The air armadas took full advantage of ideal weather in stepping up the assaults on German fighting forces and strategic targets far inland. It was described here as "a marvelous air-support campaign, getting more satisfactory every day."

British bombers based on Italy struck the Munich area during the night, a few hours after

Continued on Page 2.

DAILY MIRROR, Saturday, June 17, 1944.

Daily Mirror

JUNE 17

No. 12,636
ONE PENNY
Registered at the G.P.O. as a Newspaper.

Allies are massing strength for big blow in France

WHILE Allied forces increase their threat to the Germans in the Cherbourg Peninsula and probe forward on other sectors, General Montgomery is piling up strength for his first all-out attack.

He is patiently massing his "shock" weapon heavy artillery.

Montgomery will not attack until he is ready That is his invariable policy—and it saves lives.

The Allied air fleets have struck two big blows to back his plans.

The enemy's Channel nuisance fleet is believed to have been wiped out by the RAF's "tidal wave" attack on Le Havre. Since this bombing there has been no sign of the three torpedo boats and ten E-boats which were in the port

Sealing-off Port

Bombers are sealing off the main routes to North-West France by smashing the bridges across the Loire, which runs across country well south of the battle area.

The Americans advancing in the Cherbourg Peninsula made further gains yesterday

They are now only two and half miles from St. Sauveur, which is on the enemy's main road and rail escape route from the north.

Seizure of this position would leave the Germans with only a roundabout road running south through Le Haye. And the loss of Le Haye, which is threatened by Americans only six miles away, would almost completely cut the Peninsula off across the neck.

Panzers Rushed Up

The Germans have rushed up the 17th Panzer Grenadier Division in a last-minute attempt to hold the escape routes, and which are now within range of all types of mortars as well as field artillery.

Another American advance has been made three miles south-east of Carentan to capture a road junction.

There was little change yesterday along the central "wedge" front round to Tilly and Caen.

Allied patrols moving south of Caumont have met the Germans in force about two miles outside the town, in tank country where heavy battles were fought, until armour was withdrawn on both sides for regrouping.

The German News Agency said last night: German troops

Continued on Back Page

Midnight Communique

MIDNIGHT communique from Allied Supreme H.Q. announced:

Advances by Allied forces westward from Pone L'Abe in the Cherbourg Peninsula have continued.

Our troops have local successes in the Tilly sector, but the town remained in enemy hands.

Active patrolling has been kept up by both sides.

Adverse weather during the morning restricted air activity.

H.M.S. Ramillies yesterday engaged and silenced a battery at Beneville, on our eastern flank, after an hours' duel.

H.M.S. Nelson engaged enemy batetry north of Le Havre which had been firing into the anchorage.

Heavy bombardments in support of the armies near Isigny and Carentan carried out by U.S.S. Texas, U.S.S. Nevada and U.S.S. Arkansas.

BERLIN yesterday described the pilotless plane as Germany's "first secret weapon."

It was not until two-and-a-half hours after Mr. Morrison had made his statement in the House of Commons disclosing the existence of the plane, that German News sources referred to it.

Earlier they had said that the night's raid was made by "fast German bombers," while the German communique had said that South England and the London area were attacked with "a new type of explosive of very heavy calibre."

Hans Fritzsche, Berlin radio's star political commentator, came on the air last night especially to talk about the pilotless planes.

"What the German people have hoped for and anticipated

(Continued on back page)

NON-SENSE

One Nazi in a Midland hospital objected to the ward to which he was taken. He demanded to be moved to German-occupied England.

KING SAILS THERE

Investiture six miles behind front line

LANDED IN A DUCK—LUNCH WITH MONTY

THE King visited the battle areas in Normandy yesterday, lunched with General Montgomery at his advanced H.Q., and afterwards held an open air investiture less than six miles from the front line, where fierce fighting was going on.

He made his historic journey to France and back in the cruiser Arethusa.

The King, climbing nimbly out of the duck which brought him ashore, jumped on to the sandy beach where "Monty," in battle dress and his famous two-badge black beret, was waiting to greet him.

"Good morning, your Majesty. Welcome to France," said the General as he shook hands with the King. It was a great moment in history.

The King returned safely to a south-coast naval port last night.

He landed on a beach just west of Courselles, where the Canadians stormed ashore; and while we were in the motor launch transferring from Arethusa to the Duck, 6in. shells trom the cruiser Hawkins, which we had seen firing on our way in, tore high over the King's head, engaging a land target at a range of ten miles.

An official drawing of the German pilotless aircraft representing a wing span of 16ft., length 25ft. 4½in. Probable bomb load is 1,000lb.

More flying bomb attacks expected but —carry on!

THE raids by flying-bombs or pilotless planes which hit parts of Southern England this week "will probably continue," Home Secretary Morrison told the nation yesterday.

While exaggerated importance should not be attached to the new development, the public are urged to follow this safety advice issued by the Ministry of Home Security:—

When the engine stops and the light at the end of the machine goes out, it may mean that the explosion will soon follow—perhaps in five to fifteen seconds.

Take refuge from blast. Even though indoors, keep out of the way of blast, and use the most solid protection available.

Last night the Home Secretary issued this call to the country:

"The enemy has begun to use his secret weapon—the pilotless aircraft. The damage it has caused has been relatively small, and the new weapon will not interfere with our war effort and our sure and steady march to victory.

"The enemy's aim is clearly, in view of the difficulty of his military situation, to try to upset our morale and interfere with our work.

"It is essential that there should be the least possible interruption in all work vital to the country's needs at this time, and the Government counsel is that everyone should get on with his or her job in the ordinary way and only take cover when danger is imminent.

"There is already an efficient system for giving warning of imminent danger in factories.

"There is no reason to think that raids by this weapon will be worse than, or indeed as heavy as, the raids with which the people of this country are already familiar and have borne so bravely."

Counter-measures are being taken against the flying bomb.

Meanwhile, the usual siren warning will be given whether the enemy planes are pilotless or not.

But your radio set will give you a rough guide to the type of raider.

If the strength of your re-

Continued on Back Page

He went to paint—but how he fought

From S. L. SOLON
WITH THE ALLIED FORCES IN NORMANDY Friday

WAR Artist Captain Richards came to France to paint

He wanted to see it from the beginning, and he wanted to see it whole, so he came in with the men who got here first—the Sixth Airborne Division.

But the climate was not very suitable for painting when he got here. The airborne men were being shelled and mortared and the fighting was ferocious

Captain Richards put down his drawing pencil and took out his gun.

For several shattering hours the fight went on.

All the officers in Captain Richards's unit were killed or wounded

The artist took over the platoon and, with them held the position until relief came.

When a request came that he should return to his art the C.O. said that Captain Richards was too good a combat officer

However, now that the situation has simmered down, Captain Richards—on orders—has returned to his job as war artist.

Sunday Pictorial

June 18, 1944
TWOPENCE
No. 1,527

CHERBOURG TRAP IS CLOSING: GERMANS ON WAY OUT

TENS OF THOUSANDS OF NAZIS IN THE CHERBOURG PENINSULA FACE A DISASTER WHICH COULD COST THEM THOUSANDS OF MEN IF THEY HUNG ON TOO LONG.

Allied troops—pushing westwards—have seized a vital little town named St. Sauveur—control-point of the only remaining inland escape route from the great sea base of the peninsula of Cherbourg.

And last night, we were already beyond it—on high ground overlooking the west coast. The Germans in the peninsula have counter-attacked vainly to avoid this relentlessly closing trap

Americans, driving down a road that is constantly shelled, are at one point less than 10,000 yards from the west coast beaches.

Will they stay to defend Cherbourg to the last—as they did with such calamatous results at Sebastopol?

Already there is evidence that they are going to get out quickly. For yesterday Ninth Army Air Force planes, carrying the first bombs loaded to the plane from the beachhead, struck at German convoys trying to evacuate the Cherbourg peninsula.

Some of the bloodiest fighting has been on the Caen sector, where British troops have gained a hard-won foothold in the woods just outside this German-held town.

The weather? When our troops talk about Flaming June, they don't mean it—that way!

The fact is, Flaming June has let us down almost since D-Day

It's slowed down our advance—but, as a SHAEF spokesman said last night: "The Allies are fighting well within themselves, and our prospects—eleven days after our first landings on French soil—are improving every hour."

BATTLE FRONT LATEST—Back Page.

This Is The Price of Freedom!

They have come back to the house that was their home, here among the battlefields of Normandy. They are sad, but they know that baby Pierre will now be a citizen of a liberated France.

"You know, Smithers, I sometimes wonder if this flypaper idea of the General's isn't the answer to the whole thing."

BOMB SECRET OUT?

THE Germans' new pilotless aeroplane — the robot bomb—beat us by a few days.

For over a year some of our best scientists have been working in a key Government aircraft department to find the answer to this "secret weapon"

They had all but got the answer when the bombs began to arrive. Now work is going on at even greater pressure, though the indications are that the Germans are unable to launch these bombs on a really big scale.

Attacks went on at intervals all yesterday afternoon, following a night of raids. But the number of planes arriving was much fewer than on Friday and they had a hot reception.

Next stage of our defence will involve powerful radio transmitters mounted on lorries or railway wagons.

Experiments to beat the new device have been going on in a remote part of the countryside, and yesterday General Sir Frederick Pile, Commander-in-Chief of the A.A. Command, was on a gun-site watching our new methods.

As Captain Harold Balfour, Under - Secretary for Air, said yesterday: "We shall soon get the better of this weapon.

HOW THE BOMB WORKS—PAGE 3.

DAILY MIRROR, Wednesday, June 21, 1944.

Daily Mirror

JUNE 21

No. 12,639
ONE PENNY
Registered at the G.P.O. as a Newspaper.

Americans 3½ miles off Cherbourg in big break-through

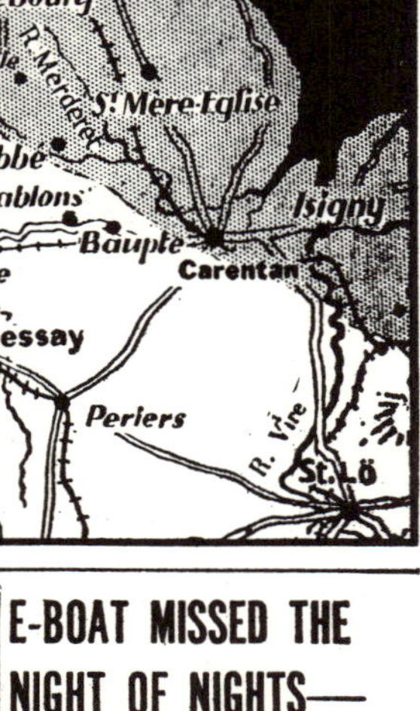

GERMAN LINES SMASHED

Midnight communique

MIDNIGHT communique from Allied Supreme H.Q. announced:—

Allied troops are attacking the outer defences of Cherbourg.

Montebourg liberated. Our forces are on three sides of Valognes, where heavy fighting is in progress.

Our positions in Tilly area firm. Very heavy fighting continued near Hottot yesterday.

Bad weather in battle area limited air operations until midday. Fighter-bombers and bombers, with fighter escort, attacked flying-bomb bases in Pas de Calais area during morning. Several hits scored on these and other military installations.

Other formations of fighter-bombers hit bridge over Loire near Nantes, destroyed railway bridge at Granville, and bombed rolling stock and motor transport at Trappes, south-west of Paris.

Fighter-bombers also successfully attacked railway trucks at number of places both north and south of Chartres.

Twelve F.W. 190s attempted to interfere with this operation. Five of them destroyed in air combat for loss of three of our aircraft.

BEACHHEAD HAS MORE PLANES THAN JOBS TO KEEP THEM BUSY

There are so many Allied planes now on the Normandy beachhead that there aren't enough targets to go round, reports a British United Press correspondent at Ninth Air Force Advance H.Q.

"We've now more planes available than we had work laid out for them," said one officer.

ALLIED SPEARHEAD PATROLS WERE LAST NIGHT FIGHTING INSIDE THE CHERBOURG DEFENCES THREE AND A HALF MILES FROM THE GREAT PORT.

Main forces were only a mile and a half behind, following up through an outer defence ring running five miles inland.

Shells from Long Tom guns were screaming over their heads into the enemy lines.

Unconfirmed reports said that St. Martin le Greard, four miles south of Cherbourg, had been taken.

An earlier dispatch from the battlefront stated that the German position had become very disorganised, suggesting that the speed of the U.S. advance up the centre of the peninsula might force a quick decision against the 30,000 trapped enemy troops.

Scrambling Back

The Cherbourg defence zone is powerful and could be strongly held by determined troops. Inside the first defence ring is a second line of fortifications two miles inland, and in the town itself are port defences with seven big bastions.

But the quality of the trapped German troops as last-ditch fighters has been doubted, and yesterday many of them were still scrambling back to the defence zone in face of advances along the whole of the American front.

Rapid progress was made on both flanks of the U.S. troops which thrust up the middle

The right wing took Valognes and Montebourg and swept up the coast well past Quineville.

On the left, troops which were a long way behind the spearheads started a sweep up the west coast.

Last night the whole line was moving to wrap itself round the Cherbourg outer defence ring.

Berlin's version of the situation yesterday was that all the German forces had "disengaged according to plan to the enlarged fortification zone of Cherbourg."

When the Allies get in the port they are likely to find a very devastated area.

Air reconnaissance has shown tremendous damage among port installations as a result of demolitions and bombardment by Allied warships.

There was no sign last night that the Germans are trying to evacuate the base.

On the British sector of the battlefront, troops which took Tilly and pushed two miles to the south-west to Hottot have held their ground in the face of strong counter-attacks launched by tanks and infantry.

They are now firmly established.

At Caen, the Germans still hold strong positions round the town but it is believed they may have evacuated the place itself because of the heavy bombardment of the past two weeks.

Confident

British headquarters are becoming more and more confident that the Germans may not be able to mount the expected counter-attack and that the Allies will be able to maintain the initiative throughout.

This is due to the bombing of enemy communications, the speed of the beachhead build up, and the activities of the underground movement.—Reuter.

U.S. NOT TO BUILD OIL LINE: WILL LEND MONEY

The U.S. Government has decided not to construct the proposed 1,200-mile oil pipeline in Saudi-Arabia.

It has, however, offered loans to private companies to help defray the costs of the project—about £4,000,000.

If such companies build the line, Britain and America will control production, much as they now regulate production in domestic oilfields.

E-BOAT MISSED THE NIGHT OF NIGHTS—AND IT'S A MYSTERY

Every night, for weeks before D-Day, a German E-boat made a reconnaissance dash from Cherbourg to the English coast and back.

Every night except one, that is . . . And that was the night before the Allies landed.

SHAEF authorities have no explanation as to why the Germans did not send the boat out that night

Veteran air crews "pin-point" hidden buzz-bomb runways

FOLLOWING up a "blanket" onslaught by American bombers, RAF and Dutch veteran air crews "pinpointed"—and pounded to rubble—buzz-bomb runways hidden in forests in the Pas de Calais yesterday.

Then, just to make sure, Typhoons swept in to send rockets hissing down on the targets.

And last night an RAF officer said: "It was quite an effort."

Almost the whole galaxy of Allied air power was called in for the great onslaught.

It was the first day of really good weather since the buzz bombs appeared, and full use was made of it:—

1—*In the morning about 500 U.S. Fortresses and Liberators plastered the "secret weapon" line, which runs from a point thirty miles south of Calais to seven miles north of Abbeville.*

2—*Two hundred Marauders and Havocs added their quota of bombs.*

3—*Later, the veteran air crews, with years of experience in precision bombing, flew Mitchells and Bostons in pin-point attacks on the carefully camouflaged runways.*

4—*Then dive-bombing Mustangs and rocketfiring Typhoons swept in.*

The "pin-pointing" crews went in through a mass of flak to hit their targets squarely.

The strength of the flak was a clear indication that the buzz-bombs had been traced to their source.

To meet the Allied attack the Germans produced another ineffective "secret weapon."

It consisted of a square

Continued on Back Page

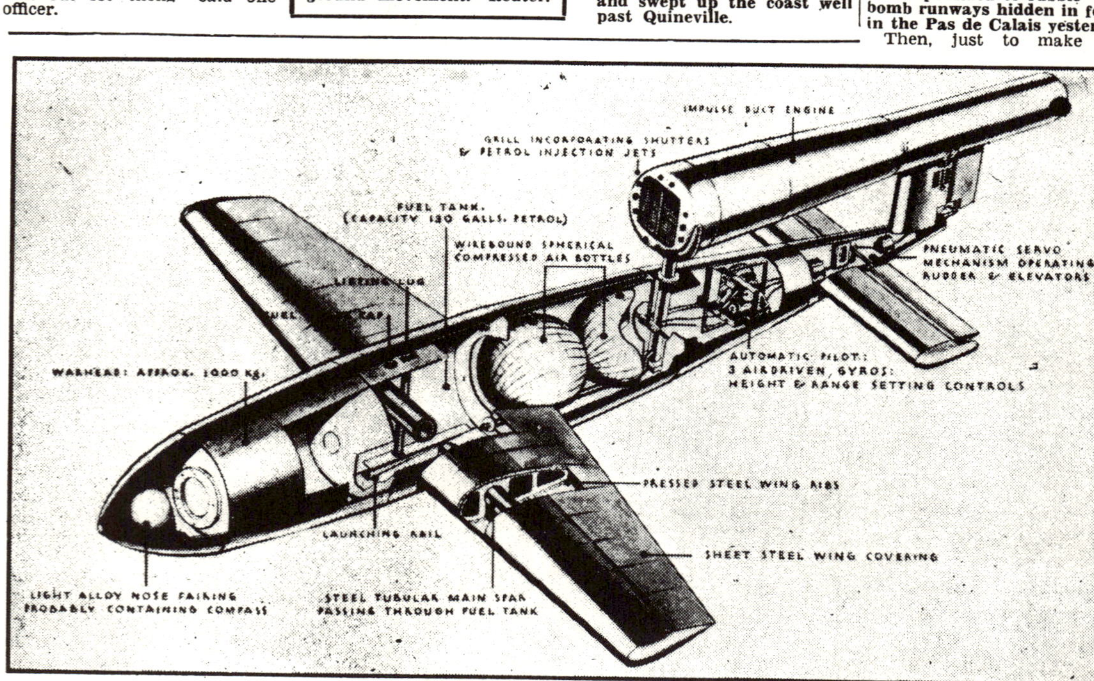

Official diagram issued last night showing how the buzz-bomb is made up.

Average net paid circulation for May exceeded
Daily---2,000,000
Sunday-3,700,000

DAILY NEWS
Copr. 1944 by News Syndicate Co. Inc. NEW YORK'S PICTURE NEWSPAPER Trade Mark Reg. U. S. Pat. Off.

★ ★ ★ FINAL

Vol. 25. No. 312 New York, Friday, June 23, 1944★ 44 Main + 12 Brooklyn Pages 2 Cents IN CITY LIMITS | 3 CENTS Elsewhere

YANKS CHARGE AT HEART OF CHERBOURG

Story on Page 3

Yanks at Cherbourg

Engineers Push Bulldozer In Wake of U. S. Infantrymen

Almost on the heels of the infantrymen, an Army engineers' bulldozer clears a path through a rubble-packed street in Valognes, on road to Cherbourg. Yesterday American troops were engaged in hand-to-hand fighting in outskirts of Cherbourg and were attacking the great port's seaward defenses from the flanks. Lieut. Gen. Bradley's landward encirclement of city is almost complete. *—Story on page 3; other pictures in center fold.*

(U. S. Signal Corps Radio-Telefoto from Acme Telefoto)

NO. 15,025 ONE PENNY * * FOR KING AND EMPIRE THURSDAY, JUNE 29, 1944

LATE WAR NEWS

MONTGOMERY SMASHES THROUGH

Rommel's Bridgehead Ring Shattered

BIG TANK BATTLE NOW RAGING

GENERAL MONTGOMERY has broken through the German holding line around the Normandy bridgehead, and throughout yesterday was engaging Rommel's crack panzer forces in the greatest tank battle since D-Day. Late yesterday the battle was still in progress, with the spearhead of the still advancing British forces less than 2½ miles from the River Orne.

The British are now driving forward on a broad front, stretching roughly from Maltot to Evrecy, and the Germans have flung in nine attacks in a desperate endeavour to halt us. Every attack has failed.

The battle which reached its height yesterday began three days ago. In those 72 hours the Germans have lost more than 60 tanks, while the British, in what one correspondent says is the "bitterest and most savage fighting" since the landing, have advanced over seven miles.

Late last night, as the battle was bursting from the wooded area around Tilly into ideal tank country, a Staff officer summed up the action: "It is a magnificent accomplishment. It is a very big battle and a highly successful one." Yet another officer said that the Germans west of Caen were "in complete turmoil."

VAST AIR ONSLAUGHT

The Germans report that Montgomery has flung in his air forces on an "unprecedented scale" in a softening-up attack covering "the whole area between Cherbourg, St. Nazaire, Orleans, and Paris." One correspondent said that "it sweeps like a hurricane ahead of Montgomery's land forces."

Behind this "hurricane of death" German tanks, manned by the best troops Rommel can find, and the British armour are shooting it out, often at less than 30 yards apart.

Up to late last night the battle had carried the British to within a mile of Maltot, a similar distance from Esquay, and about two miles from Evrecy. Advanced forces of the British thrust are believed actually to have penetrated into Esquay.

As this great thrust threatens to outflank Caen, the "hinge" of Rommel's present line, the town itself has come under a "nutcracker" assault—from Montgomery's main thrust to the south-west, from frontal pressure, and from a new attack which, the Germans report, has developed to the north-east, presumably from the British bridgehead east of the Orne. Up to early to-day no details of this new attack were available.

Resistance in the Cherbourg area has now died away, although pockets of Germans are still holding out in the extreme "horns" of the peninsula. It was estimated last night that the number of prisoners taken in the peninsula have now risen to between 30,000 and 40,000.

Our Tanks Crossed the Odon by Night

From ALEXANDER CLIFFORD
WITH THE BRITISH TANK FORCES, Wednesday.

OUR tanks are over the River Odon now. The German infantry line round the beachhead has been broken south-west of Caen. This new battle which Montgomery started three days ago is going well.

The panzers — the 12th S.S. Division—are still fighting back. Their 88mm. guns and Tiger tanks, dug cleverly in, are opposing our armour in the more open ground between the Odon and the Orne.

But our progress so far has been unfaltering.

The British tanks started across the Odon last night, after fighting their way through a whole district full of smashed, deserted villages.

The Odon is a small, narrow river not very deep but with high banks in some places. The infantry waded across easily, and the tanks found crossings where they could splash their way to the other side.

This morning their bridgehead expanded across the cornland and other tanks came in behind them.

Now the pattern of this attack looks like a long tongue issuing from the old front line of the beachhead.

The fighting to-day was not only round the tip of the freshly made salient, but along the sides of it as well. Quite a lot of Germans with tanks have been by-passed, and they are still making disconnected jabs into our flanks.

I was in a front-line village this morning when one of these side-jabs came in.

It was a wreck of a village—a sleepy little place which no one had ever heard of in peace-time, but now a mere figment on an operational map.

Bits of the sagging, splintered houses were still dropping into the streets, splashing into a mire of mud that looked like thick mulligatawny soup. There was the smell of death all round.

An old old lady was picking her way through the mud with a perambulator full of china she was saving, and the tin-hatted traffic policeman held up a full battery of guns to let her across.

She nodded and smiled at him with a pathetic courtesy.

The Germans were ranging the countryside with sudden deluges of shells. We had dodged one at a crossroads only a little way back.

Another had just fallen on the edge of this village, and a truck with some ammunition in it was blazing slap in the middle of the road we wanted to use.

Its casually exploding shells added a fresh, bewildering motif to the bedlam of noise all round us.

The batteries of 25-pounders were so well concealed that one drove along in a perpetual state of

BACK PAGE—Col. FOUR

'Only a Thin Crust Left'

The following brief message, written on Saturday by Ronald Clark, British United Press war correspondent, was delayed by censorship. It is typical of all correspondents' stories received in London last night—unanimous in sober but complete confidence.

From RONALD CLARK
WITH ADVANCED ALLIED FORCES.

I HONESTLY believe that the Allied prospects on the beachhead are the best since the invasion.

Vast loads are coming ashore for the next vital phase.

After 17 days on the beachhead I firmly believe that only a thin, tough crust of the German Army now remains to be beaten.

That conviction rests on the lack of major air and artillery attack against the vast concentration on the beachhead, the lack of more than tactical counter-thrusts, the slight extent of the artillery fire in the front line, and the fact that Poles, Russians, and Czechs, forced to assist the Germans, are appearing on an increasing number of fronts.—B.U.P.

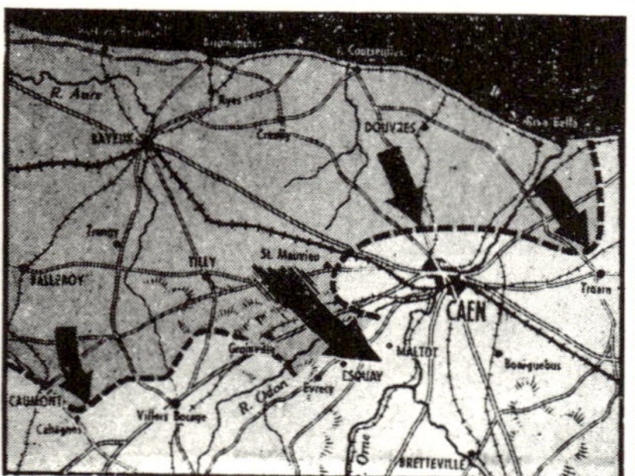

THE MINE KILLER

HERE is the first picture—an official photograph—of Britain's secret battle-winner, the flailing tank. Those whirling chains in front flail the ground, setting off buried land mines in front of the German defences, clearing a path for the infantry and armour. The tank shown here is the Crab, an adaptation of the Sherman tank. It is in use in Normandy now.

THE Crab is only one version of the flailing tank. A picture of another type, the Baron, is in the BACK Page. Other models include the Scorpion and the Marquis.

Dempsey is C-in-C of 2nd Army

Lieut.-General Dempsey.

Now in France

THE announcement that 47-years-old Lieut.-General Miles Christopher Dempsey is in command of the Second British Army in Normandy clarifies the commands of the invading forces.

It is now apparent that General Montgomery has two separate armies under his command in the 21st Army Group—the British Second Army and the American Seventh Army Corps under General Omar Bradley.

General Dempsey is General Omar Bradley's opposite number.

The Second Army has not been named before. Other British armies so far identified are: First Army, which served in Tunisia; the Fifth (partly American) and the Eighth, now fighting in Italy; the Ninth, in Syria and Transjordan; the Tenth, in Persia and Iraq; and the 14th, in Burma.

In the BEF

General Dempsey, who holds the C.B., D.S.O., and M.C., commanded the famous 13th Corps of the Eighth Army in North Africa.

At a moment's notice he was dispatched to the Middle East in December 1942, with the rank of acting lieut.-general, to take over the corps. This fought from Mareth to the Enfidaville region.

Then General Dempsey took his corps through Sicily into Italy.

As a colonel, General Dempsey commanded his battalion of the Royal Berkshires in the original B.E.F. in France.

His rapid promotion is an index to his abilities. He was lieut.-colonel at the outbreak of the war; colonel and acting brigadier on November 20, 1939, acting major-general in June 1941, and acting lieut.-general in December 1942.

3 Mutineers to Die

From Daily Mail Correspondent

CAIRO, Wednesday.—First death sentences for the recent Greek mutiny have been passed by a Greek naval court at Alexandria on three seamen, who were also found guilty of murdering an officer.

IT BEATS MINES TO DEATH

The 'Flail Tank'

A BRITISH secret weapon, it was disclosed last night, has helped us win a score of battles, from El Alamein in Egypt to Tilly in Normandy.

It is the "flail" tank, and it is used to clear a path through minefields.

Across the front of the tank is fitted a steel cylinder to which are attached a number of lengths of chain several feet long. As the tank moves forward the cylinder revolves rapidly, and the free ends of the chains beat continuously on the ground.

This beating, or "flailing," sets off anti-personnel mines as well as anti-tank mines that may be buried in the ground, and clears a path several feet wide for other tanks and troops to follow.

Land mines, the Germans thought at Alamein, were the answer to any possibility of assault, and they sowed them generously in front of our positions (writes the Daily Mail Services Correspondent).

They forgot that, even as far back as 1914-18, we had used steam rollers to trample on the buried mines of those days.

Destroyed Every Mine

We went ahead with their land mine technique in the desert, and at first they succeeded in a manner that surprised themselves. We suffered terribly at Tobruk and at Knightsbridge by the skilful use of enemy mines.

But all the time scientists at home were working on the problem.

A South African found the answer.

He designed the Scorpion, the first "flail tank," and named it after one of Egypt's best-known "inhabitants."

A number were made up from Matilda and Valentine tanks as a temporary expedient to break through the many German minefields from El Alamein to Tunis.

The Scorpion was very successful. It is reported to have destroyed at El Alamein 100 per cent. of the mines in its path. Even mines buried 3 deep did no damage except to blow away a chain flail, replacement of which was simple.

One tank, in one "run" destroyed 17 mines without any damage to the tank or its crew.

Now the Crab

While the battles in N. Africa were proceeding, experimental work went on in Britain to perfect the flail device. The first type made here was called the Baron, to be followed later by the improved Marquis, and lastly by the Crab, now in use in Normandy, which incorporates the best points of the three previous types.

On the Crab—usually an adaptation of the Sherman tank—the flails are driven by the tank engine itself, as opposed to the method used on the Scorpion, of driving the flails by an independent engine.

Flails, first used thousands of years ago for thrashing corn, were used as weapons in battles of the Middle Ages. They consisted of short staffs to which spiked iron balls were attached by means of a chain and were effective weapons against armour.

The modern version is designed to help our armour against one of the most difficult types of obstacle in modern warfare. It played a part in clearing the invasion beaches of mines.

New Blitz on the Bomb Lairs

Fighters escorted Halifaxes of Bomber Command to make a further big attack on military installations in the Pas de Calais yesterday.

The fighters saw flak around the targets die away as the first wave of bombers dropped their shattering loads. This attack followed the 1,000-planes blow overnight at the robot lairs.

On Road to Beat Robots.—Page THREE.

DEJECTED

MAJOR-GENERAL STATTLER, Von Schlieben's second-in-command at Cherbourg, sits dejected during his interrogation at Allied H.Q. in Cherbourg. He surrendered when the Americans stormed the arsenal, one of the last centres of resistance.

Gun Salvos Over the Strait

Long-range guns on the French coast at Cap Gris Nez and Wimereux, near Boulogne, fired across the Strait of Dover for about 45 minutes yesterday afternoon.

Nearly 50 rounds were fired, generally in salvoes of four. The shells fell in the vicinity of Dover. Later another shell warning was sounded in the south-east coast area.

RAF Wipe Out an Enemy HQ

Pinpoint Blitz

A SQUADRON of R.A.F. Typhoons have wiped out a German Corps H.Q. in Normandy, in a brilliant pin-point attack.

The H.Q. was in a château at St. Sauveur Endelin. Twenty-eight Typhoons were given the job of blowing it up.

Eight had to find the target and hit it. Four rocket-firing planes were to follow, and 16 dive-bombers had the task of finishing off anything that happened to be left.

The rocket-planes and dive-bombers had little to do. The first eight planes dropped their bombs from roof-top height and the other waves pounded the smoke.

Flight Lieutenant E. B. Wallace, of Cardale, Manitoba, said: "We went in after the first flight, led by Wing Commander Baldwin, had skittled their bombs into the house.

"We released our bombs at nought feet. I saw two disappear into the house, and then, 11 seconds later, a third and fourth. The house disappeared."

DEWEY NAMED BY 1,056-1

To Fight FDR

From Daily Mail Correspondent

NEW YORK, Wednesday.—Governor Thomas E. Dewey, of New York, was at the Chicago Convention nominated to-day as Republican candidate for the American Presidency by a vote 1,056 to 1. The single vote went to General MacArthur.

Governor John W. Bricker, of Ohio, was nominated as candidate for the Vice-Presidency after Governor Warren, of California, had refused to allow himself to be named.

How Dewey was chosen.—BACK Page.

Lt-Col Rocke: MPs Ask More Questions

WHEN M.P.s asked questions yesterday about Lieut.-Col. C. Rocke, formerly of the British Embassy in Rome, Major Henderson, Financial Secretary to the War Office, in the House of Commons yesterday referred them to an answer given the previous day.

Mr. Driberg (Ind., Maldon) asked what action was being taken, saying that Lieut.-Col. Rocke had broadcast propaganda for the Italian Fascist Government during the present war and had now established contact with British Forces in Italy.

Major Sir Jocelyn Lucas (C., Portsmouth S.) asked what steps had been taken to arrest Col. Rocke.

After Major Henderson had referred the questioners to the previous day's answer, Sir Jocelyn Lucas asked: In view of the fact that Col. Rocke stated quite recently that he hoped he had been able to be of some help to us during the war, could not the Minister state whether he had been working for us?

Major Henderson: I have no information about that.

Mr. Driberg: Would it not be perfectly easy to check the records of this colonel of what he broadcast from the B.B.C. monitor service?

Major Henderson: No doubt that and all other relevant information could be considered when the time comes to take a decision.

Mr Driberg: Has not the time come to treat people like these and William Joyce as traitors?

Major Henderson: In this country it is customary to collect all the evidence together before a person is dealt with under penal law.

Capt. Bellenger (Lab., Bassetlaw): Did the Minister not collect evidence when the War Office decided to withhold this officer's retired pay in 1940?

Major Henderson: It might be, but a good deal has happened since then. We wish to get the relevant evidence before we take a decision.

'JOHNNY' MADE SCORE 32

2 'Kills,' then Lunch

Wing Commander "Johnny" Johnson shot down his 32nd enemy plane before lunch yesterday to tie with the score of Group Capt. ("Sailor") Malan.

Johnson led two squadrons of Spitfires from a Normandy airfield and ran into a bunch of German fighters over Villers Bocage.

In the dog-fights which followed he shot down two of the six "kills" by his Spitfires.

New Recorder

Mr. Frederick William Beney K.C., 54-years-old Recorder of Rye, has been appointed Recorder of Norwich. He succeeds Sir William Ellis Hulme - Williams.

Weather in the Strait

State of Sea.—Choppy, then moderating.

Weather. — Warmer during afternoon, threat of rain later. Highest temperature 68 deg., 61 at nightfall. Visibility good. Wind: S.W., fresh to strong. Sky—high broken cloud, becoming overcast.

Barometer. — Steady rise continuing.

Red Army Sweeping On: Minsk 60 Miles

4 ARMIES CLOSE IN

SWEEPING new advances along the whole White Russian front brought Red Army spearheads last night less than 60 miles from Minsk.

Successive Moscow announcements revealed that four Russian columns, spanning 200 miles of country, are racing unchecked for this gateway to East Prussia, Northern Poland, and the Baltic States.

Capture of Osipovichi, big German traffic centre 58 miles from Minsk, was reported by Marshal Stalin in an Order of the Day.

It means that General Rokossovsky's forces have emerged on the road and railway to the White Russian capital 28 miles beyond Bobruisk, where battles for the annihilation of five trapped enemy divisions are continuing.

In the north Soviet forces leapt 20 miles ahead in a single day, pierced enemy fortifications and seized the lakeside fortress of Lepel.

NEW LINE GONE

A third great prize fell to General Zakharov in the centre of the front. Another Order of the Day announced that his men stormed their way into Mogilev, last bastion of the shattered Fatherland Line.

Now Zakharov's tanks and infantry are streaming across the Dnieper on a 75-miles front after piercing the second enemy defence line on its western bank and capturing the river towns of Shklov and Bikhov.

During the 24 hours of street battles for Mogilev the 12th German Infantry Division was wiped out and its commanding officer, Major-General Wagner, was taken prisoner, together with his staff and the garrison commander, Major-General Hermannsdorf.

In yesterday's actions, the Russians took over 1,500 inhabited places, including Krugloe "in the Minsk direction" and Kholopenichi, 25 miles north-east of Borisov.

Simultaneously with these gains in the northernmost corner of the line, a new threatening advance is developing towards Polotsk, enemy base guarding the roads into the Baltic States.

HEADED OFF

Bulk of the German defenders in White Russia are contained in a 500 square miles triangle with its apex at the gateway city, and they are facing disaster.

Half of Germany's armoured columns are in the east—the other 50 per cent. are facing the Allies on other fronts—but they are mostly locked south of the Pripet Marshes.

So the enemy troops trying to stem the Russian advance must fight with little effective tank support.

Germany is sending "major contingents" to the aid of the Finns, declared Martin Hallensleben, German News Agency military correspondent, last night.

News of Lord Lascelles

Daily Mail Radio Station

THE German radio from Calais broke into their programme in English last night to give a special message to the Earl of Harewood in Yorkshire. The call was made, the radio announcer stated, on behalf of Lieut. Viscount Lascelles, Lord Harewood's elder son, who was taken prisoner in Italy on June 19, after being severely wounded.

The message to Lord Harewood stated that the Viscount's condition was still satisfactory on June 23.

Lord Lascelles, son of the Princess Royal and nephew of the King, was said by the Germans to have been fighting with the British 6th Tank Division when he was captured. He is 21 years of age.

TOKIO IN RANGE OF U.S. FLEET

Washington, Wednesday.—Most of the southern part of the Japanese islands, including Tokio, are now within range of American fleet operations, according to maps released to-day by Mr. James Forrestal, Secretary of the Navy.—Reuter.

P-PLANE DOWN IN STREET

Several people were slightly injured when a flying-bomb fell in a street in Southern England last night. No one was killed.

Danes Continue Big Walk-out

From Daily Mail Special Correspondent

STOCKHOLM, Wednesday.—Danish workers, following their "open revolt" demonstration, are continuing to "take time off" from factories.

Many factories and workshops in Copenhagen closed down for hours to-day as a protest against the German eight o'clock curfew.

SUNDAY EXPRESS

JULY 2 1944 · BLACK-OUT MANCHESTER 11.26 p.m. to 5.0 a.m. · Founded by LORD BEAVERBROOK · Moon  rises 6.16 p.m. Sets 3.48 a.m. · TWOPENCE

ROMMEL TAKES OVER AT CAEN

British troops prepare for a mass attack by tanks

Men from Russia among 7 panzer divisions

FIELD-MARSHAL ROMMEL, IT WAS STATED AT SUPREME HEADQUARTERS LAST NIGHT, HAS NOW ASSUMED PERSONAL COMMAND OF THE GERMAN ARMIES IN THE NORMANDY CAMPAIGN.

He will therefore be responsible for directing the seven panzer divisions engaged in the Caen-Tilly area against the British Second Army.

It is believed he will mass his panzers and throw in large formations.

Our forces in the salient are being regrouped, and tanks are standing by in hull-down positions to meet this new threat.

German units which infiltrated into the shoulders of our Odon bridgehead early yesterday have been thrown out, and the position is firm.

North of the River Odon we are mopping up isolated pockets of German tanks and infantry which are still holding out in our salient between the road and the river.

German troops which were fighting in Russia as recently as March have been identified in the Caen area.

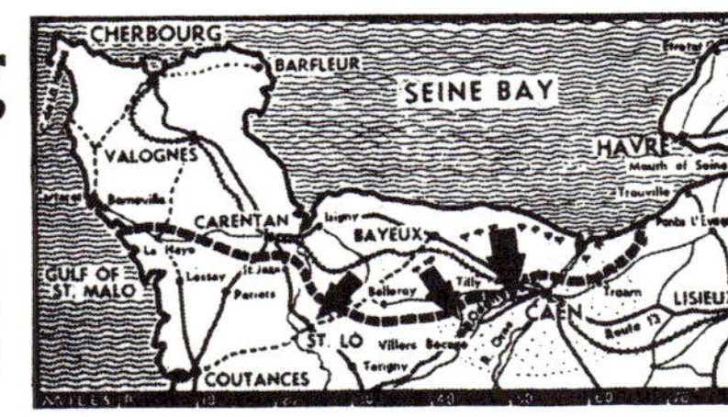

Dempsey's men hold all attacks

FROM the British Tilly-Caen front in Normandy yesterday it was reported that Rundstedt is quickening the tempo and intensity of his small-scale counter-attacks against our bridgehead despite extravagant and mounting losses.

But non-stop attacks by crack panzer formations—tanks and infantry—against General Dempsey's salient around Evrecy have failed to shift the strong British forces there, says Reuter's special correspondent at Supreme Headquarters of the Allied Expeditionary Force.

Beaten down and then thrown back, cut off after infiltration and destroyed, the Germans have gained no ground at all from this thrust into our territory, which has reached to and still holds the now legendary Hill 112 dominating the immediate area.

MONTY CALLS THE TUNE

Among new arrivals bolstering Rundstedt's defence are German troops who may have come from Russia.

The battle is in true Montgomery style, and is being played to his tune. It is a grinding-down process, in which Rommel is meeting a steady drain on his infantry and tanks. The British Second Army alone has destroyed 142 tanks since it landed.

Latest news received is that the Second Army forces over the River Odon are consolidating the newly-won positions while finally liquidating in the rear the strong pockets of resistance which were originally by-passed.

Until this phase has been completed there is little likelihood of any big-scale advance, and in any case Evrecy is as good a place to destroy Rommel's armour as anywhere else.

On no part of the front is there any movement of size at the moment.

North of Caen, where at one time British forces were within two miles of the city, the battle appears to have quietened down after shifting back to near Breville, four miles north-east of the town and on the bank of the Orne Canal.

THE GERMAN FORCES CORNERED IN CAP DE LA HAGUE IN THE CHERBOURG PENINSULA, HAVE NOW SURRENDERED, AND FOR ALL PRACTICAL PURPOSES ALL RESISTANCE IN THE PENINSULA HAS ENDED. AMERICAN PATROLS ARE NOW SEEKING OUT STRAGGLERS IN THE WOODED COUNTRY NEAR THE SHORE LINE.

Larry Lesueur, an American radio commentator, said early yesterday: "Only about 1,500 men out of the four

HOW THE 'CAB-RANK' WORKS

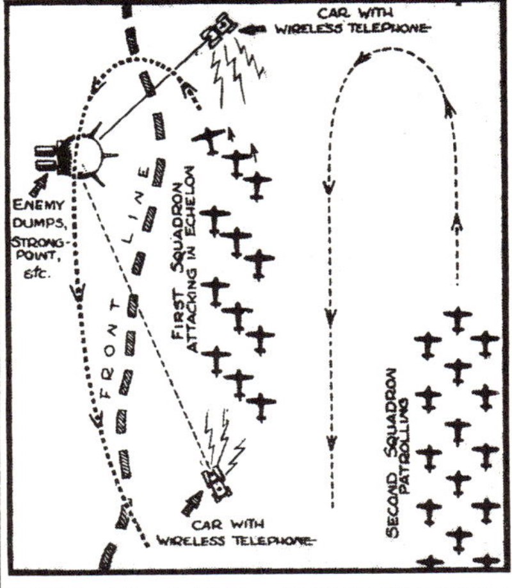

THIS front-line sketch by a Sunday Express artist shows how Air Vice-Marshal Harry Broadhurst's miniature air force in Normandy uses his "cab-rank" or merry-go-round" technique in advanced areas against enemy tanks, parks, convoys, troop concentrations, gun positions, fuel and ammo dumps, and other vital targets.

Reconnaissance vehicles equipped with radio-telephones watch every move. They are Broadhurst's high-speed spotters and in constant touch with his advance echelon of the Second Tactical Air Force.

One of them has just located an enemy strongpost and signalled its map reference. Response to the call is immediate—a matter of split seconds.

One by one the patrolling Typhoons swoop down from the "rank" with bombs, rockets and blazing automatic guns. Then with a fast climbing turn they resume their places on the rank ready for the next summons.

A squadron of Broadhurst's bomb-carrying Spitfires maintains constant vigil while the Typhoons refuel and rearm.

Never before has air-ground support been so close, quick and devastating, British Army leaders declare.

Diminishing circle

MAP shows Caen, Minsk, and Leghorn almost equidistant from Berlin.

Cromwell tank in action

A German report

THE British are using Cromwell tanks in the Caen battle, according to Guenther Weber, German war reporter.

Weber said that in fighting south-west of the town German tanks penetrated one and a-half miles into the British line and shot up 12 Cromwells.

DE GAULLE WILL CONTROL NEWS

The French Provisional Government have made plans to take control of all newspapers as France is liberated, said Morocco radio yesterday.

Radio and cinemas are also covered by a series of measures adopted by the Provisional Government.

'I'm glad we are broke'

—SAYS MR BEVIN

MR ERNEST BEVIN, Minister of Labour, said in Birmingham yesterday that after the war Britain would still be a leader.

"Britain is going to take her place, not above, but equally, with the other great nations of the world, he said.

"But to do it—and we are broke, it is no use beating about the bush. We have spent everything in this struggle and I am glad we have—I beg of the trade unions, the employers, civic authorities, and public officials, to carry on in the great objective which I think is a bigger victory to win than the military one.

NO DOCUMENT

"If you do not go through the first decade after this war with concentrated effort both in this country and with the United Nations I defy any living statesman to build a peace that will not lead to a recurrence of this trouble.

"At the Teheran Conference, Marshal Stalin, President Roosevelt, and Mr Churchill arranged the vital dates for victory, but there was no document, no elaborate signed agreement.

"I hope that those three great nations will always be able to work with the same degree of confidence."

RUSSIA'S OFFER TO HER POLES

RUSSIANS who have served in the Polish Army in Russia or have helped this army have the right to adopt Polish citizenship under a decree published in Moscow yesterday.

The decree applies to "inhabitants of the western regions of the Ukrainian and White Russian Soviet Socialist Republics, and to Soviet citizens of Polish nationality of other regions of the U.S.S.R."

The decree covers Poles who have taken Soviet citizenship since 1939, and the ancient Polish colonies in Siberia who have maintained their national language and customs for generations.

People of Polish descent who went to Russia from foreign countries may also adopt Polish citizenship.—Reuter.

Train-buster-in-chief takes over

Wing-Commander Gordon Panitz, of Southport, Queensland, train-buster with 17 trains to his score, has taken over command of a second Australian Mosquito fighter-bomber squadron.

He successfully attacked six goods trains in about ten minutes on his first daylight expedition. Another time he shot up the slipways and hangars of a German seaplane base, strafed a launch, fired a small ship, and destroyed a Junkers 88.

GERMANS FACING BIG MINSK TRAP

Tanks speed through the gaps

RED ARMY divisions last night were advancing steadily towards north Poland and Lithuania after pouring through the three gaps which have been torn in the German line at Vitebsk, Mogilev, and Zhlobin.

Marshal Rokossovsky's tanks and shock troops are driving along the high road to Warsaw after storming the German stronghold at Slutsk. Other units are pushing to the north-west in a deepening and outflanking movement on Minsk, the last big German-held base before Vilna.

Another great encirclement plan is taking shape through the marshes and forests of White Russia as Red Army units close in on Minsk from the north, east, and south.

Fierce battles are developing on the approaches to Minsk, but the Germans are being pushed back on both flanks, and the whole enemy grouping before the city is being herded into a huge salient running from Borisov in the west to Slutsk in the north.

There is no exact information on the distance the Russian spearheads are from the city, but latest reports reaching Moscow put them only 25 miles away.

Many surrender

Soviet correspondents have reported that hundreds of Germans are surrendering before they can reach Minsk. The Red Army troops are having some difficulty in moving up for a direct blow at the city because the roads are clogged with prisoners.

On the northern sector of the offensive the Russians are over the old Polish border west of Polotsk, the German base about 16 miles from the old Polish frontier, which guards the approaches to the Baltic States.

The Russian forces have flowed round it in a great flood and its garrison appears to be doomed.

The Germans lost all hope of holding their White Russian line when the Russians burst through the defences based on the Beresina River.

General Chernakhovsky's forces north of Borisov smashed across the river almost unopposed, thanks to the assistance they received from partisans who controlled the great forest stretching from Borisov to Lepel and held an important bridge which the Germans were unable to destroy.—Reuter and B.U.P.

Russians may force German fleet to battle in Baltic

Sunday Express Naval Correspondent

NOW that the Finns have decided to stay in the war the chances of a naval action in the Baltic are decidedly enhanced.

German troops in Finland must be supplied by sea. It is evident that before long the whole of Estonia will be in Russian hands, denying to the enemy the short sea passage across the Gulf of Finland.

Convoys will thus have to go by sea all the way from Stettin or Gdynia to Finnish ports, more especially Oulu, on the Gulf of Bothnia, supply base for Dietl's army.

This is one of the reasons for the arrival at Turku (Abo) of a German squadron said to include the heavy cruiser Admiral Hipper, a pocket battleship, possibly another cruiser, and at least three destroyers.

Not easy

Doubtless this force has been ordered to safeguard convoys for Finland from attack by Russian warships from Kronstadt.

But their task is not going to be an easy one. Similar measures were taken by the enemy in the north of Norway, but Soviet submarines, motor torpedo-boats, and planes contrieved, nevertheless, to inflict heavy damage on German convoys.

It is believed that the Germans intend to occupy the Aaland Islands, belonging to Finland. The strategic position of this group is highly im- approaches to both the Bothnian and Finnish Gulfs.

German forces in the Baltic comprise two pocket battleships, two heavy and four light cruisers, two old coast defence ships, and some destroyers, motor torpedo-boats, and submarines.

Air Arm, too

Against this the Russians can muster two old battleships of 23,000 tons and three or four cruisers, with an equal or greater number of destroyers, motor torpedo-boats and submarines.

In addition there is the Soviet Fleet Air Arm, which has distinguished itself on many occasions against the German Navy in Estonian waters.

B.U.P.'s Stockholm correspondent also reports that the occupation of the Aaland Islands by the Germans is likely.

A high German officer, he says, is expected to set up his headquarters at Mariehamn, capital of the islands.

Bombs hit two more hospitals

TWO more hospitals in southern England were among buildings hit or damaged by flying bomb blast during Friday night and early yesterday.

Seven out of 30 patients were killed when the wing of one hospital received a direct hit in the darkness. Search was still going on last night for others. Two wards were wrecked.

Most of the patients at the other hospital near which a bomb exploded in daylight were casualties from other flying-bomb incidents. They included children and some who had been admitted only a few hours before.

None of them was hurt, though the roof of one ward collapsed.

Crowd escapes

A woman owes her life and those of her four children to a change of mind. Until flying bombs started coming over she had no faith in surface shelters.

She altered her opinion and went to one for the first time on Friday night. Her home was wrecked.

A Baptist church suffered considerably from blast when a bomb fell near. The minister's home was among those damaged.

When warning of the approach of a flying bomb was given at a sports meeting spectators followed the advice of the announcer to throw themselves flat on the ground. A few seconds later the bomb fell close by.

Windows in the area were broken, but no one was hurt.

Danube mined for hundreds of miles

HUNDREDS of miles of the River Danube have been covered by R.A.F. Liberator and Wellington minelayers.

An Australian radio operator, Flying-Officer Neville Rasmussen, said: "The first time we did the mining we just flew up and down the river as we pleased.

"Next time there was a 'reception committee,' and ack-ack in places.

"That first time there were ships and barges all the way. Two or three trips later we saw just two barges. The river has to be swept every time one of our lads goes over—even if not a single mine is dropped."

The flow of German supplies to the armies facing the Russians has been seriously interfered with by this Allied all-out offensive against communications. But what is perhaps even more important is the disruption of the upstream traffic of oil, wheat, chrome, and other materials consigned to Germany.

Florence an 'open city'

Hitler's order as Allies near it

A SWIFT advance by the Allies all along the front brought the Fifth Army last night to within 16 miles of Leghorn and 35 of Florence.

As they pushed on towards the Gothic Line, on which these two cities stand, the German radio announced that Hitler had declared Florence an open city.

Florence, capital of Tuscany, is rich in works of artistic and historic interest, with libraries, galleries, and museums—"irreplaceable treasures," said Berlin—but as it stands at present it is within the German fortification system stretching from Leghorn across the peninsula to Rimini.

Latest battle reports say:—

General Clark's Fifth Army, making Leghorn its next big objective, has passed through Cecina and pushed on across the river three miles north-east of the town.

Over on the Adriatic coast, Allied forces are again pressing forward hard on the heels of the Germans, who are withdrawing from their Chienti River line to a new line along the Musone River, only ten miles south of the port of Ancona.

They control it

In the inland sector, General Juin's French troops, after taking two more towns, now dominate the whole area south of Highway 73. They have pushed a two-prong drive to within four miles of Siena, the nearest point reached in the direct advance towards Florence.

A combat team composed of American soldiers of Japanese origin is fighting with the Fifth Army.

Medium bombers yesterday continued to attack communications in northern Italy, particularly along the important Pisa-Rimini railway lines.

Ten heavily-laden barges, believed to be loaded with fuel and explosives, were set on fire by coastal Beaufighters east of Novi-Sad, on the Danube.

Fighters and fighter-bombers gave the battle-weary Germans no rest, spraying the retreating army with bombs and bullets.

Hungary bombed

ALLIED H.Q., ITALY, Saturday.—Up to 500 heavy bombers took part in yesterday's attacks on communications in Hungary, and airfields and a harbour in Yugoslavia.

Good bombing was reported on Banjaluka airfield and Split harbour, on the Adriatic, and on the Barc railway bridge and the Kapsovar railway yards in Hungary.

Cloud obscured the results of attacks on military targets in the Zagreb and Budapest areas.

Enemy fighters in some strength intercepted the fighter-escorted heavies, which fought them off after shooting down 11.—Reuter.

World war news

GERMANS LOSE 11 PANTHERS IN NEW 'JAB'

Eleven Panther tanks knocked out in new German "jab" against point of British salient.

Many German dead are lying in poppy fields round small towns. More prisoners taken.

RADIO Page Seven

First time in, but they fought like veterans

THE British troops who smashed back Rommel's big counter-attack in a four-hour battle between the Odon and Orne had never been under enemy fire before.

They were the untried product of Britain's battle schools, but they showed they were equal to the best Rommel could put against them.

Split into little groups under junior officers when German tanks and infantry bit into their positions, they fought back determinedly, smashed the attack, and retook the lost ground.

'OFTEN DO BETTER'

It was a feat worthy of a famous division, yet their division is new, and so far has not been officially identified.

Its newness may have something to do with its success. A brigadier said: "There is a tendency for divisions with great reputations rather to rest on their laurels, so that new divisions eager to earn fame often do better."

Already the Canadian Third Division and the U.S. 29th—both unseasoned formations—have distinguished themselves in the bridgehead.

Another senior officer commented: "These new divisions fight just as well as seasoned troops, and are perhaps a little quicker off the mark. But they pay a heavier price in casualties—they have not yet learned all the tricks of how not to get hurt."

In the stiff fighting in the woods north of Caen, too, the new boys are doing well. A tank officer there said: "Most of my lads are under 21, and new to fighting like this. They have put up a grand show."

SPECIAL SCHOOLS

All this is giving great satisfaction in those military circles where the battle school was evolved. In Britain, the United States, and Canada the toughening process is much the same—after initial training the troops are sent to special schools where they fight mock actions in realistic—sometimes fatally realistic—conditions.

They use live ammunition, and live ammunition is used against them. Machine-gunners fire over their heads as they advance.

Artillery and mortars lay a barrage around them. Hand-grenades are tossed on their flanks, and land mines are exploded in their path.

It is hard on the nerves, but prepares them for the real thing.

20 Mustangs rout 60 Hun fighters

When a force of 20 Mustangs, led by the Polish pilot, Wing-Commander Skaliski, D.F.C. and two bars, was returning from operations in northern France last week 60 German fighters were seen over the Channel.

Wing-Commander Skaliski ordered his force to attack. A series of dog-fights followed, in which the Germans lost six planes down and four probables.

The attackers lost only one plane.

Leningrad took this

During the siege of Leningrad the city was hit by 150,000 heavy German shells and more than 100,000 large bombs. Two and a-half million square yards of housing space was demolished, but it is expected that 950,000 will be restored this year.

More Beauforts

Ten thousand Australians now make Bristol Beaufort torpedo bombers.

Montgomery to Harris: 'Thanks'

General Montgomery sent this message last night to Air Chief Marshal Sir Arthur Harris, Air Officer Commanding-in-Chief R.A.F. Bomber Command:—

"My grateful thanks to Bomber Command and to you personally, for your contribution to the tactical battle in Normandy last night.

"It was a most inspiring sight for the Allied soldiers in France to see the might of Bomber Command arrive to join in the battle. Your action will not be forgotten by us or the enemy. Please thank all your pilots for me."

'Attack on Guam repelled'—Tokyo

Tokyo said last night: "The Jap garrison of Guam (former U.S. base in the central Pacific) yesterday repelled three enemy cruisers or large destroyers attempting to shell our airfield from the sea."—Reuter.

Germans loot radios

About 160,000 of the radio sets confiscated by the Germans in Norway just after the occupation have been exported to Germany.

Vichy quislings closely guarded

Rigorous security measures are being taken to protect Deat, Darnand, and other Vichy quisling Ministers, even against their own wishes German radio stated yesterday.

The decision follows the assassination of Henriot, Vichy Propaganda Minister.

Formosa bombed

American Liberators bombed Takao, a port on the island of Formosa, on June 29 and damaged dock installations, it was announced in Chungking yesterday.—Reuter.

BRACKEN WILL OPEN FLYING BOMB SHOW

VERGELTUNGSWAFFE—otherwise Hitler's "revenge weapon No. 1," known to southern England more familiarly as the flying bomb and other names—is on view in London.

A full-scale model based on latest information from the Air Ministry occupies pride of place in the Daily Express exhibition, the Battle of France, to be opened tomorrow by Mr Brendan Bracken, Minister of Information, at Dorland Hall, Lower Regent-street, London, S.W.1.

Cleverly reconstructed, the model measures 25ft in length with wing spread of 16ft, and has sections which open to show parts of the interior mechanism.

Life-size pictures

Round the walls are life-size photographs telling the story of the Battle of France from D Day onwards. These will be added to as the latest pictures arrive from the battle front.

General von Schlieben and Rear-Admiral Hennecke, captured in the fall of Cherbourg, stand outside the hall—as over life size cut-out silhouettes.

And inside are two more models, this time of the men who are helping to beat the other Germans still there—a Commando complete down to knuckledusters, and a paratrooper.

Samples of some of the weapons and equipment our men are using are there, too—from mortars and machine-guns to odd-looking motor scooters and folding bicycles—just some of the things that are among our surprises for the Germans.

The exhibition opens tomorrow at 11.30 a.m. and afterwards from 10 a.m. to 7 p.m. daily, including Saturdays. Sunday hours are 2 p.m. to 7 p.m.

Admission: — Civilians, 1/- (children half price). Forces in uniform, 6d. All proceeds go to Service charities.

The Evening News

NO. 19,481 LONDON, THURSDAY, JULY 6, 1944 ONE PENNY

FLYING BOMBS KILL 2,752, INJURE 8,000: VERY HIGH TOLL IN LONDON—Premier

BLACKOUT 11.3 p.m. to 5.7 a.m. Moon rises 10.40 p.m. Moon sets 7.9 a.m.

HITLER CALLS 'THROW IN ALL RESERVES'

Generals Warn of Collapse in East

HITLER is to-day reported to have ordered his generals to throw in all reserves against the Red Army as it races ever nearer Germany's frontiers.

According to a Stockholm report quoted to-day by Moscow radio, he flashed the instructions to his commanders in the field after General Kurt Zeitzler, Chief of the German General Staff, had visited Hitler's H.Q. to tell him that the German Army was faced with a superiority which it could not match.

It is said that at a special conference military leaders emphasised the grave danger of an Eastern Front collapse.

Counter-Blows Fail

Some of these reserves appear to have already been thrown in.

Russian reports to-day say that in the Baranovichi direction the Germans are launching frequent counter-attacks, and other German counter-attacks came west of Molodechno.

Swept Aside

But the Red Army is sweeping the Germans away in its drive to the west, said an *Izvestia* report.

Red Army tank columns are closing on four key bases of the final German defences east of the Baltic and East Prussia, Dvinsk and Vilna, northern bastions of the German fortress-chain running through Grodno down to Brest-Litovsk, and the railway towns of Lida and Baranovichi.

Massed Soviet bombers are out pounding Vilna, Baranovichi and Lida as the tanks, cavalry, and infantry race forward against the outer defence before the towns.

The Germans encircled east of Minsk are to-day in their death agony as big forces of Soviet artillery and aircraft pour a hail of shells and bombs on them in a battle to clear the last remaining areas.

At one point in a forest fighting ceased after what the *Red Star* calls "a real butchery" of the enemy.

Thousands of Germans lay dead among the trees and hundreds were marched off to prison camps.—Reuter and B.U.P. messages.

2,754 Bombs Fired: 100 to 150 a Day

DEEP SHELTERS TO OPEN

MR. CHURCHILL, in his eagerly-awaited speech on the flying-bomb raids, revealed in the Commons to-day that about 2,754 flying bombs—between 100 and 150 a day—have been launched against this country in the past fortnight.

Up to 6 a.m. to-day 2,752 people have been killed and about 8,000 injured and detained in hospital. This was practically one death per bomb. A very high proportion of the casualties has fallen on London.

Mr. Churchill revealed that 50,000 tons of bombs have been rained on flying bomb sites in France—prefabricated so they could be built quickly—on experimental stations and rocket targets. A hundred firing sites have been destroyed.

"If it had not been for these Allied bombing operations, the bombardment of London would have started perhaps six months earlier on a very much heavier scale," said Mr. Churchill. The head German scientist was killed in one of our raids, he added.

"We Shall Not Fail"

A special committee has been set up on all counter-measures for dealing with the flying bomb, Mr. Churchill announced.

Here are other points made by the Premier: It has now been decided to make use of deep shelters.

There will be no compulsory evacuation scheme for children in London, but the Government are encouraging people who have no essential work to leave. It would help if they did.

The Premier ended: "What of the future? Is this attack going to get worse? Will the rocket bomb come? Will more destructive explosions come? Will there be greater ranges? I can give no guarantee that any of these evils will be finally prevented before the time comes when the soil from which these attacks come has been finally liberated.

"London will never be conquered and will never fail."

Weather Against Us

Here is Mr. Churchill's speech in full:

THE time has come to give a fuller account of the flying bomb attacks. A wider field of discussion can be opened, but I would enjoin upon the House and on the public outside to watch their step in anything they say, because a thing which might not strike one as being harmful at all might give some information to the enemy which would be of use to him and detrimental to us.

It would be a mistake to underrate the serious character of this particular form of attack. It has never been underrated in Government circles.

The probability of such an attack has been under continued intense study for a long time.

During the early months of 1943 we received through our many and varied intelligence services many reports that the Germans were devising a new long-range weapon with which they proposed to bombard London.

FEARED ROCKET

More Shelters Open

At first our information led us to believe that a rocket weapon would be used. Counter-measures were studied by the Chiefs of Staff and the War Cabinet.

Shelter provision began to be made increasingly, and is now being intensified. These shelters are by no means ill-adapted to withstand the blast effect of the bombs at present being used.

The enemy took all possible precautions to conceal his designs. Nevertheless, as a result of searching investigation, we had by July, 1943, succeeded in locating a number of the sites.

The main experimental station was located, and the full strength of Bomber Command was sent out to attack these installations.

Very great damage was done, and a number of German scientists, including the head scientist, who were all dwelling together in a so-called "Strength Through Joy" establishment, were killed.

RAIDS DELAYED

Sites Attacked

These raids delayed by many months the development and bringing into action of both these weapons. About this time we had also located in the Pas de Calais the first of the large sites which appeared to be connected with the firing of a long-range rocket.

These sites were heavily attacked as long ago as September, and have been given continued treatment since by the heaviest weapon carried by the British and American Air Forces.

Other structures in greater numbers were discovered between Havre and the Pas de Calais. About 100 of the smaller sites were found all along the French coast between Havre and Calais, and we concluded it would be firing points for jet-propelled missiles smaller than the rocket.

All these sites were continuously bombed since last December. If it had not been for our bombing operations in France and Germany and counter preparations, the bombardment of London would, no doubt, have started perhaps six months earlier and on a very much heavier scale.

The enemy felt, among other impulses, the need of having something to boost and carry on the war and also in order to steady neutrals and satellites and persuading public opinion.

SITES PICTURED

Thousands of Photos

Up to 6 a.m. to-day 2,752 people have been killed by flying bombs and about 8,000 have been injured and detained in hospital. The number of flying bombs launched up to 6 a.m. to-day was 2,754.

The firing points in France have been continually attacked for several months and the total weight of bombs so far dropped on these and rocket targets in France and Germany, including Pennemunde, have now reached about 50,000 tons.

The number of reconnaissance flights now totals many thousands and the scrutiny of tens of thousands of air photographs has been a stupendous task.

There has been progress for a

Turn To Back Page

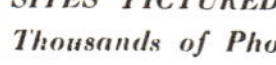

Evacuation Has Been Going On Since Monday

"Evening News" Reporter

SCHOOLCHILDREN have been leaving London since Monday under a re-opened Government evacuation scheme, it can now be revealed.

Registrations began last week. The area of evacuation covers practically all Greater London.

In some areas, registrations average 700 a day. But in others only a score or so of names have been put down.

Three Classes

The scheme applies to three classes:

1.—Unaccompanied children between 5 and 16;
2.—Mothers with children under 5; and
3.—The aged and infirm, who are expected to find their own billets.

Eventually about 15,000 will be leaving daily.

Destinations

About 5,000 children left four main stations before midday to-day—bound for Yorkshire, the Midlands, Lancashire, Cheshire, and North Wales.

The children marched from their homes or schools to assembly points, where they were picked up in buses.

One teacher was in charge of every ten children. Each child was labelled with an address. Nearly all carried suitcases.

They were given milk on the trains.

Did Not Sign

Just before the final train of the day left, parents arrived with children, but as the yhad not been registered for evacuation, the parents were told that it was impossible to include their children in the official evacuation parties until later.

More big parties are to leave to-morrow and Sunday. Five trainloads will leave Euston to-morrow between 8.30 a.m. and 1.30 p.m.

Little Londoners travel North—"Evening News" picture at Euston to-day.

REAL SUMMER

In the Straits

TEMPERATURE was soaring in the Straits of Dover to-day, with the sun shining brilliantly and every promise of a real summer's day. A light southerly breeze just rippled the calm water, from which a [illegible] haze arose.

Visibility at ground level was restricted but improving, and the sky above was cloudless. Shade temperature was 68. The barometer has now been steady for 24 hours.

WHEN BOMBS COME

The Thieves Break In

"We are having complaints of various petty larcenies by thieves who walk into houses when people have gone to shelters," said a detective to-day when William Charles Jeffrey, 44, labourer, was sentenced to a month's hard labour for being on enclosed premises for an unlawful purpose.

OUR PEACE TERMS

'Mr. Stimson Tells the Pope'

Herbert Matthews, the *New York Times* Rome correspondent, reports that Mr. Henry Stimson, U.S. War Secretary, and Mr Myron Taylor, the U.S. Special Envoy to the Vatican, "talked to the Pope primarily of the peace that is going to be dictated to Germany, but they have not come to Rome to negotiate that peace."

Matthews said it was widely believed in Rome that the Germans would make a peace effort through the Vatican, and perhaps soon. "With the Allies and the Russians driving ahead the time is approaching when the German leaders will have to think of peace," he said.—Reuter.

WARM U.S. WELCOME

For General de Gaulle

A warm welcome is planned for General de Gaulle on his arrival in Washington to-day to show him that, despite the policy of the U.S. Government towards recognition of the French National Committee, the highest respect is due to him personally, says A.P.

WOUNDED EXCHANGE

Madrid Knows Nothing

Nothing is known in Madrid of a reported further exchange of wounded prisoners-of-war which it was said would take place in Barcelona on July 28

The British Embassy, the Spanish Foreign Ministry and Dr. Arbenz, the Madrid delegate to the International Red Cross, disclaimed all knowledge of such an exchange, says Reuter.

DON'T WE ALL

When I married I was just as other men: I hoped for the best: *London court witness.*

"NORMANDY BREACH IN GERMAN MAIN LINE"

Big Air Battles Flare Up

The Germans officially announced this afternoon that south-west of Carentan the Allies have breached the German main line.

FIERCE air battles against strong formations of German fighters were fought in the skies over the whole Normandy battle front yesterday, it is announced at Supreme H.Q. to-day.

The Luftwaffe was beaten. Thirty-five of their planes were shot down and [illegible] destroyed on the ground for the [illegible] fighters.

On land the Americans, after taking the railway station at La Haye du Puits, are battling for every foot of ground as they drive on south. The Allies hold firm at Carpiquet against new German attacks. Here are war reporters' stories of the fighting:

LA HAYE NAZIS "SURRENDERED"

THEN THEY FIRED ON ALLIED TROOPS

BLOODY hand-to-hand fighting has been going on during the last few hours for La Haye.

I have been among the forward assault troops, says a B.U.P. war correspondent. They are advancing steadily, but they are paying the price.

Youngsters I knew a few days ago as lieutenants and captains are now acting as captains, majors—even lieutenant-colonels.

Many of those youngsters I knew are dead to-day through Nazi treachery in its most cruel and vicious form.

The Germans are not fighting cleanly. They are resorting to every trick in the German military dictionary. They are not respecting the Red Cross. They have killed several stretcher bearers who were carrying wounded.

Desert Trick

An old Western Desert trick was used against a group of our engineers. As the engineers were repairing a bridge Germans approached them with their hands up.

Then the Germans suddenly flopped down on to their faces and a machine-gun, concealed behind them, opened up and mowed down our men.

The battalion colonel told me: "These Germans are a slick bunch of rogues.

"One boy was shot at close range by a sniper precisely at a point where six Germans had just surrendered. It seems to have been prearranged."

I watched some scenes of the battle from the village of Bolleville, on the Barneville-La Haye road. I could see the smoking remains of four German tanks, and then I heard a cascade of small arms fire, with the deep, dull roar of the artillery thudding behind as American and German shells sighed overhead.

CAREFULLY TRAINED

The man with commonsense is the husband who knows he has married the right woman.—London witness to-day.

AIRFIELD BATTLE GROWS GRIMMER

THEY ARE FIGHTING IN HANGARS AND HOUSES

CANADIANS thrusting at the Carpiquet airfield, the aerodrome of Caen, are to-day involved in fighting intense as anything the Allies have experienced anywhere.

German reaction to the Canadian advance has been exceptionally violent.

The Carpiquet-Verson area is, however, a real "hot spot."

Rommel has massed so many troops along the Tilly-Caen front that saturation point has been reached where the fighting is fiercest. At these spots there is a concentration practically unsurpassed even in the last war. Rommel can pack in no more men.

A shell-pocked stretch of runways—a stretch of ground measuring a few hundred yards—is all that divides the Canadian and German troops in the Carpiquet air base area.

Dug-in tanks are still being employed in its stubborn defence, and hangars and houses in the vicinity are heavily defended.

ROUEN CUT OFF

Roads and Railways Bombed

Paris radio said to-day: "Following recent Allied bombing around Rouen, normal rail and road traffic has been rendered impossible, thus compelling German army vehicles to carry food supplies to the city. German troops have been detailed to undertake repair work of roads and rails leading to Rouen.

JAP ENVOY DIES

Sakamoto, Japanese Minister to Switzerland, has died, the Swiss radio said to-day.

GOOD OLD BERT

Wife at Tottenham to-day: My husband's popularity is making my husband a man of means. His drinks and entertainment cost him nothing.

NAZIS FROM PALESTINE

Two hundred Germans have arrived at Istanbul from Palestine, to be exchanged against 65 Hungarian Jews, says Exchange.

THEIR CHOICE

Two [illegible] two U.S. [illegible] Queen of Braintree (Essex) Holiday Week.

MIGHTY AIR FLEET GOES OUT

FRONT-LINE TOWNS AWAKE ALL NIGHT

After a night of almost non-stop Allied air activity over the Continent, big fleets of our planes headed for the flying bomb bases again to-day.

IT was officially announced to-day that R.A.F. Lancasters made a deep penetration through fighter-defended areas in France in the night to attack the railway marshalling yards at Dijon, more than 250 miles from the nearest point on the coast.

This was to block yet another route which the Germans, faced with the disorganisation on the railways further north, could use to bring supplies and reinforcements from Germany in a long detour towards the battlefield.

A great weight of high-explosive bombs was dropped.

Other heavy bombers attacked military installations in Northern France.

Squadrons of Mosquitoes went to Germany to attack industrial objectives, including a synthetic oil plant in the Ruhr.

Kiel Bay Attacked

Hundreds of bombers passed over Folkestone to-day on their way to the Continent, and later, the south-east coast rocked with big explosions apparently coming from the Pas de Calais area.

At the same time Berlin radio reported that U.S. bomber formations, strongly escorted by fighters, were over North Germany to-day.

The Germans reported that the Kiel Bay area was the target.

Never before during the war have people in the front line towns in the Straits of Dover area experienced such a night of Allied air activity as during the night and again to-day.

For an hour around midnight a vast armada of Allied machines passed over this coast for the Continent in hundreds.

MR. A. G. WALKDEN

Knocked Down by Car

Mr. A. G. Walkden, Labour M.P. for South Bristol, whilst on his way to the House of Commons to-day, was knocked down by a car and taken to Westminster Hospital. He is suffering from shock, but his condition is not regarded as serious.

RACES ABANDONED

Salisbury Decision

Messrs. Weatherby announced to-day that racing will not take place at Salisbury on Saturday next.

There will be racing in the north at Pontefract.

It was stated when the list of racing fixtures was issued that altered circumstances might necessitate the abandonment of fixtures even at the shortest notice.

BALLOON IN THE CART

A barrage balloon adrift was shot down by military at Gayton, Norfolk after anchoring itself to a farm cart.

BOUGHT £1,000,000 SHIPS

Mr. James Childs Gould, former millionaire shipowner, has died at 62 at his home in Coulsdon. He was the son of a Cardiff working mason, began work at 14 for 4s. a week, and during the last war bought a merchant fleet for £1,000,000. See Talk of the Day: Page Two.

LATEST

RED ARMY 10 MILES FROM VILNA

German radio says Russian spearheads now about 10 miles east of Vilna.

RUSSIAN LANDING, SAY FINNS

Finnish communique says Russians succeeded in occupying strongpoints at Aevraepaeae. Finns evacuated Teikari Island in Viipuri Bay.—B.U.P.

U.S. HEAVIES HIT FLYING BOMB BASES

H.Q. United States Strategic Air Forces in Europe states: Large forces of Flying Forts and Liberators of the Eighth Air Force to-day attacked enemy targets in North-West Germany, airfields in France and military installations in Pas de Calais, including flying bomb launching platforms.

CHINA: "GRAVE SITUATION"

General Chiang Kai-Shek admitted in Chungking to-day that China's military situation was grave.—A.P.

JAPS USE GAS

U.S. Expert Saw It Used

CHUNGKING, Thursday.

DEFINITE confirmation that Japs are using poison gas is given by Captain Ralph Thompson, of the U.S. Chemical Warfare Department.

He has just returned to Chungking from Hengyang, the "Bomb Tokio" airfield centre taken by the Japs a few days ago. He says that the Japanese used gas in this operation composed of a mixture of mustard gas and lewisite.—B.U.P.

TO FIGHT HARWICH

The Allied Ex-Services Association announce that Mr. Norman F. Hidden (Common Wealth) is to contest Harwich in the General Election, fighting on the Allied Ex-Services Association platform.

R-BOATS ROUTED

Two Sunk in Channel Fight

LIEUT.-COMMANDER D. G. BRADFORD, D.S.C., R.N.V.R., ace commander of "little ships," has given the Germans another Channel hiding.

A considerable force of enemy craft operating from Havre were routed on Tuesday night when they attempted to break through our patrols, says a S.H.A.E.F. communique.

The first contact with the enemy was made off Cape De La Heve by coastal forces of the Royal Canadian Navy commanded by Lieutenant-Commander A. Law, R.C.N.V.R., and a brief engagement followed, says the communique.

Shortly afterwards a group of nine E-boats and R-boats was sighted by another patrol commanded by Lieutenant-Commander D. G. Bradford, D.S.C., R.N.V.R.

The enemy was attacked with torpedo and gunfire. Two R-boats were sunk and a third damaged in this action.

A Second Attempt

A further attempt was made by the enemy, who had by then been reinforced, to break out to the west, but he was again intercepted by Lieutenant-Commander Law's force. After a brief engagement the enemy retired to Le Havre.

About an hour later two enemy M-class minesweepers were intercepted by Lieutenant-Commander Bradford and attacked. Hits were observed on one minesweeper before the enemy made good his escape to harbour.

GERMAN WOUNDED

'In Same Wards as British'

The Secretary for War is to be asked to-morrow by Wing-Commander E Errington (Con., Bootle): "Whether he is aware that wounded German prisoners in military hospitals in this country have been put in the same wards as British wounded, and that this is resented by the latter, and whether he will give an undertaking that this will not occur again."

STOCK FIGURE

A husband at Acton Matrimonial Court to-day: I know for a fact that my wife got £1 10s. when she pawned my suit, because it has been pawned so many times before.

TICKETS NEEDED FOR SHELTERS

BUILT NEAR TUBES

"Evening News" Reporter

THE deep shelters which Mr. Churchill disclosed are now to be used for their original purpose for the first time number eight.

They were authorised at the height of the 1941 blitz in anticipation of heavier bombing in 1942.

This did not mature, and with the exception of one or two being used for Government purposes they have been allowed to remain ready for service as shelters.

They are all built adjacent to London Transport tube stations but are separate from them and have their own entrances and exits.

Dormitories hold tiers of bunks divided into sections to house families in privacy.

Restaurants, sick bays, and modern sanitation are available. Admission will be by ticket only, issued by the local authority.

Four are north of the river and four south. They are 100 feet below ground and have 8,000 bunks in each.

BOMB STORIES

"BELIEVE it or not, old man, I got down as flat as a pancake."—By Gittins.

The Communique: Navy Foils E-Boat Raid

Here is to-day's communique from Supreme H.Q.:

ALLIED troops have taken the railway station at La Haye du Puits, and are pushing on to the South with the enemy contesting every foot of ground. our positions at Carpiquet have been held. Enemy attacks continue.

Fierce combats with strong formations of enemy fighters, which were engaged in varying weather over the battle area and to the South and East, marked our air operations yesterday afternoon and evening.

Considerble numbers of our fighters and fighter-bombers, vigorously supporting our ground forces, joined in the air battles which took place along the entire front.

Notable air victories were scored in the area bounded by Chartres, Rouen, Caen and Argentan by our fighters out to attack road and rail transport.

They also attacked tanks at Carpiquet airfield and special targets indicated by ground commanders close behind the enemy lines at St. Lo, Vire Falaise, Periers, and Dreux.

At least 35 enemy aircraft were shot down during the day and four more were destroyed on the ground. Fifteen of our fighters are missing.

During the night heavy bombers attacked the railway yards at Dijon. All our bombers returned safely. Light bombers also hit railway junctions and bridges at Villedieu, Hyenville and Granville.

During Tuesday night a considerable force of enemy E-boats and R-boats attempted to enter the Eastern Anchorage. The enemy was intercepted, brought to action and finally driven off by light coastal forces. Two enemy R-boats were sunk and a third severely damaged.

Daily Mail

NO. 15,032 ONE PENNY ** FOR KING AND EMPIRE FRIDAY, JULY 7, 1944

LATE WAR NEWS

HITLER DISMISSES VON RUNDSTEDT

Gives 'Health Reasons' as Excuse

'HEDGEHOG' KLUGE GETS THE JOB

RUNDSTEDT, in command in France at the time of the Normandy landings, has been sacked by Hitler. He has been succeeded by 62-years-old Field-Marshal von Kluge, veteran of some of the greatest battles on the Russian front.

Berlin announced the sacking of von Rundstedt in this statement from Hitler's H.Q.:

"Field-Marshal von Kluge has taken over the Supreme Command in the West from Field-Marshal von Rundstedt, who is unable to carry out his duties for health reasons.

"In a cordial letter, Hitler has expressed his thanks to Field-Marshal von Rundstedt, who has distinguished himself in the most difficult situations.

"He has also intimated that Field-Marshal von Rundstedt will be employed in other special tasks."

It is certain that this important announcement would not have been made unless von Kluge had already taken over in France, which suggests that the dismissal of Rundstedt was decided on as soon as he failed to hold the Normandy beaches.

Von Kluge, now C.-in-C. to Rommel, is Germany's defence expert, with his reputation based on his success in holding "hedgehog" positions on the Russian front. His offensive successes include the great sweep through to Moscow, when he was halted at the gates of the Soviet capital. His failures include the German attack on the Kursk salient.

Kluge, a tank enthusiast, has long disagreed with Rundstedt over the Normandy defence system, and his influence with Hitler may have been the deciding factor in the dismissal of Rundstedt, which undoubtedly represents a victory for the Nazi Party over the High Command. Both Rundstedt and Kluge have one point in common—both are soldiers first and foremost without undue interest in Nazi politics. But von Kluge is a favourite of Hitler.

It may be significant that since von Kluge took over the Normandy fighting has been characterised by ever-hardening German opposition and an increase in the enemy's efforts to hold and smash back the Allied advance.

THE NEW MAN

Field-Marshal von Kluge. *Irreverent German soldiers call him "Melancholy Baby."*

Caen: The Bombers Join in the Battle

THE full weight of the Allied Air Forces has been flung into the battle of Normandy, and throughout yesterday R.A.F. and U.S. bombers and fighters were pounding at the richest military targets ever offered to an air force.

The pick of these targets was in the Caen area, where Rommel has so massed his armour and infantry that he has reached saturation point, and is unable to deploy any more reinforcements.

At some parts he has a division to less than three miles of front—a density unequalled elsewhere, and as great as in the trench battles of the last war.

On the Allied side, men and tanks are equally closely packed.

As the Allied Air Forces batter at dumps, guns, and panzers, the land forces of this sector are for the moment idle. Both sides are waiting for the inevitable, gigantic clash for this is a "springboard" battle for position, and sooner or later one side or the other must strike.

Cut Off

The Caen front was cut off from the rest of France during yesterday's raids. Three hundred Havocs and Marauders smashed the five railways feeding the battle area, and also destroyed two bridges in the town itself.

Most of the ground gained in this week's Anglo-Canadian attack is still held by the Allies, although the Germans have established a footing in Carpiquet aerodrome.

In the American zone, the advance round La Haye du Puits is steadily continuing.

American troops have withdrawn from La Haye itself, and are now driving forward between the town and the sea—an effort to by-pass and encircle it.

This thrust is already a mile south-west of La Haye. Good progress is also being made in the assault on the forest of Mont Castre, a pivotal point for the Germans on this sector and one that is being strongly defended. The forest dominates La Haye, and U.S. troops are already menacing its last key points.

South-west of Carentan, the Americans yesterday made their biggest advance of the day—1,500yds. gain that brought them to the village of Culot.

KLUGE IS HITLER'S FAVOURITE

Even Though He Missed Moscow

VON KLUGE—pronounced "Klooga," and meaning, literally, "clever"—has a nickname with the German Army.

He is called "Melancholy Baby." His headquarters in Poland, in France, in Russia—in triumph and in disaster—are houses of gloom.

He is one of the men to whom Hitler has stuck in spite of failure. Kluge is "the man who missed Moscow." He swept through Bialystok, Minsk, and Smolensk in 1941, only to be halted at the gates of Moscow.

His subsequent success in fortifying and holding the "hedgehog defences" of Veliki Luki, Rzhev, Orel, and Vyasma gave him a great reputation in Germany, where the Nazi Press hailed him, as they had hailed Rommel, as the apostle of "victorious defence."

Created the 'Wall'

He directed the abortive German offensive in the Kursk salient, which petered out in 10 days.

As commander on the White Russian front, he had to face the big Russian offensive launched against the Fatherland Line last October.

Von Kluge, who is 61—Rundstedt is 67—comes of an old Prussian family. Mild and somewhat scholarly in appearance, brisk and decisive in manner, he has especially studied anti-French strategy.

Von Rundstedt, tall and spare, cold and unemotional, devoted to his country and his caste, is the true heir to the traditions of Germany's "General Staff."

The son of a general, he has seen 52 years of military service under Empire, Republic, and the Nazis. He has kept aloof from the Republic as well as from the Nazis, but he has always obeyed orders.

It was Rundstedt who deposed the Prussian Social Democratic Government in 1932 under the orders of President Hindenburg and Chancellor von Papen.

3 Successes

It was Rundstedt who stood ready to act in the same way against Hitler in 1933 if Hindenburg should give the order.

He has been in charge of the defences of France, Belgium, and Holland since 1942. Germans regard him as the creator of the "Atlantic Wall."

In this war Rundstedt has achieved three outstanding successes. In 1939 he led the Southern Army Group which took Cracow and Warsaw and decided the speed of the Polish campaign; in 1940 he led the army group which crossed the Meuse, broke through the French lines, and wheeled to the Channel ports.

In 1941 he commanded the Southern Army Group in Russia, which, by its advance to Kiev, brought Marshal Budenny's forces into grave danger. Normandy was his first great failure.

PANZERS DARE NOT MOVE

From G. WARD PRICE

SHAEF, Thursday Evening.

AFTER putting up a comparatively weak resistance to the American forces that managed to avoid encirclement in the peninsula are fighting with unexpected stubbornness.

They are holding on between the

BACK PAGE—Col. EIGHT

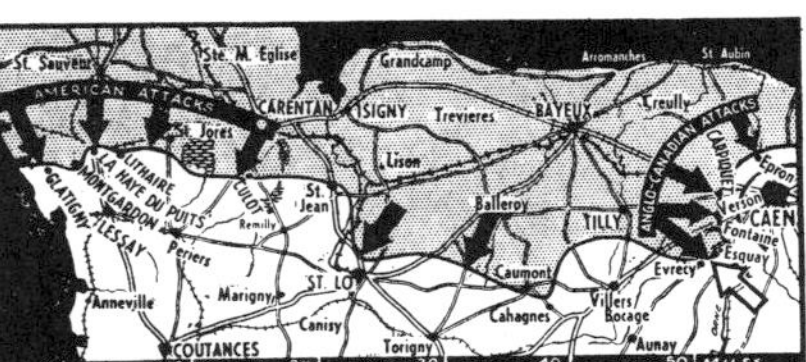

We are Only Possible Government

—GOEBBELS

DR. GOEBBELS seemed to find it necessary to reassure himself and his readers in his weekly article in Das Reich on the question of Germany's future Government.

Not once, but several times in his article, Goebbels returned to the theme: "All Germany is behind the Government. No other Government is possible.

"There is no other opinion in Germany other than that of the German Government," he claimed. "No other Government could be formed in Germany even under enemy pressure.

"No public could be found for any war opinion other than that of the German Government, which has shown in the past that it is ready for anything.

"A people is most dangerous when it has burned its bridges and has nothing to lose," Goebbels added.

"This war can no longer shake us. We have lost too much already. The last reserves are laid bare."

'Disappointed'

Goebbels went on to declare:

"The big military operations the Allies have prepared for this spring and summer have not led to any decisions. The enemy is disappointed. He has underestimated the military power of Germany.

"Our enemies have no choice. If they want to pursue their aim, other than to attempt to take Europe from us yard by yard. They cannot hope for our weakness."

He ended with a lament on the Bolshevik menace.

"A great horde is running against the European Continent from the east," he said, "and this Continent has nothing better to do but to bleed itself in internal fighting, and thus to open the door into Europe with its own hand."

'U.S. Used Winged Bombs'—Berlin

German radio said yesterday that American bombers, in their attacks on Cologne on May 28 and on Hamburg on June 18, released some "winged bombs in the shape of small gliders."

"This winged bomb," said the announcer, "was totally different in conception and effect from the German V.1 (the flying bomb), which has effective range regulators which guarantee accuracy."—*Reuter.*

Mail to France

Five tons of mail for British Service men were flown to France yesterday morning and distributed before nightfall. The mail will now be flown from England before breakfast each morning, and letters home will be the planes' cargo for the afternoon return trip.

Three-week Report on London

Morale, Damage and Defence

Co-inciding with brilliant weather in the Strait and terrific heavy bomber attacks on Pas de Calais bases, Southern England had a lull in flying-bomb attacks yesterday.

By Daily Mail Reporter

NOW that Mr. Churchill has revealed the facts about the flying bomb, it is possible to answer some of the questions that all England—and the rest of the world—has been asking in recent weeks.

For the benefit of non-Londoners, here is a review of the past three weeks. The first question generally asked is:

What is the damage like?

YOU have to look for it. It is indiscriminate damage, because this is an indiscriminate weapon.

The main impression is of glass. Going through London casually, you will see, maybe, the effects of a couple of incidents in a day—blown-out windows, with people still at work behind them; very many little houses with slates off, and some small houses wiped out altogether.

Unless it is a strong, modern building, the place that gets the actual hit is liable to be brought down to its foundations. But when the bomb falls in a modern, well-built thoroughfare of big shops and offices, it is seldom that anything more than the windows and a bit of the roof go.

How are Londoners taking it?

AS you would expect. They don't like it, and they don't pretend that they do. But the great mass of them are getting on quietly with their jobs and making their own personal dispositions for getting a reasonable amount of sleep.

This is a different reaction from the "blitz" reaction. Then there was a definite sense of backs-to-the-wall defiance, and a deep pride in the fact that "we were alone and could take it."

This new form of attack has aroused anger at its military pointlessness, bitterness over the casualties among women, children, and old folk, and a marked hardening of feeling against the Germans and all their works—a feeling that the Germans may have cause to rue later on.

People, too, are warier than in the blitz days. There is no false shame about going down on one's face in the street when a flying bomb "cuts out" overhead.

This time it is the reaction of the veteran soldier, who has learned that only a fool takes unnecessary risks.

Londoners certainly feel better now that the Prime Minister has let the rest of the world know that London really is taking it again.

Reaction is often summed up in the philosophical remark: "Well, they tried shelling Paris before they packed up last time. This looks like the beginning of the end for Germany."

How do Londoners compare it with the blitz?

THERE are two views on this. Some people find it more unnerving than the blitz.

Their argument is that in the blitz days you knew more or less at what hours it was coming, got into the habit of sheltering at night, and felt secure during the day, thanks to the protection of the R.A.F fighter squadrons.

The other side think that the flying bomb ordeal is much less worrying than the blitz days. They argue that you can hear them coming in plenty of time; you can judge just about where they are going to fall, and if you use your head you have plenty of time to take cover and get away from the main danger—which is flying glass.

With all the roar of the London traffic, how can people hear them coming?

THE roof spotters of London now co-operate. They signal from roof to roof the direction of the next bomb.

Signals fly up from the roofs away down to the south, and the roof spotters are becoming so expert at charting the course of approaching bombs that, by sounding whistles, or local klaxons, they can

BACK PAGE—Col. THREE

BERLIN SAYS 'OUR RETREAT MUST GO ON'

BERLIN declared last night that the Germans will have to abandon yet more territory to the Red Army. "The Russians," said Martin Hellensleben, German News Agency's chief correspondent, "are out to roll up our entire front." Their intentions, he added, "reveal as much large-scale planning as they show methodical strategy." The drives on Dvinsk and Vilna aimed at clearing the Baltic shores, to make way for an attack on "German territory proper." "The Russians," he admitted, "have learnt a lot during the war."

Kovel Falls to New Push South of Pripet

Into Poland

CAPTURE of Kovel, announced in a Stalin Order of the Day last night, brings the Russians nearer to Brest-Litovsk and Lublin, and increases the peril to Pinsk. Farther north a German report says the Russians have driven to within 10 miles of Vilna, on the road to East Prussia and the Baltic coast.

NEARER VILNA: BERLIN

THE Red Army have launched a new drive against the Germans south of the Pripet Marshes. Marshal Rokossovsky, extending the eastern front to a width of 350 miles, has captured Kovel and is thrusting on to the west.

Fall of this fortress junction on the direct line to Warsaw was announced in an Order of the Day from Marshal Stalin last night.

Rokossovsky's First White Russian Army are attacking on a 200-miles sector ranging from Kovel to Baranovici, which is now only ten miles ahead of his troops.

Evacuation of Kovel was reported by Berlin on Wednesday. And yesterday the Germans predicted a new all-out offensive by Marshal Zhukov south of the city to back Rokossovsky's new blow.

At the northern end of the front desperate enemy counter-attacks have failed to hold the Red Army from Vilna, gateway to East Prussia and the Baltic. Soviet spearheads, according to Berlin, are within ten miles of the fortress city.

General Chernyakhovsky is tearing gaps through the German reinforcements of tanks and infantry which have been flung in to hold this northern bastion of the last defence line before Reich soil.

Regiment Surrender

The Soviet communiqué showed that his troops, broadening the scope of their attack, have swung round Lake Naroch and advanced 50 miles in 48 hours along the main highway to Vilna, now within range of heavy guns.

Aim of the Russians is first to outflank the defences which run south-west to Grodno, Bialystok and Brest-Litovsk, and isolate the two enemy armies still garrisoned in the Baltic States.

Then the stage will be set for another smashing thrust to the west—on the narrowing front between Vilna and Baranovici.

Another 5,000 German troops have been wiped out in the pocket east of Minsk. The 195th Regiment of the 78th Assault Division surrendered en masse to the Russians.

'Hold or Die'

The communiqué reported that General Bagramyan, in his sweep forward to Dvinsk, northernmost bastion of the East Prussia defence line, has seized 150 more places.

Along the whole front German resistance is growing. Into the battle, which has moved to less than 120 miles of East Prussia, veteran Wehrmacht units are fighting with orders to hold out or die on the approaches to their Fatherland.

Enemy armoured trains have appeared on the sector before Vilna, but they cannot prevent the Soviet air hammering of their ammunition and fuel wagons throughout the area.

We Shell the Enemy with Her Picture

"TONI" is the Allies' new secret weapon on the Italian front. She is Broadway actress Virginia Robinson. Her photograph is fired at the Germans by the thousand, and she broadcasts daily to the Germans in excellent German, telling them, between music, facts that should make them doubt Hitler.

E. PRUSSIA WILL BE 'SCORCHED'

Germans Prepare

From WALTER FARR

STOCKHOLM, Thursday.

THE Germans to-night are reported to be making frantic preparations for the defence of East Prussia and the southern part of Poland in anticipation of new Russian advances.

The evacuation of civilians from Königsberg, which has for years been used as an overflow town for Berlin bombed victims, has already begun.

Hitler's H.Q., which used to be in Königsberg, has long since been removed. German military spokesmen throughout to-day warned that "any day now the Germans may expect to have to fight in defence of the soil of Germany itself."

They talk of a "deepening crisis" and of the "supreme effort needed to avoid catastrophe."

Blitz Coming

The Germans say they must expect savage Russian air attacks on such places as Königsberg, and on Berlin, in the near future. They have ordered a scorched earth policy in the east. It involves blowing up all factories in Poland and, if necessary, in East Prussia.

The German order is: "Leave not a single house standing. All cattle must be removed to Germany. Every effort must be made to gather in the harvest early in the threatened areas.

"All men in areas now coming within the combat zone, regardless of nationality, must be gathered into the labour battalions and removed to Central Germany."

MORRISON TO HEAR MPs

On Robot Plans

By Daily Mail Political Correspondent

London M.P.s are to meet Mr. Herbert Morrison, Home Secretary and Minister of Home Security, immediately to discuss various problems arising out of the flying-bomb raids and to put numerous suggestions before him for the consideration of the Government.

This will be the first of a series of meetings of this kind, maintaining direct contact between the people of London and the Government, and obviating questions in the House of Commons which might reveal information useful to the enemy.

Plans for opening deep shelters, which Mr Churchill announced in his speech, are being hurried along but will not be completed for some days. The delay will not be longer than is necessary to make certain arrangements.

Smokes to Normandy

Troops in Normandy are soon to be given an overseas address, and friends will be able to send duty-free cigarettes and tobacco.

PLANES SINK 4 R-BOATS

Brest Trawler 'Kill'

No fewer than 28 attacks were made against enemy E-boats and R-boats in the Channel area early yesterday morning by Albacores and Beaufighters of R.A.F Coastal Command and Fleet Air Arm Swordfish.

It is estimated that four E- and R-boats, which were operating off Boulogne Dieppe, and Ostend, were probably sunk and nine others possibly damaged. Two R-boats were sunk off the beaches on Tuesday night.

The Canadian destroyer Qu'Appelle (Commander A. M. McKillop, R.N.) with other destroyers intercepted four armed enemy trawlers off Brest shortly after one o'clock yesterday morning. In an hour's fight three of the enemy were set on fire. It is believed they sank, but the fourth escaped into Brest.

Shop Prices Fixed for Plums

The Food Ministry to-day announce maximum prices for plums, taking effect on Sunday.

Ordinary varieties will be 4d. to 5½d. a lb., according to area, greengages 8d. and 9d., dessert Victorias 10d., and damsons 6½d. to 8½d. a lb.

LONDON SIRENS DURING NIGHT

An Alert was sounded in the London area during the night.

PLANES SINK 9 JAP SHIPS

Pearl Harbour, Thursday.—U.S. carrier planes sank nine Japanese ships, probably sank six, and damaged at least 21 vessels during an assault on the Volcano and Bonin Islands.—A.P.

PLANE HITS HOUSES

A woman, her three-years-old son, and an R.A.F. pilot were killed when a plane crashed on houses at Huddersfield last night.

2

ALL TROOPS IN GOOD HEART

Says Eisenhower

General Eisenhower, in a statement issued to SHAEF last night on his return from the battle area in Normandy, said he found the fighting men of all the forces in good heart and exceedingly fit for the difficult tasks they faced.

"Within the area of the Second British Army there is constantly evidenced an admiration for the work of United States forces, while throughout the American flank there is universal and grateful appreciation of the vital and important tasks the British troops have been so brilliantly performing.

"By sea, air, and land we are waging this campaign as a single combat team."

LONDON'S LOSSES STAGGER U.S.

Daily Mail Special Correspondent

NEW YORK, Thursday.

AMERICA is angry at the civilian slaughter in London from flying bombs—as angry as she was when the daily news of London's blitz made it clear that for the Nazis, even in those early days, it was "total and indiscriminate" war.

This time, too, it's a more personal anger, for many Americans who heard the news to-day are relatives of those brave American rescuers to whom Mr. Churchill paid tribute.

They really feel now that when Germany bombs London she is also bombing America. That was a rather pretty "hands-across-the-ocean" thought in the days of the blitz—now it has become hard reality.

The extent of the casualties and damage done by the flying bomb amazed America. The general belief was that they had dropped mainly in the southern counties and that only a few had reached London.

People had no idea of the real seriousness of the weapon or of the long "back-room" battle which our scientists had been waging with the German inventors.

Expressions of complete surprise crossed the faces of the crowd who watched the casualty list flash out over the electrical news ticker which girdles Times-square.

"Why, it's as bad as the blitz," was the usual comment.

Americans are glad that Mr. Churchill gave such a frank statement and made no attempt to minimise the destructive power of the new weapon or of the difficulties which we had experienced in finding counter-measures.

The flying bomb has done more than anything could have done to destroy any complacency in America that the war in Europe is won.

The Daily Sketch

2 Pages of Pictures

No. 10,970 ★★ THURSDAY, JULY 13, 1944 ONE PENNY

ROMMEL IS PULLING OUT OF THE PENINSULA

Wounded Abandoned

ROMMEL is pulling out from the base of the Cherbourg Peninsula. In places his troops have retreated so fast that they have abandoned their dead and wounded.

American troops, following almost unopposed behind the retreating Germans, are within $2\frac{1}{4}$ miles of Lessay, near the western coast. Steady shelling kept enemy rearguards on the move.

More Villages Captured

On the way the Americans took the hamlet of La Croutte and the villages of Angoville-sur-Ay and La Bourdonnerie, which represents an advance of more than 2,000 yards.

One German first-aid station seized on top of an important ridge east of St. Lo had several German wounded inside it and a number of dead outside.

In a desperate move to halt some of the American advances yesterday the Germans were discovered using "sniper artillery," risking 88 mm. guns in the front line where they fired directly on their target.

Important Heights Taken

More advances have been made in the St. Lo area.

Left flank forces, driving along the Bayeux-St. Lo road, are only one and a half miles from the outskirts of St. Lo. Two useful ridges have also been taken.

"We are now looking down the Germans' throats," said an Army spokesman.

St. Endre de l'Epine has been by-passed, isolating the German garrison in the town, and the Americans have swept through La Calvaira.

The column pressing on St. Lo from the north beat down a determined German armoured counter-stroke at Le Honnet d'Arthenay and destroyed more than 20 tanks.

Small but Steady Gains

Rommel, fearful of General Bradley's intentions, appears to have made this attack as a means of defence.

SHAEF's communiqué last night said that steady Allied pressure in all the main areas continues to force the enemy slowly back. Our gains have been small but widespread, and the enemy has suffered heavily in unsuccessful counter-attacks.

"Montcastre Forest is in our hands," the communiqué adds. "South-west of

Turn to Back Page, Col. 3

When General Montgomery arrived in Caen he was given an enthusiastic welcome by the French civilians. Outside the Abbey he stood up in his car to acknowledge their cheers.

New Breakthrough Takes Soviet 20 Miles Nearer the Baltic

THE Russians have broken through on a front 93 miles wide east of the Latvian border, and are advancing on to the Baltic after a 20-mile push in 48 hours.

In two days fighting General Yeremenko's forces, spearhead of the new Soviet assault, have captured Idritsa, German base and railway junction, and 1,000 other places.

Idritsa is 48 miles north-west of Novo-Sokolniki and 90 miles north-west of Dvinsk.

The new attack represents a frontal assault against the Latvian border from the east, synchronised with the more southerly drive around Dvinsk in the rear of the Latvian defences.

With General Yeremenko's Second Baltic Army now in action, five powerful Russian armies are storming to the west on to the Baltic capitals and East Prussia on a front nearly 500 miles long.

General Yeremenko's vanguards are only 22 miles from the Latvian border which is already closely threatened by the forces of General Bagramyan, pressing on in the Polotsk and Dvinsk areas, south of Novo-Sokolniki.

The new thrust opens out the whole Russian advance, bringing in new areas and accentuating sharply the threat to the German northern garrisons.

Switched From Crimea

This is the first time General Yeremenko has been mentioned as in command of an inland sector. He was last in the Crimea, where, in command of a maritime army, he developed the coastal threat which led to the seizure of Sevastopol.

Soviet advances on all the fronts were reported in the routine Russian communiqué.

It announced the capture of Zelva, a town only 15 miles east of Volkovysk railway junction which stands almost on the main German defence line between Bialystok and Grodno.

Here, Marshal Rokossovsky's columns are driving straight for this last German line before East Prussia.

Final Vilna Battles

To the north, General Chernyakhosvky has captured Novy Dvor, 28 miles north-east of Grodno and 72 miles from East Prussia, and Nacha, 47 miles from Grodno and 83 miles from East Prussia.

While the final battles are raging inside Vilna, where the Germans are being wiped out in heavy fighting in the centre of the town, Soviet tanks and cavalry have entered Trokai, a district centre of Lithuania, 13 miles to the west.

Nearly 300 more places were captured in the Vilna and Lida areas.

To the north, General Bagramyan, forcing the Drissa River, is intensifying the threat to Dvinsk.

TURKEY ON WAR 'BORDERLINE'

TURKEY has been on the borderline from time to time, and it might be that she was again, said Mr. Cordell Hull, U.S. Secretary of State, when asked yesterday about reports that Turkey may join the Allies.

Conversations were reported to be taking place in Ankara between Turkish, Russian and British delegates, and the Turkish radio announced that the Turkish Ambassador to Berlin returned to Ankara yesterday.

The Parliamentary Group of the Turkish People's Party met on Tuesday night in secret session to hear a statement by M. Sarajoglu, the Premier and Foreign Minister.

In some quarters in Ankara it is believed that Turkey will enter the war on the side of the Allies before the end of the summer.—THE DAILY SKETCH Listening Station, Reuter, A.P.

Hitler Talks To His Generals For 3 Days

HITLER is holding a meeting of his Supreme War Council, with high officers from different fronts attending, according to Vichy reports reaching Madrid.

The meeting, it is said, began on Monday and is still going on.

Marshal von Kluge, the German C.-in-C. in France, who is one of those present, is reported to be expecting to have to use reserves now in Germany to meet additional Allied landings.

One decision already made by the council was to move Hitler's headquarters in Russia back to the West.

Paris An Open City?

German troops are also to be withdrawn from certain Balkan countries and Norway to build up reserves for the main fronts.

Laval is sounding opinion among German and neutral diplomats on the possibility of having Paris declared an open city, according to other reports reaching Madrid.

The report says that the French envoy to the Vatican has been instructed to invite the Pope to support the plan.—B.U.P.

FLY-BOMB LAIRS IN BELGIUM?

From VICTOR LEWIS,
Daily Sketch' Air Correspondent

GERMANY is believed to be using a small group of new flying-bomb launching sites to continue the attacks on London and Southern England.

They are probably located in Belgium, but some could even be as far north-east as Holland if they were placed at the extreme limit of what is believed to be the maximum range of the flying bombs.

The severe pounding to which the Pas de Calais sites have been subjected by Allied bombers may have necessitated this switch.

It is known that several of the sites in France have been wrecked and a great many more so damaged that they will be out of action for some time.

Lancasters Hit Ramps

Lancasters of Bomber Command yesterday afternoon resumed the attack on flying bomb installations in Northern France and returned without loss.

Flying bombs crossing the South coast yesterday by various routes, were chased by fighters which made many "kills." In one district the robots were reported at more frequent intervals than usual.

A train carrying flying bombs was derailed when the Vaucour railway bridge on the Metz-Verdun line was blown up by French patriots, say authoritative French sources.

German troops were immediately drafted to the spot to prevent anyone from approaching the wrecked train.

The King and Queen watch fly-bomb shoot.—Page 3.

Brixton Tank Busters Bust Twelve

TANK busters from Brixton, Croydon and Stepney, in their first real engagement with the enemy, have played a part in one of the most outstanding feats of tank destruction yet seen in Normandy.

In a lunch-hour fight with Panthers, ten men—the crews of two 17-pounder anti-tank guns—destroyed 12 Panthers for certain.

The scrap took place when a battery of British anti-tank gunners were supporting Canadian Highlanders to capture Buron, the Canadians' second objective in the Caen attack.

These troops had already fought their way through the village, but it remained to be cleared.

While four of the tank-busters covered the road north of the village, four others covered the southern outskirts just as the Germans were heavily counter-attacking.

The Brixton Busters, with their comrades, were on the two leading guns.

They took five Panthers by surprise and wiped them out.

The guns then moved half-a-mile up the road and surprised seven more Panthers, which also were destroyed.

One of the two Brixton guns was hit by enemy fire and three of the crew slightly wounded.

STILL CLOUDY

After an overcast day, with faint glimpses of blue sky and the sun, there was little change in the weather in the Straits of Dover last night. There was a light westerly breeze. In the previous 12 hours the barometer showed no change.

GUAM HIT AGAIN

American planes bombed three towns on the west coast of Guam and the airfield and Japanese installations on Roto Island, stated a U.S. Navy communiqué yesterday.

TIMELY WORDS OF FAITH

The Lord will hasten it in his time.

Isaiah, 60, 22.

Daily Mail

NO. 15,042 ONE PENNY ** FOR KING AND EMPIRE WEDNESDAY, JULY 19, 1944

LATE WAR NEWS

CAEN: THE BIG BREAK-THROUGH

Mightiest Air Blow of All Time Launches the Great Offensive

ARMOUR NOW SWARMING INTO OPEN COUNTRY

THE great Battle of France has begun. Supported by the mightiest air force ever engaged in a land battle, General Montgomery yesterday hurled the British Second Army against the line of the Orne. In a few hours this splendid fighting machine burst across the river and broke through the German front into the plain beyond. Hundreds of tanks crossed the Orne bridges and last night heavy fighting was in progress.

General Montgomery gave the news for which the whole nation has been patiently waiting in the following communiqué, issued from his headquarters exactly six weeks after the Allied landing:

"Early this morning British and Canadian troops of the Second Army attacked and broke through into the area east of the Orne and south-east of Caen. The attack was preceded and supported by a very great weight of air-power organised by the Allied Expeditionary Air Force.

"The town of Vaucelles, lying on the south side of the Orne opposite Caen, is being cleared of the enemy, and strong armoured and mobile forces are operating in the open country farther to the south-east and south. Heavy fighting continues. General Montgomery is well satisfied with the progress made in the first day's fighting of this battle."

More than 2,100 bombers—1,000 R.A.F. "heavies," 600 American Liberators, and 500 "mediums"—and hundreds of light bombers dropped 7,000 tons of bombs on the German divisions facing our troops.

This greatest air operation in history, directed by the Allied Air Commander-in-Chief, Air Chief Marshal Sir Trafford Leigh-Mallory, was completed in three hours for the loss of only nine aircraft. There was no sign of the Luftwaffe.

All day hundreds of fighters, fighter-bombers, and rocket-firing planes ranged over the battlefield and many miles beyond in support of the advancing troops.

On the American front the Germans were reported to be withdrawing last night after being driven out of St. Lo, a communications centre only second in importance to Caen, yesterday afternoon.

Greatest Air Armada Opens the Battle

By **COLIN BEDNALL**, Air Correspondent

THE greatest assembly of air power ever known in a land battle poured down the colossal weight of more than 7,000 tons of bombs on the German divisions immediately ahead of General Montgomery's break-through within the space of three hours.

More than 1,000 R.A.F. heavy bombers, more than 600 United States Liberators, 500 medium bombers, and hundreds of light bombers were employed.

The Luftwaffe never offered the slightest resistance.

Of the vast Allied armada employed only six R.A.F. heavy bombers, two U.S. heavy bombers, and one medium bomber—a total of nine aircraft—were lost in the entire operation.

Worked to a most intricate schedule this paralysing air assault was directed in all its phases by the Allied Air Commander-in-Chief, Air Chief Marshal Sir Trafford Leigh-Mallory, who flew over the battle area while it was in progress.

SPECIALLY FUSED

Of the grand total of bombs dropped, the R.A.F. heavies delivered no less than 5,000 tons. It was the first time so many of them had been used directly against the German Army in the field and the first time such a large force had been employed in daylight.

Their attack was the opening of the air assault. It was timed to begin at 5.45 a.m., but actually started five minutes earlier. It finished dead on schedule at 6.26.

In the planning of the operation a great amount of attention was given not only to the selection of targets and the timing of the attacks but also to the type of bombs employed.

The R.A.F. heavies, for instance, had three main targets. One of these was close to our own advancing troops, so instantaneous fuses were placed on the bombs so that the craters dug would be as small as possible to our own forces.

At two other targets, not directly in the path of our own forces, but directly in the path of the enemy forces, delayed action fuses were employed, so that the bombs would penetrate some distance into the ground before exploding.

In this way they tore up huge craters capable both of blocking the way to enemy vehicles and also blanketing the view of his guns.

TARGET FOR 500

The main object of the R.A.F. heavies, however, was to destroy or put out of action the German defences, guns and troops which had been holding up our own ground forces.

A foremost target was the steel works at Mondeville, in the eastern suburbs of Caen, which the Germans had turned into an extremely powerful strong-point. It had great numbers of mortars, which kept up continuous fire against our troops.

Here, also, the enemy had strongly fortified himself with anti-aircraft and anti-tank guns. Great numbers of enemy troops, too, were reported to be in position there.

The Mondeville steel works had

BACK PAGE—Col. THREE

The Enemy Knew Nothing

And Initiative is Firmly Ours

From **WARD PRICE**

SHAEF, Tuesday Evening.

THIS day, exactly six weeks after the landing, has seen the start of the second act in Normandy. The British and Canadian troops have attacked and broken through into the open country beyond the suburbs of Caen.

In Vaucelles, Caen's little satellite town across the River Orne, where are the main railway station and important factories, docks, and warehouses, our infantry are clearing fortified buildings and strong-points.

At the same time, tanks and armoured cars are pressing the enemy farther to the south east and south.

The news has caused as much satisfaction at SHAEF as it must have caused consternation to the enemy. For it proves several important points which the recent immobility of the front in Normandy has obscured.

Full Initiative

The first is that the power of taking the offensive lies with us and not with the enemy. Never since the brilliant success of the landing on June 6 has Rommel been able to break through our lines as we, in Montgomery's own words, have done to-day.

In view of the fact that all our guns, tanks, ammunition, and stores as well as troops, have so far had to be landed on open beaches exposed to the sweep of the up-Channel seas under weather conditions almost malignantly unfavourable, whereas the Germans were waiting for us on their own chosen ground, this retention of the initiative by the Allied Supreme Command is a most significant factor.

The second outstanding feature is that we have been able to conceal our intentions from the enemy. Large concentrations of troops and tanks must have been going on these last few days.

Great dumps of ammunition have been built up under cover, and yet the break-through is proof that the Germans did not detect our intention in time to move up reserves or troops from other parts of the front to block it.

Out of the Maze

Thirdly, we have pushed forward from that cramped salient between the Rivers Odon and Orne, and are also out of the built-up area of Vaucelles, immediately to the south of Caen.

If we can hold on to these gains, we should now be able to deploy and use our armoured divisions in open country on the lines for which they have been trained, instead of fighting in a Hampton Court Maze of hedgerows, lines of poplar trees, and orchard-girt farms.

Von Kluge and Rommel must be worried men to-night. General Montgomery speaks of "the first day's fighting of this battle." That phrase will sound cryptic and ominous in their ears.

Does "this battle" mean that another battle is about to begin on some other sector of the front?

AND SUN IS STILL SHINING

By Daily Mail Reporter

THE run of fine weather which began (in the Strait of Dover) on Sunday yesterday appeared firmly established.

Brilliant sunshine lit the sea throughout the day. The sky was clear and the sea rippled by a fresh wind from the east—not a rainy quarter.

The barometer remained high and steady for the third day running. Visibility was perfect—ideal conditions both for our air forces streaming out to France and for the A.A. gunners waiting to deal with any visitors the enemy might send over from his side.

Maximum temperature during the day was 72 degrees. Last night the wind veered slightly to the north-east and freshened.

For three days, in fact, the weather conditions can be summed up in the words—sunnier and sunnier.

REPATRIATION IS DROPPED

Till Trains Turn Up

LISBON, Tuesday.—All arrangements for the transfer in Lisbon of British and German civilian repatriates appear to have stopped, at least temporarily.

The British Embassy in Lisbon has no information on the whereabouts of the two trains carrying the British contingent.

Madrid reports yesterday said they were at Sete, on the French Mediterranean coast, where they had been held up for a week, during which time the passengers had not been allowed to leave the trains.—*B.U.P.*

Viscount Templewood

Sir Samuel Hoare, British Ambassador in Spain, on whom the King recently conferred a viscounty, has taken the title of Viscount Templewood of Chelsea, in the County of Middlesex.

ST. LO STORMED BY U.S. ARMOUR

From **WILLIAM HALL**, With U.S. Forces in Normandy, Tuesday.

THE eight-day battle of St. Lo is over, with the town in our hands. To-night, on the greater part of the American front, the Germans are withdrawing, striving desperately to shorten and strengthen their lines. Our ceaseless hammering is beginning to tell.

The general advance on this sector goes on, with American patrols finding difficulty in keeping touch with the enemy rearguard.

The final break into St. Lo was sensational. A mechanised U.S. task force swept through weary German infantrymen in the outskirts and burst into the town. At the head of the column, perched in a small weapons carrier, rode a high American officer.

His men went in with Wild West whoops that echoed and re-echoed through the streets.

At times the Germans laid flailing artillery fire on the approaches to the town, but that was more to protect their fleeing infantry than to stay our entry.

It is fairly certain that to-day German dead far outnumber the prisoners we have taken. Those taken alive have been dazed and shaken. They told grim stories of the battering they have received, and finally admitted that their losses have been great.

Tanks Break Through

GENERAL DEMPSEY'S troops have smashed the German line south of Caen and crossed the River Orne.

THE whole Normandy battlefront. In addition to the British break-through in the East, the Americans have captured St. Lo, important road centre.

Caen in relation to Paris.

THE greatest and most fantastic air operation of all time is described below by a Daily Mail correspondent on the spot. He describes the bombing from the time the first lone marker plane appeared, and says:

'It Was Terrifying To Watch'

LONE PLANE BEGAN IT

From **COURTENAY EDWARDS**

LEBISEY, NEAR CAEN, Tuesday.

USING the air weapon as a mighty bulldozer, thousands of British and American bombers to-day battered the German lines in front of hundreds of Allied tanks which crossed the Orne and drove into the area south-east of Caen.

It was the greatest, most fantastic air bombardment of all time. I watched the bombing standing in a jeep at the side of the Orne valley, opposite Colombelles and less than a mile from its sprawling factories.

These factories, used by the enemy as an observation post and the scene of bitter fighting in the past two weeks, lay on the fringe of one of the areas flattened by the R.A.F. steamroller.

It was a terrifying spectacle. I hope I shall never be called on to witness anything like it again.

Try to recall the most violent thunderstorm you have ever seen, multiply that by 100, add an earthquake—and you may get some idea of what the German troops on the other side of this river went through this morning.

The attack, the greatest air operation ever planned, began at 5.35 a.m. Within a few minutes a huge black cloud of smoke and dust had spread like an evil blight across the entire countryside, blotting everything from view, including the new crescent moon and the sun, just risen like a great blood-red ball.

A tremendous artillery barrage was synchronised with the air bombardment. The noise was deafening. The ground shook. The weather — prime factor in the operation—was perfect, with just a few fleecy clouds high up in an otherwise clear sky.

Had it been otherwise, the attack would have been postponed and the tanks would not have moved. It will go down in history as the most perfectly co-ordinated air-land assault ever launched.

SEALED OFF

Never before has the air-power of two nations been linked in a single battle to the same extent that the armadas of Britain and the U.S. were joined to-day.

The R.A.F.'s Bomber Command alone dropped 5,000 tons of bombs. They used about 1,000 four-engined Lancasters and Halifaxes. The U.S. Army Eighth Air Force sent some 750 Fortresses and Liberators.

Six hundred two-motor medium bombers of the U.S. Army Ninth Air Force were also sent in to [illegible]

And all day to-day hundreds upon hundreds of British and American fighters, fighter-bombers, and rocket-fighters have ranged over the battlefield and for hundreds of square miles around in an incredible display of air power.

The idea behind that tremendous initial bombardment that staggered us just now was a simple one—to paralyse the German defences, and to seal off the entire area so that reinforcements could not reach the Hun.

With this object the R.A.F. heavies went in first and pounded the enemy positions.

PINNED DOWN

It was like several Cassinos rolled into one, only most of the bombs fell, not in built-up areas, but amongst enemy fortifications, gun positions, pillboxes, tank laagers, and other strong points.

The object was not merely to knock out these positions, but also, by cratering the ground and generally stunning the enemy troops, to prevent any movement by them.

Colombelles, whose tragic fate I witnessed just now, was one of the built-up areas which came within the sweep of the R.A.F.'s scythe-stroke.

The American heavies, using precision-bombing methods, were detailed to deal with other fortified positions, most of them more isolated than the targets shattered in the R.A.F.'s saturation bombing.

The third phase of this bulldozer bombing was carried out by hundreds of medium bombers of the U.S. Army Ninth Air Force, which attacked other isolated gun positions and strong-points and also carpeted the area with fragmentation bombs.

These were scattered in such numbers and in such density that they were calculated to kill every German in the area.

The whole operation was planned with mathematical exactness. "Yet details were not worked out until last week-end," an air vice-marshal told me to-day.

PERFECT TIMING

The operation called for perfect timing and an enormous amount of detailed organisation. From hundreds of airfields each aircraft had to take off at exactly the right moment.

Perhaps it is no exaggeration to say that the R.A.F. and U.S.A.A.F. officers toiling in operation rooms and control towers played as big a part in the success of the battle as the air crews themselves.

R.A.F. Pathfinders going in ahead of the main bomber force to light up the target areas brought off one of their finest achievements. On their accuracy depended the success or failure of the operation.

Air Chief Marshal Sir Trafford Leigh-Mallory, the Allied Air Commander-in-Chief, flew over the battle area while the bombing was in progress. He was piloted by Air Vice-Marshal Harry Broadhurst.

BACK PAGE—Col. FOUR

'Shuddering, Blazing Nightmare'

This is how another correspondent, Harold McMillan, of the B.U.P., described the scene:

IN the wildest flights of imagination no man could envisage this thing.

Volcanic gouts of evil-looking yellow flame spat like automatic fountains from the ground, to make a dullish glare that spread for miles through the gloomy curtain thrown up by the first few hundred bombers.

Now the blazing, shuddering nightmare reached its ghastliest peak. Heavy bombers in stately order came in upon the scene as the whole horizon erupted, with cascades of bombs gouging into the bowels of the earth.

There is the earth of the battlefield, the debris and human remains, wrecks of villages, fumes of smoke-bombs—chaos in every sense of the word.

Still the bombers come and still the bombs fall.

The crescendo of the crash of bombs drowns out even the roar of a thousand bombers. That is how mighty it is.

Hit Bridge, Then Ten Planes

Lightning fighter-bombers about to dive-bomb a railway bridge crossing the Eure, ten miles east of Evreux, yesterday were attacked by over 50 F.W.s and Me.s.

Two squadrons of Lightnings jettisoned their bombs and attacked the German planes; the third Lightning squadron demolished the bridge, and then joined in. Ten of the enemy were destroyed, six probably destroyed, and 11 damaged. Three Lightnings are missing.

AIR CREW RECRUITS FOR ARMY

Some Even Going to Civilian Jobs

By Daily Mail Air Correspondent

THOUSANDS of young men who set their hearts on becoming R.A.F. pilots after the Battle of Britain and who, after years of training and study, were finally accepted for air-crew duties are now, by War Cabinet decision, being drafted into the Army and even civilian roles.

This, like the similar redrafting of naval personnel made known by the *Daily Mail* Naval Correspondent yesterday, is official recognition of the fact that our man-power needs to finish the war can now be measured.

Air crews take so long to train for action that it is probable that many now beginning their training in the R.A.F. will not complete it in time to meet the enemy.

By transferring to the Army, recruits will have a much better chance of getting into action.

Those given civilian rôles will do work of vital national importance.

On Fatigue

Although bitterly disappointed at losing air-crew status, many will nevertheless welcome a clear-cut decision on the surplus.

This arose first through the rapid retreat of the Luftwaffe from open combat. Both the R.A.F. and the U.S.A.A.F. found they required nothing like the fighter pilot replacements expected.

Hundreds of even fully trained air crews have had to wait months for posting to operational squadrons.

They have been given all manner of jobs to fill in time. Trained pilots on full time fatigue duties could be found at many R.A.F. stations.

The surplus mounted still more rapidly, too, when, with a reduction of training, large numbers of instructors also became available for operational squadrons.

In addition to air crew recruits, a large part of the R.A.F. Regiment is also being surrendered.

The Air Ministry announcement of this decision says:

"The Royal Air Force is most reluctant to lose the services of the airmen volunteers affected, many of whom will have had services in the A.T.C., but the highest strategical demands of the war must naturally transcend all other considerations, and it is in this spirit that these young men are being asked to accept this new situation."

Tojo Gets the Sack

General Tojo, the Jap Premier, has been relieved of his post of Chief of the General Staff.

The change was announced a few hours after he had broadcast the news of the loss of Saipan, in the Marianas—the nearest point to Tokio yet reached by the Allies.

See BACK Page.

DSO FOR MAN NAZIS NAMED

'Blockade Buster'

Acting Tempy Commander Sir George Binney, R.N.V.R., named by the Germans as "the brains" behind the blockade-running attempt by ten Norwegian ships from Gothenburg to Britain in March 1942, has been awarded the D.S.O.

Last night's *London Gazette* said the award was "for outstanding leadership and skill."

He is a 43-years-old bachelor and was knighted in 1941 for "special services in the supply of valuable war materials." In 1942 he was assistant commercial attaché at the British Embassy in Stockholm.

43 Die in Paris Prison Mutiny

BERNE, Tuesday.—Forty-three inmates of the Santé Prison in Paris were killed during and following a mutiny on July 8, according to a Paris dispatch to the *Petit Dauphinois*. Fifteen died in a sharp fight with their guards. The others were tried and executed.—*A.P.*

Hungary to Stop Expelling Jews

BERNE, Tuesday.—Admiral Horthy, Hungarian Regent, has promised the International Red Cross that no more Jews will be deported from Hungary, it was learned here to-day.

He authorised the Red Cross to direct the evacuation of Jewish children to countries willing to receive them, and the evacuation to Palestine of any Jews possessing visas.—*A.P.*

Brazilians Join '5th'

WASHINGTON, Tuesday.—The War Department announces that a Brazilian expeditionary force has arrived at Naples to join the Allied Armies on the Italian front.—*B.U.P.*

21 Miles Now to Lvov

New Soviet Drive, 130-Miles Front

THE Red Army is now only 21 miles from Lvov, greatest base the Germans still hold in South Poland.

A great new drive has carried the Russians 32 miles deep into the shattered enemy lines. Soviet tanks and assault troops are pouring through a breach 130 miles wide.

This break-through, made by Marshal Koniev's First Ukrainian Army, was announced by Marshal Stalin in an Order of the Day last night.

In three days 600 places have fallen to the advancing Russian forces. They have stormed Krasnoye, railway junction 25 miles from Lvov, and Kamenka, 21 miles north-east of the bastion city.

Fifty-three Soviet generals are in command of the massed tank, artillery, cavalry, and air force units which are driving on for Lvov itself.

German sources, which reported the offensive last week-end, have admitted that Soviet spearheads have already crossed the River Bug

DE GAULLE SEES ALLIED ENVOYS

Gen. de Gaulle yesterday received the British, Canadian, and Yugoslav representatives, according to Algiers radio.

RAIL TOWN BOMBED

Bomber Command planes yesterday attacked the railway centre at Vaires, on the outskirts of Paris, an important centre for supplies to the Normandy front.

2

and reached points due north of the city.

Berlin last night stated that the Germans are again in retreat westwards, racing to escape encirclement by Koniev's troops.

Opening of a third Soviet thrust against Brest Litovsk, this time from the south east of this bastion city in the German line defending East Prussia and Central Poland, was reported by the German News Agency.

"The Soviet offensive has now spread to the Kovel area, where a new major attack began yesterday," it was stated.

"The whole front from Tarnopol via Luck to the Kovel area is now on the move."

This means that Russian forces are now advancing on Brest

BACK PAGE—Col. FIVE

Newcastle Journal
North Mail
No. 30,590
Friday, July 21, 1944. ONE PENNY
6 A.M. EDITION

Their Fuhrer went to the radio this morning to tell German people of another "1918 plot"

HITLER SAYS, "OFFICERS TRIED TO KILL ME"

4th blow at Robot Caverns

NUMEROUS flying-bombs were shot down on Wednesday night and yesterday, when the numbers sent over were smaller during the preceding 24 hours.

Lancasters, with fighter cover, continued the counter-offensive with a fourth attack on the F-bomb depot in the caves at Thiverny, near Paris.

Fortunate escapes from F-bombs include those of a family of five who were rescued uninjured from a garden shelter buried in debris, and of two men and their wives, neighbours, who decided to spend the night in their shelter. They had not done so previously, and an F-bomb demolished both houses.

MORE THREATS

Writing in "Das Reich" Goebbels again implies that the F-bombs are designed to persuade us to stop bombing Germany.

Threatening new horrors, he adds: "German scientists' discoveries have all been completed. Some of their results are still being tested; but the majority are in use."

Terrorist No. 1

HIMMLER, Europe's Terrorist No. 1, is now Commander-in-Chief of the German Home Army.

Reich home army put under Himmler

SENSATIONAL moves in Germany following the attempted assassination of Hitler yesterday were announced in a six-minute broadcast by the Fuhrer himself early this morning.

He told the German people and the world that a small clique of officers in Germany, as in Italy, had attempted to repeat "the 1918 stab in the back."

Suggesting serious dissension in the German High Command, he warned German leaders and ordinary soldiers in the field not to obey these "usurpers."

At the same time he made Gestapo Chief Heinrich Himmler, already Minister of the Interior, Commander-in-Chief of the German Army in Germany to create order "once and for all."

Although denying that the conspirators came from the Wehrmacht, he disclosed that the bomb with which his assassination was attempted was placed by Colonel Graf von Stauffenberg.

Hitler also announced that General Guderian, the great tank expert, would become chief of his personal staff in place of Jodl, injured in the assassination bid and now in hospital.

Grim threat

"All resistance has to be broken immediately," Hitler declared, and added the grim threat, "All criminal elements will be ruthlessly exterminated."

"Every decent soldier will understand my actions," he added. "What would happen to Germany had the attempt succeeded cannot be imagined."

He regarded his escape "as a confirmation of the task imposed on me by Providence to continue on the road of my life as I have done hitherto."

Doenitz, for the Navy, and Goering, for the Air Force, also spoke.

Doenitz described the people responsible for the assassination plot as "a clique of mad generals."

"A small clique of mad generals having nothing in common with our brave army, has attempted this murder, in cowardly faithlessness committing the most dastardly treachery against the Fuhrer and the German people," he said.

The German Navy, through Doenitz, swore allegiance to Hitler, and the Luftwaffe did the same through Goering. Both oaths were recorded over the radio to the people of Germany.

Air force 'on spot'

Goering said, "The task is the extirpation of the traitors which will give the Germans strength. The Luftwaffe is on the spot."

Telephone communication between Berlin and Stockholm was cut at 7.40 last night.

Colonel Count von Stauffenberg, whom Hitler named as the man who placed the bomb, is not well-known outside the pure military caste in Prussia.

He is believed to be a member of an old Prussian Junker military family with a long traditional career in the German Army.

He represents a class of German officer of the younger type that resented the conduct of the war by the Nazi Party.

He has seen service in Russia. He has also served as a junior staff officer, and presumably this status gave him the facility and the status to attend a momentous gathering of Nazi and Wehrmacht generals.

"Slight burns"

First announcement of the attempted assassination was given last night in an official Berlin announcement, which said it was made with high explosives and that Hitler escaped with "slight burns and concussion." The announcement said:—

"Achtung. We are broadcasting an important announcement. Attempt to murder the Fuhrer. The Fuhrer not hurt."

"An attempt on the life of the Fuhrer was made with high explosives to-day. The following persons on his entourage were severely injured.—

"Lieut.-General Schmundt, Colonel Brandt, Lieut.-Colonel Borgmann, Collaborator Berger.

"Slighter injuries were suffered by Colonel-General Jodl as well as the Generals Korten, Buhl, Bodenschatz, Heusinger, Scherff, and Admirals Voss and von Puttkamer.

"Hitler received light burns and concussion but no injuries. He at once began to work again.

"He then received Mussolini for a long meeting previously arranged.

"Shortly after the attempt Marshal Goering came to Hitler."

The German Radio later corrected the list of injured, deleting the name of Lieut.-Col. Borgmann from the list of those gravely injured and adding it, and the name of Naval Captain Assman, to the list of the slightly injured.

[Reuter messages.]

"Hitler: Is the death plot a propaganda frame-up?" and stories of previous attempts on the Fuhrer's life in Page Two.

HITLER AT HIS HEADQUARTERS

HITLER, with some of his generals, studies the map of the Russian front.

Allies push on to Gothic Line

IN blinding rainstorms and through deep mud, the Fifth and Eighth Armies are driving on to close the last gap before the Gothic Line proper.

They have pushed the Germans back to the north bank of the Arno and have crossed the Esino River 10 miles beyond Ancona. Fifth Army patrols are less than nine miles from Pisa.—Reuter.

From AUBREY HAMMOND
"Newcastle Journal" War Correspondent

ROME, Thursday.

Polish troops are mopping up west and south of Ancona, where the Germans, taken by surprise, left much valuable material behind, although the city was thoroughly mined and demolished and the harbour was found full of sunken ships, including King Victor's yacht.

Progress is being continued in many sectors of the Italian front, but torrential rain has interfered with our forward movement.

The fact that the dominating terrain south of the River Arno gave our artillery observation over the valley forced the enemy to withdraw to the north bank.

In the central Fifth Army sector prisoners say they had been completely bewildered by our sudden breakthrough and that numerous isolated units had been wiped out.

SIX TOWNS FALL

Elements on the right sector, where advances up to three or four miles took place and six towns were taken, reached within three miles south of Castel Fiorentino, which is the junction of the roads to Florence and Empoli.

On the Eighth Army's front the coast road beyond Ancona was cut at Torretto and other forces were along the banks of the Esino from the river mouth to six miles inland, a bridgehead having been established ten miles west of Ancona and south of Chiaravalle. Italian troops moved from captured Santa Maria Nuova towards Jesi.

Coming north from Arezzo our troops arrived around Laterina and Castiglion, both north of the Arno River.

Elsewhere the Germans stubbornly defended the town of the same name, while stiff fighting went on for Montevarchi, 15 miles down the river from Arezzo. North-west of the city we reached Gello, and in the western sector an advance was made to the north and west of Radda, which was taken.

Captured German documents show anxiety about the shortage of equipment and interior arms and ammunition, and all available troops, including the slightly wounded, are ordered to comb the countryside for salvage to the last round of ammunition.

CAEN IS JUMPING OFF PLACE

From H. S. WOODHAM
"Newcastle Journal" Military Correspondent

GENERAL EISENHOWER'S HEADQUARTERS,
Thursday Night.

THE position in the area south and south-east of Caen is that after three days of fighting the Second Army has secured the battle arena it has been seeking, but the battle has yet to be won.

Are we satisfied then with this advance of about six miles after this terrific air and ground effort?

It is difficult to give a confident answer without knowing or disclosing what is General Montgomery's aim, without saying whether the offensive has a limited objective or whether it is to be pushed to the utmost and the farthest skill and endurance can take it.

But from the information at my disposal the answer is that the progress is satisfactory.

SEMI-CIRCLE

Our forces are firmly established in a semi-circle South of Caen which at its deepest point is about five miles from the centre of the city. This is a good jumping-off place for the second phase of the struggle.

There has not yet been any large-scale armoured fighting. Note the words "large scale."

The British armour has been mainly opposed by anti-tank weapons and strong-points, so that the big armoured fight in the plain is a thing of the future, presumably the near future.

Rommel is said to have five and a half divisions of infantry and armour at least facing us below Caen, including a newly identified division of infantry—the 272nd.

His armour is ready and waiting for the big test, and the fact that it has apparently been withdrawn behind the long anti-tank screen north-west of Vimont does not indicate reluctance to engage but that Rommel probably does not consider the proper moment has arrived.

Rommel is fighting a holding battle and it is going to be lengthy and gruelling.

The first round has gone to Montgomery, for by the capture of Caen and St. Lo the Allies have now got the termini of 15 good roads. The first round also suggests that Montgomery, as usual, is able to surprise his old enemy.

Infirmary has to draw on "reserve"

The annual report of Newcastle Infirmary for 1943 says that during the year 16,106 patients were admitted to the general wards, against 14,442 in 1942, an increase of 1,664. The average length of stay of each in-patient was 12.03 days, compared with 12.5 in the previous year.

The service had again been maintained only by drawing on reserves and borrowing from the bank the money not otherwise provided. The seriousness of this position had been repeatedly brought to public notice.

New out-patients numbered 113,144, against 106,617 in the previous year, an increase of 6,527.

The income for the year was £29,004 short of the sum required to pay the ordinary expenses.

The total subscribed income for the year was £114,709 11s. 5d., an increase of £12,460 1s over the amount received in the previous year.

REDS OPEN NEW ROAD TO WARSAW

Nazi-held cities outflanked

THE Russians are storming over the last five miles to Lvov. Moscow officially reported last night the capture of Doroshev, only five miles to the north of this great city, which is the key to the Carpathian Passes and Southern Poland.

Simultaneously, Marshal Koniev has pressed past the city and captured Rava Russka, 30 miles to the north-west of the highway to Lublin.

Further north, Marshal Rokossovsky, who captured Kovel a fortnight ago, has opened a new offensive and in three days has advanced 31 miles through a gap 93 miles wide.

PRUSSIA—8 MILES

These two army group commanders—their successes recorded in two Orders of the Day from Marshal Stalin and the routine communique—have outflanked both Brest-Litovsk and Lvov and opened up a new break-through threat to Warsaw and the San, the next river line west of the Polish Bug.

On the Baltic Front, said one German report, the Red Army has fought its way to Augustov, 40 miles north-west of Grodno and only eight miles from the East Prussia border.

Moscow reports make no reference to this sector, but indicate important developments in Lithuania where, driving north from Utena, the Russians have captured 80 places and have cut the westbound railway from Dvinsk to Memel at a town called Ponevezh, 90 miles along the line from Dvinsk.

400 PLACES TAKEN

Rokossovsky's new offensive between Brest-Litovsk and Lvov has already captured 400 places including Maloryta, 27 miles south-east of the former on the railway to Kovel, Lubomil, 30 miles west of Kovel on the railway which crosses the Bug to Chelm and Lublin, and Opalin, 42 miles north-west of Kovel, on the river's eastern bank.

Beside sharpening the threat to Brest-Litovsk—which, like Lvov, is threatened from three sides—this new thrust to the river seems likely soon to link up with Koniev's forces standing on the waterline in the Sokal area for a joint drive on Lublin and Warsaw from the south-east.

Lvov was already partly outflanked from the south by forces working their way round in the direction of the Galician fortress city of Przemysl, which changed hands three times in the first week of Hitler's invasion three years ago.

[Including Reuter.]

OVER REICH

The German Radio reported at 7 o'clock last night enemy raiders over North-West Germany, Thuringia and Hanover. Paris long-wave radio broadcast air raid warning signals at 7.30.

Midnight communique

Infantry thrusts gain more ground

COMMUNIQUE No. 90 from General Eisenhower's H.Q. last night said:—

A series of infantry thrusts to the east and south of Caen have steadily extended the area which is firmly in our hands.

Bourguebus and Frenouville have been freed of the enemy and we are in possession of the villages of Bras and Hubert Folie and of the ridge to the north of St. Andre-sur-Orne.

Enemy attempts to counter-attack were repulsed and our threat to Troarn was increased by an advance towards St. Pair, on the high ground to the south of the town.

North-west of St. Lo Allied troops advanced to the line of the Vire and also improved their positions to the south of the town.

TANK TRAINS HIT

Visibility limited air operations over the immediate battle area from midnight until noon, but several successful attacks were made in North-East France.

Near Amiens, two trains loaded with enemy tanks were effectively bombed by our fighter-bombers, which also damaged a bridge over the Somme, and destroyed railroad rolling stock at Abancourt and at Sable-sur-Sarthe, north-east of Angers.

A highway bridge at Gisors was attacked, and rail lines were cut in several places north of Laval and Le Mans and south-west of Dreux.

Escorted light bombers hit the rail centre at Chaulnes, near Amiens, destroying much rolling stock.

Coastal aircraft attacked enemy surface craft in the Channel. One enemy aircraft was shot down near St. Quentin. Two of our fighters are missing.

Hitler's six-minute speech

THE FULL TEXT

HITLER'S speech in full was as follows:—

German men and women, an attempt on my life has been planned and executed.

The reason why I am speaking to you to-day is so that you can hear my voice and know that I am unhurt and healthy.

A very small clique of criminal officers, ambitious and without conscience, planned to do away with me and to take command of the German Wehrmacht.

The bomb, which was placed by Count von Schauffenberg, exploded two metres from my right hand side. It has hurt a number of my collaborators. One has died. I myself am not hurt—only a few scratches and some burns."

WORK AND SORROW

Ever since I entered the Wilhelmstrasse I have fulfilled my duty to the best of my ability and conscience.

When it became clear to me that war was inevitable the times which followed were times of work and sorrow.

At an hour in which the Germans are in the middle of grave battles a very small group—just as in Italy—believed that they could give us a stab in the back as in 1918.

This time they made a very serious mistake. The contention of these conspirators that I was already dead has been easily disproved.

The circle from which these conspirators spring is a very narrow one. It has nothing in common with the German armed forces and in particular with the German Army.

It is a very small clique of criminal elements who will now be mercilessly exterminated.

HIS ORDERS

At this moment I therefore issue the following orders:—

No civilian authority is allowed to accept orders from any other authority belonging to this group.

No military authority, no troop leader, and no soldier is to follow any orders given by these usurpers.

On the contrary, it is everybody's duty to arrest suspicious elements and to slay them immediately.

So that definite order may be brought about I have appointed Reichminister Himmler C.-in-C. of the armies at home. Into the general staff I have called General F Guderian in order to replace the Chief of the General Staff. I have also appointed a second well-tried general from the Eastern front to be his colleague.

All other authorities will be unaffected. I am convinced that the appearance of this very small and treacherous clique of conspirators has created at last the atmosphere at home which the front is needing.

GRATEFUL TO GOD

It is impossible that at the front hundreds of thousands, nay millions, of good men are giving their all, while at home a very small clique of miserable, ambitious creatures is trying to deny us our success.

This time, however, we shall render the accounts as we National Socialists have been accustomed to.

I am convinced that every decent officer, every brave soldier will understand this.

What the fate of Germany might have been had the plot to-day succeeded hardly anybody can imagine. I am grateful to Providence and to the Almighty, not because He has preserved my life—my life is sorrow and work for my people—I am grateful because He gave me the possibility to carry this burden and carry on with my work as my conscience guides me.

Every German at home has, therefore, the duty to intervene ruthlessly and to arrest all suspicious characters and, in the case of their resisting, to slay them immediately.

WILL CARRY ON

Orders to this effect have been given to the forces. They will be carried out promptly in that sense of obedience for which the German Army is known.

My old comrades, however, will gladly rejoice at the news that once again I was able to escape an attempt on my life which would have brought terror to the German people.

From this, too, we recognise the hand of Providence that I have to carry on with my work and that I shall do so."

* * *

Grand Admiral Donetz, Commander-in-Chief of the German Navy, and Reich Marshal Goering, Commander-in-Chief of the Luftwaffe, broadcast messages also to the men under their command.

British are fighting in Troarn streets

GERMANS REPORT NEW ALLIED ATTACK

ALLIED troops were yesterday fighting in the streets of Troarn and Bourguebus, focal points of the battle south-east of Caen, while up to half-a-dozen villages have been occupied.

At Troarn, seven miles east of Caen, a tank spearhead is blasting resistance from the crossroads beyond the station near the heart of the town. They smashed through to the crossroads shortly before noon yesterday.

At Bourguebus, on the main Falaise road, five miles south of Caen and the most southerly point yet mentioned, Allied armour is in action.

The German News Agency said last night that Bourguebus, together with the localities of Emieville, Frenouville, and Soliers had actually fallen in a new Allied attack.

"British and Canadian divisions have gone over to a new general attack on a broad front from the Colombelles-Toufreville-Sanneville area," the Agency said.

"After a laborious and costly advance averaging about a mile and a half the attack petered out, but the localities of Emieville, Frenouville, Soliers and Bourguebus, all in this area, were lost to the Germans."

CONSOLIDATING

This German report does not fit in with a despatch from Reuter's special correspondent yesterday afternoon. "The tempo of the fighting east of the Orne has slackened in the past few hours. British and Canadians are consolidating their gains and strengthening their new forward line."

No major counter-attack has developed, although Rommel has a considerable force of armour which he may yet commit in a concerted counter-thrust.

As it is, Rommel has attempted no more than expensive frittering tactics which cost him so much in personnel and equipment between the Odon and the Orne.

The battle area east of the Orne is charred and covered with German dead.

After cleaning up Faubourg de Vaucelles Canadian and British troops gave the Germans no chance to move up armour before driving south.

When the Germans recovered from their "bomb-happy" state on Tuesday they found a solid wall of armour bearing down with great force and violence.

PANZERS RECOILED

The remnants of the panzer divisions met the full blast of the attack. They recoiled, and the Allied force stormed through Fleury-sur-Orne, Ifs, Cormelles, Hubert-Folie, Le Poirier, Soliers, and Frenouville.

The Germans used anti-tank guns effectively against our armour and laid thick minefields round the approaches to their positions.

The small village of Ifs gave the Canadians a lot of trouble, but they swept through the built-up area and swung right to the high ground behind Fleury.

Another Allied force came through Fleury and up the forward slopes of Hill 67.

The Germans are anxious over the loss of Hill 67, which gave the Allies observation over their positions to the south and south-west across the Orne to the woods in the direction of Maltot—pivot of the last German resistance in the tongue of land at the confluence of the Orne and the Odon.

It is caught now in a pincer thrust, which threatens to cut off the garrison.

Latest

"CONSPIRACY HAS COLLAPSED"—NAZIS

German News Agency states officers' conspiracy completely collapsed. Ringleaders have either been shot or committed suicide. Von Stauffenberg among those shot.—Reuter.

Black - out - to - day, 11.28 p.m. to 4.57 a.m.

Sun rises to-day, 5.55 a.m.; sets, 10.28 p.m. Rises to-morrow, 5.57 a.m.; sets, 10.27 p.m.

Moon rises to-day, 7.2 a.m.; sets, 11.14 p.m. Rises to-morrow, 8.9 a.m.; sets, 11.39 p.m.

To-day's Text

Selected by the Rev. John W. Titherington, Heaton Road Baptist Church, also (Hon.) Free Church Chaplain to the Miner Trainees.

A Salute to the Evacuees, and to homes that receive them.

I WAS a stranger and you entertained me.
—St. Matt 26-35 (Moffat).

AND whosoever shall give to drink unto one of these little ones a cup of cold water only in the name of a disciple verily I say unto you, he shall in no wise lose his reward.
—Matt. 10-42.

He was commended

Chief Petty Officer and Mrs. Wilkinson-Ferguson, of 67, Weldon Crescent, High Heaton, have been informed that their son, Apprentice Officer, William H. Wilkinson-Ferguson, M.N., has been commended for good service while his ship was under fire.

W.M. WILKINSON-FERGUSON

Wilkinson-Ferguson, who is 21 years of age, has served in the M.N. for three years.

RUSKIN'S HOME

Mr. John Howard Whitehouse, the educationist, who has devoted many years to the study of Ruskin, has offered Ruskin's old home, Brantwood, in the Lake District, to Oxford University.

VICHY VICTIM

M. Pierre Vienot, Ambassador in London of the French Provisional Government, died in London yesterday, aged 47.

Mme. Vienot, who is believed to be still in France, was informed of her husband's death in a special broadcast last night. His illness was thought to be the cumulative result of his many months in Vichy gaols.

RECOGNISED

The Egyptian Government has decided to recognise "de facto" the Liberation Committee as the provisional Government of France.—Reuter.

DOENITZ

These mad generals believe they can free us from our struggle

ADMIRAL Doenitz in his broadcast said:—

"Men of the Navy, holy rage and measureless wrath fill us over the criminal attempt which was to have cost our beloved Fuhrer his life. Providence willed it otherwise.

"These mad generals, these villains, are only the tools of our enemies whom they serve in a spineless, cowardly and false sort of cleverness.

"In reality, their stupidity is boundless. They believe that by the annihilation of the Fuhrer they can liberate us from our hard but inexorable fateful struggle.

"And in their disproportionate and trembling narrow-mindedness they do not see that by their criminal act they would lead us into horrible chaos and deliver us defenceless to our enemies.

"Extermination of our people, enslavement of our men, hunger and nameless wretchedness would be our lot.

"Our people would live through an unspeakable time of tragedy, infinitely more gruesome and burdensome than the hardest times they can possibly experience through our present struggle.

"We shall make these traitors innocuous. The Navy stands faithful to its oath in proving loyalty to the Fuhrer and ready to do or die and struggle unreservedly.

"It accepts orders only from me, the Supreme Commander of the Navy, and from its own military leaders, so as to evade the possibility of any misleading situation through the issue of forged instructions.

"It will ruthlessly destroy everyone unmasked as a traitor."
—Reuter.

Average net paid circulation for June exceeded
Daily---2,075,000
Sunday-3,700,000

DAILY NEWS
Copr. 1944 by News Syndicate Co. Inc. NEW YORK'S PICTURE NEWSPAPER Trade Mark Reg. U. S. Pat. Off.

FINAL

Vol. 26 No. 23 New York, Friday, July 21, 1944★ 32 Main+4 Brooklyn+4 Kings Pages 2 Cents IN CITY LIMITS | 3 CENTS Elsewhere

GENERALS REBEL, TRY TO KILL HITLER

Fuehrer, Hurt by Bomb, Names Himmler to Put Down Revolt

Story on Page 3

F. D. R. NOMINATED ON FIRST BALLOT

Story on Page 2

COMPLETE NEWS—MAGAZINE SECTION—COMIC FEATURES

New York Post

FOUNDED 1801, VOLUME 143, NO. 210.

TWO SECTIONS

NEW YORK, TUESDAY, JULY 25, 1944

36 PAGES

TERROR OF DEATH HAUNTS HITLER

16 Captured Generals Appeal To Germans to Give Up

Stories on Pages 2, 17

WE OPEN BIG PUSH IN FRANCE

Story on Page 3

Average net paid circulation for June exceeded
Daily---2,075,000
Sunday-3,700,000

DAILY NEWS
Copr. 1944 by News Syndicate Co. Inc. NEW YORK'S PICTURE NEWSPAPER Trade Mark Reg. U. S. Pat. Off.

★★★★ FINAL

Vol. 26. No. 29 New York, Friday, July 28, 1944★ 32 Main+4 Manhattan Pages 2 Cents IN CITY LIMITS | 3 CENTS Elsewhere

ENTIRE NAZI EAST FRONT COLLAPSES

Reds Take 6 Big Enemy Bases In War's Greatest Victory

70,000 OF FOE FACE U.S. TRAP IN FRANCE

Stories on Pages 2 and 3

Daily Mirror

JULY 28

No. 12,671
ONE PENNY
Registered at the G.P.O. as a Newspaper.

Great break through by American tanks

ROMMEL ARMY FACES TRAP

GOVT. WILL BE EXPERT PACKER AND REMOVAL MAN FREE FOR EVACUEES: THEY'LL JUST HAND OVER A LIST AND THEIR KEYS

WOMEN who have been evacuated from danger areas to the provinces will soon be able to cook with their own saucepans, use their own towels and bed-linen and wear a change of their own clothing.

The Government is going to act as "expert packer and removal man" for them. All they will have to do themselves is to make out a list of what they require and hand over their keys. And it won't cost them a penny.

Mr. Willink, Minister of Health, has drawn up the scheme. Local authorities, mainly the L.C.C., are to put it into force.

The idea is to overcome, as far as possible, the shortage in the reception areas of towels, sheets and all the other household goods that make a place a home.

"It is only natural that householders, although willing to do all they can to help evacuees, are finding it difficult to provide such things as household linen," a Ministry of Health official said yesterday.

"The evacuee mother will fill in a form giving her home address, how access to her home can be obtained, and listing the articles she requires for herself and her children.

"Only Necessaries"

"This form will then be sent to the evacuating authority that sent her away, who will then arrange for the articles to be collected and dispatched to the billet.

"The scheme will be confined to goods which are considered to be strictly necessary—towels, bedding, cooking utensils, essential clothing, cots, perambulators, and light articles of furniture, such as small cupboards."

Details of the scheme have already been sent to local authorities, and it is hoped to bring it into operation in a few days.

Evacuated mothers are, however, being encouraged to make their own arrangements wherever possible for articles to be posted on to them by a neighbour.

TO TALK ON PEACE

British, U.S., Russian and Chinese representatives will meet next month to discuss an international security organisation. Mr. Cordell Hull, U.S. Secretary of State, said yesterday. Mr. Stettinous, U.S. Under-Secretary of State, will lead the U.S. party.

Berlin reported last night that a new major offensive had been launched on the British front in Normandy. There was no Allied indication of this.

AMERICAN armoured forces thrusting west of St. Lo are within five miles of Coutances, enemy rear hub town near the coast, threatening to trap seven German divisions, cabled Reuter's special correspondent with the U.S. First Army last night.

Striking at the north of the threatened pocket, other American forces have taken Lessay and Periers, important enemy road centres.

The message said: Coutances is within artillery range and an effort is being made to close the trap on the Germans in the Periers-Lessay area, where about half the entire German force on the American front, including the Second S.S. Panzer Division and the 17th S.S. Panzer are fighting.

The Germans are frantically trying to withdraw from the pocket north of Coutances and their resistance, except for the rearguard, is described as "disorganised and chaotic."

The breakthrough was described by an American spokesman last night as "complete."

IT HAS AT PRESENT REACHED A DEPTH OF TWELVE MILES AT ONE POINT SOUTH OF THE MAIN ST. LO - PERIERS ROAD.

This report followed official news that U.S. tank columns, surging through the breach in the enemy defences west of St.

Continued on Back Page

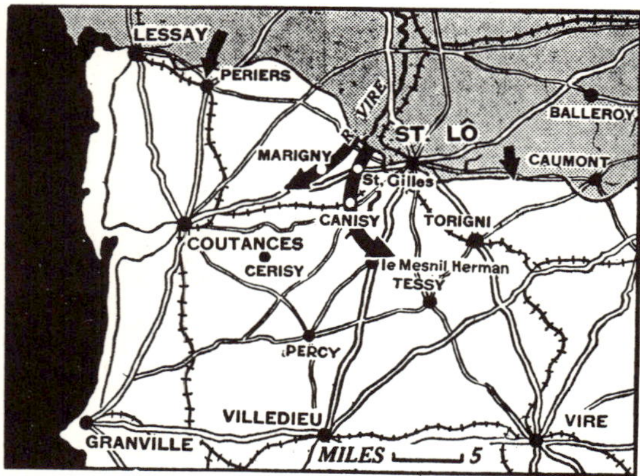

Midnight Communique

MIDNIGHT communique from General Eisenhower announced:—

Allied armoured thrusts in the western sector continue to make rapid progress.

One column has cut road from St. Lo to Percy in neighbourhood of Le Mesnil Herman. Another has advanced four miles to south-west of Canisy.

A third has driven some distance west from Marigny down the Coutances road.

An advance of some 2,000 yards has cut the Periers-Lessay road between St. Lo and Caumont. Advance troops, after occupying Berigny, have reached outskirts of Notre dame d'Elle. Other forces have reached Mouffet.

Enemy has made no further effort in Caen sector.

Strong counter-attack by enemy towards Verrieres repulsed last night.

Enemy shipping off Pas de Calais coast was attacked by coastal aircraft today.

Moscow bid by Polish P.M.

POLISH Prime Minister Mikolaczyk is on his way from London to Moscow to discuss Russo-Polish relations with the Soviet Government.

The decision that M. Mikolaczyk should go to Moscow—a courageous one on the Premier's part—was taken at a meeting of the Polish Cabinet called to consider the situation caused by the setting up of an "opposition" Government in Poland—the Polish Committee of National Liberation—with Russian approval.

Diplomatic relations between Russia and the Polish Government in London were severed many months ago.

While Russia has recognised the new Polish Committee, Britain continues to recognise the Polish Government led by M. Mikolaczyk.

Britain hopes that an understanding may be reached and unity restored, but the problems are complex and deep-rooted.

There was a further complication last night, revealed by M. W. Banaczyk, Polish Minister of Home Affairs, in a broadcast from London.

He said the Polish Government in the present situation was forced to disclose, despite the danger of German reprisals, that the Polish Vice-Premier and three Ministers and other Government officials are already working with the underground movement in Poland.

"These men will come into the open at the proper time and in the place where they are in office," he said. "Their names are known to the British and American Governments.

"The Polish Government believes that these men, who for five years have been leading resistance and work of the Polish Underground State, will be recognised as rightful representatives of the legal State authority, and of the will of the nation."

NORMANDY FRONT IS "EXPLODING" IN NEW ATTACK, SAYS BERLIN

THE German Overseas News Agency's war correspondent in Normandy, reported last night:

"The Allies have launched a new major offensive on the whole British front, including the most southerly points at Caumont, and over the invasion front generally.

"The Normandy battle is on the threshold of a new and decisive phase. Grim fighting is raging everywhere.

"Strong British groupings launching new thrusts under cover of a deep gorge north of Verrieres have managed to gain ground, but the Germans are counter attacking.

"Big British concentrations of tanks and motorised forces south of Caen are at present being shelled.

"It may be assumed that Montgomery can now put fifty divisions in the field, including very strong new tank groupings. The British Second Army alone is estimated to possess 1,500 to 2,000 heavy tanks, and the U.S. First Army probably has the same.

"The Allied strip of land on the Normandy coast now resembles a blazing boiler whose safety valves are inadequate to prevent a great explosion."

Our troops ordered—don't eat French food: Cafes and shops ban

From GEORGE McCARTHY, "Daily Mirror" Chief Correspondent

FRANCE, Thursday.

THE food of Normandy is to be rationed and stored—to feed the people of Paris and the great cities of France when they have been liberated.

Since the Allies arrived there has been meat, butter and cheese in abundance. These have been available to the French without ration cards, and British troops visiting the towns have gone back to the fields and orchards bearing armfulls of cheese and parcels of excellent butter.

All that is to end.

From August 1 the British troops will not be allowed to eat meals in restaurants, or to buy foodstuffs in the shops.

The civilian population is to be rationed. They will, however, still be allowed plenty to eat. For instance, the meat ration will be five times that permitted during the German occupation.

The food saved by these restrictions will be carefully hoarded to relieve the acute shortage now known to exist in the big cities.

Many fewer cattle are to be

Continued on Back Page

6 Soviet victories—Baltic Nazis cut off

ALONG a 600-mile front from the gates of Czechoslovakia to the Baltic Republics, the Soviet forces yesterday dealt Hitler's routed legions six staggering new blows.

These were the victories, announced in five orders from Marshal Stalin, which made it the greatest day of victories in history.

The Red Army, in a lightning forty-mile thrust, have struck to within eighty miles of the Baltic, taken the Lithuanian road and rail centre of Shavli, and cut the last retreat line of all the Germans in Estonia, Latvia and northern Lithuania.

Troops of the second Baltic Front, smashing on towards Riga, the Latvian capital, have captured Dvinsk, last big enemy bastion barring their advance.

With Dvinsk has fallen Rezekne, an important rail and road centre, forty-four miles to the north-east.

The beginning of a wedge which may soon cut off Warsaw from East Prussia has been driven into the German position by the capture of Bialystok, 100 miles north-east of Warsaw.

Lvov, encircled for several days, has been cleared of the enemy.

The road to Czechoslovakia, through the Tartar Pass, was opened up when Soviet troops stormed into Stanislov, the big base guarding the Carpathian approaches.

Stalin's Order No. 5, announcing the capture of Shavli, was strategically the most important of all.

The railways from Riga to East Prussia and Kaunas are now cut. Only minor escape routes are left open for the German 16th and 18th Armies, under General Lindemann, holding the Baltic.

Thus, the German Baltic Army group is faced with complete disaster.

TUESDAY, AUGUST 1, 1944

Latest Prices

BLACK OUT 10.34 to 5.39 | Moon Rises 7.25 p.m. Full Moon Aug. 4 | Sets 3.44 a.m. Radio Page 4

LATE NIGHT

THE STAR

No. 17,507 ONE PENNY

ALLIES LINK UP & DRIVE SOUTH

Nazi Lines Pierced By New Thrusts

MORRISON'S ALERT-WITHIN-ALERT

New Klaxon Warning

3 BLASTS—TAKE COVER

A NEW klaxon warning system, to tell the public of immediate danger during flying-bomb attacks, is to be introduced at once.

This was announced in Parliament today by Mr. Morrison, Minister of Home Security, who told M.P.s :

"The Government have considered the desirability of introducing a special warning, in the London area, in addition to the alert sounded on air raid sirens, to indicate the near approach of a flying bomb.

LINKED TO FACTORIES

"Of the various methods examined, the most practicable would appear to be to make audible, to a wider public, the danger-warning signals sounded in factories connected to the industrial warning system.

"The amount of warning given cannot be more than about one and a half minutes. The warning signal—which will be known as the 'danger warning'—will be three two-second blasts on a klaxon, or other suitable instrument, at intervals of two seconds.

"The signal to indicate danger is passed will be a continuous blast lasting six seconds.

"Pending the installation of standard instruments, the most suitable instruments at present available will be used. The new system will be brought into operation step by step, as quickly as the necessary work can be carried out.

"Meanwhile, arrangements will be made so that, as far as possible, all unofficial warning signals for the public already in use, are made to conform with the standard warning signals.

NO VISUAL SIGNALS

"These unofficial signals will be superseded, as soon as the new system of warnings has been brought into operation.

"The Government have considered whether there should also be a system of visible signals, but have come to the conclusion that this is not desirable.

"No system of visible signals could be devised which would be seen from all parts of the streets, and there would be a serious risk of traffic accidents caused by the diversion of drivers' attention from the road. Existing visible signals will therefore be superseded when the new audible system is in operation.

"The Government wish to make it clear that the proposed system of danger warnings, although considered the most practicable, is admittedly imperfect and incomplete and subject to certain other limitations.

"It will, for instance, only be possible to provide danger warnings in areas where there are premises connected to the industrial warning system, but the system will be extended steadily as circumstances and resources allow.

"Moreover, there can be no guarantee that the danger warning will always precede the fall of a flying bomb, and there will inevitably be many warnings which are not followed by bombs in the vicinity.

"WORK MUST GO ON"

"The Government consider that the system proposed offers better prospects of success than any other, but only experience can show how far it will represent an improvement on the present air-raid warning system.

"Factories have their own internal

CONTINUED ON PAGE FIVE, Col. THREE

ENEMY 'SCORCH' WARSAW

THE Germans in Warsaw are burning and blowing-up buildings in the Polish capital, according to an "Izvestia" dispatch from the front, quoted by Reuter's Moscow correspondent this afternoon.

Such demolitions are the usual prelude to evacuation of a city by the enemy.

Clouds of smoke over Warsaw have been reported by Red Air Force pilots raiding the German defences.

On the ground Russian and Polish troops, under an umbrella of hundreds of Red-starred planes, today attacked Praga—Warsaw's "Brixton"—from three sides, says A.P.

One of the greatest artillery concentrations of the entire Eastern Front was blasted. and German defences on the edge of Praga, which faces Warsaw proper from the east bank of the Vistula.

A considerable Russian advance west and south-west of Grodno, where the Red Army have reached the immediate approaches to East Prussia, was reported by "Red Star," according to Exchange.

Earlier, Soviet units were said to be only 10 miles from the frontier.

German radio said that a number of Soviet "nuisance raiders"—probably reconnaissance planes—flew over East Prussia during the night.

The Nazis also admitted that the German troops had "shortened their lines" between the Middle Bug and Augustovo, i.e., north of Warsaw.

"This Is Stalin Speaking"

Marshal Stalin, guiding and watching over the Red Army offensive, is giving his orders personally by telephone over direct lines to the front, says a Soviet war correspondent, according to Reuter.

"The telephone rings in a general's quarters or a general's dug-out. 'This is Moscow—Stalin speaking,'" said the correspondent.

Exempt Nurses From Firewatching—M.P.

Mr. Sorensen (Lab., West Leyton) is to ask the Home Secretary if, in view of their arduous duties and long hours of service, he will exempt nurses from fire watching.

New Court Clerk

Mr. L. H. Walden, who has been at Stratford Court for more than 31 years, and for 25 years Clerk to the Justices, today shared in welcoming his successor, Mr. H. Graham Barrow, of Morpeth.

TWO GREAT NEW ALLIED ADVANCES IN NORMANDY—ONE BELOW CAUMONT AND THE OTHER BEYOND AVRANCHES, AT THE BASE OF THE CHERBOURG PENINSULA—WERE REPORTED IN LATE REUTER CABLES FROM THE BATTLEFRONT TODAY.

British and American forces have joined hands south-west of the Foret l'Eveque and are now driving south in a powerful double-barrelled thrust through Rommel's defences, Doon Campbell wrote from the Caumont area.

The forest itself has been captured, and another British column is less than two miles north-west of Le Beny Bocage after a lightning stab more than ten miles south from Caumont across the River Souleuvre.

These achievements, in which nearly half a dozen more towns and villages have fallen to the British, come after a night of successes all along the line.

East of the Orne, Canadians have

captured Tilly Campagne, below Bourgebus.

American armour has crossed the River Selune, last German defence line at the base of the Cherbourg Peninsula, at Ducey and Pontabault, wrote John Wilhelm, and the next important natural defence line for Rommel's men falling back to the south is the River Loire. Over 6,000 prisoners were captured in the American sector yesterday, he said.

Today's Allied communique reported an advance on a broad front, and afterwards Supreme Headquarters announced that British and American troops, battling through the "Normandy jungle" south-west of Caumont, had, in the past 24 hours, doubled the bulge punched into the German line.

Progress has also been made against heavy resistance in the Percy-Villedieu area, says Reuter. American

CONTINUED ON BACK PAGE, Col. FOUR

MORE RAIDS ON FLY-BOMB DEPOTS

LANCASTERS and Halifaxes of Bomber Command attacked flying-bomb launching sites and supply depots in the Pas de Calais and near Rheims during the night, it was announced in an Air Ministry communique today.

From these, and the usual mine-laying operations, four of our aircraft are missing.

There was great Allied air activity over the coast again today. Wave after wave of planes flew out.

Flying-bomb attacks on Southern England, including the London area, were resumed today.

During the night a few bombs were sent over, causing casualties and damage.

Rescue Scenes—Page Four.

Berlin Once More

Berlin was bombed again during the night, and Russian aircraft were over East Prussia today, according to German radio. There is no news of these raids from Allied sources.

Evacuated London Wives & Army Pay

Lieut.-Col. Mayhew (Con., East Ham N.) asked the War Minister in the Commons today whether the 3s. 6d, London allowance to soldiers' wives would still be paid to those who evacuated with their families into a safe area.

Sir James Grigg replied that families who had left London since June 13, when the flying bombs began, would continue to receive the allowance during their absence provided they were still paying rent and had not sublet their London homes. It was a special and purely temporary arrangement for as long as the flying bomb menace was on us. Afterwards it would be reconsidered.

MIST IN STRAITS

A fairly low ceiling of mist covered the sky in the Straits of Dover today and it was cool. The sun was expected to get through later.

A light northerly wind was blowing off shore and the sea was smooth on this side. Visibility was five to six miles.

Stole From Shelter

At Romford today, John Simpson (21), was sentenced to one month's imprisonment for stealing a suit of clothes and other wearing apparel and an identity card from an air-raid shelter at Romford.

Infantry advancing along a lane under cover of the trees after the British forces had launched their attack from the Caumont area.

Rommel Latest —'Liquidated'

According to a usually well-informed source, quoted by Reuter's Geneva correspondent, Rommel's disappearance may be connected with the recent Hitler purge.

This report says he was "liquidated" after being recalled to Hitler's H.Q.

At the same time, underground authorities in Algiers corroborated the story that Rommel had died in Normandy of wounds, and added that Gen. Stuelpnagel, commander of the German occupation forces in France, had committed suicide.

LATE WAR NEWS

No. 15,055 ONE PENNY FOR KING AND EMPIRE THURSDAY, AUGUST 3, 1944

GERMAN FRONT COLLAPSES

Allies Win Greatest Victory Since Invasion Day

TANKS NEAR RENNES IN BRITTANY DRIVE

THE German front west of Caen has collapsed. Allied tanks rolling into the interior of France are meeting virtually no opposition. American armour, fanning out in strength from the north-east corner of Brittany, is well on the way to Rennes, key to all communications to the Brittany Peninsula, and St. Malo.

British troops have broken through the German positions 15 miles south of Caumont, and an official spokesman describes the British attack as a "major success."

The outskirts of Vire have been reached and the Vire-Vassy road cut, but so speedy has been the Allied advance that the exact whereabouts of many of the forward units are not known.

Hour after hour last night reports poured in of the greatest victory since D-Day. Scores of French towns and villages have been captured, and the extent of the advance may be judged from the fact that Rennes lies about 45 miles south of Avranches, captured on Monday.

While American troops captured Villedieu British forces closed in from the east, thus placing the Germans still in the Tessy pocket in a precarious position. The British have already taken 1,500 prisoners.

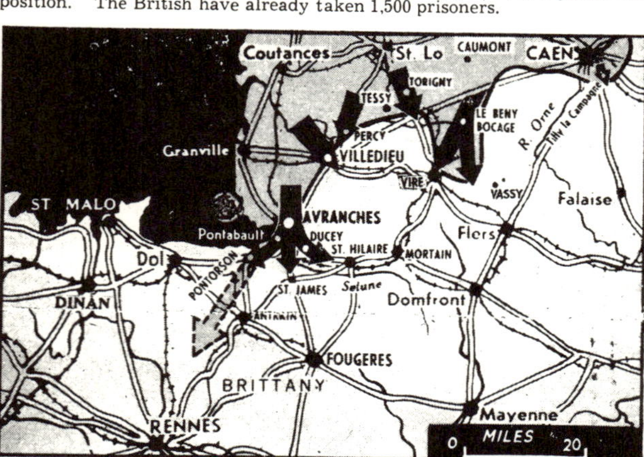

Everything Moving—and Moving Fast

Clifford's Story of the Battle

'Our Chance'

From ALEXANDER CLIFFORD

LE BENY BOCAGE, Wednesday.

THE spirit of advance was as clearly in the air to-day as the yellow dust itself.

The whole Second Army seemed to be on the move forward. You could feel the excitement in its veins. You could feel it as plainly as we used to feel it in those mad desert advances.

The situation geographically is still so untidy as to be indescribable.

But we are on beyond Le Beny Bocage, through a whole cluster of villages to the south-east. We are on beyond Jurques. We are going ahead everywhere.

Just here and there the Germans are holding and resisting.

The line of advance runs like a great hook round the west and south of the area between St. Martin des Besaces and Le Beny Bocage, and there are Germans still in it.

In woods here and there and along the bushy banks of streams, little enemy battle groups are fighting, but it is no longer an organised front.

★

I COULD list you the name of a hundred villages but they are only confusing. The important thing is this instinct of movement and success which has seized the Army. There is a feeling that a chance is being afforded to us and we are taking it.

Our mileage is admittedly not spectacular. We have made 12 or 13 miles in four days, which is not impressive beside those whirlwind advances in Africa. But this is not a country where you can overrun empty square miles.

Where each field and each lane and each farm may be an enemy strongpoint you cannot expect a dizzy speed. You must measure our mileage against the quality of this close-grained country. Then you will see why these 13 miles have bred this mood of success to-day.

Everything was moving, and moving fast, to-day.

The roads that were no-man's-land last week are peaceful and empty again now. But the roads ahead are endless tunnels of choking dust.

But you could leave these main arteries of traffic and drive sideways into a quiet, manless country. Unmilked cows grazed in the vegetable plots and chickens hopped in and out of parlour windows. The inhabitants had fled or been driven out by the Germans. The main tentacles of war had passed it by.

Along the wayside you saw all the signs of a recent rapid advance. French peasants—men, women, and children—gathered jubilantly to watch German prisoners being searched. Rommel had swept through this district a week before with an S.S. bodyguard, who had left bitter memories behind.

★

IN the next place the people were trying to shave the heads of three women who had been too friendly with the enemy. The women hid in a shop, but village tempers were roused and the crowd hunted them down.

In the end they simply had their hair clipped off, not shaved. They sneaked off home in a disgrace that will never be forgotten.

Prisoners are still straggling in from the thick, by-passed country round about.

Just beyond here to-day I saw a puzzled despatch rider trying to cope with two Germans who had surrendered to him. He was shepherding them along on his motor-bike, looking for someone to give them to.

Some way farther on a little action was in progress—one of the thousands of tiny engagements which together compose the present battle.

Some Germans had dug-in a couple of anti-tank guns beside a stream and were lying in wait there. A squadron of British tanks went clattering off down the road to see to it. Some dived left into the woods and the others went straight ahead. "The old princer movement," said someone.

The armoured car patrols took no notice. They carried on with their exploration programme while the tanks mopped up.

★

THAT is how this advance is being done. The men who are doing it down here are members of a division that is earning a great name for itself in Normandy—though for some inscrutable reason its name cannot yet be mentioned.

There had been fascinating doings at these cross-roads the evening before. First the woman who was emptying her washtub was waiting on her doorstep to warn the armoured cars about the mines the Germans had just laid outside her house.

Then two Germans came from another house and surrendered. Then two Frenchmen said they supposed they had better surrender, too, because the Germans had forcibly conscripted them.

Then a whole German patrol with armoured cars was seen approaching down the road.

A British N.C.O. with an empty pistol held them up. He got two motor-cyclists and six other Germans in a truck. The armoured cars turned off on another road and ran head on into a British tank. The tank fired its Brownings and the armoured car crews all took to the woods.

When things like that happen you can be quite sure that the battle is going well.

British Drive Reaches Vire

From G. WARD PRICE

SHAEF, Wednesday Evening.

LIKE the break-up of a log jam on a Canadian river, the front in Normandy has to-day been a scene of jostling, confused movement—all in one direction. Everywhere on both the British and American sectors the whole line is advancing, with armoured cars and tanks swooping about in front.

Along part of what was till lately a most stubbornly contested battle line, our troops have lost touch with the retreating enemy. At other points, such as the sector between Percy and Tessy in the middle, the Germans are still resisting stoutly.

This seems to be the result of the temperament of the enemy troops concerned rather than the execution of a strategic plan.

On that particular strip of front there happened to be two armoured divisions, the 2nd Panzers and the 16th Panzers. They formed the last bastion of what it is perhaps not too optimistic to call the crumbling German front.

A little to the east of the Percy-Tessy sector the ground in front of the British troops is being yielded rapidly to them.

To-day they have advanced from Le Beny Bocage due south for 12 miles.

They have cut the main road that runs east from Vire towards Falaise. They have here reached a point 35 miles south-west of Caen, in whose suburbs they were so recently penned up, and are on the outskirts of that historic granite-built cloth-making town of Vire, which stands amid a chestnut forest, deep gorges, wild cascades, and fern covered slopes on the majestic sweep of the river of the same name.

'VAUX DE VIRE'

Vire is the place from which the English word "vaudeville" is derived. In the 15th century the gay songs of a local poet, Olivier Basselin, became known as "Vaux de Vire."

This advance forms for the present a British salient in the constantly improving outline of the Normandy front.

Farther north our troops are pressing forward into Villers-Bocage after occupying Fougèrolles, two miles to the north of it, and we have cleared the Germans out of the Bois-du Homme, that formidable eminence and hide-out which until recently sheltered a whole armoured enemy division.

While resistance is thus cracking under British and Canadian pressure, the Americans on the west flank—which looks like soon becoming the "Far West" flank—are driving forward into Brittany at right angles to their former line of advance down the Cherbourg Peninsula.

The main forces of their tank divisions have already passed Pontorson, the first town on the road that runs parallel with the

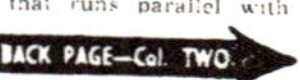

'U.S. Driving to Loire' —Sertorius

SERTORIUS, the German Overseas News Agency commentator, stated last night:—

"The American tank stabs from Avranches in a south-westerly and southerly direction, which gained a fair amount of ground after crossing the Selune, may have as an objective a break-through to the mouth of the Loire.

"The operational task of the mobile American forces advancing from Avranches, between the Selune and See rivers to the east, is clearly to roll up the German front west of the Orne, and where possible to strike it in the rear."

Another German News Agency report said that American spearheads had advanced to Pontorson, 12 miles south-west of Avranches, where they had been engaged in heavy fighting.

"Several tank divisions and formations of motorised infantry aimed at crashing through into the interior of Western France," this report said.—*Reuter.*

Rhone Valley Hit by Italy Heavies

ALLIED H.Q., ITALY, Wednesday.—Targets in the Rhone Valley, including railway yards and oil storage areas, were bombed to-day by heavy bombers from Italy. Other bombers struck at harbour installations at Genoa.—*Reuter.*

THOUGHT FOR TO-DAY

It is not easy now to be a German soldier.—*German Forces radio last night.*

He Planned the Invasion

General Moryan, who Mr. Churchill revealed in his speech yesterday, was chief of the Anglo-American planning staff for the invasion. They selected the beaches for the attack and planned the main operations of the scheme.

Flyer and WRNS Wife Killed

Two officers of the Fleet Air Arm and a W.R.N.S. officer, the wife of one of them, have been killed in an aeroplane accident at sea. They were Pilot-Officer Fretwell, of Manchester; Sub-Lieutenant Myles Jackson, of Tunbridge Wells, and his wife Daphne, a former Dublin University student, whom he had married only a year ago. Both were 22.

They had taken off from a station, and had been in the air about half an hour when the plane blew up. None of the bodies was recovered.

BLACK-OUT TO-NIGHT

	p.m.		a.m
LONDON	10.30	to	5.42
BELFAST	11.07	..	5.52
EDINBURGH	11.17	..	5.21
MANCHESTER	10.47	..	5.43
BIRMINGHAM	10.41	..	5.46
NEWCASTLE	11.05	..	5.19
LEEDS	10.47	..	5.39
LIVERPOOL	10.50	..	5.46

R.A.F. Did Knock Out Rommel

'Injured in a Car Crash'—Berlin

BERLIN has at last admitted that Rommel has been injured and that for the time being he is "out of the war."

The German News Agency announced last night:—

"Field-Marshal Rommel met with a car accident as the result of an air raid in France on July 17.

"He suffered injuries and concussion. His condition is satisfactory, and his life is not in danger."

Rommel was first reported wounded last Saturday. Prisoners captured on the American sector said he was hurt when Allied planes strafed his car in the Lisieux area.

On the same day a French woman was quoted by front-line correspondents as saying that she nursed him after the attack and actually saw him die.

Flood of Rumours

On Monday the German News Agency issued an ambiguous message intended by implication to mean that the German field commander was fit and well.

This did not serve to halt the flood of rumours about Rommel's fate, and messages from the United [illegible] reports "so circumstantial that they make sense," that he died after receiving serious chest injuries from the strafing plane.

19 Canadians Murdered

By S.S. Captors

MR EDEN announced with regret in the Commons last night that an officer and 18 men of the Canadian forces, taken prisoner in Normandy, had been murdered while in custody by the 12th S.S. Reconnaissance Battalion of the 12th S.S. Panzer Division, under the direction of certain of their officers.

The Swiss Government had been asked to lodge a strong protest with the German Government demanding an immediate searching investigation, the punishment of those responsible, and an assurance that orders would be issued to prevent a recurrence.

Full story—BACK Page.

OLD MASTERS WERE SAFE

Dulwich Gallery Hit

Only about 100 of the less valuable of the collection of 600 paintings were in Dulwich College Picture Gallery, London, when the building was severely damaged by a flying-bomb recently.

All the masterpieces had been removed previously to a secret place of security.

It is considered that the damaged pictures can be restored.

During a recent raid a flying-bomb exploded within a few feet of the *Daily Herald* building in London. No one was hurt.

Surrounding buildings were extensively damaged.

Exchange Ship is Recalled to Port

LISBON, Wednesday.—The Drottningholm carrying 900 British internees from camps in France and Germany who have been exchanged for German internees from South Africa, put out to-day, but at the last minute was signalled to heave to because of a hitch regarding her safe conduct.

She is expected to sail at dawn on Friday.—*Reuter.*

Berlin is Angry With the Turks

'Broke Their Pact of Friendship'

AN angry communiqué announcing Turkey's decision to break with Germany as from midnight last night was broadcast from Berlin last night.

It stated: "The Turkish Government has to-day communicated to the Turkish National Assembly its decision to break off diplomatic and economic relations with Germany.

"After violent discussion at a secret session of the Turkish People's Party yesterday, the Turkish National Assembly has to-day accepted the Government's decision.

"By this act Turkey has abandoned her traditional policy of friendship with Germany and of neutrality as a condition of her independence, thereby breaking her treaty of friendship with Germany.

'Despite Warning'

"Despite the warning of the Reich Government, the Turkish Government has yielded to pressure by England, America, and Russia and has chosen a way which deprives it of free and independent action.

"The Foreign Office has informed the Turkish Chargé d'Affaires this afternoon that his mission in Germany has ended, and has requested him to leave Reich territory forthwith."

The break, writes the Diplomatic Correspondent of B.U.P., was described in diplomatic circles yesterday as "a diplomatic defeat of the first order for Hitler and his arch-conniver Von Papen," who have spent the entire war trying to keep the Turks in line with the interests and solidarity of Hitler's Balkan coalition.

That Turkey has now made the plunge after months of wavering indecision is a tribute to the Allied military position as it stands at present.

Turkey, on her side, is now obviously qualified for participation [illegible]

Turkish Statement

"The friendship that unites Turkey with Britain induces her to present to the Grand National Assembly the British and American proposal to break off economic and political relations with Germany," said M. Sarajoglu, quoted by the German News Agency.

"In order to meet the difficulties which would arise from this decision, economic and financial help were asked for," continued M. Saraioglu.

"Following a positive answer to this request given by our British allies, our Government informed the British Ambassador that the Government would pass to the National Assembly the decision taken by the Cabinet to break off diplomatic and economic relations with Germany as from the night of Wednesday to Thursday.

London Satisfaction

"This positive answer was received with great satisfaction in London. Two days later, the British Ambassador in a signed letter to the Foreign Office stated that this positive decision of the Turkish Cabinet was real proof of the friendship and agreement between Britain and Turkey and expressed also the importance of Turkey's participation in the decisions she is about to take.

"Friends, the decision you are about to take is not the decision for war. This will depend on the attitude taken by the opposite side. I am sure that the decision taken by an assembly which has the fate of Turkey in its hands will be great and historical and will ensure the future happiness of the country."—*B.U.P.* and *A.P.*

Lord Hardinge of Penshurst Dies

Lord Hardinge of Penshurst, a former Viceroy of India, died at his home at Oakfield, Penshurst, Kent, yesterday, aged 85. He had been ill for some time.

He was the first baron, being elevated to the peerage in 1910, when he was appointed Viceroy of India after a distinguished career in the diplomatic service. He is succeeded by his son, Sir Alexander Henry Louis Hardinge, who was private secretary to the King until last year.

New Luftwaffe Chief

Lieutenant-General Kreipe has been appointed Chief of Staff of the Luftwaffe in succession to Colonel-General Korten, who was killed during the attempt on Hitler's life.

Pick-a-back Plane, Robot Tank Are 'Secret Weapons'

TWO new German "secret weapons" were described in Reuter despatches from Normandy yesterday. They are:—

The "pick-a-back-plane" an ME. mounted on a JU 88, the nose of which is filled with high explosive; and

A **robot tank**, V 1., bigger than those used unsuccessfully in Italy.

One of the "pick-a-back" planes was shot down recently by a night fighter and caused a "colossal explosion" as it hit the water.

The plane can be operated by one man instead of five. It has not yet been used on any scale, but its potentialities to the personnel-starved Luftwaffe are most attractive.

Captain R. C. Lewis, of London, said: "The JU 88 is remotely controlled by the pilot of the ME."

If flak is encountered the pilot can set the JU on a pre-determined course and detach himself.

The robot tank, which made its appearance on the Canadian front, has a driver who takes it as far as he can, gets out, and directs it by wireless.

The tank is supposed to jettison a quantity of explosive, turn round, and waddle back. It is slightly larger than a Bren-gun carrier.

Six actually jettisoned their explosives, four seemed to mill about aimlessly as though they were out of control, and two were knocked out by mortars.

• • •

Partisans Join Warsaw Battle

20,000 ATTACK NAZIS

AS the Russians develop their flanking movements around Warsaw the German defenders face a grave threat in the capital itself by the sudden appearance of 20,000 Polish Partisan troops who have engaged the enemy in street battles in four parts of the city.

The Partisans are led by General Bor, who is in contact with the Russians in the suburb of Praga on the north-east side of the capital.

The Polish Forces Press Bureau in London says the four main areas where fighting is raging are Kercelak, Belvedere-square, Pulawska, and the Avenue of Polish Forces—all in the western part of Warsaw.

Strong Russian forces have crossed the Vistula south-east of the city and established a second bridgehead, according to a German High Command broadcast last night.

Moscow claims that the Germans have lost about 570,000 men in the last month—equal to their losses between August and November 1918.

The Red Army is now building up its strength in readiness for the onslaught on East Prussia.

The Germans are being forced back to their border fortifications.

Yesterday's German High Command communiqué admitted that in heavy fighting between the forest of Ugustow and Memel they had lost the localities of Kalvarija and Vilkaviskis.

The latter place is only 12 miles

BACK PAGE—Col. FOUR

'Break With Germany'

Next Finn Move

MARSHAL MANNERHEIM, newly appointed President of Finland, is to take the oath of office on Friday. His first step towards peace, according to a National Broadcasting Company report from Stockholm yesterday, is likely to be a break with Germany.

M. Eero Vuori, head of the Finnish trades unions, was named in the same report as likely to become the new Premier, as he is believed to have been a powerful factor in crystallising the activity of the "peace opposition" and is known to be acceptable to the Soviet Union.

The Swedish *Aftonbladet* reported yesterday that the Russians had offered the Finns substantially the same peace terms as those of last February.

Meanwhile, the paper said, the Germans have now concentrated a third of all their forces in Finland round Aabo (Turku), on the west coast, and it is believed that they will occupy the Aaland Islands (between Finland and Sweden) if Finland tries to make peace.

Optimism is the keynote of Finnish Press comments on Ryti's resignation. Most of them hope Finland will be able to retain her independence.—*Reuter* and *B.U.P.*

LATEST

WARSAW DRIVE: RUSSIANS TAKE 200 PLACES

Russian communique announces capture of 200 places north and west of Siedlce in drive on Warsaw.

More than 100 places taken north of Kovno. Town of Vilkaviskis, near East Prussian border, captured.

Sunday Pictorial

August 6, 1944
TWOPENCE
No. 1,534

BIG NEWS!

Russians Are Fighting On German Soil—Montgomery Bursts Through

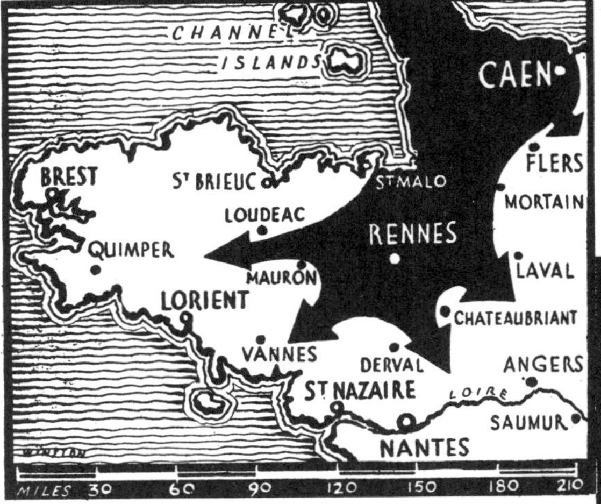

THIS MORNING WE BRING YOU NEWS OF TWO EVENTS THAT WILL RANK AMONG THE MOST IMPORTANT IN THE HISTORY OF THE WHOLE WAR. THEY MARK THE FINAL TURNING OF THE TIDE AFTER NEARLY FIVE YEARS OF WAR.

In the west Montgomery's two-fisted blows have struck home. American tanks have not only reached the outskirts of Brest, at the tip of the Brittany peninsula, but have reached the River Loire and cut the peninsula in two.

That is not the only news of great importance. In the East the Russians have smashed across the frontier of East Prussia—and for the first time the Allies are fighting on German soil. The whole story is told on the back page.

Montgomery has burst through the German defences. Our whole line is on the move, and the road into France becomes clear. And in Italy, Florence has fallen.

The beachhead fight in Normandy has become the Battle of France.

Reeling under Montgomery's attack, the Germans, while attempting to hold a hinge in the Caen area, are swinging back their whole front.

For the moment there is no settled front.

In the Caen sector, held by British and Canadian troops, our tanks are rolling eastward. The enemy in twenty-four hours have abandoned fifty square miles even in this vital area.

But even more spectacular is the way American tanks are sweeping through Brittany. The great peninsula, with its vitally important ports of Brest, Lorient and St. Nazaire—all U-boat bases—is cut off.

Pushing along the Channel coast the Americans are in St. Malo, though the town is not yet entirely captured. Fall of St. Malo means the cutting-off of the Channel Islands.

Berlin admits that the Americans have got six armoured and motorised divisions out into open country in Brittany.

Berlin also says that fifty-four Allied divisions are now in France. If this figure is correct it means we must have something like 650,000 men

"This settles the matter," commented Berlin. "Normandy is of decisive importance."

AS THE MAP SHOWS THE GERMANS FACE DISASTER

Fuller Says—

IT WILL NEED A MIRACLE TO SAVE ROMMEL NOW

The Germans in France are facing disaster, says Major-General J. F. C. Fuller, one of the world's leading tank experts and "Sunday Pictorial" Military Correspondent. Here, in his last night's commentary on the news, he explains that for Rommel to retrieve the position it is necessary for him to perform one of the most remarkable withdrawals in the whole history of war.

HISTORY I think will decide that the supreme event of the last few days is the collapse of the German front in Normandy. Because in strategic importance it exceeds all the great happenings in Eastern Europe—the assault on Warsaw, the occupation of the Gulf of Riga and the invasion of East Prussia. For tactically it has opened the long sought Second Front in the West.

Since the initial landing and until a few days ago, the Allied forces in Normandy occupied no more than a bridgehead. Now that bridgehead has vanished, and in its place we see a true base established from which operations are in full swing.

The Normandy door—the door to the whole of Western France—has been burst in at its lock—Avranches. Its centre, south of Gaumont, has been smashed, and what now remains of it is precariously swinging on its hinge—the Caen area.

Yet, even more important than this bursting, smashing and swinging, is that a gap has been created in the German strategic front in the West—a gap extending from the Gulf of St. Malo to the Mediterranean.

This is no exaggeration. For if, as has been proved, the Germans have not force enough to hold a front of a hundred miles, it certainly may be assumed that they have not force enough to hold one of greater length unless they can place between them and their enemy an obstacle of such strength that it will lend power to their waning numbers.

Only one such obstacle exists within reach. It is the river Seine—the magnet which all but certainly will draw them eastwards. And the more it does so, the wider grows the gap.

Can the Germans withdraw to it? Or can they be prevented from doing so? These, so it seems to me, are the two vital questions which must be answered by the Allied Command before they commit their forces to the next step.

As regards the first: Should Rommel, or whoever is now directing the German forces in Normandy, successfully carry out this retirement, then, indeed, it will be one of the most remarkable retreats in history.

Can this withdrawal be prevented? Here we touch on future operations and the answer must therefore be left to the future. Yet one thing may be mentioned. It is this:

Should the answer be that we can stop the retreat and do so, then the decisive moment in the Battle of France is approaching. Because the final overthrow of Rommel will follow, and that will knock the foundations from under the feet of every other German army corps, division and brigade now in France.

That is why I have stressed the importance of the winning of the strategic gap. For once Rommel and his army are annihilated that gap becomes France.

Begins Today

No woman in this war has had an adventure to equal that of Alice Leone Moats, young American authoress, noted for her daring and audacity. Unknown to anyone she made her way through Spain to the Pyrenees and then got the French to smuggle her to Paris.

For five weeks she moved among the Gestapo—to bring out an astonishing story of life under the German heel. She has written it all down and the "Sunday Pictorial" has secured the exclusive rights in Britain to tell it—the story of a girl the whole German Army could not stop. Miss Moats' narrative—

ON PAGE 4

AND CHEERS FOR THE BOYS DOING IT!

Sunday Graphic
No. 1,531 (E) SUNDAY, AUGUST 6, 1944 TWOPENCE

U.S. TANKS REACH BREST

Only 18 Miles From St. Nazaire: Full Story On Back Page

Normandy Tonic

The campaign in Normandy is going well—in fact magnificently. This is reflected in General Montgomery's wholehearted laughter as he relaxes for a few moments with his men. George Formby, of ENSA, was responsible for the General's amusement

FOUR PAGES OF LATEST NORMANDY PICTURES INSIDE

Daily Mail
NO. 15,058 ONE PENNY * FOR KING AND EMPIRE MONDAY, AUGUST 7, 1944

LATE WAR NEWS

MONTY SWINGS EAST—FOR PARIS

British and Americans Sweeping On in Dual Threat

THE STAFF VIEW OF FRANCE:

'Hitler is Facing the Big Crisis'

IN NORMANDY, Sunday Night.

A SENIOR staff officer at General Montgomery's H.Q. said to-night: "My view is that the next two or three weeks may be the most critical of the war.

"It does look as if Germany is going to be faced with tremendous disasters in many places and a terrible time ahead."

The officer disclosed that the Allied campaign in Normandy is going almost exactly to the schedule planned in London several months ago.

"We were supposed to get to Brest on D plus 50," he said. "This did not include the complete cleaning up of the Brittany Peninsula—that was expected to take up to D plus 60."

That was the plan before February. To-day is D plus 60.

The officer backed up General Montgomery's policy of building up large reserves before cracking through the German defences.

"While it meant that the earlier stages of the campaign had to be slower, one hopes that the later stages of the campaign may be quicker than we expected," he said.

ELIMINATED

"We have made contact with 35 enemy divisions. As a result of recent operations about 13 divisions have been virtually eliminated.

"From the remaining 22 approximately 11 are facing each army. We reckon we have five panzer divisions against us and about three against the Americans.

"It is a major naval disaster for them if they lose the operational value of the Brittany ports. The whole of their naval strategy will have to be reorientated."

The officer said that two things—the security of the beaches and the need to accumulate forces and supplies—had so far influenced the course of events, and went on:

"It was a very trying period for General Montgomery at first.

"You and I probably felt things were going very slow during that time and wondered if it was not possible to quicken things up and change the original plan.

"But the C.-in-C. kept his plan, and I think he was very wise that he did not try altering it to any marked degree.

12 HOURS OUT

"I remember similar sort of conditions on a smaller scale during the Battle of Alamein. He had complete confidence the whole time that the battle would turn out completely successful.

"Actually, General Montgomery did say in his final pep talks that he thought it would be a dog-fight for ten days. It was actually 9½ days.

"Unquestionably the enemy has decided to fight this battle out here, and any reserves he can produce are endeavouring to get along here on push bikes and on foot and on railways as far as they are allowed.

"It is frightfully difficult to see how these reinforcements can be sufficient to enable him to retrieve the situation—a situation where he has a very big open flank. It is very difficult to see how he could set up and fight it out with any success.

"In this movement of the reserves from the north and south I think one can say that if they had arrived ten days ago the situation might have been different.

"One thing is certain about his policy in Brittany—the enemy has decided on a policy of trying to hold key points and ports. That seems to be his plot. He is pulling into these fortress areas.

"When one pulls into a fortress area there is a normal strategy, and one expects that one thing he might do is to try and come up from the south and relieve the fortresses, and start the war again in Brittany.

"But his forces may not be sufficient to enable him to do that."

The officer estimated that the British had recently taken about 2,500 prisoners—a total of 15,000: U.S. prisoners had risen by 30,000 to over 80,000.—*Reuter*.

A BRITTANY 'DUNKIRK' IS UNDER WAY

Line Wheels for Paris

THE line of the front in France has changed in a week from West to East to North to South as the British Second Army and powerful U.S. forces wheel towards Paris. The Americans are outflanking the German line at Laval, and rolling wheatfields now lie before them almost all the way to the French capital. Brittany is cut off, over-run.

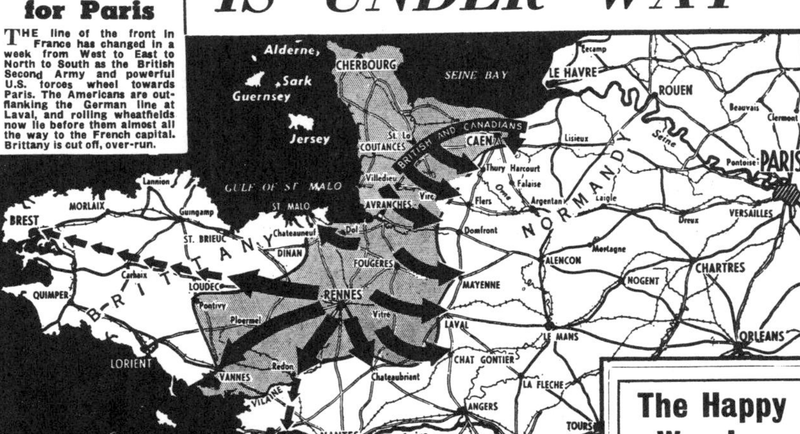

GENERAL MONTGOMERY has begun the race for Paris. Evidence last night all went to show that he has set the British and American armies the task of reaching the French capital and rolling up the German front before the enemy can recover from the mighty blows dealt to him last week.

The entire British Second Army has wheeled eastwards and is pressing hard on the heels of the German divisions as they fall back behind the River Orne.

Many miles to the south strong American forces have also swung eastwards. They have reached the towns of Mayenne and Laval, along two main roads to Paris, and Château-Gontier, 17 miles south of Laval, on the way to Le Mans.

These forces are outflanking, and promise to continue to outflank, the German front. Ahead of them, along almost the entire 150 miles to Paris, lies flat, open country.

Behind the Germans as they retreat is the broad River Seine, with all its bridges destroyed. The enemy's situation, in the words of Alexander Clifford, cabling from the front last night, is very ugly.

The German News Agency reported last night that several American tank and infantry divisions had already reached Laval and were being reinforced ceaselessly.

NAVY WIPE OUT CONVOY

In the west the whole of the Brest Peninsula is being overrun. Last night brought the news of the first German attempt to escape by sea and its interruption by the Navy. One entire convoy of seven ships was wiped out off St. Nazaire and another chased back into port.

An Admiralty communiqué said the first convoy, which was escorted, was sailing south when it was intercepted by the cruiser Bellona and four destroyers, Haida, Tartar, Ashanti, and Iroquois. Both convoy and escort were destroyed.

Damage inflicted on the second convoy before it escaped into St Nazaire is not known. The British ships suffered only a small number of casualties. This action suggests that the Navy's blockade of the Brest Peninsula will be as complete as the blockade of the Cape Bon Peninsula in Tunisia.

Brest, Lorient, and St. Nazaire were finally sealed off from the rest of France when an American column driving south from Rennes and Redom reached the Loire somewhere between St. Nazaire and Nantes. Another force reached the big town of Vannes, between St. Nazaire and Lorient.

There was no report last night that the column which reached the outskirts of Brest on Saturday has penetrated into the port. Explaining the almost complete absence of resistance in the peninsula, the German News Agency said that defence forces were being concentrated round the most important towns.

So far the only points where real opposition has been met are Château Neuf, seven miles south of St. Malo, and around Dinan, which has been by-passed.

Supreme Headquarters expect the rounding up of considerable numbers of prisoners in the peninsula, but they will probably be of the labour battalion type.

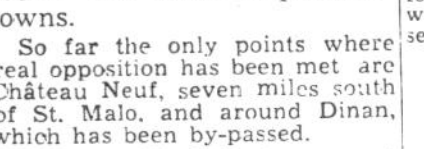

BATTLE FOR VIRE

At Rennes the Americans have captured one of the best airfields in France. Luftwaffe officers got out so hurriedly that they left behind suitcases half-packed.

Last night the Germans were fighting most stubbornly in the area of Vire, where the British and American sectors link.

Vire now stands at the tip of a German salient.

The Americans are thrusting towards it from the west after capturing most of the Forest of St Sever.

British troops were last reported to be 1,500 yards north-east of the town, and also to the south-east.

This represents the British right wing. Farther north infantry, tanks, and rocket-Typhoons yesterday afternoon attacked Mount Pincon.

BACK PAGE—Col. TWO

U-BOAT PEN—DIRECT HIT

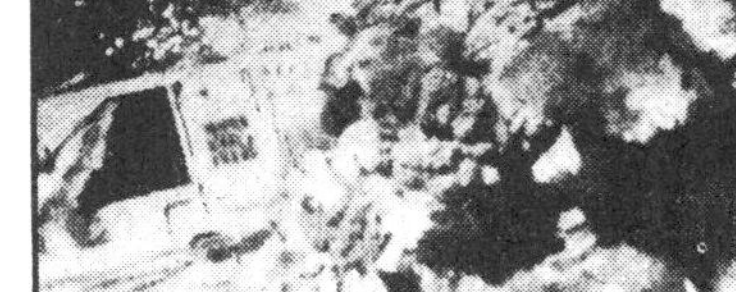

A DIRECT hit by an R.A.F. 12,000lb. bomb—nearly six times the size of a German flying bomb—on the "bomb-proof" U-boat pens at Brest on Saturday. On the left is a pen ripped open by an earlier bomb. The picture was taken from one of 16 Lancasters in the raid. Five scored direct hits, and the near misses of the remainder set up a tidal wave which probably undermined the pens and may prevent U-boats escaping before Brest is taken.

Elation is Sweeping the Front

Ugly for Rommel

From ALEXANDER CLIFFORD

BRITISH FRONT, Sunday.

EXCITEMENT is mounting in the British Second Army again. Things have got moving once more over the week-end. Our advance is regaining speed.

Some of the wild, confused exhilaration of the American situation is overflowing into our front. The crumbling of the German left wing is starting to infect the right wing.

There is no very big news yet. On paper it still looks as though we are facing a solid German front from Vire to the sea, north of Caen.

The actual list of enemy divisions against us is still impressive. It still seems, superficially, that we are plodding patiently while the front facing the Americans has collapsed into a series of mad pursuits.

But there are facts enough to account for this new instinct of success which you can breathe in the air here. Villers Bocage and Aunay-sur-Odon—two road junctions which the Germans desperately defended—have been yielded to us.

BACKS TO SEINE

The fighting has reached Mount Pincon, which is Normandy's highest and most strategic hill. We have had time to harden our own grip on the immediate situation. The Americans are swinging round deep down to the south of us.

If you fit the British front into the Allied picture as a whole you will see that the Germans now have a shrinking bridgehead west of the Orne. It is threatened from every side, except the south-east.

The left flank is hanging in thin air. Not so far behind them is the bridgeless Seine. Rommel's substitute is up against a situation which is suddenly looking very ugly.

The process of events on the British front is much clearer now. The break-through we made in the centre of the German line a week ago was more effective than we knew. But the Germans managed to conceal the fact for a time.

At first we had that unmistakable feeling that things were going well. The advance leaped swiftly forwards. The divisions against us were not first-class, and everything seemed prosperous.

But the German divisions could

BACK PAGE—Col. FOUR

The Happy Warrior

Portrait of a Victor

HE'S bearded, soiled, and tired from days of non-stop battle, but completely happy as, pipe in mouth, he marches on through Villedieu. For he is a victor, taking part in the great American advance.

'BRITTANY, RISE FOR THE LAST BATTLE'

A CALL to the people of Brittany to rise against the Germans was broadcast by the Provisional Government of the French Republic from Radio Algiers last night. "Workers, peasants, officials, employees, the time has come for you to take part, with or without weapons, in the last battle," said the speaker.

"All those of you who belong to the F.F.I. have already received your battle orders and are at your posts.

"All those who were unable to join the battle before must now obey the following orders, which will ensure the success of the uprising."

People who were unarmed were told to try to capture arms from the enemy, to form small mobile units, and to join the F.F.I. formations.

The broadcast ended: "The hour of uprising also approaches for other regions of France. Men of Brittany, the whole of France will follow you in your insurrection."

A Vacancy Will Shortly Occur...

From a Berlin radio broadcast last night:

"The greater number of men to-day are clean-shaven. Most great men were beardless. Even Frederick the Great, King of Prussia, was clean-shaven.

And the Führer?

"The moustache is not worn by officers; it is the sign of the little corporal. In fact, ever since the last century, people wearing moustaches in Germany were more often than not politically suspicious."

STALIN LAUNCHES NEW FORCES

Red Armies Close Ring on Warsaw

Germans Fire City

RED Army tanks and infantry have closed the ring on the eastern suburbs of Warsaw, which lie across the Vistula.

This has been achieved by a break-through to the river banks north of the city. It means that the German defenders, now under crossfire from north, east, and south, must withdraw to the main city.

There the Polish underground army is continuing the battle.

Luftwaffe planes, carrying out a ceaseless bombardment, have set fire to the city behind the German infantry as they strive to check Marshal Rokossovsky's advance with "suicide" counter-attacks.

Mountain Battle

That was the scene in the Polish capital last night, when the Russians, closing in for the big assault, had rushed up artillery and mortars to pound the suburb of Praga, where the Germans were holding out east of the Vistula.

At the southern end of the battle-front yet another Soviet army has joined the offensive.

This was disclosed by Marshal Stalin when he announced that General Petrov, commander of the Fourth Ukrainian forces, has stormed into Drohobycz, a centre of the Polish oil area and stronghold guarding the Carpathian passes.

Capture of this town—18 miles west of Stryj, which fell on Saturday to Marshal Koniev—is the first news for months of General Petrov, who was in charge of the troops which liberated the Kuban with General Tolbukhin.

Below Warsaw, the Soviet communiqué reported, the Russians are continuing to expand their bridgehead over the Vistula.

Map in BACK Page.

JAP CONVOY WIPED OUT

U.S. Raid Bonin

From Daily Mail Correspondent

NEW YORK, Sunday.—A U.S. task force raiding the Bonin and Volcano Islands, 750 miles east of the Japanese mainland have sunk at least 17 Jap ships, possibly sunk six more, and damaged others.

The raiders practically wiped out an escorted convoy at one point. Their total "bag" of ships sunk included five destroyers or escort ships, five cargo ships, and a tanker.

A number of Jap planes were also destroyed. Sixteen U.S. planes were lost.

Lorient, Toulon U-Pens Bombed

Bomber Command in daylight yesterday evening sent a force of Lancasters with fighter cover to attack with 12,000lb. bombs the submarine shelters at Lorient, one of the most important U-boat bases in the Brest Peninsula.

Earlier in the day a force of Liberators and Fortresses struck at the U-boat pens at Toulon.

Battle Over Bomb Lairs.—BACK Page.

British 'Beyond Florence'

German controlled Paris radio said last night that the British, "with immense artillery and armour, have pushed on beyond Florence."

No amplification of this message, which suggests that the Arno has been crossed and that the whole of Florence is in Allied hands, was given.

Germans Shell Florence.—BACK Page.

RAF Fighters at Russian Bases

British and U.S. fighters operating from Russian bases yesterday attacked railway targets in Ottenia—where the frontiers of Yugoslavia, Rumania, and Bulgaria meet. This is reported by the German News Agency, quoting a Rumanian communiqué.—*Reuter*.

Papen on Way Home

ISTANBUL, Sunday.—Von Papen, German Ambassador to Turkey, following Turkey's action in breaking off relations with Berlin, started his journey back to Germany from Istanbul to-night.—*B.U.P.*

R A F Out Last Night

Large forces of R.A.F. heavy bombers crossed the east coast at dusk last night, heading east.

Weather in the Strait

State of Sea.—Practically calm

Weather.—Sunny and warm all day. Maximum temperature, 78 deg., 60 deg. at 10.30 p.m. Visibility limited by haze to about 10 miles. Wind, N.E. light to fresh.

Barometer. — Steady after slight fall.

Hitler Pleads for Security

'THEN I CAN WIN WAR'

HITLER has appealed to his Reich leaders and gauleiter to give him security on the home front. He promised them that he will "finish with" his military foes if in the Reich itself there is "absolute security, blind confidence, and faithful collaboration."

His appeal was made on Friday—its terms were only disclosed last night—when the gauleiter were summoned to his H.Q. Hitler again thanked fate for his escape from the generals' plot, adding that no person could lead Germany better than he could.

According to the version of his speech put out by the German News Agency, Hitler has now discovered that the generals' plot was a continuation of "sabotage" that had been going on ever since the Nazis took power.

"I am not afraid of the fighting against the exterior enemies," declared Hitler. "At the end we will finish with them.

"All I need is the conviction that in our rear there is absolute security, blind confidence, and faithful collaboration.

"That is the primary condition. The mobilisation of all the forces of our people, which is taking place to-day, could not have been undertaken if the criminal dealings of the eliminated saboteurs had continued.

"I am only thankful to fate for leaving me alive so that I can continue this struggle. I believe that the nation needs me, that it needs a man who will not capitulate in any circumstances, but will continue to bear the flag of faith and confidence. I also believe that no other person could do that better than myself."

Terboven, the German Commissioner for Norway, broadcasting on Oslo radio yesterday, said that the officers expelled from the Army will probably be tried by the People's Court to-morrow.

He added: "What has been maturing since 1933—the type of 'soldier-pure-and-simple'—has ceased to exist. From now on there will be only one type—the National Socialist soldier, officer, and general."

LATEST

SURRENDER OFFER AT LORIENT

Brittany, Sunday.—German troops in Lorient offered to surrender to American troops. They insist on surrendering to Americans rather than French. U.S. troops are on the way to Lorient from Vannes.—B.U.P.

3

Army Leave Is On Again To-morrow

By Daily Mail Reporter

THE ban on Army leave and free travel for troops on home stations, imposed nearly six months ago, is to be lifted to a limited extent to-morrow.

To cope with the expected increase in traffic the railway companies have planned extra trains, but none of these will be scheduled in the ordinary timetables.

Issue of seven-days leave passes for troops stationed in Britain was stopped in preparation for D-Day. Only "embarkation leave" has been granted.

The ban also applied to the Navy, except for men returning from long cruises, and to the R.A.F., but not to air crews and airmen on airfields engaged in "ops" against enemy territory.

Home in 'Civvies'

Troops have been granted the usual weekly 24-hours pass, but have not been allowed to move outside a radius of ten to 25 miles from their stations. No free travel vouchers have been allowed.

An Army officer told me: "This will be good news for the Forces. There has been some discontent because soldiers with nothing but their Army pay allege that others in better circumstances have been going home in civilian clothes for their 24-hours leave and paying their own fares."

Rumanians Fight Hitler Youth

Daily Mail Radio Station

Serious clashes between the Hitler Youth organisations and Rumanian students in the streets of Bucarest were reported by Moscow radio last night.

The Germans are reported to have demanded that the Rumanian students should step off the pavement and walk in the roadway when a Hitler youth came their way.

U.S. Shut Naval Base

From Daily Mail Correspondent

GEORGETOWN, British Guiana, Sunday.—The U.S. naval base in British Guiana is being closed, and the personnel and supplies moved to the base in Trinidad.

INTO OCCUPIED FRANCE—AND OUT — The Exclusive Story of the American Girl Who Did It! — *Start It Today! On Page 2*

8 GERMAN OFFICERS HANGED BY HITLER

5¢

NEW YORK Journal-American

AN AMERICAN PAPER FOR THE AMERICAN PEOPLE

Daily 5 Cents, Saturday 5 Cents in New York City; 10 Cents Elsewhere | SUNDAY, 10 Cents in New York City and 50-Mile Zone, 15 Cents Elsewhere

No. 20,663—DAILY TUESDAY, AUGUST 8, 1944 In Two Sections—Section One

7TH SPORTS WALL ST. SPECIAL

100 Miles from Paris

Nazis Doom Marshal, Generals

LONDON, Aug. 8 (AP).—Field Marshal Erwin von Witzleben and seven other German army officers were hanged today, Berlin announced, after a trial in which they confessed plotting to kill Hitler and surrender Germany to the Allies.

This brought to 16 the announced deaths of alleged conspirators in the Berlin-proclaimed plot which culminated in the July 20 bomb explosion at a Hitler headquarters.

Today's executions took place two hours after conclusion of the trial of von Witzleben and the seven others, all of whom had been expelled previously from the army.

In Nazi Germany, "just punishment" usually means death.

An official account of yesterday's trial, broadcast by DNB, disclosed the alleged plot against Hitler had been hatching since last Summer.

Col. Count Claus von Stauffenberg, named by Berlin as the actual assassin, was declared to have brought explosives into Hitler's presence twice before July 20—but to have refrained from letting them go because Gestapo Chief Himmler was not with Hitler—"he was to be finished at the same time."

TRY 3 OTHER GENERALS.

Three former generals and four lesser officers were tried with von Witzleben, who was quoted as testifying that he and Col. Gen.

Continued on Page 2, Column 4

Biddle Bars Prosecution For PAC Tie

By DAVID SENTNER,
N. Y. Journal-American Washington Bureau

WASHINGTON, Aug. 8.—Attorney General Francis Biddle today turned down the demand of Rep. Dies (D.-Tex.), chairman of the House un-American Activities Investigating Committee, to prosecute under the Hatch Act Federal employes working politically with the CIO Political Action Committee.

Dies had termed the PAC, previously labeled by his committee as Communist-controlled, the "political arm of the New Deal," and made public the names of 15 former Government officials now prominent in PAC activities.

Telephone calls and telegrams were listed between 77 Government officials and PAC leaders by Robert E. Stripling, chief investigator for the Dies Committee, who referred to the plans of Sidney Hillman, head of the National Citizens PAC and CIO-PAC to raise two separate campaign funds of $3,000,000 each to support the Roosevelt-Truman ticket.

The action of Biddle in rejecting Dies' demand came as no great surprise to members of the Dies Committee who stepped up their plans to hold a sub-committee inquiry into PAC activities. Biddle previously had ruled that CIO-PAC fund-raising was no violation of the law.

Biddle, acknowledging receipt of the Dies letter calling for prosecution of the alleged offender under Section 9 of the Clean Politics Act, declared that violations of this clause was not a criminal offense and therefore "would not come within the investigative or

Continued on Page 2, Column 6

Finn Peace Cabinet Due

STOCKHOLM, Aug. 8 (AP).—An announcement was expected today on the formation of a new Finnish cabinet which presumably will be called upon to negotiate peace with Russia.

Nazis Rush Reserves

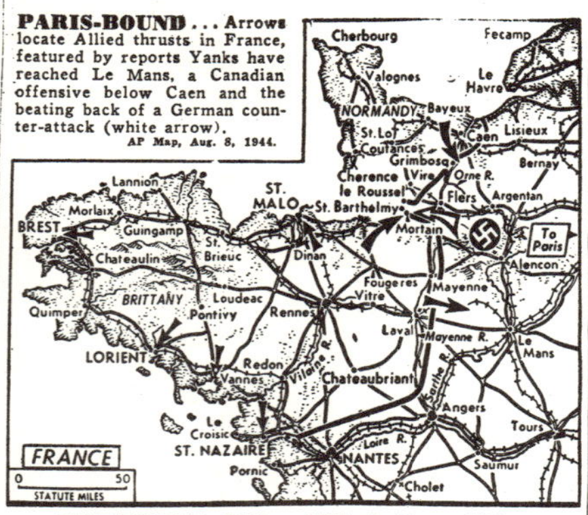

PARIS-BOUND . . . Arrows locate Allied thrusts in France, featured by reports Yanks have reached Le Mans, a Canadian offensive below Caen and the beating back of a German counter-attack (white arrow). *AP Map, Aug. 8, 1944.*

SUPREME HQ., Allied Expeditionary Force, Aug. 8 (AP)—Allied troops, advancing in two powerful surges at the wings of a 130-mile front, drove today to within a little more than 100 miles of Paris.

The Germans desperately rushed in forces from southern France.

Canadian troops hammered four miles into the main enemy line below Caen, and Americans on the southern flank struck toward Le Mans, only 110 miles from the French capital. Advance elements already were reported in Le Mans, a road and rail hub.

The doughboy drive left behind to the northwest the wreckage of the Germans' abortive but still-writhing counter-attack in the Mortain area.

The exact sector where the Allies were a little more than 100 miles of Paris was not specified.

At the northern end of the Allied front the Germans' stout Caen hinge, loosened by an unprecedented 1,000-plane RAF bombardment totaling 6,700 tons last night, was battered again in daylight by 600 U. S. heavy bombers which loosed about 1,800 tons of bombs.

BOMBERS IN ACTION.

Some 400 other bombers today beat up airfields at Romilly sur Seine, 55 miles northwest of Paris, and at Le Perthe, northwest of Romilly. They also bomber the platforms from which robot bombs are hurled at England.

Canadian-British troops stormed over the Orne River in a four-mile advance. They punched through a once-impregnable anti-tank screen, seizing strongpoint villages by the dozen.

On the Breton Peninsula, U. S. troops battled against stubborn resistance for the northern port of St. Malo, fought on the outskirts of Brest, and threw a concentrated attack against Lorient.

Berlin radio acknowledged Americans had broken into St. Malo at one point.

The Germans rushed in rein-

Continued on Page 2, Column 2.

THE WEATHER

Partly cloudy; slightly warmer. Sun rises, 5:58 a. m.; sun sets, 8:04 p. m. High tide at Governors Island, 12:30 a. m. and 12:50 p. m.

HOURLY TEMPERATURES

4 a. m.	70	9 a. m.	72
5 a. m.	70	10 a. m.	74
6 a. m.	70	11 a. m.	75
7 a. m.	70	12 Noon	77
8 a. m.	70	1 p. m.	77

(Complete Weather Report on Page 16)

TODAY'S INDEX

The Journal-American has the largest circulation of any evening newspaper in New York City.

ALLIED PRINTING TRADES UNION LABEL COUNCIL NEW YORK 230

It is the only New York evening newspaper possessing the three great wire services—ASSOCIATED PRESS—INTERNATIONAL NEWS SERVICE—UNITED PRESS

(PHONE YOUR NEWS TIPS TO CORTLANDT 7-1212)

Yanks Bomb Shanghai, Wreck Port

CHUNGKING, Aug. 8 (UP).—The Central Chinese News Agency reported today that American B-24 bombers attacked Shanghai at noon, causing great devastation in the harbor area.

Shipping in the Whampoa River also was severely bombed. The dispatch described the harbor and the river shipping as being "disastrously hit."

Earlier today the Japanese Domei news agency had reported a single B-24 had bombed Shanghai but claimed only "very slight damage" was caused.

Leaders Praise Inter-Faith Rally

Appeal for rescue of Europe's remaining Jews from Nazi sentence of death.—See Page 22.

"—For action at this moment so that America may raise its voice in protest and lift its hand to release this yoke of persecution and bondage laid upon these suffering human beings—"

"—Our nation leading the fight for a democratic world also must recognize its responsibilities to a valiant people and use every means within its power to save from massacre the remaining Jews in Nazi-occupied Europe—"

"You are to be congratulated on your efforts to organize public opinion against these atrocities—"

"— I cannot believe that the Nazis are unable to distinguish right from wrong, or that the American people are able to accept such horrible wrongs as those of the Nazis without wanting to cry out in protest —."

These messages, received today

Continued on Page 17, Column 4.

Late Gen. McNair's Son Killed in Action

WASHINGTON, Aug. 8 (INS).—Halfway around the world from the spot where his father, Lt. Gen. McNair, was killed by an American bomb July 27 in France, Col. Douglas McNair, 37, followed his parent in death on Guam, the Army has disclosed.

The War Department said it has just received word of the death of the younger McNair.

German Prisoners Say: Himmler Assassinated And Goering Wounded

ON THE BRITISH FRONT IN FRANCE, Aug. 8 (AP).—A newly captured German intelligence officer asserted today that Heinrich Himmler, German Gestapo and SS chief, has been assassinated and that Reichsmarshal Herman Goering was wounded in a new outbreak against the Nazi hierarchy.

(There was no confirmation of this report. The officer's report was based on second-hand information and therefore is subject to reservation. In this connection, the British Radio said today a German lieutenant taken prisoner in France related he had given a "pep talk" to his troops and "for want of other good news" had told them that Himmler was dead.)

Nine other captives, all Austrians, declared they could corroborate the assertion of the intelligence officer.

"We heard that (Marshal Erwin) Rommel was wounded in the head by bomb fragments on the Normandy front, but was recovering," one of the Austrians said. "The best news came Sunday when we heard that Himmler had been killed and that Goering was wounded in the attack on Himmler."

The British first heard the story of the alleged assassination from the Austrians. The German intelligence officer, who had been kept apart from the Austrians, was asked:

"I suppose Himmler is stronger than Hitler these days?"

"No, Himmler is dead," the Nazi intelligence offer asserted, "he was assassinated. I heard it at my headquarters Sunday. All our officers are talking about it."

Doom of Hitler, War's End Near, Reporter Says

By KINGSBURY SMITH
European Manager, International News Service.

Forty-eight hours ago I stood on the battlefields of Normandy.

Today I am in New York after flying the Atlantic.

That in itself is a portent of how near the future wars of Europe will be to America.

I left the battle of France with a firm conviction that the sand is rapidly running out of Hitler's hour-glass of destiny.

I also came away with the conviction that, surprised as the Germans may be by the swift American breakthrough across the base of the Brittany peninsula, they have seen nothing compared with the blow that is going to strike them like a bolt of lightning.

It now seems quite possible that the decisive battles of the American and British armies in Western Europe will be fought in the Norman countryside.

There is a sense of victory in the air in Normandy. You can see it in the eager faces of the American fighting men moving up the dusty Norman roads to the front lines. You can notice it in the barely restrained optimism of the American and British commanders.

The German is on the run in France.

He may stand and fight ferociously and stubbornly here and there, but his own faith in victory has vanished.

He fights now only because of fear; fear of what will happen to him if he surrenders; fear of what will happen to a defeated German army.

There is little doubt in the minds of American and other Allied officers and men in France that the European war will be over by Christmas.

It could end within a few weeks if the present retreat of

Continued on Page 2, Column 7.

Nazis Scorching East Prussia

(Map on Page 2.)

MOSCOW, Aug. 8 (UP).—The Germans burned houses, farms and other installations along the East Prussian frontier today in the first application of the "scorched earth" policy to their "holy" soil as Red armies closed in along a 215-mile siege arc.

Civilians already have been evacuated from areas east of Konigsberg—a further sign that the Nazi command feels the Red Army is about to smash across the border into Germany's eastern-most province.

Two more Russian armies—the 1st Baltic and 2nd White Russian—were revealed to have joined in the mounting battle for East Prussia as Gen. Cherniakhovsky's 3rd White Russian Army bogged down five to 10 miles from the border in the face of heavy resistance from reinforced Nazi troops.

Col. Gen. Zhakarov's 2n Army pushed 15 miles northwest from Bialystok and captured Knyszyn, 32 miles south of the East Prussian border, and Gen. Bagramian's 1st Army at the northern end of the front sent two spearheads crashing toward Memel and Tilsit.

The battle for Warsaw roared on without a letup or decisive change.

Von Papen in Berlin

The German-controlled Paris radio said today in a broadcast that Franz von Papen, former German Ambassador to Ankara, arrived in Berlin last night.

TODAY ON ALL WAR FRONTS

August 8, 1944.

FRANCE—Allied units 100 miles from Paris.

RUSSIA — Germans apply "scorched earth" policy to delay Russian penetration into East Prussia.

ITALY—British in furious battle near Florence.

PACIFIC—Yanks closing trap on Jap garrison at Guam; sever foe's supply line in Wewak area, British New Guinea.

NEWSPRINT RATIONED

make it last!

The severe shortage of newsprint makes it difficult to print enough papers to meet the demand. Save valuable paper by buying your Journal-American from the same newsdealer daily. Then save old copies for waste paper collection. Remember, waste paper makes containers for ammunition and medicines.

The Daily Sketch

NEWS AND PICTURES

No. 10,992 ★★★ TUESDAY, AUGUST 8, 1944 ONE PENNY

1,000 HEAVIES STRIKE MASSIVE MIDNIGHT BLOW SOUTH OF CAEN

135 Tanks Smashed In Day's Battle

LAST night from 11 o'clock onwards more than 1,000 R.A.F. Lancasters and Halifaxes attacked the hinge of the German line just south of Caen.

Many thousands of tons of bombs were dropped in an attack which was the closest support yet given to the army by heavy bombers.

This massive new air blow came at the end of a day in which our planes scored the greatest victory over tanks during the war.

Mortain Is Recaptured

One hundred and thirty-five German tanks from elements of four crack panzer divisions were destroyed by 9 p.m., mainly by R.A.F. rocket-firing Typhoons, when Von Kluge launched his first major offensive in the direction of Avranches in a desperate bid to split Normandy from Brittany.

The attack was made on a seven-and-a-half mile front between Mortain and Sourdeval, and was the largest co-ordinated blow against the Americans. Divisions for it had been drained from various sectors of France.

In the early stages of the attack the Germans penetrated to a depth of about three miles in the area of Cherence le Roussel, five and a quarter miles north-west of Mortain.

Mortain fell to the Germans, but at midnight it was reported at Allied headquarters that they had been driven out of the town, which was again firmly in American hands.

Crack Divisions Mutilated

The German divisions hurled in were the Lehr, Second S.S., Second Panzer and 116 Panzer. Loss of 135 tanks means that the Allies have wiped out nearly a whole armoured division.

The Germans appear to have thrown into action the armour which they switched from the Caen hinge-sector.

The wing achieving the great success of the day was that commanded by Wing Commander Charles Green, D.S.O., D.F.C., who discovered the German concentration while out on reconnaissance. He is a 29-year-old ex-London stockbroker.

The biggest battle took place where the Germans had penetrated three miles in the Cherence area, five and a quarter miles north-west of Mortain, where tank-versus-tank fighting took place, involving at least 30 to 40 German tanks.

The Germans launched their attack at the obvious spot, writes Reuter's correspondent at Allied Supreme Headquarters, and it seems likely that the Americans are well prepared to deal with it.

Through the 20-mile-wide Avranches - Mortain corridor run the two vital roads supplying the American forces over-running Brittany and thrusting east towards Paris. One goes through Avranches and the other ten miles east through Brecey.

We Hold Counter-drive

If the Germans broke through here and cut these roads it would put the American armoured spearheads in an awkward spot.

The American advance east of the Mayenne is still going forward on a 50-mile front between Laval and Domfront.

At the northern end of the front British forces have cut across the River Orne on a two-mile front.

The hotly contested town of Vire has fallen to British troops, and they have also captured 1,000ft.-high Mt. Pincon.

American forces punching out westwards into Brittany have met stiff resistance in isolated parts.

They have reached Auray, 20 miles from Lorient. St. Brieuc was taken in a drive along the northern coast, and St. Malo is isolated from the south.

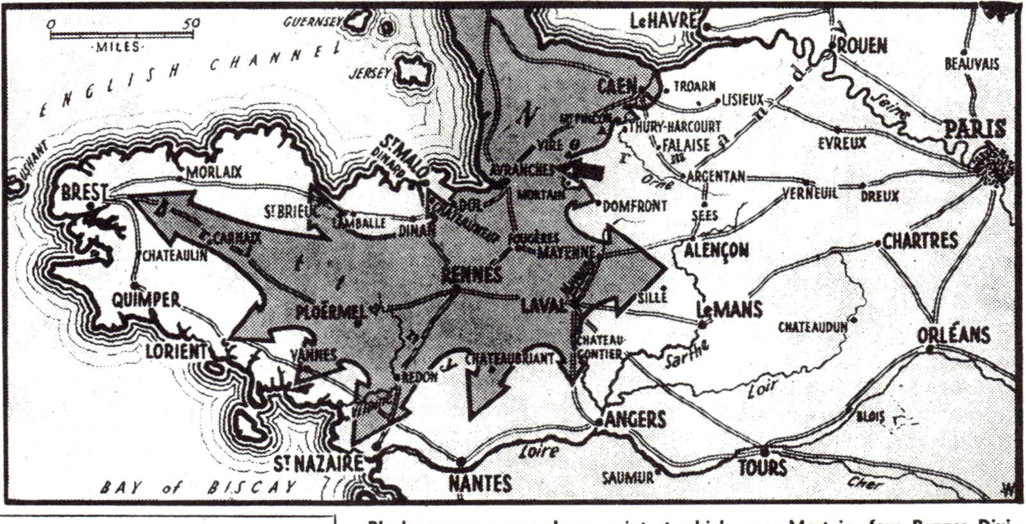

Black arrow on map shows point at which, near Mortain, four Panzer Divisions tried to drive a wedge between our armies in Normandy and Brittany. Above Caen our tank spearheads are pushing forward.

JEEP RUNS INTO TANK BATTLE

From WILLIAM MAKIN, Kemsley Newspapers War Correspondent with the American Army in Normandy

MOTORING back to H.Q. from the St. Mogo battle last evening, I directed my jeep through what was pleasant open country which the Germans had evacuated without much of a struggle some days ago. Suddenly a roar overhead showed several British Typhoons diving low.

Their rocket-guns were shooting and we heard the sound of ack-ack guns in reply. I suddenly realised that I had run into another battle in this extraordinary warfare which seems to flare up at the most unlikely places.

Farmer Stared

We took to the ditch and then saw American tanks going into action against German tanks looming out of the thick grass. It was a tank battle reminiscent of the Western Desert.

The tanks lurched at each other, spitting fire through neatly stacked hay-bundles. A farmhouse was ablaze and the farmer stood there staring in amazement, pitchfork in hand, at this sudden eruption of war in his acreage.

Turn to Back Page, Col. 3

French Army Fight In France Soon

"THE hour of revenge has come," said General de Gaulle, broadcasting last night from Algiers.

"Soon a powerful French Army, battle-trained and well equipped, will deploy on the inter-Allied front in France.

"Everybody must fight. *Frenchmen, rise and into battle.*

"The Battle of France, France's battle, is extending and accelerating."

Referring to the work already being done by the Resistance Movement, General de Gaulle revealed that paratroops as well as the F.F.I. (French Forces of the Interior) had been in the field of battle since June 6.

The regiment of paratroopers was dropped over Brittany and gathered round it more than 6,000 resisters.

On the proposal of General de Gaulle the regiment has been awarded the Croix de la Libération.

Big Part In Offensive

A decree announcing the award said the regiment destroyed many lines of enemy communications, and had played a large part in the success of the Allied offensive.

General de Gaulle also revealed that the number of Germans killed in Brittany by French troops from June 6 until last evening exceeded several thousands.

Those who had surrendered could also be counted in thousands.

In the Eastern Rhone more than 10,000 Germans had fallen into the hands of the F.F.I., while in the Vercors alone two German divisions had been tied down as a result of the activities of the Maquis.

Germans Quit S.W. France

GERMAN forces in South-Western France have begun a full-scale evacuation, said an Associated Press message from Irun, on the Spanish border, last night.

Only a handful of the Gestapo and gendarmes are left to cover the French-Spanish frontier, the report added.

This is the second report within a few days from the Spanish frontier of such a withdrawal.

'Supreme Alert' Call To Norway

THE following message was broadcast last night by the B.B.C. to the people of Norway:

"From now on the people of Norway must be in a state of supreme alert.

"No help must be given to the Germans, no work be done for them by Norwegians. Those patriots who seek help must be given every possible assistance by the rest of the population."—THE DAILY SKETCH Listening Station.

WOMEN DIG EAST PRUSSIA DEFENCES

HUNDREDS of thousands of men, boys and women have been rushed to the East Prussia border to build new fortifications in a bid to keep out the Red Army.

As they dig they can hear the thunder of Russian guns, and Dr. Ley, chief of the German labour front, has gone to speed up their efforts. The diggers include, according to Berlin, the professors and students of Koenigsberg University, who marched out in a body to help.

Berlin also says that the Germans have fallen back several miles before stopping the Red Army at Wirballen, a mile from the East Prussia border.

Moscow has not yet announced the crossing of the frontier, but last night's communiqué reported the cutting of the rain road from Bialystok to the East Prussian town of Lyck with the capture of Knyszyn, north-west of Bialystok.

In the Baltic States the Germans are gradually being split up for final annihilation.

North-west of Kaunas more than 40 inhabited places have been taken, one of which, Pograutse, is 38 miles from Kaunas and 50 miles east-north-east of Tilsit.

New Offensive

To the south the Russians are 30 miles beyond the Vistula and less than 30 miles from the main railway running south-west into Silesia, Germany proper.

More than 60 places have been captured in the fighting for the widening of the bridgehead over the Vistula south-west of Sandomir, the existence of which is officially announced by Moscow for the first time.

A big new offensive by Red Army troops of two fronts appears to be developing in the approaches to the Carpathians.

For the third night running Marshal Stalin announced the capture of more important places in this area. On Saturday night it was Styrj. Sunday night it was Drohobycz.

Last night there were two places: Sambor, the hotly-contested railway junction; and Boryslav, the oil town just south-west of Drohobycz.

The two Russian fronts involved in these captures are the First White Russian front—which took Sambor — commanded by Marshal Koniev, and the Fourth Ukrainian front, under General Petrov.

All the towns captured on that part of the Russian front which directly faces the Carpathians and the borders of Czechoslovakia

GLASS IS SET FAIR

A starlit sky with some haze and a light southerly breeze in the Straits of Dover followed a day of unbroken sunshine yesterday with blue skies and a calm sea—perfect holiday weather.

The sun sent the shade temperature up to 75 in the afternoon. During the day the barometer lost a point, but the glass is set fair.

TIMELY WORDS OF FAITH

The Lord is my rock, and my fortress, and my deliverer; my God, my strength, in whom I will trust; my buckler, and the horn of my salvation, and my high tower.

Psalms, 18, 2.

DAILY MIRROR, Wednesday, August 9, 1944.

Daily Mirror

AUG 9

No. 12,681
ONE PENNY
Registered at the G.P.O. as a Newspaper.

MONTY SENDS IN HIS TANKS

Armour strikes out from four-mile wedge driven in south of Caen

From GEORGE McCARTHY
"Daily Mirror" Chief Correspondent
SOUTH OF CAEN, Wednesday, a.m.

THE Germans last night were being steadily hammered out of the famous hinge of their whole Normandy front.

After an attack by more than a thousand Fortresses and Liberators the great Canadian and British advance south of Caen leapt forward again yesterday afternoon

Our armour, breaking out of the positions the infantry had consolidated during the night, swept to the south.

They captured Cintheux—nine miles south-east of Caen—and were soon astride the main road to Falaise.

Infantry were following on. To the west, British troops who threw a bridgehead over the Orne were engaged all day in bitter fighting to prevent German troops from moving to oppose the Canadian breakthrough.

Now no help appears to be coming to the desperate enemy forces south of Caen.

●

Reports at SHAEF early today stated that the Allied wedge was four miles deep and that the fighting was the heaviest of the whole Normandy campaign.

Battlefront comment of a Canadian staff officer was: "The hinge of the German line is loosening, though it hasn't by any means been yanked off the door yet."

With American armoured columns getting "wound up" for new thrusts toward Paris, Montgomery's savage blow at the Germans' bomb-battered Caen hinge position threatens a new crisis for Von Kluge.

The German commander, despite the heavy casualties already sustained by his tanks, persisted yesterday in his attacks at the Allied corridor between the Normandy and Brittany fronts.

Once again he was held—and the development of the Allied offensive south of Caen showed that his panzer effort had failed entirely to check Montgomery's plans.

The British and Canadians took eight villages in their attack.

Some of them—such as May sur Orne and Tilly la Campagne—had defied the Allies for weeks.

The enemy troops, dazed by the preliminary bombing of a thousand RAF heavy bombers, found our troops had driven forward three miles in the opening assault.

Then the Germans recovered enough to start fighting back.

Continued on Back Page

Great idea, say the troops

British and Canadian infantry in the offensive south of Caen, think the new armoured troop-carriers which took the "first wave" into action are a great idea which saved many lives.

Developed from four experimental models, the carriers are armoured-plated lorries—some with sand between the plates as additional protection.

Working almost non-stop for two days, 250 REME men finished the job only on Thursday. Many of the lorries had to be fitted with new engines.

U.S. ADMIRAL'S SUICIDE AFTER D-DAY "COMBAT FATIGUE"

REAR-ADMIRAL Don Moon, 50-year-old commander of a U.S. Task Force in the invasion of Normandy, has committed suicide, it was announced in Washington last night.

"Admiral Moon's death apparently followed combat fatigue," said Mr. Forrestal, U.S. Navy Secretary.

One of the youngest of the U.S. Admirals, Admiral Moon leaves a widow and several children.

One who knew him told the *Daily Mirror* last night: "He commanded the task force which attacked the Cherbourg Peninsula during the invasion.

"Though the waters were heavily mined, he carried out the operation at great speed and at low cost."

PALESTINE HIGH COMMISSIONER WOUNDED IN CAR AMBUSH

SIR Harold MacMichael, High Commissioner in Palestine and Transjordan, was attacked and slightly wounded by terrorists who ambushed his car on the Jerusalem-Tel Aviv road yesterday.

Lady MacMichael was unhurt, but two members of the High Commissioner's staff were seriously wounded.

The High Commissioner is shortly being succeeded in his office by Viscount Gort, and was on his way to a farewell function when the ambush occurred.

The car was under police escort. The terrorists opened fire from the side of the road.

The police are believed to have made a number of arrests.

Sir Harold had been High Commissioner since 1938. He is sixty-one.

His wife to who he was married in 1919, was Miss Nesta Stephens, daughter of the late Rev. J. Otter Stephens.

Sir Harold MacMichael

Hun 'plotters' hanged: Firing squad plea fails

DEATH came to eight former German war chiefs yesterday, two hours after the Berlin People's Court had sentenced them to be hanged for plotting the death of Hitler, according to a German News Agency statement on the trial last night.

In their last hours, five of these men pleaded to be shot instead of hanged, and their pleas drew a sharp retort from the President, who said testily:

"You wanted to blow the Fuehrer to pieces, and now you ask for honest bullets. That is really the limit."

The pleas for death before a firing squad came from Field-Marshal Riven von Witzleben, Colonel - General Hoeppner, Major-General Stieff, Captain Klausing, and Lieut.-Colonel Bernadis.

No protest at the sentence came from the remaining conspirators Lieut.-General von Hase, Reserve Lieut.-Colonel von Hagen, and Reserve Lieut. Count Yorck von Wartenburg.

By order of the court, the estates of these men will be confiscated by the Reich—they had already been expelled from the Army and wore civilian clothes during the trial.

Count von Wartenburg is said to have stated that the conspirators had planned to make immediate contact with the Allies if the plot had been successful

He also, said the German report, disclosed that Colonel-General Beck, former Chief of the General Staff, was to be chief of the Government, and Goerdeler, former Burgomaster of Leipzig, for whose arrest a reward of 1,000,000 marks has been offered, was to be Vice-Chancellor.

General Hoeppner was to be Commander-in-Chief of the Reserve Army, and Wartenburg himself was to be Secretary of State in the Reich Chancellery.

And Von Witzleben: "In the first instance we intended to get the Fuehrer into our hands, but not by means of an attempt on his life.

"We agreed to await a moment when the Fuehrer was travelling with the least possible entourage, to kidnap him. We thought that a live Fuehrer would be of more use to us than a dead one."

The prosecuting counsel, demanding the death penalty for all the accused, said they planned, after killing Hitler, "to rule the German people with measures dating back to the Eighteenth Century, with martial law and police truncheons.

"They are typical reactionaries," he added.

The German News Agency, which originally said Beck committed suicide, stated last night that Colonel-General Fromm, former C.-in-C. of the German Home Forces, personally shot General Beck during the arrests of the conspirators.

DOCTOR, IN PYJAMAS, TENDS VICTIMS OF BUZZ-BOMB

THE Germans sent more buzz-bombs over the Southern Counties yesterday. Damage and casualties were caused in the early hours.

Nurses, volunteer first-aid workers, and a doctor worked in pyjamas covered with dust after a buzz-bomb had wrecked a church and damaged shops and houses

Rescuers in one district were guided by the barking of a

Continued on Back Page

P.M. VISITS FRANCE

Mr. Churchill has made a flying visit to Normandy to receive first-hand information of our recent advances from General Montgomery and the American General Bradley.

First (but last) in queue

By Your Special Correspondent

TEIGNMOUTH bus runs once an hour from Torquay, and Mr. Eric Troward, who works in Torquay, always found the trippers from Teignmouth beat him to it.

He lives at Marden, ten miles from Torquay, too far to walk, and he can't get out much before six, so he couldn't make the queue with any chance of being among the lucky for the six o'clock.

He advertised for a man to be his stand-in; turn up in the queue as soon as the five o'clock bus went, and draw a fee of eighteenpence an hour.

Thirty-eight men answered the advertisement. He took the first, because he didn't expect a second.

The stand-by is George Simpson, 40, bachelor—nobody to worry because he is always out at teatime—invalided out of the Army after the doings at Dunkirk, in Tunisia and Italy, and fixed up with a firewatching job at a shop.

"I stand in the queue five nights a week, and that 7s. 6d. comes in handy," says Mr. Simpson.

LATE WAR NEWS

NO. 15,060 ONE PENNY ★★ FOR KING AND EMPIRE WEDNESDAY, AUGUST 9, 1944

CAEN ADVANCE: TANKS TAKE OVER

Infantry Drive a Wedge Five Miles Deep

BIGGEST BATTLE SINCE D-DAY NOW RAGING

IN the greatest attack since D-day British and Canadian tanks were last night thrusting in force down the road to Falaise—the shortest but most heavily defended road to Paris. They struck out from a five-miles-deep wedge which the infantry had driven into the maze of German gunpits and stronpoints during the previous 12 hours. At the other end of the front American columns driving eastwards from Mayenne and Laval were unofficially reported to be only 100 miles from Paris. Rommel's drive to split the American Army at Avranches has ended disastrously. After being driven from Mortain, which they captured on Monday, the panzer divisions yesterday lost Barentan, six miles farther east. A new development reported by the Germans late last night was an Allied airborne landing at the mouth of the Loire "to support tank-borne infantry racing to the area."

CLIFFORD CABLES FROM THE FRONT:

They Must Hold Us Now or They're 'Done'

From ALEXANDER CLIFFORD

NORMANDY FRONT, Tuesday.

FROM the Orne to the Loire the whole French front is reeking with battle to-day. With everything else crumbling, the hinge of the German line is now being battered loose by the biggest attack of all.

All the terrible weight of a full-scale Anglo-Canadian attack has been flung against it south of Caen. That is the new factor which has made this the most tremendous fighting day since D-Day.

Rommel is facing his most critical hour. The whole German front in France from end to end is at stake. From east to west this is what is happening now:

Canadian and British troops and tanks, supported by literally thousands of bombers, have broken sheer into the German lines south of Caen. They fought through the night and gained their immediate objectives on time.

PANZERS MEET DISASTER

The German divisions fighting east of the Orne are at the same time threatened from farther down the river. British troops have made and established a firm bridgehead across it round the village and wood called Grimbosq. They were fighting to enlarge it all to-day.

Farther south and west comes the wooded, hilly area whose vital keypoint is Mount Pincon, which we captured over the week-end. There we are mopping up the Germans from copse to copse and from ridge to ridge.

Then the front falls away in a confused zone of armoured patrols until it comes to Vire, which we hold. From here it runs to Mortain, where Rommel has suffered a disaster which is without parallel of its kind in this war.

What the Germans were trying to do there was so typically Rommel that it is impossible to believe that he did not conceive the plan.

It lines up exactly with his "dash to the wire" in November 1941, when he tried to throw the British Army into confusion in Libya by sending a marauding tank force right back to the Egyptian frontier.

Here in France he decided to cut the American Army in half by recapturing Avranches. He collected a handful of panzer divisions and sent them racing west.

PERFECT TIMING

Somewhere between Domfront and Mortain they were spotted. And then there began an all-day battle between tanks on the ground and rocket-firing Typhoons in the air.

The results are staggering. Eighty-four tanks in flames and 33 damaged. Over 200 lorries either flaming or smoking or damaged. The Typhoon pilots flew 1,014 sorties.

It is a stupefying blow to the enemy's tank strength. And it could not have been more perfectly timed. For in addition to everything else the panzers were in entirely the wrong place.

The whole German Army was for the moment off balance. And it was at this moment that we launched our great new attack against the hinge—the Caen sector.

It was launched with all the fanfare and elaboration of an opera first night. It had every refinement which our attacking technique has yet invented. And it had several new features never tried before.

It jumped off from a starting

BACK PAGE—Col. FIVE

Tanks Push Down Road to Falaise

Let Loose in Force

From WILLIAM WILSON

OUTSIDE ROCQUANCOURT, Tuesday.

POWERFUL Allied armoured formations poured across the fields south of Caen this afternoon under the fire of German heavy guns.

They were exploiting the night's deep penetration into the German positions defending the road to Falaise.

The armoured forces, made up of British and Canadian units, advanced in steady columns on both sides of the Caen-Falaise road.

They raised great trails of dust at which the German heavy guns fired spasmodically as they passed the villages of Tilly-la-Campagne, Rocquancourt, and Fontenay-le-Marmion.

Occasionally the armour halted as the shellfire came close to allow the dust to die down. When the shelling stopped, the tanks resumed their advance after only slight delays.

At 12.30 p.m. a large force of Fortresses began a bombardment of the German positions immediately ahead of us—a second defence line running from the Orne through Bretteville-sur-Laize and St. Sylvain.

★

INFANTRYMEN said they had a fairly easy time last night. One grinning Scotsman pointed up in the air and said, "That's what we like to see. We don't give twopence when they are around."

Smoke and dust rose ahead of us as bombs from succeeding waves of bombers tore up the German positions. Guns opened up again and the tanks went forward.

During the morning fighting had consisted mostly of mopping up and consolidating.

Tilly, which has caused the Canadians two weeks' trouble and considerable casualties, was surrendered at 11 a.m. to-day by a major whose command had been reduced to 70 fanatical Hitler youths.

The major and his men held out all night against heavy attacks. About 10 a.m. he sent his wounded towards our positions with a message that he would surrender with the survivors of his force if we would send an escort for them.

The officer directing the attack was afraid that it might be a trick and refused to send an escort. He did, however, cancel the barrage which was about to be laid down on the shattered village.

An hour later the major and his 70 youthful Germans, many of whom appeared to be only 17 or 18, filed out of their battered positions and marched to the British lines just outside the village.

All that is left of Tilly is a cluster of smashed walls, many standing only shoulder-high in the rubble-filled streets.

★

Reuter correspondents with the Canadians, Charles Lynch and Ross Munro, cabled:

OUR armour has been turned loose in force down the road to Falaise. Tanks drove almost half-way to that town before running into opposition.

They made contact with the enemy at Cintheaux east of Bretteville-sur-Laize and nine miles south of Caen. Falaise lies 11 miles farther south.

Another tank force engaged 20 big German tanks in the area between St. Aignan and St. Sylvain—about a mile east of the main road.

The Allied armour thundered for-

BACK PAGE—Col. FOUR

WE BREAK INTO ST MALO

Refugees Flock From Dinard

American forces have broken into St. Malo at one point, the German radio reported last night.

From JOHN HALL

OUTSIDE ST. MALO, Monday (delayed).

THE siege of St. Malo drags on, but to-day, the third day of battle, American troops edged a little closer and won bridgeheads through the perimeter defences.

They advanced towards an inner defence line, and to-night there is fighting going on near the town.

Dinard, the holiday resort across the estuary of the River Rance from here, has now been drawn into the battle.

This morning we were shelled by guns close to Dinard, and at the same time refugees came pouring out of the town. They said they had been ordered to leave by the Huns.

Some among them had escaped from St. Malo by rowing across the estuary. They came in small groups, each with a leader, carrying a white flag, frightened and exhausted by tramping with heavy packs under a burning sun.

A few more refugees from St. Malo escaped to-day. They told me that there are still nearly 20,000 civilians left in St. Malo, St. Servan, and Paramé, most of them very young or old people.

Appeal Spurned

They have good supplies of water, but the Germans have plundered their food reserves.

There are a few citizens of Eire remaining in St. Malo and Dinard, but no British people. The British colonies in both towns were broken up by the Germans soon after the occupation, and the people sent to Germany.

A week ago the German commander of the garrison here was asked by the mayors of St. Malo, St. Servan, and Paramé to avoid fighting in the three towns, and save them and the citizens from bloodshed and destruction. The appeal was spurned.

As I write heavy gun duels are in progress. Heavy shells falling at a crossroads behind me come from naval fortifications on the islet of Cezembre.

Town Damaged

We bombed Cezembre yesterday, and to-day its fire is lighter, but the noise of battle is the greatest I have heard since that memorable morning of July 25 near Pont Hebert, when a great fleet of American aircraft opened the door for this sensational drive.

It seems inevitable that St. Malo must be severely battered. In the early hours of this morning troops well behind the lines heard the sound of a terrible explosion coming from the direction of St. Malo jetty.

So far it is not confirmed whether our gunfire had hit an ammunition dump, or whether the Huns were carrying out demolitions

At some points American patrols held their fire to allow streams of refugees to get clear.

ADMIRAL DIES OF 'FATIGUE'

Led U.S. Invaders

WASHINGTON, Tuesday.—Admiral Con Pardee Moon, who commanded a naval task force in the invasion operations in Normandy, died on Saturday, it was announced here to-day by Mr. James Forrestal, United States Navy Secretary.

Mr. Forrestal said Admiral Moon apparently took his own life as the result of battle fatigue.

Admiral Moon's task force attacked the Cherbourg Peninsula during the invasion, although the waters were heavily mined. The operation was carried out with great speed and at low cost.—*Reuter.*

'Kesselring Gives Up Command'

ZURICH, Tuesday.—An unconfirmed report published by the *Libera Stampa* of Lugano to-day states that the Fascist Marshal Graziani has taken over command of all troops in Italy from Field-Marshal Kesselring.

Kesselring, it is added, has been badly wounded and left Italy after informing Hitler he was unable to continue in command.—*Reuter.*

1,000 Fight on in Florence—BACK Page.

Papen Back in Berlin

Von Papen, who was German Ambassador to Turkey, arrived in Berlin yesterday after visiting Sofia and Belgrade, reports Paris radio.—*A.P.*

Climax Reached in Polish Talks

MOSCOW, Tuesday.—The next stage in the talks which Polish representatives, including the Premier, M. Mikolajczyk, are holding here will, it appears, make or break the negotiations.

Meetings were not resumed this morning as both sides are considering the new prospects.—*Exchange.*

Allies Trap Fleet of U-boats

Atlantic Battle Nearly Over

GERMAN U-boat warfare in the Atlantic has been cut more than 75 per cent. by the break-through into Brittany, and the Battle of the Atlantic is virtually finished, naval authorities said at SHAEF last night.

About 100 U-boats are expected to be captured in the three great U-boat bases of Brest, Lorient, and St. Nazaire, or to be left stranded in the Atlantic without any home base.

The submarine menace has been choked off at its roots at the very moment when it is of the utmost importance to the Allies to have an uninterrupted flow of shipping to the French battlefront.

It is probable that the U-boats in the Brittany bases are attempting last-minute escapes, but their chances are slim.

Admiral Doenitz will probably now have bases available for fewer than 50 submarines, only 25 of which can be at sea at once. And with these he must cover the whole Atlantic.

C-in-C Hit in Ambush

Sir Harold MacMichael, High Commissioner of Palestine, was slightly wounded when terrorists ambushed his car and fired shots from the side of the road.

A fortnight ago it was announced that Viscount Gort, Governor and Commander-in-Chief of Malta, was to succeed him as High Commissioner and Commander-in-Chief of Palestine and High Commissioner of Transjordan.

With Lady MacMichael Sir Harold was motoring to a farewell function under police escort when the attack was made.

Two members of the High Commissioner's staff were seriously injured.

It is believed that arrests have been made.

'U.S. Scandal' in Burma

From Daily Mail Correspondent

NEW YORK, Tuesday.—The Senate Military Affairs Committee to-day planned an investigation into the six months' accumulation of reports of conditions among U.S. Army forces in Burma.

Senator Robert Reynolds, chairman of the committee, said he expected the inquiry "to reveal and end a particularly ugly and distressing scandal, leading to punishment for all guilty persons."

German Oil Plant Hit from Russia

MOSCOW, Tuesday.—U.S. Eighth Air Force bombers flew from bases in the Soviet Union yesterday to attack the German synthetic oil plant at Tresbinia, 20 miles west of Cracow.

Announcing this to-day, a U.S. communiqué reports that the raid was made in unusually good weather and fires and explosions were seen. Bombers and escorts destroyed four German planes.—*Reuter.*

Hitler's Court Hangs Field-Marshal

2 HOURS AFTER TRIAL

EIGHT of the men who tried to kill Hitler were last night hanged in Germany. They were Field-Marshal Erwin von Witzleben, four generals, and three other Wehrmacht officers. They died two hours after the Reich People's Court had found them guilty.

Their trial in Berlin disclosed that the murder plot was hatched in 1943. Since then at least four attempts have been made to assassinate the Führer and once a bid was made to kidnap him.

After pouring out the fantastic story yesterday, the German News Agency reported that the Wehrmacht purge is by no means ended. Three more generals and other officers have yet to be tried.

The eight who have been hanged were:

Field-Marshal von Witzleben—if the revolt succeeded he was to have been C.-in-C. of the German Army.

Colonel-General Hoeppner—rebel chief of the Home Army, who signed orders for Nazi leaders to be arrested before he himself was seized.

Major-General Stieff—one of the originators of the murder plan in the summer of 1943.

Lieut-General von Hase—leader of the Wehrmacht units which joined the revolt after the attempt on Hitler failed.

Lieut.-General Bernardis—who was formerly on the General Staff.

Captain Karl Klausing—described as "a puppet in the conspirators' hands."

Reserve Lieut. Count Yorck von Wartenburg—to have been Secretary of State in the re-formed Reich Chancellery; and

Reserve Lieut. von Hagen.

'Honour' Denied

The condemned men were denied the "honour" of being shot. "Such a shameful act cannot be punished by an honest bullet," said the crimson-robed President of the Court, Dr. Freisler, as he pronounced sentence.

In a day of running commentary on the trial scenes, Berlin claimed that every officer admitted his guilt.

Fresh details revealed of the plot in the German News Agency's obvious propaganda report were these:

1. For the whole of July 20—when the murder bid was made—the rebel generals sat in the Bendlerstrasse [offices of the German High Command].

2. They gave orders for the seizure of radio stations and the arrest of Nazi Ministers: for a cordon to be thrown round the Wilhelmstrasse, and public buildings occupied: for the arrest of all leaders of food and arms production: and for concentration camps to be flung open.

3. A strong force of rebel shock troops was sent to capture Goebbels when it was thought Hitler was dead.

4. Mayor Goerdeler of Leipzig, on whose head the Gestapo

BACK PAGE—Col. TWO

Field-Marshal von Witzleben.
His Nazi salute rejected.

'Himmler is Dead,' say Prisoners

Göring Wounded?

From ROGER GREEN

NORMANDY FRONT, Tuesday.

A NEWLY captured German Intelligence officer to-day told his captors that Himmler had been assassinated and Göring wounded in a new outbreak against the Nazi hierarchy.

Nine other captives, all Austrians, corroborated the statement.

One Austrian said: "We heard that Rommel had been wounded in the head by bomb fragments but was recovering. Then the best news came on Sunday, when we heard that Himmler had been killed and Göring wounded in an attack on Himmler."

'Assassinated'

The British first heard the story of the alleged assassination from the Austrians. I approached a German intelligence officer who had been kept apart from the Austrians, and said to him: "I suppose Himmler is stronger than Hitler these days?"

He replied: "No, Himmler is dead. He has been assassinated. I heard it at my headquarters on Sunday. All our officers are talking about it"—*A.P.*

There is no further confirmation of this story, which should be accepted with reserve for the present. But whether true or not, it is significant of conditions in Germany that reports of this kind should be accepted by German officers and men without apparent surprise.

GERMANS QUIT THE SOUTH

In Farmers' Carts

MADRID, Tuesday.—German forces in Gascony, south of the Garonne, are streaming northward in a disordered mass in horse-drawn wagons requisitioned from French farmers, say first-hand reports received here to-day.

The Nazis left only a covering force of Gestapo, gendarmes, and Customs guards to hold the Pyrenees frontier west of Toulouse and the southern wing of Hitler's Atlantic Wall.

All the way north the Germans were harassed and ambushed by French Partisans.—*A.P.*

Two Russian Armies Race for Riga

TWO Russian armies have smashed German counter-attacks with massed tanks and infantry and have now begun the assault against Riga, capital of Latvia.

In three days' fighting the enemy lost 6,000 dead as they tried in vain to check the advance. The Red Army smashed 89 tanks and self-propelled guns

Now General Bagramyan's forces, 20 miles from Riga, are racing across flat, unobstructed country. Marshal Yeremenko, 70 miles, has an even plain before him, too.

These new thrusts, disclosed in the Soviet communiqué last night, are matched by a general swing westwards by the Russians and retreats by the Wehrmacht along most of the eastern front.

Another important Russian gain on the northern front is the capture of Krustpils, railway junction controlling east-west lines north of Dvinsk and the Baltic.

Main gains on the southern sectors were made west of Sandomir, where the Russian bridgehead is broadening over the Vistula.

In the approaches to the Carpathians another oil town has fallen—Dobromil, 14 miles south of Przemysl.

NEW PANZER BLOW STOPPED DEAD

SHAEF reports repulse of very heavy German counter-attack against British bridgehead over the Orne. Enemy suffered severe losses in this operation, particularly in armour.

MANY HURT IN MONTREAL CLASH

Montreal, Tuesday.—Many people were injured—including three with revolver wounds—in an election-day clash between hundreds of people in rival gangs in Montreal to-day.—A.P.

2

Germans Machine-gun Swiss Holiday Girls

From Daily Mail Correspondent

GENEVA, Tuesday.

MORGINS, a Swiss winter sports station in the Canton of Valais, was bombed and machine-gunned by three German planes which came from the direction of France yesterday afternoon.

Flying low, a German bomber, accompanied by two fighters, dropped two bombs, one of which pulverised a soldiers' rest châlet and damaged a number of dwellings.

Then the fighters dived, firing their machine-guns along the village street.

Half of a châlet where a number of young girls were on holiday fell into a torrent. Three girls were injured and the rest fled panic-stricken into an adjoining forest.

Among 20 people injured were two Swiss soldiers.

Later in the evening the Luftwaffe returned and bombed the village of Vacheresse, on the French side of the border.

The attacks were no doubt intended to be against the French Resistance Forces, who now completely control the Val d'Abondance area of the Savoy. Afraid to venture their troops into these mountainous regions, the Germans have been obliged to call in the Luftwaffe.

During the last few days Allied planes, in broad daylight, have been clearly seen from Switzerland dropping large quantities of arms and supplies in this French district. A small proportion was captured by the Germans, but the greater part safely reached the Maquis.

Warsaw Calls for Ammunition

Resistance by the Polish underground movement in Warsaw is dying out because of lack of ammunition, states a message from Polish underground army leaders, received last night by the Scottish Committee for Polish Freedom.

The Polish underground army and the Vice-President acting in Poland asked for ammunition on August 2 from the Russians and the British Government in London. The Russians did not send any, and London sent supplies once only, but not enough. Since then, it is stated, everything has stopped.

'Glass' Falls in the Strait

State of Sea.—Calm.

Weather.—Banks of mist after sunshine, much cooler. Maximum temperature, 71 deg.; 58 deg. at 10.30 p.m. Visibility restricted. Wind, S.E., light.

Barometer.—Steady after another slight fall.

MONDAY, AUGUST 14, 1944

Latest Prices

BLACK OUT	Moon Rises 3.7 a.m.	Sets 6.49 p.m.
9.55 to 6.15	New Moon Aug. 18	Radio Page 6

LATE NIGHT

THE STAR

No. 17,518 ONE PENNY

EISENHOWER CALLS TO ALL HIS FORCES

"Opportunity For A Major Victory"

'MAKE THIS WEEK MOMENTOUS'

GENERAL EISENHOWER, FROM HIS ADVANCED COMMAND POST IN NORMANDY, TODAY ISSUED THE FOLLOWING ORDER OF THE DAY: "ALLIED SOLDIERS, SAILORS AND AIRMEN—THROUGH YOUR COMBINED SKILL, VALOUR AND FORTITUDE, YOU HAVE CREATED IN FRANCE A FLEETING, BUT DEFINITE, OPPORTUNITY FOR A MAJOR ALLIED VICTORY, ONE WHOSE REALISATION WILL MEAN NOTABLE PROGRESS TOWARDS THE FINAL DOWNFALL OF OUR ENEMY.

"In the past, I have, in moments of unusual significance, made special appeals to the Allied forces it has been my honour to command. Without exception the response has been unstinted and the results beyond my expectations.

"Because the victory we can now achieve is infinitely greater than any it

has so far been possible to accomplish in the West, and because this opportunity may be grasped only through the utmost in zeal, determination, and speedy action, I make my present appeal to you more urgent than ever before.

"I request every airman to make it his direct responsibility that the enemy is blasted unceasingly by day and by night, and is denied safety either in fight or in flight.

"I request every sailor to make sure that no part of the hostile forces can either escape or be reinforced by sea, and that our comrades on the land want nothing that guns and ships and ships' companies can bring to them.

"I request every soldier to go forward to his assigned objective with the determination that the enemy can survive only through surrender. Let no foot of ground, once gained, be relinquished, nor a single German escape through a line once established.

"With all of us resolutely performing our special tasks we can make this week a momentous one in the history of this war—a brilliant and fruitful week for us, a fateful one for the ambitions of the Nazi tyrants."

ESCAPE GAP IS CLOSING

Nazi Retreat May Become A Rout

THE German Seventh Army in the Vire-Mortain area has been forced into a general withdrawal in daylight, it was announced from Supreme Headquarters this afternoon.

The withdrawal is covered by strong rearguards, and the enemy is strongly protecting his northern flank from the pressure of the British and Canadian armies.

No Sign Of Collapse

There is heavy movement eastward throughout the battle area.

There is no sign of collapse in the Vire-Falaise area. Every inch of ground there is being fiercely contested, and will be while the Germans are struggling to get out through the narrowing escape gap. The next few days will show whether the German retirement is to become a rout.

It is now revealed that substantial American forces moving northwards from Le Mans through Alencon have reached the vicinity of Argentan.

Gap Narrowed

This northward movement is now meeting increasing resistance, but is still making progress.

The exit gap through Falaise has been narrowed to between 30 and 40 kilometres (18 to 25 miles), and it is still shrinking.

The Allies have made gains in the Vire area up to three miles, but there has not been much progress in the neighbourhood of Mortain itself.

Further south, we have crossed the river Varenne between Domfront and Mayenne and established a bridgehead.

More small advances have been made in the British-Canadian sector between the Orne and the Laize.

The enemy still holds Thury Harcourt, but we have moved forward a little in the drive on Conde against very strong opposition.

East of the Vire there have also been slight advances stubbornly opposed. Indeed along the whole British front opposition is still stiff.

Two Towns Taken

"Further progress was made East of the River Orne, where Allied troops entered Clair Tizon and Donnai," said today's communique from Gen. Eisenhower's H.Q.

"South of St. Pierre la Vieille, the advance continued along the high ground on each side of the road to Conde.

"South-east of Vire, ground was gained in heavy fighting. Further south, towards Mortain, our forces, following the German withdrawal, encountered mines and long-range artillery fire.

"In Brittany, the Allied attack on Dinard continues to meet strong resistance, and remnants of the German garrison of St. Malo still hold out in the citadel.

"Slight advances have been made by our units in the vicinity of Brest. There has been no change in the situation at Lorient."

A Berlin military spokesman stated: "While strong American tank columns are driving on from the area north of Alencon, the German lines south of Caen have been taken back several hundred yards to a new defence line."

All-Out Air Blows On Battle Zone

ALLIED air forces, in the greatest strength since D-Day, are harassing von Kluge's withdrawal through the Falaise Gap.

Under brilliant skies throughout the week-end, and again today, great forces of fighters and bombers of all types have been ranging over France.

Allied aircraft which are taking part in the mammoth blitz range from fighters to four-engined bombers.

A high Staff Officer at United States First Army headquarters described the Allied operations as an "all-out effort."

Our planes were again over Falaise today, combining with the Army to deal a smashing blow at enemy vehicles on the road as they tried to pull out of the gap.

The air section of today's communique from General Eisenhower said: Highways and road junctions on both sides of the Seine from Paris to the sea and westwards to Lisieux and Regles were attacked by heavy and medium bombers.

Medium bombers also attacked rail bridges at Peronne, Beautor, Doullens and Cherisy, rail facilities at Corbeil, and enemy gun positions in the Falaise area.

A railway bridge over the Seine at Le Manoir, U-boat shelters at Brest, an oil storage depot for U-boats at Bordeaux, and gun positions at St. Malo and on the Ile de Cezembre were other targets for heavy bombers.

From these operations 14 heavy and two medium bombers are missing.

Fighters, fighter-bombers and rocket-firing fighters provided cover for the ground forces, and bombed and strafed tanks, motor transport, strongpoints, and troop concentrations in the battle zone.

Fighters also ranged over North-Eastern and Central France, attacking locomotives, railway cars, motor transport and canal barges, while other fighters provided escorts for bombing missions.

Light bombers last night continued their attacks on transport targets behind the enemy's line.

The Allied Air Forces flew about 5,500 sorties yesterday.

NEW CLUES IN £500 MYSTERY

New clues to the mystery of the £500 box of florins which vanished from Euston station on Friday were being followed up today by Scotland Yard.

The box, weighing about 140lb., was part of a consignment from the Bank of England to the Bank of Scotland.

How it vanished is a mystery. It is believed that the theft was carefully planned and the box snatched away while the attention of officials was distracted for a few seconds.

"Sea Fight Off Guernsey"

German radio today reported a naval engagement south of Guernsey just after midnight between a German minesweeper unit and "enemy" destroyers and MTBs.

It added that several hits were scored on the destroyers, and said the German vessels suffered minor damage and casualties.

Sunshine In Straits

In the Straits of Dover today there was a light northerly wind, cloudless sky and bright sunshine. The sea was slight, and visibility was about 10 miles. Barometer was rising.

SPAIN HEARS MYSTERY BANGS

Explosions in the distance from the direction of France are being heard on the Franco-Spanish frontier from time to time, says Reuter.

What they are cannot be said for certain. Guesses are: Guns, the Germans blowing up stores, or, French patriots at work.

It is asserted from many sources that the coastal guns near Biarritz have been dismantled and wooden dummies set up in their place.

Custom officials at the frontier nowadays wear worried looks, and the Gestapo are active throughout South-Western France.

Big Air Armada Out Again

HUGE formations of Allied planes flew out over the Channel again today.

There were two main fleets, each of which must have included hundreds of planes. One headed east and the other south-east.

They took more than an hour to cross the coast.

The German air raid service announced this afternoon: "**Allied bomber formations are over South-Western Germany and Western Bavaria. Other raiders are over Pomerania.**"

And an Air Ministry communique said: "A force of Mosquitos of RAF Bomber Command attacked Hanover during the night. Mines were also laid in enemy waters.

"From these operations one aircraft is missing."

New Hungary Call-Up

Female labour service in Hungary has been made compulsory, according to Budapest radio.

DAILY MIRROR, Tuesday, August 15, 1944.

Daily Mirror

AUG 15

No. 12-686
ONE PENNY
Registered at the G.P.O. as Newspaper.

GAP CUT DOWN TO 12 MILES: HUN ARMY 'PINNED'

HE SAW A NAME IN WOUNDED LIST—IT WAS HIS SON, "LOST" 17 YEARS

LOOKING through a list of the patients at a military convalescent home in the Midlands, Corporal Harry Holden, RAMC, saw his own name—with a difference.

It had "Captain Wilfred" in front of it.

He checked up and found that Captain Holden, who had been in an airborne regiment and was wounded a few days after D-Day, was his twenty-seven-year-old son, whom he had not seen for seventeen years.

Father and son were overjoyed to meet again, for Captain Holden had thought his father to be dead.

"When my son is better we are going to celebrate in London in spite of buzz-bombs," said Corporal Holden.

Seventeen years ago, when his mother died, Wilfred was adopted by his father's sister and taken to Australia. His father and aunt lost touch, and he heard his father had died.

He came to England at the outbreak of war to join up.

It's been a happy reunion in more ways than one. Corporal Holden has given his son £50 which he has kept in trust for him since 1935. It was left him by an uncle.

FIGHTER PILOTS CAPTURE 300 NAZIS WITHOUT A SHOT

THUNDERBOLT pilots flying over France yesterday captured more than 300 Germans without firing a shot.

Captain J. R. Willingtham tells how it happened.

"We were strafing trucks when we noticed a small group looking up at us and waving white flags.

"We buzzed them several times, without shooting, and pretty soon there were several hundred. We looked for our infantry, but there wasn't a doughboy around.

"The Germans formed into columns of four and started marching down the roads toward our lines, while we shuttled back and forth over them — but our ground liaison officer told us the infantry said the credit was all ours."

Fighter-bombers yesterday renewed their attacks on transport in France which, in two previous days, had destroyed or damaged nearly 600 locomotives, more than 6,000 rail cars and 900 military vehicles.

By 1 p.m. the fighters had increased their score by twenty nine locomotives, 301 rail cars and twenty-two military vehicles.

ALLIED armies smashing from north and south toward Falaise had last night cut down the escape gap for the German Seventh Army to twelve miles and put the enemy routes under gunfire.

Von Kluge yesterday called off all full-scale attempts to scramble out of the shrinking pocket. The Allied planes' bag of military trucks and tanks dropped to a moderate figure.

The German forces still in the pocket are either virtually trapped, or the enemy Commander has ordered them to fight it out. In any case, many of his troops are "pinned" by the Allied pressure.

Some German armoured units are believed to have escaped, but battlefront reports early today said that the bulk of the 100,000 men of Von Kluge's Seventh Army were still in the pocket.

On the north, Canadian troops thrust to within three miles of Falaise. On the south, American armour was fighting toward the town from Argentan,

New assault tactics helped the Canadians to break into the enemy's heavily defended gun belt

Allied artillery blinded the German gunners with a barrage of smoke shells. Then over 700 RAF bombers roared in

On the Canadians' right flank, British troops drove to within two and a half miles of one of the enemy's main escape roads.

And at the western end of the pocket American forces swept forward seven miles from Mortain.

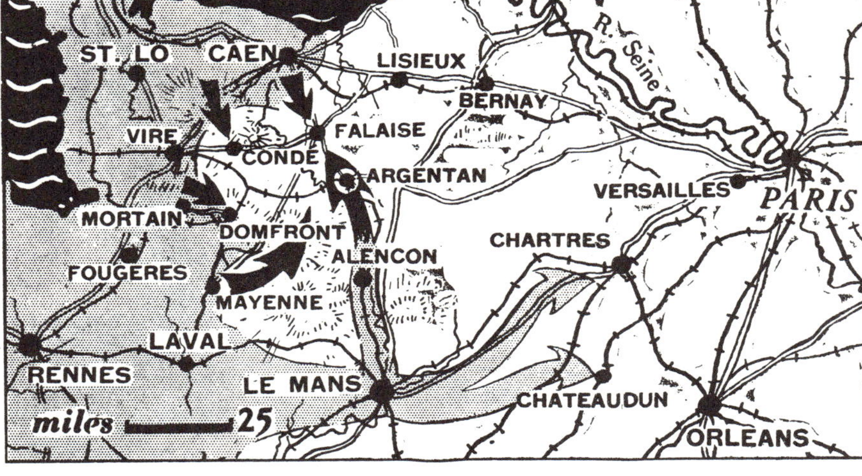

Smoke, tanks, bombs in shock attack

From GEORGE McCARTHY "Daily Mirror" Chief Correspondent

NORTH OF FALAISE, Monday.

IN the perfect noon of an ideal summer day, the Canadian Army today launched a new attack towards Falaise.

Armour and lorried infantry raced across the fields under cover of a great curtain of smoke which our 25-pounders had laid in a concentration of fire that had lasted for more than an hour.

In just over sixty minutes after the offensive opened, the armour reported that they had crossed the Laizon River and were advancing against little opposition.

In one area the concentration of tanks and transport had been met, but they had withdrawn before our advance.

Just two hours after the battle began the RAF's heavy bombers sailed into the attack. In a cloudless blue sky waves of hundreds of Lancasters and Halifaxes, led by their pathfinders, appeared over smoking fields.

IN 105 MINUTES THEY DROPPED 4,000 TONS.

Their task was one of the most difficult our heavy bombers have ever been asked to perform. They had to pinpoint targets immediately to the right of the advancing Canadians, an exacting daylight test of the precision of their aim.

From a General's armoured car parked behind a miniature haystack I watched the battle open. Two miles away, along an irregular ridge, the smoke shells from our guns were bursting.

Then, in the dip below us, the tanks moved up, their tracks spraying yellow dust behind them. With them moved the infantry mounted on Priests—self-propelled guns specially adapted to carry foot soldiers.

As they advanced the smoke barrage went ahead so

Continued on Back Page

ANOTHER ARMY

The Third U.S. Army is now operating in France with the First U.S. Army, which is now commanded by Lieutenant-General Courtney Hodges. The commander of the Third Army has so far not been named.

"All out now"—Eisenhower

General Eisenhower yesterday called on all our forces in France for a supreme all-out effort for a major victory.

This week can be **"momentous in the history of war—a brilliant and fruitful week for us, a fateful one for the ambitions of the Nazi tyrants."**

In a special Order of the Day addressed to Allied soldiers, sailors and airmen, he said:

"Through your combined skill, valour and fortitude you have created in France a fleeting but definite opportunity for a major Allied victory, one whose realisation will mean notable progress toward the final downfall of our enemy.

"Because the victory we can now achieve is infinitely greater than any it has so far been possible to accomplish in the West, and because this opportunity may be grasped only through the utmost in zeal, determination and speedy action, I make my present appeal to you more urgent than ever before.

"I request every airman to make it his direct responsibility that the enemy is blasted unceasingly by day and by night, and is denied safety, either in fight or in flight.

"I request every sailor to make sure that no part of the hostile forces can either escape or be reinforced by sea, and that our comrades on the land want nothing that guns and ships and ships' companies can bring to them.

"I request every soldier to go forward to his assigned objective with the determination that the enemy can survive only through surrender.

Secret column breaks Hitler tank division

First news of one of General Bradley's "secret columns" came in a dispatch from a British United Press correspondent yesterday.

This column, striking forty miles north east from Mayenne, created an inner ring of U.S. armour closing in on elements of five German Panzer Divisions which were holding out east of Mortain. The dispatch said:

THE famous Adolf Hitler S.S. Division has been cut to ribbons by a U.S. armoured column, which liberated twenty towns and villages in twenty-four hours.

The advance is the nearest thing to a man-made tidal wave. The nerves of the German prisoners have been completely shattered by their ordeal.

As we advance, the woods and fields on both sides of us are full of bewildered and shell-shocked Germans

The column advanced along the road from Mayenne and passed through the towns of Ribay and Javron. It was only then that the column encountered heavy German resistance, with fighting lasting several hours.

BUZZ-BOMBS CAUSE FEWER DEATHS NOW

Many houses have been damaged by flying bombs in every period of twenty-four hours over eight weeks, but fatalities per bomb are down to something like one-third compared with the first fortnight, said Mr. H. U. Willink, Health Minister, at Birmingham yesterday.

Note: Last figures of flying bomb casualties given by Mr. Churchill on August 2 were: Projectiles launched, 5,340; persons killed 4,735, injured 14,000.

There was a lull during daylight in buzz-bomb activity over Southern England yesterday. An alert was sounded in the London area, and there was some damage and casualties.

BIG DRIVE FOR PRUSSIA IS ON

THE battle for East Prussia has started. Marshal Stalin last night announced the fall of Osowiec, eighteen miles south of the East Prussia border, and gateway for a Soviet advance into the Masurian lakes district.

As the Order of the Day was issued it was stated in Berlin: "The offensive against East Prussia has started in earnest."

Arms and munitions from the Allies in the West have reached the underground forces in Warsaw during the last forty-eight hours, according to information reaching Polish circles in London last night.

This assistance, while still on a very small scale, is said to have enabled the forces of General Bor, C.-in-C. of the Polish home front army, to inflict heavy losses on the Germans and to hold their own.

In an order to units of the Home Army outside the capital General Bor last night ordered all available well-armed units of the Home Army to make immediately for the capital by forced marches.

TUESDAY, AUGUST 15, 1944

Latest Prices

BLACK OUT 9.53 to 6.16 | Moon Sets 7.41 p.m New Moon Friday | Rises 4.1 a.m. Radio Page 5

LATE NIGHT

THE STAR

No. 17,519 ONE PENNY

LANDING IN S. FRANCE

"The Operation Is Going On Extremely Well"

A NEW Allied landing in France was announced today in a special communique from Advanced H.Q. Italy, which said: "American, British and French troops, strongly supported by Allied air forces, are today being landed by American, British and French fleets on the Southern coast of France."

Latest news is that " the operation is going extremely well."

No indication of the exact place of the landing has yet come from official Allied sources, but an American broadcast from Allied Force Headquarters this afternoon said it was made on a coastline of about 100 miles between Nice and Marseilles, and the German News Agency said it was made at Bormes, 25 miles east of Toulon.

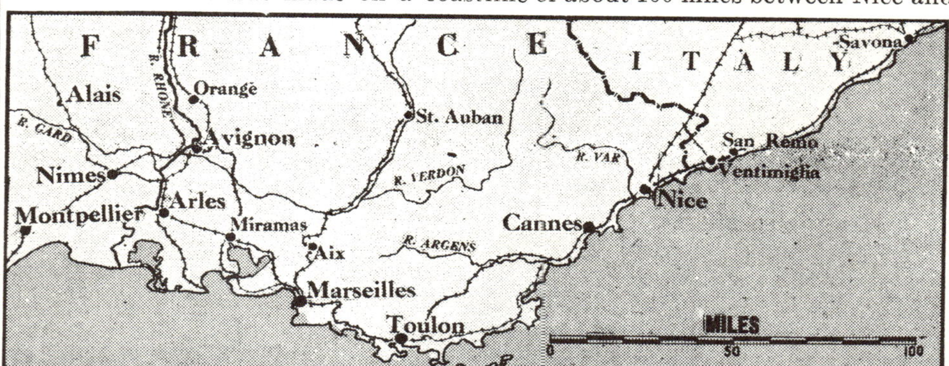

The airborne force which took part in the landing was the largest ever dropped in any Allied operation.

In a broadcast on the landing Chester Morrison, NBC correspondent, said: " There was a minimum of German opposition when the first wave of infantry landed at a place which I can only describe at the moment as a beach in the South of France.

" Paratroops were landed two miles inshore before dawn.

" In less than an hour one company of the first wave had reached its first objectives.

" Seven waves with 2,000 men or more had landed before 10 o'clock.

" At dawn the aerial bombardment began. 'H' hour, the hour of infantry attack, was 8 o'clock.

" At ten minutes to seven a heavy naval bombardment began.

" Fire was poured into shore positions where primary objectives were neutralised."

It is understood that the Allied forces taking part in the landing are commanded by General Devers, of the U.S. Army.

Soon after the landing the Supreme Commander Mediterranean Theatre of War, General Sir Henry Maitland Wilson, broadcast to the people of France a proclamation in which he said:

" The armies of the United Nations have landed in Southern France. Their objective is to drive out the Germans and join up with the Allied armies advancing from Normandy.

" French forces are participating in these operations side by side with their allied brothers in arms, by sea, land, and air.

" The Army of France is in being again, fighting on its own soil for the liberation of its country with all its tradition of victory behind it. Remember 1918.

" All Frenchmen, civilians as well as military, have their part to play in the campaign in the south. Your duty will be made clear to you. Listen to the Allied radio.

" Read notices and leaflets; pass on all instructions from one man and woman to another.

" Let us end the struggle as quickly as possible so that all France may resume again her free life and that conditions of peace and security may come. VICTORY IS CERTAIN.

" Long live the spirit of France and all that it stands for."

Sir Henry Maitland Wilson made his proclamation in French.

David Brown, of the Mutual Broadcasting Corporation, sent out this report: " Supported by a tremendous fleet fo warships of all types

CONTINUED ON BACK PAGE, Col. TWO

ALLIED CHIEFS

General Sir H. Maitland Wilson (left) and Lieut.-Gen. J. L. Devers, who is understood to be in command of the forces landed in the South of France.

Ambassador-Major

Mr. William Bullitt, former U.S. Ambassador to Paris, has joined the French Army, and has been given the rank of major, to take part in military operations on French territory, said a BUP cable from Algiers today.

Kenya Rice Record

Rice growing in the Tana River valley of Kenya is steadily increasing, and a bigger crop than ever is hoped for this year, says Reuter. In eight years the rice production figure has been increased twelvefold.

PINCERS CLOSE ON FALAISE OUTLET

THE Normandy escape gap is closing and the Canadians are now fighting only 2½ miles north of Falaise.

An Allied spokesman said this afternoon: " The bag is more closed round the Germans today than it was yesterday.

" There is still no sign of any panic in the German Army—they are still making an orderly withdrawal. We have evidence that some armoured elements have escaped beyond Falaise.

" More than 1,000 prisoners were taken yesterday on the Canadian front."

" Advances were made yesterday on both sides of the Falaise-Argentan gap," said today's communique from General Eisenhower.

Over The River

" Allied troops attacking towards Falaise from the north quickly gained their first objectives, and, having crossed the River Laison, are now firmly established within 7,000 yards of the town.

" On the other side of the Gap, the thrust northward from Le Mans and Alencon has reached the vicinity of Argentan. Pockets of resistance left behind in this advance are being mopped up near Alencon.

" Inside the Normandy pocket advances were made. Between the Laize and the Orne an advance of some 5,000 yards brought our forward elements to the vicinity of the village of nnoeil.

" In the Orne Valley, Thury Harcourt was cleared of the enemy. North of Conde the village of Proussy was taken, and our troops are approaching St. Denis de Mere.

" Farther west, Allied troops advanced to within a mile of Vassy and south-east of Vire an advance of a mile has brought us to a point about one mile from Tinchebray.

Pushing To The East

" Other units advancing south of Vire are moving along the Gathemo-Tinchebray road against moderate resistance.

" Troops pushing eastwards from Mortain have reached Ger. Along the southern boundary of the pocket our columns moving from the Barentan area are approaching Domfront, and units which reached Ranes are encountering increasing resistance.

" In Brittany, fighting is still in progress at St. Malo, where the situation remains unchanged, and at Dinard, where we have made advances towards the port. At Brest and Lorient there is nothing new to report."

Supreme headquarters announced later this afternoon that a considerable advance along the road from Vire has reached a point about a mile short of Tinchebray. We are still steadily advancing in the Vire-Mortain sector against slightly increased resistance.

There is considerable enemy road movement eastwards in the pocket. There is not, however, any question of a routed army pouring out of the pocket on the escape routes.

There is a weakened resistance by the enemy in St. Malo, where the position is coming more comfortably under our control. The Americans are in Dinard, where there is not now very much organised resistance.

[Great Air Onslaught Over The Battle Front.—See Page Three.]

BERLIN AGAIN

MOSQUITOS of RAF Bomber Command, carrying 4,000lb. block-buster bombs, made a swift attack on Berlin just before midnight, Air Ministry News Service announced this afternoon.

One of the pilots said when he returned: " The weather was very clear. As we approached Berlin the enemy switched on searchlights, scores and scores of them. Flak was pretty heavy, and they also had quite a lot of fighters up over the target."

All our planes returned safely.

Radio reports say that other targets in the French Riviera and near Paris were also raided.

The attack on the Continent was resumed early today.

Big forces of Allied planes flew out over the coast, and later Berlin radio reported that U.S. planes, with strong fighter escort, were over South-West Germany.

No. 15.069 ONE PENNY

Daily Mail

FOR KING AND EMPIRE

SATURDAY, AUGUST 19, 1944

LATE WAR NEWS

DECISIVE BATTLE OF FRANCE HAS NOW BEEN WON

Kluge's Beaten Army is Being Pursued—and Destroyed

From ALEXANDER CLIFFORD

NORMANDY, Friday.

WE have won a decisive victory in Normandy. The German Seventh Army is now in full retreat. You can state this tremendous news as simply as that to-day. Overnight the situation has suddenly become sharp, clear, and overwhelmingly important. The Germans here are defeated. This is what has, in fact, happened.

Most of those German divisions are, after all, still trapped in the pocket. Only yesterday did the Germans themselves recognise the extent of their plight. The gap is now down to three or four doubtful miles. The panzer divisions are trying to fight their way through it in a tremendous running battle.

You can call the victory decisive without hesitation. It does not mean that the Germans will immediately cease fighting. It does not mean that this particular battle will not drag on for a few days yet. It does not even guarantee a big bag of prisoners in the end.

But it does mean that the best German divisions are irretrievably mauled and disorganised. It means that they can never again bring a really serious force against us in Western Europe. It means they will probably never again be able to organise any sort of a front in France.

All our thrust is north-east now. The British and Canadians on the left and the Americans on the right are heading straight for the Seine. Between our stretching arms the Germans who fight their way out of the little pocket find themselves being still embraced and funnelled towards the bridgeless river.

The clue to to-day's situation is that the Germans never really knew they were trapped. They thought they could counter-attack against the Americans and shoulder off that whole southern flank. They thought they could break the trap instead of merely escaping from it.

But something happened at midday yesterday. Someone suddenly got the true facts. A fantastic scramble to leave the pocket began. The German defeat was abruptly and glaringly revealed.

All yesterday afternoon German vehicles began to appear in the lanes and fields between Falaise and Argentan.

They were all wildly striving to get east, every man for himself. The Seine ferries started to operate in daylight for the first time.

WHITE FLAGS

The tanks began to shoot their way east. The news spread from unit to unit.

Right in the middle of the pocket they began to hand out white flags and tablecloths to the air forces.

They could not really surrender because the units all around them were not surrendering. So the air force told them to keep right on waving or they would be bombed.

The adjutant of the Ninth Panzer Division went out to reconnoitre a route for a counter-attack. He found to his astonishment that his maps were marked utterly wrong. His route lay through Allied territory. Then he was rocketed by Typhoons. In supreme bewilderment and discouragement he surrendered.

The Air Forces were out attacking the gap all yesterday afternoon and again to-day. Stubbornly and desperately the mobile German forces passed on.

This at last is a disorganised retreat. It would be a rout-if we allowed it to be.

THREE BLUNDERS

To get the full flavour of this victory, to realise why the crisis has crystallised so suddenly, you must add up the three big blunders the Germans have made since D-Day. And you must keep in mind all the time their fatal blind spot—their lack of information.

Their first blunder was that they did not bring down enough strength at the beginning. They knew their best chance was to seal us up in Normandy.

But they were terrified of another landing somewhere else. So they did not have enough troops here, and we broke out at the western end.

Their second blunder was when the pocket was forming. They sought to put matters right by a wild, spectacular drive back to the sea at Avranches. That failed, and the pocket became a terrific fact.

Their third blunder was the idea that they could break this trap instead of simply escaping from it. They thought the whole solution was to counter-attack at Argentan and swing back the whole American advance.

CRUCIAL FACTOR

Back of it all—the crucial factor—is their lack of information. They cannot send up reconnaissance planes, their patrolling has never been good, they get nothing from prisoners. They simply cannot find out what is happening.

They could not possibly tell how strong the Americans were in the places they captured down south. They hopelessly miscalculated.

They did panic a week ago when the pocket was first formed. They started to rush out their rear headquarters, their administrative units, their civil affairs departments, and so on.

That was when hundreds of lorries suddenly appeared on the roads and were so devastatingly attacked from the air.

It is an enormous thing—far bigger than the mere liberation of Paris.

Incidentally, if you are impatient for that, remember these points:—The Americans already have supply lines of fantastic length. Paris, when it is captured, will have to be fed. From every point of view the conduct of the war must come first.

Whichever way you like the Germans' difficulties multiply.

We have seen enough in this campaign to teach us the conditions

BACK PAGE—Col. SEVEN

THE DRIVE FOR PARIS—

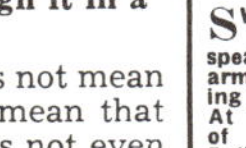

SWEEPING forward from Dreux and Chartres, spearheads of General Patton's armoured columns are operating in the vicinity of Paris. At Trun, 10 miles south-east of Falaise, Canadians and Polish troops are reported to have linked up with Americans from Argentan, thus closing the ring round the remnants of von Kluge's army in the Falaise pocket.

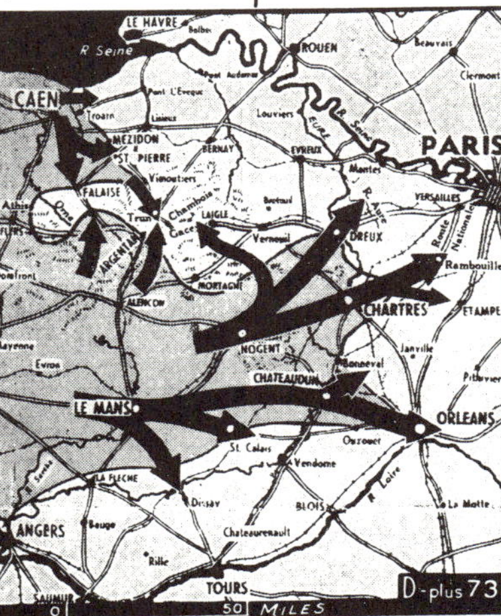

Tanks Are Swinging North Again

WHILE General Patton's armoured columns are pressing nearer Paris, another pincer move is shaping against the shattered German panzer army in Normandy.

According to Berlin strong formations of Patton's Third Army have swung north to Gace and Laigle, on the main road to Evreux, in "an attempt to encircle the Seventh German Army." Allied sources were again silent yesterday on the movements of the speeding tank columns.

Sertorius, the German commentator, revealed the Allied armoured thrust to the Laigle region. Coupled with the drive on Paris, he said, the move indicated the considerable scale of forces being employed on the Allied wing. He spoke significantly of "elastic defence."

The German-controlled French radio stations of Paris and the Vichy network went off the air yesterday as Patton's columns swept towards Paris.

The Germans spoke of fighting at Rambouillet, 22 miles from the city, and at Etampes, 30 miles to the south, while a Berlin message to Stockholm reported American patrols 12 miles from the French capital.

★

BERLIN reported that Patton's main thrust was being made along the main west road which runs from Paris through Versailles to Chartres. Many towns in the rear of the speedy tank columns are being liberated. One is Vendome, about 40 miles south-west of Orleans.

Indications of a breach between the Wehrmacht and the S.S. are reported by war correspondents at Allied headquarters.

The S.S., who are doing all they can to keep themselves intact at the expense of the Wehrmacht, are "Hitler fanatics," and it is not without interest that the leader of the Seventh German Army, which is in course of destruction, is Hausser, an S.S. officer.

The confusion has been caused by the efforts of the S.S. to leave the Wehrmacht "holding the baby." In their desperation to save what they can, the Germans have put up planes of their carefully hoarded Luftwaffe in larger formations than have been seen for some time.

★

PILOTS of the R.A.F. Tactical Air Force and Ninth Air Force on Thursday had their most successful day against the German ground forces retreating towards the Seine. They struck with cannon, machine-gun, rocket, and bomb, and when darkness called a halt to their efforts, Typhoons, Spitfires, and Mustangs had established their record-scoring day since D-Day.

The final count showed 570 vehicles and 19 tanks destroyed.

Late yesterday the Germans put up F.W.s in formations of 40 and more in an attempt to strafe our pursuing armour and infantry.

Mustangs shot down seven and shot up several hundred soldiers south-west of Compiègne.

Between the old Falaise gap and Trun fighters found concentrations of 400 to 500 vehicles and just beyond Argentan fighter-bombers bombed and shot up three big German columns destroying about 100 vehicles.

After a morning attack by a small force of Liberators which bombed the airfield at Roye, near Amiens, other Liberators, with Fortresses, attacked enemy airfields near Nancy-Essey, St. Dizier, and Romilly-sur-Seine.

Other heavy bombers hit the Woippy air engine works near Metz and fuel depots in Eastern France. Marauders struck seven miles south of Paris at a fuel depot at Valenton.—*B.U.P.* and *Reuter*.

—And the Man Who Leads It

GENERAL ("Blood and Guts") Patton, in command of the Third United States Army which is approaching Paris. In this picture he is talking to a French boy "somewhere in France."

LAVAL FLEES FROM PARIS

May Go to Germany

With Allied armies driving from north and south the "rats" in France have started deserting the sinking ship.

Laval, Darnand, and other Vichyites have fled from Paris to Metz, and will go to Germany with others of their kind when the Germans retreat across the Rhine, says a resistance leader who crossed into Allied territory in Northern France yesterday.

The Vichy Government is "giving consideration" to the question of moving, said a German official spokesman yesterday.

In Paris everybody is awaiting the arrival of the Allied armies. Only the collaborationists are getting out before the coming storm.

Italians Here Can Go to the Pictures

But 'Pubs' Barred

ITALIAN "co-operators," the new name for Italy's prisoners of war in Britain, may now talk with civilians and visit private houses if invited.

They can visit cinemas at the discretion of their commanding officer, but must not enter public-houses or use public conveyances except on duty.

More than 60,000 of the prisoners of war have been formed into units which have done work of great value to the Allied war effort. About 6,000 are employed on maintenance work on British railroads, 2,000 have so far been placed at the disposal of the Air Ministry, and some have taken the place of British pioneer units.

Their good behaviour and discipline have justified the privileges granted.

Co-operators may now exchange part of their pay into sterling and buy in local shops. Previously their pay was in token money, and could only be expended in the camp canteen.

WARSAW AID FROM R.A.F.

1,750-miles Flights

R.A.F. and South African night bombers from Italy have been dropping weapons and ammunition to Polish patriots in Warsaw since the uprising started at the beginning of August.

The round trip of 1,750 miles through areas strongly defended by night fighters was made by more than 100 aircraft. Twenty bombers have been lost in the operations.

More than half of the total of the "Warsaw Express" planes have fought through all hazards, coming down to low levels and flying at slow speeds to ensure accuracy in dropping supplies.—*Reuter*.

Earlier this week General Bor, C.-in-C. Polish Home Army, sent a message to the R.A.F. thanking them for the supplies which were dropped to Warsaw patriots on Sunday night.

German Papers Late

From Daily Mail Correspondent

LISBON, Friday.—For the past two days no German newspapers have appeared on the Lisbon news stands. It was customary for the German newspapers, including *Das Reich*, Goebbels's paper, to arrive in Lisbon from Berlin punctually every day by air.

CANDIDATE WOUNDED

Lieutenant C. H. Johnston, prospective Liberal candidate for North Edinburgh, has been wounded while serving with the 51st Highland Division in Normandy.

Mr. Roosevelt said yesterday that he was to have another meeting with Mr. Churchill soon.

3 Powers Agree on Germany

FDR and Premier to Meet Soon

WASHINGTON, Friday.

PRESIDENT ROOSEVELT stated to-day that a general understanding had been reached between Russia, Britain, and the United States regarding the occupation of Germany.

He also told journalists that he was going to confer with Mr Churchill soon.

The understanding on Germany, he said, was arrived at regardless of how or what date the Reich capitulated.

The three Powers had entered into discussions and everything was proceeding satisfactorily.

'Must Be Occupied'

Understanding on specific details had not yet been reached. These concerned sections of the country each Ally would occupy.

He added that it would be just as easy to reach agreement with China regarding the occupation of Japan. He had nothing on paper with China, but had discussed such an occupation.

The Allies, however, were determined not to allow Germany or Japan to quit until their homelands had been invaded and completely occupied

The President appeared to be most emphatic as he gave correspondents the news of his impending meeting with Mr. Churchill. But he declined to give any details.

It would be the tenth meeting between President and Premier during the war.

President Roosevelt also revealed yesterday that the question of combining the United States Army and Navy Commands was being studied, and everyone was agreed upon it.

He explained, however, that nothing would be done until after the war.—*Reuter* and *B.U.P.*

GAS MAY BE NAZIS' V3

Stockholm Report

NEW YORK, Friday.—The Germans intend to start using gas this month, according to John Scott, the Stockholm correspondent of the United States magazines *Time* and *Life*.

"A week's careful checking and perusal of published and unpublished evidence from Germany," he writes in *Life*, "has convinced me that Germany's 'V3' is gas, and that it is scheduled for use late in August.

F-Bomb Depot Bombed

Lancasters of R.A.F. Bomber Command, wtih fighter cover, yesterday attacked a flying-bomb storage depot at L'Isle Adam, about 15 miles north of Paris.

This is the second V-weapon depot to be attacked at L'Isle Adam. The other has now been almost entirely destroyed.

Liberator Sank 2 U's in 22 min.

Saved Normandy Convoys

Crew Awards

By COLIN BEDNALL, Air Correspondent

MORE than ten weeks after the invasion began the Admiralty has permitted the Air Ministry to tell for the first time this morning the story of an air success against U-boats, which massed in terrifying strength to smash the invasion.

A Liberator captained by 21-years-old Flying Officer K. O. Moore, of Vancouver, definitely destroyed two U-boats in 22 minutes. So much was thought of this feat that the young captain was awarded an immediate D.S.O.

Two other members of the crew were given the D.F.C. and a third the D.F.M.

An official account of this one episode states: "Thousands of Allied troops now fighting for the liberation of Europe owe their safety in the English Channel to the crew of the Liberator."

The Admiralty is known to be withholding from the public many other accounts by official and accredited observers of superb work by R.A.F. Coastal Command in breaking the enemy's submarine threat to the invasion. The fact that it was given operational control of the U-boat war still enables it to do so.

Together with another correspondent I flew on these operations about two months ago at the invitation of the Air Ministry. The Admiralty, nevertheless, impounded the stories and has refused repeated requests for their release since.

No Reasons

No security reasons have been given for the suppressions. This form of censorship can be applied under the conditions by which official "facilities" are granted, but it is the only occasion, in my experience, on which it has been applied.

The fact that a Liberator encountered—let along destroyed—two U-boats in 22 minutes provides a clue to the nature of the submarine threat which was broken.

"Before we took off," said Flying Officer Moore "my squadron commander said there were so many U-boats attempting to reach the invasion forces that we ought to see one an hour on the average.

The first submarine sighted was fully surfaced. There were about eight German sailors on deck "running like hell to man the guns."

Straddled

Depth-charges straddled the submarine perfectly. "It seemed to jump into the air and explode," said Flying-Officer Moore.

"One of the crew said 'Let's get two submarines.' I told him to be patient. Almost immediately the navigator, who was adjusting his bomb-sight, shouted that there was another U-boat ahead.

"It was a smaller one and also fully surfaced. It made no attempt to avoid a fight. It put up a flak barrage in the shape of a fan. We flew straight through the flak and got another perfect straddle.

The D.F.C.s for this action were awarded to a wireless operator-air gunner, Warrant-Officer W. P. Foster, of Ontario, and the navigator, Warrant-Officer (now Pilot-Officer) T. J. McDowell, of 5, Nursay-avenue, Kilmarnock, Ayrshire. The D.F.M. was won by Sergeant J. Hamer, also a wireless operator-air gunner, who comes from King Harold-road, Shrub End, Colchester.

Russians Storm Big Vistula Stronghold

TROOPS of the First Ukrainian front, having forced the River Vistula in the area of Sandomir, as a result of stubborn fighting have advanced up to 30 miles, extended the captured bridgehead on the western bank of the Vistula to a front of 74 miles wide, and yesterday captured by storm the town of Sandomir, an important stronghold of the German derences on the left bank of the Vistula.

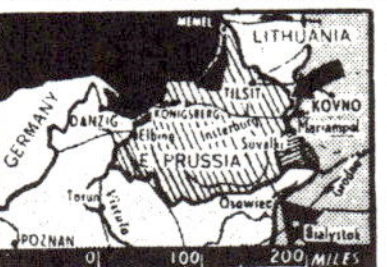

This was announced last night by Marshal Stalin in an Order of the Day to Marshal Koniev.

The Order mentions 21 infantry generals, six artillery generals, six tank generals, six Air Force generals, two generals of Signals, and two generals of sappers.

It ordered a salute of 20 salvoes from 224 guns at 11 p.m. last night, Moscow time.

Although there is as yet no news of an actual move by Red troops over the frontier of East Prussia the Germans are already dying on their own soil as the Russians attack along the Sesupe River line.

Frontier forts are under bombardment, but the Germans are fighting fanatically for every yard of ground before the full tide of the Soviet offensive.

Among the retreating enemy are remnants of the crack S.S. tank division "Greater Germany," which lost 100 tanks in a day.

Road to Koenigsberg

The path to the Insterburg Gap, the shortest and most convenient route to Königsberg, is opening up despite desperate resistance by picked German storm troops.

Big battles are going on in four other vital sectors of the front—on the approaches to the Tallinn-Riga line west of Lake Pskov, around Siauliai, before Warsaw, and across the Vistula 120 miles south of the Polish capital.

Huge armoured and infantry forces are meeting, but the Red Army is everywhere holding its ground or steadily advancing

The Wehrmacht is throwing in everything available, but indications are that the Red Army is on the eve of inflicting some of the most telling blows on German military power since the war began.—*Reuter*.

MAQUIS STORM A GARRISON

550 Germans Give In

GENEVA, Friday.—A communiqué issued by General Koenig to-day says that the French Forces of the Interior are waging open war in the Creuse Department. They surrounded the capital of the department, Gueret—100 miles south of Orleans and 75 west of Vichy—and forced the German garrison, 550 strong, to surrender.

The *Neue Zürcher Nachrichten* states that the resistance of the Wehrmacht in Upper Savoy can be said to be broken. The Maquis is completely controlling the region between the cantons of Valais and Geneva, and also between Mount Saleve—close to Geneva—and the Rhone.

The Maquis are making a strenuous effort to seize the Alpine road passes in the Grenoble region, from which Allied tanks advancing from the South would be able to overrun the Lyons region.—*Reuter*.

Two-way Drive for Toulon

FALL 'EXPECTED SOON'

THE Riviera invasion continues to go well. Allied reports last night stated that advancing spearheads were closing in on Toulon. Algiers radio said fighting was going on in the neighbourhood of the great naval base and on the airfield at Cannes.

Berlin stated that "the enemy is trying to extend his hold on the coastal zone by making new landings on both sides of Toulon."

"Fall of Toulon is expected soon," declared a Reuter correspondent, who described the pace of the Allied advance as sensational.

Sertorius, German military commentator, declared: "Enemy tanks have been landed on a large scale, mainly on the western sector roughly from St. Raphael to the Hyères Bay."

The drive for Toulon is along two main roads—along the coast through Hyères and inland through Cuers to the north-east.

On the eastern flank the Germans speak of Allied troops pressing northward from Cannes.

In the centre the advance has reached a depth of 25 miles. The beachhead includes more than 65 miles of main Riviera railways.

RESISTANCE IS CRUMBLING

From EDWIN TETLOW,

GENERAL WILSON'S H.Q., Friday.

THE Riviera invasion has turned out to be one of the most successful Allied operations of its kind since the war began.

Our assault force went through the "impregnable" wall of the European fortress like a sword piercing butter. The German defenders—or more accurately the ersatz Germans scraped up from

BACK PAGE—Col. FOUR

LATEST

'FINAL NAZI CATASTROPHE' —EISENHOWER

General Eisenhower, who visited advanced lines in Normandy, predicted "final catastrophe for the Germans" at Press conference.

RUSSIANS TRAP THREE DIVISIONS

Three German divisions encircled north of Sandomir, says Russian communiqué. Big tank attack repelled east of Praga, the Warsaw suburb.

'More Troops in Florence Area'

Praegner, the German military correspondent, said last night that both the Americans and British troops are being reinforced in Italy "in a big way," especially with artillery and tanks.

The concentration of new forces is most notable in the Florence area.—*Reuter*.

"Eighth" over the Arno.—BACK Page.

The Daily Sketch — NEWS AND PICTURES
No. 11,003 ★★ MONDAY, AUGUST 21, 1944 ONE PENNY

ALLIES EXTEND BRIDGEHEAD BEYOND SEINE

Our Tanks Across, Says Berlin | Patrols 6 Miles From Paris

GENERAL PATTON'S American forces have crossed the Seine about 30 miles north-west of Paris, between Vernon and Mantes, and have made important new advances west and south-east of the capital.

Berlin admitted the crossings of the river in a radio announcement yesterday, and last night the High Command said the Americans had brought up reinforcements "to extend the bridgehead on the east bank."

Strong airborne forces landed on the far side of the Seine and were joined by tanks which crossed the river, the announcement added.

Now the Americans are ranging for miles along the west bank, in an area where the Germans were frantically massing barges, some capable of carrying 500 men and originally intended for invasion of England, to ferry across the river the forces threatened by encirclement.

Between Vernon and the sea, however, the enemy have managed to cross the Seine in considerable numbers. They are using any sort of craft they can lay hands on. At one point men were seen swimming across.

De Gaulle Meets Eisenhower

Many of these men, and others taking cover in a forest south-west of Rouen, were caught yesterday by about 60 Marauders, who rained fragmentation bombs on them. Fires and explosions were seen in the forest area.

Indication of the imminent liberation of Paris was given in an official announcement last night that General de Gaulle and General Koenig, Commander-in-Chief of the French Forces of the Interior, yesterday visited the Supreme Commander's H.Q. (Full story is on Back Page).

Latest news of the threat to Paris is that the Americans are in the neighbourhood of Versailles, only six miles from the city boundary, cables Seaghan Maynes, Reuter correspondent.

At the same time the right wing is swinging round Paris in a great by-passing movement, and threatening the road centres controlling the main routes to the Channel ports, the German frontier, Switzerland and Southern France.

Patrols operating to the south-east are near Melun and Fontainebleau, twin road junctions 21 and 26 miles from Paris, where most of the strategic highways link up.

Turn to Back Page, Column 3

5-Abreast Tank Bid To Escape

From RICHARD McMILLAN, B.U.P. War Correspondent Beyond Trun

TRAPPED Nazi tanks made a last bid to break out of the box yesterday.

They advanced five abreast from the Forest of Gouffern and raced over the high ground to the highway between Trun and Chambois.

Some of the tanks succeeded in cutting the road, but they were caught by our fire from three sides and knocked out.

The remainder of the attackers were forced back into the bag, which is now closely sealed again.

Panzer Losses

The road from Trun to Vimoutiers is one of the most grisly sights of the battlefield. It is jammed tight with broken transport and corpses of horses.

First reports show that the Germans have already lost 500 tanks in the Battle of the Gap. At the present rate of destruction the total losses may reach between 700 and 1,000.

Another B.U.P. correspondent cabled:

Germans are still trying to filter in twos and threes through the Allied forces enclosing the box.

Unable To Surrender

Many are surrendering, but surrender itself is not easy.

Any German who wants to give in has to run the gauntlet of heavy fire before he can give himself up.

There is still known to be one group of Germans at the edge of the box who want to surrender, but are unwilling to move from their present positions because of the fire they would have to face to reach our lines.

They sent an emissary asking for an escort; but that would have meant virtually stopping the battle and allowing hundreds of other Germans to make their way out.

"Send flame-throwers and smoke them out," was the reply of a Canadian officer. "If they want to surrender they can come in themselves. We'll let them come in, but we won't go for them."

Eight German trucks, loaded with ammunition and petrol, suddenly rolled into Trun yesterday and began unloading, apparently unaware that the place was in Allied hands.

We let the Germans unload and then they were taken prisoner.

AIR BLOWS CREATE JIGSAW

From LAWRENCE FAIRHALL, Kemsley Newspapers Correspondent With R.A.F. in France

WHAT the Allied air forces are doing to-day can best be described as the destruction of an army from the air.

Clouds of dense black smoke are rising from the thousands of wrecked transport and tanks belonging to German divisions caught like rats when they attempted to run the gauntlet of Allied air power towards the Seine.

The roads leading from Trun to Vimoutiers are littered with a crazy jigsaw pattern of smashed enemy trucks, horse-drawn vehicles, motor-cycles, staff cars and tanks.

It is a terrible and ghastly experience of the effectiveness of air power.

Since three o'clock on Thursday afternoon when the full weight of this air blitz hit the Germans, nearly 5,000 transports and more than 400 tanks have been destroyed or damaged.

By 8 o'clock yesterday evening the day's bag was nearly 200 transport and 45 tanks destroyed or damaged in spite of the unfavourable weather conditions.

Most of the destruction was done when tanks, trying to break out of the box, were caught "flat-footed" by rocket-firing Typhoons.

Careered All Over Place

Prisoners report that as the Allied planes stepped up their attacks, so did the confusion among their officers and comrades caught in the gap become greater.

Commanders lost touch with their units, which careered all over the place aimlessly.

Every heavy vehicle which could move was towing something. Every truck, lorry and tank had sentries sitting on their mudguards or turrets to give warning of air attack.

As in the air during the battle of Britain, it is the Spitfires which are taking the heaviest toll of the enemy on the ground.

Three-quarters of the enemy motor transport destroyed has fallen to Spitfire pilots.

On occasions they have even deprived the rocket Typhoons of their prey, the tanks, by scoring flamers with cannon fire.

Lieut.-General Patton, who always packs a couple of pistols in his belt, producing a new weapon acquired since his arrival in France to show to Lieut.-General Omar Bradley, who commands the 12th Army Corps.

Toulon Sea-Air Blitz As French Near Port

From AUBREY HAMMOND, 'Daily Sketch' Correspondent at Mediterranean G.H.Q.

FRENCH armour and infantry were last night closing in on Toulon, the great naval base, following a devastating sea-air bombardment.

The invasion fleet poured shells into the port's defences, while Marauders and Thunderbolts struck 15 times within a few hours to paralyse the shore batteries.

Up to noon fighters had destroyed 36 motor transports, 12 railway cars, two locomotives and two barges in the area.

The triumphant advance of the Seventh Army continues and official announcements record nothing but "success and further progress." Prisoners now number more than 12,000.

Advancing ten miles further in their drive to the west and north-west, Allied forces have crossed the Durance river at several points, and by reaching the outskirts of the city of Aix, 15 miles north of Marseilles, they look like constituting a serious threat to that great port.

An advance of several miles has also been made south-west from St. Maximin.

4,285 Sorties Flown

Lieut. - General Devers, Deputy Supreme Commander; Lieut.-General Eaker, M.A.A.F. Commander; and Major-General Cannon, Commanding the First Tactical Air Force, have made a first-hand air survey.

An indication of the Allied air supremacy in this theatre can be gauged by the fact that during every minute of H-Day, from midnight to midnight, three of our planes were crossing into enemy territory.

An all-time record for the theatre of 4,285 sorties were flown by M.A.A.F. aircraft.

★ ★ ★

Algiers radio last night said that the Allies had captured Peyrolles, on the Durance, 36 miles north of Marseilles, and that a French column were five miles from Toulon.

H-Day "Lost" Paratroops Are Fighting Back—Page 3

TIMELY WORDS OF FAITH

By works a man is justified, and not by faith only. . . . For as the body without the spirit is dead, so faith without works is dead also.

James, 2, 24-26.

WEDNESDAY, AUGUST 23, 1944

Evening Standard
37,424 BLACK-OUT 9.37 p.m.—6.29 a.m. MOON rises 11.30 a.m., sets 11.8 p.m. ONE PENNY
FINAL NIGHT EXTRA ●

THE PEOPLE OF PARIS HAVE FREED THEIR CITY

Fifty Thousand Patriots and Thousands of Unarmed Citizens Arose—And the Men of Vichy Fled

THE ILE DE LA CITE BECAME FORTRESS

The liberation of Paris by French patriots was announced in a communique from General de Gaulle's Headquarters to-day. It followed a statement from the Headquarters of General Koenig, Commander of the French Forces in France, saying:

"ON SATURDAY, AUGUST 19, IN THE MORNING, THE NATIONAL COUNCIL OF RESISTANCE AND PARIS COMMITTEE OF LIBERATION, IN AGREEMENT WITH THE NATIONAL DELEGATE AND REPRESENTATIVE OF THE PROVISIONAL GOVERNMENT OF THE FRENCH REPUBLIC, ORDERED A GENERAL INSURRECTION IN PARIS AND THE PARIS REGION.

"The F.F.I., to the strength of 50,000 armed men, and supported by several hundred thousand unarmed patriots, immediately went into action.

"The Paris police, who were already on strike, took possession of the police prefecture and turned the Ile de

la Cite (an island in the middle of the Seine) into a fortress, against which the German attacks broke.

"Yesterday, after four days' fighting, the enemy had been defeated everywhere.

"The patriots occupied all the public buildings.

"Vichy representatives were arrested or had fled.

"So the people of Paris played a major part in the liberation of their capital."

The Ile de la Cite is situated in the heart of Paris. The cathedral of Notre Dame and the Palais de Justice are situated on the island, which is joined by a bridge, to the Ile de St. Louis.

It is understood that the first news came in a broadcast from a radio transmitter under the control of the F.F.I., which appears to be situated either in Paris or very near the city.

Paris has been in German hands since 7 a.m. on June 14, 1940, when German motorised units moved in

(Continued on Back Page, Col. One)

50,000 PRISONERS

The Falaise pocket has now yielded between 40,000 and 50,000 prisoners to the Allied armies which trapped the German Seventh Army in it ten days ago, cables Ross Munro, Reuter and Canadian Press war correspondent.

The Canadian Army have captured 18,000 prisoners since their first operation launched down the Falaise road on August 8.

It is expected that the total will reach 25,000 when all are counted.

Swiss Break With Vichy

Swiss radio announces that the Swiss Government have withdrawn their diplomatic representation from Vichy, following a statement by Marshal Petain that he has been compelled by violence to leave Vichy, and is, therefore, no longer effective Chief of the French State.

The people of Belfort, French fortress town near the Swiss-German frontier, greeted Laval with whistles and shouts of "A bas Laval" and with curses when he returned there last night, said Reuter's correspondent, cabling from the Swiss Frontier to-day.

CHURCHILL AND BADOGLIO CONFER

Mr. Churchill conferred with the Italian Premier Bonomi and Marshal Badoglio yesterday, says Associated Press from Rome.

Straits Sun After "German Weather"

It was warm and fine in the Straits of Dover to-day, with a temperature of 72 deg. in the shade at noon. There was a gusty, variable wind, which made the sea choppy.

The sky was cloudy, but there was a good deal of sunshine. Visibility across the Channel was restricted to a few miles by mist.

AND HERE IS TO-DAY'S GREAT NEWS OF

THE BATTLE OF FRANCE, 1944

This is the picture of France to-day as Allied armies sweep north, west, south and east. Advances are being made in all parts of the country.

General Maitland Wilson's army in the south are only 240 miles away from General Patton's vanguards striking 60 miles south-east of Paris.

A NEW ALLIED LANDING HAS BEEN REPORTED AT BORDEAUX, FOURTH BIGGEST CITY IN FRANCE, AND IN NORMANDY BRITISH AND CANADIANS HAVE ADVANCED ANOTHER 17 MILES.

HERE ARE THE SPEARHEADS POINTING AT THE CRUMBLING HEART OF THE GERMAN ARMY.

NOW IN FULL PURSUIT

From LESLIE RANDALL
Evening Standard War Reporter

WITH THE SECOND ARMY, Wednesday.

The Canadians have had a particularly good day, and have taken 7000 prisoners.

The Germans made a feeble effort to hold Lisieux, but found it was useless, and pulled out.

There is now only one line on which they can possibly make any sort of a stand before they reach the Seine.

That is the line of the river Risle, and we do not expect that it will give us much difficulty.

The advance along the coast was made by the Dutch and the Belgians.

Deauville fell into their hands

(Continued on Back Page, Col. Four)

1—Grenoble Reached

Grenoble, city of 100,000 people in the French Alps, commanding the important mountain passes of Eastern France, has been reached by American troops thrusting up from the Riviera.

The implications of the advance are tremendous. Grenoble is only 25 miles from the Maquis-held Savoy province and only 80 miles from the Swiss border.

Meanwhile Lyons, the Manchester of France, is only 34 miles away from American spearheads in the heart of the Rhone Valley industrial belt.

The reaching of Grenoble was announced in to-day's Allied communiqué, which said that American troops of the Seventh Army had made a swift advance northwards of 140 miles in eight days.

Algiers Radio says French and Allied reconnaissance units have reached the gates of Avignon.

Fighting is going on in the inner suburbs of Marseilles.

2—North: 17 Miles On

Advances up to 17 miles were made yesterday, followed by a steady surge forward to the Seine by the entire Allied front. It was the best day of the whole Normandy campaign.

The longest British advance was due west of Gace, where they had already turned their line at the River Touques, which the Germans had hoped to hold.

British tanks covered 17 miles and swept into L'Aigle, on the River Risle, against only spasmodic opposition, says British United Press correspondent, Edward Beattie.

Correspondents at Supreme Headquarters say the Germans are attempting an "inland Dunkirk" across the Seine to save what they can out of the wreck.

Air observation has disclosed that the German retreat is taking on all the characteristics of a rout, with more confusion than has yet been seen.

3—'Bordeaux Landing'

The Allies are reported to have made another landing in France—in the Bordeaux area, in the south-east.

This announcement was made at 4 a.m. to-day by the French military authorities at Hendaye.

Messages received at Irun, Spain, say the landing was made just south-west of Bordeaux, near Arcachon.

Arcachon is 35 miles from Bordeaux.

There has been no official confirmation of the landing yet.

4—Sens: Railway Cut

General Patton's spearheads, which have reached Sens, have cut the main Paris-Marseilles railway.

Behind this vanguard General Patton's columns are coming in from Orleans, liberating towns and villages every hour in a great fanning movement outflanking Paris, reports British United Press correspondent, Virgil Pinkley.

With Sens in their hands, the Allies can now strike swiftly to the east on Troyes, and then Nancy, on the roads to Metz, 150 miles away.

THE WEATHER
Today: Showers, ending before noon; later clearing and cooler
Temperatures Yesterday: Max., 86; Min., 69
Detailed Report on Page 21

NEW YORK Herald Tribune

LATE CITY EDITION

VOL. CIV No. 35,711

THURSDAY, AUGUST 24, 1944

THREE - CENTS In New York City

Romania Joins Allies, Turns Guns on Germans; Paris Frees Itself, U.S.-French Troops Sent In; Marseille and Grenoble Fall, Nazi Rout Grows

Paris People FreeOwnCity In4-Day Fight

Rise on Call of Resistance Chiefs, Drive Off Nazis and Vichy's Officials

Prefecture of Police Turned Into a Fort

Battles in Rue de Rivoli, at Bastille, Concorde; Koenig Expected Today

By Eric Hawkins
From the Herald Tribune Bureau
Copyright, 1944, New York Tribune Inc.

LONDON, Aug. 23.—Paris has been freed by its own people after four days' fighting in which several hundred thousand unarmed citizens and 50,000 armed men of the resistance forces routed the Nazi garrison troops and occupied the city's principal buildings. It is the first Allied continental capital to be wrested from the Germans.

Announcing the liberation of the city after fifty months of German occupation and tyranny, a special communique issued today by General Joseph Pierre Koenig, commander of the French Forces of the Interior and newly appointed military governor of Paris, said the Germans were "defeated everywhere" in fighting which began last Saturday.

The great mass of Paris patriots went into action, the communique said, when a general insurrection in the capital and the Paris region was ordered by the resistance leaders in France, in agreement with a representative of General Charles de Gaulle's provisional government.

Police Seize Prefecture

The Paris police, who had been on strike for nearly a week, took possession of the Prefecture of Police on the Ile de la Cite, which was transformed into a fortress against which German attacks broke, while other patriot forces seized all public buildings, according to the communique, which added that representatives of the Vichy regime in Paris either fled or were arrested.

With their bridgehead over the Seine near Mantes, American forces were thirty miles west of the capital, while to the southeast they were broadening their sweep as they pressed on, it was stated. It was thought probable that the territory overrun by General George S. Patton's fast moving forces extended to the outer environs of Paris at points north of Corbeil.

The news of the freeing of Paris was first broadcast by a radio station near Paris which presumably had been seized by the patriots. This was followed by a triumphant broadcast from Algiers accompanied by "La Marseillaise" and the announcement that gun salvos, church bells and street parades were to celebrate the event during the day.

Koenig's Communique

General Koenig's communique followed early this afternoon.

It said:

"On Saturday Aug. 19 in the morning the National Council of the Resistance and Paris Committee of Liberation, in agreement with the national delegates and representatives of the provisional government of the French Repub-

(Continued on page 4, column 2)

Story From Paris: Nazis Asked Truce To Withdraw Army

Patriots' Chief Rushes to Bradley With the News; He Orders Troops In

By Charles Collingwood
Columbia Broadcasting System Correspondent

PARIS, Aug. 23 (By Radio via London).—The 2d French Armored Division entered Paris today after the Parisians rose as one man to beat down the motley, terrified German troops who had garrisoned the city.

It was the people of Paris who won back their city. It all happened with fantastic suddenness.

The American Army was occupied with the drive through Evreux to the mouth of the Seine, after which it was planned to invest Paris.

Yesterday a Frenchman burst into Lieutenant General Omar N. Bradley's headquarters. He was the chief of the Forces of the Interior in Paris, and he had a staggering, incredible story to tell.

He said he had concluded an armistice with the German forces in Paris. The people of Paris had

(Continued on page 4, column 5)

Nazi Admiral Yields French Hospital to American Patient

Sends Him Out in Auto to Get U. S. Troops Before Partisans Can Arrive

By Homer Bigart
By Wireless to the Herald Tribune
Copyright, 1944, New York Tribune Inc.

AIX-EN-PROVENCE, France, Aug. 22 (delayed).—Rear Admiral Karl Eyerich entered a private room of the German marine hospital near here at 3 p. m. Sunday and gravely laid his sword on a cot where a captured radio operator-gunner of an American bomber crew was recuperating from a broken leg.

Although the Americans had not yet captured Aix, Admiral Eyerich said he feared French Partisans would break into the hospital and harm 300 German patients and his staff of seven doctors and twenty-eight nurses.

"I yield my command," the admiral said, "but on one condition. You must go out and find Americans and bring them here quickly."

The sergeant, a tall, slight youth from Cleveland, nodded weakly.

(Continued on page 8, column 2)

French Enter Marseille in Circling Move

Great Port Is Captured With Little Resistance; Snipers Are Mopped Up

Fresh Gains Made In Toulon Fighting

Patch's Army in 100-Mile Dash, Is Only 230 Miles From Forces at Sens

By Homer Bigart
By Wireless to the Herald Tribune
Copyright, 1944, New York Tribune Inc.

MARSEILLE, France, Aug. 23.—French troops entered Marseille in triumph this morning, receiving from France's greatest port and second city a welcome that outthundered the heavy guns of the German garrison still holding out in Fort St. Nicolas.

Fewer than 3,000 Germans were believed to be besieged in the ancient fort commanding the entrance to Vieux-Port, but there were scattered groups of snipers in other parts of the city and it was not until 7:32 that French tanks rumbled down the famed Rue Cannebiere.

Partisans had already mopped up the district around the Palais Longchamp and the zoological garden, and had seized the prefecture, releasing scores of political prisoners. They had rounded up several hundred Germans. I saw four Partisans leading forty Germans at rifle-point down a narrow alley, while thousands of spectators whistled and hooted.

Americans Reach Grenoble

By Russell Hill
By Wireless to the Herald Tribune
Copyright, 1944, New York Tribune Inc.

ROME, Aug. 23.—General Jean de Lattre de Tassigny's French corps, tasting at last the sweet fruits of victory for which they have waited, hoped, prepared and bled for four years, entered Marseille as liberators today.

This great news followed the announcement earlier in the day that a column of American armored forces in a sensational 100-mile drive north through the Alpes de Provence had reached Grenoble, for two years the greatest center of the French resistance move-

(Continued on page 2, column 5)

Americans Drive On East For Germany

Push From Sens Opposed by Planes Only, Border Now 150 Miles Away

Annihilation Battle Rages in Normandy

Evreux Seized in Thrust From South; 3d Army Fighting South of Paris

By The Associated Press

SUPREME HEADQUARTERS, Allied Expeditionary Force, Aug. 23.—American armor hammered out fresh gains south and southeast of Paris today, while to the northwest of the capital—now fully in control of French patriots—Americans and Canadians claimed a tightening stranglehold on remnants of the German army still below the River Seine.

Allied fighters and fighter bombers harried the Germans' frantic efforts to withdraw across the river by any possible means.

The latest advance south of Paris saw armored reconnaissance units drive more than fifteen miles east of Sens, while others passed through Corbeil and Melun, and still others gained positions between Orleans and Sens.

Evreux Is Captured

Chief prize in the drive on the lower reaches of the Seine was Evreux, which the Americans freed, while a parallel American advance neared Conches, farther west. Resistance everywhere was light, except where the Germans slowed the Canadian advance in the forty-five-by-thirty-mile pocket by blocking further bridgeheads across the Touques River.

[A Belgian communique said Belgian troops fighting beside the Allies had advanced twelve miles along the Channel coast, overcoming stiff resistance as they fanned out above Deauville, and inflicted heavy losses on the Germans.]

"The main battle for France is already over," reported Harold Boyle, Associated Press correspondent, who watched American tanks drive fifteen miles east of Sens to within 150 miles of the German border with no sign that the Germans were rallying.

Truckloads of prisoners streamed back in the wake of the American advance, but there was not a single smoldering enemy vehicle to indicate the enemy had put up a determined fight, said his dispatch, datelined "En Route to Berlin."

Only swarms of German war-

(Continued on page 2, column 3)

A British Haul of Prisoners From the Normandy Pocket

These Germans were captured in the Falaise-Argentan area by British troops during the liquidation of the pocket in which a large portion of the German 7th Army was cut to pieces by the Allies

Associated Press wirephoto from Signal Corps radio

Aranha Forced Out in Brazil by Pro-Argentines

Army Officers' Pressure on President Vargas Blamed; Called Severe Blow to U.S.

By Joseph Newman
From the Herald Tribune Bureau
Copyright, 1944, New York Tribune Inc.

BUENOS AIRES, Aug. 23.—Oswaldo Aranha has been forced to resign as Foreign Minister of Brazil by a group of army officers who opposed his foreign policy on the ground that it established too close relations with the United States and blocked Brazilian recognition of the Argentine government, according to well informed persons who have arrived here from Rio de Janeiro.

They reported that on Aug. 11 Aranha was named vice-president of the Society of Friends of America, an organization for the promotion of closer relations between Brazil and the other American countries, especially the United States. The following day the headquarters of the society, of which Jefferson Caffery, American Ambassador to Brazil, is honorary president, were closed by order of

(Continued on page 16, column 1)

Security Plan Gains in Capital; Hull Sees Dulles for 2½ Hours

Roosevelt Tells Big-Three Conferees of Need for Early Agreement; Hull to Meet Senate Group; Dewey Representative Reports 'Progress'

By Bert Andrews

WASHINGTON, Aug. 23.—The prospects of bi-partisan cooperation on the issue of an international security organization were enhanced today by a host of developments in which the on-the-scenes role of President Roosevelt was matched in importance by the proxy representation of Governor Thomas E. Dewey, Republican Presidential candidate.

As one important move in the effort to clear the way for a political campaign minus bitter cleavage over foreign policy, it was learned tonight that Cordell Hull, Secretary of State, had invited the bi-partisan group of Foreign Relations Committee Senators to confer with him at 10 a. m. Friday so he can tell them of the proceedings up to date of the "Big Three" conference at Dumbarton Oaks.

This action, which was also designed to smooth the path for eventual Senate acceptance of the final distillation of the views of the United States, Russia and Great Britain, and of China after China is called in, for the China-Britain-United States phase of these discussions, came as the climax of the following happenings:

1. President Roosevelt met with the forty-two delegates to Dumbarton Oaks and urged upon them the importance of an early agree-

(Continued on page 13, column 1)

Two Red Armies Drive 60 Miles Into Romania

Vaslui and 2 Bessarabian Bastions Fall; Konev's Men Take Dembica in Poland

By The Associated Press

LONDON, Aug. 24 (Thursday).—The Soviet offensive that knocked Romania out of the war roared through its fourth day yesterday, capturing Vaslui, 140 miles northeast of the Ploesti oil center; the two big Bessarabian bastions of Tighina and Cetatea-Alba, on the west bank of the Dnestr, and more than 400 other towns.

Disregarding developments on the political front, the 2d and 3d Ukrainian Armies deepened to as much as sixty miles the holes they have ripped in the German-Romanian defenses and advanced to within 167 miles of Bucharest.

Romania still was garrisoned

(Continued on page 2, column 3)

King Michael Breaks Ties With Hitler

Soviet-American-British Armistice Accepted, He Announces Over Radio

Will Fight Hungary For Transylvania

Moscow Asserts Germans Are Shooting Down Retreating Romanians

By The Associated Press

LONDON, Aug. 24 (Thursday).—Romania announced last night that she was switching from the Axis to the Allied side in the war, and a subsequent Soviet communique reported that shooting had broken out between retreating Romanian and Nazi soldiers on the eastern front.

Acceptance of armistice terms offered by the Soviet Union, Great Britain and the United States was announced in a proclamation broadcast from Bucharest.

The early morning broadcast Russian communique told of clashes on Romanian soil between the Romanians, ordered by King Michael to cease hostilities against the Red Army, and the Germans. Romanian prisoners were quoted as saying that the Germans were firing on the Romanians and blocking their withdrawal.

"A large number of Romanian officers and men have thus been killed," said the communique, "in armed clashes between the retreating Romanian detachments and German frontier detachments in several places."

The King's Proclamation

A proclamation by twenty-two-year-old King Michael, read over the Bucharest radio, said all hostilities against the Red Army, as well as Romania's state of war with Britain and America, would cease "from this moment." Russian armies were stabbing into Romania to within 167 miles of Bucharest and threatening the Ploesti oil fields as the announcement went on the air.

The text of the King's proclamation, as recorded by the British Ministry of Information, follows:

"Romanians! In the difficult hour of our country I have decided for the salvation of the fatherland on immediate cessation of hostilities with the United Nations, and I call upon the government of the national union to fulfill the determined will of the country, to conclude peace with the United Nations.

"Romania has accepted armistice terms offered by the Soviet Union, Great Britain and the United States.

"From this moment all hostilities against Soviet armies and the state of war with Great Britain and the United States will cease.

"The United Nations have guaranteed the independence of Romania.

Orders the Army to Fight

"Any one who opposes the decision we have taken and who takes justice in his own hands is an enemy of our nation. I order the army and the whole nation to fight with all means and at the cost of any sacrifice against him.

"All Romanians must rally around the throne and the government; he who does not assist the government and resists the will of the nation is a traitor to the country.

"The United Nations have recognized the injustice of the dictate of Vienna under which Transylvania was torn from us.

"At the side of the Allied army and with their help we will cross the frontiers unjustly imposed upon us at Vienna."

There was no immediate official confirmation of the royal procla-

Morgan and Kuhn, Loeb Named With 47 Railroads in Trust Suit

From the Herald Tribune Bureau

WASHINGTON, Aug. 23.—Collusive and illegal actions, some dating since 1932, to fix rates and retard improvement of service and equipment was charged today by the Department of Justice in an anti-trust law suit against the Association of American Railroads, forty-seven Western carriers and their chief executives, and the New York banking houses of J. P. Morgan & Co., Inc., and Kuhn, Loeb & Co. Also named as defendants were the officers and directors of the American Railroad Association, the Western Association of Railway Executives and thirty-one other individuals.

Attorney General Francis Biddle, now on the west coast, disclosed through his office here that the civil complaint under the Sherman anti-trust act, said to be one of the largest anti-trust suits in history, had been filed against the railroads in the United States District Court in Lincoln, Neb. He said that the act applied to railroads despite the fact that many aspects of their business are subject to regulation by the Interstate Commerce Commission.

"The Supreme Court has held that 'the commission has no power to enforce the Sherman act as such,'" said the Attorney General, who had made a number of statements recently that this and other suits would be filed. "Consequently, it is the duty of the Department of Justice to take action against these practices which so vitally affect the people of the Western part of the United States and the national economy as a whole."

Wendell Berge, Assistant Attorney General, explained that some of the Western railroads had wanted to lower rates and install new services but had been dissuaded by the association, which

(Continued on page 16, column 1)

U. S. Plane Falls Afire, Kills 54, 35 of Them Children, in England

By The Associated Press

LONDON, Aug. 23.—Fifty-four persons, including thirty-five children, all under five, were killed today when a flaming American bomber plunged into a church school infants' department in the quiet Lancashire village of Freckleton.

It was feared thirty or forty other persons may have been trapped in the ruins of a snack bar across the street. None had been reached by rescue parties when darkness fell.

Eight American soldiers were among those killed, including three members of the plane's crew. The death toll was expected to reach seventy-five in Britain's worst accident of the kind.

The United States Strategic Air Force announced that the bomber, a Liberator, crashed after it was caught in a sudden storm. The pilot was among the three crewmen killed. Other members of the crew were injured. Identification of these casualties was withheld.

Another Liberator, accompanying the plane, continued on a local flight.

The plane smashed through the top of the school building, where forty-one children under five, many of them refugees from robot-bomb attacks, were assembled. It

(Continued on page 10, column 1)

News on Inside Pages

Office Help

The Daily Telegraph

and Morning Post

No. 27,832 LONDON, SATURDAY, AUGUST 26, 1944 Printed in LONDON and MANCHESTER PRICE 1½d.

LONDON LATE EDTN.

Gen. de GAULLE ENTERS LIBERATED PARIS

LAST GERMANS SURRENDER AFTER ULTIMATUM

ALLIED TANKS IN DAY OF STREET FIGHTING

GREAT FORCE REPORTED ON WAY TO CITY

The remaining Germans in Paris surrendered last evening after Gen. Leclerc, commander of the French Second Armoured Division, had sent their commander an ultimatum telling him to cease resistance, which had become useless.

Gen. de Gaulle entered the liberated city at 7 p.m. and was received at the Prefecture of Police and at the Hotel de Ville, the Town Hall, by the new Prefect. In a brief speech he said: "I wish simply and from the bottom of my heart to say to you, 'Vive Paris.'"

These announcements were broadcast from Paris after a day of fighting in the city against scattered points of German resistance.

In these operations French Forces of the Interior were joined by tanks and infantry of Gen. Leclerc's force, advance units of which entered Paris late on Thursday night.

Terms of surrender were laid down at a meeting at the Montparnasse station between Gen. Leclerc and the German commander.

Detailing their provisions, the Paris broadcast said: "The order will be given to German commanders to cease fire and hoist the white flag. Weapons will be collected and surrendered intact, and men will be assembled without weapons at specified points until new orders are given."

The terms also provided that any German who did not lay down his arms would not be covered by the laws of war and would be treated as a franc-tireur.

When captured German officers were led from the Hotel de Ville, added the radio, the police had to prevent a crowd from lynching them.

REJOICINGS AMID GUNFIRE

This swift climax came after a day during which exultant Parisians sang and danced in beflagged streets to the accompaniment of shelling and machine-gun fire as enemy points of resistance were being reduced.

From planes that flew over Paris and its environs yesterday came reports that a great force of American tanks and troops was converging on the city.

"The roads to Paris," said one observer, "are flooded with a mighty force. I saw convoys stretching unbroken over many miles. It was a solid mass of guns and tanks, with armoured cars out in front.

"As I got near Paris some of the forces were deploying into the woods. The towns and villages through which this immense armament is passing are lined with French people cheering."

EYE-WITNESS ACCOUNT OF ENTRY INTO PARIS

From PETER LAWLESS,
***Daily Telegraph* Special Correspondent**

PARIS, Friday.

After a day and a night of heavy fighting the Second French Armoured Division entered Paris during the night, and Gen. Leclerc with his headquarters tanks entered by the Porte D'Orleans at 9.55 a.m.

From Sceaux to the heart of the town the streets were lined and progress was frequently interrupted by the wildly enthusiastic crowds, whose flower missiles were at times dangerous.

There was a sensational break in the tumultuous scene when firing was opened from a top floor window in the Boulevard Raspail and grenades were thrown. Return fire was immediately opened from tanks, armoured cars and by the French Forces of the Interior, who were everywhere in evidence.

Never can so many people have got out of jeeps so quickly to take inglorious cover on the street—and a jeep is not easy to get out of.

TRIUMPHANT DRIVE
City's Gratitude

The pandemonium soon died away, the crowd miraculously reappeared and the triumphant procession was continued to the Gare Montparnasse, where we are at present halted in a vast sea of cheering, singing French people.

Their reiterated phrase was "merci, merci," and if there was ever any doubt as to the nature of the Allied welcome it was very quickly dispelled, for never was there a more spontaneous, profounder demonstration of gratitude than I have experienced on the exhausting drive.

Every pause has been filled with hand-shaking and wholesale embracing by both sexes, and even the protection of a pipe does not save one's face from contact with bearded garlic.

MOTOR-CYCLIST FIRST
Meeting With F.F.I.

The first soldier to enter the town was a motor-cyclist on reconnaissance. He got in last night at 21 hours and met members of F.F.I. They put him on top of a car and conducted him in triumph to the mairie of the 14th Arrondissement.

F.F.I. and troops of the Second Armoured Division entered at several points to the south of the town and crossed the Pont Austerlitz and penetrated Boulogne-Billancourt and western suburbs. At 21.20 ten tanks made their way slowly through an enormous crowd up the Boulevarde Henri Quatre.

Before leaving the Germans carried out wholesale destruction. Amongst buildings destroyed are Le Grand Palais, Ministry of the Marine, factories and the railway at Nantgerre and Viaduct Nogent.

It is apparent that the armistice asked for by the Germans was not observed by either side. The difficulty of notifying irregular troops of F.F.I. and the natural foulness of the enemy were causes.

The Paris Press has been free since Sunday.

The last few days were a nightmare with Germans issuing from various points to spread carnage and destruction.

The Gare de l'Est, Austerlitz, Nord and Lyon were all German strongpoints, as also were the Grand Palais, Invalides, Concorde, Madeleine, Louvre, Chambre des Deputies. F.F.I. strongholds were Mairies of Arondissement.

STIFF OPPOSITION
Artillery Sent Up

The French division's advance started yesterday morning from south and south-west. It met stiff opposition and artillery in unexpected strength, so that artillery was rushed up. Fighting was particularly severe at Le Noble and Antony.

At Sceaux, where I spent the night on the road, strong resistance was met at cross-roads.

The morning paper Le Liberation carries the banner. "Is sont arrivés," and the messages of the King and President Roosevelt.

The bells of Notre Dame des Victoires rang for the first time since June 14, 1940. In a few minutes all the bells of Paris were ringing, with the sinister rumble of artillery in the background.

The grave deep notes of Notre Dame contrasted with the tinkling bells of the little églises de quartier, the tocsin of St. Germain Lauxerrol and St. Jullen le Pauvre.

All new chief officials have taken up posts during the last few days, but with assumed names.

The advance guard of the French division reached the centre of Paris before 10 o'clock and went to the Hotel de Ville. Officers immediately called at the Prefecture de la Seine.

There were still plenty of German snipers about, so that the first French officer to report to M. Serat, Prefect of Police, was accompanied by a detachment of French troops.

Having been leading shouts of "Vive la France," and singing the Marseillaise, and celebrating in my jeep the liberation of Paris, I have now received a message from a woman cyclist, who went to the Hotel Scribe for me, that that part of the town was not yet liberated.

As I write, with the population breathing on me and jogging my arm, the occasional clatter of hostile and Allied machine-gun and rifle fire is still heard. Paris for some days yet will be no place for relaxation.

Gen. de Gaulle is to announce the Republic from the Hotel de Ville. The paper L'Aube carries a capital cartoon of Hitler at a gaming table seeing Paris raked in by a croupier.

Every mother wants her child to be kissed, and the latest addition has just been firmly placed on my typewriter.

The Metro has not been working since Saturday. There is water and electricity but no coal.

Gen. Leclerc has sent tanks to the gardens of Luxembourg to clear the neighbourhood of the Senate. He is reported to have gone to the German commander asking him to surrender the town.

LAST ACT IN LIBERATION

RACE AGAINST FAMINE

Over the barricades flung across streets with world-famous names the Battle of Paris died out yesterday.

From the reports, confused and sometimes contradictory, the picture did not clear until the evening.

Then it emerged that the Germans, counter-attacking against the liberating patriots of the French Forces of the Interior, were still active in a number of areas and pockets in the city early in the day, aided by tanks and artillery.

But a vanguard of Gen. Leclerc's Fighting French regulars, racing against both the threat of the Germans and the rapidly-growing menace of famine, had entered the city early. By the evening a war reporter was able to broadcast: "The liberation of Paris is a fact."

There followed a stream of messages from the freed city, giving these highlights:

Prisoners.—Hundreds of German prisoners were marched through the streets of Paris to-day. There were 600 Germans who had held out in the Chamber of Deputies who surrendered to the F.F.I. and Allied forces.

Symbol.—Fighting French leaders burst through a German cordon to reach the Arc de Triomphe and lay a tricolour bouquet on the grave of France's unknown warrior, beneath the arch. Capt. Maurice Shuman, London spokesman of the Fighting French, said: As we entered Paris the tricolour bouquet was thrown into our car. We decided to place it on the grave of the unknown warrior.

"The Germans fired at us," said Capt. Shuman. "I saw a French soldier fall to the pavement, and a French nurse carrying the flag of the Red Cross run out to help him. The Germans fired and killed the nurse."

DANCING WITH JOY
Amid the Fighting

Under Fire.—"The French are dancing with joy at the arrival of our advancing column amid actual fighting, at the risk of their lives," said a Reuter correspondent.

One battle front photographer who was risking his life to get pictures of the troops fighting into Paris said: "Even if I get out alive, the pictures will look 'phoney,' because of these crazy civilians running about as if the tanks were not firing."

Generals Meet.—Gen. de Gaulle met Gen. Leclerc in the Montparnasse district of Paris.

The Price.—More than 1,000 French patriots are lying unburied in the streets, killed in hundreds of skirmishes throughout the city.

The Grand Palais in the Champs Elysees was set on fire and burnt out on Tuesday. The death-roll is believed to be heavy, as a circus was playing there at the time.

CHEERING & FIGHTING
Crowds Follow Battle

The cheering and the fighting overlapped. Late last night there was still sniping. A typical account was thus broadcast by Paris radio at 9.40 p.m.

"Crowds in the streets followed the battle, taking cover only when shells actually came their way. Many people kept up running commentaries on the telephone to their friends to keep them informed, and made appointments to celebrate victory together. This was a real Fourth of July for the people."

(Continued on P. 4, Col. 3)

This Morning's War News

France

Gen. de Gaulle enters liberated Paris; last Germans surrender after ultimatum; Allied tanks in day of street fighting; great force reported on way to city. (P1)
Eye-witness account of entry into Paris. (Pp 1 & 4)
Pétain is at chateau near Belfort. (P1)
Thrust beyond Antibes; Rhone delta cordon. (P1)
British use new flame guns. (P3)
Allied pacts with France. (P3)

Russia and Balkans

Rumania declares war on Germany after Nazis beaten in Bucharest battle; Germans surrendering all over country; organised resistance to Russians ceases in Bessarabia. (P1)
Bulgaria's fall expected this week-end. (P1)
Germans' 25 divisions. (P4)

Air

German oil hit again by 2,000-plane raid. (P3)

Mr. Churchill

Visit to the Pope. (P3)

Italy

Allied thrust; 10 miles to Gothic Line. (P3)

THE APPROACH TO PARIS

Two scenes from the outskirts of Paris which epitomise the Allied entry into the capital. Top: Welcoming crowds greet our forces two miles outside the city. Below: Troops advancing warily three miles away from Paris. An ammunition dump hit by French shells is seen burning.

THRUST BEYOND ANTIBES: RHONE DELTA CORDON

FROM OUR SPECIAL CORRESPONDENT
ALLIED H.Q., MEDITERRANEAN, Friday.

It was officially announced late to-night that American troops have occupied the coastal town of Antibes, seven miles east of Cannes. They are now well beyond it in a drive towards the foothills of the Maritime Alps and the city of Nice.

Prisoners now total 20,000 said to-day's communiqué.

Americans pushing westwards to throw a cordon round the Rhone delta are in the vicinity of the ancient towns of Arles and Tarascon, 33 and 12 miles south of Avignon, key point in the Rhone Valley. The German strategic reserve in the South of France was formerly stationed at Avignon.

Bitter fighting continues in the port area of Toulon, where the German garrison have now no hope of escape. Further west French forces are mopping up isolated enemy pockets in Marseilles, mostly near the harbour.

FLYING COLUMN

Allied planes have bombed the only remaining railway bridge over the Rhone at Avignon.

A flying column, with some armour, is operating ahead of the main Allied forces, it was revealed to-day. The activity of this column, which made the spectacular 150-mile drive to Grenoble, is again shrouded in secrecy.

The main body of American troops has moved north to consolidate the hold on the Grenoble area in co-operation with men of the Maquis.

Hundreds of British and American-owned villas returned to Allied hands yesterday when Cannes, Mougins and Grasse were occupied.

RACE FOR SEINE CROSSINGS

TYPHOONS HAMMER FLEEING ENEMY

With British, Canadian and Belgian troops sweeping on as much as 20 miles in 24 hours at some points, operations yesterday in the fast-dwindling Lower Seine pocket had developed into a race for the river crossings.

The weather having improved, R.A.F. rocket-firing Typhoons were hammering the retreating Germans wherever they could find them.

Airborne troops, fighting as infantry, by capturing Honfleur, dominated the mouth of the Seine and increased the threat to the Germans at Le Havre, five miles away across the estuary. They advanced three miles beyond Honfleur along the coastal road.

British patrols, pushing on after the capture of Bernay, reached Brionne and met Americans who had advanced north from the Evreux area.

LINK UP SOUTH OF ROUEN

Canadian and British forces under Gen. Crerar, driving ahead rapidly after crossing the Risle, linked up with American units on the Seine south of Rouen late yesterday.

The first contact was made at La Haye Malherbe, about seven miles south-east of Elbeuf. Strong formations of armour and infantry followed up the reconnaissance units.

A famous British armoured car unit operating north of the Canadians also raced east, says Reuter, and linked up with other Americans at St. Armand de Hautes Terres, five miles south-west of Elbeuf.

Allied troops were right up to the Risle river for 10 miles north of Brionne to St. Philbert. Between there and the coast they were across all three roads leading out of Beuzeville and were pressing ahead.

POCKET 15 MILES DEEP

The pocket was being reduced so rapidly that the Allies were not stopping to count their prisoners. It had been compressed to an irregular area extending approximately 15 miles west from Elbeuf to Brionne and 20 miles from there to the coast near the mouth of the Risle. The base along the Seine measured about 28 miles in a straight line.

The only news from Allied sources of the operations of Gen. Patton's American Third Army south-east of Paris was that Montereau, at the confluence of the Yonne and the Seine, had been occupied and further gains made.

END OF WAR BY OCTOBER

A U.S. FORECAST

From Our Own Correspondent
WASHINGTON, Friday.

Mr. Clifton Woodrum, chairman of the House of Representatives committee on post-war military policies, told the committee in Washington to-day that the Army's tentative estimate was that October would see the end of the war against Germany.

Mr. Roosevelt at his Press Conference said he was about the only person who had not predicted the date of the end of the war.

Asked about the probable period between the collapse of Germany and the collapse of Japan, he said that anything he could say would be speculation on his part.

MR. CHURCHILL LEAVES ROME

Mr. Churchill, looking very fit and in excellent spirits, left Rome on Wednesday evening for an unknown destination.

During the day he had had a conversation with the Pope, and an "off the record" talk with war correspondents.

Mr. Churchill's Visit to the Pope—P3

RUSSIANS TAKE TARTU

ESTONIAN BASE

An Order of the Day by Marshal Stalin last night, addressed to Gen. Maslennikov, stated that troops of the Third Baltic Front yesterday captured by storm the town and large road and railway junction of Tartu [Dorpat]. The Order described the town as an important German stronghold covering the roads to Central Estonia.

POPE TO BROADCAST

It was officially announced in Vatican City yesterday that the Pope will broadcast next Friday evening, states A.P.

LORD ELLESMERE

The death was announced yesterday of the Earl of Ellesmere, one of the wealthiest landowners in Great Britain and a prominent member of the Jockey Club. He was 71.

Obituary—P3

LATE NEWS

12 NAZI DIVISIONS TRAPPED

Soviet communiqué says 12 German divisions surrounded south-west of Kishinev, Bessarabia. More than 13,000 surrendered. Rest being wiped out.

100,000 ENEMY DEAD IN RUMANIA

Moscow states enemy lost 40,000 killed on Second Ukrainian front Aug. 20-25. In same period 60,000 enemy killed on Third Ukrainian front. Russians captured 195 tanks, 1,051 guns. 105,000 prisoners taken.

ROBOT SITES BOMBED

In daylight last evening Lancasters and Halifaxes of R.A.F. Bomber Command attacked flying bomb launching sites in Northern France.

U.S. PATROLS IN TROYES

Correspondents at Shaef stated just before midnight that U.S. patrols were as far east as Troyes, 90 miles south-east of Paris.

Continuous air attacks along Seine. U.S. Ninth Air Force up to 6 p.m. destroyed 41 enemy planes. 3

Black-out (London) 9.30—6.34
Moon rises 2.51 p.m.; sets 12.16 a.m. to-morrow.

BULGARIA'S EXIT EXPECTED THIS WEEK-END

TURKISH REPORT

ANKARA, Friday.

The Bulgarian Regents, Prince Cyril, brother of the late King Boris, Filov, the former Prime Minister, and Mikhov, former War Minister, to-day received M. Bagrianoff, Prime Minister, Lt.-Gen. Ruzev, War Minister, and M. Draganoff, Foreign Minister.

The collapse of Bulgaria is believed to be imminent. Diplomatic circles here express the opinion that the country will probably surrender to the Allies within the next few days, possibly even this week-end.

Armistice negotiations reported to have taken place are believed to have entered their final phase.

A special Bulgarian emissary returned to Istanbul on Tuesday after seeing M. Bagrianoff at Sofia on the previous day. He is believed to have brought with him a positive answer to certain Allied demands.—Reuter.

BULGAR PEACE ENVOY

"INFORMAL TALKS"

By Our Diplomatic Correspondent

As long ago as last April, Britain and the United States reached agreement on the conditions upon which Bulgaria would be allowed to conclude an armistice.

The arrival of the Bulgarian emissary Moushanov in Ankara in an entirely informal capacity reopened the subject, but his credentials, which stamped him as being an accredited representative of his Government and giving support to the proposals he carried with him, did not reach London until a few days ago.

Moushanov's proposals are now before the British and American Governments for examination and have been forwarded to the Soviet Government, which is not at war with Bulgaria, for its information.

Bulgaria is not being allowed any latitude for bargaining and her conditions now being examined are not regarded as counter-proposals. She will have to take the road indicated by Britain and America or suffer the consequences.

SPAIN INTERNS NAZI SHIPS

FRENCH BORDER CALM

From Our Own Correspondent
MADRID, Friday.

At least six German merchant vessels and warships are interned in northern Spanish ports, it is now possible to reveal. Nazi troops and officials similarly sought refuge in Spain during the last few days and have been disarmed and interned.

French collaborationists and other refugees, including women and children, who crossed the border at various points between the Atlantic and the Mediterranean are being looked after by the Spanish authorities.

The whole Pyrennean border is reported to be quiet on both sides. The French, it is stated, have taken charge of all frontier posts except that on the Oloron-Jaca road, where a few Germans, forced back by the Maquis, are still expected in Spain.

MR. EDEN ACTING AS PREMIER

TWO LEADERS ABROAD

By Our Political Correspondent

Mr. Eden, the Foreign Secretary, is acting as Prime Minister pending the return of Mr. Churchill from Italy. He took charge when Mr. Attlee, the Deputy Prime Minister, left for Algiers.

This is the first time that both the Prime Minister and Deputy Prime Minister have been absent from the country at the same time. It is also the first time that Mr. Eden has been acting Prime Minister.

Agreements between Britain and America and the French Committee of National Liberation to regulate arrangements for the control of liberated France were completed yesterday.

Details—P3

4 Years Ago To-day

Four Eire villages bombed by German raider. Dublin protested to Berlin.

3 Years Ago

Iranians offered only token resistance to the advancing Anglo-Soviet army.

1 Year Ago

King Boris of Bulgaria reported seriously ill in Sofia after visit to Hitler's H.Q.

NAZIS BEATEN IN BATTLE FOR BUCHAREST

RUMANIA DECLARES WAR ON GERMANY

ENEMY SURRENDERING ALL OVER COUNTRY

After the defeat of the German garrison in Bucharest yesterday, in a fierce battle, the new Rumanian Government declared war on Germany.

This was stated last night by Bucharest radio.

The radio added: "According to the latest news, the last German strongholds in the country are giving in. Whole groups of German soldiers are laying down their arms and surrendering to our troops. A real Rumanian victory is on the march."

The radio said that the German Legation had been informed that the Rumanian Army would take no hostile action against Germany and would allow the German troops to withdraw. The Germans promised that they would take no hostile action.

Later they attacked and tried to disarm the Rumanian forces. The Germans also machine-gunned and bombed civilians.

All German attacks were beaten back by the Royal Guards. German guns and lorries were destroyed and German prisoners taken. At 11 o'clock the capital was completely freed.

The German garrison surrendered.

The radio added: "Germany has placed herself in a state of war with Rumania and the Rumanian forces have been ordered to disarm all German forces and thus liberate Rumania."

FIGHT FOR AIRFIELD

Another version of the broadcast said:

"After a mass bombardment by dive-bombers German troops attempted to capture the Baneasa airfield [near Bucharest], but all their attacks were repelled by Royal Guards regiments with very heavy losses to the Germans.

"Big German guns and vehicles are littering the roads leading from Baneasa to Bucharest.

"At 11 a.m. Baneasa village and airfield fell into our hands. The capital was thus completely liberated from the German formations, many of which were completely wiped out."

Cairo messages said that the Russians now control Rumania and Bessarabia as far south as the Danube, either by direct occupation or by co-operation with the Rumanian troops.

This was borne out by the German Overseas News Agency, which said the Russians were now fighting in the Danube Delta.

Hammer, the German military spokesman, said: "Owing to the attitude of the Rumanian soldiers the Russians have won cheap victories."

BATTLE WITH S.S. AT PLOESTI

• In the Galatz area two German divisions are reported to face superior Rumanian forces. It is believed that the Germans will try to scuttle their Black Sea fleet at Constanza. The port is thought to be still in Rumanian hands.

Stockholm and Algiers reports say that Rumanian troops are attacking German S.S. troops guarding the Ploesti oil wells, and street fighting is going on in the town.

Rumanians and Hungarians were stated to be fighting in the towns of Brasov, Cluj, Maros-Vasarheli and other border areas. The German News Agency said the postal, telegraph and telephone communications between Rumania and Hungary had been suspended.

Moscow Despatch—P4

TEQULOUET TELOUQUET TEQOUTEUL QELUTOUET

Daily Mail

LATE WAR NEWS

No. 15,076 ONE PENNY FOR KING AND EMPIRE MONDAY, AUGUST 28, 1944

PATTON'S TANKS 90 MILES FROM GERMANY

U.S. Troops Reach Marne: 15-Miles Drive from Paris

FOUR Allied armies were last night pouring across the Seine on a front of 200 miles to begin the great drive for the frontiers of Belgium and Germany. On the right wing American spearheads were reported at Vitry, only 90 miles from the nearest point in Germany.

Striking out from their bridgehead at Melun other American forces have reached Lagny, on the Marne, 15 miles from the centre of Paris.

Another attack was launched from the bridgehead at Mantes, north-west of Paris, and here Americans were reported to be advancing against little or no opposition.

Between Mantes and the sea the British and Canadian armies have three bridgeheads over the Seine. They are extending their hold along the east bank, piling up guns, tanks, and supplies.

"We shall probably break through and go a long way once we have collected all we want on the east side," said one of General Dempsey's senior staff officers.

At the same time a pitched battle is being fought out at the approaches to the city of Rouen, which bestrides the Seine at the top of one of the great loops in the river.

The Germans are trying desperately to keep the Rouen bridges open for their troops still west of the Seine, but the Canadians are across the river at Ponte de l'Avehe, 10 miles to the south, and the fall of the city appears to be imminent.

LEAVING LE HAVRE

Between Rouen and Dieppe the Germans are reported to be hastily evacuating the whole of the Havre Peninsula and the Seine Inferieure district to the east of it.

That is the broad picture of the Allied drive to the east.

News of the arrival of American advance guards at Vitry was given by Algiers radio. They are apparently part of the column which reached Troyes.

SHAEF revealed last night that this force had swung 12 miles north-east of Troyes. To reach Vitry they must have advanced another 25 miles.

Vitry is 45 miles south-west of the historic battlefield of Verdun.

It is on the great road east from Paris through Sezanne to Nancy, Strasbourg and the Rhine. At Nancy it links up with the converging highway through Sens and Troyes.

If the Americans continue in a north-easterly direction their advance will bring them to the Saarbrucken area.

North-west of Paris the three British and Canadian bridgeheads over the Seine are at Vernon la Roche, Guyon, and Pont de l'Arche.

RIVER SLAUGHTER

While the bridgeheads are being extended hundreds of guns drawn up behind the west bank of the river farther north are hammering the German "Dunkirk."

The enemy are trying desperately to evacuate their armour and infantry. Great numbers of craft of all kinds, choked with material, have been smashed by our shell-fire and by the bombers.

Some of the German armour has been ferried across, but a great deal has been destroyed, and thousands of infantry have been slaughtered.

The Germans appear to be very thin all along the line of the Seine. There are nests here and there, but there is no semblance of a prepared defensive line on which they could hope to make a real stand.

A German High Command statement last night said: "Massed Allied forces are relentlessly pushing after the German forces withdrawing towards the lower Seine.

"Other Allied columns, backed by a tremendous artillery barrage and a smoke-screen, crossed the Seine at Vernon and La Roche Guyon.

"American forces which were aiming at sweeping rapidly north from Mantes have been stopped.

"Constant Allied reinforcements are, however, pouring into this sector, and Allied superiority in armoured forces is increasing.

"American tank columns operating in the area east of Sens have swung north and north-east."

ALLIED forces have crossed the Seine south of Rouen and are heading for the rocket coast.

AMERICAN forces are advancing beyond Paris and have reached the Marne.

HITLER LOSES 25 GENERALS

Rommel a 'Probable'

BRITISH HEADQUARTERS, FRANCE, Sunday. — Twenty-five German generals and one admiral have been killed, wounded, captured, replaced, or have just disappeared in Western France since D-Day, it was announced late to-day.

The list, which was read out by a staff officer, included Field-Marshal Rommel, who was described as "severely wounded and probably dead."—*A.P.*

Lord Templewood in France Again

MADRID, Sunday.—Lord Templewood, formerly Sir Samuel Hoare, the British Ambassador to Spain, has again crossed into France by car for an inspection tour.

He rode over the International Bridge at Hendaye, where organised Maquis forces are now stationed.—*Reuter.*

Still Sunny in Strait

State of Sea.—Choppy.

Weather.—Warm and sunny with some increase of wind in the afternoon. Maximum temperature: 81deg. Visibility: Fairly good. Wind: S.W., fresh. Sky: Clear.

Barometer: Going down gradually.

MIDNIGHT WAR DIGEST

SEINE AREA: From Rouen to the sea the Allied armies are forcing the river crossings. In places they are miles beyond them. Reports say that the Germans are abandoning Le Havre and its peninsula. East of Paris American troops are clearing the area between the rivers Seine and Marne. In Paris itself the last German strong-points are being mopped up.

EAST: Sweeping through Troyes United States armoured columns were last night reported at Vitry le François, 45 miles south-west of Verdun and a bare 90 miles from the German frontier.

SOUTH: Toulon and Marseilles have been largely cleared of Germans, although strong-points are still holding out. Berlin reports a tank battle in the Rhône Valley, where the Americans are apparently trying to cut off the enemy's retreat. American patrols which reached the Swiss frontier during the week-end are reported to be continuing their advance northwards.

An American Keen on Security

From Daily Mail Correspondent

NEW YORK, Sunday.—A waiter at a New York night club put a whisky and soda before a guest last night and said: "It's O.K., Buddy. It's on the house. Just fix that Security Conference so that it stays put."

The guest was one of the British delegates to the Security Conference at Dumbarton Oaks, Washington, who with others was taking the week-end off to see the sights of New York.

Warsaw to Paris: 'We Fight On'

Daily Mail Radio Station

A message to liberated Paris, "from the heart of a battle-scarred Warsaw," was sent last night by the Polish patriots fighting in their capital.

"German guns and howitzers, German flame-throwers and bombs, German machine-guns and hand-grenades will not break our spirit," it said. "Like Paris, we shall not submit to the evil, but rise in triumph on the day of liberation."

Doenitz's Last Hope

Berlin-controlled Hilversum radio last night appealed to young Dutchmen to join the German Navy. Special recruiting centres have been set up in Dutch ports.

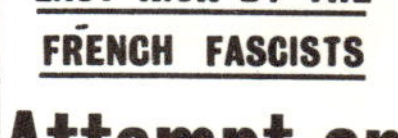

RUHR DAY-RAID R.A.F. LONGEST

R.A.F. heavy bombers, Halifaxes, made their longest daylight flight into Germany yesterday when they attacked synthetic oil plants at Homberg-Meerbeck, in the Ruhr.

They were escorted by Spitfires. They made their first long-range daylight flight for two years to join the United States heavies in their onslaught on the enemy's oil.

By striking in the daytime the R.A.F. Halifaxes would be able to drop block-busters on installations which have already been heavily attacked.

Medium forces of Eighth Air Force Flying Fortresses and Liberators, escorted by Mustangs and Lightnings, also attacked military targets in North-West Germany and the German-held Danish peninsula yesterday, stated a communiqué from United States Air Force Headquarters.

14 Missing

There was no enemy opposition to the bombers, but the escort shot down one German fighter and destroyed another on the ground during strafing operations on the way home. From this operation three bombers and eleven fighters are missing.

Thunderbolts bombed and strafed targets in the Metz and Saarbrücken areas. Preliminary figures show the Thunderbolts destroyed or damaged 12 planes, 116 locomotives, 440 railway cars including 65 fuel cars, and an ammunition train and 41 motor vehicles.

Largest night raid—BACK Page.

AEGEAN 'NOOSE' TIGHTENS

Sea, Air Blockade

ALEXANDRIA, Sunday.—Since the Allies lost their foothold on the Dodecanese Islands last October, air and sea operations have been tightening the blockade on these eastern flank garrisons of the Balkans.

These attacks have been pressed home with such great effect that out of the 51 fairly big ships—totalling more than 82,000 tons—which the enemy had in this area 32, totalling 62,000 tons, are believed to have been sunk.

The lion's share of this siege has fallen to Coastal Command of the R.A.F., which has put in 76,000 flying hours since the blockade began. British submarines, however, have been the top scorers. So far they have sent to the bottom seven tons in every 30 sunk. Surface craft have chalked up two tons in every 50.—*B.U.P.*

Strike Threat If Hungary Fights

STOCKHOLM, Sunday. — A new radio station calling itself the Hungarian Independence Station Kossuth, has called on Hungarian soldiers and workers to revolt against the Germans, says the Stockholm paper *Allehanda*.

If a new Government able to negotiate with the Allies is not formed in Hungary by to-day, says the station there will be a general strike throughout Hungary.—*B.U.P.*

Chinese Shell Japs

CHUNGKING, Sunday. — Chinese artillery inflicted heavy casualties on the Japanese when Tangyang, north-east of the Yangtse River port of Ichang, was shelled all day.—Reuter.

LAST KICK BY THE FRENCH FASCISTS

Attempt on Life of De Gaulle

Shots In Notre Dame

BY attempting to assassinate General de Gaulle in Nôtre Dame Cathedral French collaborationists and knots of still resisting Germans made a last attempt to throw Paris into confusion during the week-end.

The great cathedral was crowded to the doors in thanksgiving for the city's liberation when shots rang out from the roof.

Worshippers flung themselves on the floor, dodged behind pillars, and took cover behind pews.

Simultaneously firing broke out between the cathedral and the Place de la Concorde, seething with people who had been unable to get into the service.

Here, too, the crowds flung themselves flat while rifle and machine-gun bullets sprayed over their heads.

Such was the press in the cathedral that the would-be assassins appear to have escaped. The shots were not many. General de Gaulle was not injured and there were few casualties.

Hunt for Fascists

Outside in the Place de la Concorde the firing was more serious. Killed and wounded are believed to run into hundreds.

One shot rang out, then another, but at first the crowd, inured to this kind of thing by days of street fighting, took little notice.

Then machine-guns started to chatter viciously.

"I watched people run and fall in panic as bullets sprayed into them," said an American broadcaster.

"Then our own guns opened up, firing just over our heads. Tank guns also started firing.

"For half an hour there was a pitched battle and 1,000,000 people lay flat and prayed aloud as bullets spurted in their midst."

A great hunt for Fascists is on. There is still some shooting in the streets. Householders have been ordered to keep their doors locked and see that nobody gets on to the roof.

Luftwaffe Back

Death came to Paris again yesterday morning, when the Luftwaffe attacked the city for the first time since June 1940.

Incendiaries were showered down on the Latin quarter, the districts round the Gare de l'Est, the Arc de Triomphe, and the Bois de Boulogne, in the neighbourhood of the Porte d'Orleans, and Montrouge, north of the Gare St. Lazare, and the Butte Montmartre.

The industrial districts of St. Denis and Sceaux outside the city were also bombed, with casualties and much damage to property.

Later in the morning German fighters sprayed the streets of the capital with bullets.

Apart from these raids there is amazingly little damage. The only real signs of fighting are around the Tuileries, where in the Hôtels Continental and Crillon the Germans had their headquarters.

It was at the Continental that the German Staff surrendered. They

BACK PAGE—Col. TWO

As the Sniper Fired

THIS was the scene in the Place de l'Hôtel de Ville when a sniper—said to have been a French Fascist—opened fire as General de Gaulle crossed the square during his ceremonial entry into Paris. The crowds who a second before had been cheering madly threw themselves down, but several were hit.

A CIVILIAN, believed to be the sniper, being carried away by gendarmes after the firing ceased.

4 U-boats Hit by R.A.F.'s Lone Patrols

STRIKING successes against U-boats by R.A.F. planes on individual patrols were announced last night.

A Sunderland, two Halifaxes, and an R.A.F. Liberator attacked four U-boats. And every one of the aircraft returned safely to base.

Despite intense flak and eight hits the Sunderland kept up the assault and damaged its U-boat.

For his bravery the Sunderland's captain, Flight-Lieutenant C. G. D. Lancaster, of Woldingham, Surrey, has received a bar to the D.F.C.

Cat-walk Crawl

When a Liberator was seriously damaged in a night battle with a U-boat the depth-charges could not be jettisoned as the release gear was hit. The flight engineer, Sergeant K. B. Bettany, of Porth, Glamorgan, released them by hand and worked for three-quarters of an hour to do so. He had neither 'chute nor Mae West.

Until the depth-charges were away the captain and co-pilot had to stand on the rudder control to keep the Liberator on an even keel. But the rear gunner kept on firing and scored hits.

'Heavies' Go Out Again

Big forces of Allied heavy bombers were seen crossing the East Coast heading towards the Continent yesterday evening. The thunder of their engines filled the air for three-quarters of an hour.

V2 No Worse Than V1: News from Russia

By Daily Mail Reporter

VALUABLE information about the secret rocket device which the Germans refer to as V 2 is reported to have been given to the British Government by Soviet Russia. This information would enable British experts to form definite conclusions about the potentialities of V 2.

In certain circumstances it seems that this additional secret weapon will be no more serious than V 1.

In addition the information will enable the British Government to make preparations to deal with it.

In their recent advance in Poland the Russians came across a place at which the Germans had been testing this rocket. Their experts, on the instructions of Marshal Stalin, immediately set to work to discover all they could. The information was sent to London with the least possible delay.

Long Lull Broken

A few flying-bombs early yesterday morning broke the longest lull in Southern England since the bombardment began.

There were two attacks—one during the hours of darkness, the other in the early morning. The first attack was on a very small scale, but the second was more concentrated and of short duration.

Observers on the coast reported that in this attack the Germans took advantage of a mist which suddenly sprang up in the Channel.

Berlin is disregarding the lull. Without interruption the German radio announced in every news broadcast last night: "London is still subjected to continuous bombardment."

CHEVALIER IS SHOT—PARIS

F.F.I. Still Doubtful

Maurice Chevalier, the French actor and film star, was killed by French Patriots on Friday, says a Reuter report from Paris, but French headquarters in London last night would not confirm it.

"If the report is true," said a French spokesman, "it would be the first time on record that men of the Resistance Movement have shot a collaborator without giving him a trial.

"Men of the F.F.I. always arrest collaborators and bring them before a judge."

"Gayest Man in Europe"—Page TWO.

Mission Ended

MADRID, Sunday.—The Spanish Government has instructed its Embassy in Vichy to consider its mission ended since the Government to which it was accredited has ceased to function, it is learned in Madrid.—*B.U.P.*

Bulgaria Gets Allied Terms

NO NEUTRALITY POSE

By **WILSON BROADBENT,** Diplomatic Correspondent

ALLIED armistice terms, which this week-end have been sent to Bulgaria, will demand her complete surrender. Bulgaria will not be allowed to adopt an attitude of neutrality. She will have to surrender all the territories which she has seized since the war started.

Passage through her territory for Allied troops should they require it will also be demanded.

The terms have been drafted by the European Advisory Committee in London, on which sit representatives of Britain, the United States, and Soviet Russia.

This is the body which has drawn up terms for the unconditional surrender of Germany.

The terms to Bulgaria will be handed to an emissary who is waiting in Istanbul, and will be taken by him to Sofia.

GALATZ TAKEN BY RUSSIANS

WITH the capture of Galatz, the big port at the head of the Danube delta, the road into the Balkans is wide open to the Russians.

In an Order of the Day Marshal Stalin last night announced that the port was stormed by General Tolbukhin's army from Besserabia.

This was the second Order to tell of big Soviet successes. The first, to General Malinovsky, disclosed that his Second Ukrainian tank and infantry forces have stormed into Ramnicul-Sarat and Focsani, both heavily fortified enemy strongholds on the road to Ploesti, the oil centre, now only 58 miles ahead.

German reinforcements were flung into the battle with orders to fight to the last man. Kuban Cossacks took a heavy toll.

Among the dead in the trap south-west of Kishinev, said the routine Russian communiqué, were three German generals. Four more were captured.

The communiqué also told of a mass Soviet air raid on Illait in East Prussia. Fires could be seen for 120 miles.

Fierce battles in and near Ploesti itself were admitted last night by Colonel von Hammer, Berlin military correspondent.

He reported that the position of the Wehrmacht forces in all Rumania had become "extremely perilous," and he blamed the "unhindered advance of Soviet tank and motorised columns."

"Strong German forces are involved in fighting of extreme fury with far superior Russian forces both east and west of the Pruth" admitted Von Hammer.

"Other Soviet tank columns have penetrated into the German rear communications between the Pruth and the Sereth.

"The German battle force in this sector is now falling back to the Carpathian passes."

MANY TRAPPED

Ankara reports state that 10 and possbly 11 Wehrmacht divisions are trapped in South-Eastern Rumania as a result of the armistice.

German bombing of Bucarest and other cities has so enraged the Rumanians in Transylvania that they have started a campaign to exterminate German civilians estimated to number 1,000,000.

Bucarest radio states that Rumanian forces have encircled the Germans sent to attack the city, and the last nests of enemy resistance inside the capital have been cleared.

All Germans in the area have been ordered to report to the police. Any saboteurs will be shot on the spot.

Masses of Germans are surrendering to the advancing Russian armies, who have also taken over five full Rumanian divisions, as well as other units.

Meanwhile, on the Polish front, Berlin reported that powerful Soviet attacks have been launched from the Vistula bridgeheads south of Warsaw, and also north-east of the city.

It was claimed that all the assaults were held.—*B.U.P.* and *Reuter.*

Forts Into Air Liners

STOCKHOLM, Sunday.—Five Flying Fortresses which made a forced landing in Sweden have been lent by the American Government to the Swedish Government temporarily, said the Swedish radio to-night. The Swedish Government has converted three of them into air liners. —*Reuter.*

LATEST

ROCKET BASE BOMBED

Lancasters and Halifaxes with fighter cover made two attacks on large concrete structure at Mimoyecques, in the Pas de Calais, believed to be connected with German long-range rockets.

FUEL DUMPS AT RHEIMS HIT AGAIN

Two fuel dumps north-west of Rheims bombed last night for third time in 30 hours by Marauders and Havocs. Radio installation at Boulogne also hit.

GERMANS LOSE 21 DIVISIONS

In Balkan Collapse

Daily Mail Radio Station

A British staff officer speaking from London gave to the German forces last night the following balance-sheet of the situation in the Balkans.

"Twelve German divisions are lost in Rumania. The Sixth and Eighth armies doomed—a disaster greater than that of Stalingrad.

"Nine divisions in Greece and the Ægean Islands are cut off from the homeland and must be written off.

MONDAY, AUGUST 28, 1944

Evening Standard

37,428 BLACK-OUT: 9.26 pm to 6.37 am. MOON: Rises 5.7 pm; Sets 1.31 am. ONE PENNY

FINAL NIGHT EXTRA ●

Nazis Make No Big Effort to Oppose Seine Crossings

THEIR ONE ANXIETY—TO GET OUT OF FRANCE

Still 20,000 in Trap West of the River

From LESLIE RANDALL, Evening Standard War Reporter

ELBEUF (on the Seine), Monday.

We are now over the Seine in several places. The Germans are making no great effort to oppose our crossing of the river. Their troop movements are still eastward.

THEIR ONE ANXIETY IS TO GET RIGHT OUT OF FRANCE BEFORE THEY ARE ENCIRCLED AGAIN. THEIR MANPOWER SHORTAGE IS SO ACUTE THAT THEY HAVE ALMOST NO OTHER TROOPS FOR THE DEFENCE OF THE FATHERLAND.

They have few to spare in Germany to send to the Maginot Line. That, no doubt, is the reason why there are no reports of any great activity improving the defences there.

The places where we are over the Seine are at Pont de l'Arche, at Elbeuf, east of Louviers, and Vernon.

We have considerably enlarged our bridgehead at this last place, and elements of our armour are now over the river.

The Germans have five depleted divisions — three infantry and two Panzer—left on this side of the Seine—a total altogether of about 20,000 men. They are bottled up in the three loops of the river between the Foret de Bretonne and the Foret de Rouvray.

FINE TARGETS

The two principal remaining places where they are trying to escape by the ferry service are at Rouen and Duclair. Our air force are pounding them day and night.

The masses of motor transport offer splendid targets, and an enormous number of vehicles have already been destroyed.

The Germans are still trying to get across the river by daylight, so desperate is their plight. Yesterday our airmen sank eight barges full of troops. Particularly at Rouen, we hope to inflict "another Chambois" on them.

The Canadians who have crossed the river at Elbeuf are now only seven miles from Rouen. The Germans still on the west side of the river here look like being caught in a trap from which there will be no escape.

LITTER OF WRECKAGE

Here at Elbeuf you can see what happened to the Germans of the broken Seventh Army, when they reached the Seine.

The ferry at Elbeuf is on a stretch of the Seine where there is a big open space used as a cattle market and recreation ground. The scene there to-day tells its own grim story.

That open space is littered with the wreckage of the camouflaged carts and covered wagons of the German horse-drawn transport columns.

The horses are lying there dead, with their legs stuck up in the air at grotesque angles. This cattle market was the slaughter ground of Germans hemmed in by our

(Continued on Back Page, Col. Three)

MORE V2 SITES ARE CAPTURED

Allied troops clearing the area west of the Seine have come across an increasing number of V-2 sites in varying stages of construction, says Harold Mayes, Reuter correspondent with the Tactical Air Force in France.

It appears that one of the large regions the Germans intended for the use of this weapon is being mopped up in good time.

There is an early prospect of reaching a considerably larger area of sites across the river.

30-HOUR BOMB LULL ENDS

Flying-bomb attacks were renewed early this afternoon after a lull of 30 hours. A.-A. defences went into action on several points of the coast of Southern England.

Several of the bombs came in lanes well to the east. An Alert sounded in the London area.

Allied Non-Stop Air Blows Go On

Forces of Allied bombers were heard crossing the East Coast, heading towards the Continent, to-day for nearly an hour.

Bomber Command Mosquitoes last night kept up the air offensive against Germany, which went on almost non-stop throughout the week-end when they attacked Mannheim, the much-bombed Rhineland chemical and industrial centre.

HUNDREDS OF KISSES FOR EISENHOWER

An American commentator broadcasting from Normandy this afternoon said that General Eisenhower had returned to the fighting fronts to-day after his visit to Paris.

Robert Reuben, Reuter's special correspondent, adds: General Eisenhower was nearly mobbed by excited Parisians at the Arc de Triomphe.

Throughout his tour he got the now customary exuberant welcome from the women of Paris—hundreds of kisses and embraces.

Another Marne Town Captured

Allied forces are moving steadily eastward between the Seine and the Marne, and the Germans appear to have abandoned the Marne line, says a reporter at Supreme Headquarters.

Allied troops have advanced 11 miles to capture Meaux, the second town on the Marne to fall—probably by pushing eastwards from Ligny, which fell yesterday. They met no sign of organised resistance.

Allied forces are moving in the direction of Chateau Thierry, one of the great battlefields of 1918.

Meaux was one of the towns through which the British forces passed in the 1914 retreat from Mons, but the tide turned at that moment, and the only Germans who reached there were a few patrols.

North-east of Nogent-sur-Seine Villenauxe has been reached.

To the north-west General Eisenhower's forces have begun to burst out from the Mantes bridgehead, and have pushed a little way east against varying resistance.

Enemy groups are being mopped up in the area of Troyes, and also on the Seine north-west of Paris.

These groups vary immensely in strength. Some are as big as 1000 men.

Allied attacks at Brest have made progress up to 1000 yards and the town is now closely invested.

65,000 Prisoners Taken by "3rd"

It was learned to-day that since Third Army headquarters became operative in France the U.S. Third Army have taken 65,000 prisoners and killed 16,000 Germans

It is also stated that the U.S. First Army have been taking an average of 2000 prisoners a day for the past four days.

CORNERED GERMAN IN PARIS HOLDS THE WHITE FLAG

The battle of the Chamber of Deputies barricades is over. The leader of the 500 Germans hugs a pillar with one hand while the other clutches the white flag. Other Germans peer through the bars at the Frenchmen with the Tricolour as their beaten leader discusses surrender terms.

Other pictures from Paris—PAGES FOUR, FIVE and BACK.

26 KILLED AS 'PLANE FROM U.S. CRASHES

Twenty-six people were killed when a Sky Master mail airplane from America crashed at Prestwick, Ayr, early to-day.

Fourteen were passengers seven were members of the crew, and five were occupants of a house which was demolished.

It is believed that the airplane circled twice before crashing. Visibility was bad.

Prestwick, which lies at the end of an Atlantic ferry route, is one of the world's busiest air junctions. Through it have passed many "priority" passengers on missions of national importance.

Four houses were demolished and Civil Defence workers and members of the U.S. forces were still searching the debris at dawn.

Five of the dead were in a house in Hillside-avenue on which the airplane crashed. One of the victims was William Kenneth Snowden, 22, of London, who was employed at the airfield.

Two families in two of the houses escaped unhurt.

One of the rescued was Mr. Alexander Haswell, who is stationed in Sussex, and was on ten days' leave. His five-year-old daughter Irene was killed.

Nazis Battered in Rhone Retreat

American forces of the Seventh Army have reached the Rhone river in the vicinity of Montelimar, 75 miles north of Avignon and 150 miles north-west of Marseilles.

For several days, says to-day's communiqué, in a series of actions, they inflicted heavy losses on the Germans, who had been attempting to ward off a serious threat to their east flank.

Altogether 15,000 German troops are attempting a wholesale withdrawal from the south of France, chiefly up the eastern bank of the Rhone, says David Brown, Reuter's correspondent.

The American forces driving north from Avignon and west of Grenoble, he adds, have severely battered and hacked the remnants of the 19th Army trying to escape.

30,000 Prisoners

French troops are maintaining a fast pace in clearing up the Marseilles and Toulon areas. More than 7000 prisoners have been taken in and near the two cities, increasing the total for the southern France campaign to more than 30,000.

On the eastern coastal flank of the bridgehead, American forward elements have advanced to the Var River, which enters the Mediterranean about five miles west of Nice.

The naval communiqué says landings are continuing.

The F.F.. in Cannes, says Reuter, dealt promptly with some 60 male and 40 female French Gestapo spies and informers. Most of them were apprehended and shot.

A LONDON SINGER SHOT

A London singer, Mr. Thomas R. Lloyd, 38, of Adelaide-road, Hampstead, was injured by a revolver shot to-day while talking to a friend in the street.

He was hit in the right shoulder, but his condition is not serious.

Six shots are alleged to have been fired by another man. Mr. Lloyd's friend was unhurt.

No arrest has yet been made.

Sun After Rain in the Straits

After mid-day rain and drizzle fell heavily in the Straits of Dover for a time, and visibility was very poor, but by 2 p.m. the sun was out again, the clouds breaking and rising higher.

The wind was blowing quite hard from the south-west, and the sea was choppy.

French Control For Paris

From PHILIP GRUNE
Evening Standard War Reporter
PARIS, Sunday.

Paris is to be handed over to the French within the next few days.

American troops who are now in the town with the French will move out, and control will be taken over by the French only.

Though much of the initial stages of the entry into the capital were carried out by the U.S. Reconnaissance Corps, the main force was French.

American infantry were brought into the heart of the city to take care of snipers, but they will be withdrawn when official handing over is made known.

Parisians spent a happy week-end, despite disturbances and street battles in places like the Place de la Concord and the Rue Royal. It is now stated the United States First Army alone have been taking an average of 2000 prisoners a day for the past four days.

The Germans made several counter-attacks in the suburbs during the week-end, but none was successful.

I understand that Germans cut off in the suburbs were mostly paratroopers, some of whom took part in the rescue of Mussolini after the capitulation of Italy.

Hastings Beach To be Opened

The central part of the beach at Hastings and St. Leonards, stretching from Hastings pier to Warrior-square, will be opened again to the public to-morrow.

The covered walk along the lower promenade will also be re-opened.

Miles 0 25 50 — DIEPPE — AUMALE — NEUFCHATEL — BEAUVAIS — R. Aisne — SOISSONS — COMPIEGNE — REIMS — EPERNAY — CHALONS — VITRY — FECAMP — YVETOT — DUCLAIR — ROUEN — PONT DE L'ARCHE — R. Seine — GISORS — MERU — SENLIS — CHATEAU THIERRY — R. Marne — MEAUX — SEZANNE — LE HAVRE — BOURGACHARD — PONTOISE — PONT AUDEMER — ELBEUF — LOUVIERS — VERNON — MANTES — POISSY — LAGNY — PECY — VILLENAUXE — PROVINS — ROMILLY — TROYES — NOGENT — HONFLEUR — L'EVEQUE — TROUVILLE — R. Risle — LE NEUBOURG — R. Touques — BERNAY — EVREUX — R. Eure — VERSAILLES — PARIS — MELUN — MONTEREAU — BROGLIE — LISIEUX — ORBEC — DREUX — CORBEIL — FONTAINEBLEAU

News Chronicle

No. 30,671 FRIDAY, SEPTEMBER 1, 1944 ONE PENNY

Eisenhower gives the facts of victory: 400,000 German casualties, including 47 divisions destroyed, mauled or trapped; in material the enemy has lost 1,300 tanks, 2,000 guns, and 3,500 planes

ALLIES CROSS MEUSE AND SOMME

O'Connor drives 60 miles in 48 hours to take Amiens

THE British are over the Somme; the Americans are over the Meuse and driving on Sedan and Charleville.

The German front, it was stated in dispatches from the war fronts last night, is completely broken and the battle of France is rapidly drawing to a close.

Robert Reuben, Reuter's special correspondent with the First American Army, cabling last night, said: The German front has completely broken and the battle has turned into a rout. The Germans are fleeing so fast that it is becoming most difficult for the American forces to maintain contact. "It has turned into a pursuit instead of a battle," said a military official.

So disorganised is the German retreat that in one bag of 400 prisoners an American division captured elements of 64 different units. Prisoners have poured into American camps at the rate of about 2,000 a day, and this would be much higher if contact could be maintained.

There is no doubt that the battle for Northern France is over. Prisoners taken by the First U.S. Army to date run to 115,520.

And in Picardy the great German retreat is turning into rout, reports Richard McMillan, B.U.P. war correspondent.

With three deep thrusts by armoured flying columns, the advancing British Second Army is covering 40 miles a day at some points.

Three bridges

Amiens is ours. Last night we had three bridges over the Somme.

It now seems impossible for the enemy to hold on to a line anywhere, and it looks as though it may not be long before the Channel coast with the flying bomb sites will fall to us.

Gen. Dempsey's brilliant master-stroke appears to make the German defeat in France as complete as it can be.

South-west of the thrust to Amiens the Canadians have swung a right hook round Rouen and are now about 20 miles from Dieppe.

Westward the Belgians have crossed the Seine at Quilleboeuf, 18 miles from Le Havre, and other forces are over at Duclair and Caudebec.

London
FLYING BOMB SITES
Rotterdam
ENGLAND
HOLLAND
Dover
Flushing
Boulogne
Lille
Brussels
BELGIUM
Mons
Cologne
GERMANY
Dieppe
Amiens
Rouen
Beauvais
Coblenz
Frankfort
Rheims
Sedan
L'BURG
SIEGFRIED LINE
Paris
Marne
Chalons
Verdun
Nancy
Mannheim
Orleans
Troyes
St. Dizier
MAGINOT LINE
Stuttgart
Loire
Le Creusot
Basle
FRANCE
SWITZ'D
Geneva
Clermont Ferrand
Lyons
Grenoble
Milan
Valence
Turin
ITALY
Genoa
Miles
0 25 50 75 100
Montpellier
Beziers
Narbonne
Marseille
Toulon
Nice
G. OF GENOA
G. OF LIONS
Leghorn

Field-Marshal Montgomery

GEN. MONTGOMERY, described yesterday by Gen. Eisenhower, Supreme Allied Commander, as "one of the great soldiers of this or any other war," has been promoted Field-Marshal.

Gen. Montgomery is one of the few generals who have been made Field-Marshal without having been Chief of the Imperial General Staff, the highest Army appointment.

★

Other honours announced last night included:

C.B.E. for Brig. Fitzroy Maclean, M.P. for Lancaster, who has been liaison officer with Marshal Tito's army in Yugo-Slavia.

M.B.E. for Maj. Randolph Churchill, M.P., son of the Prime Minister, who was also attached to Tito's army.

C.B.—Lt.-Gen. Patton, Commander of Third United States Army in France, and Maj.-Gen. Manton S. Eddy, for their work in North Africa.

Eisenhower's tribute to Montgomery: Back Page.

Two Nazi armies shattered: two more cut up

THE extent of the German defeat in France was made known last night by Gen. Eisenhower in a report to the Combined Chiefs of Staff covering the period from D-Day to August 25.

The German Seventh Army and the newly-formed Fifth Panzer Army have been decisively defeated, dragging down with them the bulk of the First and Fifteenth Armies.

Twenty infantry divisions and five Panzer divisions were destroyed; 12 more infantry divisions and six Panzer divisions were badly mauled. Altogether the enemy lost in killed, wounded and captured over 400,000 men, of whom 200,000 are prisoners.

OVER 200,000 PRISONERS

Here is what Gen. Eisenhower announced in his "factual report":

The equivalent of five Panzer divisions have been destroyed and a further six severely mauled, including one Panzer Grenadier division. The equivalent of 20 infantry divisions have been eliminated and a further 12 very badly cut up and have suffered severe losses. Included in this total of infantry divisions are three of the enemy's crack parachute divisions.

In addition, one parachute division and two infantry divisions have no hope of escape from the fortress ports of the Brittany Peninsula in which they are marooned. One infantry division is isolated in the Channel Islands.

Total enemy casualties amount to over 400,000 killed, wounded and prisoners of war, of which over 200,000 are prisoners of war; 135,000 of these prisoners have been captured since July 25. The total continues to mount.

2,000 GUNS TAKEN OR WRECKED

One thousand three hundred tanks and over 20,000 motor transport have been captured or destroyed. About 500 assault guns and 1,500 field and heavier artillery guns have been captured or destroyed. In addition the enemy has suffered very heavy losses in coast artillery equipment.

The German Seventh Army and newly formed Fifth Panzer Army have been decisively defeated, and into this defeat have been drawn the bulk of the fighting strength of the First and Fifteenth Armies.

Three Field-Marshals and one Army commander have either been dismissed or incapacitated by wounds. One Army commander, three Corps commanders, 15 divisional commanders and one fortress commander have been either killed or captured.

In the air the Luftwaffe has taken a fearful beating. Since June 6, 2,378 German aircraft have been destroyed in the air and 1,167 on the ground. In addition, 270 aircraft were probably destroyed and 1,028 aircraft were damaged in the air.

300 SHIPS SUNK OR DAMAGED

At sea the enemy has been unable to interfere seriously with the invasion forces. Losses to Allied shipping have been small.

Of the enemy's naval forces, some 300 vessels have been sunk or heavily damaged by Allied action. In addition, a number of enemy merchant ships have been sunk and the Germans have been forced to scuttle, in their harbours, large numbers of all types of shipping, both naval and mercantile.

The sustained work of mine-sweepers has resulted, within three months, in a "mine-bag" off the French beaches which totals one-tenth of all mines swept in five years in all theatres of war.

Allied team work has again demonstrated its ability to overcome the most adverse kind of conditions in defeating the enemy.

Russians enter Bucharest

THE Russians are in Bucharest. They entered the Rumanian capital yesterday after routing the German troops in the Ploesti region and south of Ploesti.

This new success was announced in an Order of the Day to Gen. Malinovsky, commander of the Second Ukrainian front. Thus, it said, the German threat to Bucharest from the north was removed.

Twenty-three generals were named. Seven of them were tank generals. Moscow celebrated with one of the big salutes—24 salvoes from 324 guns.

7,000 more captives

Moscow's night communique disclosed that in the drive to Bucharest 250 places were liberated.

Over 7,000 Germans were captured, including Major-Gen. Stingel, Commander of the 76th Infantry Division, who was commandant at Jassy.

West and south of Constanza the Russians drove on towards the Bulgarian fontier and occupied several towns, including Medgidia.

Tanks beaten back

North-east of Warsaw German infantry and tank attacks were repulsed. Before the Germans could recover the Russians counter-attacked and captured the towns of Aleksandrov and Radzymin, 9 and 12 miles north of Warsaw respectively, considerably improving their positions.

It is known that the Germans are making a major effort to defend the German border by a stand on the Vistula rather than on the Oder, and they are throwing in many of their picked divisions from the reserves of the High Command, including such crack panzer units as the Death's Head, Hermann Goering, Viking and Westlands S.S. divisions.

Carpathian clashes

In the Eastern Carpathians between Poland and the central plain of Rumania the Russians are still driving towards Hungary.

Fighting in the Carpathian passes was admitted by von Olberg, German military commentator. "Soviet attacks were repulsed in the Ujitso and other mountain passes as well as in the Bistritsa valley," he said.

Almost the whole of Slovakia is held now by Czechoslovak forces, while Marshal Tito is striking northwards towards the Danube, the Save and Belgrade to meet the Red Army.

News Chronicle Moscow Correspondent, Reuter, B.U.P. and A.P.

Germany's oil position: Back Page

Ploesti oilfields will survive

Although the Germans wrought heavy damage to the Ploesti oilfields, they failed to destroy them. The wells are burning, flames rise to hundreds of feet, but the Russians, with the aid of Ploesti men and women, are winning the battle with the fire.

Poles send off their proposals to Moscow

By VERNON BARTLETT

THE Polish Government's proposals for a solution of the Soviet-Polish crisis were sent to Moscow yesterday. Since there are no diplomatic relations between the two Governments, Sir Archibald Clark-Kerr, the British Ambassador, will act as postman and will deliver the document to Mr. Molotov.

The most important proposal deals with the future relationship between the Polish Government here and the Committee of National Liberation in Lublin.

Both would disappear. Instead, there would be a new Government appointed by the President of the Republic on the advice of Mr. Mikolajczyk, the present Prime Minister. This Government and also a National Council—a kind of token Parliament—would be established in Warsaw and would prepare for elections to be held at the earliest possible moment.

The Communists

The London proposals refer only obliquely to the Committee of National Liberation. They concentrate instead on the Polish Workers' Party, the war-time equivalent of the Communists, and they propose that this party should have the same representation in the new Government and the National Council as each one of the other four political parties represented in the present Government in London.

Claims put forward by the Com-

Continued Back Page B

LATE NEWS

BULGARIA SEALS FRONTIER

Istanbul, Thursday. — Bulgaria today sealed the Turkish-Bulgarian frontier.

LONDON BLACK-OUT
9.17 p.m.—6.43 a.m.
Moon rises, 3.31 p.m.; sets, 8.11 a.m. tomorrow. Harvest Moon tomorrow.

De Gaulle meets the workers

From WILLIAM FORREST
News Chronicle Special Correspondent

PARIS, Thursday.

THREE members of the Provisional Government of France are now in Paris with the head of the Government, Gen. de Gaulle.

They are M. Massigli, Foreign Minister; M. Le Troquer, Commissioner for the Liberated Territory, and M. Cérat, Commissioner for the Occupied Territory.

Two other Ministers, M. d'Astier (Interior) and M. Jacquinot (Navy), are with the French forces in the South. The remaining Ministers are on their way to Paris from Algiers.

When all have arrived it is expected that Gen. de Gaulle will reconstruct his Cabinet so as to include representatives of the resistance movement who have remained in France throughout the occupation.

Gen. de Gaulle has had his first official meeting with the leaders of the French workers.

Taking over factories

A delegation from the Confédération Générale du Travail (the French T.U.C.) called on the head of the Government and discussed measures for organising war production.

Among the measures demanded by the C.G.T. is the confiscation of factories whose owners have fled with the Germans.

Gen. de Gaulle said that such a step would be perfectly legal since it was authorised by a law of July, 1939.

De Gaulle made a very favourable impression on these trade union leaders who have organised the underground struggle of the French workers.

M. Saillant, who acts as secretary of the C.G.T. in the absence of Léon Jouhaux, held captive in Germany, said: "I believe France has found in de Gaulle the artisan of her resurrection."

The Velodrome d'Hiver, the largest stadium in Paris, is being used as a detention camp for arrested collaborators.

Every day brings to light new

Continued Back Page A

Germans planned to stand on Somme

From S. L. SOLON
News Chronicle War Correspondent

WITH THE BRITISH FORCES, Thursday.

THE German plan to maintain an organised retreat to the Somme has been smashed. Tonight a high officer on Gen. Montgomery's staff disclosed that a captured German document revealed the enemy's intentions to be:

1. The German Army was ordered to withdraw in four stages to the Somme, where a strong defensive line was to be established and held.

2. German rearguard units were to delay the Allied forces until such a line could be organised.

3. The withdrawal was to take place between August 29 and September 2.

That, in contrast to the impossible orders issued to the German Army in the past 60 days, appeared to be a realistic and logical counter-measure to the situation in which an army obviously has not the forces to stand and fight.

The answers

This was the Allied answer:

1. The Germans were given no opportunity to reorganise their forces north of the Seine and build their first stage defence line.

2. The Germans were outflanked, cut apart and still further disorganised.

3. In the past 48 hours the British and Canadian troops have made the swiftest gains since the landings.

The advances have been spectacular. British troops which yesterday advanced from the Vernon bridgehead through Mandeville have today taken Grandvilliers, Haut Mesnil, Catheux. They crowned this magnificent 60-mile advance in two days by taking Amiens.

Amiens is 22 miles south-east of Abbeville. That is the only gap in this rapidly formed lower Seine pocket now open to the Germans. All the enemy coast defences, all the islands of resistance still holding out—and the total may add into several divisions—is now in danger of being completely cut off. Another British column advancing through Beauvais has reached Brouinlieu—an advance of 40 miles in 24 hours.

Moving north

Enemy vehicles have been seen moving north of Amiens, but the German transport problem is extremely critical.

Canadian troops are in Rouen.

In a number of towns we have seen French flags flying, although we have not actually reached them, and that may indicate that the French Forces of the Interior have taken them over.

The weather over there

Battlefield weather yesterday:

Thundery cloud in patches; frequent heavy rain squalls sweeping the front.

[In the Straits last evening a westerly wind was blowing at almost gale force and seas were heavy. The barometer showed a slight rise.]

P-planes from Belgium

Halifaxes and Lancasters of R.A.F. Bomber Command, with fighter cover, yesterday attacked long-range weapon supply depots in Northern France

IT is believed that the enemy was using a new northerly flying-bomb base yesterday.

Most of the bombs which were launched in a series of short attacks appeared to come over the French coast between Calais and Dunkirk.

Observers think that most of them were discharged from sites in Belgium.

If the enemy attempts to continue the bombardment from Belgium (writes an Air Correspondent) it will mean that the bombs will have a greater sea distance to cover, and our aircraft patrol will have more time and space in which to attack them.

Free from A.A. fire

Our aircraft would also have an opportunity of tackling the bombs free from enemy A.A. fire.

South-Eastern and Eastern England are within range of flying-bomb attacks from the Belgian coast in the Ostend area, but clearing the Pas de Calais will rob the enemy of numerous sites that were prepared for constant and intensive attack on this country.

He is not likely to be so well prepared in Belgium and will not be encouraged to make expensive installations there in view of the threat of the advancing Allied armies.

From other sites yesterday only a score or so of bombs came over in ten hours. Formerly a similar number usually came over in one hour.

Japan's turn next, says Roosevelt

From Our Own Correspondent

NEW YORK, Thursday.

AT their forthcoming meeting President Roosevelt and Mr. Churchill will determine the role of Britain in the conquest of Japan when Germany is defeated.

These decisions, and decisions on the plans for the Allied occupation of Germany, which, it is expected, will also be reached at the forthcoming meeting, will enable both countries to complete their arrangements for demobilising some fraction of their armed forces.

Hungary asks for our terms

—Istanbul report

HUNGARIAN circles in Istanbul have received a report that Hungary has approached the Allies for armistice terms. There is no indication that such a step has been undertaken in Turkey.

It was officially stated in Cairo yesterday that the Bulgarian delegation there is segregated until the Allied terms are presented to them. There is no question of negotiations.

There is no disposition on the Allied side to treat the Bulgarians as any other than representatives of an enemy Power.

Bulgaria aids Nazis

A Tass message from newly-captured Constanza to Moscow—where the Rumanian armistice delegation now is—reports that 48 hours ago 23 armed German ships arrived in the Bulgarian Danube port of Rustchuk to join others already sheltering there, and were not disarmed or interned.

Other German warships and submarines are reported to have taken refuge in the Bulgarian Black Sea ports of Varna and Burgas, and the Bulgarians have already helped the Germans to scuttle several of them.

Others are stated to have been accepted by the Bulgarians as part of the settlement of German trading debts.

No effort is being made by the Bulgarians to intern or to evict German units which are in partial control of their country.

News Chronicle Moscow Correspondent and Reuter

DR. GOEBBELS THINKS AGAIN ABOUT SECRET WEAPON "MIRACLES"

GOEBBELS'S latest warning on secret weapons is addressed to the German people.

It would be foolish, he told them in his weekly article in "Das Reich" yesterday, to expect a sudden change in the war situation overnight as an immediate result of the use of new weapons.

Dr. Goebbels said: "We must summon all our strength to overcome the enormous difficulties before us.

"The enemies of Germany are set on forcing a decision favourable to them this year, and the development of Germany's new arms, which would offset the vast Allied superiority in men and material, cannot come with such a speed as to be immediately effective.

"That is the dilemma which confronts us.

"However, Germany does not mind being slow in coming on, since we know that soon a more favourable situation must arise.

"Of course, we do not intend to serve up a new miracle weapon by which alone we could hope for a turn in the fortunes of war.

"We must look at all the facts of total war. It is just as wrong to assume that modern war is only a question of morale as it is wrong to think that it is a question of technical development alone.

"It cannot be denied that at present our morale is far higher than our technical war potential. We must bring the latter up to the standard of the former.

"It is not so much that we shall acquire a number of new miracle weapons which will turn the tide.

"Rather, the German method of conducting the war will assume different aspects.

"Our enemies will then need as much time to catch up with us as we needed time to catch up with them.

"It will be foolish to think that this change in our favour will take effect from one day to the next immediately our new weapons appear.

"It will take effect relatively slowly and we must have some patience."

Goebbels's new caution is in striking contrast to the confident assurances with which Hitler has tried to sustain the morale of his troops.

A typical recent prophecy was that of District Leader Reineking, of Heepen, on August 13: "The world will be amazed when our new weapons are released. England will then either capitulate or perish."

Only a few days ago a "secret weapon" article in Hitler's newspaper, "Voelkischer Beobachter," said: "We have never been closer to victory than we are now."

8TH ★★★★★★★★★ Sports Complete
Wall Street Financial News

BROOKLYN EAGLE

WEATHER—Cloudy, showers tonight; partly cloudy, warm, less humid tomorrow.

103d Year. No. 240. DAILY & SUNDAY • (Copyright 1944 The Brooklyn Eagle, Inc.) • BROOKLYN, N. Y., FRIDAY, SEPTEMBER 1, 1944 • Entered at the Brooklyn Post-office as 2d Class Mail Matter • 3 CENTS IN NEW YORK CITY ELSEWHERE 4 CENTS

OPEN BATTLE FOR BELGIUM

BULLETINS

1,000 U. S. Fliers Leave Romania

Bucharest, Sept. 1 (U.P.)—More than 1,000 of the 3,000 American airmen shot down in the last year's air "Battle of Ploesti" passed through here today in a great mass evacuation staged by the U. S. 15th Air Force.

HULL DENIES ANY NAZI PEACE TALK

Washington, Sept. 1 (U.P.)—Secretary of State Cordell Hull said at his press conference today that the United States had not received any surrender or peace offer from Germany.

Continued on Page 13

BASEBALL—Local Teams

Giants	0	0	0	0	0	0	1	0	■	— ■
Dodgers	0	0	6	0	2	0	0	0	■	— ■

Batteries—Feldman, Lombardi; Herring, Owen.

Senators	1	0	0	2	0	0	2	■	—
Yankees	0	0	0	0	0	4	■		—

Batteries—Thesenga, Ferrell; Roser, Garbark.

BELMONT RESULTS (Saratoga Meeting)

1—Sea Base 11.10-5.40-2.90, Patricia P 8.60-3.70, Pilate's Echo 2.30 (1:21½)
2—Bay Magic 27.10-13.30-6.00, Morani 13.30-6.50, More Wine 4.70. (1:51)
DAILY DOUBLE PAID $165.70
3—Be Faithful 2.70-2.30-2.40, Super Fortress 6.20-4.30, N'ecase 5.70. (2:22)
4—Extra Base 6.40-3.70-3.10, Little Flyer 4.00-3.10, Abignonia 5.10. (2:53½.)
5—Elkridge 4.50-3.20-2.60, Bridlespur 7.90-3.50, Invader 3.10. (3:24)
6—Bon Jour 4.60-3.10-2.50, Great Rush 7.20-3.80, Eternity 2.90. (4:03½)

SEVENTH RACE—
1—Night Glow
2—Dora Dear
3—Resplendence
4—Dare Me
5—Directory
6—Sea Frolic
7—Free Air
8—Sticky Kitty

FIRST 3 SECOND 5 THIRD 1

Charts, Entries, Selections, Baseball on Page 17

Dodgers Score 6 Runs in 3d

The Dodgers scored six runs to chase Harry Feldman from the hill in the third inning of the game with the Giants today at Ebbets Field.

Mickey Owen passed his physical examination today and was accepted for military service. He will remain with the Dodgers until called.

Game in Detail

FIRST INNING—Rucker popped to Stanky. Galan took Hausmann's fly. Ott filed to Olmo. No runs, no hits, no errors, none left.
Bordagaray filed to Medwick. Owen

Continued on Page 17

7-INNING BOX SCORE

GIANTS	A.B.	R.	H.	O.	A.	F.
Rucker, cf	3	0	[illegible]	1	1	[illegible]
Hausm'n, 2b	3	0	0	2	1	6
Ott, rf	3	1	2	1	0	[illegible]
Medwick, lf	0	0	0	1	0	[illegible]
Sloan, lf	2	0	0	1	0	0
Lombardi, c	3	0	1	1	0	0
Kerr, ss	2	0	0	4	0	[illegible]
Reyes, 1b	3	[illegible]	0	8	1	0
Jurges, 3b	2	0	0	1	2	0
Feldman, p	1	[illegible]	0	1	0	0
Hansen, p	0	0	0	0	1	[illegible]
Gee, p	0	0	0	0	3	0
Mancuso	0	0	0	[illegible]	0	0
Luby	1	0	0	0	0	0
Totals	23	1	3	21	9	1

DODGERS	A.B.	R.	H.	O.	A.	E.
Bordagaray, 3b	4	1	[illegible]	[illegible]	0	0
Owen, c	4	1	3	2	[illegible]	
Galan, lf	4	0	0	1	0	
Walker, rf	2	2	0	1		
Olmo, cf	3	2	1	4	[illegible]	
Schultz, 1b	4	0	2	6	[illegible]	0
Stanky, 2b	3	0	1	4	4	
Brown, ss	3	1	1	3	2	0
Herring, p	3	1	0	0	1	0
Totals	3)	8	11	2	7	0

Betz, Osborne Gain in Net Play

Defending champoin Pauline Betz of Los Angeles and second seeded Margaret Osorne of San Francisco gained the semi-finals of the national amateur women's singles tennis championship today

Continued on Page 17

Marlboro Results

1—Cominch. 4.60, 2.40, 2.30; Sunbee. 5.50, 2.30; Electric, 3.00. Off time, 2:32.
2—Nepolee, 4.30, 2.50, 2.20; Well Alright, 3.20, 2.80; Sharp Reward, 2.80. Off time, 3:05½.
DAILY DOUBLE PAID $9.50

Dade Park Results

1—Felicity, 3.20, 2.40, 2.20; Lady Discovery, 2.60, 2.40; High Batts, 2.40. Off time, 4:01.

Thistle Downs Results

1—Coboriation, 1st; Viva Voce, 2d; Lucky Lettie, 3d.

Detroit Results

FIRST RACE—
1—Blue Imp
2—Connecticut
3—Kiss-Kiss
4—Lochlea
5—Virginia Van
6—Big Boso
7—Ebony Bee
8—Tack Force
9—Nancy Lee
10—Gold Queen
11—Way Cloud
12—Reigh Veil

FIRST SECOND THIRD

Two Chinese Executed

Special to the Brooklyn Eagle

Ossining, Sept. 1 — Yun Tieh, 24, and Lew York Hing, 19, Chinese immigrants, died in the electric chair last night at Sing Sing prison for the strangling of Marjorie Jasey, 18, during a robbery in Manhattan in January, 1943.

KENNEDY NAMED TO U. S. BENCH

Federal Prosecutor Picked by Roosevelt To Succeed Campbell

Washington, Sept. 1 (U.P.)—President Roosevelt today nominated United States Attorney Harold Maurice Kennedy to be Federal District Judge for the Eastern District of New York, succeeding the late Marcus B. Campbell.

Kennedy, who was Assistant Attorney General in N. Y. State in 1939, has been U. S. attorney for the Eastern District since Aug. 4, 1939

Served Under Amen In Borough Probe

Mr. Kennedy has been United States Attorney for the Brooklyn-Long Island district since his appointment in 1939. He had served before that, as special assistant under John Harlan Amen in the investigation of corruption in public office and in 1928 was chief counsel for the ambulance chasing investigation.

As United States Attorney he has prosecuted 42 espionage cases, said to be the largest number of such prosecutions in any district, three Japanese propaganda cases and many others. He received a high commendation from Secretary of the Navy Knox, as well as from Edward Stetinnius, assistant Secretary of State, and Lord Halifax, British Ambassador, for handling of a ship libel case in such a way as to permit the ship involved to sail on scheduled with her convoy.

Mr. Kennedy is a member of the law firm of Delatour, Kennedy & Miller, 185 Montague St., of which the other partners are Hunter Delatour and Walter A. Miller.

He was a naval lieutenant in World War I and is a member of Old Glory Post, American Legion, and the Legion's 40 and 8. Mr. Kennedy's son, Robert A. Kennedy, was football captain of Poly Prep and recently was awarded the Yale Cup.

Advised of the nomination, Mr. Kennedy said: "It's an honor one could not refuse."

Garden State Results

1—Belmatch, 25.20, 10.80, 6.10; Opalocka, 24.10, 14.40; aSoma Lassie, 5.70. Off time, 2:36½.
aArcher-Taylor entry.
2—Anamosa, 8.10, 3.50, 4.20; Whetstone, 7.20, 5.30; Tintrel, 6.70. Off time, 3:10.
DAILY DOUBLE PAID $164.10
3—Sting Les, 5.90, 3.30, 2.40; Lanceron, 3.00, 2.20; Rosa Azteca, 2.50. Off time, 3:38.
4—First Admiral, 5.00, 3.10, 2.80; aLanlast, 4.50, 3.30; Blue Kilts, 4.20. Off time, 4:07½.
aStanley entry.
FIFTH RACE—
1—Squadron
2—Legation
3—Saxon Paul
4—Hard Cracker
5—Brenner Pass

FIRST SECOND THIRD

Naragansett Park Results

1—Quakertown, 10.20, 5.60, 3.60; Down Six, 30.00, 17.80; Halcyon Boy, 7.40. Off time, 2:32½.
2—Canopus, 10.80, 8.40, 6.60; On High, 17.20, 10.20; Mossy Lake, 8.20. Off time, 3:04½.
DAILY DOUBLE PAID $432.40
3—West Fleet, 10.40, 6.20, 3.80; Hazard, 8.20, 5.20; Jes Lov Me, 3.80. Off time, 3:33½.
4—Peraliage, 36.00, 13.40, 8.40; Dear Miss 10.40, 7.60; Missmenow, 17.00. Off time, 4:05.
FIFTH RACE—
1—Captain's Aide
2—Friend Or Foe
3—Railroader
4—Jamoke
5—Damask Rose
6—Boysan
7—Eaglestone
8—Prince Puck

FIRST SECOND THIRD

Washington Park Results

1—Troop Train, 4.20, 3.00, 2.80; Lostahat, 4.40, 3.40; Big Me, 4.20. Off time, 4:08.
SECOND RACE—
1—Sales Talk
2—Roger's Boy
3—Lone Ace
4—Stage Door
5—Rex Avis
6—Recalling
7—Broadhead
8—Early N Smart
9—Free Miss
10—Bright Reigh
11—Mismark
12—Jack K
13—Running Sue
14—Infinity Flirt
15—Free Style
16—To A Tee

FIRST SECOND THIRD

Verdun Falls, Yanks Push On

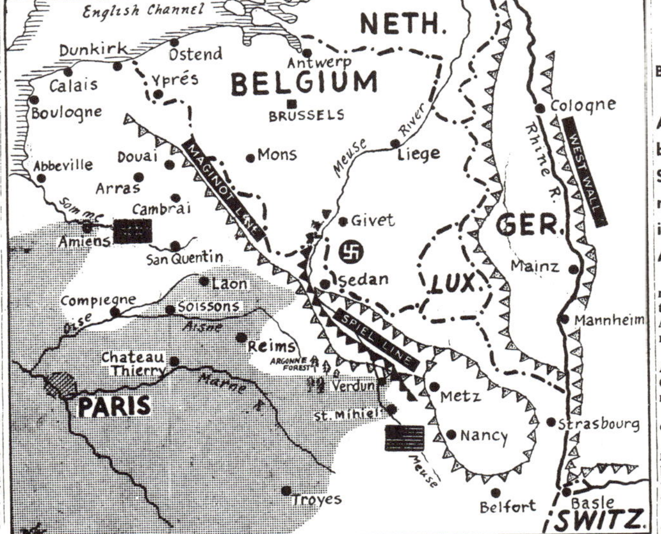

THE WAR TODAY—Mighty Allied armies rolled toward Belgium and the Reich today, snapping up formidable Verdun in stride, crossing the Meuse River and aiming at Hitler's inner defenses. Soon the vaunted Westwall or Siegfried Line will be tested. Eagle's war map based on information available at 2 p.m., Brooklyn time.

BULLETIN

Supreme Headquarters, A. E. F., Sept. 1 (U.P.)—Two American tank armies opened the battle for Germany and Belgium along a 100-mile front tonight, capturing Verdun and St. Mihiel and breaking into the historic Ardennes Gap above Sedan.

By VIRGIL PINKLEY

Supreme Headquarters, A. E. F., Sept. 1 (UP)—American troops were reported to have opened the battle of Belgium in the Ardennes Forest north of Sedan tonight, while the U. S. 3d Army's tanks and riflemen surged past the fallen fortress of Verdun in a lightning drive that Berlin said had broken into Alsace-Lorraine only 25 miles from Germany.

Attacking under a mighty aerial barrage that littered the roads to the Rhineland with enemy dead and the wreckage of thousands of Nazi transport vehicles, the American 1st and 3d Armies pounded in on Germany and Belgium along a front of more than 50 miles.

German resistance melted away under the paralyzing American thrusts that stabbed at Belgium and the Ardennes Gap on the north and sprawling iron and steel centers of Lorraine at the southern end of the line.

(American troops have captured St. Mihiel, historic scene of bitter fighting in the first World War.)

The outer works of the Maginot Line, where some military men thought the fleeing Germans might stand and fight, were breached and overrun by fast-rolling American drives across the Meuse below Sedan and beyond Verdun in little more time than it took to drive through them.

The United Nations radio at Algiers broadcast a front report that units of the American 1st Army had reached the Belgian border at an undisclosed spot north of Sedan.

Headquarters spokesmen had no confirmation of the report, but it appeared likely that the Yanks already had smashed across the border and were sweeping forward through the same Ardennes Gap in which the Nazi hordes came in the Summer of 1940 to conquer France.

On the Canadian right flank, the British 2d Army drove 21 miles beyond Amiens to capture Hebuterne, 12 miles

Continued on Page 2

SOVIET TANKS DRIVE TO BORDER OF BULGARIA

Thousands of Foe Pocketed in Sweep 35 Mi. Past Bucharest

By HENRY SHAPIRO

Moscow, Sept. 1 (U.P.)—Soviet tanks and mechanized cavalry swept 35 miles beyond Bucharest, liberated capital of Romania, to the Danube River border of Bulgaria today in relentless pursuit of Germany's fleeing, decimated Balkan legions.

Other elements of Marshal Rodion Y. Malinovsky's 2d Ukrainian Army to the north already had swung west through the Transylvanian and Carpathian Alps toward Hungary and a junction with Marshal Tito's partisan army in Yugoslavia.

(Tito's Partisans have gained control in the Bioce-Brusi sector of western Serbia, cutting all enemy communications between Serbia and Bosnia, a communique to London said.)

Reach Danube

Front dispatches disclosed that a Russian armored column had

Continued on Page 13

79 BORO, QUEENS, L. I. MEN IN CASUALTY LISTS

The War Department today announced the names of 69 Brooklyn, Queens and Long Island men wounded in action in the Asiatic, Central Pacific, European, Mediterranean and Southwest Pacific areas and the Navy Department announced ten local casualties.

The complete latest casualty lists for this area are on Page 15.

Greek King in London

London, Sept. 1 (U.P.)—King George of Greece arrived in London today to confer with British leaders.

Nazis Seize Budapest As Balkans Seek Peace

Troops March Into Slovakia to Battle Guerrillas—Bulgar Cabinet Reported Out

London, Sept. 1 (U.P.)—German troops were reported occupying the seething Hungarian capital of Budapest today and an unconfirmed Berlin broadcast said the entire Bulgarian cabinet had resigned in the midst of its peace negotiations with the Allied powers.

With Patriot oands in open revolt against the Nazis in Slovakia and the Hungarian people reportedly clamoring for peace, there were signs that Berlin had recovered from the initial shock of the Balkan uprising and was taking drastic counter-measures.

German troops marched into Slovakia to battle the Patriot forces and a United Nations radio broadcast from Algiers said they also had assumed complete military control of Budapest.

The German D. N. B. news agen-

Continued on Page 13

REPORT GOERING FIRED

London, Sept. 1 (U.P.)—Neutral dispatches to London said today Adolf Hitler had relieved Marshal Hermann Goering of his post as the Reich's air defense chief and was preparing to proclaim a "general people's war" to defend Germany.

A Berne dispatch said Hitler intended to call up every German civilian able to carry arms, including women and children. Stockholm reports said Deputy Nazi Party Leader Martin Borman had replaced Goering as ARP Director.

Oysters 'R' in Season

The lowly oyster came back into prominence today just because there nappens tc be an R in September. You know, of course, that this is SeptembeR 1.

Peace May Need Aid Of Force, Says Pontiff

By HENRI GRIS

London, Sept. 1 (U.P.)—Pope Pius XII, addressing the world by radio on the fifth anniversary of the beginning of World War II, said tonight that the "threat of armed force might have to be enforced even after the cessation of hostilities to preserve the peace" but that postwar settlements must be based on "justice for all."

"The social policy of the future will have to protect personal property," His Holiness asserted. "Small and medium property in agriculture, industry and commerce must be encouraged and guaranteed. In the future the private property of everybody must be insured. Private property must not overshadow general property but must be a part of it."

The Pope foresaw a "great economic struggle" which will start when the war—now at a "decisive point"—ends.

He expressed horror at the violence now sweeping the earth and appealed to the victorious nations to insure peace that would uphold the "fundamental rights of all peoples."

"We are appealing even to those who do not belong to the family of our Church to reconsider collaboration with all nations of a Christian civilization because there can be no advantage to humanity without a basis of Christianity," His Holiness said.

"In the midst of so many ruins of souls some honest people have remained pure and are now preparing for the great work of reconstruction in the world.

"All men are waiting for the end of the war. The promises made by statesmen must be fulfilled."

Laval Still Clinging To Nazis Victory Hopes

By United Press

Pierre Laval was reported by the Tokyo radio today to be still faithful to Franco-German collaboration and to be confident of final German victory.

The broadcast, reported by the United Press in San Francisco, said Laval made the declaration at a meeting in eastern France with Marshal Petain and Vichy cabinet members.

Senator Norris, Ill, Growing Weaker

McCook, Neb., Sept. 1 (U.P.)—Physicians attending former Senator George W. Norris said today he was "growing steadily weaker."

Norris, 83, suffered a cerebral hemorrhage Tuesday. The physicians said his temperature was above normal and his condition continued critical.

WHERE TO FIND IT

DAILY MIRROR, Tuesday, September 5, 1944.

Daily Mirror

SEPT 5

No. 12,704 ONE PENNY Registered at the G.P.O. as a Newspaper.

INTO HOLLAND—BRITISH TRAP 100,000 HUNS

370 buzz-bombs in week but mothers come back

"During the week which ended at six o'clock this morning, it is estimated that the enemy launched some 370 flying-bombs against this country, making a total of approximately 8,070 flying-bombs launched since the attacks began," said an Air Ministry statement last night. Up to midnight last night, London's "no-bomb lull" had lasted 100 hours—the longest lull since buzz-bombs began.

THOSE who have been evacuated should stay in their present quarters until we tell them it is safe to return," said a Ministry of Health official.

"Those who return to the south before they get such advice from the Ministry will do so at their own risk, and will receive no assistance from the Government."

The registration scheme for those who wish to be evacuated is still open, and yesterday arrangements were being made in Solihull, Birmingham, for the arrival of 800 children and mothers from London today.

Yet, despite this, London-bound expresses leaving Birmingham yesterday carried a considerable number of families joyfully returning to the capital.

And in London itself a steady stream of returning mothers and children has been growing in the last forty-eight hours.

Many have come back laden with prams, pots and pans and bedding laboriously sent to them a few weeks ago.

At King's Cross a particularly large number were seen yesterday returning from the North.

At St. Pancras the afternoon train from Nottingham was crowded. Many children carried gas masks.

At Euston the numbers were not so great, "but the trickle from the north and Midlands is steady," said an official.

Gestapo terror mounts to hide crack in Reich

By Your Diplomatic Correspondent

THE Gestapo, in desperation at the approach of defeat, have begun a reign of terror in Germany.

Astonishing reports are reaching neutral diplomats in London from their opposite numbers in Berlin. It is clear from these that in many parts of the Reich the ordinary forces of law and order have ceased to exist, and that the armed Nazi gangs are operating against the civil population.

From one source I learned that the German generals condemned to death after the plot against Hitler's life were not hung, as reported in the communiques, but were garrotted.

This was done slowly so as to last about eight minutes, and a film was made by the Ufa company from beginning to end of the executions.

This film has been shown to high officers at every military station in Germany and on all fronts, as a warning of what they can expect if they attempt to defy the Nazis.

Neutral opinion is that the long expected break within the Reich has come at last. If civil war has not actually broken out in Germany there is ample evidence that it is very near.

Swiss reports say there have been large-scale arrests by the Gestapo throughout the Reich of people who tried to dodge the new mobilisation decree.

Nearly 2,000 men and several hundred women have been arrested in Berlin.

GENERAL DEMPSEY'S 38 miles a day tanks, racing 232 miles in six days, have smashed into Holland.

Last night they were at least seven miles over the border after sweeping right across Belgium in less than forty-eight hours.

This lightning drive was announced by the Dutch Premier in a broadcast to the people of Holland.

Dutch officials in London said we had reached Breda, once Rommel's H.Q., thirty miles from Rotterdam.

By liberating the great Belgian port of Antwerp in a twenty-five-mile advance from freed Brussels, Monty's men have given Hitler a Dunkirk of his own.

But he has no gallant fleet of little ships to rescue the 100,000 Huns thought to be trapped between the Rivers Somme and the Scheldt with their backs to the sea.

Monty's successes mean also that 300 miles of the Siegfried Line from Aachen to the Swiss frontier is now directly threatened by Allied armies.

Brussels was captured after one of the most terrific forward drives of the war. One British column did seventy miles in

Continued on Back Page

'INTO GERMANY'—TWO REPORTS

ALTHOUGH security silence still blankets all official news of the Allied drives towards Germany, Charles Collingwood, American radio correspondent in Paris, broadcast last night:

"Although no official information was available in the French capital, it is reported that American troops have entered Germany and may have reached the Rhine."

Algiers radio, quoting Associated Press, reported that Allied troops had reached the German frontier in Belgium at two points ninety miles apart.

SCORCHED EARTH—IN GERMANY

ONCE again in this war the "scorched earth" order has gone forth—only this time it is to the people of Germany.

In a call to a "People's War," to be printed by the entire German Press today, the German people are told:

"Workers and peasants must leave lathe and plough, every village and every farmhouse must become a nest of resistance.

"The enemy must not find a single cornstack to feed him, and every road must be destroyed in his path."

Whether the German people will carry out these suicidal orders in the face of the invading Allied armies is a different matter.

They may lead to the final dissolution of Nazi authority in the immediate rear of the battle areas.

Evacuation of Alsace is in full swing. Krupps factories, Siemen's works and aircraft works are packing their most important machines for transit to Germany.

Roads to the Rhineland are jammed with columns of lorries loaded with food from Alsace, including potatoes and grain.

HG 'demob' plan ready: But it's too early yet

THERE will be no more Home Guard parades—soon. An outline plan for the "standing down" of the force is ready and local details are to be worked out.

But for the present the Home Guard is officially considered necessary.

This is revealed in a letter sent by the War Office to formations and Home Guard units and released for publication yesterday.

"The success on the Continent," the letter says cautiously, "points to the possibility" of the time when all danger is passed being "near."

"It is therefore necessary to have the machinery ready for the standing-down of the Home Guard in order that the detail can be worked out and thus result in smooth and quick operation when the time comes," the War Office says.

"During the last months," the letter says, "the Home Guard has performed a vital service by enabling the regular forces to leave this country and by providing protection against the danger of potential enemy interference. This danger has not yet disappeared.

"The Home Guard has also given the most valuable service in assisting the Civil Defence organisations and the public in connection with the attacks by flying missiles. This danger also has not yet passed."

"May stop work each Sunday as Home Guard protest."—Back Page.

MORE BRITONS ON THEIR WAY HOME

Nearly 3,000 Allied prisoners of war and internees, including 800 British civilians, will be exchanged at Goteborg, Sweden, this week.

Exchanged Germans—2,345—will be taken to Goteborg in the Swedish ships Gripsholm and Drottningholm, and the British Arundel Castle. The ships are due to leave Goteborg with their Allied passengers on Sunday.

BRUSSELS ENVOY

Sir Hughe Montgomery Knatchbull-Hugessen, Ambassador at Ankara, has been appointed Brussels Ambassador.

"WELCOME"—DUTCH PREMIER

PROFESSOR GERBRANDY, Premier of Holland, addressing his people by radio last night, welcomed the Allies to Holland. He said:

Now that the Allied armies, in their irresistible advance have crossed the Dutch frontier I wish to extend a hearty welcome to them on behalf of you all.

You will prepare for them the reception they have earned, as soldiers in the cause of freedom.

The hour of liberation has struck. Soon the moment will come when the Queen will return in your midst to govern in justice and peace.

General Eisenhower also addressed a message to the Dutch. It was an instruction to the people of Rotterdam to preserve their harbour. He called on owners and workers in factories to protect all industrial installations.

The message was followed by a radio intimation that it should not be regarded as a general call to armed resistance in Rotterdam.

Average net paid circulation for August exceeded
Daily---2,050,000
Sunday-3,700,000

DAILY 

NEWS

Copr. 1944 by News Syndicate Co. Inc. NEW YORK'S PICTURE NEWSPAPER Trade Mark Reg. U. S. Pat. Off.

Vol. 26. No. 62 New York, Tuesday, September 5, 1944★ 36 Pages 2 Cents IN CITY LIMITS | 3 CENTS Elsewhere

BRITISH FREE ANTWERP AND BRUSSELS

Story on Page 3

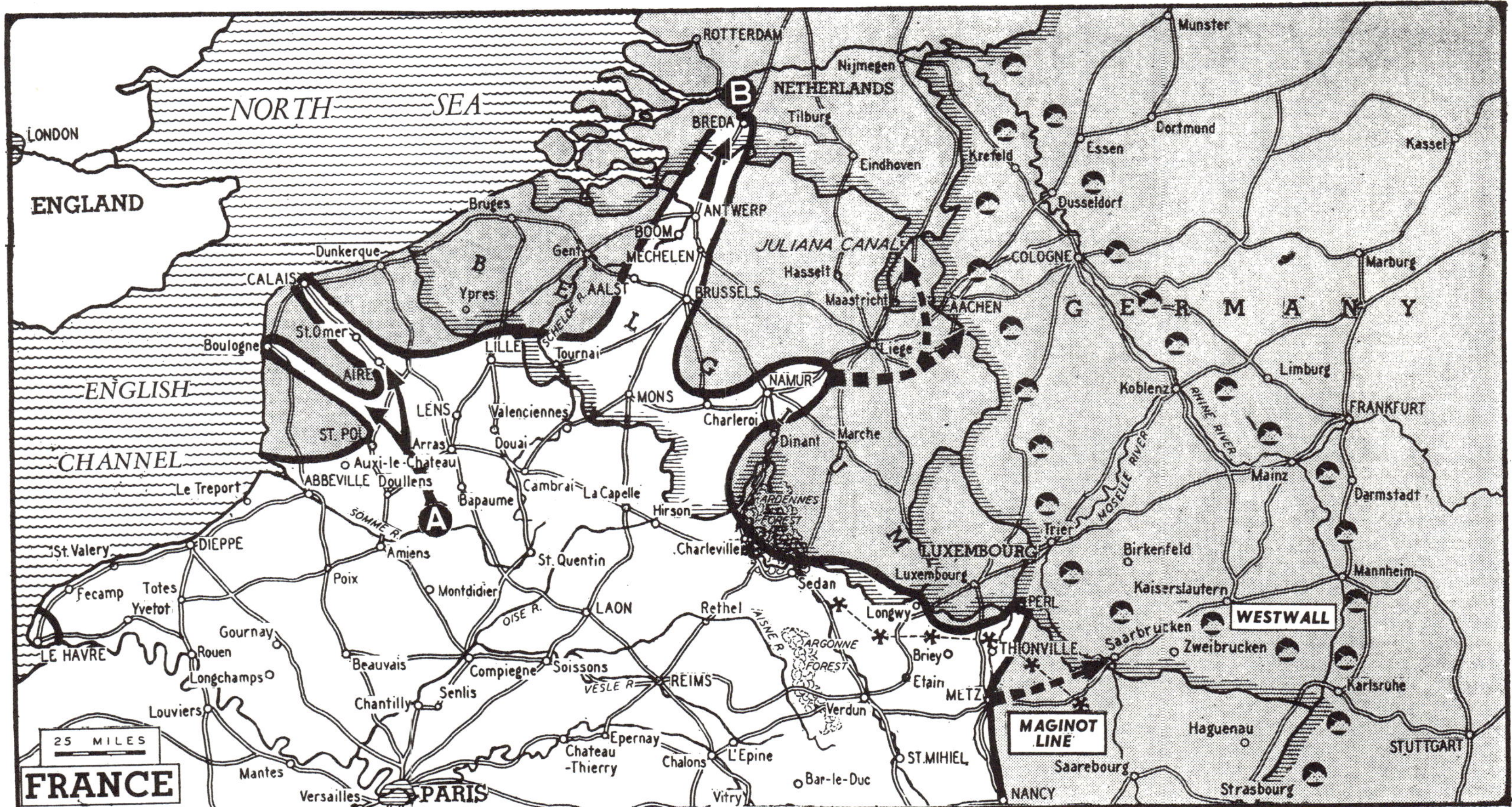

(NEWS map by Staff Artist)

Nazis Reel Back. Canadian and British forces (A) cutting into coastal pocket in which 100,000 Germans were trapped, drove into Calais and Boulogne. Meanwhile, British 2d Army smashed across Netherlands frontier to take Breda (B). Yanks (broken arrows) were reported probing German defenses around Aachen and Saarbrucken. —*Story on page 3*

News Chronicle

No. 30,675 WEDNESDAY, SEPTEMBER 6, 1944 ONE PENNY

SIEGFRIED LINE BATTLE BEGINS

Allies reported to have taken Aachen and Saarbruecken

REPORTS received in London last night indicate that the battle for the Siegfried Line has now begun.

1. Messages from Berne say that Aachen and Saarbruecken have been captured;

2. Paris radio reported that American tank forces, passing through Belgium, have reached the German frontier at many places and that other tanks are approaching the Siegfried Line;

3. A report from the French frontier says that American tanks have reached the outskirts of Strasbourg and that fighting is reliably reported to be taking place on German soil around Saarbruecken; and

4. Between 500 and 750 heavy bombers of the U.S. Eighth Air Force, escorted by up to 500 fighters, yesterday attacked targets at Karlsruhe, Stuttgart and Ludwigshafen.

For Karlsruhe this was the second raid in 24 hours. Mosquitoes were over early yesterday morning.

Targets for the Forts and Liberators were rail yards and repair shops at Karlsruhe; the Daimler-Benz aero engine and motor transport factory at Stuttgart, and industrial targets at Ludwigshafen.

Behind the Siegfried Line there are signs of panic among the German people.

FLEEING FROM FREIBURG

Reports from the Swiss frontier say that since Monday thousands of the inhabitants, together with evacuees from the bombed areas, have been fleeing from Freiburg to the east.

Streams of lorries and vehicles of all kinds, loaded with household goods, are moving from the Belfort area and Alsace and are crossing the Rhine at Weil, where the goods are entrained for transport deeper into Germany.

Late last night Supreme H.Q. broke its three-day silence on the progress of the U.S. Third and First Armies.

The Third Army was reported at Nancy, Commercy, St. Mihiel and north of Rethel.

The First Army has taken Namur and has reached Charleroi, Dinant and Givet.

On the other fronts in Belgium the news is good, although the advances yesterday were slower.

The weather over there

The weather yesterday morning was not quite as good as was expected. There was five-tenths to eight-tenths cloud in the coastal areas, but it was slightly better inland. A considerable improvement later in the day was anticipated

[Weather improved in the Straits last evening. Cloud was high and broken and visibility good.]

FRANCE.—The Canadians are within three miles of Boulogne. At one point they are by-passing the port. Polish forces are reported near St. Omer. The drive on Calais and Dunkirk goes on.

The general position is that three German divisions are being pressed against the coast, perhaps even on to the beaches of Dunkirk.

Thousands of the enemy are surrendering, mainly to the Canadians.

In daylight last evening Lancasters of Bomber Command dropped over 1,000 tons of bombs on enemy troop concentrations in Le Havre. Another force of Lancasters attacked gun emplacements in Brest.

BELGIUM.—Antwerp remains the farthest point in the British advance known to be firmly held. The port and industrial facilities are in good condition, and when the coast of the Dover Straits and the mouths of the Scheldt have been cleared Antwerp will be of the highest value.

The forward area of the advance is now a firmly held wedge point through Antwerp and broadening out to Alost and Louvain in the rear. The bridges over the Dyle River at Louvain are intact, but there is still some enemy resistance in the town.

HOLLAND.—According to one report the British are now 17 miles over the frontier.

Thunderbolt and Lightning fighter-bombers of the Ninth Air Force, continuing their attacks on enemy motor and horse-drawn transport in Belgium and Germany on Monday, carried out operations in a vast triangle bounded by Mons, Antwerp and Cologne.

During the day 211 motor trucks and 194 horse-drawn vehicles were destroyed, according to still incomplete reports.

The leader of one Thunderbolt group said that in Holland "the back-to-Germany movement was in full swing. Bands of soldiers, trucks, troop trains and even civilians were all headed in one direction."

The Prime Minister of Luxemburg announced yesterday that Allied troops had entered his country.

Ronald Walker cabled last night: Wehrmacht disintegration complete

THE RETREAT HAS BECOME A ROUT

News Chronicle War Correspondent

PICARDY, Tuesday.

ALTHOUGH the Germans are still fighting furiously at localised points, there can be no doubt that the retreat of the German army has become a rout.

I cannot quote the author of the following sentence, but I pass it on as a statement made with a detailed knowledge of what is happening in Northern France and Belgium: The distinegration of the German Army is complete.

The Germans, who for years have been schooled into collective thinking, are now thinking individually. Their single thought is how to get back to Germany. Their last hope is the safety of the Siegfried Line.

This is the immediate picture: but if you take the long view there is the spectacle of Germany faced with the final, major disaster.

At the Eastern approaches to Germany are the armies of Russia. The armies of Britain, America and Canada, with contingents of Poles, Norwegians, Belgians and French have arrived at the Western approaches.

East or West

Inside Germany the enemy may be able to assemble sufficient troops to defend either the East or the West; but not both.

Which is it to be? That question will soon be answered.

I have used the word disintegration. Perhaps these figures of the existing strength of three German divisions will show how far-reaching is this collapse.

One division has been reduced to three officers and 90 other ranks, equipped only with infantry weapons—rifles and machine-guns. Another has only 800 men with infantry weapons. A third has ten officers and 140 other ranks.

The normal strength of a division is around 12,000 men.

Another interesting and significant fact has come to light.

Left to fight

German divisions, or what is left of them, retreating along the Channel coast have been ordered to hand over their arms and equipment to holding troops and to make their way back to Germany as best they can.

The holding troops are ordered to fight rearguard actions to enable their comrades to escape.

And these retreats are at the other end of the scale of the former German triumphal progress. These soldiers are often ragged and hungry, with their boots in tatters. They live like the mercenaries of old, on the country through which they pass. They have no means of communication.

For the first time the German Army is starved of equipment. Its tanks, guns, lorries, carts and equipment are scattered wholesale along the roads and in the fields, burned out and wrecked. The train of supplies from Germany has ceased.

Air power

We are now realising in full the fruits of our overwhelming air power.

Close support given by the medium bombers, fighters, fighter-bombers and rocket-firers have knocked from the hands of the German Army the weapons on which they depended.

On D-Day these did not lack quality; but already there was a lack of quantity. But now there is no more, or very few.

This is the direct result of our long-range strategic bombing of German industrial centres which has so reduced supplies of essential equipment that the German forces have been forced to live on the fat of their stocks.

These stocks, so far as we can find out here, have been exhausted, and little else remains.

In this way the heavy bombers of the R.A.F. and the U.S. Army Air Forces have contributed directly to the sweeping victories of the Allied armies in France.

Into the Reich

Apart from using a few air bases in Holland, it is evident that the Luftwaffe has retreated right into Germany.

As a contributing factor in trying to slow up the forward progress of the Allied forces it has ceased to exist.

As we race forward we get nearer and nearer to England. These rapidly-changing conditions have changed the nature of our air operations and have introduced problems for us.

The ground forces are no longer asking for air support. They have no need to. Furious German resistance sometimes consists of 40 or 50 odd men or less fighting to their last bullet.

More often than not our forward patrols race on and meet with no resistance, to be followed up by the main contingent. These in turn leave behind them in the woods small parcels of German troops, who are either tracked down or finally come out voluntarily and disconsolately.

Because the ground forces no longer need air support—although they may ask for it at any time—the R.A.F. Second Tactical Air Force has been left to operate more or less independently during the past few days.

They patrol for enemy movement on the ground with some success and for enemy movement

Continued Back Page A

Rumours

Rumours multiply and spread as the war in the West reaches its climax. Here is last night's crop, gleaned from Sweden to Spain:

"RIOTING IN THE REICH"

THE Stockholm "Tidningen" printed last night a story of a Nazi garrison's mutiny near Berlin; and rioting in several Reich cities, with crowds of women and soldiers shouting, "We want peace and down with Hitler."

S.S. Guards fired on the demonstrators, killing several, the Stockholm accounts say.

"PRIMAVERA IS RIBBENTROP"

HERR PRIMAVERA, the priority-passenger in the big blacked-out plane that flew from Berlin to Barcelona may have been Ribbentrop, Nazi Foreign Minister, it is rumoured in Madrid.

Von Papen, ex-envoy to Turkey; Funk, Reichsbank president, and Curtius, former Foreign Minister, are also said to be in Lisbon, probing the chances of sanctuary "pending peace moves."

"PEACE—NO; IT'S STILL WAR"

BRUSSELS radio repeated the rumour that the Nazis had surrendered, quoting "foreign broadcasts." But Supreme Headquarters were still unable, late last night, to state who first put out the report.

More of such rumours can be expected (writes the Political Correspondent). They must be treated with the utmost caution.

London peace rumours: Page Three

Tirpitz is bombed again

The German battleship Tirpitz was one of many targets hit when the Fleet Air Arm made its greatest attack on Norway last month.

Last night's Admiralty communique said that the Tirpitz was attacked with large and medium bombs, and hits were claimed, but smoke-screens hid results.

A destroyer and a tanker were set on fire, a flak ship blown up and 16 other vessels, including a U-boat, damaged.

Four enemy planes were shot down, four destroyed on the water and others on the ground.

Our losses were a frigate and 11 planes.

Full story Page Three

Bombarded Warsaw has no light

Gen. Bor, C.-in-C. Polish Patriot Army, stated in a communique yesterday on the fighting in Warsaw:

"Since daybreak on Monday the enemy has been carrying out a concentrated bombardment of the city by heavy artillery and from the air. The main power station is destroyed and the whole city is without light.

"We succeeded in evacuating all our troops with their arms and equipment, as well as the slightly wounded and the prisoners, when we were forced to abandon the Old Town."

Vernon Bartlett on Polish Government Crisis: Back Page

Greeks form Unity Government

Cairo, Tuesday.—M. Papandreous, Greek Prime Minister, has now completed a National Unity Government which has decided to disavow the Naza - inspired "security battalions" in Greece and to make an appeal to the Greek people by radio and leaflets dropped from plane to abandon internecine strife.—Reuter.

The old lady with the umbrella

Seen in Brussels:

An old Belgian lady dressed all in black, busily prodding with her umbrella three German prisoners who were being led through the streets.

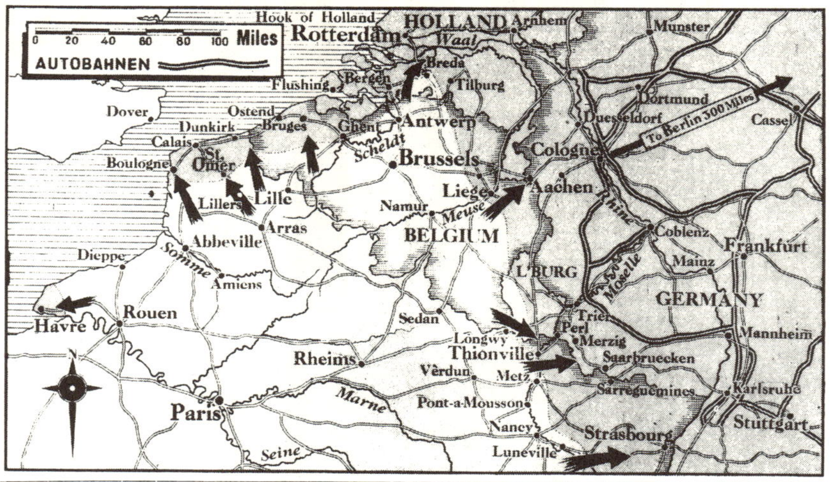

80 journalists are arrested in Germany

BERNE, Tuesday.

THE "Journal de Geneve," quoting German reports, discloses that more than 80 reporters and editors, suspected of opposition to the Nazi regime, have been sent to concentration camps.

The newspapermen include the staffs of the three main German news agencies—D.N.B., Europa Press, and Transocean.

The report added that several thousand members of old Prussian, Brandenburg, Silesian, Westphalian, and Bavarian families have also been interned since July 20.

Bacon ration cut to 4oz.

THE bacon ration is to be reduced from six to four ounces a week on September 17, reverting to the normal quantity after a temporary increase.

Nazis flee—by hearse

Two hearses and a steam-roller were included among road vehicles in which German soldiers tried to escape from Northern Belgium.

This indication of the Nazi desperation in their attempts to get back to Germany was brought back by an American Thunderbolt group. They had the hearses and the steam-roller in their "bag" on Monday.

THE LAST RESERVES

By DITTMAR

Dittmar, principal spokesman of the Nazi High Command, devoted his weekly broadcast last night to Germany's final effort in the time of crisis.

He went back to the Romans for an example—to the triarium which in the battle groups then formed the last reserves of a formation.

"Our position," he said, "has in the past few days undoubtedly become such that the decision now is undoubtedly in the hands of these last reserves."

Dittmar in full: Back Page

Budapest radio reports sudden disturbance"

The municipal gasworks of Budapest, the Hungarian capital, are out of order because of "a sudden disturbance."

Budapest radio last night asked the entire population of Budapest, Kispest and Ujpest to shut down their gas meters, as no gas will be available until further notice.

Ujpest and Kispest are industrial suburbs of Budapest, and together have a population of over one million.

Budapest was bombed yesterday.

'Phone to Ireland restored

The public telephone service between Great Britain and all parts of Ireland has now been restored.

Lord Haw-Haw is still silent

What has happened to Lord Haw-Haw (William Joyce)?

Last night, for the seventh successive night, he was not heard at his usual time on the German radio. "Views on the News," Joyce's special feature, was read by a deputy.

When he last broadcast Joyce said: "I am going away on a tour of duty." That was on August 30, the day the British Second Army was making its great thrusts beyond the Seine.

Brussels raided

Brussels, Tuesday.—The Luftwaffe dropped several bombs on Brussels yesterday in a tip-and-run raid soon after the German Army had lost the city.—B.U.P.

Sweden shuts door to Nazis

Terrible deeds committed

STOCKHOLM, Tuesday.

SWEDEN will refuse asylum to war criminals and send back to their own country for justice any who "slip through" Sweden's frontiers, Gustav Moeller, Minister of Social Affairs, announced tonight.

Noting that Sweden's frontiers have been open to all refugees, Mr. Moeller said:

"During this war, however, there have been committed terrible deeds of a nature that hardly anybody previously would have thought possible in a world calling itself civilised.

"Such deeds have been committed above all in the occupied countries.

Cannot be justified

"It is probable that many people, knowing that they are responsible for actions which have shocked the minds and sense of justice of ordinary people, and which cannot be justified by the requirements of war, will try to escape to neutral countries, including Sweden, in order to elude punishment.

"It should not be concluded that Sweden will be open or prepared to grant asylum to those who, by their actions, have defied the conscience of the civilised world, or betrayed their own country.

"It can be taken for granted that Sweden will close its frontiers in the face of a large or small invasion of such 'political' refugees."

This was Sweden's first public pronouncement regarding her attitude toward war criminals since the United Nations in 1943 appealed to the neutrals to close their borders on them.

Mr. Moeller revealed that Sweden is at present harbouring 61,000 refugees, including 5,000 from Nazi Germany, Austria and Czechoslovakia.—News Chronicle Correspondent and A.P.

No refuge for them in Argentina

The Argentine Minister in Washington, Rodolfo Garcia Aras, said yesterday that rumours that Argentina might become a refuge for the Nazi leaders are "totally unfounded."

Swiss radio quoted an official announcement yesterday decreeing that all frontier posts are to be mobilised. Announcements to this effect have been posted in all towns concerned.

It has already been reported that the Spanish Ambassador in Washington, Senor Juan de Cardenas, had stated that "no one has ever contemplated providing a hiding-place in Spain for the enemies of the Allied countries."

136 children die on roads

The number of children killed on the roads in July was the highest ever recorded in this month with the exception of July, 1941, states the Ministry of War Transport.

Fatal accidents to child pedestrians numbered 10. In addition 30 child cyclists were killed.

These were more than a quarter of the total road deaths for the month. Casualties to children and adults together totalled 511 killed and 10,302 injured. In July last year the figures were 384 killed and 9,502 injured.

Japs driven from town on Chindwin

KANDY, Ceylon, Tuesday.

THE Fourteenth Army have pushed to the Chindwin River and occupied Sittaung without opposition.

A conservative estimate gives the number of Japanese dead as 1,000. Many were found lying in motor vehicles, in which they had fled before the Allied advance but were prevented by lack of petrol from reaching the Chindwin.

The bodies of hundreds more who starved trying to reach the river have been found in the jungle.

Thirty miles upstream from Sittaung patrols have reached Thaungdut, which is also clear of Japanese.

CALAIS STORES BURNING

FOR over 40 hours up to last night the enemy had been making continuous demolitions in the coastal area of the Pas de Calais.

Yesterday at Deal rumblings and earth tremors were heard and felt all day.

It was judged from the sounds that the enemy w's destroying stores and dumps as well as carrying out demolitions. Both flashes and flames could be seen through the pall of smoke above the French cliffs.

Allied air forces were adding to the destruction.

At times, too, the distant sound of artillery fire was distinct.

LATE NEWS

RESISTANCE STIFFENS

U.S. Third Army H.Q., Tuesday night.—German High Command preparing to contest any further advances into Alsace-Lorraine and towards the Rhine by Gen. Patton's armour, cables Eric Downton, Reuter's Special Correspon-

LONDON BLACK-OUT
9.6 p.m.—6.52 a.m.
Moon rises 10.43 p.m., sets 1.13 p.m. tomorrow. New Moon, Sept. 17.

Russians have declared war on Bulgaria

RUSSIA has declared war on Bulgaria.

A Note complaining that Bulgaria had violated her neutrality by aiding the Germans was handed to the Bulgarian Minister in Moscow last night by Mr. Molotov, Soviet Commissar for Foreign Affairs.

Since Bulgaria's action could only be regarded as participation in the war against Russia, said the Note, Russia had no alternative but to declare war.

"The Bulgarian Government even now refuses to break with Germany, and carries out a policy of so-called neutrality, on the basis of which Bulgaria continues to render Germany direct help against the U.S.S.R., rescuing Germany's retreating forces and giving them a base on Bulgarian territory for a new centre of German resistance."

Out for Warsaw

Last night's Moscow communique announced the capture of Wyszkow, about 30 miles north-east of Warsaw, with 150 others places.

It looks as if the all-out attempt by the Russians to achieve a decision in Central Poland has started with the offensive opened by Gen. Zakharov, north-east of Warsaw, Moscow dispatches said last night.

One of the war's hardest tank battles has been fought to a standstill in this region, after the German High Command had massed its armoured forces with the determination to hold Warsaw and deny the Russian armies a chance of breaking through towards Danzig.

The new thrust by Gen. Zakharov's Second White Russian Army has crossed the River Narev, south-west of Lomzha, and gained an important hold on the Warsaw-Rastenburg (East Prussia) highway. It threatens to split the German front between East Prussia and the Polish capital.

Russian forces are pouring over the pass from Ploesti to the captured road and rail hub at Brasov, important city in Hungarian-occupied Transylvania (cables Paul Winterton, News Chronicle Moscow Correspondent).

Road to Vienna

The road to Vienna lies before them.

With the Russians moving up from the south the enemy has no chance of holding the Carpathian passes for long.

Once again he has no alternative except retreat. Nor can he hope to hold Hungary: it has hostile forces closing in on three sides, and must soon go the way of other satellites

Budapest radio said last night that hostilities had broken out on the Hungarian-Rumanian frontiers. "Hungary has taken the necessary measures to throw back the Rumanian troops which had penetrated Hungarian territory," it said.

NEWS YOU CAN'T GET ELSEWHERE

PM Daily

FIVE CENTS

(Copyright, 1944, by Field Publications)

VOL. V — No. 71

Thursday, September 7, 1944

Scattered Showers, Warm

COMPLETE EDITION

Germans Stop Running

Page 4

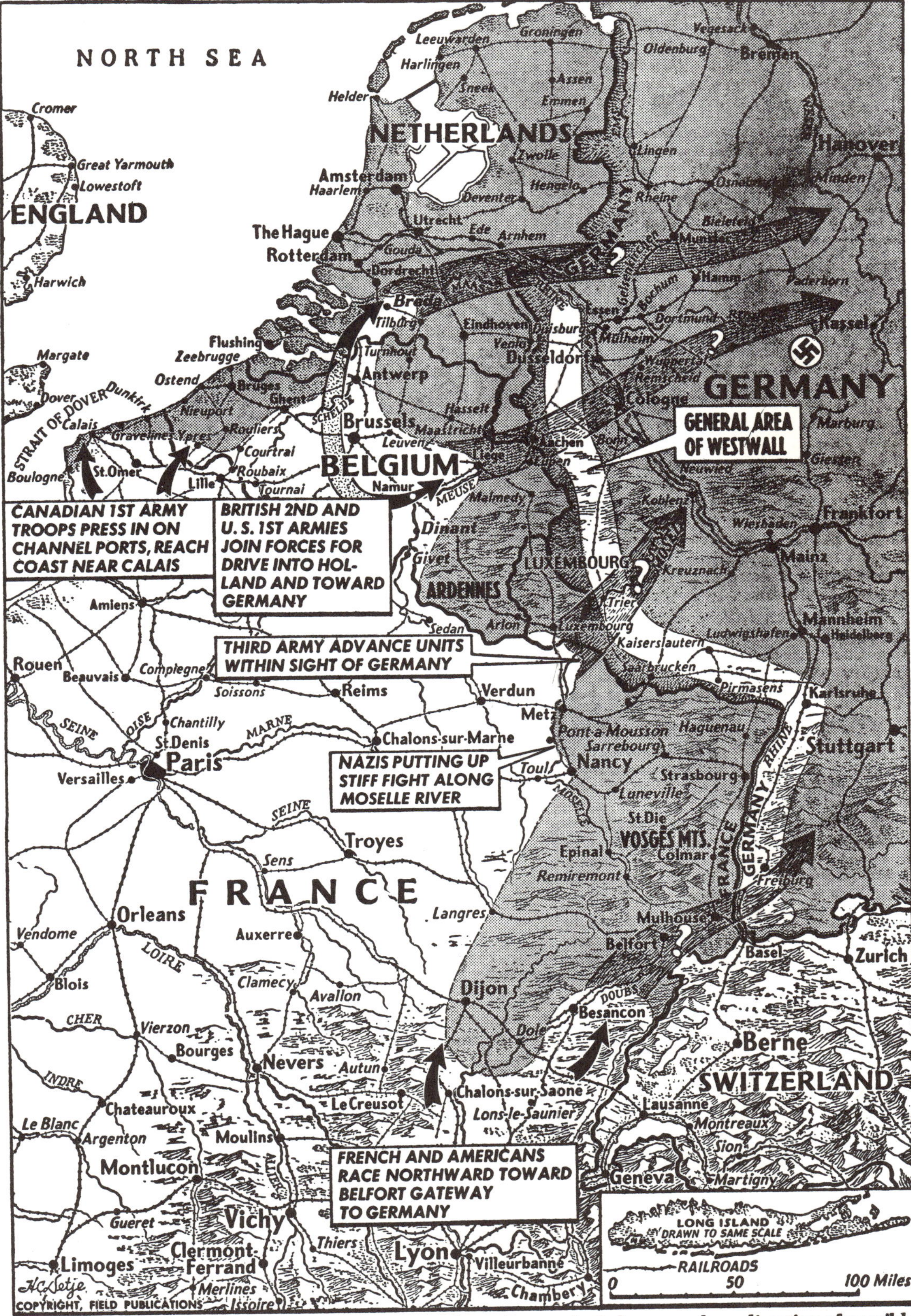

Map shows today's battlelines on the Western front. Large shaded arrows show direction of possible Allied thrusts into Germany.

25 German Divisions Face Balkan Trap

Page 7

German Problem First for FDR-Churchill

Page 9

By Ralph Parker:

What War Is Like to Jap Civilians

Page 7

PM TELLS YOU MORE NEWS IN LESS TIME

DAILY MIRROR, Thursday, September 7, 1944.

Daily Mirror

SEPT 7

No. 12,706 ONE PENNY Registered at the G.P.O. as a Newspaper.

BLACK-OUT OFF

From Sunday week, Sept. 17

FIRE GUARD

Ends Tuesday in most areas

HOME GUARD

No compulsion from Monday

C.D. CUTS

Workers switch to Forces or factories

BY BILL GREIG

HERE is the cheeriest home news Britain's long-suffering civilians have had since the war began five years ago.

The black-out is to end on September 17—a week on Sunday—when Double Summer Time ends. On that date street lamps will be lit once more and you will no longer have to obscure completely the lights from your windows—except in certain coast areas.

Peace-time curtains will do, unless they are very flimsy. The test will be: can objects in the room be seen from the outside?

But don't throw your black-out material away. If the sirens should sound you must be ready to black-out completely again.

Pre-war street lighting will be allowed in districts which have the "master-switch" system. Elsewhere, the lighting will be like that in side-streets before the war.

Fireguard duties will be abolished over a large part of Britain from Tuesday. Daylight guards are abolished everywhere, but in London and in parts of East and Southern England night guards will still be needed.

Over most of Britain whole-time Civil Defence workers are to be switched to the Army or essential work. Many part-timers will be released. For those who remain, maximum hours for duty and training will be cut to twelve a month.

Compulsory drills and training for Home Guards will end as from Monday next—including aid to Civil Defence. Home Guard duties still required will be left to volunteers. The H.G. call-up is suspended.

FULL DETAILS: BACK PAGE.

25,000 prisoners at Mons: Calais entered: Moselle is crossed

As the Pas de Calais battle nears its climax, Allied troops making for the Siegfried Line are crossing the River Moselle in the face of bitter resistance. Twenty-five thousand prisoners, including two divisional generals, have been taken in the Mons pocket in Belgium.

CANADIAN troops were reported last night to have penetrated into Calais and to be less than a mile from Boulogne in the battle to free the south coast of England from the menace of the German cross-Channel guns.

The roar of the battle could be heard in Dover Straits towns. At times big explosions shook English soil, and the German guns fired more salvos of hate across the Channel.

"Hell-fire-corner" had a shell warning from 1.50 p.m. to 3.40 p.m. After a five-hour lull more shells came over as the glow of Calais fires lit up the clouds.

Meanwhile, British troops of the Canadian First Army were carrying out one of the toughest tasks since Caen.

After crossing the mouth of the River Seine in make-shift boats, they were faced with the job of cracking the "suicide" defence of the great port of Le Havre.

Among the British units are the Royal Scots Fusiliers, the Duke of Wellingtons and the King's Own Yorkshire Light Infantry.

Soon after the German garrison had rejected another surrender ultimatum, RAF Lancasters dropped more than 1,500 tons on the port last evening.

Lancasters and Halifaxes bombed Emden, the nearest haven for German ships fleeing from the Channel ports.

Allied bombers made two one-hour attacks on the port of Brest, on which more than 3 000 tons have been dropped since last Friday.

Here is a round-up of the news from other fronts last night:—

CENTRAL FRANCE.—Allied troops are now only forty miles from the Belfort Gap.

BELGIUM.—British troops have reached Ghent, inland port on the Scheldt. Capture of both Antwerp and Louvain has put the British Second Army ahead of schedule.

HOLLAND.—British were said to be "in sight of Rotterdam." Berlin denied that Breda or any other Dutch territory had been occupied.

Govt. plan for cradle-to-grave insurance

By Your Political Correspondent

THE Cabinet is to issue next week its own "Beveridge" scheme, the result of two years' struggle between Ministers of different views and parties.

I understand that it will create a new Ministry of Social Services, to administer a scheme expected to cost £500,000,000 a year at first and £700,000,000 in the years to come.

The main proposal is an all-in insurance scheme, to which everyone will have to contribute, covering them for

Unemployment and sickness.

Family allowances.

Maternity benefits.

Funeral assistance.

The family allowances, which will be paid without means test, will be 5s. a week for each child, as announced by Sir John Anderson more than a year ago.

Continued on Back Page

BBC instructs Nazi slaves

THE 10,000,000 foreign workers inside Germany were advised to leave the towns, hide, collect news and await the arrival of Allied armies by a staff officer of Allied H.Q. who broadcast in the B.B.C. European service last night.

His message was the second broadcast during the day to the workers inside Germany.

Watch the behaviour of the Germans, they were warned; be ready to give details about their crimes and render impossible the destruction of factories and plants, particularly of oil depots which may serve the Allies.

ONLY "IKE" CAN ACCEPT PEACE BID

By Your Diplomatic Correspondent

NO peace overtures from Germany have been made to any of the Allied Governments. Reports of mysterious visitors in London, Lisbon and elsewhere have no foundation in fact.

So far as is known, not one German of any standing has succeeded in leaving his country since the attack on Hitler.

We have, in fact, made it clear to the Germans that there is only one man with whom they can deal, and that is General Eisenhower.

He is empowered by all Allied Governments to accept unconditional surrender if offered by the German High Command.

He would, if necessary, deal with Kluge, his "opposite number" in the West, but only if assured that the surrender included also the armies fighting against Russia.

Meanwhile we are taking no risks of any of the Nazi leaders slipping through our hands.

THURSDAY, SEPTEMBER 7, 1944

Evening Standard

37,437 BLACK-OUT 9.3 p.m to 6.53 a.m. MOON rises 11.10 p.m., sets 2.30 p.m ONE PENNY

FINAL NIGHT EXTRA ●

LONDON'S 80 DAYS: THE FIRST FULL STORY

8000 Fly-Bombs Came Over: Only 9 p.c. Reached London in Last Days: Fighters Got 1900; Defences Had 2000 Balloons, 2800 Guns

AMERICANS ARE THRUSTING INTO THE ARDENNES

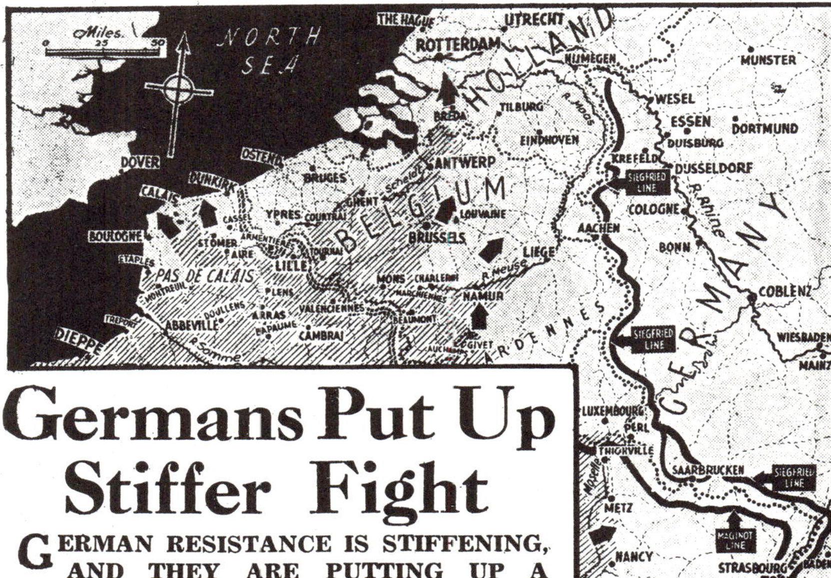

Germans Put Up Stiffer Fight

GERMAN RESISTANCE IS STIFFENING, AND THEY ARE PUTTING UP A DETERMINED FIGHT AROUND NANCY, METZ, CALAIS, BOULOGNE AND LE HAVRE.

Elsewhere the German withdrawal is continuing, say reporters at Supreme Headquarters to-day.

But there are increasing signs that a considerable force of German troops has still to be engaged and defeated either on or before the Siegfried Line.

A new threat to Germany is developing from a drive by the American First Army, who have pushed a column across the Meuse and through the Ardennes Forest beyond Auchamps, 11 miles north of Charleville.

Other columns of the First Army, who crossed the Meuse at Namur, are operating south-east of Namur and north-east of Givet.

This drive across the Meuse is developing well, but reports that our troops are at Liege and Aachen are premature.

"LITTLE CASSINO"

Indications are increasing that General Patton's forces thrusting on to Germany from the Verdun area will face their heaviest fighting within the next two weeks, adds Robert Richards British United Press war correspondent.

"Little Cassino" is the next objective before our assault troops. This is the German position in the hills overlooking the village of Pont à Mousson on the Moselle.

Troops are pouring across the Moselle to build up the bridgehead for the next step to Germany. Petrol armour and supplies have to be brought up before the commander can hit the Germans a real blow and follow up without halting.

PORTS BATTLE

The Germans are still fighting hard for the Channel ports.

Boulogne and Calais are now closely invested. We are in the outskirts of Boulogne, and reconnaissance elements have reached the outskirts of Calais all round the port but no direct assault has yet been launched against either place

Charles Lynch, Reuter correspondent says that advance Canadian spearheads are seven miles west of Dunkirk. Polish troops became the first units of the Canadian Army to cross the Belgian frontier, driving to Ypres and beyond.

The foulest weather since D-Day, with cold rain and fog, failed to hold up the advance as troops by-passed Calais and raced east towards Dunkirk, Ostend and Zeebrugge.

Fanatical resistance continues at Brest and Le Havre.

Communiqué—PAGE THREE.

TERRIBLE CRISIS, SAYS GOEBBELS

"There is no need to be bowled over with astonishment that neutral countries and part of our camp following, too have begun to get wobbly in face of the dramatic sweep of events in the world war situation," says Goebbels in his weekly article in Das Reich, quoted by Reuter.

"A people which defends its freedom can rely only upon itself and its own strength in times of terrible crisis, and this strength suffices in most cases to safeguard the nation's liberty.

"Total Effort"

"That is why it is our duty to pursue the tasks of the people's total war effort with a gravity and zeal as if life itself were at stake. And indeed our national existence is in the balance and with it the personal existence of every single one of us.

"If our enemies now are racing against time, they are forced to do so by dire necessity.

"They see no other way out of the dilemma of a miscarried military policy, which sooner or later must bring about the gravest conflicts among them."

The V-Sign in the Sky

The last rays of the setting sun last night caused a large unmistakable V-sign to appear, says Reuter from Wellington, New Zealand.

'NAZI LINE SHORTENED IN SOUTH'

The Germans this afternoon admitted that their troops in Southern and South-Western France "have been taken back to a shorter line."

They say the German air force have had to help their troops, "often evacuating their wounded by air and dropping arms and ammunition."

French troops moving due north up France have covered 75 miles since they were last checked at Lyons.

They are now well within 25 miles of Dijon.

Reuter's correspondent David Brown says General Patch's Seventh Army are rolling on unchecked towards the Doubs Valley and the Belfort Gap

They have reached the town of Arbois on the road to Besancon after taking Poligy on the way

Arbois adds Reuter, is 25 miles north-east of Lons-le-Saunier, reported occupied by the Americans yesterday

The French and Americans between them have liberated another large segment of Eastern France between the Saone River and the Swiss frontier

PATTON AND PATCH LINK NEAR BORDER

An American commentator, broadcasting from Southern France this afternoon, quoted by Reuter, said: "General Patton's 'Will o' the Wisps' and the Seventh Army (General Patch's forces from Southern France) have joined forces very close to the German border.

"It is not permitted to name the exact point of the junction, but the battered German 19th Army are apt to be caught by it roughly in the region of Belfort."

Berlin asserted to-day, says Reuter, that the German armies in Southern France had got back and joined the main German armies in the north.

"The Battle is Over," Says Duncan Sandys

THE FIRST FULL STORY OF BRITAIN'S BATTLE WITH THE FLYING BOMB, IN WHICH 92 PER CENT OF THE FATAL CASUALTIES WERE IN LONDON, IS REVEALED TO-DAY.

Mr. Duncan Sandys, M.P., Chairman of the Flying Bomb Counter-measures Committee, revealed that during 80 days' bombardment 8000 flying bombs were launched, of which 2300 reached the London area.

THE STORY TELLS OF A GUN BELT WHICH STRETCHED FROM MAIDSTONE TO EAST GRINSTEAD SO AS TO SCREEN LONDON, AND HOW IT WAS DECIDED LATER TO MOVE THE ENTIRE A.-A. BELT DOWN TO THE COAST SO THAT THE GUNS SHOULD HAVE AN UNINTERRUPTED FIELD OF VIEW.

In the first week 33 per cent were brought down and the same proportion reached London, whereas in the last week 70 per cent of the bombs were brought down by the defences and only nine per cent reached London, the others being inaccurate or erratic.

"Except possibly for a few last parting shots, what has come to be known as the Battle for London is over," said Mr. Sandys, who disclosed that bombs were also launched from aircraft, Heinkel 111 being specially adapted.

"As was noticed by many people, a small proportion of the bombs came in by night from a due easterly direction.

"This puzzled us a little at first; because so far as we knew there were no firing sites either in Belgium or Holland. However we very soon obtained information that these flying bombs were being launched not from the ground, but from aircraft.

"Specially adapted Heinkel bombers were carrying the bombs pick-a-back and launching them from the air over the North Sea. These bombs proved less accurate than those fired from the land.

OUR INTRUDERS

"To meet this new form of attack additional guns were rapidly sent to the Thames Estuary, and intruder squadrons were sent out each night to patrol over the Dutch and Belgian coasts.

"At the same time attacks were made on the airfields from which the launching airplanes were operating.

"These counter-measures have reduced the scale of airborne launchings to very small proportions.

"This form of attack can, of course, be carried on from airfields in the heart of Germany.

"We cannot, therefore, as yet assure the public that flying bomb attacks will cease altogether. We can, however, be reasonably confident that the scale of attack will be very small."

A RECORD BAG

The record bag was on August 28, when out of 101 bombs which approached the coast of England 97 were brought down by the defenders and only four reached London.

"More than 8000 flying bombs have been launched at an average of 100 a day. Of these 2300 got

(Continued on Back Page, Col. One).

100 Times More Light In Streets

Evening Standard Reporter

The new "half lighting" which becomes legal on September 17 is 100 times stronger than the "star" lighting which has previously been allowed, it was learned to-day.

But there will be no "flash up" all over the country, or even all over London. Lamps which have fallen into disrepair, shortage of labour and shortage of materials will make the great light up a gradual affair.

One of the difficulties facing lighting authorities is that certain materials have to be bought from specialised firms and this is likely to take some time. Labour supplies, it is pointed out, are "an unknown quantity" depending on many priority factors.

London authorities quickly moved to "action stations," and while workmen overhauled installations many emergency conferences were held to perfect the capital's plans.

Westminster City Council and **Battersea** Borough Council have already given a lead. Westminster have already begun work on the new half-lighting, and Battersea, said Mr. H. F. J. Thompson, the chief engineer, to-day, has all the necessary equipment. Only the labour supply is needed.

A start has been made to light up Piccadilly Circus, but Westminster City Council, whose system is partly gas and partly electricity has no master switch plan. Piccadilly can therefore be expected to be lit like a side street.

At Armistice

A leading official in the gas industry said to-day that preparations for the re-establishment of full lighting at the conclusion of an Armistice are well advanced

"There is no doubt that the streets in the West End of London will be pretty bright on armistice night."

Master Switches

Among the cities with a "master switch" are Leeds and Glasgow They will benefit by having almost a pre-war standard of lighting.

Curtains

The Board of Trade have already arranged for mills making black-out material to switch to the production of ordinary curtaining

The Board's officials are considering whether the material, already off the coupon, can be sold without coupons for other purposes.

Batteries

More radio high-tension batteries, now scarce, may be one result of the dim-out. Manufacturers, who expect to make far fewer torch

(Continued on Back Page, Col. Six)

The "Reply" Cost A Shilling

An ingenious range-finder, so simple that the whole device cost little more than one shilling, was the complete answer to fly-bomb night fighting, said Mr. Duncan Sandys, chairman of the Flying Bomb Counter-Measures Committee, to-day.

It was produced by 56-year-old Sir Thomas Merton.

(See Londoner's Diary.)

We Know Quite a Lot About V2

Mr. Duncan Sandys, asked about V2 to-day, said:

"I am a little chary of talking about V2," he replied. "We do know quite a lot about it.

"In a very few days' time I feel that the Press will be walking all over these places in France and will know a great deal more then than we do now."

A.A. DIARY

Here is the week by week toll taken by the A.-A. guns after the belt had been moved to the coast:

First week	**17 per cent**
Second week	**24 per cent**
Third week	**27 per cent**
Fourth week	**40 per cent**
Fifth week	**55 per cent**
Sixth week	**60 per cent**
The last week	**74 per cent**

"The people of London owe much to the men and women of the A.-A.," said Mr Sandys. "And in particular to General Pile, to whose energy and personal leadership these achievements are in large measure due."

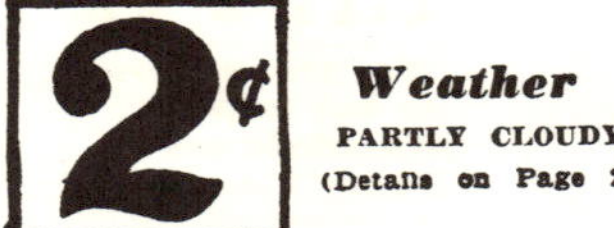

5c Elsewhere in U. S.
3c in Suburbs

Vol. 21. No. 68. R NEW YORK, MONDAY, SEPTEMBER 11, 1944 FINAL 6 A. M. ★★★★

U.S. ARTILLERY POURS SHELLS INTO GERMANY

1st Army 6 Mi. From Aachen, Crosses Luxembourg Border

CHURCHILL IN CANADA FOR TALKS WITH F. D.

Stories on Pages 2 and 3

CITY 6 A.M.

The Sheffield Telegraph

TELEGRAPH—No. 27,809. FOUNDED 1855. TUESDAY, SEPTEMBER 12, 1944 One Penny INDEPENDENT—No. 28,032. FOUNDED 1819.

LARGE PART OF MAGINOT LINE CAPTURED INTACT

ALLIES ENTER GERMANY

U.S. 5 MILES OVER BORDER 'IN REASONABLE STRENGTH'

AT SIEGFRIED LINE

GENERAL HODGE'S First Army troops have crossed the German border in "reasonable strength" some miles north of Trier, it was officially announced at Shaef late last night. They are about five miles inside Germany, and in contact with the Siegfried Line. The entry into Germany was preceded by heavy artillery bombardment.

The crossing was made by troops which had swept across Luxembourg. Trier is in the heart of the Siegfried Line defences, and the Allies are probably probing the crust of Germany's fortress chain. At Shaef it was indicated that once in General Hodge's men intend to stay in.

The report that there was an artillery barrage before their entry is an indication that their advance is being made with full artillery support and quite probably with an adequate air cover. It is the first time Allied troops have fought on German soil since 1940.

LORRAINE TOWN FREED

American forces driving across Lorraine yesterday captured a large part of the Maginot Line intact.

Reuter's correspondent at General Patton's H.Q., cabling this news last night, also reported that U.S. infantry took Aumetz, the first Lorraine town to be liberated.

Aumetz is about ten miles south-east of Longwy and a few miles south of the Luxemburg border. Further south the Moselle battle reached a new pitch, with crack German troops fighting back strongly against the Allied forces engaged in the major operation of forcing the river and smashing through the Lorraine gap.

The Germans have been flung back across the Moselle below Liverdun. They had established bridgeheads in this area and held them for 24 hours. These have now been wiped out.

Third Army troops continue to hold three bridgeheads over the [illegible] last night.

General Patton's most important gain, however, was the capture of the strong fort of Villey le Sec in the outer defences of Nancy. This means that the outer lines protecting the fortress are now breached and the way lies open for a direct attack on the city itself.

NEW THRUST FROM LIEGE

The Allies are now within range of the Siegfried Line all the way south from Aachen to Trier, and their positions there diverge along the more southerly stretch of the Moselle, writes a correspondent from Shaef.

North and east of Liege German resistance is strongest, but east of Liege the Allies have pushed forward and occupied the town of Herve. South-east and south of Liege they have reached the area of Theux, which is about 15 miles from Liege.

There was strong German reaction in the area of Bastogne to the Allied drive to within about four miles of the German border. There is increasing resistance from Luxemburg down to Mersch.

In fierce fighting north of the Albert Canal the British drove the Germans out of the Heichel cross-roads yesterday some distance to the east of Bourg Leopold.

They destroyed a number of self-propelled German 88 mm. guns and some tanks and drove north to the area of De Groote, crossed the Escaut Canal, and sent their patrols up to the Dutch border.

There is considerable evidence of German confusion along the Siegfried Line. They are apparently uncertain where the Allied blows are likely to fall and there are signs that the German soldiers are becoming increasingly dispirited.

Turn to Page 4

PREMIER WAS SEASICK

THE President, before leaving for the Citadel, called out to Mr. Churchill: "Hello! I'm glad to see you. Eleanor (Mrs. Roosevelt) is here. Did you have a nice trip?"

Mr. Churchill replied: "Well, we had three beautiful days, but I was frightfully sick."

When the President said "I have lost some weight," Mr. Churchill rejoined, "I have lost some colour."—Reuter.

WAR IN JAPAN PLANNED

CHATEAU FRONTENAC, QUEBEC, Monday.

WITHIN two hours of their arrival at the Citadel here, Mr. Churchill and President Roosevelt were busily engaged in drawing up the agenda for the coming campaign against Japan.

Conference officials say the agenda is so complicated that it requires detailed discussion by the two leaders to ensure that each segment will dovetail into a master plan which will ultimately bring the war to the Japanese mainland.

The release by the British and U.S. delegations of Stalin's message, declining to come to the Quebec conference on the ground of military preoccupation at home, confirmed that this conference would be carried on without Russian participation.

Therefore the British and American leaders were limited to the consideration of their own resources—confidently considered to be more than enough for Japan.

But a dispatch from Moscow, saying that foreign observers there foresaw continued Three-Power co-operation "elsewhere" after the defeat of Germany, contributed to the generally genial atmosphere here, despite the absence of Soviet representatives.

"Victory Everywhere"

When Mr. Churchill and President Roosevelt arrived in Quebec they had five minutes' animated conversation at the Wolfe Cove Station, before entering separate cars and driving through flagged streets to the Citadel.

A crowd was waiting when Mr. and Mrs. Churchill's train, named the "Bonaventure," arrived from Halifax, Nova Scotia.

The Prime Minister, wearing Trinity House uniform and smoking a cigar, smiled broadly at the crowd and, giving the "V" sign, told them: "Victory is everywhere."

Among those welcoming Mr. Churchill were Mr. Mackenzie King, the Prime Minister of Canada, with whom he and the British Chiefs of Staff will also confer.

Tour Was Preface

Mr. Stephen Early, the White House secretary, told the Press: "The conference opening to-day was preceded by the necessary tour of Pacific bases which President Roosevelt undertook recently and on which he has already reported to the American people.

"It is almost exclusively a military conference and there may be a dearth of news, but we will do our best to keep you informed."

Mr. Cordell Hull, U.S. Secretary of State, has not planned at present to go to Quebec, it was announced to-day.—Reuter, A.P., B.U.P.

Our Political Correspondent writes:—

The Prime Minister will not be back from Quebec in time for the reassembly of Parliament on September 26th, and so Members will have to wait a little longer to hear from him another statement on the war and upon his mission.

Bulgars Free British

Sixty-nine British soldiers, including 48 officers, who were prisoners of war in Bulgaria have been released and have arrived in Istanbul, said Turkish Radio last night.—B.U.P.

To-day's Prayer

By the Rev. George Braithwaite, Wortley Vicarage, Sheffield.

O HEAVENLY FATHER, help me this day to think what is good and do what is right. Put far from me all bitterness and discontent, and draw me into the sunlight of Thy love. Teach me to know Thee by knowing others, to serve Thee by serving others, and to worship Thee in thankfulness of heart and peace of mind. And to bring me into the way of happiness that leadeth to eternal life. Through Jesus Christ our Lord. Amen.

WOODHAM

AID FROM ALL SIDES

From H. S. WOODHAM,
"The Sheffield Telegraph" Military Correspondent
Supreme Headquarters, Monday night.

THE Germans are making a determined stand as the Allies approach the Reich frontiers.

Reinforcements have been brought in from North Holland, Denmark, and Italy—about two divisions in each instance.

The fact that Kesselring, who is so hard-pressed in Italy, has been compelled to send help to France is some indication of the apprehension felt by the German High Command about the effects of an Allied crossing of the frontiers.

It is possible that more troops may be brought from Denmark. Here there were four divisions, and if these are all rushed to France they may be replaced in Denmark by units from Norway, who will in turn be replaced by the divisions withdrawing from Finland.

Suicide Resistance

This progressive reinforcement of the Western Front may go on until all the German troops have left Finland and have got to Norway.

The divisions sent to the southern borders of Holland are not crack troops, but they should be able to put up a good fight for a short time.

The suicide resistance at the Channel Ports is another part of the plan to hold up the Allies for, until our supply position improves greatly, it may be impossible for us to exert the maximum pressure against the enemy.

The third factor is the increased resistance put up by the Luftwaffe. To-day the German fighters have been up in hundreds.

Rockets Strike at Shipping

Rocket-firing Beaufighters of R.A.F. Coastal Command, escorted by Mustangs of a Polish squadron of A.D.G.B., attacked a formation of enemy naval auxiliary ships off the Friesian Islands on Sunday night, stated an air communique last night.

Explosions occurred on two of the ships, one of which probably sank. A third was set on fire and two others were damaged by cannon-fire. One Beaufighter is missing.

More Shells

Enemy guns at Cap Gris Nez opened fire across the Straits of Dover yesterday afternoon, but sent over only a few shells.

Coastal towns in the vicinity of Dover had their third shell-fire warning since midnight. Allied shipping appeared to be the target.

We Need Ports For Last Blow

BRITISH IN LE HAVRE OUTSKIRTS

From MATTHEW HALTON, "The Sheffield Telegraph" War Correspondent.

With the 1st Canadian Army, Monday.

THE first Canadian Army with its British, Canadian, and Polish troops is now fighting a stiff battle for the Channel ports.

Their battle line is from the mouth of the Seine to the mouth of the Scheldt.

The supply problem is becoming ever more vast, ever more intricate, and before dealing Germany the *coup de grace* we have to solve this problem. We need the ports.

So once more our fighting men are in a roaring of guns and a moaning of mortars. Once more the infantry, the tanks, the sappers have to wade into powerful positions through the deepest of steel.

*

After a great exhilarating pursuit of a broken army from Normandy to Holland these men are in hot battle again.

On the right wing of the First Canadian Army Canadian troops now have a bridgehead across the Ghent canal and should possess Bruges.

In the centre British and Canadians are attacking towards Dunkirk, Calais, and Boulogne. On the left British troops are fighting in the outskirts of Le Havre.

A full-dress British attack [illegible] went in last night.

*

The first men took the high ground dominating the port. Other units then had to go through most formidable minefields.

The attack ran into trouble. New gaps had to be made under murderous fire. The battle continued to-day.

Numerically the German garrisons in the ports are not strong. There are about 5,000 in Le Havre, about 3,000 in Calais, 5,000 in Boulogne, 2,000 in the strong-points between Calais and Boulogne, and about 10,000 in Dunkirk.

But these towns are powerfully defended with terrific minefields and large numbers of guns and mortars, and the garrison soldiers are largely good troops specialists and marines.

Best Day For British

BRIDGE SEIZED INTACT

From DOON CAMPBELL

With British 2nd Army near Dutch Frontier, Monday.

THIS has been the British troops' biggest and best 24 hours of the campaign in the West.

Second Army armour and infantry have entered the "inner porch" of the Dutch frontier [illegible] a fighting officer, "Have got stuck into the Germans and fairly slaughtered them."

At forward H.Q. I was told that more Germans had been killed and more of their equipment destroyed to-day than was the case in the whole 200 mile run to Brussels.

It was not a day of sweeping advances through diluted and uncoordinated opposition: it was a fight for a road junction, for a cluster of houses and, finally, for a vital canal bridge.

General Dempsey's men rushed the bridge, and British tanks were on the far side before the Germans had time to react.

This was the canal to which Prince Bernhard of the Netherlands referred yesterday when he said, "If we cross the Escaut canal we are more or less on the Dutch frontier."—Reuter.

North-South Link-up Near Dijon

IT was announced last night at Third Army Headquarters that elements of the Third Army made contact with elements of the Seventh Army near Sombernon, 16 miles west of Dijon, yesterday.

Third Army units have started a new attack south of Nancy. Heavy counter-attacks forced several U.S. units to withdraw across the Moselle near Corny, but other units have already established a new bridgehead.

The official announcement of the link-up says that first contact was established between the armies when two officers shook hands at an undesignated point.

Last night also came the news that French troops have completed the occupation of Dijon.

U.S. troops have reached the outskirts of Vesoul, 30 miles west of the Belfort Gap.

New "Bag" Forming

About 12 miles north of Besancon the Americans are encountering strong resistance beyond Rioz.

The northward thrust to Vesoul has cut the second of two main roads leading directly into the Belfort Gap—the first through Besancon is already cut—and the only possible escape for the German 19th Army now is through a long network of minor roads into the Gap from the north-west.

These are being lopped one by one by Allied shears swinging across the entrance of the Gap and pocketing what will possibly turn out to be an appreciable bag of German troops.

The French troops who drove into Dijon have further cut down the escape corridor for the battered remnants of the German 19th Army between the Doubs and Ognon Rivers.

Grand Duchess in the Queue

As news sellers were distributing newspapers announcing the liberation of the city of Luxemburg, a large car drew up at a news theatre in Piccadilly yesterday.

The Grand Duchess of Luxemburg, accompanied by a woman friend, stepped out and joined the queue waiting to enter the theatre.

France Visible

After another beautiful autumn day, with sunshine from dawn to dusk, a fresh and cool easterly breeze blew through the Straits of Dover at nightfall, and there were white-capped wavelets. The sky was starlit, with not a cloud in sight.

All day the French coast showed up clearly.

Swiss Train Gunned by U.S. Fighters?

Swiss Radio last night quoted a communique declaring that three American fighter planes machine-gunned a Swiss train between Basle and Zurich, wounding several passengers, though none seriously.

BRITISH ARMOUR, headed for Holland, passes the Town Hall at Louvain, Belgian town just before the Albert Canal.

RED ARMY PINCERS THREATEN HUNGARY

KROSNO, 84 miles east of Cracow, first main objective in the new Russian drive south-east of Cracow, has fallen to the Russians, according to Berlin reports.

Krosno is also 45 miles west of Przemysl and only 17 miles from the nearest part of the pre-war Czechoslovak border in the Carpathians.

The threat to Hungary is growing (writes "The Sheffield Telegraph" Military Correspondent). According to German sources a powerful Russian force is driving south of Przemysl into the passes of the Northern Carpathians leading to Slovakia.

These passes take the armies through hilly country and then descend into the Hungarian plain, where the going is easier.

The rising in Slovakia may result in some of these passes falling into the hands of the Slovakian Partisans.

Clearing the Roads

In the south the Russian advance through the heart of Rumania is taking their troops towards the Southern Hungarian border, so that there is a prospect of Hungary being gripped between the northern and southern pincers.

The clearing of the roads through Transylvania into Hungary was carried a stage further by the capture of Sighisoara by the Russians and Rumanians yesterday, says B.U.P.

Russians and Rumanians captured more than 200 places, including the town of Medias, 22 miles west of Sighisoara, and Petrosani.

At Petrosani they are approaching the Vulcan Pass.

Nearing Lomza

General Zakharov's troops are continuing their attacks on the Narev front in Northern Poland, and have taken 30 more places.

Moscow's communique reported an advance to within 2½ miles of Lomza, main base defending the southern approach to East Prussia.

The situation in Yugoslavia is moving to a climax with the German garrisons being pinned down by the swift thrusts of Marshal Tito.

Armistice terms for Rumania are being worked out in Moscow between M. Molotov, Sir Archibald Clark-Kerr the British Ambassador, and Mr. Averell Harriman, the U.S. Ambassador, and the Rumanian delegates.

Warsaw Poles' Heavy Losses

A communique from General Bor, C.-in-C. of the Polish Home Army, discloses that the losses among the Polish defenders of Warsaw's "old town" during one month's fighting were 80 per cent., and losses among staff personnel were even heavier.

All those soldiers of the home army who were still alive were evacuated in the withdrawal from the "old town." At that time they totalled 1,300 armed soldiers.

Paulus Joins Free Germans in Moscow

From "The Sheffield Telegraph" Listening Station:

One German field-marshal and 13 German generals have joined the Free German Committee in Moscow during the past four weeks, said a broadcast by the committee last night.

The field-marshal was Paulus, of Stalingrad.

Polish Corps' Two Months' Record

The Polish Corps fighting with the Eighth Army in Italy has, between June and August, advanced 230 kilometres, fought seven decisive battles, captured the towns of Soimo and Ancona, and against heavy opposition crossed the Cesano and Metaro rivers, it was announced yesterday.

Luftwaffe Up: 175 Down

WORST HOME DEFEAT

SHAEF, Monday.

TO-DAY the Luftwaffe joined in the Battle of Germany on a large scale—and suffered their greatest defeat of the war over German soil. They lost 175 fighters.

They threw great formations of fighters, including jet-propelled planes, with up to 100 in each formation, against the 1,000 heavy U.S. bombers which attacked oil plants at Merseburg, Lutzkendorf, and Misburg. The mighty aerial battle raged all over Central Germany from Hanover to Leipzig.

But the German challenge had been anticipated, and the fighter escort of 800 was easily more than double the number sent on similar missions of late.

Of the American force 48 bombers and 29 fighters are missing. The escorting fighters destroyed 130 of the German planes.

The American fighters destroyed 42 more German planes on the ground by strafing aerodromes. Four bombers and about half of the missing fighters are believed to have landed safely in France and Belgium.

Havre Hit Again

Strong forces of R.A.F. Halifaxes and Lancasters again attacked the German garrison and forts at Le Havre, on which 5,000 tons of bombs were dropped yesterday.

On Sunday night a force of our Mosquitoes attacked Berlin without loss.

Meanwhile, over the battle area our rocket-firing Typhoons and Spitfires are again co-operating with the Army with deadly effect.

Nine waves of Marauders and Havocs of the U.S. 9th Air Force from British bases renewed their support of General Patton's Third Army with heavy attacks on large-calibre guns and emplacements on the Moselle and a Nazi headquarters in Metz. One Havoc is missing.

A ferry crossing between Flushing and Breskens, which was being used at high pressure by the Germans, was severely damaged without loss by the accurate bombing of Mitchells and Bostons of R.A.F. 2nd T.A.F. Among the squadrons taking part was a Mitchell Squadron of the Royal Dutch Naval Air Service.

Germans Move Out of Greek Islands

The Germans have begun to get out of the islands off Greece. They evacuated Chios on Sunday after destroying their entire stock of ammunition and food supplies, reports Turkish Radio quoting the paper "Ulus."

They have also begun to evacuate Lesbos and Lemnos, according to other information quoted by the radio.

The German troops taken off the islands are being concentrated at Salonika.—B.U.P.

Biggest Day R.A.F. Raid on Germany

THE R.A.F.'s heaviest daylight attack on Germany was made last evening by Halifaxes and Lancasters on three synthetic oil plants in the Ruhr.

In addition to major attacks for the first time on oil plants at Castrop Rauxel and Kamen, near Dortmund, there was a return attack on the largest synthetic oil plant in the Ruhr at Nordstern.

No cloud was over the targets and all three plants were accurately marked by the Pathfinder force.

Flying Officer P. J. Gray, from St. Albans, who was in the Kamen attack, said, "Explosions occurred in rapid succession, and black smoke rose to a height of over two miles. There was intense flak, but no fighters were seen."

Bombers streaked out over the coast of East Anglia after dusk last night towards Germany. The noise of their engines was heard continuously for over an hour.

Deutschlandsender said shortly after 11 o'clock that two "bomber formations" were over Germany and a third was approaching.

LATE WIRES

BLACKOUT
To-day—9.00 p.m. to 7.05 a.m.

JAP CONVOY WIPED OUT

Carrier-based aircraft of the U.S. Pacific Fleet have struck at Mindanao in the Philippines, destroying entire Japanese convoy of 52 ships. Sixty-eight aircraft were destroyed.—Reuter.

COMPLETE NEWS
PLUS
PICTURE MAGAZINE
PLUS
COLOR COMICS
5¢

Week-End Edition

New York Post

FOUNDED 1801, VOLUME 143, NO. 255. COPYRIGHT, 1944, NEW YORK POST.

NEW YORK, SATURDAY, SEPTEMBER 16, 1944

Official:

SIEGFRIED LINE COMPLETELY PIERCED

With the U. S. 1st Army Invading Germany, Sept. 16 (AP)—The whole Siegfried Line is in direct peril today from several breakthroughs made by American infantry south of Aachen, placing our forward troops beyond the lines of the last fixed fortifications in that area. Tanks at the same time smashed forward east of Aachen. The deepest penetration of Germany is about 12 miles.

American patrols have been going into Aachen itself, although the town is not yet in 1st Army control.

(Earlier Story, Page 3)

"Daily Herald," Monday, Sept. 18, 1944.

CURTAIN TIME
7.39 p.m. to 6.10 a.m.
Moon Rose 7.16 a.m.
Moon Sets 7.55 p.m.
Lighting-up Time: 8.9 p.m.

Daily Herald

No. 8915 MONDAY, SEPTEMBER 18, 1944 ONE PENNY

STOP PRESS

STOCKHOLM A.A. FIRE

Stockholm, Monday.—"Foreign" planes flew over Stockholm last night. A.A. defences went into action.—Associated Press.

AIRBORNE ARMY CAPTURES DUTCH TOWNS NEAR REICH BORDER

Thousands Of Paratroops Landed Before AA Guns Opened Fire

From STANLEY WOODWARD, "Herald" War Reporter, Somewhere In Holland, Sunday

MEN of the First Allied Airborne Army, who landed behind the German front line in Holland to-day from a great sky-train of more than a thousand gliders, troop-carrying planes and towing planes, had cleared the enemy from several Dutch towns before nightfall.

Strong units swooped down near the German border, and by night English and American troops were established. The strong fighter and bomber support made the move a success. Losses from flak were small.

It is as yet too soon to assess the tactical situation, but the landing has definitely gone according to plan.

Mortar, machine-gun and artillery fire are going on around us.

We have seen the first prisoners. They looked fit, surly and bewildered. And some of them are unusually young.

The planes and gliders landed with their loads or dropped their paratroops right to time table.

I travelled with them in the fourth glider and landed with them in a turnip field near a house, outside of which a Dutch family greeted us in their Sunday best.

I am writing this from my half-dug foxhole in a little wood near that turnip field.

On the way over it seemed that all the gliders and aircraft in the world were gathered together.

BRITISH ADVANCE

AS the enemy began to rush troops to the areas of Holland menaced by the Allied air landing, General Dempsey's Second Army launched a big offensive from its main bridgehead on the Escaut Canal.

The attack was preceded by a barrage from hundreds of guns. When the barrage lifted, tanks lumbered across followed by British infantry.

Tommies rode on top of the tanks and in carriers. Ahead of them a creeping barrage swept forward 200 yards per minute, while more infantry stalked the woods and fields on both sides.

The landing in Holland was the greatest airborne invasion ever known—and it took the Germans by surprise.

Not a Nazi plane was in the sky when the aerial armada crossed the coast, and clouds of paratroops, followed by glider-borne units, were dropping on their objectives before the enemy's A.A. guns opened fire.

At first, German resistance on the ground was light, but later reports said that stiff opposition had developed in many places.

Jeeps, Tanks, Guns Landed

Supreme H.Q. is maintaining secrecy about the area where the assault from the air was made. But a broadcast to the people of Holland revealed that our troops were landed south of the Rivers Rhine and Lek.

Berlin said that a strong landing was made at noon on the north bank of the Rhine near Nimejen, and that other landings were near Tilburg and Eindhoven, and near the mouth of the Rhine. The German News Agency said later that landings were still taking place.

British, American, Polish and Dutch troops took part in the landing, which began at noon. Some of the gliders probably carried light guns, jeeps and light tanks.

"Everyone in Holland seemed to have been to church," said a fighter pilot.

"They had been walking home in their Sunday best, but everybody was standing in the streets. You could almost see their open mouths.

"The gliders went down as if they were parking. There they were parked together, wing-tip to wing-tip, in straight lines, just like cars in a garage.

"They were all bang in the right spot, and unloading was going on. In one place I got right down and saw the local people in their Sunday best lending a hand with the unloading.

"In another landing zone, the troops were already leaning over an orchard wall talking to a crowd of girls."

Weather conditions were ideal. Low clouds provided cover for the unarmed, unarmoured troop-carriers, but over the zones where paratroops were to drop and gliders to land the clouds lifted and gave perfect visibility.

Enemy Positions Pounded

The paratroops were in action with the enemy long before the last of the gliders had reached the target.

Fifteen hours before the landing the Allied air forces opened a terrific attack on enemy positions in Holland.

Late on Saturday afternoon, Marauders and Havocs bombed Dutch dykes, to impede German concentrations and reinforcements. At night, Lancasters and Mosquitos hit Dutch airfields.

Yesterday morning 850 Fortresses bombed gun positions over a wide area and Mosquitos strafed barracks. The Forts operated in sections with six to 12 bombers in each, and each section was allotted different gun-sites.

Just before the landings began, United States fighters, flying low to draw enemy fire, swarmed down on enemy gun positions in a day of "suicide" flying.

The fighters, carrying fragmentation bombs and extra ammunition, swooped down to roof-top height to draw the guns' fire and then silenced them with bombs.

At the same time, Spitfires, Mosquitos, Mitchells and Bostons attacked the barracks, bombing and strafing the soldiers' quarters, and rocket-carrying Typhoons attacked flak ships.

IT WENT OFF WITHOUT A HITCH

From WAR REPORTERS
With First Allied Airborne Army, Sunday.

WAYFARERS in a certain part of Holland to-day saw the most tremendous sight of the war, tight, low formations of sky trains stretching for miles, all round them—above, below and at their sides—fighters forming an armoured aerial tunnel.

Then thousands of multi-coloured parachutes glittered in the bright noon-day sun, gliders, released from their tow planes, drifted gently to earth.

An Army of Liberation dropped from the skies; an army fully equipped, its own supplies dropping with it, to launch a new blow at the Reich and to harass the retreating Germans in their rear.

More than a thousand British and American troop carriers took part in the operation.

Germans Caught Flatfooted

By the time the last of them and the last gliders reached the dropping zone hundreds of the earliest arrivals had set up their equipment and were ready for action.

It was aerial D-Day. It had been expected for some time.

Since this First Allied Airborne Army was formed other plans for its operation had had to be scrapped because our ground troops had advanced quicker than was expected or because the weather closed in.

But when it was eventually carried out—H-Hour was 1 p.m.—it caught the Germans flatfooted. The great sky armada was over the drop area before they could man their guns.

By the time the second and third formations of the C.47 Douglas transport planes began to drop their human loads light flak was shooting up.

Late arrivals saw some planes burning down below and others had crash-landed.

Suicide For Any Nazi Plane

But the fighter escort did a smashing job in snuffling out the German gun positions, and the percentage of troop-carrier losses was the lowest of any airborne operations.

Only a matter of minutes before the first troop-carrying planes arrived bombers hammered the area.

A building—believed to be the Luftwaffe H.Q. in Holland—was ablaze. One of our Mosquitos had scored a direct hit.

★ Continued on Back Page

'GOING WELL' REPORTS ARE COMING IN

From STANLEY BISHOP
"Herald" War Reporter at S H A E F, Monday, 1 a.m.

GOOD radio contact was established last night between the Airborne Army in Holland and Supreme H.Q., and progress reports have begun to filter through.

But it must be, of necessity, some time yet before the first tactical picture of the initial successes can be given.

We must expect a delay of perhaps from twelve to twenty-four hours before the situation can be assessed.

So far everything has gone well and according to plan in the air and on the ground.

Until dusk last evening Allied fighter bombers and fighters were working ahead of the airborne advance, attacking enemy gun posts and defence positions, and breaking up transport columns wherever they were found.

At Heart Of Reich

The attack is being made in the area where the enemy hoped his flank was secure, anchored on the waterways of Holland and the North Sea.

As the operation develops, the right flank of the German armies will be turned.

The new invasion, linked with the advance of the British 2nd and the Canadian 1st Armies from Belgium, is an immediate thrust intended for the heart of the Reich.

CALL TO START RAIL STRIKE

THE Dutch Government, in a broadcast to Holland last night, called for a general strike of all the railway workers "to impede enemy transport and troop concentrations as much as possible."

"The Government," said the broadcast, "is fully aware of the great responsibility which it is taking, but after careful consultation with the High Command it is of the opinion that in the given circumstances this act is of such primary military importance it can no longer be delayed.

"It wishes all faithful and courageous patriots to ensure the carrying out of this action to the best of their abilities."

700 TONS ON A GUN POSITION

In daylight last evening a strong force of Lancasters attacked an important gun position and the German garrison on Walcheren Island in the mouth of the Scheldt.

Nearly 700 tons of H.E. bombs were dropped in a highly concentrated attack.

Rings show landings reported by the Germans.

A GUNNER in an escorting aircraft had a front-seat view of part of the huge Allied air fleet as it sped on its way for the airborne assault on Holland.

GERMANS THROW HOME GUARD INTO FRONT LINE

BATTALIONS of Germany's Home Guard, ranging from boys of 15 to men of 65, were flung into the line with paratroop units yesterday in a vain effort to stem another advance on the German frontier.

This attack was opened after American units had crossed the Meuse in force north of Maastricht.

United States officers said that extreme measures to take forts and pillboxes were mostly unnecessary.

"Our shells scared the daylight out of the German kids and the old men. They would scatter into the woods, and when we began shelling the woods they would run into the fields, only to be mown down or taken prisoner by our machine-gunners."

As Aachen's garrison fought pitched battles against Americans driving in from north and south, a Third Army spearhead struck past Stolberg, six miles east of the city, to a point only 25 miles from Cologne and the Rhine.

The spearhead troops broke right through the second defence chain in the Siegfried Line.

Big guns, rolling up in support, were in position when the Germans launched a furious counter-attack—the most serious since the Normandy breakthrough.

Cottage Pillboxes

Salvo after salvo crashed on the enemy, silencing his guns and scattering his tank and infantry formations.

Despite Luftwaffe support—30 Messerschmitts strafed and bombed Allied units—the counter-attack was beaten off.

Fast-moving American motorised units pressed on to capture still more fortified zones.

A war reporter with them cabled:—

Just in front of us is a row of little concrete cottages which are catching the special core of the fire.

They look very homelike, pretty little places, and you almost look for vines around the doors until suddenly you see that the "windows" are machine-gun apertures. They are pillboxes, complete with friendly little gable roofs.

These pillboxes are the last fortified line in this area behind the main Siegfried Line—which we have already broken.

Like Madmen

The Nazis are struggling like demented men.

Three times they counter-attacked in broad shoulder-to-shoulder lines, screaming hoarsely as they came forward and falling in unbroken rows before our tanks and guns.

The drive into the Schnee Eifel forest, north-west of Prum, has met strong opposition.

In the Moselle Valley our troops are now across the river in strength.

Metz is reported to be almost completely encircled, and the units that took Chateau Salins and Luneville have now linked up on a 20-mile wide front east of Nancy.

Seventh Army troops are rapidly wiping out the pocket south of Epinal.

Clear And Cool

Straits weather last night: Clear and cool, light easterly breeze. Barometer steady and high.

20,000 Nazis Surrender Without Fight

TWENTY THOUSAND German troops, with their commander, General Elster, surrendered to a 24-year-old American officer on Saturday without firing a shot.

They had been cut off at Beaugency, near Orleans, by the junction of the Third and Seventh Armies.

Lieut. McGill, the American, said yesterday:—

While we were operating 50 miles south of the Loire, F.F.I. units told us that the enemy column was willing to surrender, but would like us to send out two battalions for a token battle—to make it look good."

That was impossible.

I drew up terms of surrender, and told two officers—one Belgian and one British, both of whom spoke German—to visit the German general.

Air Watch

I also called for air support to come immediately in case the whole thing proved to be a false alarm.

If our airmen saw a white panel on the ground, they were to know that surrender was making progress; if they saw a red colour they were to strafe the German column.

As it turned out, General Elster agreed to the terms sent over.

But he insisted on formal surrender to an Allied general, and this ceremony was carried out later.

He handed his revolver to General Robert Macon, commander of the 83rd Infantry Division, a unit of the new Ninth United States Army.

Our Heavy Guns In Action

British heavy guns fired across the Straits of Dover in the morning and in the late afternoon yesterday.

Just before dusk the enemy replied with fewer than a dozen shells, including a three-gun salvo.

Men In Charge

The man in command of the Allied Airborne Army is Lieut.-General Lewis H. Brereton.

His deputy-commander is Lieut.-General F. A. M. Browning, British Army.

The Two Men, by Stanley Bishop —Page 2

FORWARD INTO GERMANY—MONTY

THE triumphant cry now is: "Forward into Germany!"

This was Field-Marshal Montgomery's message to his men broadcast last night. He said:—

The Allies have removed the enemy from practically the whole of France and Belgium, except in a few places, and we stand at the door of Germany.

By the terrific energy of your advance northwards from the Seine you brought quick relief to our families and loved ones in England by occupying the launching sites of the flying bombs.

We have advanced a great way in a short time, and we have accomplished much.

The total of prisoners captured is now nearly 400,000, and there are many more to be collected from those ports in Brittany and in the Pas de Calais that are still holding out.

"Immense Losses"

The enemy has suffered immense losses in men and material. It is becoming problematical how much longer he can continue the struggle.

Such an historic march of events can seldom have taken place in such a short space of time.

You have every reason to be very proud of what you have done.

Let us say to each other "This was the Lord's doing and it is marvellous in our eyes."

And now the Allies are closing in on Nazi Germany from the East, from the South and from the West.

Their satellite Powers have thrown the towel into the ring and they now fight on our side.

Our American Allies are fighting on German soil in many places. Very soon we shall all be there.

Useless Order

The Nazi leaders have ordered the German people to defend their country to the last and dispute every inch of ground.

This is a very natural order, and we would do the same ourselves in a similar situation. But the mere issuing of orders is quite useless. You require good men and true to carry them out.

The great mass of the German people know that their situation is already hopeless, and they will think more clearly on this subject as we advance deeper into their country.

They have little wish to continue the struggle.

But whatever orders are issued in Germany and whatever action is taken on them, no human endeavour can now prevent the complete and utter defeat of the armed forces in Germany.

Their fate is certain and their defeat will be absolute. Good luck to you all—and good hunting in Germany.

Fly-Bombs Over

Two flying bombs which crossed the East Coast last evening fell in Southern England.

The first damaged two cottages and smashed a considerable area of glass in a market garden.

CANADIANS FIGHTING IN BOULOGNE

CANADIAN troops yesterday received the order: "Capture Boulogne!"

An all-out offensive was launched. By 6 p.m. the outer defences were breached, and by 9.30 p.m. the suburb of Wimereux was captured.

The attack went in with tremendous support from hundreds of Halifaxes and Lancasters which blanketed the outer defences with 3,500 tons of high explosives in little over four hours.

There was large-scale artillery support as flail tanks, flame-throwers and armoured troop carriers advanced against strong gun positions and pillboxes.

Infantry stormed the entire north-eastern defence line, and quickly secured positions dominating the whole town.

Coast Watchers

Many people lined the cliff tops along the South-East Coast of England to watch the battle, which became fiercer after nightfall as R A F bombers went out again to blast enemy strongpoints.

Flares were dropped in and around the port.

The Germans seemed apprehensive of a sea attack as well, for they constantly swept the sea with powerful searchlights, the beams reaching well beyond mid-Channel.

At other times they threw their searchlights on to the cliffs farther to the east, apparently to spot any troops preparing for a flank attack.

Germans Raid Rome

German planes yesterday raided Rome for the first time in strength, and dropped bombs on the outskirts.

DAILY MIRROR, Wednesday, September 20, 1944

Daily Mirror

SEPT 20

No. 12,717
ONE PENNY
Registered at the G.P.O. as a Newspaper.

BRITISH REACH THE RHINE

THE BRITISH SECOND ARMY HAS REACHED THE RHINE. IT IS ONLY THREE MILES FROM THE REICH FRONTIER.

Thrusting thirty-seven miles yesterday, our tanks are on the outskirts of Nijmegen,

There the Huns are fighting desperately to hold the last bridge over the Rhine, called the Dutch Waal at this point.

Monty's tanks advanced more than fifty miles in less than forty-eight hours, linking up with the air invaders all the way, in this bound across Holland from the Belgian border, according to Allied front line reports last night.

And Berlin said: "The battles in Holland overshadow all other events on the western front. It may be expected that the Allies will intensify their offensive."

By reaching Nijmegen, General Dempsey's men have made their second big link-up with the air invaders.

They had already contacted paratroops near Eindhoven, and SHAEF last night confirmed German reports that another landing was made at Nijmegen.

Monty's tanks drive 37 miles in a day

Also confirmed was the German story of a landing at Arnhem, on the northern branch of the Rhine delta and ten miles from the Reich.

Yesterday, third day of the invasion of Holland, airborne reinforcements and supplies were still pouring in, protected by fighters.

The Luftwaffe steered clear.

About 700 Flying Forts attacked the railway centres of Hamm and Soest, east of Dortmund, through which enemy reinforcements must pass to reach the invasion zone by the most direct route.

According to a front-line correspondent, everything in our great cross-Holland sweep is going better than "according to plan."

British, American, Polish and Dutch airborne troops are well dug-in and are beating off strong opposition.

The enemy still holds the towns of Best and Helmonde in strength.

These towns are on either side of the British wedge driven northward from Einhoven. But it appears unlikely that the enemy will be able to develop a serious threat to our wedge.

Heavy fighting is going on in the Nijmegen area. The Germans have dug themselves in and brought up tanks.

The slim finger of the British thrust passes through Eindhoven, crosses the Wilhelmina Canal where a blown bridge was rebuilt last night, and continues across the River Maas at Graves, eight miles south-west of Nijmegen.

This swift drive was possible because the air invaders prevented the enemy from blowing up the bridges across the many waterways.

News from the other fronts was scanty last night.

In Belgium a heavy counter-attack against the British bridgehead over the Escaut Canal north of Gheel has been repulsed, according to SHAEF at midnight.

The First U.S. Army, which has taken 180,000 prisoners since D-Day, has made yet another crossing into Germany—just beyond the Dutch town of Sittard.

Sittard, about twenty miles north-west of Aachen, and one mile from the German border, has been captured. Aachen is now completely surrounded.

NORTH SEA
WILHELMSHAVEN
HAMBURG
GRONINGEN
BREMEN
AMSTERDAM
ZWOLLE
THE HAGUE
OSNABRUCK
HANOVER
LEIDEN
HOLLAND
UTRECHT
NIJMEGEN
ROTTERDAM
MUNSTER
TILBURG
BREDA
EINDHOVEN
ANTWERP
ESCAUT CANAL
SCHELDT
ALBERT CANAL
KASSEL
R. RHINE
DUSSELDORF
GHENT
MAASTRICHT
GERMANY
COLOGNE
BRUSSELS
AACHEN
BONN
NAMUR
LIEGE
EUPEN
50 MILES

British Second Army has reached the Rhine—and linked up with airborne forces—at Nijmegen, three miles from Germany.

Copenhagen in full revolt—battle raging outside Danish royal home

FULL revolt has broken out in Copenhagen, Stockholm reported last night.

In other Danish cities fighting has been going on between Danes and Germans since noon yesterday.

Late yesterday afternoon German-controlled Danish radio reported a clash in the square outside the royal palace at Amalienborg, in which King Christian recently took up residence.

German marines are said to be attacking the castle, where they are reported to be trying to disarm 160 Danish policemen who are defending the castle, helped by the population.

The Swedish paper "Dagens Nyheter" says that King Christian, his wife, Queen Alexandrina, and the Crown Princess Ingrid are besieged in a cellar.

The German-controlled broadcast said a detachment of the marines was "peacefully passing when they were attacked by Royal Guards and fighting took place, with losses on both sides."

Ferry and air connections with Sweden have been broken and a general strike proclaimed in Copenhagen as from 1 p.m today is already in operation.

Dead bodies are reported to be seen everywhere in the Danish capital.

The revolt followed an attempt by the Germans to disarm the Danish police, alleged by German authorities to be collaborating with illegal organisations.

Motor Cars Banned

In connection with this move the Germans decreed that anyone found in possession of firearms would be shot.

The trouble apparently began last Thursday night when Germans fired on crowds in City Hall-square, Copenhagen. The Danish Freedom Council called a 48-hour general strike in protest.

The Germans used their typical cunning to disarm the police at Elsinore. They sounded an air raid alarm at eleven o'clock yesterday morning—the signal for all police to turn out to duty stations.

Having got the police into the open and split up into small groups, the Germans pounced on them and took over their duties.

THEY WANT LEOPOLD AGAIN

KING LEOPOLD is to return to the throne of Belgium.

M. Pierlot, Belgian Prime Minister, speaking at the first meeting of the Belgian Parliament in liberated Brussels yesterday said so.

"We are looking forward to welcoming home our war prisoners, political prisoners, King and Princes," he said.

As the Chief of the State, King Leopold will resume and exercise his constitutional prerogatives and the monarchy will remain, added M. Pierlot.

M. Pierlot also revealed that the Government of Belgium has contracted for three million tons of food supplies for the first six months after the liberation of Belgium.

COST OF LIVING

Official cost of living index figure was unchanged on September 1 compared with August 1. It was 102 points above the July, 1914, figure.

GERMAN RAILWAY YARDS ATTACKED

Strong forces of Flying Fortresses yesterday attacked railway marshalling yards in Western Germany (including Hamm) east of the Rhine, and industrial targets at Wiesbaden, in Western Germany.

No enemy fighters attacked the bombers, ten of which are missing.

...Then the phone bell rang

Mr. P. Dupong, Prime Minister of Luxemburg, with three of his Ministers, was to have left Britain for his native land today. A farewell party had been planned.

But an hour or two before the time fixed for the party the phone bell rang at the Luxemburg Legation in London. The trip had been postponed "for the time being." The "farewell party" was off, but the "Daily Mirror" was told Mr. Dupong, Mr. Joseph Bech, his Foreign Minister, Mr. Victor Bodson, Minister of Justice, and Mr. Pierre Krier, Minister of Labour, will leave for Luxemburg "very shortly."

U.S. HONOURS "MAD MIKE," MAN WHO "NURSED" EXPLOSIVES TO STEM JAPS

THEY call him "Mad Mike" in Burma.

Under General Wingate he specialised in blowing up bridges and trekking through the jungle nursing loads of explosives, which he treated as tenderly as his beard.

Last night it was announced that "Mad Mike"—31-year-old Brigadier James Michael Calvert, D.S.O.—had been awarded the coveted U.S. Silver Star.

An Irishman and one of "Wingate's Follies," the seasoned jungle fighters carrying on the Wingate tradition in battle with the Japs, he once engaged a strong enemy force and compelled it to withdraw before completing the railway demolition job he was on with. He won his D.S.O. for that.

His home is at Seaton, Devon, and he's unmarried.

His father, Mr. Hubert Calvert, of Bramble Hill, Seaton, told the *Daily Mirror* last night:

"He isn't even engaged. He's far too busy thinking about fighting to think of anything like that.

"He was in Shanghai, and saw the Japs butcher the Chinese. He determined straight away to get into the fight against them.

Always a soldier, "Mad Mike" has held every rank in the British Army from private to brigadier, with the exceptions of sergeant-major and first lieutenant.

Cut off once after attacking the Japs with a Commando unit of stragglers, he marched with the Japanese Army for several days disguised as an Indian refugee and escaped by swimming the Chindwin River.

In a recent exploit recounted by his father last night, he and his men made a landing and formed a road block.

They were without air support because bad weather prevented ammunition and food being dropped, but "Mad Mike" got his force out.

For four weeks he and his men held a second road block, despite daily attacks by fanatical Japanese who lost 3,000 men.

Finns give up Petsamo

DETAILS of the Russo-Finnish armistice terms were given by Von Born, acting Finnish Prime Minister, in a broadcast last night.

The Finns are to withdraw immediately to the 1940 border, the Porkhale Peninsula and a fairly large land and sea area, are to be leased to the U.S.S.R. for fifty years and Petsamo is to be given up.

Aerodromes in South and South-West Finland are to be placed temporarily at the disposal of the Allies.

The Finnish merchant fleet is also to be placed at the disposal of the Allies, and the Finnish Army will return to a peace-time footing.

German forces in Finland are to be disarmed and Finland, over six years, is to pay an indemnity of £75,000,000.

More came back—to die

MRS. CHUMLEY had three daughters. Jean, thirteen years old, Joan, who is nine, and five-year-old Margaret.

She'd just had a baby, too—a son, John Jeffrey.

Wisely, two months ago, she packed the three daughters off to safety, in Birmingham.

Things got quieter. Government spokesmen were optimistic. And Mrs. Chumley wanted her daughters home.

So she fetched them back on Friday. There was a joyous family reunion.

Yesterday morning, when the Chumleys were asleep, a buzz-bomb fell in their garden. The house was demolished.

Rescue workers dug feverishly for two hours. They could hear a child crying for help.

Then, in the wreckage, they found the remains of a bed. There was little fair-headed Margaret, her mother's arm around her.

Her father was dead. Her sisters were dead. Her little baby brother was dead. Her mother, who had so eagerly brought them back from the evacuation area, was dead.

The whole family, with the exception of Margaret, had been wiped out.

One of the rescue workers said: "We could hear Margaret before we could see her. After about two hours we got through the wreckage. The bed seemed as if it had fallen from the floor above and had collapsed under the debris.

"Arms and legs of children were showing through.

"Her mother's arm, which was around her, had saved Margaret.

"We propped her up and she was as brave as could be all the time as we took the debris away.

V1 OVER FRANCE

Buzz-bombs are being used by the Germans apparently against the Allied rear installations in the Meuse Valley.

DAILY MIRROR, Friday, September 22, 1944.

Daily Mirror

SEPT 22

No. 12,719
ONE PENNY
Registered at the G.P.O. as a Newspaper.

DEMOBBING—FULL PLANS

Pay rises for long service | New call-up of deferred men

By BILL GREIG

HERE is the news for which the country has been waiting . . . how the men and women will be demobbed, what will happen to the men now deferred, the new rates of pay for the Services. Main points are:

After the ending of the war with Germany and while that with Japan continues, young men now deferred will be called up and also men reaching military age, while at the same time demobilisation will begin.

Men and women from the Forces will replace those called up so that there will be no loss of output.

Demobilisation priority will be based on age and length of service. (See Key Chart on Back Page.) Neither overseas service, marriage, size of family, nor having a job waiting will count.

Certain skilled men will be released out of their turn to assist in restarting industry and building houses. They will not be allowed to go back to their old jobs but will work where directed.

No man will be forced to leave the Forces out of his turn and all will be able to volunteer for further Army service. Those leaving out of their turn will lose certain benefits.

Service pay rates are increased as from September 3 by 1s. for the first three years of service for privates with 6d. for each succeeding year up to five. N.C.O.s and officers receive proportionate increases.

Japanese campaign pay will range from 1s. a day increase for a private to 11s. for senior officers. This also applies to troops in India and naval men serving ashore.

The cost of these increases will be £100,000,000 a year.

DEMPSEY'S 2nd BRITISH ARMY REACHES THE LAST RHINE CROSSING—LINKS UP WITH PARATROOPS AT ARNHEM, SAY NAZIS

GENERAL DEMPSEY'S Second British Army, bursting across the southern arm of the Rhine delta over the captured Waal bridge at Nijmegen, have reached the northern arm—the Lek, last big water barrier to the outflanking of the Siegfried Line

This sensational admission was made by Berlin last night. Dempsey's men, it was stated, have linked up with the isolated British paratroops in heavy fighting at Arnhem, on the Lek.

This reported ten-mile thrust found no confirmation at SHAEF, where it was stated at midnight that there was still hard fighting at Nijmegen.

Air scouts have spotted German transports moving east out of Arnhem.

Allied front-line messages said the spectacular battle for the concrete bridge at Nijmegen ended in our favour soon after the harried Germans had loaded it with dynamite intending to destroy it.

But before they could do so they were surprised by American airborne troops who crossed the river to the west and closed in from behind while British tanks made a frontal attack.

More reinforcements, including Polish paratroops, and supplies were flown to the airborne army yesterday

Thunderbolt escorts destroyed twenty German planes in air fights. Four Thunderbolts are missing.

"RED ARMY IS INSIDE WARSAW"—ANNOUNCE HUNS

THE Red Army has entered the western suburbs of Warsaw, the German News Agency announced last night within twenty-four hours of their earlier admission that small parties of Russian troops had crossed the Vistula and are fighting in isolated pockets around the city area.

This unconfirmed statement followed a denial by Polish official circles in London that Polish commando paratroops had been dropped on the city, as reported in an earlier German broadcast.

On the Baltic front the Russians were yesterday rolling on another capital, Tallinn, pursuing the Huns through the Estonian countryside "like an avalanche."

One Estonian unit is in the forefront of the advance, passing their burning homesteads set on fire by the Germans.

The capture of the key railway town of Rakvere, fifty-five miles from Tallinn, was announced in last night's Soviet communique.

The Red Army drive through Western Rumania is now only twelve miles from the Hungarian frontier.

HUNS SWITCH TO HOLD DEFENCES IN GOTHIC LINE

KESSELRING was reported yesterday to be moving troops from the west coast of Italy to bolster up his defences in the central Gothic Line, after the Fifth Army had captured four more mountains guarding the route into the Lombardy Plain.

The Allied drive smashed a way toward the mountain village of Santa Lucia which forms part of the Futa Pass defences.

Eighth Army troops continue their hard-driving advance against most bitter resistance between the San Marino Republic and the Adriatic with Greek forces now within a mile of Rimini.

Bulldozers earth up Huns in pillboxes

BULLDOZERS are earthing up Siegfried Line pillboxes containing "No surrender" Germans, according to a Reuter war correspondent last night.

Deadly house-to-house fighting was raging last night in Stolberg, ten miles east of Aachen. The Allies have taken valuable high ground on the eastern edge of the town.

The Press liaison officer at Hitler's H.Q. broadcast: "Northwest of Aachen, in the Maastricht salient, Allied columns forced their way forward but were halted west of Geilenkirchen, twelve miles north of Aachen."

Most of the port of Boulogne has been cleared. About 6,000 prisoners have been taken so far.

In Belgium, south of the Scheldt, progress in driving the trapped Germans back to the estuary is quickening.

Poles have closed up to the Scheldt mouth from north of Antwerp to Terneuzen and have taken 1,300 prisoners.

BELGIAN REGENT

The Belgian Parliament yesterday approved the decree appointing Prince Charles Regent in the absence of King Leopold.

DEMOBBING

Service and age the key: marriage does not count

GENERAL demobilisation does not start till Japan is beaten, but piecemeal demobbing starts when Germany is beaten.

Man (and woman) power will have to be re-arranged, between the Services and the factories as the military situation develops, and the call-up will continue, even while men are being released from the Forces to return to industry.

The Fifty and Overs will be out first, if they want to go.

Age and length of service will count together for the others. Two months service gives a man the credit of an extra year on his age.

Thus a man of twenty-four, with five years' service, a man of thirty, with four years' service, a man aged thirty-six, with three years' service, a man aged forty-two, with two years' service, and a man of forty-eight, with one year's service, will all be equal in the demobbing Age, plus service.

RARE EXCEPTIONS

to this will be certain specialists, such as some builders, wanted urgently for reconstruction. They will be demobbed out of turn, but some men now exempt as munition makers will be called up.

No man will be released from the Forces if the military situation is such that he ought to stay in, and, again,

(Continued on Page 2)

CALL-UP

I UNDERSTAND that it is not intended to go high in the age limits in the new call-up of men for the war in Japan. In most cases they will be below 30, but the final decision will not be taken until it is clear how many men will be required, writes Your Political Correspondent.

As they leave the munitions factories and the office desks those workers will be replaced by men who have had Army service and are being released in their groups.

The call-up of boys for the mines will continue, and it is not anticipated that many miners will have to be released as specialists as most of them were called up in the early days of the war. They will therefore be among the first out, but their numbers may not give all the workers required.

Almost all the skilled men to be released under Class B—that is men essential to restart-

Building to have any priority that is going

ing the country's industry—will come from the building and allied trades.

They will not be allowed to pick and choose their jobs but will go where directed.

A few teachers may also be released, but most of them will have to wait until the builders have got the schools ready.

No employer will be allowed to ask for any particular man.

Mr. Bevin is determined that the system which operated after the last war when employers brought out relatives and friends first will not happen again.

This, of course, applies only to the men released as specialists out of their turn.

PAY

By Your Political Correspondent

7 shillings a week extra for those below sergeant with three years' service

NEW long-service-pay rates for the Forces come into operation as from September 3, Japanese campaign rates on November 1.

It will be impossible for the authorities to cope with the new rates at once, and men should not expect to receive new rates and back money immediately. Some weeks may elapse or even longer in certain theatres of war.

I understand that the Chancellor of the Exchequer has ruled that War Service increases are to be subject to income tax, but not the special pay for the Japanese campaign.

Women will receive two-thirds of the War Service increase and of the Japanese pay and full Far East allowance. This allowance takes the place for all ranks of additions now made because of service in certain areas.

Under the War Service increase a private soldier who was in the Army on September 3, 1939, and will, therefore, have completed five years' war service, will be entitled to three increments—the first 1s. for completing three years' service, the second and third 6d. each for completing his fourth and fifth years.

Thus he will be entitled to another 2s. a day on top of his present pay which is 4s. 9d. or 5s. a day.

For other ranks the rates are:—

7s. a week below Petty Officer and Sergeant, after three years' war service, with an additional 3s. 6d. a week for each subsequent year's war service.

10s. 6d. a week for Petty Officers and Chief Petty Officers, Sergeants and higher N.C.O.s and Warrant Officers of the Army and RAF after three years' war service, with an additional 3s. 6d. a week for each subsequent year's war service.

15s. 9d. a week for officers be-

(Continued on page 2)

LATE LONDON EDITION

No. 5,265 [Estab. 1843] Registered at the General Post Office as a Newspaper — Telephones: Central 3030 — SUNDAY, SEPTEMBER 24, 1944 — Telegrams: Worldly, Fleet, London — PRICE TWOPENCE

Certified Net Sale Exceeds **4,000,000** *Copies Per Issue*

NEW ALLIED AIRBORNE LANDING

Great Bid to Relieve British Troops Isolated in the Arnhem Area

THOUSANDS PUT DOWN DESPITE LUFTWAFFE AND GROUND DEFENCE

THOUSANDS of new glider-borne men and paratroops, both British and American, with supplies, were landed in Holland yesterday afternoon in support of the British Second Army's drive to relieve the British airborne force which has now been heroically holding out in the Arnhem area for the past seven days.

This dramatic news, officially issued by S.H.A.E.F. last night, brings fresh hope that the gallant force, isolated on the north side of the River Lek, will soon be liberated. Earlier their position had been reported as critical, though their commander had radioed that the men were in high spirits and would continue to hold out.

The new landing was successfully carried out, despite strong opposition from enemy ground defences and the Luftwaffe, fighter planes of the R.A.F. and U.S. Eighth Air Force providing full support for the tug-planes and gliders.

Some units of General Dempsey's Second Army were said last night to have reached the south bank of the River Lek, and it was reported that only the river, which is a quarter of a mile wide near Arnhem, now separates the two forces.

Two hundred German tanks supported by S.S. troops made a desperate attempt on Friday evening to cut the Second Army's supply corridor, but rocket-firing Typhoons broke up the attack and cleared the threat to our main highway to Arnhem.

SKYTRAIN STRETCHED FROM ENGLAND TO HOLLAND

PILOTS of the Dakotas which carried the paratroops and towed the gliders to Holland reported on their return that gun flashes and ground movement indicated that the isolated airborne troops were still offering heavy opposition to the Germans.

It was the sixth day of similar missions over Holland, and the glider procession was one of the longest of the week.

Observers reported that the "skytrain" stretched from airfields in Southern England to the coast of enemy-held Holland.

The Dakotas with their glider-trains skimmed over the enemy-held terrain at 500ft. levels for more than 45 minutes, meeting only occasional bursts of flak, says a Reuter correspondent.

But once over the landing zone the sky filled with flak and small-arms fire as the gliders cut loose from the tow-ships.

The gliders went down safely, however, through the ground fire, landing from all directions amid clouds of dust as their noses skidded across the ground.

U.S. Eighth Air Force fighters knocked out enemy gun positions and engaged enemy planes in dog-fights before and during the arrival of the air transports.

At least 27 German planes were shot down by Thunderbolts and Mustangs.

One group of 30 German fighters were within striking distance of the Allied transport planes when Thunderbolts tore in, broke up the enemy formations, and accounted for 19 of them.

WHERE THEY ARE HOLDING

There was no report from Allied sources last night as to the positions occupied by the British airborne heroes north of the River Lek, but Capt. Sertorius, the German radio military commentator, declared:

"*The larger part of the town of Arnhem has been cleared of enemy forces, and the remainder of the British First Airborne Division is compressed in the suburb of Oosterbeek (four miles west of the centre of Arnhem) and in the forest north of the town.*"

At one time during the week it was reported that our airborne troops held the road bridge over the river to Arnhem, and yesterday correspondents with General Dempsey's Second Army reported that the bridge was still intact.

Whether our men still hold it, however, is not clear.

But whatever has happened in the Arnhem area, or may still happen, the gallant resistance and endurance of our airborne men will go down to history as one of the epics of the war.

Meanwhile, in an attempt to smash our corridor, infantry and 200 Panther tanks launched a powerful attack on the main highway north of Eindhoven, between Uden and Veghel.

In the words of a senior staff officer: "The enemy achieved a certain amount of success."

But then the rocket-firing Typhoons went in, and what looked like a grave peril to the British rear was soon wiped out.

A senior staff officer said subsequently: "British troops have now cleared the threat to the highway, though Germans are lurking in the woods and attacking the Second Army's soft-skinned vehicles."

Now Allied troops and armour are pouring northwards from Nijmegen for the final all-out attack that will carry them over the Lek.

On developments within the next 24 hours may depend the success or failure of the whole airborne operations.

The German troops know that they are defending the gateway to Berlin, 300 miles away.

The German High Command fear a breakthrough to the Ruhr, for once General Dempsey is across the river, the wide open plains of Germany lie ahead and nothing can stop his armour from hacking its way through to the Ruhr and on to the heart of the Reich.

The furious bloody fighting now raging over this stretch of Holland may well be the decisive action in the Battle of Germany.

NEARER AND NEARER

AIRBORNE MEN WILL NEVER QUIT

Here are the latest messages from correspondents with the gallant airborne troops north of the river:—

Alan Wood (Friday, 5 p.m.).—The British Second Army is getting nearer and nearer to where we are.

Already many of the shells overhead are from Second Army guns landing on Germans behind us, and in front is something which we hope is their armoured cars firing.

In spite of the savagery of the fighting there is still some chivalry about it. British and German wounded—it makes no difference—come in alike to our field dressing stations.

Once a German came in offering us terms of surrender, and one of our colonels promptly rushed out and planted the Airborne flag in front of his H.Q.

Though our men—some of them—are hard put to it not to fall asleep over their guns, they go on fighting and go on attacking.

And one day perhaps the world will learn the full story of what they have done here.

"When it's over," said a sergeant, "I'd like to see these men flown back to England and march through London just as they are now, with six days' dirt on them."

Meanwhile my personal thanks to four of them—Signalmen Cull, Butcher, Noon, and Hardcastle, the wireless operators who get these dispatches away and keep us in touch with England.

Stanley Maxted (Friday 4 p.m.).—On this sixth day in this mortar and shell-riven pocket the airborne troops are hourly becoming more amazing to me.

This morning enemy loud speakers again blared out in clumsy English asking these men to surrender.

It was a silly thing to do. It made these chaps hopping mad. You should have heard their language.

The guts of these airborne chaps is wonderful.

The hate has started again. As I write it seems that there is no point of the compass from which we cannot get mortared or shelled or machine-gunned or sniped.

One part of the perimeter is held by sergeants — the glider pilots, every one of whom is a sergeant or staff-sergeant.

The Medical Corps are on the job right round the clock. Theirs is a particular sort of courage.

Some 943 prisoners have come in to-day—just Germans who have had enough and are stunned by the cold ferocity of men who don't know what quit means.

The artillery of the Second Army has come into range and engaged enemy targets to-day. It was sheer music. We hope the orchestra swells. We are pretty sure it will.

LATEST NEWS

AIRBORNE MEN CROSS RIVER

Stated at S.H.A.E.F., at midnight, that some patrol elements from the airborne force north of the River Lek, at Arnhem, have crossed to the south bank and contacted other airborne troops operating with General Dempsey's armoured units.

GERMANY'S TWILIGHT

"THIS IS IT," SAID NAZI GENERAL

One more German general has learned the inevitable lesson.

Major-General Ferdinand Heim, commander of the garrison at Boulogne, told Canadians who were taking him off to captivity yesterday:—

"*There comes an evening in every campaign—this is the twilight.*"

Already 10,000 prisoners have been taken from Boulogne; a total of well over 12,000 is expected.

Contrary to German Radio claims, no major operation has yet begun against Calais or Dunkirk.

The Americans' advance into Germany is now being measured in tens of yards, said James Cassidy, a radio reporter, broadcasting from inside the Reich last night.

First Army troops are mopping up the last German stragglers in Stolberg, but there is little movement elsewhere on the front from Geilenkirchen to the southern end of the German-Luxemburg frontier.—Reuter, B.U.P., and A.P.

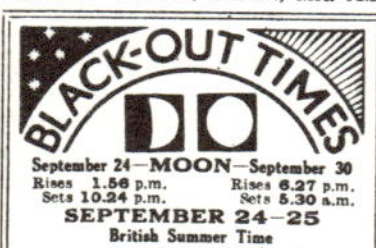

BLACK-OUT TIMES

September 24—MOON—September 30
Rises 1.56 p.m. Sets 10.24 p.m. — Rises 6.27 p.m. Sets 5.30 a.m.

SEPTEMBER 24-25
British Summer Time

	START	FINISH
London .	7.25	6.20
Dover .	7.20	6.15
Norwich .	7.20	6.15
Southampton	7.30	6.26

Lighting-up Time for Vehicles is half an hour after Black-out Time.

Radio Programmes on Page 5

THE OTHER DEMOB. PLAN

Heart Torn Out of the Gothic Line

'EIGHTH' HEAD FOR PO VALLEY

ALLIED prospects of isolating and destroying a substantial portion of the German armies in Northern Italy brightened yesterday with the clearing of the skies over the Adriatic battle area and the beginning of the Eighth Army's long-awaited thrust into the Po Valley.

American troops, driving through the Apennines, were able to see the Po Valley from advanced hillside positions late yesterday, and a major commanding one formation told his men: "The Gothic Line has been smashed down the middle."

Although the exact location of these positions cannot be disclosed because of military security, it seems safe to say the smash has carried Fifth Army troops over some of the tallest peaks in Italy to where the broad Lombardy Plain—at the gateway to which lies Bologna—is unfolded before them.

They tore the heart out of the Gothic Line at a point where it was probably deepest in its bulwarked defences.

At the same time the assault—the chief part of which was carried out by one of the mightiest artillery concentrations in military history—chewed up a large part of what was left of Kesselring's weary Wehrmacht so badly that prisoners said some entire battalions were as low as 60-man strength.

General Leese's front has now been advanced to the Marecchia River line from Rimini inland. From a well-established bridgehead beyond the river the Eighth Army is driving forward—but General Alexander's H.Q. maintain silence on the depth of the penetration made beyond the river.

BITTER FIGHTING

To the west Fifth Army troops have reached the crest of the Central Apennines.

But they face bitter fighting in the rugged Futa Pass, the 2,963ft. defile carrying the main highway over the mountains, before the last 20 miles to Bologna.

At the Marecchia bridgehead Allied troops have a foothold three miles wide and two miles deep in the entrance to the Po Valley, and additional crossings have been made farther inland, north-west of Verucchio.

In the central sector, near the village of Santa Lucia, the battle for high ground east of the pass provides another example of the outflanking technique used so successfully in the mountains of Tunisia, Sicily, and South Italy.

German artillery is active, but there is evidence that much of the shelling is from self-propelled guns, indicating that the fixed defences are already largely passed in this grim scramble up the precipitous slopes through the toughest defence belt the Germans have been able to devise.

To some extent, too, the Germans appear to be disorganised, though still fighting stubbornly.

SHORT OF FOOD

There are signs that the mountain defenders are running short of rations, and as they are forced back from the crests they are abandoning quantities of equipment which it would be impossible to move over the roads.

As a result of Allied successes on the Adriatic it was reported from Bari last night that German and Italian Fascists in the Istrian Peninsula just across Jugoslavia's north-western frontier have been mobilising the people for defence, holding invasion exercises, and displaying other signs of nervousness.

Invasion drills were held in Trieste and citizens of Gorizia have been called up for the construction of defence works.

The partisans, besides gaining control of much of the Dalmatian coast below the peninsula, have been active in the frontier zone, capturing an airport five miles from Fiume on the east side, and besieging Clana, just across the border.

Three formations of Mitchell bombers blasted the German-held Italian cruiser Taranto at La Spezia, leaving her in flames from hits across the bows, amidships, and astern.—Reuter and A.P.

German Carve-Up: Dramatic U.S. Report

NEW YORK, Saturday.—A plan for the permanent division of Germany is now under consideration by President Roosevelt and the U.S. Cabinet, according to the "Wall Street Journal."

The newspaper, an unsensational one, says that the plan is as follows:—

1.—East Prussia and the Polish Corridor to go to Poland.

2.—Germany west of the Rhine to go to France.

3.—The separation of what was left of Germany into two States, north and south. These would not be federated, but would be maintained as completely separate entities.

The "Wall Street Journal" continues that the plan was drawn up by a special committee headed by Mr. Henry Morgenthau, Secretary to the Treasury, and that the reason Mr. Morgenthau visited Quebec was to confer upon it with Mr. Churchill and President Roosevelt.

Further provisions of the plan, according to the newspaper, are as follows:—

The bulk of German industry, such as steel, chemical, and synthetic fuel would be transferred to countries which Germany stripped, such as France, Russia, and Belgium.

Germany, in effect, would be left with little more than a civilian goods industry like textiles, food manufacture, etc.

The Ruhr Valley to be supervised by the Allies.

All education to come under Allied control, and schools to be closed until new textbooks are prepared.

Universities, with the exception of medical schools, to be closed indefinitely.

The plan, drawn up by the Treasury, is not yet the official policy of the U.S. There is much opposition to some aspects of it, such as the division of Germany into two States, but it is significant of the trend of thinking in North America.

It is notable that the "New York Times" declares, on what it describes as "unquestionable authority," that President Roosevelt insists on a hard peace by which the whole of the German people will learn by bitter experience that they have been beaten and what the consequences of defeat are.

The newspaper adds that President Roosevelt took the matter into his own hands three weeks ago when he found evidence of softness in one Army manual prepared for the guidance of U.S. troops in Germany.

He let it be known that he considered the manual "pretty bad."—B.U.P.

CABINET "SPLIT"

HULL AND STIMSON OPPOSE THE PLAN

Washington, Saturday Night.—Morgenthau plan has split wide open the President's Cabinet Committee on German peace policy.

It has failed to win support from Mr. Cordell Hull, and is violently opposed by War Secretary Stimson.

For the time being, the dispute has so interfered with Departmental work on detailed arrangements for the post-war control of Germany that the Three-Power planning by the U.S., Britain, and Russia on a long-range German policy is virtually stalled.

When President Roosevelt presented the Morgenthau Plan to the Prime Minister at Quebec Mr. Morgenthau and Mr. Eden were present; Mr. Stimson and Mr. Cordell Hull were not.—A.P.

STRAITS: CLOUDY

After a finer day with sunny periods the sky clouded over in the Straits of Dover last night and looked threatening.

Visibility was excellent from coast to coast before dusk, and the sea continued smooth with only a light westerly breeze.

£500 FOR AN ARMISTICE DAY CARTOON

WITH ten days still remaining before the closing date, a record entry now seems assured for the "News of the World" Armistice Day Cartoon Competition.

As already explained in the general conditions governing the competition,

A cash prize of £500 will be awarded for the best effort; and Eight cash prizes of £50 each for cartoons whose merits most nearly approach those of the winner.

Special classes have been arranged for children, divided as follows:—

1.—For Boys and Girls under 18: Ten Cash Prizes of £10 each.

2.—For Boys and Girls under 12: Ten Prizes to the value of £10 each in National Savings Certificates.

It is essential that juvenile entrants should state their age, and in all cases name and address should be written on the back of the cartoon.

The general closing date for the competition is Wednesday, October 4.

In addition to the prizes already enumerated there will be a special prize of **£100** for the best Cartoon submitted by a member of H.M. Forces serving overseas, whose entry, by reason of his or her service, is not received in time to take part in the main competition. *In their case the closing date will be December 31 next.*

Thus the total prize money will be £1,200.

The Cartoons should be addressed to:

The Editor,
"News of the World,"
30, Bouverie-street,
London, E.C.4,

and the words "**Armistice Day Cartoon**" clearly written in the top left-hand corner of the envelope or wrapping.

The Cartoons will be judged by the Editor of the "News of the World," whose decisions must be accepted as final.

Russians Drive For Hungary

Great New Assault by Land and Air

AGREAT new land and air assault on Hungary was launched by Russia yesterday, while at the same time the Russian drive for East Prussia was kept up relentlessly.

As the Russians swept to the borders of Hungary crowds of people thronged the streets of Hungarian cities and towns clamouring for peace, according to reports reaching Ankara.

It seems more than likely that Hungary will soon follow the example of Italy, Finland, Bulgaria, and Rumania, and beg for terms to get out of the war. More than 36,000 Hungarian soldiers are said to have deserted during the past week.

An Order of the Day from Marshal Stalin last night announced the capture of Paernu (or Pernov), last "Dunkirk" port left to the Germans in Estonia, and 850 more inhabited localities.

The twofold blows the Russians are now striking, north and south, may decide the fate of the whole vast East Front battlefield. These are the roads the Russians are taking to the Reich:—

1. Along the Baltic shore: Where three Soviet army groups, after a brilliant string of victories in the last two days, are striking through the Baltic States in a drive for East Prussia and Germany, and are smashing German panzers at an almost unprecedented rate.

2. In Central Europe: Where Marshal Malinovsky's army group, after a triumphant sweep across the Transylvanian Alps, is on the borders of Hungary, in a great thrust across the Central European plain to Budapest, Vienna, and beyond.

In the north three army groups—those of Marshal Govorov, General Maslennikov, and General Bagramyan—have struck forward in offensives from the shores of the Gulf of Finland to the Baltic hinterland around Riga.

TANKS MOWN DOWN

During the past week Soviet guns and armour have destroyed more than 500 Tigers and panzers on this battlefield. Just over a month ago, in the same battle-scarred country, the Russians knocked out 1,800 German tanks.

In six weeks the German High Command have lost more than 2,300 of their much-needed panzers—the equivalent of at least ten armoured divisions at present German strength.

Farther north the liberators of Leningrad, under their famous commander Marshal Govorov, are on the march to Germany.

Hitler's "Nord Group," penned along the Baltic shore, is dragging out its last day.

Marshal Govorov's intervention, which was postponed for many weeks by the German defence of the Baltic-Lake Peipus isthmus, is already bringing the Germans face to face with an ignominious splash in the sea, mass surrender, or one last desperate stand against overwhelming odds at Riga, the Latvian capital.

Govorov's forces are now pursuing the Germans with shells, bombs and bullets in all directions in Estonia.

Hitler has been reinforcing his Baltic forces up to the last minute. One regiment arrived straight from Berlin, where it had been engaged in the removal of bomb wreckage.

Marshal Govorov's forces may be one of the main armies assigned to the invasion of East Prussia.

PLENTY OF ARMOUR

His march southward towards Riga is already well under way, and he has powerful forces of tanks and self-propelled guns to deal, if necessary, with the great enemy armoured group concentrated south-west of Riga.

These forces have been trying to break through into Central Latvia and Estonia before Marshal Govorov could succeed in forcing his way on to the Baltic battlefield through the German defence zone between the Gulf of Finland and Lake Peipus.

General Bagramyan beat off the attacks just long enough for Govorov to complete his own preparations.

It is significant that the Germans at Telgava, south-east of Riga, made a supreme effort to break through several days ago, and gained ground slightly. But this was too little and too late.

Far to the south of these great Baltic moves the Russians are poised on the Transylvanian—Hungarian border for the strike towards Budapest.

Soviet military commentators report that "the Red Army has begun storming Hungary by land and air," but give no further details.

The commentators seem to imply that recent Soviet promises to knock out Hungary will be kept far quicker than the Horthy Government had expected. A Hungarian communique last night admitted the loss of the town of Arab. "after heavy fighting."

The Hungarian Magyars are leaving a trail of fire and ruin on the threshold of their native plains, according to a front-line dispatch to "Red Star," the organ of the Soviet Army, and the local population says that the Hungarians have been behaving in an even worse manner than the Germans.—Reuter and B.U.P.

THE RACE FOR BERLIN

The Red Army is just ahead of its Western Allies in the race for Berlin, according to distance figures given in "Red Star," quoted by Moscow Radio and Reuter.

"Our Allies," the paper says, "are 328 miles from Berlin, and the Red Army is now destroying the last of Hitler's forces 316 miles from the German capital."

British Only Five Miles From Tiddim

KANDY, Ceylon, Saturday.—The 14th Army, who drove the Japanese southwards from Imphal, are now on the last lap to Tiddim, important road and track junction in North-west Burma.

They have occupied Tongzang, the last village before Tiddim, and are now within five miles of this immediate objective.

The capture of Tongzang was accomplished by the encirclement of the village by troops of the Fifth Indian Division, who established a road block behind the Japanese.

When the Japanese saw the danger they tried to break through, but it was too late.

In a final attempt 60 Japanese attempted to rush the road block in lorries, but were beaten off and withdrew into the jungle.

In a hospital captured at Tongzang were 90 Japanese dead.

As Allied task forces complete their blockade of the Philippines, the Japanese on the island have ordered martial law to prevent the Filipinos from rising in support of General MacArthur.

The invasion is expected to begin soon after the springboard bases on which we landed to the east and south-east are put into shape.

Meanwhile the softening-up attacks by carrier-borne planes continue. The Japanese air force in the Philippines has been ripped to pieces by the terrific Allied air assault.—Reuter and B.U.P.

ARMADA OUT AGAIN

HEAVY BOMBERS GO FOR THE REICH

After a spell of comparative inactivity, R.A.F. heavy bombers thundered out from East Coast bases in strength at nightfall last night.

They travelled in a long procession in the direction of Germany.

Between nine and ten o'clock the German air-raid service went into action with reports that "an enemy bomber formation is over Western Germany"; "fast enemy fighter formations are over and approaching North-West Germany"; and then, "two bomber formations are over West Germany."

Both Emden and Munchen-Gladbach were badly devastated in Bomber Command's recent attacks, stated the Air Ministry's News Service last night.

Reconnaissance photographs after the daylight attack on Emden on Sept. 6 show that 80 per cent. of the fully built-up areas was either destroyed or severely damaged, and three ships sunk in the harbour.

Photographs of Munchen-Gladbach after the night attack on Sept. 9 disclose three-quarters of the fully built-up area either destroyed or badly damaged. Munchen-Gladbach was one of the main centres of the Rhineland textile industry and a key traffic centre to the south-west of the Ruhr, not far behind the German lines.

THE QUEBEC STORY

MARSHAL STALIN INFORMED OF DECISIONS

Marshal Stalin was yesterday told of the decisions reached at the Quebec Conference by the British Ambassador in Moscow, Sir Archibald Clark Kerr, and the U.S. Ambassador, Mr. Averill Harriman, Moscow Radio announced last night.

M. Molotov, Commissar for Foreign Affairs, was present at the meeting.—B.U.P.

MORE FLYING BOMBS

Two flying bombs which crossed the East Coast shortly after dark last night landed in rural areas of Southern England.

NO. 15,103 PRICE 2 FR. 50

Daily Mail

CONTINENTAL EDITION

THURSDAY, SEPTEMBER 28, 1944

LATE WAR NEWS

THE NEWSPAPER FOR THE ALLIED FORCES IN FRANCE

EPIC OF SKY MEN

THE AGONY OF ARNHEM

TO-DAY The Daily Mail is able to print pictures taken from the inside that show the Agony of Arnhem. The photograph above—radioed from a neutral source last night—is of exhausted and wounded parachutists captured after their great fight against odds.

PARATROOPS in action, firing on the nearby enemy with a 3-inch mortar, while themselves are under heavy fire. The Airborne men brought this picture back with them when the survivors were finally withdrawn. Other pictures on BACK Page.

ONE of the airborne photographers wrote: "We are completely surrounded. Our perimeter becomes smaller every hour. Now it is a matter not of taking pictures, but of fighting for our lives. If the land forces don't contact us soon, then we've had it."

230 HOURS OF HELL

From RICHARD McMILLAN, B.U.P. War Correspondent

WITH BRITISH ARMY BEFORE ARNHEM, Wednesday.

STRUGGLING through a hurricane barrage of fire from 88mm. guns, tank cannon, and machine-guns, the last survivors of the noble band of British Airborne troops who held the Arnhem bridgehead for nine days were ferried over to our lines during Monday night.

I saw the tragic but heroic cavalcade of bloody, mudstained, exhausted, hungry, and bearded men flood up from the river bank into our lines after going through 230 hours of hell.

Many were stretcher cases. Many were wrapped in blankets. Some hobbled with sticks. All were so completely exhausted that they could hardly keep their eyes open. They were beaten in body, but not in spirit. "Let us get back again; give us a few tanks and we will finish the job," they said.

Every one of them had a story to tell of terror by day and by night, of ceaseless enemy attacks with flame-throwers, tanks, and self-propelling guns firing high explosive and armour-piercing shells.

Captain Bethune Taylor, of Landsdowne-place, Cheltenham, wearing a beard like a French poilu's, told me his story of the tragic adventure as he struggled against sleep.

"Most of the division dropped on Sunday," he said. "I—a gunner—dropped on Monday. It was easy. A bit of flak hit our glider, but we landed west of Oesterbeek, and took up positions.

"There were odd snipers, but they did not cause much trouble, and we started moving towards the bridge. One brigade began to move down the railway lines.

"It ran into the first tough opposition. Eighty-eight millimetre guns were at the road and rail crossing and they forced this section back.

FIREWORKS BEGIN

"That was the beginning of the fireworks. The next day the situation began to deteriorate. We were forced to take up new positions.

"We scooped out some earth in a cabbage patch and got our guns going. We took a bit of a bashing that day—from 88mms., from tanks, and machine-guns.

"We were told to withdraw, and at nightfall we did so, with tanks following us up. We then got into a field in the middle of a wood. The German tactics were to send in tanks followed by infantry. The tanks fired then turned away, leaving the infantry.

"We usually managed to clean up the infantry, who were not too good. But then the Germans brought in flame-throwers and self-propelling guns. They gave us more than we gave them. They also sent over fierce fire from mortars.

"The weather was fine, with odd spots of rain. We had two days' food, with an extra day's food for the whole division. The resupply seemed to work well.

"We marvelled at the amazing

BACK PAGE—Col. FIVE

'Break-out' Order to Survivors

From ALAN WOOD, Representing the Combined Press

WITH ARNHEM AIRBORNE FORCE, Tuesday.

THIS is the end. The most tragic and glorious battle of the war is over, and the survivors of this British airborne force can sleep soundly for the first time in eight days and nights.

Orders came to us yesterday to break out from our forest citadel west of Arnhem, cross the Rhine, and join up with the Second Army on the south bank.

Our commander decided against a concerted assault on the Germans round us. Instead, the plan was to split up into little groups, 10 to 20 strong, and set out along different routes at two-minute intervals, which would simply walk through the German lines in the dark.

Cheeky patrols went out earlier tying bits of white parachute tape to trees to mark the way. To hinder the Germans waking up to what was happening, Second Army guns laid down a battering box barrage all afternoon.

The first party was to set off at 10 p.m.; our group was to leave at 10.4 p.m. They went round distributing little packets of sulphanilamide and morphia. We tore up blankets and wrapped them round our boots to muffle the sound of our feet in the trees.

Waited for Boats

We were told the password—"John Bull." If we became separated, each man was to make his way by compass due south until he reached the river.

Our major is an old hand. He led the way, and linked our party together by getting everyone to hold the tail of the parachutist's smock of the man in front of him, so our infiltrating column had an absurd resemblance to some children's game.

It was half-light, with the glow of fires from burning houses around, when we set out. We were lucky; we went through a reputed enemy pocket without hearing a shot except for a stray sniper's bullet.

Another group met a machine-gun with a fixed line of fire across their path. Another had to silence a bunch of Germans with a burst of Sten fire and hand grenades.

Another had to pause while a German finished his evening stroll

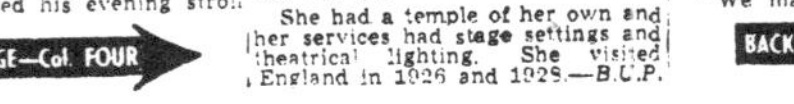

BACK PAGE—Col. FOUR

'Jet' Planes Beat the Fly-bombs

BRITISH jet-propelled aircraft fought "with success" against the flying bombs, it was announced last night.

This is the first statement about our jet-planes since January last.

Reports from the south-east coast areas during the heavy flying-bomb attacks stressed that the two fighters most successful against them were the newest Spitfire and the secret Tempest.

The statement last night was issued simultaneously in Britain and America.

It added: "Details of the jet-propelled aircraft and their engines must still remain secret, but research scientists, aircraft technicians and workers in both Britain and America may take pride in their work."

About Germany's jet-planes, the Ministries say: In spite of their high speed and rate of climb, they have shown themselves to possess poor manœuvrability.

'Hot Gospeller' Dies

OAKLAND, California, Wednesday.—Aimee Semple MacPherson, the "hot gospeller" evangelist, died at Oakland to-day of heart disease She was 53.

She had a temple of her own and her services had stage settings and theatrical lighting. She visited England in 1926 and 1928.—B.U.P.

Arnhem Gave Us Nijmegen

2,000 Men Safe Out of 8,000

TWO thousand troops of the First British Airborne Division were evacuated from the Arnhem bridgehead out of 7,000 to 8,000 dropped in the area, according to an American broadcast from Paris last night.

The speaker said the figure may be higher. About 1,200 wounded were left behind in the care of the Germans and British doctors who stayed with them.

The Germans claimed that they held 6,450 prisoners, including 1,700 wounded, and that British killed numbered 1,500.

At SHAEF last night it was emphasised that the Arnhem operation must not be regarded as a failure.

Without it we could never have hoped to capture the even more vital Nijmegen bridge, where the Waal is twice as wide as the Lower Rhine at Arnhem.

The British troops prevented the Germans from moving south at speed to Nijmegen, and forced them to send their reinforcements by a roundabout route through Emmerich. When they reached Nijmegen they were too late.

Two to three days is regarded as the fighting span of airborne troops. The First Division held out for nine days.

Bad weather eventually made withdrawal necessary.

★

A correspondent with the British Second Army has given his reasons for the failure of General Dempsey's spearhead to relieve the airborne forces.

After the weather he blames the difficult, canal-intersected Dutch countryside, where our tanks had to keep to elevated roads and were consequently good targets for hidden German 88mm. guns.

The epic of the airborne invasion of Holland began on Sunday, September 17.

While American formations were securing the bridge at Nijmegen, British troops, dropped 10 miles deeper behind the German lines, fought their way into Arnhem and for a time controlled the bridge there.

But the Germans, acutely sensitive to this grave threat, rushed up some of their best units and finally the gallant little band controlling the bridge was overcome.

From then on the rest of the British force held out grimly on a stretch of wooded high ground about three miles to the west of Arnhem.

General Dempsey's men struck north from Nijmegen in a determined effort to relieve them, but only a few patrols and limited quantities of supplies got across the Rhine.

German troops lining the north bank in strength prevented an effective link-up.

Enemy Retreat in Holland Begins

BRITISH 2ND ARMY H.Q., Wednesday.

MORE than 100,000 Germans in West Holland are in process of organising a mass getaway. They are attempting to withdraw north and then eastward through the 25-miles gap between Arnhem and the Zuider Zee.

The gap is their only hope of escape.

The British corridor from Eindhoven to west of Arnhem bars all other west-east routes to the Reich.

The Luftwaffe yesterday made an all-out attempt to aid the withdrawal by an attack on the great Nijmegen span bridge, across which all Allied transport must pass to Arnhem.

From five o'clock onwards last night the German planes used everything, from bullets to a pick-a-back glider bomb, in the attack.

Allied traffic was halted for a short time while débris was cleared round a 20ft. hole near one of the approaches.

The British corridor continues to broaden. General Dempsey's forces are making steady progress in the two-flank advance west and east of it.

Canal Line

British and Canadian troops on the west hold a firm line along the Antwerp-Turnhout canal.

They have mopped-up a six-mile stretch of territory.

Farther north on this flank there is very stiff fighting in the woods to the west of Oedenrode—where 48 hours ago the Germans momentarily cut the corridor highway.

The Germans are fighting well to hold this flank to make possible the general withdrawal from West Holland.

East of the corridor two re-equipped German divisions, the 107th Panzers and the 10th S.S., have had 150 of their 200 new tanks smashed by the British armour, and opposition to our thrust is diminishing.

Meanwhile, in their offensive against Calais the Canadians have cleared the whole area west and south-west of the town.

The Germans have withdrawn into the town itself and, protected by water inundations, are offering heavy opposition.—*Reuter.*

Throughout the British south-east "hell-fire" area bills were posted yesterday carrying this message from Mr. Herbert Morrison to the townspeople: "Every sympathy with the gallant citizens in the concluding stages of their ordeal. Hold on! I am assured by the competent military authority that the end of your trial will not be long delayed."

Everybody In Insurance For Injuries

By Daily Mail Political Correspondent

EIGHTEEN million people are affected by the Government's revolutionary plan for reforming the laws on workmen's compensation which have been in existence in various forms for the past 50 years.

Complete details of the Government's proposals are issued as a White Paper to-day.

All who work for their living and receive wages or a salary are eligible for all benefits. They will be placed on the same footing as ex-Service men.

Disability will be assessed by medical boards, and compensation will be awarded on the basis of medical reports without recourse to the law courts.

Once an award has been made it will be permanent and will not be varied not even should the recipient earn extra money.

A new principle is introduced whereby compensation will not only be paid as in the past, to those who lose their earning power, but also in future to those who "lose their health, strength, and power to enjoy life."

Outline of Scheme: Page THREE.

Rainstorm in the Strait

Sea.—Little disturbance.

Weather.—Fine until 6 p.m., when there was a rainstorm. Maximum temperature, 66 deg., 52 deg at 7.30 p.m. Visibility fairly good. Wind west, light; sky overcast.

Barometer.—Steady.

THE 'CARPET BAGGERS'

Commons Question

Mr. J. H. Wootton-Davies (Con., Heywood and Radcliffe), in a Parliamentary question to the War Secretary next Tuesday, will ask:

"What principles are being applied by the Supreme H.Q. of the Allied Expeditionary Force with regard to granting permission to business men of Allied nationality to go to France for the purpose of re-establishing their trade connections, and whether he can give an assurance that British business men will be given facilities in this respect not less favourable than those accorded to other Allied nationals."

'Civil Air' is to Have a Minister —But a Junior

By COLIN BEDNALL

THE Government, I am reliably informed, is more or less agreed on the appointment of an Under-Secretary for Air (Civil Aviation).

As the title implies, it is intended that this junior member of the Government should devote himself exclusively to the needs of the future Merchant Air Fleet—but still under the ægis of the Air Ministry.

The announcement is intended to convince the reassembled Parliament of the Government's good faith.

Parliament's reaction, it is expected, however, is more likely to follow the first thoughts of those already aware of the new proposal.

★

IT is thought, in fact, that only one of two reasons can really be responsible for the appointment now of an Under-Secretary for Air (Civil Aviation).

The first is that the Lord Privy Seal, Lord Beaverbrook, at any moment will show himself to be weary of the frustration involved in representing the present Government on Civil Aviation. Some sort of ready stop-gap for the exasperated Lord Beaverbrook may, therefore, be considered desirable.

The other more cynical explanation advanced is that the appointment is a convenient way of ensuring political suicide for some gentleman not held in very great affection by his colleagues.

Nowhere in aviation circles is it now expected that Parliament will tolerate the continued administration of Civil Aviation by the Air Ministry. Many reasons for this view are being advanced. Some of them are considered to be a little unfair to a Ministry which after all won the aerial Battle of Britain and the aerial Battle of Germany.

One fact, however, is not disputed. If the Air Ministry is to continue with its task of ensuring superiority in military aviation, it cannot, and will not, give a fully sympathetic attention to a serious rival. The rival, of course, is Civil Aviation.

★

THE Government's failure on Civil Aviation is known to be much more the result of high Cabinet policy than the inadequacy of any one of the confusing number of Departments now charged with responsibility for it.

To blame the Air Council, for instance, for the lack of the air-liners wanted for the peace or even for insufficient numbers of British military air transports is a waste of breath.

The Air Council — and this apparently may be something of a revelation—is not constituted to deal with Civil Aviation.

Aviation circles fear, in fact, that astute political organisers might be delighted to see Parliament launch itself once again into an endless discussion around such "red herrings."

The Government has an embarrassing list of *specific* charges to answer. They can be listed in their full array, if necessary.

ALBANIA FORCES PRESS ENEMY

Partisans Link

From EDWIN TETLOW, Daily Mail Special Correspondent

SOUTH EUROPEAN H.Q., Wednesday.

ALBANIA, pocket kingdom on the Adriatic, occupied by Mussolini five years ago, is the newest war front.

Picked Allied troops have landed secretly in a sea and air invasion, and are already fanning out on a wide stretch of country.

Partisans have linked with them and the joint forces are now engaging the Germans, prodding them on into a general withdrawal from the south-west Balkans.

The landing is the fruit of months of "cloak and dagger" stabs at enemy garrisons on the Adriatic seaboard.

British and Allied troops have been ashore for weeks, living in caves and in mountain hideouts, training Partisans and leading them in resistance and sabotage against the Germans.

The Allied invasion has come as the climax to their operations.

In addition to the landings on the Albanian mainland troops are ashore on the islands off Yugoslavia. No Allied mention is made of operations in Yugoslavia itself, but the Germans report landings along the whole Dalmatian coast.

The Allied troops now in Albania can count on the help of some 20,000 Albanian guerillas. In addition, Yugoslav Partisans of Marshal Tito's command have been operating with the Albanians in recent weeks, and it is possible that these forces have been strengthened.

General Tolbukhin's Russian troops in Bulgaria are also only 165 miles from the northern Albanian coast, and an Allied drive inland might result in a link-up which would cut off the five German divisions in Greece.

Heavy fighting is already raging in Macedonia, west of the Belgrade-Salonika railway, the Germans' main escape route from Greece, and between Leskovac and Nigh, farther up the line, between Yugoslav Partisans and the enemy.

FRENCH GOVT. TAKE RENAULT WORKS

The French Government have decided to requisition the Renault works at Billancourt as part of the policy of purging firms which aided the Germans.—Reuter.

RIGA: NEW SOVIET ADVANCE

Soviet communique announces more progress in the drive on Riga. Over 200 places captured.

SATURDAY, SEPTEMBER 30, 1944

Evening Standard

37,457 DIM-OUT 7.11 p.m. to 6.30 a.m. MOON rises 6.27 p.m., sets 5.30 a.m. ONE PENNY

FINAL NIGHT

All Cross-Channel Guns Captured: Dover Hears the Liberation News by Loudspeaker

THE CAPTURE OF CAP GRIS NEZ AND THE SILENCING OF ITS LAST CROSS-CHANNEL BATTERIES WAS ANNOUNCED IN TO-DAY'S SUPREME HEADQUARTERS COMMUNIQUE.

Dover heard of its liberation shortly after 10 o'clock to-day. Loud speakers in the town gave them the following message:

"The Mayor has received official information that all the long-range guns on the other side of the Channel have now been captured."

The message was also broadcast in the caves, where many people have been sheltering during the fierce bombardment of the last month. There were cheers all through the town.

The scene to-day and the four years' ordeal are described on PAGE FOUR.

HITLER TELLS CALAIS: 'HOLD'

'Pocket Goering' Says: 'We Fight to Last Man'

The attack on Calais was restarting at noon to-day, after the 24-hour armistice for the evacuation of civilians.

From SAM WHITE

CALAIS, Saturday.

THE GERMAN GARRISON AT CALAIS WILL FIGHT TO THE LAST MAN IN ACCORDANCE WITH ORDERS ITS COMMANDER HAS RECEIVED FROM HITLER.

This was stated by the German commander himself, Colonel Schroeder, at the outset of the astonishing conference he had with the general commanding the British assault forces yesterday by the side of a demolished bridge some eight miles from Calais.

The conference was held at Schroeder's rcquest and was part of the truce

Schroeder's first words dispelled any hope that he intended to ask for terms of surrender.

After returning the British general's salute with a stiffly raised arm, he said:

"I wish you to understand, General, I have received orders from my Fuehrer to fight to the last man, and that is what I intend to do.

"The sole reason for my suggesting this truce is to find a way for evacuating the civilian population from Calais."

"WONDERLAND"

Schroeder himself, about whom very little is known, except that he arrived to take over the garrison a few days ago, looks like a pocket edition of Goering.

Chubby, excitable, dressed in a smartly-cut but shabby jacket and breeches shaped like butterfly wings, he gesticulated continuously, and once commented on the conference: "This is like something out of Alice in Wonderland." But it was Schroeder's aides who attracted most attention. They were all young, all "wasp waisted," but the arm of one was missing, another had a wooden leg, and the third was disfigured by a badly burnt ear.

The British general's last words to Schroeder were, "Well, colonel, I hope you will enjoy to-morrow's bombardment by our heavy bombers."

Schroeder smiled and said, "C'est la guerre."

How soon can the city be expected to fall?

Obviously it is not going to be an easy job. Calais is ringed by mines, inundations and a long tank trap around the western perimeter of the city.

If, however, Schroeder thinks he can repeat the performance of the commander of the Le Havre garrison and drive out in his car to surrender when he thinks he has delayed the Allies sufficiently, then he has got another think coming to him.

Urquhart, of Arnhem Goes Home To-day

Major-general [illegible] Urquhart, D.S.O., commander of the First Airborne Division, who escaped from enemy hands at Arnhem, was expected home at Chudleigh, South Devon, to-day.

Mrs. Urguhart said to-day that her husband telephoned her last night.

"He sounded very cheerful, well and in good form," she said, "and told me he would be home as soon as his men were landed safely."

THE TREK OUT

German Drivers Wanted To Surrender to Canadians

From WILLIAM WILSON, British United Press War Correspondent

NEAR CALAIS, Saturday morning.

Twenty thousand French civilians have started the great trek from Calais where two armies are preparing the field for the battle that is being resumed at noon to-day.

Crowds of French men, women and children poured down the main road out of the town, loaded with whatever of their belongings they could hastily scrape together—as much as they could carry in suitcases on bicycles and in pushcarts.

A f w lucky one travelled in cars, crammed to overflowing with a cargo of Frenchmen and their belongings. Others, less lucky, went in ambulances. They were the casualties from the battles that had raged near their homes.

Even the Germans did what they could to get the civilians away. They provided 20 or 30 cars and lorries to speed up the great trek.

German drivers brought them to the assembly point outside Calais and turned over the cargo of humanity to the Canadians, who took the loads on as far as possible along the road to the edge of the canal, where there is a ruined bridge.

On Foot

There the civilians piled out and the trek went forward on foot—across an improvised bridge to Ardes, where Canadian and French vehicles were waiting to take the people on to refugee centres.

But the German drivers who brought the civilians out of Calais refused to go back when their task was finished, although they were under orders to do so from their own officers. They created an awkward situation, because the Canadian officers were not allowed to take them prisoners during the truce.

"Ye've been waiting three weeks for a chance to get away," two Germans who spoke English told me. "We're not going back now. Nine men out of ten in the Calais garrison feel the same way and only the commanders want to fight."

All the Same

I asked them if all the other drivers felt the sam eway, and they replied eagerly: "Yes, we'll ask them. You'll see for yourself then."

I'm damned if I know what

(Continued on Back Page, Col. One)

AN ARNHEM SMILE

Sgt. John Bonome, of Twickenham, one of the glider pilots who fought in the Arnhem battle, grins with pleasure at being back in England again.

Cloud After Sun in Straits

During the morning in the Straits of Dover there were sunny periods, but the sky clouded over towards mid-day with a high ceiling of broken cloud.

Across the Straits the French coast showed through the haze, and the sea was smooth

Montgomery's Armies in "Slogging Match" Along the Whole Front

NIJMEGEN IS STILL SECURE

FIELD MARSHAL MONTGOMERY'S ARMIES ARE TO-DAY FIGHTING A SLOW, UNSPECTACULAR SLOGGING MATCH ALONG THEIR WHOLE FRONT, SAYS WILLIAM STEEN, REUTER'S CORRESPONDENT.

Everywhere German opposition is stiff, and repeated counter-attacks have to be beaten off.

Nijmegen rests securely in British hands in spite of vicious German attempts to recapture it. Luftwafre attempts to bomb the vital bridge have been equally unsuccessful.

The British Second Army have also further expanded their own Holland salient.

To-day's Supreme Headquarters communiqué stated:

"Our troops are advancing steadily on a six-mile front west of Turnhout in face of stubborn opposition.

"German counter-attacks against our Nijmegen salient were repulsed north of Best and in the vicinity of Nijmegen.

"Allied forces advancing towards Hertogenbosch from the south-east are within four miles of the town.

"Fighters are fighter-bombers closely supported our ground forces and attacked transportation targets in Holland.

"There was considerable opposition in the air, and, according to reports so far received, 31 enemy aircraft were shot down by our fighters, four of which are missing."

FOREST FIGHT

Desmond Tighe, Reuter's correspondent with the British Second Army, cables to-day:

"An enemy counter-attack near Bemmel, in the Nijmegen area, has been held by the British.

"The Germans are stubbornly shelling Best, which is in Allied hands, six miles north-west of Eindhoven, from a mile away.

"There is very fierce fighting in the Reichswald Forest, where American airborne troops, with British armour, staged a counter-attack after an enemy local gain yesterday south-east of Nijmegen.

(Continued on Back Page, Col. Four)

WIDENING BREACH IN SIEGFRIED LINE

From DREW MIDDLETON

With the American 1st U.S. Army near Stolberg, Saturday.

Yard by yard, hardy veterans of some of the finest divisions in the American Army are widening the breach in the Siegfried Line in one of the bitterest battles of the war.

This is exacting, strenuous fighting, the like of which has not been seen since Lieut.-general Omar Bradley broke the German positions around St. Lo.

Though many of the Germans and Italians opposing the American First Army are composed of convalescents and comparatively old soldiers, we must fight for every inch, and fight with troops some of whom fought almost continuously for almost four months.

Rhine Crossings

Behind cleverly comprised defences, the Germans are refitting and regrouping field divisions for the coming battle for the Rhine crossings. Though their strategic situation is grave, the Germans on this front are far stronger tactically than they were a fortnight ago.

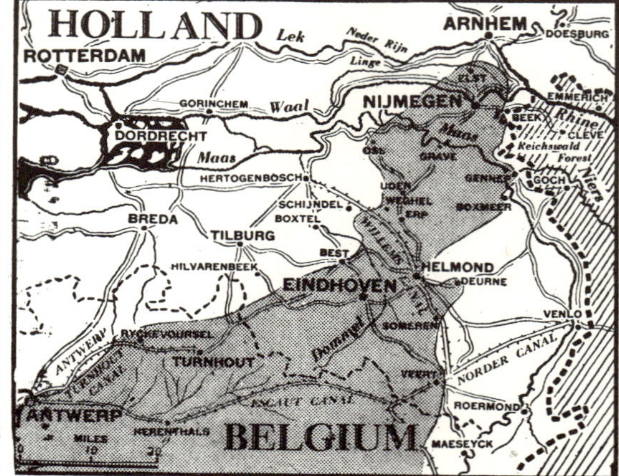

Two-Hour Stream Of Bombers

"Allied bomber formations are over Western Germany and others are heading for Western Germany," said German radio to-day.

A fairly strong force of R.A.F. fighters, most of them Spitfires, went out over the Straits of Dover to-day. They were flying in distinct squadron formation and went up the Channel as if on their way to Holland in six groups.

East Coast observers saw wave after wave of heavy bombers, fighter-bombers and fighters go out for nearly two hours.

GUNS POUND WARSAW NON-STOP

Soviet guns are roaring unceasingly before Warsaw, smashing the enemy's fortifications on the other side of the Vistula, says Reuter.

The Polish capital is still burning.

The Germans are keeping up fierce machine-gun fire across the Vistula from tall buildings in the city and at the same time they are making a systematic attempt to raze Praga by shellfire.

The Red Army in the Baltic are drawing ever tighter the ring round the Latvian port of Riga, while at the southern end of the Russian front three spearheads are thrusting at the heart of Hungary from both sides of the Carpathians, says Reuter.

Among 30 places captured by the Russians in the increasingly difficult country north-east of Riga is the German strongpoint of Eikazi, about 27 miles from Riga and five miles north-west of the railway town of Segewold.

In the Szecho-Slavakian sector the Red Army are fighting dizzy mountain battles where sudden thunderstorms are transforming paths into torrents and sending huge boulders crashing across the roads.

THE TWINS COME HOME TOGETHER

After 4 Years In Germany

John and George Holness, brother privates in the Buffs, 24-year-old twins, of Selsey, Kent, have been repatriated after being together during more than four years of capitivity.

They enlisted together in 1939, went to France, and were captured together at St. Valery in June 1940.

They shared the same prison camps. The brothers were not wounded, but after working for nearly four years in coal mines in Germany and Poland they have suffered in health.

Daily Mail

LATE WAR NEWS

NO. 15,108 ONE PENNY ** FOR KING AND EMPIRE WEDNESDAY, OCTOBER 4, 1944

RUHR PARALYSED BY RAF BOMBING OF EMS CANAL

Reich 'Moat' Battle

Push Beyond Siegfried

From **JOHN HALL,** Daily Mail Special Correspondent

RIMBURG, Tuesday.

ONCE again the Siegfried Line has been cracked open. An American First Army spokesman was able to announce to-night that a definite new breach had been made north of Aachen.

We are now through the fortified zone both north and south of Aachen.

The German mining town of Ubach was captured late this afternoon, after a battle in which 39 pill-boxes were smashed.

This carries the new attack four miles from its starting point, and American forward troops now face open country where pill-boxes give way to minefields, anti-tank ditches, and trenches prepared by community digging.

Fight for Castle

Besides Ubach a number of coal-mining villages, which are almost continuous, like some of those in South Wales, were captured.

So far the attack has yielded between 500 and 600 prisoners.

Red men fought for Ubach—Americans and Huns, plastered from foot to head with red clay that sticks and cakes and turns men and guns to the colour of the soil.

Continuous rain has made the new American assault a battle of mud. This afternoon the battlefront looked like one of those Flanders scenes from the First World War winters.

Scores of pill-boxes were knocked out in bitter street - fighting this morning. The Americans rushed them in platoons, ignoring the concentrated fire from the embrasures.

It was supremely heroic fighting, and it was made more desperate for the Americans because Hun mortar teams lobbed patterns of bombs just in front of the pill-boxes.

But this afternoon I was assured by an American staff officer that casualties have not been heavy.

Toughest Fight

One of the toughest fights has been not for a pill-box but for an old German schloss — Rimburg Castle, which stands on the frontier near the town of that name. It was by-passed late yesterday, but so much sniper fire came from it that an assault was ordered.

The castle, owned by a nephew of Field-Marshal von Brauchitsch, former German Commander - in - Chief, stands on rising ground in a woodland and is surrounded by a wide moat behind which is a high wall.

Firing slits that were made for bows and arrows were used by the Hun defenders. The Americans formed an assault group, rushed the narrow bridge over the moat, and smashed in the schloss doors.

That was just before dusk last night. Darkness did not end the fight. All through the night the Americans probed from room to room, killing, wounding, and capturing.

By dawn to-day the remaining Huns had been penned in the west wing of two floors. Half a dozen hand grenades sent crashing through the windows brought them

BACK PAGE—Col. TWO

THREE big developments on the Western Front were reported last night: 1. The Dortmund - Ems Canal, main bottleneck in Germany's water system, has been breached by 96 Lancasters, paralysing the Ruhr and loosing flood waters deep in the rear of the Siegfried Line (see picture). 2. Another force of Lancasters yesterday smashed the sea wall on Walcheren Island, guarding the Scheldt estuary, and left the North Sea pouring in to engulf the big German guns. 3. U.S. troops breached the Siegfried Line north of Aachen.

THIS was how the Dortmund-Ems Canal looked on Monday, nine days after the R.A.F. had smashed its banks with 12,000-pounders and many smaller bombs and emptied it in a blow comparable with that on the Mohne and Eder dams in May 1943. Both branches of the canal, which here flows high above the surrounding country, are dry, and on the lower branch a barge can be seen on the canal bed. Arrows show where 12,000-pounder direct hits let the water flood out over the countryside.

96 Planes Did It in 40 Minutes

NINETY-SIX Lancaster bombers, led by Wing Commander G. W. Curry, of West Monkseaton, Northumberland, have delivered the most important air-attack of the war against German communications, it was officially announced last night.

Their five-ton bombs tore great gaps in the embankments of the Dortmund-Ems Canal, draining it dry and practically isolating the Ruhr. The attack was made ten days ago, but it was not until yesterday that air reconnaissance was able to confirm the complete success of the operation.

At one blow the main bottleneck in the vast and vital inland waterway system of Germany was entirely severed. The economic and military effects of this will be enormous and far-reaching.

While the Dortmund-Ems Canal is dry—and so far there is no sign that the Germans have begun the long and difficult task of repairing the damage—the Ruhr is completely isolated by waterway both from the North Sea and from Berlin and Eastern Germany.

No Rhine traffic can now reach the North Sea, because the Rhine itself is cut at Nijmegen and almost certainly impassable for heavy traffic at Arnhem.

The canal was attacked at a place where it was highly vulnerable. This was the Glane By-Pass, north of Münster. Here the waterway has been doubled, and both sections flow above the level of the surrounding country between embankments and over the River Glane.

BARGES GROUNDED

The river is camouflaged, because it would otherwise be easy to find the by-pass by looking out for the point where canal and river cross.

The 12,000lb. bombs have made huge gaps in the embankments alongside both sections of the canal.

To prevent such a danger, safety gates were built across the two arms of the canal, but the bombs fell so as to make these gates useless and let the water out from both sides.

Reconnaissance photographs show long lines of barges lying on the bottom of the empty waterway.

When the embankments have been repaired the enemy will be faced with the problem of pumping water from a lower level into the long stretch of canal which has been drained.

The attack lasted only 40 minutes, from 9.35 to 10.15. At the same time the industries of Munster, not many miles away, were raided Fighter opposition was intense, and the canal was also guarded by flak and searchlights. Bomber Command losses that night were 22 aircraft, of which 14 were lost in the attack on the canal.

Long before the war 11,000,000 tons of freight were carried each year to and from the Ruhr on the Dortmund-Ems canal.

Water traffic has increased greatly since then with the growing strain on the German railways and shortage of oil for road transport.

Some stretches of the canal carried three times as much traffic in 1943 as before the war. Now oil is shorter than ever, and the railway system still more strained, so that the waterways have become even more important.

They were the only communications in Germany which had so far escaped serious attack, and the interruption of traffic now is a far more serious matter than it would ever have been before.

Gateway to N. & N.E. — MUNSTER — Ems canal — Dortmund- — Lippe — Glane — Concentrated Factory Area — Gateway to N. & S. — DORTMUND — HAMM — Gelsenkirchen — Oberhausen — BOCHUM — Mohne Dam — Sorpe Dam — Gateway to E. & S.E. — ESSEN — Mulheim — Ruhr — Rhine — DUISBURG — Gateway to N.W., W. & S.W. — Wuppertal — DUSSELDORF — 0 10 20 Miles — Kiel — Emden — BERLIN — HOLLAND — MUNSTER — DORTMUND — BOCHUM — DUISBURG — DUSSELDORF — BELGIUM — RUHR — Leipzig

INQUIRY ON COAL BY 6 EXPERTS

THE Minister of Fuel and Power, Major Lloyd George, has appointed a technical committee of mining engineers, under the chairmanship of Mr. Charles C. Reid, Production Director at the Ministry, with these terms of reference:

"To examine the present technique of coal production from coal face to railway wagon, and to advise what technical changes are necessary to bring the industry to a state of full technical efficiency."

Five mining engineers will serve with Mr. Reid.

All kinds of problems are awaiting technical investigation—notably the mechanisation of the mines. Experts feel that further developments will not only increase production but decrease the number of accidents and make mining a more attractive occupation.

Major Lloyd George said in the House of Commons yesterday that coal output per miner has fallen by 5 cwt. a week mainly owing to an increase of 25 per cent. in voluntary absenteeism.

Sky Clears in the Strait

Sea.—Practically calm.

Weather.—A good deal of sunshine during the day, but heavy cloud at times. Sky cleared at dusk and wind dropped. Maximum temperature 64deg., 46deg. at 7.30 p.m. Visibility restricted, hazy. Wind west, light.

Barometer.—Steady.

Carriers Can Become Our Crack Liners

SUPER "Woolworth" aircraft-carriers, which have been completed in British shipyards for the air blitz against the Japs, may become luxury liners in the keen competition for sea - passenger traffic after the war.

These ships are carrying out in reverse the policy of converting merchant ships and fast tankers into small aircraft-carriers for convoy escort duty.

They were primarily designed for service with the Navy, but can be converted in a few months into liners, so that the Government's guarantee to restore Britain's merchant fleet to full strength can be fulfilled.

The design of their hulls and engines follows modern passenger-ship practice. As soon as they can be freed from naval duty they will return to the yards that built them.

'Carpet Bagging': Eden to Speak

The Government, through Mr. Anthony Eden, the Foreign Secretary, will make a considered statement in the House of Commons to-day on the question of American business men in uniform being given facilities to travel to Paris.

This matter was first ventilated by *The Daily Mail* and has roused considerable discussion.

A question was put on the Order Paper by Miss Irene Ward Conservative member for Wallsend, which asks Mr. Eden to reply to the allegations "that American officers are conducting private business interests in Paris."

RAF 'SINK' A DUTCH ISLAND

Sea Swamps the Enemy Guns

LAST night the North Sea had engulfed the fortified Dutch island of Walcheren after pouring through a great breach torn in the massive sea wall by 12,000lb. bombs.

The blow was struck yesterday by the R.A.F. to swamp German long-range batteries on the island which bar the way to shipping moving up the Scheldt estuary to Antwerp.

Most of the island is below sea level, and Air Marshal Harris waited for the highest tides before he sent out his planes.

Wave after wave of Lancasters, between 1 p.m. and 3 p.m. yesterday, dropped their cargoes on the great dike.

They breached it near West Kapelle, and engulfed the German garrison. Guns and defence posts were quickly under several feet of water. They will be inundated at every high tide.

200ft. Thick

The dike was 200ft. thick at the base, and crews report that a huge gap some several hundred yards wide was torn in it. They saw the sea surging in and stretching out over the island.

Flying Officer H. Ellis, a bomb aimer, of Tottenham, said: "I saw the sea pour through the gap, fill bomb craters, and then reach the town of West Kapelle, 700 yards from the shore."

Photographs taken within an hour of the attack showed an area 1,000 yards by 700 yards flooded.

All the Lancasters attacked from below cloud base at 5,000ft.

Not one bomber was lost.

'Pram' Wrecks Tanks

Daily Mail Special Correspondent

WITH THE EIGHTH ARMY, Italy, Tuesday.—Hitler's latest secret weapon on this front is a "perambulator" in which the "baby" is a gun firing a rocket which will penetrate 6in. of armour.

Germans who have seen the "perambulator," presumably a reply to the bazooka, wheeled into action have named it the "Little Doll."

New Civil Air Policy 'Forced' on Cabinet

By **WILSON BROADBENT,** Political Correspondent

THE Government's continued shilly-shallying over the formulation of a definite policy, designed to enable Great Britain to assume her place as a foremost civil air Power after the war, reached a climax yesterday with these developments.

1. The Prime Minister announced in the House of Commons that Lord Beaverbrook, Lord Privy Seal, was no longer responsible for civil aviation policy, the Civil Aviation Transport Committee, of which he has been chairman, having completed its inquiries and tendered its report.

2. Lord Londonderry received a request from the Government to postpone the debate on civil aviation which he had intended to open in the House of Lords to-morrow, and agreed to do so for one week.

3. Mr. Churchill received a deputation of members of Parliament, who made representations to him arising out of reports that an Under-Secretary is to be appointed to the Air Ministry to take charge of civil aviation matters.

Obviously, a point has been reached where the Government realise that the persistent anxieties of those who are deeply concerned about Britain's position in the future air age must be set at rest.

A statement with this object in view can therefore be expected from the Prime Minister in the very near future. But I was warned last night not to expect too much.

There are to be Cabinet discussions in the next few days at which civil aviation policy will be thrashed out. These will be vital discussions, and as regards some of the personalities concerned, they may be critical.

It is clear that the Government are feeling the pressure of opinion from inside as well as outside. It may be that Lord Beaverbrook has at last produced a spark.

Restive

Mr. Churchill's intimation to the House of Commons yesterday, which was carefully worded as if purposely to hide some of the most vital facts of the situation, came as a surprise to most members, but not to those who have interested themselves in the Government's failure to produce a policy.

As *The Daily Mail* disclosed last Thursday, Lord Beaverbrook has become increasingly restive at the continued delay in obtaining the Cabinet's agreement to a specific air policy.

He is said to feel that all his efforts are being rendered futile, and that without a policy it is useless for him to continue to represent the Government as spokesman on civil aviation.

It was anticipated that he would be Thursday's spokesman for the Government, but as the Government asked for a postponement, probably Lord Beaverbrook felt that he could not undertake the task.

It seems that Lord Beaverbrook's views are now before the Cabinet

BACK PAGE—Col. FOUR

Soviet Take 'Bomb Berlin' Isle

Moscow announced last night that the Red Army has captured Dago, one of the two Baltic islands guarding the entrance to the Gulf of Riga. It was used in 1941 as a "Bomb Berlin" base.

Other Russian forces yesterday made new crossings of the Yugoslav border.

Vast Nazi 'Maquis' Organised

To Fight on From Salt Caves

Daily Mail Special Correspondent

GENEVA, Tuesday.

REPORTS of the organisation of a vast Nazi "Maquis" in Germany to carry on guerrilla warfare are confirmed to-day by the "Journal de Geneve." Preparations, the paper states, are far advanced.

The centre of the "Maquis" is in the neighbourhood of Garmisch - Partenkirchen, in the Tyrolean Alps, and work on communications between Berchtesgaden and Garmisch is in progress.

The innumerable salt caves in the region, stretching from Obersalzburg to Wels and Steyr, with their

CONFIDENCE VOTE FOR BELGIAN GOVT.

Belgian Government yesterday received vote of confidence of 128 votes to six, reports Belgian national radio.

FOOD REACHING PARIS

Almost 4,000 head of cattle, besides large quantities of milk, potatoes, and flour have arrived in Paris to help out the food situation, states the Prefect of the Seine Department broadcasting over the French National radio.—B.U.P.

2

subterranean passages, are meant to shelter vast numbers of Nazis.

Already many war factories are installed in them and vast stores of materials and food are being accumulated.

Hitler, Himmler, and Bormann, inspired by the exploits of the French Savoy Maquis, will make their last stand in the area with their most fanatical followers.

Meanwhile the *Journal* reports that the world will be "stupefied" when it becomes known just how many Germans have disappeared since April 1.

For months, it adds, the German people have been dumb. Their silence is sepulchral in cafés, cinemas, trains, and streets.

General Eisenhower's call to the foreign workers in Germany to rise was followed immediately by the creation of a vast concentration camp in the Breslau area. It is equipped with modern gas apparatus.

LATE WAR NEWS

NO. 15,117 ONE PENNY ** FOR KING AND EMPIRE SATURDAY, OCTOBER 14, 1944

AACHEN'S DEFENDERS CRACKING

CLIFFORD SUMS UP THE CAMPAIGN

'This is Still an Army of Retreat'

Wrecking as it Falls Back

From **ALEXANDER CLIFFORD**, Daily Mail Special Correspondent

WITH THE BRITISH ARMIES, Friday.

THE fighting to tidy up the shapeless British Front in Holland is growing stiffer.

The newest development is the drive eastward which the Second Army has started from half-way up its great salient.

The attack went in near the village of Overloon, and it is still going on in the soggy fields and damp woods of that flat, dreary countryside.

Both here and down on the Scheldt the Germans are resisting strongly and methodically. They are determined to prevent us from reshaping the front the way we want it.

They know that when we do we shall be in a position to launch another full-scale offensive.

It is true that the great thrust up to Arnhem was 80 per cent. successful and 20 per cent. failure, but from the point of view of the next operation it is the 20 per cent. of failure that must be considered.

We could not follow through immediately and complete the drive as originally planned, so we must start afresh and plan things anew.

The Arnhem semi-success left us with this salient thrusting up like a great thumb into Holland.

It was a promising position if it could be quickly exploited, for it threatened all the Germans in Western Holland.

But it could not be quickly exploited. Now it is an awkward shape that must be rationalised and simplified.

★

SO we were engaged in a large-scale mopping-up operation, with the emphasis for the moment on these two points—the mouth of the Scheldt and the area towards the Meuse east of Eindhoven.

The Germans have had plenty of time to get their breath and regain their balance. Their resistance is now fully planned.

They have sorted out their jumbled divisions and have distributed new equipment and arms.

They have got their supply routes organised to suit the new circumstances. They have finally got complete control of their own army again.

Realising the value of Antwerp to us, they have planted this garrison each side of the mouth of the Scheldt so that we cannot use the river.

It is the same tactics as the Berlin High Command has used all along—to try to embarrass us by denying us ports. They hope that with the bad weather of winter our armies here will be semi-blockaded.

The German garrisons on the Scheldt are having a very unpleasant time.

The dikes have been bombed, and their gun positions have been bombed, and their supply routes are being bombed all the time.

By land they are cut off. But they still have possible escape routes, and they show no signs of panicking. They have no doubt been ordered to hold out there till they die.

They are putting in strong counter-attacks both there and on the Overloon front.

These are simply counter-thrusts designed to throw the next phase of our operation off balance and do as much damage as possible.

They are always on a local scale, and their function is basically defensive. But they are now stronger and more co-ordinated than they have been for some time.

The Germans can now switch troops quite systematically from one part of the front to another.

They have had time to lay minefields and map out their defence plans. They have recovered very cleverly from the mess they got themselves into at Falaise.

★

IN Holland they are gradually ruining the country for us. They know well enough that they are going to lose it and they themselves don't want the harbour installations anyway.

So they are methodically wrecking them. They are gradually moving out their more static establishments and administrative headquarters. Things like prisoners' camps are being liquidated and the occupants being sent back to the Reich.

The whole Dutch flooding system is being carefully controlled.

For us it means much stiffer resistance than we have had since Normandy. The weather, as usual, is against us.

The low-lying Dutch fields become just so much mud in the autumn.

The leaves are falling from the trees, and the woods are squelchy and treacherous underfoot.

The days get progressively less good for flying. The whole rhythm of warfare is being forced to slow down yet in spite of all these defensive advantages—to which must be added the new fanaticism of the Germans when fighting for German soil—we still retain the initiative and we still advance.

That is the measure of our superiority and our guarantee of success.

All their stupendous efforts have not provided the Germans with an army that can do more than retreat.

Col. Reitz Very Ill

Colonel Reitz, High Commissioner for South Africa in London, who was taken seriously ill a few days ago, has been removed to hospital.

Americans Battle Into Centre of Flaming City as Relieving Tank Column is Wiped Out

Defeat and on their own soil

HERE is one of the most eloquent pictures that has yet emerged from the war. These are German soldiers captured in battle on their own soil; held prisoner in a German town, guarded by the bayonets of an invading army.

They sit around a courtyard in Aachen. They are young men; their uniforms do not bear the stains of prolonged battle; it is clear that they gave up the fight in its early stages.

Almost every man in the group might present a model for a study in dejection. This is the proud German Army in its twilight.

64 Panzers Destroyed

THE battle for Aachen is swiftly drawing to its climax. American troops have smashed their way into the city proper, and last night were driving forward against heavy small-arms fire. The city's escape gap has been narrowed to half a mile, and early to-day indications were that the defence of the town has begun to crack. This weakening of resistance follows the virtual wiping out of a German armoured force massed near Wurselen for the relief of the city. This force was attacked by artillery and dive-bombers; 64 of its tanks were destroyed. On the British front General Dempsey has broadened his assault towards the Maas, east of Nijmegen, and is now attacking on a four-miles front. Around the Scheldt pocket, where the Canadians continue to make steady progress, waterways have suddenly filled with enemy barges and small boats—a possible prelude to an attempt to evacuate the encircled garrisons.

INSIDE THE CITY

Suicide Men Fight on

OUTSIDE AACHEN, Friday Evening.

AMERICAN troops broke into Aachen proper at 9.30 this morning, and to-night the infantry, fighting from house to house, are driving deeper and deeper into the city against moderate resistance from small arms fire. So far little or no artillery opposition has been encountered.

At least half of the city is destroyed; more and more of it is being blasted into destruction at this moment

On all sides there is the thunderous roar of American guns pounding the city. Thunderbolts race overhead on their way to strafe and dive-bomb.

Fires are burning all around; machine-guns beat a tattoo of death against almost every building.

But still fighting on are fanatical little nests of German machine-gunners and riflemen. Every target they see is greeted with a hail of fire.

How Attack Began

War correspondents followed the troops into the city. They saw few civilians, these were huddling in their basements to escape the pulverising American fire.

For half an hour before the attack from Aachen-Forst began, Allied mortars blanketed the German-held area immediately in front of the American positions. Light artillery covered the area beyond that, and heavier guns operated at longer range.

Tank destroyers followed the infantry in, and tanks blasted out German machine-gunners at point-blank range.

The first batch of prisoners taken were well fed and husky.

They were confident, too—sure that Germany will win the war.

The next batch were found in a street, hands in the air.

The first impression of the city is the great devastation. Down long, straight streets were endless rows of blown-out window casements, of smashed houses, of broken roofs.

Next one saw tall men in German grey standing in the middle of the street, with the shorter Americans guarding them.

Two women were in one group of prisoners.

They were taken to the basement of a nearby house where about a dozen men and women were huddled content to be out of the shellfire.

One woman said that they had been ordered to go to the station a month ago to be evacuated.

But when they got there they were told that no more trains were running

So far American casualties in this attack have been definitely light. — *Messages from Reuter, B.U.P., and I.N.S.*

Taking No Chances

From Daily Mail Correspondent

GENEVA, Friday. — Visitors to Berchtesgaden now have to pass through a special chamber where they are X-rayed to see whether they are carrying arms, according to reports reaching here.

And Outside

ARMOUR IS BLITZED

From **JOHN HALL**, Daily Mail Special Correspondent

IN GERMANY, Friday.

HITLER is hurrying his attempts to ensure that the soil of the Reich is purged of invaders.

During the past few days he has been rushing the massing of forces between the Rhine and the territory held by the American First Army north and south of Aachen. It is a long time since the Huns exhibited so much recklessness in massing forces—moving troops and armour and artillery in daylight along roads covered by American artillery and strafed by aircraft.

TUDDERN Waldenrath Geilenkirchen Ameln Alsdorf Schaufenberg JULICH Wurselen AACHEN DUREN Stolberg FOREST Hurtgen EUPEN Hammersdorf Roer Gemund 0 10 20 MILES

He paid for it again to-day—paid for it so heavily that the expected blow was not delivered.

In good weather the American Air Force swooped on columns of armour and infantry, blasting tanks with rockets and strafing infantry with cannon fire.

Near Wurselen these units were caught assuming battle order. Dive-bombers and rocket aircraft pounded them again and again; a heavy concentration of artillery threw tons of high explosives at them.

Dazed Captives

The German losses were very heavy. Dazed prisoners reported that of one group of 43 Tiger tanks only eight survived; 29 out of 35 smaller tanks were destroyed.

And the dead, they said, lay in piles.

Despite this slaughter of men and materials, the Americans are not discounting the possible force of any eventual blow.

"The mauling we have given him by air and artillery has thrown out of gear his plans for quick attack," I was told, "but the main threat remains—and we are ready for it."

The Germans have been most active to-day trying to hold open the pincers round Aachen, but to-night the gap was only a half-mile wide as a result of slow, hard-won progress by the Americans against dug-in tanks, artillery, and small arms fire.

Berlin Says 'General Attack Soon'

SERTORIUS, the German commentator, last night again forecast an early Allied offensive on the Western Front.

"Eisenhower's armies are at present fighting for favourable jumping-off grounds for the new general assault against the Reich, which is expected to break shortly.

"Fresh troops have been concentrated in the immediate rear of the First U.S. Army.

"It seems not unlikely that they are no longer earmarked for the Battle of Aachen, but for other objectives, possibly for a grand-scale attack in the sectors on both sides of Geilenkirchen.

"The expected attack by the Second British Army from their Nijmegen bridgehead having so far failed to materialise, tension is mounting." —*Reuter.*

£12 10s. WHEN WRENS LEAVE

Clothes Gratuity

Modified arrangements for paying of plain-clothes gratuities to Wren ratings leaving the Service come into force on Monday.

Mobile ratings will be given a plain-clothes gratuity of £12 10s. Immobile ratings will be given the same gratuity provided they have served at least 12 months.

Payment of this gratuity is to be made before discharge.

COAL STOCKS ARE DOWN

Over 3,000,000 Tons

There was a net fall in coal stocks during the year ended June last of 3.3 million tons, states the *Board of Trade Journal.*

In the second quarter of this year, coal production was abnormally affected by disputes, particularly in Yorkshire, which were estimated to have resulted in the loss of 587,100 tons, compared with 227,100 tons in the corresponding quarter last year

The net costs of production for the first quarter this year were £62,500,876, wages accounting for £45,916,608

CAUSE FOR DEJECTION

HERE is good reason for all Germans to be dispirited now. Shaded area shows the vast territories lost by the Germans since Stalingrad and the ever-narrowing territory left to them.

EDEN CONFERS WITH POLES

Four-Power Talks

MOSCOW, Friday.—Mr. Eden conferred with M. Mikolajczyk, the Polish Prime Minister, and members of his delegation in Moscow to-day.

Earlier the Polish leaders called on M. Molotov, the Russian Foreign Minister, and Mr. Harriman, U.S. Ambassador to Russia, had seen M. Mikolajczyk.

Mr. Churchill and Marshal Stalin did not meet to-day, but preparations for the next meeting are being made.—*B.U.P. and Exchange.*

U.S. Planes Hit 63 Jap Ships

From Daily Mail Correspondent

NEW YORK, Friday.—Three hundred and ninety-six Japanese planes were destroyed and 63 enemy ships sunk or damaged in a two-days assault on Formosa and Pescadores, a communiqué from Admiral Nimitz announced to-day.

There was no indication of the size of the task force employed, but the tremendous damage done indicated that probably over 1,000 carrier-borne planes were engaged. American losses were 45 aircraft.

Molotov Sees Mikolajczyk

MOSCOW, Friday.—M. Mikolajczyk, Prime Minister of Poland, conferred briefly to-night with M. Molotov, Russian Commissar for Foreign Affairs, and representatives of the Polish Committee of National Liberation at their headquarters.

M. Mikolajczyk declined to comment on the meeting but said he hoped to see Marshal Stalin and Mr Churchill later.—*A.P.*

170 Raid Deaths in September

Civilian air-raid casualties in this country during September were 170 killed or missing (63 men, 80 women, and 27 children); 360 in jured and detained in hospital (130 men, 194 women, and 36 children)

During August 1,103 people were killed and 2,921 injured.

ROOSEVELT SILENT ON MOSCOW

News Kept Secret

From Daily Mail Correspondent

WASHINGTON, Friday.

PRESIDENT ROOSEVELT this morning received a long, confidential dispatch from Moscow, and reading it made him three-quarters of an hour late for his Press conference.

But when the reporters asked him if he had any comment to make on the progress of the Churchill-Stalin talks, he replied, "No," though he said he was being kept fully informed.

The President was vaguely non-committal when asked if the Prime Minister was acting as spokesman for the United States as well as for Britain in the present talks.

But though he said that, of course the Premier could not act as spokesman for the U.S. Government, he did not deny that he was able to give Stalin Washington's views on vital U.S. problems now being discussed.

It is still reported persistently here that the President will meet Stalin himself in the near future, but Roosevelt's reply to a question on the subject was that he just did not know.

Reports of Tension

There is a certain amount of mystery about the Stalin-Churchill meeting. Isolationist politicians and journalists are already making capital out of the reports that there is tension between Roosevelt and Churchill and between Stalin and Churchill.

Meanwhile it is learned here that the U.S. Administration's interim plan for the occupation of the Reich has now been finally agreed on.

The first plan is for the initial occupation of Germany up to the time when the armistice is signed or all German resistance has been overcome without surrender.

This plan, already in operation in the occupied areas of Germany, is simply military rule based on the Eisenhower dictum that "We come as conquerors, not as oppressors."

Reich in Three

An important part of this plan is that Allied troops will not fraternise with Germans in the slightest degree as they did in 1918.

The second phase of the interim plan will come into operation when the British, Russian, and American troops have completely occupied Germany.

The country will then be divided into three areas.

The third or long-range plan is still the subject of anxious debate, and little headway has been made in this direction.

In the last analysis it is agreed that the formulation of such a plan will depend on whether the German people show signs of being educable into a way of life in which they will present small danger to the rest of the world, or whether the assumption that they can ever be wooed away from militarism and love of power is untenable.

Fly-Bombs Come in from NE

Flying bombs were launched against Southern England during the night. One flew inland with fighters in pursuit.

Several robots were discharged by their parent planes and they met a very heavy barrage as they crossed the east coast, flying in from the north-east. At least one was blown up.

Gale and Rain in the Strait

Sea.—Rough.
Weather.—Gale and more rain after sunny early in morning, rainstorms in afternoon. Temperature at 10 p.m., 53 degrees.
Barometer.—Low, falling.

Hungary Drive Imperils Reich

RUSSIANS TAKE RIGA

Soviet troops have crossed into East Prussia. Von Olberg, German military commentator, admitted this last night. He said that east of Tilsit the Russians "at no place entered German territory to any major extent."

A THREAT of intense gravity to Germany's "back door" is developing rapidly on the great plains of Hungary. Soviet troops are less than 50 miles from Budapest and battling forward to menace the Reich.

The Hungarian capital is reported in chaos. And the armies of Hungary are either trapped in Transylvania or streaming north before the conquering Russians.

Once Budapest is taken, the road to Vienna—and the Reich—will lie open, with no natural obstacles to bar the way.

Reports that Hungary is seeking peace were backed up by an *Izvestia* statement last night that the Germans were quitting Budapest.

The fate of Budapest may be decided by a great tank battle now raging near Derecen. The Germans are showing anxiety about the outcome of the clash.

Last night's Soviet communiqué reported the capture of 50 more places in Northern Transylvania and more progress in Yugoslavia.

Far to the north the Red Army has captured **Riga**, important naval base and capital of Latvia.

Marshal Stalin announced this last night in an Order of the Day.

Big Soviet successes were recorded on other sectors of the front.

North-east of **Warsaw** the Germans have abandoned the strong-point of Rozan.

FINLAND: German troops, estimated at 60,000, are trapped in Northern Finland by a Soviet landing six miles from Petsamo.

The Germans have lost their main escape route by sea, and must either cross into Sweden and be interned, or move into Northern Norway through wild, frozen country.

Yugoslavia: Swiss radio, quoting a Yugoslav communiqué, said last night that Marshal Tito's Partisans had penetrated into Belgrade.

Cleft Chin Case: Girl Dancer of 18 Held

With U.S. Soldier

By Daily Mail Reporter

AN 18-years-old dance hostess and an American soldier were last night charged with the murder of "handsome" George Heath, the man with the cleft chin who was found dead a week ago in a ditch near Staines, Middlesex.

The girl, Elizabeth Marina Jones, of King-street, Hammersmith, is to appear to-day at Feltham Police Court.

The soldier was charged by Scotland Yard detectives in the presence of American military police and will be dealt with under U.S. procedure before a court-martial.

The soldier had been detained by the police since last Tuesday; the girl was arrested yesterday afternoon.

Precedent

This double charge of murder involving a British subject and an American soldier has set a precedent.

By agreement with the British Government any American soldier accused of a civil or military offence, including a charge of murder, is dealt with by the American authorities here.

Scotland Yard have, I learn, furnished the American authorities with a full report of their investigations and statements taken during the inquiries

The proceedings before the Feltham court to-day will be brief.

Heath was found dead in a ditch at Knowle Green, Staines, Middlesex, soon after 6 o'clock last Saturday morning. He had been shot, and the police took impressions of tyre marks of a car found near by.

Investigations showed that Heath ran a one-man car-hire service, and three days later his grey Ford V 8 was found abandoned in a cul-de-sac off Fulham Palace-road, Hammersmith.

He was last seen in the West End late on Friday.

MRS. CHURCHILL ON AIR

Mrs. Churchill will broadcast a two-minutes talk on the "Aid to Russia" Fund flag day after the nine o'clock news on Monday.

TRAPPED AMERICANS FIGHT WAY OUT

Near Aachen, Friday.—German tanks isolated two American infantry battalions for 12 hours to-day. The Americans rejoined the main forces after fighting from house to house.—B.U.P.

RUSSIANS BEGIN WARSAW PUSH

Powerful Russian forces are preparing to cross the Vistula and storm Warsaw, according to German broadcasts. Russian artillery yesterday opened a massive bombardment of the German positions across the river.

SUNDAY EXPRESS

OCTOBER 15 1944 | BLACK-OUT (London) 6.38 p.m. to 6.55 a.m. | Founded by LORD BEAVERBROOK | Moon Rises 5.7 a.m., Sets 6.2 p.m. | TWOPENCE

BRITISH CAPTURE ATHENS AFTER LAND, SEA AND AIR ATTACK

Planes fly tons of food and medical supplies to the Greek capital

Sky men take airfield: No opposition

BRITISH TROOPS YESTERDAY OCCUPIED ATHENS AND THE PIRAEUS (THE PORT OF ATHENS) AND FOOD AND MEDICAL SUPPLIES ARE NOW BEING FLOWN IN TO THE POPULATION OF THE GREEK CAPITAL.

The supplies are being dropped by American troop-carrier planes which, after towing gliders and landing a large force of British paratroops on airfields near Athens, returned to the airfield on the Peloponnese Peninsula in Southern Greece where the food and medical equipment had been piled up for quick transport.

Late last night a shuttle service was moving hundreds of tons of necessities to the capital.

According to the first eye-witnesses of the Allied occupation, says Reuter, there was no opposition when the Allies landed. The Germans had all pulled out and Athens and its airfields were in the hands of Greek Patriots when the paratroops dropped.

News of the capture of Athens and the Piræus was given in a special communiqué from Allied Mediterranean Headquarters, which added:—

"The occupation was carried out by British and Greek troops, who were transported, landed and supported by ships of the Royal Navy, which included units of the Greek Navy.

Airborne troops lead

"British airborne troops carried in aircraft of the US Army Air Forces played a leading part in the operation.

The operation was greatly facilitated by preliminary operations carried out in the Ægean by a mixed force of cruisers, carriers and destroyers of the Royal Navy, operating under the command of Rear-Admiral Troubridge and later under the command of Commodore G. N. Oliver, also by the action of the Land Forces Adriatic under Brigadier Davy in the Peloponnese, and the Balkan Air Force under the command of Air Vice-Marshal Elliott.

"The evacuation of enemy garrisons by air from the islands in the Ægean has also been gravely hampered by the successful attacks carried out on airfields in Greece by the American Fifteenth Air Force under the command of Lieut.-General N. Twining.

"General Sir Henry Maitland Wilson, the Supreme Allied Commander, has appointed Lieut.-General Scobie as the Land Task Force Commander in Greece."

Kinsman of Nelson

"Naval forces engaged are commanded by Rear-Admiral Manfield and Air-Commodore Harcourt-Smith is in command of the Air Forces in Greece."

Rear-Admiral Troubridge, who is 48 and a direct descendant of Nelson's famous captain, commanded the British naval force at Oran. He afterwards received the American D.S.M.

Commodore Oliver, who has 29 years' service in the Royal Navy, was decorated with the American Legion of Merit for the support given by his ships to the land forces in the Tunisian campaign.

Air Vice-Marshal Elliott, aged 48, was appointed A.O.C. Balkan Air Force in August after being in charge of air operations at Gibraltar. He commanded a night-fighter station in the blitz of 1940-41.

HUNGARY PREPARES TO QUIT WAR

NEWS reaching London last night indicated that Hungary is on her way out of the war.

As Soviet troops swept across the 50 miles of plains separating them from Budapest, it was reported by Paris radio that Hungary had accepted preliminary terms for an armistice.

At the same time British United Press reported from Ankara that two Hungarian delegations were leaving Budapest this week-end to meet Allied officials.

One delegation, said the report, would go to Rome and the other to the Red Army front in an attempt to reach Marshal Malinovsky, the Soviet C.-in-C.

Malinovsky's troops, driving towards Budapest, are now fighting a great tank battle on the plains near Debrecen.

In the Balkans the Germans' situation is growing worse every hour.

Marshal Tito's radio said last night: "Troops of the Red Army and of Marshal Tito's Yugoslav Army of Liberation are fighting in the streets of Belgrade."

Far to the north thousands of Red Army men and hundreds of tanks are streaming out along the borders of East Prussia, which may be invaded at any hour.

Loss of Riga, the Latvian capital, captured almost unscathed by the Russians, has changed the entire situation in the Baltic Sea, says Reuter.

The Russians are now driving non-stop beyond Riga in pursuit of the shattered German forces which are being pressed back towards Libau and Windau.

Last night's Soviet communiqué reported that the Russians advancing south of Riga had reached the main railway connecting the Latvian capital with the important junction of Mitau along its whole length, after smashing German positions along the River Kekava and beating off a series of counter-attacks.

The communiqué also reported the capture of a place just under two miles south-east of Belgrade.

PINNER ITALIANS MOVE OUT

To 'new barracks'

THE Italian co-operators who have been billeted in modern villas at Pinner are leaving.

All yesterday they were loading their kits and bedding on Army lorries which left, with men standing on the tailboards and the roof, for what they describe as their "new barracks" at Rayners Lane, Middlesex.

By nightfall all but a few had gone. The remainder will leave today.

Their departure only two weeks [illegible] protests by residents of this pleasant estate.

Quite inoffensive

Mr. W. T. Collins, of Woodnall Gate, who got in touch with Sir Reginald Blair, M.P. for Hendon, said: "We shall be glad to see them go. The houses are not suitable for billeting prisoners of war."

Other residents, on the other hand, said they were sorry they were going. One woman said: "They are quite inoffensive."

At the bottom of the road a group of Italians in British battle-dress with the Italy flash, and others in Italian uniform, were playing with local children or chatting to their mothers.

The houses at Pinner are not to stay empty. The Sunday Express understands that the War Office is handing them over to the Harrow Urban District Council to re-house bombed-out families.

The prisoners billeted in Chiswick houses will move out early next week.

A Ministry of Works official said alternative accommodation had been found for those which did not involve private dwellings.

U.S. GENERAL IS PRISONER

The U.S. War Department disclosed in Washington last night, says Reuter, that the first American general has been captured by the Germans.

He is Brig.-General Arthur W. Vanaman. He was first reported missing in action over Germany on June 27 while acting as an observer on a bombing attack.

Coast watchers see fly bombs downed over sea

For the fourth night in succession the Germans launched an airborne flying bomb attack against Southern England last night.

Coast observers saw brilliant flashes out at sea, believed to be due to the destruction of bombs coming in from the north-east.

P.M., Stalin agree on Poles

Man-to-man talks

IT is believed in Moscow, says Duncan Hooper, Reuter's special correspondent, that there is no fundamental disagreement between Marshal Stalin and Mr. Churchill on the Polish question.

The gulf between the Polish Government in London and the Lublin Committee remains deep, however, and any bridges that may be built must be of the firmest if they are to last.

Mr. Churchill and Marshal Stalin are said to be talking to each other as man to man.

Both relish an argument. If they do argue, it is only because of the very earnest attempt each makes to get a full appreciation of the other's viewpoint.

Mr. Churchill, Mr. Eden and the British Ambassador, Sir Archibald Clark-Kerr, conferred with the Polish Prime Minister, Mr. Stanislaw Mikolajczyk, the Polish Foreign Minister, and the Speaker of the Polish National Council in London, Professor Grabski, yesterday.

Mr. Churchill fit

The ground is rapidly being cleared for a meeting between M. Mikolajczyk and his group and the representatives of the Polish Committee.

Mr. Churchill keeps fit and sleeps soundly for six hours every night. He takes an occasional nap in the daytime when he has time.

He begins work immediately after breakfast, often taken in bed, while he reads telegrams and newspapers—London newspapers reach him daily.

After breakfast he lights his first cigar. (The Norwegian Ambassador in Moscow sent him a box of Coronas soon after his arrival.)

He has a Russian cook and, in addition to food supplied by the Soviet authorities, has English extras such as tea, bacon and marmalade.

Last night he was given a great ovation when he attended a gala ballet performance at the Bolshoi Theatre.

Meat supply assured

The United States is now in a position to assure most of the United Nations of a meat supply, a high official in Washington told Reuter yesterday.

Labourer's £561 a year, free of tax in U.S. Army cookhouse

WHEN George Rice, Irish labourer, working in an American Army cookhouse, was charged at Trowbridge yesterday with being in unlawful possession of American Army property which included half a dozen pork chops, suits and underclothing, he said his wages were £561 a year, free of tax.

Rice was fined £10, and told by Major Eric Mackay, the chairman, that he received handsome payment for what he did in the war compared with what the boys got who fought the battles.

Invasion committees disbanded

INVASION COMMITTEES in South-West England, regarded in the early days of war as one of Britain's most vulnerable invasion points, are to be disbanded.

The South-West Regional Commissioner, Sir Hugh Elles, has told committees in the area that their continuance is no longer considered necessary.

Plymouth Emergency Committee, acting upon the commissioner's intimation, yesterday disbanded the city's invasion sub-committee.

ACLAND STANDS DOWN

Too busy to fight

SIR RICHARD ACLAND, M.P., finds that as leader of Common Wealth he is too busy to remain in Parliament—even as a Common Wealth member.

That was the explanation he gave yesterday when he announced that he is standing down as prospective candidate for Waterloo (Liverpool).

Sir Richard said: "To look after the constituency properly would require at least one full week's work every month. Building up Common Wealth needs all my time.

"We shall probably offer the support of our party to Waterloo's Socialist candidate, Mr. Frederick Osborne."

Sir Richard added that following a request from the Common Wealth national committee for a meeting to discuss terms on which, subject to certain conditions, it might affiliate with the Socialist Party, the reply indicated that "possibly some of their members might be willing to meet Common Wealth to explore the situation quite informally."

Captain Malcolm Bullock has been Conservative member for Waterloo since 1923.

Bitter fighting on roofs and in sewers of Aachen

By MONTAGUE LACEY: Aachen suburbs, Saturday

THERE is tough street fighting now in ancient Aachen. The Germans are on the rooftops and down in the sewers.

They are using pill-boxes camouflaged as hen houses, as they resist our entry with machine guns, pistols and hand grenades.

It is slow, tedious and dangerous work, but the Americans are going about it in a business-like manner.

We learned our lessons in the street fighting in North Africa, and then in Sicily and in Italy. Unless street fighting is conducted on slow and careful lines, the advantage is always with the defender. And, as I see it now, we are going to take Aachen with the minimum of casualties.

There is no need to do otherwise. The city has no military value for us except as a traffic channel, and we are not in need of that at the moment.

The battle of Aachen, put in its proper perspective, is a minor affair compared with the battle that is brewing to the east of the town, where we have made a major breach in the German defences.

Badly mangled

Here, for the last three days, the Germans have been gathering some of their best troops and their heavy tanks and armour for a decisive battle. But already this is a badly mangled force, and we have been able to hold them off before their offensive can get launched.

It is estimated today that more than 80 tanks have already been knocked out. That is a bad blow for the enemy.

THE GERMANS HAVE ALSO BEEN USING THEIR BROKEN LUFTWAFFE IN PENNY PACKETS ON THIS SECTOR, AND THIS IS A SIGN THAT THEY TAKE THE SITUATION SERIOUSLY. WHEREVER THEY HAVE THROWN IN THE REMNANTS OF THEIR AIR FORCE YOU CAN BET THAT IS THE PLACE THAT IS HURTING THEM.

They have to come out in the dark, however. For most nights this week they have come over our lines strafing and dropping anti-personnel bombs.

Fine days

With today we have had three continuous cold, bright, sunny autumn days, and it is impossible to estimate just what this fine weather has meant to us. I guess the prayer of all the soldiers here who go to church tomorrow will be for more fine weather.

There are chaplains right up to the front lines, and I write this near a farm barn that is being got ready for a service tomorrow. Even the chaplain has come out to have a look at the swarms of planes that are overhead.

There are vapour trails all over the sky made by our bombers, and the fighters are so high above them that you cannot see them. It seems as they weave their patterns in the sky that they will soon block out all the blue that is left, and leave us overhead a canopy of man airmade clouds.

But there are no clouds to cloak the enemy's movements. Bombs

BACK PAGE. COL. THREE

Rome banker sent to jail for 30 years

DR. VINCENZO AZZOLINI, former governor of the Bank of Italy, was yesterday sentenced to 30 years' imprisonment, at the close of the sixth day of his trial, for collaborating with the Germans, by handing over to them gold reserves of the bank.

The trial took place in the Corsini Palace, before the High Court of Justice.

Azzolini remained calm while Judge Lorenzo Maroni, after donning a black and gold velvet cap, read out the sentence.

His emotion showed only in his flushed face, and he stumbled at the door as Carabinieri led him from the courtroom.

The prosecutor had asked for the death sentence, but extenuating circumstances were allowed, and this saved Azzolini's life.

The court took two hours to reach a decision. The judges were four professional magistrates and five so-called popular judges, all party men.

The trial was held in conditions of notable fairness for Azzolini.

A curious feature of the case which has aroused comment in London, was the intervention in it of the supposedly neutral Bank for International Settlements.

'Observations'

A telegram was sent by Mr. Thomas H. McKittrick, American president of the bank, to the court and to high Italian Ministers expressing thanks for Azzolini's action in saving the bank's gold and, according to messages from Rome, "adding observations in his favour."

It seems likely that this action will intensify the demand for the liquidation of the bank. Opposition to its continued existence was reflected at the Bretton Woods conference, when the Norwegian delegates urged that the Governments of the United Nations should appoint a commission to examine the management and transactions of the bank during the war.

NIGHT RAID ON GERMANY

German radio said last night: "Small formations of fast bombers are over Western Germany."

17 airmen saved

An airplane returned to Edmonton, Alberta, yesterday after rescuing 17 stranded American airmen in the Hudson's Bay region and flying them to Churchill, Manitoba, says Exchange.

Shell-shocked in June

In international match yesterday

NINETY THOUSAND football fans saw England beat Scotland 6—2 at Wembley Stadium yesterday

This was the largest attendance at Wembley since the war. The maximum pre-war capacity was approximately 100,000.

There were more cars than in previous matches, and police checked carefully. Many of the cars were driven by Servicemen with a recreational petrol allowance.

King Haakon of Norway shook hands with both teams before the match.

There was a surprise change in the Scottish team when Willie Shankly, the right half, failed to come through a test on his knee, and an "unknown" player, Robert Thyne, a sergeant in the R.E., was brought in at right half.

Thyne, who was playing in Scottish junior football a few years ago, was wounded and shell-shocked in France in June. He has only played a few games for his club, Darlington, since recovering.

Thyne, who is 23, was wired for originally to deputise for Baxter, the Scottish centre half and captain, whose mother is seriously ill.

When Shankly was reported unfit Thyne was put in at right half. He had never played in this position before.

Frank Butler's report of the game—PAGE SIX.

Air Minister back

Sir Archibald Sinclair, Air Minister, returned to London last night after a two-day tour of British and American air bases in France and Belgium.

War latest

BOMBERS RAID JAP BASES

Allied bombers raided Japanese installations at Amboina and Ceram, dropping 130 tons of bombs, General MacArthur's communiqué announced.

GREAT NIGHT ARMADA OUT

Observers in Southern England last night reported that the greatest night air armada they had ever seen was flying out towards the Continent.

RADIO—PAGE 7

DE GAULLE: ALLIES ARE NEGLECTING FRANCE

GENERAL DE GAULLE, in a broadcast to the French nation recorded last night, asserted that "the other great Powers are treating France with neglect" in planning the peace.

He said: Several weeks have already elapsed since the enemy was driven from the greater part of France.

Joy and pride in liberation do not prevent the French nation from courageously assessing the hard reality of its circumstances nor from measuring clearly the conditions of its salvation.

Frenchmen know that the war in which they have been taking a major part is not going to end yet.

The enemy has re-established his front from Breda to Belfort.

He is stubbornly resisting in the Italian peninsula, he is fighting savagely in Poland and the Baltic countries. He is preparing to fight to the end in the interior of his own territory.

Our tasks

Germany will be beaten only by renewed and bloody exertion, in which France wants to and must take the greatest possible part.

Many a Frenchman may well be amazed at the kind of neglect with which the other Great Powers are at present treating France in regard to the conduct of the war and the preparations for peace.

The country is fully aware of what has to be done.

First of all we must work. Whatever the difficulties, each has his allotted task.

Of course, it would be easy to enumerate all that is lacking and to stress the shortcomings of others, but things will not get better, unless everyone pulls his weight.

Then, it will be necessary for the national effort to develop within the national set-up. From top to bottom all must take their full legal responsibility.

For the present we have to take things as they are, and recognise that in our difficulties we must above all rely on ourselves, and understand that our greatness will tomorrow, as in the past, spring not from the good will of others, but only from our own endeavours.

FRANCE'S TRAITORS GOING 'TO THE GUILLOTINE'

HEADS of Frenchmen who helped the Germans are falling with increasing rapidity

Many have been guillotined or shot. The military court at Montpelier reached 15 death sentences a day a week after the liberation. Marseilles averaged 20 death sentences a day in one month.

The charges vary. Yesterday a woman was sent to prison for 20 years with hard labour at Perigueux because she bought furniture looted by the Germans. At Limoges the mistress of a German officer got five years.

Thirty death sentences have been passed on traitors in Paris. Most have already been carried out.

Prominent among those condemned was Du Truch, Vichy Prefect of Lozere Department, who was tried before a court-martial at Mende, found guilty of collaboration, and shot on Friday.

Other provincial courts-martial or civil tribunals are now busy trying French agents of the Gestapo or leading Vichy collaborators. In Brittany and Southern France the courts are working at top speed.

Most of those already condemned are of Corsican or Italian origin who, before the German occupation, were notorious figures in the French underworld of dope smugglers, white slave traffickers and blackmailers.

Heavy tribute

Many of them had made fortunes by first exacting heavy tribute from Jewish and other political refugees from the Nazis in return for pretended protection. Later they denounced their victims to the Gestapo.

But while the provincial courts are working overtime, Paris newspapers accuse the Paris courts of red tape and delay.

Thus Bony and Lafont, although self-condemned as heads of the French Gestapo, are still untried.

Of 6,000 suspects interned at Drancy, a former German concentration camp near Paris, nearly 200 are released daily on the ground of insufficient evidence.

The first sitting of a special tribunal created in Paris to try crimes of anti-nationalism and collaboration is now announced for next Wednesday.

Stephane Lauzanne, former editor of the Paris morning newspaper Le Matin, who for over 20 years wrote virulent anti-British editorials, and during the German occupation was effusive in his praise of Hitler, will be first in the dock. He is expected to receive the death sentence.

Other Frenchmen to be tried by the same tribunal are General Pinsard, the organiser of the anti-Bolshevist Legion, and the three self-avowed assassins of Georges Mandel.

DAILY MIRROR, Saturday, October 21, 1944.

Daily Mirror

OCT 21

No. 12,744
ONE PENNY
Registered at the G.P.O. as a Newspaper.

The men who killed Rommel

This is the man who led the death hunt on Rommel, Wing-Commander J. R. Baldwin, D.S.O., D.F.C. and bar (hand on map), photographed with the men of his wing on a French airfield in July.

AACHEN FALLS

Allies take first big German town—now only heap of rubble

AACHEN—or the great heap of rubble that was the first big German town to be besieged by the Allies—has fallen.

Mopping up was completed at 3.30 p.m. yesterday, it was announced at U.S. First Army headquarters last night.

Victory in the face of bitter resistance came seven days after the Allies entered the city—eighteen days after the first encirclement stroke.

The U.S. First Army is now astride the direct railway line to Cologne, forty-five miles away.

Yesterday morning scores of prisoners marched out of the debris that once housed 155,000 Germans to join the 10,000 already in the cages.

Artillery and dive-bombers completed the job the heavies began, and now I doubt if there are 300 habitable buildings left in the city (says a British United Press war correspondent).

●

BRITISH and Canadian troops, with strong tank and air support, began at dawn yesterday an offensive to speed up the operations aimed at allowing us to use the great Belgian port of Antwerp.

The drive, north of Antwerp, was made in the direction of the German defence line between Bergen-op-Zoom on the coast to Roosendaal, ten miles inland.

Canadians using flame-throwers advanced several miles in the first few hours.

Infantry rode on the back of tanks.

The German pocket on the other side of the Scheldt has been nearly halved.

German troops in one sector are under the complete control of N.C.O.s. Their officers disappeared three days ago.

D-DAY BOYS GET LEAVE OVER THERE

D-Day boys are getting their first leave—but they won't be able to come home.

Forward area troops who have endured some of the fiercest fighting in the last few weeks, many of them veterans of the beaches of Normandy, are getting forty-eight hours behind the line.

Most of them are being billeted at quiet hotels in Brussels, where they can get the comforts of "civvy life."

The thing the men of the Army of Liberation want most is sleep and hot baths—but entertainments and club attractions are also provided for them in the Belgian capital.

It is intended that the men shall get forty-eight hours' leave every six months.

STALIN SEES CHURCHILL, EDEN LEAVE MOSCOW

MR. CHURCHILL and Mr. Eden left Moscow yesterday and were seen off from the airport by Stalin—the first time he has conferred such an honour on visiting dignitaries since war began.

PHILIPPINES HEROES ARE BACK—HEADING INVASION

WITH every living member of the ill-fated garrison who escaped from Corregidor with General MacArthur in 1942—and plus the greatest striking force ever assembled in the Pacific—MacArthur is back in the Philippines.

Yesterday afternoon General MacArthur reported to President Roosevelt that the invasion—known as "A" day—was making splendid progress.

Spearheads of the attack columns are pushing inland on the island of Leyte towards the city of Tacloban.

Sixth Army troops, who pushed their way on to the island in hundreds of assault boats, were protected by a force of more than 600 ships.

With the American vessels were two Royal Australian warships, Shropshire and Australia, as well as Australian transports.

Heavy tanks went ashore in the sixth assault wave. Japanese air opposition was practically absent.

—and what they can remember!

EIGHT RAF Typhoon men share the credit for ending the career of Field-Marshal Rommel with their cannons, it has now been established after weeks of research by the air and military intelligence services.

Their names—and what they can remember about what seemed a trivial exploit—were revealed in Brussels last night. They are:

Wing-Commander John Baldwin, D.S.O., D.F.C., of Bath, who won a bar to his D.F.C. by chasing Nazi planes round and round the Eiffel Tower in Paris;

Flying Officer C. E. Hall peacetime London estate agent;

Flying Officer Pete Langville, of St. John's, New Brunswick;

Pilot Officer B. Lenson, of Talbot Court, Kingsbury-lane, London;

Flight Lieutenant R. W. Davidge and Flight Lieutenant W. A. Switzer, both of Epsom, Alberta;

Flying Officer J. W. Darling, of York-road, Aldershot; and

Warrant Officer A. E. Sugden, of Outremont, Montreal.

It was on the afternoon of July 17 that eight dive-bombers led by Wing-Commander Baldwin set off on a bombing and strafing mission near the village of Dozule, east of Caen.

Wing Commander Baldwin said: "There was no difficulty in finding the target, a German Headquarters building.

"The pinpoint on our map looked like a farmhouse. We scored ten hits on it with 500-pounders and then, as we seemed to have a lot of petrol left, I decided we would carry out an armed reconnaissance of the area with cannon.

"East of Caen and south of Coburg, near a villaged called Dozule, I spotted two dispatch riders, one biggish armoured car, another motor transport, a staff car and a smaller armoured car.

"This indicated somebody

Continued on Back Page

Nurse the Huns drowned

THIS is the story of a pretty, twenty-seven-year-old girl, Marie Jarman, whose life was devoted to nursing the sick and whose death story silenced the few "be kind to the Germans" delegates at the Trades Union Congress at Blackpool yesterday. The story was related by her father, Mr. C. Jarman, general secretary of the National Union of Seamen.

The Congress listened in tense silence as he cried: "It makes me sick when I hear people protesting the moment we try to pin responsibility on the criminals — particularly the German criminals.

"There are some crimes which have been committed at sea for which no reparation or atonement can be made in material terms, such as the sinking of hospital ships," he said.

"My own daughter was lost in one of them, trained as she was as an Army nurse to minister to Allies and enemies alike, without a chance of saving her life or the hundreds of others who perished with her.

Mr. Jarman told of cases in which U-boat commanders had machine-gunned seamen after they had taken to their boats when their ship was sunk and had chopped off the fingers of men clinging to rafts.

"So far as the seamen are concerned we indict the whole of the German people. They have exulted over the sinking of hospital ships, over the flying bombs, and all the atrocities they have committed. We are not fighting a nation of normal human beings but a nation of maniacs."

When Mr. Jarman left the conference room, he told the *Daily Mirror* of the telegram which arrived at his home in Nelson-road, New Malden, Surrey, early this year.

He and his wife thought their daughter Marie was still nursing wounded Germans in a hospital overseas.

When they opened the telegram they read that she, and many other nurses, had been drowned when a German

Continued on Back Page

DAILY EXPRESS

No. 13,851 | Black-out 6.21 pm to 7.9 am | MONDAY OCTOBER 23 1944 | Moon rises 1.53 pm sets 10 pm | One Penny

This is the home-made invasion harbour—*First picture*

They call it Port Winston

A MIGHTY feat of engineering is pictured above . . . a feat that has revolutionised modern warfare.

"Port Winston," they call it in the Merchant Navy. It has a harbour as large and impregnable as Gibraltar—secretly prefabricated in Britain by thousands of workers, and towed in sections, with the components for a sister port, to the open beaches of Normandy.

The story was told in full in the Daily Express of Monday last.

These artificial harbours, assembled by the Navy and the Army, made possible an invasion without an established port and completely bewildered the enemy . . . After the violent June gale, the harbour designed for the U.S. Forces was abandoned. Salvage was used to reinforce the British harbour.

The vast pre-fabrication work for the staggering Operation Mulberry had to be completed in seven months. "Port Winston" is Harbour B (B for British) at Arromanches. It now takes anything from 7,000-ton Liberty ships to coasters, unloading direct into ducks, lighters and causeways. On its beaches squadrons of tank landing ships and flotillas of ramped craft run up to discharge their cargoes with every tide.

And here is the key

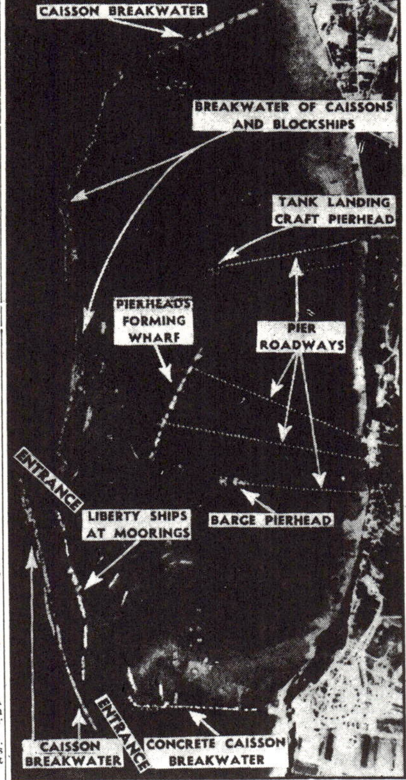

How they made the ports : Story in pictures, Page Three

SCHELDT BIG GUN FORTRESS FALLS

New British attack is 'going nicely'

WITH the whole of Field-Marshal Montgomery's front in Holland and Belgium set ablaze yesterday by a sweeping new British assault, it was revealed late last night that German big-gun batteries at the Scheldt entrance barring the way to Antwerp had been silenced. Here are the front highlights:

1 Canadian infantry captured the fortress town of Breskens, in the Scheldt pocket, and stormed beyond it to Fort Frederick, where they seized coastal batteries.

2 The British advanced steadily all day yesterday from two directions on the heavily defended town of Hertzogenbosch in an offensive which opened before dawn. It was reported last night to be "going very nicely."

3 North of Antwerp Canadian and British tanks and infantry liberated the town of Esschen, 12 miles from the starting point of their attack.

4 The Americans opened two new battles. North-east of Aix-La-Chapelle they were in bitter struggle for the town of Wuerselen. To the south, General Patton began an assault into the country east of Nancy, which was flooded by Allied dam-busters.

Through water, mud and mines

From JOHN REDFERN: Breskens, Sunday

GETTING the Germans completely off balance, the Canadians today won the vital town of Breskens, to the north of the Scheldt pocket, captured a lot of prisoners and guns and, according to a German officer, killed off the enemy's fortress commander.

This man-sized programme was carried out with great dash by units, who, because of past experience, call themselves the "Concrete busters," professional fortress breakers.

Once we were inside Breskens enemy resistance seemed to collapse.

According to a German officer prisoner, Captain Bollmein, the commander of Breskens garrison, was shot by a Canadian rifleman as he started with a section to retrieve some of his men who had just been captured.

He was killed a few yards from a zig-zag anti-tank ditch four miles long, which traced the perimeter of Breskens' main defences.

The rest of his rescue party was captured.

Swam across

Two crossings of this anti-tank ditch yesterday afternoon ensured the capture of Breskens town. The first men over had to swim for it in 12 freezing feet of water—with mines waiting for them on the opposite side.

They lurched on, slithering about in mud more than a foot deep and fought the Germans on the perimeter from trench to trench until they reached the houses in the town.

The ditch is 25ft. wide. Our men had to get over without any cover, but a heavy artillery barrage kept down the heads of the Germans, some of whom found us on top of them before they realised what was happening.

All night the Canadians continued fighting. Shooting from windows and doors, they confused the already startled garrison, who had never expected the anti-tank ditch could be jumped like that. Patrols also pushed out towards the harbour.

Ate between shots

Behind them, in absolute darkness, engineers worked on a ramp for supplies over the ditch. They lifted mines and used German sappers' material lying about.

At nine this morning, without a rest, the infantry attacked again. They ate between shots in ragged fighting in the deserted streets. Again the Germans largely relied on shelling. They called on their three heavy batteries at Flushing to support them.

At noon today, when the Canadians were all over the place and also cleaning up eight pill-boxes on the southern perimeter, a report came to one brigade headquarters that on the edge of the

→ BACK PAGE, COL. FOUR

CHURCHILL FLIES BACK

May speak in House this week

MR. CHURCHILL is back from Russia. He landed at an airfield near London just before dusk yesterday.

Last night he met Ministers, and he will tell Parliament probably this week of his talks in Moscow, but at present it is not intended to have a debate.

Mr. Churchill will now give his attention to the controversy over the compensation clauses of the Blitz Bill, on which some Conservatives threaten to vote against the Government on Wednesday.

Mr. Eden did not return to Britain with him, though they left Moscow together. Mr. Eden is having talks which he feels he must hold himself.

The Premier wore Air Commodore's uniform when he landed and looked fit and very cheerful.

A kiss from Mrs. Churchill . . . Last night's picture.

As he stepped from his four-engined plane Mrs. Churchill hurried forward to embrace him.

There, too, to meet him was Lord Swinton, the New Minister of Civil Aviation, who arrived only yesterday by air from West Africa.

Before leaving by car, Mr. Churchill, smoking a cigar, shook hands with his crew and gave the V sign to airmen and A.T.C. cadets who saw him land.

Also back in London are the members of the Polish mission to the Moscow talks.

Moscow radio said last night: "The Moscow talks continue to be Topic No. 1 in the Press and with the man in the street. They have shown there can be no difficulties in the relations among the great Powers which cannot be overcome by good will and respect for each others opinions."

Paris trial No. 1

PARIS, Sunday.—Georges Suarez, accused of collaborating with the Germans as political director of the newspaper Aujourd'hui, will be tried tomorrow when the first series of Paris "purge" trials begins.—Express News Service.

RUSSIANS REACH NORWAY

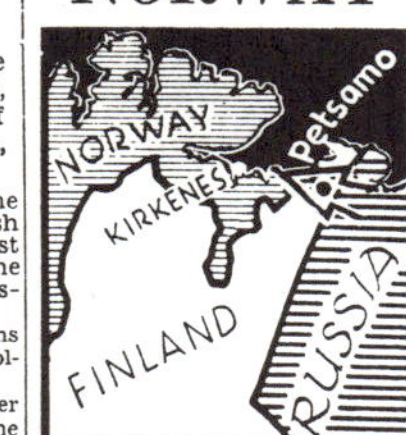

RUSSIAN troops driving the Germans out of Northern Finland have reached the border of Norway, it was announced last night.

They have captured the Pechenga (Petsamo) nickel mines and cleared the area.

'I cannot say Sieg Heil . .'

AIX-LA-CHAPELLE, Sunday.—After he had signed the document of surrender yesterday, Colonel Gerhard Wilck, commander of the German garrison at Aix, addressed his defeated troops. He said :—

"The American commander has told me that I cannot give you the 'Sieg Heil' or 'Heil Hitler,' but we can still do it in our own hearts.

"Dear German soldiers: This is a painful occasion. I have been forced to surrender as ammunition and food are exhausted.

"I have seen that further fighting would be useless. I have acted against my orders which were that I should fight to the last man.

"I wish to remind you that you are German soldiers and to ask you always to behave as such. I wish you all the best of heart and a quick return to our Fatherland when hostilities have ceased so that you may help in the rebuilding of Germany."—Exchange.

3 Germans escape from prison camp

Three German prisoners escaped from a Colchester camp on Saturday and were still free last night. They are Hans Bilstein, aged 18, bearded and 6ft. tall, Corporal Helmut Schwidienski, aged 24, who is wearing jackboots, and Lance-Corporal Ernst Blank, aged 46.

Ford fly-bombs?

NEW YORK, Sunday.—After reconstructing a German flying bomb engine from parts sent from England, Ford engineers are building a jet propulsion engine for robot bombs. — Express News Service.

Civilians can fly to Paris

To do business of national importance

By BASIL CARDEW

THE London-Paris airway is open again to civilians—but only if their business is urgent and of national importance.

This, the biggest air transport concession made since the war began, was announced by the Home Office last night.

Civilians who wish to travel to the interior zone of France, including Paris, now taken over by the de Gaulle Government, no longer need military permits, but only exit permits from the Home Office and French visas from the Consul-General, Bedford-square.

Exit permits will be granted only when the traveller has the backing of the Government Department under which his business normally comes.

Even then transport may not be immediately available.

Only a few seats in the cross-Channel aircraft are at present being held for civilians.

Two transport services have been operating to Paris for some weeks—one by Transport Command, R.A.F., the other by U.S. Air Transport Command.

No sea crossing

The British service has been lent personnel from British Overseas Airways Corporation, who are temporarily wearing R.A.F. uniform. It is reasonable to suppose that B.O.A.C. will soon take over part of the London-Paris schedules, and eventually the lot.

It is probable that British travellers will go by R.A.F. planes and Americans by U.S. aircraft.

No one will be allowed to travel to any part of France still in the war zone; and no sea transport for civilians is yet available.

Last week I travelled by the British route, which was then controlled by Shaef. The service operated from a Paris airport to one on the outskirts of London.

More than half the seats in the plane were empty.

Flying bombs at front

SHAEF, PARIS, Sunday Night.—A number of flying bombs have been seen in the First U.S. Army sector of the front during the day.

It is not stated where they fell, but it is possible that the Germans may be using them for the first time as a front-line weapon.

Cloudy

Straits : More settled, but cloudy.

CHIEF FOR BIG SWITCH-OVER

Will do the job for nothing

By TREVOR EVANS

THE man who will get Britain back from war production to peacetime production starts work at the Board of Trade today.

He is Sir Charles Bruce-Gardner, 56-year-old chairman of the Ministry of Aircraft Production's Production and Efficiency Board. And he goes to the Board of Trade as Chief Executive for Industrial Reconversion.

On a commercial basis this job might be worth £50,000 a year. Sir Charles will do it—as he has done his M.A.P. job—for nothing.

He will decide the priorities of all major industries for raw materials and man-power to satisfy :—

Plan dropped

1—Demands of our overseas customers for the goods we propose to export;

2—Demands of our own people for goods which they have been denied during the war.

For six months, Mr. Dalton, President of the Board of Trade, has been accumulating records of the needs of Britain's industries. Sir Charles will transform these blue-prints into working models.

First it was planned to move a whole team of experts from M.A.P. to the Board of Trade for this job. But Mr. Dalton dropped the idea of "rule by committee" in favour of control by one man, known for his power of detached decisions.

Some of the men who were intended for the committee are joining Mr. Dalton's business men's brains trust. They include :—

Sir Thomas D. Barlow, Director-General of Civilian Clothing;

Lord Forres, member of the Industrial and Export Council;

Sir Cecil Weir, Director-General of Equipment and Stores, Supply Ministry;

Captain Spencer Freeman, Principal Director, Regional and Emergency Services Organisation, Ministry of Aircraft Production;

Sir Kenneth Lee, Director-General, Raw Materials Controls, Supply Ministry, and

Sir Charles Innes, expert in Indian industrial affairs.

This brains trust, which meets once a week, will continue to advise. But final decisions will be taken by Sir Charles.

Sir Charles, in 1938, became executive chairman of the council of the Society of British Aircraft Constructors at £15,000 a year. He became the spokesman of the British aircraft industry.

After he joined Lord Beaverbrook at the Ministry of Aircraft Production he became responsible for the dispersal of aircraft factories.

He resigned in 1941 to return to the Aircraft Constructors' Society, but in May last year again joined M.A.P. as Controller of Labour Allocation and Supply.

It's Fighter Command again

Express Air Reporter

PILOTS of the R.A.F. who wear their jackets with the top button undone, showing they fought with Fighter Command, will be toasting the Air Ministry today.

It is announced that Fighter Command is to be reborn after a "death" of nearly a year.

The unwieldy title of Air Defence of Great Britain, A.D.G.B. for short, is dropped, and Fighter-Command, under 50-year-old Air-Marshal Sir Roderic Hill, reverts to the control of the Air Ministry.

SHOT DOWN 800

The decision has been taken on grounds mainly sentimental, but also because A.D.G.B. has become chiefly offensive now.

Fighter Command's name disappeared last November, when Air Defence of Great Britain, title of our defensive air force before the war, was re-created.

A.D.G.B. was a component of the Allied Expeditionary Force. Its planes shot down 800 German planes, two-thirds of them at night.

Fascist boss hid in cupboard

ROME, Sunday.—Police have found Giulio Sarrocchi, former Fascist boss, hiding in a bathroom cupboard in a flat. He was dragged out half naked to await trial.—Express News Service.

LONDON C.D. CUT IN TWO

But fire watch goes on

Express Staff Reporter

CIVIL DEFENCE is to be cut by half in the London area, it is announced today, but there is to be no change in the existing Fire Guard arrangements.

"In London and the likely target areas," says the Ministry of Home Security, "although daylight manning is no longer required, it is still necessary that Fire Guards should be on duty at night to deal with any enemy attacks.

"For the present, therefore, Fire Guards in these areas will still be required to continue the good work they have so long performed.

"The Fire Guard Orders and the statutory obligations under them are still in force."

Civil Defence cuts are to be made in the Eastern, Southern and South-Eastern regions, as well as the London area.

Reason: "The progress of the war makes it no longer necessary to maintain the same scale of preparation as hitherto in these regions."

In the Eastern, Southern and South-Eastern regions the number of whole-time workers will be reduced by from one-third to two-thirds. In some areas only a small nucleus of whole-timers will be retained.

Released workers need not do part-time service, and will be eligible for all the benefits that may be made for whole-time workers under final demobilisation

Take jobs earlier

Arrangements in each service and the areas to which they are applicable will be decided by the regional commissioners concerned.

So that councils and local officers of the Labour Ministry may have as long as possible to choose people for release and to place them in employment, final notice of discharge will not be given until November 30, to take effect on December 30.

Workers chosen can, if they wish, accept an approved job before that date.

The order of release will be generally the same as that for the

BACK PAGE, COL. SEVEN

M. of F. TO RATION GERMANY

Express Staff Reporter

THE Ministry of Food will take over food distribution in Germany as soon as Germany surrenders, it was learned last night.

Officials who have looked after Britain's food affairs will go to Germany.

Over the week-end these men and women from food offices all over Britain were enrolling for service in Germany and Austria.

A circular from the Ministry of Food in London asked for volunteers on these conditions :—

1 Present pay plus an overseas allowance (not yet fixed) and expenses.

2 Executive and clerical staffs are eligible for appointments similar to their present one.

3 Those who speak German or Russian will get special consideration.

Regional officers have been asked to arrange German and Russian classes for their staffs.

A senior official was unable to say last night whether British or Allied food will be sent for German civilians.

Not a bomber was lost

A heavy force of Lancasters and more than 1,100 U.S. heavies blasted transport centres in Germany yesterday without a single loss.

Hundreds of fighters escorted them, and only two are missing—believed landed on friendly ground.

The Lancasters blasted the inland port and railway centre of Neuss, near Dusseldorf. The Americans bombed Brunswick, Hanover, Munster and Hamm.

No enemy fighters were met. The bombers attacked in cloud.

Moscow attacks Persia Premier

MOSCOW, Sunday.—The Russian paper Trud today attacks Mohammed Saed, Persian Premier, who refused Russia an oil concession.

It says he shows outward friendship for Russia, but tolerates Fascist elements organised by a German agent.—Express News Service.

Gibraltar ends curfew

GIBRALTAR, Sunday.—With the return of more than half of Gibraltar's evacuated population, the curfew has been lifted, and street lighting is being considered. —Express News Service.

165 runaways

STOCKHOLM, Sunday.—Sweden has interned 165 deserters from the German Army.—Reuter.

3 a.m. LATEST

FIVE NAZI SHIPS SUNK IN NORWAY

Moscow reports that Russian M.T.B.s sank two German transports, two trawlers and a patrol boat in Varanger Fiord, just beyond Norwegian border, which Red Army has reached.

4,000 NAZIS DIE NEAR BELGRADE

Moscow announced last night that 4,000 Germans were killed and 1,300 captured when Russian forces liberated Kragujevac, near Belgrade.

FRIDAY, NOVEMBER 3, 1944

FINAL NIGHT EXTRA •

Evening Standard

37,486 DIM-OUT: 6.0 pm to 7.29 am. MOON: Rises 7.47 pm. sets 12.24 pm. ONE PENNY

Resistance Ends at Zeebrugge: Scheldt Pocket Clear: Germans Report Six New Landings on Walcheren

ALL BELGIUM IS FREE

An Advance in the Aix Sector

All Belgium has now been liberated. The Scheldt pocket has been cleared, and all resistance ceased at Zeebrugge at 7.30 a.m. to-day.

PRISONERS TAKEN IN THE SCHELDT POCKET SINCE THE LEOPOLD CANAL ATTACK WAS FIRST LAUNCHED ARE AT LEAST 12,250, CABLES REUTER'S CORRESPONDENT, DESMOND TIGHE.

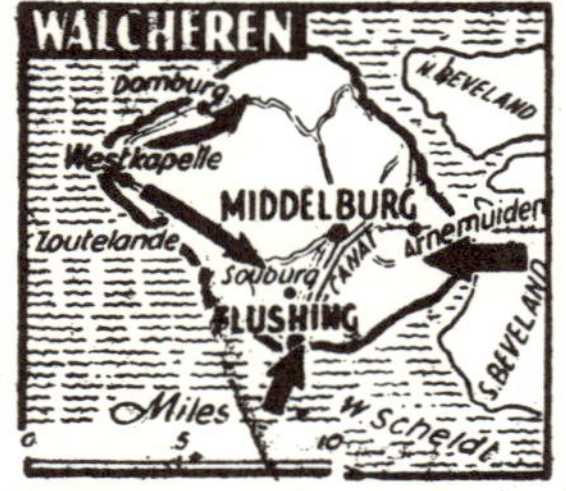

In the Scheldt Estuary, all North Beveland island is reported clear of the Germans.

An American radio correspondent says the Germans have cleared out of North Beveland and the neighbouring island of Tnolen without a fight.

On Walcheren, Flushing is nearly clear of the Germans, too. Street fighting is going on in Domberg.

Further Allied landings in the estuary were reported to-day by German radio, which specifies six landings, and claimed that three were "smashed by the German defences"

MOPPING-UP

A Reuter correspondent on the other hand says the Walcheren operations are going well

A marine Commando force is working along the coast north-east and south-east of West Kappelle and is now within two miles of the Army Commandos fighting in the Flushing region he says.

Most of the western rim of the island is now in our hands and the island's heaviest gun positions are being mopped up there one by one

U.S. ADVANCE

The new American offensive which has driven through the Huertgen Forest, south-east of Aix-la-Chapelle (Aachen), was renewed to-day and for the second day progress was made against heavy German resistance

Patrols which yesterday went north and south of Vossenack joined up beyond the village during the night says Reuter's correspondent John Wilhelm

To-day's offensive undoubtedly places the total of prisoners taken since D-Day by the American First Army at more than 200,000, far the greatest yet taken by any Allied army

The German version of the new United States attack, as given by the German news agency, is:

"American troops in the strength of two regiments yesterday morning went over to the attack south-east of Aix (Aachen).

"They were supported by strong artillery fire and numerous tanks. The attack was launched

(Continued on Back Page, Col. One)

SIEGFRIED LINE
GEILENKIRCHEN
HEERLEN
Ubach
JULICH
COLOGNE
MULHEIM
Wurselen
Eschweiler
AIX-LA-CHAPELLE
Verlautenheide
DUREN
Stolberg
R. Rhine
BONN
Hurtgen
Euskirchen
Eupen
Miles
Rotgen
0 10 20
VERVIERS

BUDAPEST "FEAR" AS RED ARMY STRIKE

The fate of Budapest hangs in the balance to-day as Soviet tanks and self-propelled guns rumble towards the outskirts of the capital.

A Red Star despatch, quoted by Associated Press, says that prisoners seized in the north-bound offensive on the east side of the Danube described Budapest as in a convulsion of fear, with merchants and industrial magnates getting out as fast as they can

Szalazi's Arrow Cross officers co-operating with the Germans, have stripped the city of all civilian motor vehicles to rush reinforcements to the front.

A Race

The battle for Budapest is becoming a race, cables Henry Shapiro British United Press correspondent.

Two tank columns are storming ahead for the honour of spear-heading the Soviet drive into the Hungarian capital

One column advancing from the south has less than 20 miles to go. Closing in from the south-east, the second column is within 25 miles of Budapest. Artillery fire can now be heard in the city

At the present rate of progress Russian tanks may be in Budapest by the week-end

The Germans are flinging in despairing counter-attacks with massed infantry supported by panzers.

According to Exchange, panic among the German troops is converting the retreat into a rout.

The first snow has fallen in East Prussia.

A fierce battle is raging round Sibenik, last remaining Yugoslav port on the Adriatic coast, where Germans who fled from the Split sector, as well as those who were pushed southward during the battle for Zara, have joined forces, and are trying to make a last stand.

With Zara, Split and Dubrovnik now in Yugoslav hands, practically the whole of the Dalmatian coast lies open to receive Allied supplies and equipment, says British United Press.

Large Business Premises Do Best Under New Scheme

HOW FIRE WATCH CUTS WILL WORK

Evening Standard Reporter

CHIEF FIRE GUARDS OF LONDON BOROUGHS WERE TO-DAY CONSULTING WITH THEIR SENIOR FIRE GUARDS ON THE BEST WAY TO CARRY OUT THE RELAXATION IN FIRE GUARD DUTIES ON BUSINESS PREMISES.

There will be no question of releasing any fire guards, the Ministry of Home Security emphasised. The reduction will be simply in the number of duties performed.

A circular sent by London Regional Civil Defence headquarters to local authorities sets out details of the scheme.

Fire guards on business premises which at present have large numbers on duty each night will come off best, but in no case will the cuts be less than the 50 per cent recommended by the Minister of Home Security.

Recommended reduction in personnel on duty each night are:

Number on Duty Now	On Duty in Future
3 to 5	3
6 to 15	3
16 to 30	6
31 to 45	9
46 to 60	12

[For each additional 15 on duty at present, add three.]

In blocks of business premises where the number of fire guards in each group is less than six local authorities, with the agreement of occupiers of the premises, will regroup teams to make the maximum cuts possible

The minimum number of fire guards on duty in each group will be three, the number required to man a stirrup pump team

The circular points out that relaxation of duties may have to be cancelled at short notice if the situation should make it necessary

From Sunday

Fire Guards on business premises will in future be known as fire watchers.

The temporary suspension of the fire guard plans will mean that fire watchers will notify the N.F.S of any outbreak of fire, either from enemy action or local causes.

Street party leaders and, in the City of London area, block commanders, will continue with their duties, but sector captains and, in the City, block leaders will not be required under the new scheme.

Duties in the City of London area will be relaxed from Sunday night. Each City sector has been asked to submit plans to the Corporation, and these will be approved next week. Until then each sector will make what reduction it considers necessary.

This will mean that men on duty where there are at present 45 or more fire guards will, in future, only have to firewatch at most about once in six weeks. For the smallest blocks where amalgamation will not be possible, the number of duties will be halved.

Bombers Over Again To-day

Germany is apparently being heavily bombed again to-day, for German radio said that "many fast bombers are approaching Bavaria."

Another formation of "many fast bombers" was reported heading for Western Germany.

Later bombers were reported approaching Bavaria and Lower Austria

The very strong force of Lancasters and Halifaxes which bombed Dusseldorf last night dropped well over 4000 tons of bombs.

Mosquito bombers raided Osnabruck. Twenty-one bombers are missing.

Mosquitoes of 2nd T.A.F., harassing German transport services, had another successful night, attacking 21 trains, more than 40 motor transport vehicles, and several tugs and barges

Beaufighters, Wellingtons and Royal Navy Barracudas, operating under R.A.F. Coastal Command, found enemy shipping unusually active off the Dutch coast during the night, and for many hours harried and attacked a variety of merchant shipping, E and R boats and minesweepers.

Five Jet-Planes

Five enemy jet-propelled fighters and four other fighters were shot down last night by the aircraft that bombed Dusseldorf.

TWO MEN IN BLACK MASKS

Two men wearing black masks, and believed to be carrying firearms, entered a shop at Enersdale-road, Hither Green, this afternoon.

They snatched £40 in notes, and drove off in a dark saloon car.

No Fly-Bombs

No flying bombs came over Southern England during the night

75 ENEMY SHIPS SUNK

American light naval forces, co-operating with British units, have sunk 75 enemy ships in the Western Mediterranean in the past ten months, says Exchange.

The vessels range from two destroyers, four corvettes and a 3000-ton merchantman, two lighters.

The H.G. Can Keep His Respirator

Home Guards are after all to retain their respirators as long as the rest of the population keep theirs.

Newest instruction regarding the collection of equipment sets this out clearly.

This girl, member of the Belgian White Brigade, who gave help to the Allies in Roosendaal shows her automatic to Allied tank crews. She rounded up many collaborators in Esschen

Battle Of Destroyers

TWO OF OURS SINK THREE OF THEIRS

Two Royal Navy destroyers have sunk three enemy destroyers in the Adriatic, it was revealed to-day.

The communiqué from Allied H.Q. Mediterranean, said: "On the evening of November 1 the destroyer Wheatland (Lieutenant Hugh Askew Corbett D.S.C., commanding) and the Avon Vale (Lieutenant Ivan Hall commanding) operating among the islands west of Pag Island in the Adriatic, engaged and sank two enemy destroyers

"About an hour and a half later a third destroyer was engaged and sunk. Some survivors were rescued and made prisoner

"Our forces suffered no casualties although the Avon Vale sustained superficial damage."

THREE BOYS IN A BOAT

Set Out to Row To London

Two boys of ten and one of 11, evacuated from London to Paignton, "borrowed" a dinghy from Paignton harbour with the intention of rowing back to London.

Before starting they thought better of it, but the boat drifted out to sea and was picked up by a ship and taken to Dartmouth.

At Paignton juvenile court to-day the lads admitted breaking into a shop and 41 other offences, including the theft of the dinghy.

The oldest boy was sent to an approved school and the other two were bound over.

He Tried to Rob Lady Jellicoe

An Arab villager who assaulted and attempted to rob the Countess of Jellicoe of some jewellery was sentenced to three years' imprisonment by the Haifa court, says Reuter.

GOVERNMENT PLAN IS A 'GIGANTIC' ONE

—Says Sir William Beveridge

Sir William Beveridge (Lib., Berwick-on-Tweed) to-day made his maiden speech in Parliament in the Social Security debate.

He welcomed the Government White Paper, and recalled, "It is nearly two years ago that I laid on the doorsteps of the Government, in Whitehall a report on social insurance—a large and rather noisy baby—but a most kindly Government took that report in, and cared for it, and I have lost sight of it." (Laughter.)

To-day by one route or another, the baby had found its way from Whitehall to Westminster, and he also had moved to Westminster.

"Admission of paternity is always a slightly delicate operation, perhaps even particularly delicate in a maiden speech," he said, amid laughter.

"I think this plan is the same baby I left on the doorstep two years ago. I wish it were my child, and would like to behave to-day as an old-fashioned father, and help its career and correct any bad features of the child."

Describing the Government scheme as "gigantic," Sir William

(Continued on Back Page, Col. Two)

£5000 Salary For New Minister

By Our Political Correspondent

While the Commons were discussing the social insurance scheme to-day, the text was published of the Bill to set up the new Ministry which is to administer the scheme.

The Bill provides for a salary of £5000 a year for Sir William Jowitt as Minister of Social Insurance, and £1500 a year for a Parliamentary Secretary to the Ministry

The new Ministry take over the functions of the Ministry of Health in regard to National Health Insurance, old age pensions, widows and orphans and old age contributory pensions, and supplementary pensions; from the Ministry of Labour, Unemployment Insurance and Unemployment Assistance, and from the Home Office Workmen's Compensation.

Daily Mail
NO. 15,146 ONE PENNY ★★ FOR KING AND EMPIRE FRIDAY, NOVEMBER 17, 1944
LATE WAR NEWS

EISENHOWER LAUNCHES HIS KNOCK-OUT BLOW

4 German Towns Ours in First Giant Onslaught

THE great offensive to burst open the gates of Germany broke out in full fury yesterday. By nightfall six Allied armies were hammering forward along the 400-miles front from Holland to the Alps. A new American army was flung into the attack, which bears all the signs of aiming at a knock-out blow before the New Year.

The greatest fury of the Allied assault was concentrated against a 50-miles belt stretching from Venlo to Aachen, the zone facing Germany's greatest industrial areas.

The north of this belt is being attacked by the British Second Army; the centre by the U.S. Ninth Army—fighting its first full-scale battle; and the south by the U.S. First Army.

The American armies attacked within two hours of each other. The First Army struck at 11 a.m.; the Ninth Army—the victors of Brest—at 12.45.

Hundreds of guns heralded the assaults with devastating bombardments. Overhead roared thousands of Allied bombers—1,200 U.S. Forts and Liberators to pound defence posts and rear communications; 1,150 planes of Bomber Command to blast the fortress towns of Duren, Julich, and Heinsberg. At least 8,000 tons of bombs were dropped.

Midnight reports suggest that the attacks are making good progress. Within two hours of the start of the battle the Ninth Army's tanks and infantry had gone forward over a mile from its position on the Dutch-German frontier and had captured the German towns of Immendorf, Floruich, Euchen, and Beggendorf.

Greatest Force

For two months the Ninth has been a "mystery" army, placed by the Germans on almost every sector of the Western Front. Yesterday the Germans discovered its real positions when its tanks smashed east in the area of Geilenkirchen to sweep across recently dug tank ditches as though they did not exist.

The launching of this assault completes the pattern of the Allied winter offensive in the West. British, American, and French forces are now pressing forward along great sectors of the rain-drenched, snow-covered battle line.

The massed might of these forces is the greatest General Eisenhower has ever employed. His troops on the Western Front outnumber the Germans, estimated at 500,000, by three to one.

In Holland, General Dempsey's troops are steadily breaking down the Venlo pocket. Throughout yesterday their advance continued, and nightfall saw them within one and a half miles of the Maas stronghold of Roermond and less than five miles from the German border.

Patrols have got to within two-thirds of a mile of the Maas at places, and the whole advance here is going faster than expected.

In 48 hours the Second Army has advanced 11 miles over a country seamed with mines and booby-traps. These are the barriers behind which the Germans are falling back to their new defences along the Maas.

Below Dempsey's army is the U.S. Ninth: then comes the U.S. First. Still farther south is General Patton's Third Army.

The Third, according to Berlin, is striking east with 700 tanks as well as completing the encirclement of Metz.

Late yesterday the Germans reported that this thrust to the Saar had penetrated into the key town of Morhange.

Around Metz itself fighting has livened up and German counter-attacks have recaptured two of the city's forts.

American assaults compensated for the loss of the Metz forts by gaining further ground in other sectors round the city.

Below Patton's forces are the French First Army and the U.S. Seventh, steadily pressing the Germans in around the Belfort Gap.

Hint of a German retreat in this area came last night with the news that the enemy had set the towns of St. Die, Corcieux, and Lescours on fire.

Final word on this six-fold attack comes from Berlin. The German Official News Agency yesterday sent a note to editors asking them not to use an article it circulated on Wednesday.

The article was entitled: "*The Fronts are Being Stabilised.*"

'SECRET 9th'

THE "Secret Ninth"—the American Army about whose position the Germans have so often speculated, arrived in England soon after D-Day, its commander, Lt.-General W. H. Simpson, arriving on D+13.

It was originally the U.S. Eighth Army, but General Eisenhower changed its number two days later so that it should not be confused with the British Eighth Army.

It was originally planned to keep the Ninth in England till October, but the speed of the Allied advance after the Normandy break-through speeded up the time-table. The Ninth took over the Brittany operation and the siege of Brest from September 5.

BOMBING SHOWS THE PATTERN

WHERE the bombs fell yesterday. This carpet, laid by 2,350 Allied "heavies," marks the pattern of attack. Along 400 miles of the Western Front six Allied armies march into battle to tear open the gateways to Germany.

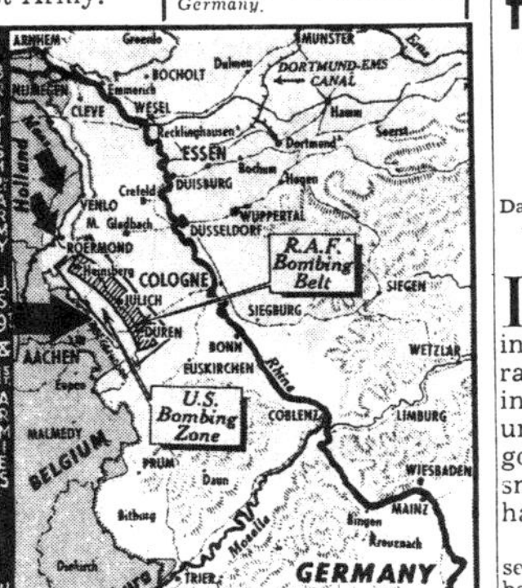

British Guns Pound at the Reich

From RICHARD McMILLAN

WITH BRITISH FORWARD TROOPS, Thursday.

BRITISH Long Toms, massed with other guns, began shelling German soil to-day. I marched with the infantry down a road leading to the German border, and saw something new which may indicate a new defeatist frame of mind among the enemy.

The walls in one village carried freshly painted signs saying "We never capitulate," over and over again.

In the badly smashed village of Heijthuyse every wall bore a slogan, obviously written by a specially assigned signwriter protesting that Germany would fight on "in spite of everything."

Our guns pounded the retreating Germans as well as lobbing shells over the frontier. Rooftops in Germany could be seen by our forward infantry as they drove on against feeble resistance.

In one village about a mile from the Maas the Germans had the surprise of their lives. In a forward trench Private Alick Armit, whose home is in Perthshire, told me about it:

"We got into the village last night," he said. "It was ablaze like daylight as hayricks and farmsteads outside it caught fire from our tracers.

"The whole skyline was a beacon like Old Nick's furnace, while the village streets looked like alleyways to hell.

Trapped

"Some Germans ran out of the farms in the lurid light and were caught by our machine-gunners. A group of German cylists came along the main road from the frontier to the village, thinking it was still in German hands.

"They dismounted in front of their billets to find that we were in occupation and that they were prisoners."

At another point a young lieutenant was leading two tanks, with infantry carried in a "Kangaroo"—a tank converted so as to carry men inside their armour plating.

The Kangaroo got separated from the tanks and a few minutes later

BACK PAGE—Col. SIX

RAF BLAST WAY FOR THE ARMY

From Daily Mail Reporter

R.A.F. BOMBER BASE, Thursday Night.

WITH the word "Go" from the Allied Command the fury of Bomber Command and the U.S. 8th and 9th Air Forces was unleashed on the string of fortified towns just in front of the armies this afternoon.

It was a repeat of the "softening up" which took place before the break-out from Caen—but on a much greater scale.

More than 1,150 Lancasters and Halifaxes attacked Duren, Julich and Heinsberg with more than 8,500 tons of bombs.

At a Lancaster base in the Midlands I spoke to the crews of squadrons who had been in the attack on Duren. The weather over the target was ideal, and crews were confident that Duren was well and truly "plastered."

Flying Officer L. Goff, of Bournemouth, said: "We bombed from 12,000ft., half-way through the attack. The eastern half of the town was covered in smoke. The bomber controller told us exactly where to aim our bombs in the western half of the town."

That bomber controller—or "master bomber"—was one of a number of experienced pilots who went on the raid in the role of master of ceremonies.

It was their job to decide when one part of the target has been bombed sufficiently.

The first day has gone well—and given good weather the area before Cologne should be "Caened" in a very short time to clear the way for the Allied Army.

NOEL MONKS, Daily Mail Correspondent with the 9th Army, sends this eye-witness dispatch telling of the great attack. On this occasion, Monks's story has been pooled with the rest of the Press.

The General Said 'Let's Go!'

Then the Massed Tanks Charged Enemy Flee

From NOEL MONKS, Daily Mail Special Correspondent

WITH THE 9TH U.S. ARMY IN GERMANY, Thursday.

IT is only two hours since our commanding general picked up the radio telephone connecting him with the various units and said "Let's go," and already three small towns are in our hands.

Men of his army needed no second bidding. They have been waiting for this for many dreary days and weeks, a ghost army entrenched in German mud, and to-day we saw them go into battle like unleashed hounds.

I saw the Germans climb up out of their mud-holes and go stumbling, blindly, hopelessly, back before our tanks and infantry, as they moved relentlessly across open sugar beet fields towards their first objectives.

The ground shook with our artillery barrage as the Ninth Army's assault got under way to a smashing start.

The mile-long tank ditches that German men and women have been digging these past weeks, as we watched them from vantage points proved no obstacle to our tanks.

Not a single German tank challenged ours as we crossed open country.

LIKE TIDWORTH

I watched the opening stages of the offensive from an observation post set up in No Man's Land for our tank commander, and it was like having the most expensive seat at the Tidworth tattoo.

Only the shell bursts and the machine-gun fire and the general hubbub of battle were real here in Germany.

Like a fleet of racing yachts coming up to the starting-line, the American tanks ploughed through the mud from their assembly points and headed out across No Man's Land sharp at 12.45 p.m., the time fixed for the general assault.

Some of them came racing past our observation post, flinging great chunks of mud into the air, their guns blazing away at the enemy positions 800 yards ahead.

Navy Seizes Two Danish Ships

Two Danish fishing vessels have been intercepted in a prohibited area and brought into port with their gear and crews by a British patrol.

The Admiralty stated last night that despite repeated warnings Danish fishing vessels continue to enter prohibited areas in the North Sea.

V2s Fall on Saar

ZURICH, Thursday.—It is reported here that misfired V1s and V2s have landed in the Saar, causing very heavy casualties, especially at Saarlautern (Saarlouis).—*Reuter.*

Moves to End the Prisoners Scandal

War Office Meet the Railways

By Daily Mail Reporter

A BETTER deal for British civilian railway passengers at the expense of hitherto pampered German prisoners of war is likely to follow the astonishing story told by Earl Poulett in the House of Lords on Wednesday.

Earl Poulett described how he and his young wife were ordered out of their railway carriage by a British officer armed with a Sten gun.

The officer wanted the carriage for two German officer prisoners. Earl and Lady Poulett had to stand in a bitterly cold corridor for five hours.

Two developments yesterday followed the ventilation of that story:

1.—War Office and railway officials met to devise methods of moving German prisoners by rail in such a way as not to inconvenience British civilians.

2.—A full inquiry was ordered by both the War Office and the L.M.S. into how the officer concerned came to order Lord and Lady Poulett out of their carriage.

In response to my inquiries yesterday both War Office and railway officials agreed that there is no ruling under which British civilians can be turned out of seats they already occupy to make room for German prisoners.

'No Authority'

At the War Office I was told:

"The guard was certainly entitled to carry firearms while escorting enemy prisoners, but whether or not he was carrying a Sten gun we do not know. It is more likely he would have had a small automatic.

"There is no reason why he shouldn't have a Sten gun if he preferred such a heavy, cumbersome way of arming himself. However, he had no authority to turn civilian passengers out of their seats, and the matter will be gone into fully."

The War Office added that there is in fact no reason why German war prisoners should not travel in the luggage van. There are only two things from which, under the terms of the Geneva Convention, they must be protected: the curiosity of the public and the wind and the weather.

I understand that as a result of yesterday's meeting new plans are likely to be worked out—either the putting on of an extra carriage for prisoners, the running of special trains, or holding prisoners over so that they are not transported in ones and twos, but only in numbers with special compartments reserved at the end of the train.

Treatment of German prisoners on the British railways has long been a cause of deep resentment on the part of civilian travellers.

There have been occasions when a train packed with standing civilians has pulled up alongside another train loaded with grinning Germans, each with a seat to himself.

Eating Chocolate

One *Daily Mail* reader relates a recent experience when 14 civilians were forced to stand, on a long journey in an icy corridor, while in each heated compartment they could see five German officers smoking and eating chocolate.

When a complaint was made to an inspector he explained that he was powerless in the matter. He did, however, see that the inside blinds were drawn so that the civilians did not have the extra humiliation of watching.

An official of the railways told me: "We are aware of these awkward and uncomfortable situations, but operationally we do not come into it at all.

"The War Office contact us and make these reservations for prisoners, and we have to do as we are asked."

'THIS MAN IS MAD'

Says Brain Expert

HERE is a new set of Hitler pictures which came to The Daily Mail last night. They make an intriguing study in the light of the latest views—published below—of Dr. William Brown, whose first public report on Hitler's mental state appeared exclusively in The Daily Mail last Saturday.

'HITLER IS UNDER RESTRAINT'

Daily Mail Special Correspondent

NEW YORK, Thursday.

A NEW report on Hitler's mental condition has been made to the British Government by Dr. William Brown, director of the Institute of Experimental Psychology at Oxford. Dr Brown, who is considered the greatest living authority, outside Germany, on Hitler's mind, is now of the definite opinion that Hitler is under restraint.

After close study of the text of Hitler's recent proclamation, Dr. Brown said:

"The German text of the proclamation shows words and phrases which Hitler habitually uses in speeches and which are peculiar to him. The German word for Almighty or 'Providence' is repeated eight times. The phrase 'to be or not to be' is repeated eight times, which is typical of Hitler's previous speeches.

"However, I don't think Hitler wrote those words recently. I think he wrote them soon after the attempt on his life in July. He must have been thoroughly frightened by that attempt.

"I believe he intended to deliver a longer address to the people a little later, and started to write part of it. But I think he went mad before he could deliver it.

"It is my view that he is now probably being kept under restraint physically and politically.

"I think his intended speech was brought up to date by our friends Goebbels and Himmler.

"They saw what we and other nations were saying about Hitler's silence last week and I think they got frightened and said to themselves, 'We must find something.'

"Then they probably rummaged through Hitler's stuff and found this undelivered writing.

"There is actually nothing new in the proclamation—nothing concerning new military developments or V2. Hitler certainly would not have missed the opportunity to mention them had he actually written the proclamation recently."

4 Deg. Frost in Strait

Sea.—Moderate.
Weather.—Coldest night of winter with 4 deg. of frost. Low banks of fog at dusk. Clear overhead. Wind, light, W.N.W. Max. temp., 41; 34 at 7.30 p.m. At 10 p.m., 28.
Barometer.—Still rising.

Women First Out of War Work

WIVES AND OVER 50's

By GARRY ALLIGHAN, Industrial Correspondent

THE full "master plan" for winding down Britain's war effort in stages has now been stated, the third part being Mr. Bevin's White Paper on demobilising 10,000,000 men and women from war work into peace production.

Demobilisation of the Services is the first part, gradual relaxing of controls announced by the Premier yesterday is the second, and the Minister of Labour's White Paper to-day is the third. It falls into three sections:

1. Young men between 18 and 25 will be called up after Germany is beaten, and if the war with Japan demands it the age limit will be raised to 27.

2. As soon as the European war ends, men over 65 and all women over 60 will be retired from war jobs.

In addition, all women, married or single, can leave industrial jobs if they have household responsibilities. Women can also leave if they wish to join husbands released from the Services.

Women over 50 without those qualifications may also retire if they wish and provided there are not strong production reasons to retain their services.

These three groups, to whom retirement is permitted, will be known as "Class K" workers.

Mr. Bevin pays a great tribute to these women workers and hopes that many of them will not exercise their right to retire if engaged on work of national importance of value to peace-time industry.

3. Certain groups of workers will be taken from their present jobs and transferred to work nearer their homes.

This concession will have priority application to "Class K" workers who do not want to retire and any

BACK PAGE—Col. FOUR

Ben Smith Tells U.S. Our Needs

NEW YORK, Thursday.

MR. BEN SMITH, British Resident Minister in the U.S., in his first public speech since his appointment, to-night appealed for understanding of Britain's post-war economic aims and for U.S. support and co-operation in world expansion of commerce.

Mr. Smith said: "Our two great countries can achieve far more by combined effort than we could possibly achieve by working independently.

"If your exporters are going to regard every British effort to regain export trade as an attack on American trade we are not going to get much farther in our joint efforts to promote world expansion of commerce, without which America certainly could not attain the three-fold increase of foreign trade which President Roosevelt recently mentioned.

"Before the war we were one of your best customers. In 1937 we took 21 per cent. of your exports."

Describing how Britain had sacrificed her exports and accumulated an adverse balance of about £3,000,000,000 overseas in the prosecution of the war, Mr. Smith outlined the three-fold objectives of British economic policy.

"Before the war just about one per cent. of the consumption of the world was represented by British exports. What we are hoping to achieve is to increase this figure to 1½ per cent.

"Our second objective is to rebuild our blitzed towns and overtake the arrears in normal house building and repairs.

"Our third objective is that we must have as much increase in civilian standards as the equitable distribution of the world's limited supplies may permit."—*Reuter.*

France Seeks No Rhine Hegemony

Daily Mail Special Correspondent

LYONS, Thursday.—M. Georges Bidault, French Foreign Minister, assured Mr. Eden in Paris that Belgium need not fear that France is striving after hegemony in the Rhineland.

3,000 LEYTE JAPS ISOLATED

About 3,000 Japanese troops are "virtually cut off" in the Limon salient on Leyte, in the Philippines, General MacArthur announces. Artillery has again bombarded Ormoc corridor.

RED PLANES SINK SHIP AT DANZIG

A German transport of 6,000 tons has been sunk by Soviet planes in the port of Danzig, it was officially announced in Moscow.

2

WEDNESDAY, NOVEMBER 22, 1944

Evening Standard

37,502 DIM-OUT 5.32 p.m. to 8.1 a.m. MOON rises 2.2 p.m., sets 11.21 p.m. ONE PENNY

FINAL NIGHT EXTRA●

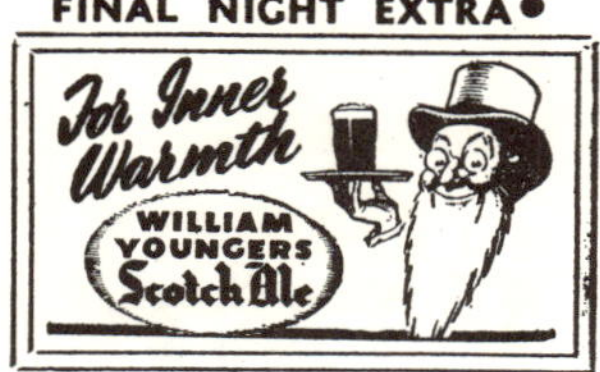

Dempsey Drives On: Stage 1 is the Break-in; Stage 2 the Dogfight

BRITISH BITE INTO SIEGFRIED "BACKBONE"

British troops of General Dempsey's Second Army, east of Geilenkirchen, have for the first time encountered the true backbone of the Siegfried Line—defences ranged in series in front of the River Roer.

WE HAVE ACHIEVED THE FIRST STAGE—THE BREAK-IN, SAYS RICHARD McMILLAN, BRITISH UNITED PRESS REPORTER.

The second stage—the "dogfights" or levering-in process—is now being carried out.

The third stage is to smash right through the series of pillboxes, and then try to beat the enemy to their next line of defence.

Charles Lynch (Reuter reporter) adds that the German pillboxes are arranged close together to command

the valley of the Wurm, which flows north-east from Geilenkirchen to join the Roer River north of Linnich.

The British have sliced diagonally into the Siegfried Line, instead of assaulting it frontally; as a result the anti-tank barriers which are arranged in a great unbroken line running from north to south, were largely ineffective in the drive on Geilenkirchen and beyond.

But the pillboxes face in all directions and must be overcome one by one. The result is savage fighting with no material change.

Farther north, in the Venlo area, the German pocket west of the Maas continued to contract yesterday and a large number of Germans have been pulled back across the Maas, leaving only a rearguard on the west side.

MAASBREE OURS

The British have captured Maasbree (just over five miles west of Venlo and five miles from the German frontier) and are also reported on the edge of Baarlo (on the Maas, about five miles south-west of Venlo).

After the capture of Helenaveen they have advanced four miles north-east to the approaches of the village of Sevenum. The Weerd factory area, 1000 yards north-west of Roermond, has been captured.

Before Venlo the British are not yet up against a firm defence line: they have not yet hit an anti-tank

(Continued on Back Page, Col. Three)

Mulhouse Is Ours

Mulhouse has been captured by armoured elements of the First French Army, reports Robert Wilson, Associated Press reporter at Sixth Army Group Headquarters.

The French took 1000 prisoners, including part of the staff of the German Nineteenth Army in this important industrial and railway city, which lies about 10 miles from the Rhine, north-west of Basle.

Meanwhile, violent street fighting rages in Belfort, and the fall of the citadel is imminent.

The French troops have also reached Colmar, 25 miles north of Mulhouse, says a Paris report.

American troops of the Seventh Army, and French troops, including General Leclerc's armoured division, have advanced eight to ten miles beyond Sarrebourg to threaten the Savern Pass, most northerly of the Vosges gateways, adds Reuter.

Progress is continuing all along the southern front with advances ranging from 13 to 15 miles in a

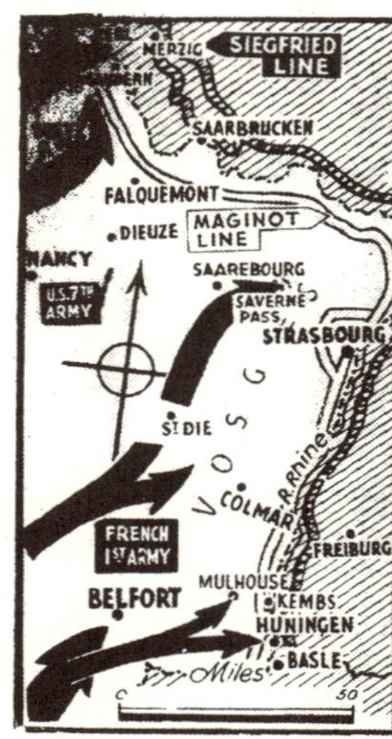

NAZIS TAKE ST. LOUIS

Evening Standard Correspondent

BASLE, Wednesday.

The Germans' vigorous counter-attack north of the Swiss border, in an attempt to trap the French forces which have passed through the Belfort gap, has so far been fairly favourable to the Germans.

Several villages held by the F.F.I. have been retaken by the Wehrmacht after fierce fighting.

Just before midnight, it was confirmed that the frontier town of St. Louis had been reoccupied by the Germans and that their advance was proceeding westward.

King Sees Viceroy's Son

Captain the Hon A. J. Wavell, son of the Viceroy of India, was received in audience by the King at Buckingham Palace to-day.

Metz General is Captured

Evening Standard War Reporter

With the U.S. Third Army, Wednesday.

General-lieutenant Kittel, who is believed to have been commander of the German 462nd Administrative Division at Metz, has been captured.

He was seriously wounded while commanding the enemy troops on the island of Chambiere, which fell yesterday, and was found in hospital by men of the 95th U.S. Infantry.

Only the island of Saulcy remains to be cleared in the Metz area, apart from five fort groups still holding out and refusing to surrender.

It is estimated that prisoners taken in the Metz area so far total 4600, of whom 1500 were captured yesterday.

3850 'PLANES HIT THE ENEMY'S OIL

GERMANY'S BOMB-BATTERED SYNTHETIC OIL CENTRES HAVE WILTED UNDER THE FULL WEIGHT OF ATTACKS BY 3850 ALLIED AIRPLANES IN LESS THAN 24 HOURS.

The latest raid in this concentrated hammering was made last night and yesterday afternoon by some of the 1500 airplanes which Air Chief Marshal Sir Arthur Harris sent over the Reich to round-off the devastation started earlier yesterday by 2350 American aircraft.

After dark Halifaxes and Lancasters went for the two Ruhr oil plants at Sterkrade and Castrop-Rauxel, where large fires were started.

The Sterkrade works, three times already put out of action and restarted production, was having its fourth pasting since soon after D-Day.

NEW TARGET

A new target, Aschaffenburg, rail town 25 miles south-east of Frankfurt, was also visited by the heavies.

The bombs which fell on it, for the first time in this war, were dropped in direct support of the advancing French Army.

Earlier, in daylight, escorted Lancasters struck at Homburg.

All the operations since yesterday afternoon, which included blows at Hanover, Stuttgart and Worms, intruder bombing and sea-mine laying, cost Bomber Command 15 airplanes.

To-day's Air Ministry communiqué says that large fires were seen, and smoke rose to a height of 10,000ft. after yesterday's concentrated attack on the synthetic oil plant at Homburg.

CATHERINE'S D.F.C.

Catherine, baby daughter of Flt. Lieut. A. J. Wingwood, of Hamilton, Bermuda, tests her growing teeth on her father's D.F.C., awarded at a recent Buckingham Palace investiture for his work on bombing missions.

Caillaux Dead

EX-PREMIER OF FRANCE

M. Joseph Caillaux, former French Premier, has died at Le Mans, said Paris radio this afternoon.

He was 81.

M. Caillaux's strong influence for many years in French politics was that he became regarded as the unchallenged master of French finance.

He it was who brought down the Blum Cabinet in June 1937, when he led the Senate attack on the Government's Finance Bill.

Caillaux long advocated an alliance between France and Germany. After Versailles, Clemenceau accused him of having had treasonable communication with Berlin.

M. Caillaux

At the beginning of 1918 he was put under arrest, and in February 1920 his trial began before the Senate.

The capital charge of treason against him was dismissed, yet it was at least made clear, said a writer at the time, that Germany had regarded him as a friend.

Found guilty of correspondence with the enemy he was sentenced to three years' imprisonment—but having been in gaol so long, he was at once liberated.

Writing in the Paris Soir in October 1939, Caillaux predicted a quick victory for the Allies.

"The Western Powers would have to display disconcerting incompetence to lose the war," he said.

First Nazi P.o.W.s Leave England For Isle of Man

The first batch of German prisoners to be interned in the Isle of Man, about 300, left Fleetwood for the island to-day. They came to Fleetwood by ordinary train and in reserved compartments under military guard.

They marched to the landing stage in single file, with three yards distance between each man. Their uniforms varied from army field grey to the darker grey of the Luftwaffe. They were plentifully supplied with greatcoats.

"VICTORIA STATION HIT" SAYS BERLIN

German radio claimed to-day that London's Victoria Station had been hit by a V2.

To-day's German communique said that heavy long-range fire continues on Antwerp and recently on the area of Liege.

New British C.-in-C. For Egypt

Lieut.-general C. W. Allfrey is to be General Officer Commanding British troops in Egypt, it was officially announced in Cairo to-day, says Associated Press.

General Allfrey formerly commanded a British formation in Italy. He is 49. He joined the Royal Artillery in 1914, and holds the D.S.O., M.C. and bar.

General Allfrey will replace Lieut.-general Robert Stone, whose next post has not been announced.

WODEHOUSE ARRESTED IN PARIS

It was confirmed in London to-day that P. G. Wodehouse, the author, and his wife, have been arrested in Paris by the French authorities.

It was stated that questions of procedure are now under discussion between competent authorities in London and the French.

Details of the charge, or charges, are not yet known.

Mr. Wodehouse and his wife were moved from Berlin to Paris by the Germans some time ago.

Mr. Wodehouse is 63. He was staying with his wife at Le Touquet when the Germans overran France in 1940.

He was interned for a time, but the Germans released him in 1941, partly, he stated later, because he had reached the age of 60, and partly on the intervention of friends in America.

P. G. Wodehouse

Mr. Wodehouse gave several broadcasts over the German radio dealing with his camp experiences, but, he declared after the liberation of France, "I refused all offers to do propaganda broadcasts."

Before returning to Paris, Mr. and Mrs. Wodehouse lived at the Adlon Hotel, Berlin, where they had to report weekly to the German Foreign Office, and in Upper Silesia.

"A Real Good Rocket Show"

A German headquarters was obliterated yesterday in a surprise attack by rocket-firing Typhoons of the R.A.F. 2nd T.A.F. from an advanced airfield in Holland.

The entire operation took only 40 minutes from take-off to landing.

The sudden appearance of the Typhoons out of low hanging cloud layers caught the enemy A.-A. so much by surprise that no guns were fired until the first section of dive-bombers had released their rockets.

Then the barrage was so fierce that half the attacking force was hit, although all the Typhoons returned to base.

The closest escape was that of a flight-sergeant who found two shrapnel holes in his radiator and another one in his windscreen.

"A complete picture of destruction," was how a squadron leader described the headquarters, which were about 10 miles ahead of our forward lines.

"When I came over," he said, "I could not see what it was. There was just a cloud of debris and dust. It was a real good rocket show."

TUESDAY, NOVEMBER 28, 1944

Evening Standard

37,507 DIM-OUT: 5.27 pm to 8.10 am. MOON: Rises 4.30 pm; sets 7.31 am. ONE PENNY

FINAL NIGHT EXTRA

Britain Mobilised 7,000,000 Women, Paid 3 Times More Income Tax, Increased Munitions 6 Times

OUR WAR SECRETS

The Farms Kept Us Going

From WILLIAM ALISON,
Evening Standard Political Correspondent

Some of the most closely-guarded war secrets of Britain are out to-day.

THE CHANGED MILITARY SITUATION HAS MADE IT POSSIBLE FOR THE GOVERNMENT TO LIFT THE VEIL, AND, FOR THE FIRST TIME TO REVEAL IN DETAIL THE IMMENSITY OF OUR ALL-OUT WAR EFFORT IN THE MOBILISATION OF MEN, MATERIAL AND MONEY.

One of the features of the mobilisation of the population is the part played by women. It runs like a thread through the narrative about man-power, and the White Paper says the high degree of mobilisation achieved has been largely due to the contribution made by women.

At the middle of this year, out of 16,000,000 women between 14 and 59 years, 7.1 millions were in the Services, whole-time C.D., or industry.

Food: We are eating more bulky and starchy food, and less meats, fats and sugar.

The ordinary consumer received only 30 shell eggs in 1943 as a registered customer.

Clothes: Rationing provides about one-half of what you had pre-war.

The clothes ration is barely adequate to cover even the minimum requirements of adults.

Houses Damaged

Houses: Of the 13,000,000 houses in the United Kingdom 4.5 millions have been damaged by enemy action, of which 202,000 are totally destroyed or beyond repair.

Income-tax: Law changes and increased earnings have raised the number of income-tax payers from 4,000,000 in 1938-9 to 13,000,000 and increased the amount paid from £336,000,000 to £1,183,000,000.

But under the "nest egg" arrangement there is £305,000,000 repayable after the war. Private savings in 1943 were five times greater than in 1938.

The income of private persons before taxation rose from £4,779,000,000 to £7,708,000,000 between 1938 and 1943. "Most of this increase," says the White

(Continued on Back Page, Col. Three)

The Work of A Poet's Son

Evening Standard Reporter

The publication of the White Paper telling the story of Britain at war must take a great weight off the mind of Sir Edward Bridges, Secretary to the Cabinet, who played a big part in its preparation.

He, the 52 years old only son of the late Poet Laureate, Robert Bridges, has known all this country's secrets since the first day of the war.

Now that so many facts and figures have officially become public, Sir Edward will be relieved of a vast number of vital secrets.

Tall, slim and scholarly—he has his father's devotion to books and classical scholarship, though he is not a poet—Sir Edward has been Secretary to the Cabinet since August 1938, when he succeeded Lord Hankey.

Sir Edward has been described as a "very efficient machine" in business. He has been a Civil Servant since the end of the last war.

Sir Edward Bridges

During that time he was head of the Treasury Division, responsible for matters of defence, and also a member of the Air Ministry Supply Committee.

Won the M.C.

He had four years' personal experience of war, for he served through the 1914-18 war, and won the Military Cross. He was a captain in the Oxfordshire and Buckinghamshire Light Infantry.

A former Fellow of All Soul's College, Oxford, he married in 1922 the Hon. Katharine Farrer, daughter of Lord Farrer of Abinger. They have two sons and two daughters, and live at Epsom.

"Sir Edward has all his father's love of scholarship, Oxford and the countryside," a friend told me to-day. "He is an accomplished painter."

STATEMENT ON CAR TAX SOON

Sir John Anderson, Chancellor of the Exchequer, in answer to several members who asked in Parliament to-day for a statement on the revision of motorcar taxation said he hoped to be able to make a statement early in the new session.

PATTON'S MEN GAIN FOUR MILES: "ABOUT TO CROSS GERMAN FRONTIER NEAR ST. AVOLD"

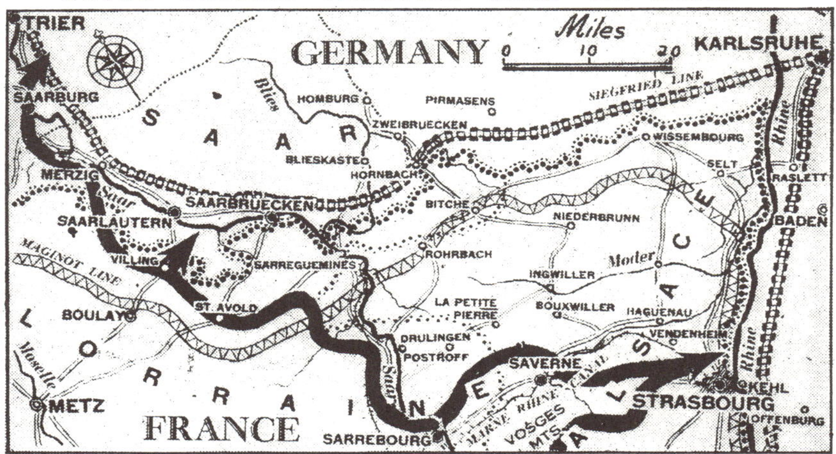

Troops of General Patton's Third Army are about to cross the German frontier north of St. Avold, says Paris radio.

Philip Grune, Evening Standard war reporter, writes: Elements of the 95th Infantry Division have made gains up to four miles on a six-mile front, and early to-day were reported at Villing, five miles south-west of Saarlauten, and only a mile from the German border.

Units of the 80th Division advanced 3½ miles to the north-east, and are now beyond the town of Seingbouse, 2½ miles from Germany.

Almost all German resistance has now been crushed in the Vosges, according to New York radio.

An unconfirmed radio report said to-day that Allied troops had crossed the Rhine north of Strasbourg; but later the French War Ministry declared that no French troops had crossed the Rhine.

FIRST ARMY: STREET FIGHTING

Street-fighting is going on in five German villages on General Hodges's First Army front — Jungersdorf, Inden, Hurtgen, Langerwehe and Graushau, says John Wilhelm, Reuter reporter.

Jungersdorf, on the eastern edge of the Hurtgen Forest, is little more than three miles from Duren. Inden, on the Inde River, is 3000 yards from the River Roer.

About 90 German soldiers are holding out in an old Teutonic castle, Schloss Frenserburg, about eight miles south of Julich.

NINTH ARMY: "NEW ATTACKS"

The German official news agency reported to-day that after bringing up reserves, the Americans yesterday started new large-scale attacks in the Aix area.

General Simpson's troops have almost reached the Roer River south of Julich, after the capture of Kirchberg which was finally cleared yesterday evening.

Earlier reports said the Ninth had already reached the Roer at two points, at Kirchberg and east of Altdorf, which has also been reached.

Merzenhausen, about a mile to the south of Barmen, is cleared, says Harold Mayes Reuter correspondent.

Two German counter-attacks launched to the south, from Flossdorf, a little over a mile north-west of Barmen, were beaten off. Fighting is still going on in Koslar, south of Merzenhausen.

SECOND ARMY: BRIDGE CLASH

A sharp skirmish took place yesterday in the middle of the wrecked railway bridge at Roermond, on the Maas, when

(Continued on Back Page, Col. One)

Pierlot May Appeal To His Country

With Brussels transport almost at a standstill, M. Pierlot, the Belgian Premier, says British United Press, is expected to make an appeal for the country's support in a statement late to-day in the Chamber of Deputies.

The Cabinet met for an hour, earlier, but a communiqué issued makes no mention of the strike.

Shouting "Down with Red Handed Pierlot" and "Bread and Coal," striking tramway workers marched through the barricaded Brussels streets to-day.

The strike is not general, but efforts are being made to extend it. Latest reports in the capital indicated that transport workers in Brabant were coming out and that operatives in several industrial undertakings had ceased work.

Resistance members at Port Namur stopped a number of trams and forced the passengers to get out, and wire and trolley poles were cut, but no serious incidents are reported. The Communications Ministry thinks that the strike will peter out before the end of the day. Other Ministries take a similar view.

SHELLS: *By Churchill*

Mr. Churchill in the Commons to-day made a statement on the shell position. He said:

"Nine months ago we opened up our shell-filling and shell-making plants again on a large scale on account of impending operations.

"The immense piling up of reserves which had occurred earlier had led to a temporary damping down. Since then further important expansions have been made.

"I am prepared to say that provided factory workers maintain and they may even improve upon the present planned output, there is no reason to suppose that the British Armies will be short of necessary ammunition to fight their battles.

"We have also very considerable reserves, the use of which depends on the varying estimates as to the duration of the German resistance."

'War Off Norway Flares Up'—Berlin

The naval war off the Norwegian coast has flared up very considerably recently, says to-day's German communiqué.

Yesterday, German convoys off Western Norway beat off several attacks by enemy bombers and torpedo-carrying airplanes, bringing down six of them.

Gale, Rain, Mist

A south-westerly gale blowing with a force of about 50 m.p.h. lashed the Straits of Dover to-day.

Conditions were very bad with high seas and, for some hours, torrential rain. Low clouds and mist made visibility very poor.

The Guns To-night

There may be night gunfire in an East Coast district to-night and for the rest of the week.

Cautionary notices to this effect have been posted.

PARIS VISIT BY TWO M.P.s STOPPED

Mr. Herbert Morrison, Home Secretary, has, it is understood, refused visas to two Conservative M.P.s who were to visit Paris.

They are Mr. Ronald Tree (Harborough division of Leicestershire) and Mr. Hamilton Kerr (Oldham).

It had been arranged, says the Press Association, that they should stay with Mr. Duff Cooper, our Ambassador to France. Both have held the post of Parliamentary private secretary to him.

The Foreign Office had agreed to the trip and seats had been booked for them to attend the French Parliament.

Both are members of the Tory Reform Committee, for which they are making a study of foreign affairs.

Mr. Morrison is likely to take the view that, pending a Cabinet decision, special privileges should not be given to M.P.s to travel to France in Service airplanes, on which there are at present heavy demands.

Unless the visit is clearly in the national interest, the official attitude is that priority should be given, for example, to business men who have urgent trade negotiations to undertake and to others with specific things to do.

BOMBERS OUT

Allied bombers were over Western Germany at 9 a.m. to-day, German radio announced.

Last night Lancasters and Halifaxes of R.A.F. Bomber Command were over Germany in great strength, with Freiburg and Neuss, railway centres and advance supply bases for the Western Front, as the main objectives.

Berlin was attacked by a force of Mosquitoes, many carrying 4000lb. bombs.

Fighter Command intruders were out over North-West Germany and Holland last night, and inflicted damage on trains and transport vehicles. Mines were also laid in enemy waters.

No aircraft is missing from this operation.

Freiburg is the nearest town of importance to the Mulhouse and Colmar sectors, where the French are advancing. It has 199,000 inhabitants.

SOME V-BOMBS

During the period from dawn yesterday up to 7 o'clock this morning there was enemy air activity directed against Southern England.

A 'Wave' Caused Dump to Blow Up

The death roll in the R.A.F. dump explosion near Burton-on-Trent has now reached about 20 killed, with 60 missing.

Nine people were killed in a cement works near the dump and the missing in the works include four Servicemen, 11 civilians and six Italians. The inquest was opened this afternoon.

"The total value of the bombs must have run into millions of pounds, and there were enough for hundreds of major raids on Germany," said a former R.E. officer engaged at the dump.

"What appears to have happened," he added, "is that one bomb exploded, and the rush of air acted as a detonator for all the bombs in the dump.

"It was this detonating wave underground which caused the 'earthquake' effect felt several miles away."

Describing the dump, the officer stated:

"It looked like an Aladdin's cave. You went from one cavern to another by passages ablaze with electric light.

"There were 90ft. of earth ceiling, which also acted as a protection against enemy raids.

"The safety regulations were comprehensive and stringent."

Like a Desert

The area surrounding the dump is like a desert. The grass is scorched, the ground is pitted with giant bomb craters, and hundreds of cattle are lying dead in the fields.

Two farms were destroyed and every house in a village was affected. But no one appears to have been killed in any of the villages which were badly shaken.

Tailpiece. — Goebbels is now trying to add the bomb explosion near Burton-on-Trent to the credit of Germany's V-weapons.

His German official news agency, in its European service, put out the following under a faked Stockholm dateline to-day:

"With reference to reports that an R.A.F. munitions depot suddenly blew up in the north English town of Burton-on-Trent, it now transpires from London that this explosion was the result of a bombardment with a German V-weapon."

Christmas Leave From Italy

TWO CONTINGENTS WILL BE HOME

The Prime Minister was asked in the Commons to-day if he could make any further statement on the possibility of granting home leave for Christmas to soldiers in the Mediterranean theatre.

Mr. Churchill said that in his statement of November 17 he expressed the hope that some men would be back from the Mediterranean by Christmas.

"The first contingent of officers and men from Italy will be here quite soon," he added. "I am not going to give the actual date. Another contingent is due before Christmas. The first contingent from the Middle East will arrive before the New Year.

"All this is in full accordance with the expectations which I authorised."

THREE IN 16 MINUTES

Lieut. A. A. Harrington, of Ottawa and Atlantic City, New Jersey, U.S.A., a young Mosquito pilot flying with the Canadian Cougar Squadron, has knocked out three German night fighters in 16 minutes over the Western Front.

His total kill is now seven destroyed, and one probable.

Harrington's navigator is Pilot Officer D. J. Tongue, of Birmingham, who has shared in all seven kills.

Daily Mail

NO. 15,167 ONE PENNY * * FOR KING AND EMPIRE TUESDAY, DECEMBER 12, 1944

LATE WAR NEWS

ALEXANDER RUSHED TO GREECE

Churchill: 'Deal With the Situation and Report'

BRITISH paratroops entering the E.A.M. headquarters in Athens, while a tank puts its nose—and gun—right inside the doorway, and a second tank stands menacingly near. Before long, the paratroops had "mopped up" inside the building, and the nerve-centre of the rebels' resistance in Athens was in British hands.

PARATROOPS ready for action in the streets of Athens, where, not long before, they had been garlanded as liberators by crowds among whom were the very people they now have to fight.

11th-HOUR MOVE SENDS MACMILLAN TOO

By **WILSON BROADBENT,** Diplomatic Correspondent

FIELD-MARSHAI Sir Harold Alexander, newly appointed Supreme Allied Commander in the Mediterranean, has been sent to Greece, accompanied by Mr. Harold Macmillan, British Resident Minister to Allied Headquarters, to deal with the situation there and to report at once to the War Cabinet.

Mr. Churchill is expected to give the House of Commons an account of Field-Marshal Alexander's findings and recommendations as soon as possible.

The British Government are determined to do their utmost to put an end to the unhappy and unsatisfactory state of affairs at present existing in Greece.

Field-Marshal Alexander has received personal instructions from the Prime Minister to end the fighting as quickly as possible, providing this can be done with the full assurance of future peace and co-operation among all the political parties.

Mr. Harold Macmillan was in London on Saturday morning, awaiting an aeroplane to take him to Washington to discuss developments in Italy with the State Department.

It was only at the last minute that he was told by the Prime Minister to cancel his plans and join Field-Marshal Alexander in Greece.

Between them they are expected to make contacts with all political elements in Athens.

Their talks will have the object of producing a working understanding which will lead to the disarmament of the various groups, and thus clear the way for the establishment of a Government of national unity, imbued by purpose and power to restore the finances and economic position of Greece.

RAF SILENCE ELAS GUN

ATHENS, Monday.

THE 75mm. Italian gun position behind the Modern Stadium, which E.L.A.S. troops have turned into a strong-point, has been silenced, apparently by yesterday's air strafing.

The gun had been shelling the centre of the city, and yesterday hit British H.Q. and killed a Greek woman outside the building.

Near the centre of the capital the British have evacuated the civil prison, taking with them a number of E.L.A.S. prisoners they had captured earlier.

TROOPS ON WAY

Colonel Napoleon Zervas, chief of the E.D.E.S. (Right Wing Militia) has indicated that he is willing to obey the general order to all guerilla forces to lay down their arms.

Reports from Salonkia said that the Left Wing E.A.M. organisation was in complete control there, and the British were working with it as being the only authority, representatives of the Athens Government having no effective power.

E.L.A.S. forces to-day commandeered six small hotels in the southern districts of Athens, barricaded

BACK PAGE—Col. FIVE

New Plans for Three Power Talk

Eden, Stettinius and Molotov

From **DON IDDON,**
Daily Mail Correspondent
NEW YORK, Monday.

AN early meeting between Mr. Anthony Eden, Mr. Stettinius, and M. Molotov is under consideration, it was learned to-day.

It is expected that the Foreign Ministers will meet some time in January as a possible prelude to a conference between Churchill, Stalin, and Roosevelt.

The necessity for the meeting is being stressed here in view of the Anglo-American clash on the policy to be pursued in Italy and Belgium.

Controversy over the British action continued here to-day. Columnist Walter Winchell, in a broadcast last night heard by millions of Americans, appealed to British correspondents here to cable a special column entitled "To the People of Great Britain," which his newspaper, the *New York Daily Mirror*, refused to print and his syndicate failed to distribute.

The controversial Winchell column in question sharply criticised the British Government's policy in Greece and other liberated countries. Winchell wrote:

"People of the United States are aware of the deepest differences between our Governments in 150 years.

'We Must Part'

"If the British Government is effecting your will it may mean the end of our friendship; if the British Government's policy speaks for you then we must part because we are not fighting for the same things.

"We doubt very much that the British Government speaks for the British people when it sacrifices our friendship—why did you send in your British tanks to surround the House of Deputies in Brussels?

"How would you like it if Belgian tanks were to surround the Houses of Parliament?

"This is a fateful hour, and the decision is with you, the British people. If your policy is the reactionary one of your Government you must go your way alone."

There was a great deal more in the same strain. At the same time the Hearst newspapers, usually anti-Churchill and anti-British, came out with front page editorials backing the Prime Minister's stand, praising his policy and saying: "He has the earnest support of the American people."

Press and public as a whole remain divided on the issue. Fifty per cent. support Mr. Churchill, 50 per cent. denounce his policy.

BELGIAN GIRLS SEND DOLL FOR PRINCESS

From **COURTENAY EDWARDS,**
Daily Mail Special Correspondent
BRUSSELS, Monday.

A DOLL for Princess Margaret Rose was among the thousands of toys which streamed into Brussels to-day for the "Toys for Britain" appeal.

It was made for the Princess by schoolgirl daughters of Belgian miners at Paturages, near Mons.

The doll is dressed as a Belgian miner, complete with black overalls, red and white neckerchief, and steel helmet.

One girl made the miner's axe, another his wooden clogs, a third his safety lamp, and so on.

With this souvenir will come a note written by the girls. It says: "To her Royal Highness Princess Margaret Rose of England, as a mark of homage and respectful gratitude.

"Never will we forget with what generosity and courage the English people fought to give back to us Belgian children the liberty and independence to which we are so passionately attached."

The Gifts Arrive—Picture in Page THREE.

BIG 6 RULE LABOUR DECISIONS

Union Votes Beat Local Parties

By **GARRY ALLIGHAN,**
Industrial Correspondent

SIX big trade unions, representing nearly 2,000,000 industrial workers, captured and controlled the Labour Party conference, which opened in London yesterday, and forced through policy declarations in opposition to the votes of every local Labour Party present.

Professor Harold Laski, presiding owing to the illness of Miss Ellen Wilkinson, attempted to give a doctrinaire Socialist basis to the conference.

But this was rapidly swept away by the "Big Six" trade unions, whose block votes throughout the day's proceedings were flung heavily in favour of a programme which they regarded as more realistic.

It was the block vote of the "Big Six" unions which swamped the almost unanimous votes of the local constituency political delegates and ensured acceptance of the national executive's policy on the general election. These six unions are:

Mineworkers' Federation, 430,000 members paying £8,600 into Labour Party funds this year.

Transport and General Workers Union, 360,000 members, paying £7,300.

General and Municipal Workers, 250,000 members, £5,100.

National Union of Railwaymen, 225,000 members, £4,300.

Distributive Workers, 200,000 members, £4,100.

Textile Workers, 120,000 members, £2,500.

Housing Demand

Deference was naturally paid to their views by the national executive, whose financial report showed that of the total revenue of £52,504 derived from regular weekly subscriptions, £46,755 came from the trade unions.

A special resolution brought forward by the executive on housing and town planning described the plans and proposals so far put forward by the Government as "totally inadequate and indicating a lack of realisation of the extent and gravity of the problem."

The resolution was passed, with an amendment calling for the continuance of rent restriction for ten years after the war.

"Labour Stays in Coalition Till Victory."—BACK Page.

Phantom Fire in West End—Flares

By Daily Mail Reporter

HUNDREDS of telephone calls to London N.F.S. headquarters last night started a rumour about a mysterious fire the reflection of which was seen in the sky for miles.

Roof spotters reported a blaze, saying it was "in the West End area."

The Daily Mail received dozens of calls. Crowds gathered in Piccadilly to watch a searchlight apparently playing on the "phantom fire."

Then the mystery was solved. A fire brigade exercise was being lit up by red flares and as a searchlight was co-operating the sky was lit up by a bright glow.

BUILDERS TO BE RECALLED

Back to London

London men in the building trade who are working in other areas are to be directed back to their home districts.

This plan to speed-up bomb damage repair is approved by the Ministry of Works who have also agreed to stocks of material held by other Ministries being set free for house repairs.

Bombed-out families will soon be installed in fashionable houses in Mayfair and Knightsbridge, where many houses now empty are to be requisitioned for homeless people.

E. Bristol Backs Cripps's Return

The application of Sir Stafford Cripps, M.P. for East Bristol, for re-admission to the Labour Party is being supported by the local Labour Party.

The national executive have been waiting for this recommendation before giving a decision. The Party split at Bristol is likely to end soon

Missing Airman Mystery

Four R.A.F. airmen baled out of an aircraft over Swansea last Saturday, and only three of them have been found.

One of them, a sergeant, had not been traced up to a late hour last night, and it is thought he may be suffering from loss of memory.

V-DEATH TOLL UP TO 716

1,511 Hurt in Month

Civilian casualties due to air attack in Britain during November were 716 killed or missing believed killed, and 1,511 injured.

Of the killed, 269 were men, 345 women and 102 children under 16. Injured were 515 men, 799 women, and 197 children.

The figures, issued officially last night, show a substantial increase over October, when 172 civilians were killed and 416 injured.

Fine in the Strait

It was almost spring weather in the Strait yesterday, with long spells of sunshine and a quiet sea. Temperature rose to 55deg., but dropped to 35 at 10.30 p.m. The barometer rose a little.

Celanese is Rebuked by 'Change

Profits 'Omission' Rocked Market

DR. HENRY DREYFUS
At once held a conference.

By the City Editor

A CONFERENCE at the headquarters of British Celanese, Ltd., in Hanover-square, W., was called last night by Dr. Henry Dreyfus, chairman of the company.

It followed the issue of a statement by the Stock Exchange during the day. No report on the meeting was issued.

Because the directors of the company announced their 15 per cent. dividend ten days before they published particulars of profits there have been wild fluctuations of shares. That is what led the Stock Exchange Committee to take the unusual step of issuing a statement.

Otherwise, the Stock Exchange might be blamed for something on which they have previously made their views very clear.

In little more than a week the shares of the company have rocketed from 33s. to 41s. 3d.—then yesterday they slumped to 36s. 3d. at one time.

Buyers first hoisted the shares because the company paid its first dividend in its 25 years' existence.

Disappointed

But the profits issued yesterday were disappointing. The report showed them to be less than the amount of the dividend, which could only be paid because of an adjustment of Excess Profits Tax paid in previous years.

Had the profits been announced at the same time as the dividend, it is contended, there would have been no false hopes or wild fluctuations in the shares to the detriment of the public.

After the close of the Stock Exchange yesterday the Committee issued this statement under the heading—

BRITISH CELANESE, LIMITED.

"Attention has been called to the fluctuations in the price of these shares in the Market between the date of the dividend announcement and the publication of the profit figures.

"The inadvertent omission on the part of the directors to publish profit figures simultaneously with the announcement of the dividend emphasises the desirability of co-operating with the policy of the Committee as laid down in the Chairman's letter of December 12, 1938."

This letter stated that in many instances there was a danger of misunderstanding, either because of vagueness in wording or because announcements are unaccompanied by preliminary figures.

Lack of the figures, it was pointed out, might establish a false market in the shares until the figures become known.

SS MEN BATTLING FOR DOOMED BUDAPEST

THE Germans yesterday flung crack S.S. troops—the best they have on the Hungarian front—into the battle of Budapest.

These troops, sworn to defend the southern gateway of the Reich to the death, are the last defence of a doomed city.

The Red Army, less than six miles from the city, are steadily closing in on three sides, and the dourly resisting Germans are being pushed back on to a city already ablaze from bombs, shell-fire, and demolitions.

The Russians are fighting their hardest battle for several weeks. Tanks and guns hoarded for this action have been flung into the line by the Germans, and the Luftwaffe has been called up to try to stem the Soviet advance.

North-west of Budapest a new threat is building up for the Germans, as Red Army men rapidly advance towards the Bratislava Gap—the gateway to Vienna. Moscow officially recorded advances of 1½ and six miles on this sector last night.

16,800 Airmen Hit the Reich

300 MILES OF PLANES

MIGHTIEST Allied air armada of the war—including 1,600 U.S. Fortresses and Liberators—swept over the Reich yesterday to hit German supply centres behind the Western Front.

Never before has the British-based U.S. Eighth Air Force sent so many heavy bombers on one mission.

More than 800 fighters screened this vast force, which carried 16,800 airmen into battle—equivalent of more than an infantry division.

In five great formations they rumbled over the English coast towards the Rhineland, making a column of aircraft 300 miles long.

Over Germany, Forts and Liberators split into three main forces to smash railyards at Frankfort, Giessen, and Hanau, all of which feed the German armies from Cologne to the Saar.

Luftwaffe fighters stayed on the ground and flak was meagre. Twelve bombers and two fighters were lost.

Earlier, R.A.F. Lancasters and Mosquitoes flew to the Ruhr to hit marshalling yards and an oil plant at Osterfeld and oil plants at Meiderich and Bruckhausen. One bomber is missing.

Italy-based heavy bombers of the U.S. 15th Air Force pounded targets in Vienna, an oil refinery at Moosierbaum, 22 miles away, and the railyards at Graz, 100 miles to the south.

HODGES MOPS UP ON ROER

From **JOHN HALL**
U.S. FIRST ARMY, Monday.

SIX more miles of the Roer river are under American control to-night. The last Germans clinging to the western bank of the river between Duren and Julich have only a toe-hold.

Duren, last big bastion before Cologne, has clearly been "written

BACK PAGE—Col FIVE

Howe Leads New Fleet in Pacific

Australia Provides British Base

From Daily Mail Correspondent
MELBOURNE, Monday.

ADMIRAL Sir Bruce Fraser, newly appointed C.-in-C. of the British Pacific Fleet, announced on his arrival here to-day that his flagship will be H.M.S. Howe, the 35,000-tons King George V. class battleship.

His augmented fleet, he said, will include battleships, aircraft-carriers, cruisers, destroyers, corvettes, and other vessels, as well as Australian warships.

The Australian ships include four "N" class and two "Q" class destroyers, and two minesweeping flotillas.

The Australian cruisers which have been in action in the Philippines will remain under the command of General MacArthur.

Australian ratings and pilots from the R.A.A.F. also would join his fleet.

Admiral Fraser could not say how the Pacific Fleet would be used until he had conferred with Admiral Chester Nimitz, American C.-in-C in the Pacific, under whom the Combined Forces of the United Nations in the Pacific will operate.

★

HIS administrative H.Q. will be in Melbourne and Sydney. The battleships will dock at Sydney and the aircraft-carriers at Brisbane.

"The building up of my command" he said, "has been possible without detracting from the combat strength of the British South-East Asia Command relative to the strength of the enemy.

"I am in full accord with the American strategy of using large numbers of aircraft-carriers.

"The country with the greatest sea power must win the war. We have that sea power. The Japanese are losing theirs.

"Field-Marshal Montgomery told me that Germans between 20 and 25 are hopeless in their outlook, cannot be changed, and the only thing to do is kill them.

"The Japanese Fleet apparently has the same idea, and the only thing to do is to sink it. This we shall surely do.

"But as the Japanese Fleet goes back, the job becomes more difficult. In the end we may find ourselves island-hopping."

Admiral Fraser said his fleet will not have to worry about any food problem. The fleet simply came to Australia and the food was waiting. The value of this assistance was tremendous.

★

PAYING a tribute to the "little ships" of the Royal Navy, he said he did not think even the Russians realise the great effort put forward by the British Navy, particularly the little ships.

"Every month last winter," he said, "we pushed through a convoy of 35 ships, which carried thousands of aircraft and motor vehicles, and thousands of tons of stores.

"In the pitch darkness of the northern waters, we met hot opposition. Some corvettes and destroyers were sunk and in those icy waters men could not live for five minutes."

Admiral Fraser got busy soon after his arrival. He conferred with the Navy Board, and will fly to Canberra on Wednesday for talks with the Australian War Cabinet before he sees Admiral Nimitz.

The Acting Prime Minister, Mr. Forde, announced to-day that at the request of the British Government, the Australian Government had undertaken to provide by next June services and supplies estimated to cost not less than £21,000,000.

This was in addition to similar needs totalling £110,000,000 to be provided this financial year for the United States in the South-West Pacific area.

"The Australian people," he added, "will give the members of the Royal Navy their most cordial greetings. Already in some capitals organisations have prepared clubs and entertainment facilities for the 'British invasion.'"

Jap Naval C-in-C Killed in Raid

Admiral Chiuchi Nagumo, Supreme Commander of the Japanese naval forces in the Central Pacific, and Commander of the force which attacked Pearl Harbour, was killed last July in an American attack on the island of Saipan, the Japanese News Agency said yesterday.—*Reuter.*

MAURA GOING TO SPAIN BORDER

Paris, Monday.—Miguel Maura, Spanish Republican leader, who hopes to unseat Franco, is leaving for the Pyrenees to-morrow to await the result of the crisis in Spain.—B.U.P.

PATCH LINKS WITH PATTON

Alsace, Monday.—General Patch's Seventh Army has linked up with General Patton's Third south of the German frontier.—Reuter.

2

PINPOINT RAID ON V2 TOWN

Every Bomb Hit

Picked pilots of a Spitfire bomber squadron made a power-dive blitz from 8,000ft. up on a V2 target yesterday—and beat their own record for pin-point accuracy

Every bomb hit the narrow target—a railway station and sidings in a thickly populated Dutch town, where V2 supply trains unload.

Elsewhere in Holland other Spitfire bombers attacked launching sites and other rocket targets.

Wreckage of rockets intended for England litters the ground at Leiden, just north of the Hague. A whole wing of Typhoon fighter-bombers swooped on a V2 train on Sunday and plastered it with 1,000lb. H.E. and 500lb. incendiaries.

Daily Mail

LATE WAR NEWS

NO. 15,175 ONE PENNY ** FOR KING AND EMPIRE THURSDAY, DECEMBER 21, 1944

25-MILE GAP IN ALLIED LINE

Crisis Hour of Rundstedt's Drive Near

HAND-TO-HAND BATTLE IN ARDENNES FOG

General Hodges was fighting hard last night to narrow the 25-miles gap torn in the U.S. First Army lines. The Germans are using up to 15 divisions—250,000 men six of them panzers, the rest Volksgrenadier.

From **JOHN HALL**, Daily Mail Special Correspondent EUPEN, Wednesday Night.

FIELD-MARSHAL VON RUNDSTEDT is trying to exploit the surprise advantages he has gained. He began the process by lashing out with armour and waves of infantry, both at the northern and southern shoulders of the offensive. All this is going on in "Hitler weather."

Heavy fog enshrouds the entire forward area. In fact, it seems to envelop the whole of Western Germany. Everything but the flying bombs aimed at our communication lines has been grounded.

The general picture is a little less unsettling, but gives no grounds for complacency. While he thrusts at the shoulders, the enemy has his "wild-cat columns" ranging westwards.

The northern prong appears to me to have been aimed at reaching towards the River Meuse, a few miles south of Liége. It has been checked. Only small units have been located near Stavelot.

There are indications that the drive is not keeping up to the time-table that planned it as a break-through. But not much importance can be attached to early failures. Every battle is a chapter of things which do not go "according to plan."

My view of a still very much confused situation is that the critical hours are fast approaching. Here we are neither pessimistic nor complacent.

Every hour General Bradley ties a little more strength into his lines. It is a cursed lot—or probably excellent forecasting by the German weather experts—that we were unable to use our air superiority.

Visibility has varied from 30 to 200 yards, but rarely more than that.

Rundstedt has thrown many divisions into this attempted break-through, and has probably a good many more available in reserve if his gamble comes off.

Only details I am allowed to report are scant—for security reasons. The Hun made his first effort to push up the shoulder of his offensive, attacking east of Malmedy.

There, paratroop infantry, supported by a force of Royal Tiger tanks, tried to dislodge American troops on a ridge. They were met by heavy fire, and there was hand-to-hand fighting in the swirling mists.

DAWN ATTACK

At dawn, with this battle still going on, the Huns launched another thrust along the northern shoulder near Stavelot, which is six miles south of Spa.

Both were full-scale attacks and were made with grim determination. American artillery saturated both areas with tremendous cannonades.

To get a general idea of what is happening along the outer fringes of the offensive, picture the rolling forest country of the Ardennes, swathed in mist, and innumerable wooded roads connecting with the great north-south roads lying through Bastogne.

It is mostly along secondary connecting roads that the Hun tank units are "wild-catting." Mostly, they are operating in small forces, four tanks and five or six armoured cars, with half a dozen armoured cars carrying infantry.

GUERILLAS OUT

Some of these columns have been using American tanks and vehicles and carrying the Allied white star marking. We have four authenticated instances of the Wehrmacht soldiers being in civilian clothes, posing as Belgian civilians and then suddenly producing "burp" guns and shooting up American command posts.

One party of paratroops in civilian clothes were on bicycles and were posing as forest workers.

I have been impressed by the way the Belgian Resistance Movement has rallied to arms again. They came out as soon as the offensive began.

Inadequately armed and invariably without steel helmets, they have helped as guides, tracking enemy units and taking part in the fighting.

MONSCHAU OURS

News agency reports of the battle last night stated:

AMERICAN troops have recaptured Monschau, two miles inside Germany, from where the Germans began their northernmost thrust towards Liége.

The town, 16 miles south-east of Aachen, was retaken after the German garrison had been surrounded.

Panzers are officially reported to have been checked short of St. Vith, although, in the thrust up from the south, they reached the village of Maspelt, four miles below St. Vith.

In the extreme southern part of the enemy drive German units which crossed into Luxemburg near Echternach have been surrounded.

Earlier reports said a major German penetration had been made in the Eifel Forest region east of St. Vith. Some American troops were encircled and the Germans advanced 20 miles.

Every type of unit in the German Army is fighting here—S.S. troops, regulars, panzer forces, and Volks-grenadier divisions.

THE ENEMY SAYS—

12 Miles from Liége

GERMAN spearheads are within 12 miles of Liége, according to the Berlin correspondent of the Stockholm *Aftonbladet*.

Captain Sertorius, Berlin military commentator, said last night: "Eisenhower has thrown his forces into the sector where the main German pressure is exerted.

"But Rundstedt, who holds the initiative, can always shift the focal points of his offensive.

"The battle has not yet reached its climax by a long way. New, bitter battles will be fought, and the first offensive phase will be quickly followed by other momentous operations.

"We must be prepared for an Eisenhower plan—that is, we must expect Eisenhower to abandon all his offensive plans in the north and south and concentrate all his available forces on the centre of the Western front."

The German News Agency last night claimed that Allied divisions have been rushed from both the Aachen and Saar fronts to hold Rundstedt's offensive. It added: "Three to four Allied divisions have been either destroyed or badly mauled."

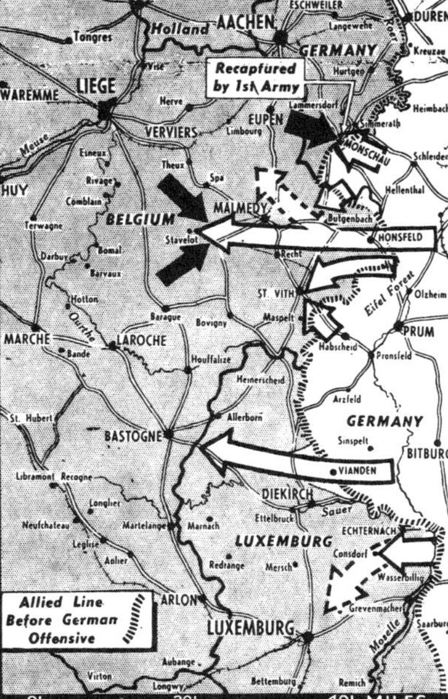

CLIFFORD SAYS:

It May Be the Last Big Battle

If We Hold Them

From **ALEXANDER CLIFFORD**, Daily Mail Special Correspondent

WESTERN FRONT, Wednesday.

IN the suddenly quickened atmosphere of the Western Front ideas are having to be revised.

An army that was supposed to be beaten has suddenly launched a blitz. And it needs explaining.

I am afraid it means handing some bouquets to the Germans. But we should not balk at that. This very counter-offensive of Rundstedt's has shown again the need for estimating your enemy correctly.

The fact of the counter-offensive has instilled vigorous new life into the campaign after the disappointment of Arnhem and the long-puzzling, tedious slog through the autumn mud. The origins of it need explaining.

But the sheer fact of it has set the air aquiver with possibilities—the possibility that we might lose a lot and the possibility that this might be the last battle of all.

That second possibility is the one that emerges most strongly from this new situation. After three days you can diagnose Rundstedt's effort as so supreme that it is almost certainly unrepeatable.

If we win this, it may not mean the immediate end of the war, but it might easily mean we should never need to fight another battle.

★

SPEAKING from the point of view of the average well-informed soldier out here, this German effort really has been a surprise.

We did know — it was all published three weeks ago—that the enemy had been swiftly creating new utility divisions. We knew he had strong new panzer formations up his sleeve waiting for an opportunity to use them. But few people expected anything quite like this.

After all, we had been winning all along the line from Normandy to the Rhine. We practically won the war in August and September. The Germans, through all that time, had barely been able to launch one serious counter-blow against us. Judging by previous form, it seemed hardly likely they would be able to launch one now.

Perhaps, on the basis of the past six months, we have tended to over-estimate the inherent weakness of the Wehrmacht. For their defeat from Normandy to the Rhine has not been a story of continuous gradual collapse. It has been the story of one tremendous collapse resulting from one enormous blunder.

That blunder, oddly enough, was the Germans' one attempt at a serious counter-offensive—when they tried to break back through to the sea at Avranches, between Normandy and Brittany, and split the Americans in two.

★

AND that did not look like a blunder to anybody when it started. It was simply a good gamble which failed, and in military science a gamble which fails is a blunder.

The result of that failure was the immediate loss of France, Belgium, and half Holland. The Wehrmacht seemed completely broken. The war looked won.

The Germans made a supreme effort of improvisation at Arnhem—which must always remain a brilliant victory for them. They got sufficient control of the situation to hold the rest of the front along the great rivers and the prepared defences. They made no more great mistakes.

And behind the scenes they prepared the great recuperative gesture which they are making now. They scraped together everything good they had.

Their modified Tiger tanks began trickling in from the factories. New and improved guns and mortars equipped the freshly trained panzer divisions. Husky youths fresh from school, with a background of tough Hitler-Jugend training, came into the line.

A brand new and militarily magnificent spearhead was fitted into the old, tired Wehrmacht.

★

IT was got into position with great stealth and with remarkable organisation.

All our tremendous bombing has not been able to prevent this army getting equipped. All our rail interdiction and attacks on communications have not prevented men and

BACK PAGE—Col. SEVEN

'Saw-Tank' Cuts Through Forests

THE Americans are now using a "saw-tank" in the West, said the German radio last night. These new tanks, mentioned for the first time by either side, cut a way through dense forests for infantry and armour.

Censure Threat for Govt. on Greece

By **WILSON BROADBENT**, Political Correspondent

MR. ANEURIN BEVAN last night threatened the Government with a vote of censure when Parliament reassembles after the Christmas recess on January 16 if the situation in Greece has not improved by then.

He declared that he and his friends would table the motion even if the Labour Party leaders refused to do so officially.

This was the only result of the emergency debate demanded of the Government by the Labour Party, in spite of the efforts of the extremists to impart some heat to the discussion.

The debate was most unsatisfactory, for it did nothing to resolve the cleavage of opinion existing in the House of Commons and the country.

Mr. Anthony Eden was most earnest in his effort to convince the Labour Party that the aims of the Government were in accordance with their expressed desires, but he failed to do so.

As Leader of the Labour Party, Mr. Arthur Greenwood went out of his way to be moderate in the expression of his views, and showed quite clearly that he had no desire to embarrass the Government.

The Prime Minister was absent from the debate, which did not attract a large attendance of members, and ended without a division.

Report.—Page THREE.

Sforza's 'No' to U.S. Post

ROME, Wednesday.—Count Sforza, who was offered the post of Ambassador in Washington in October, and whose nomination was approved by the United States, has refused to accept. He told Signor Bonomi, the Italian Premier, he would "greatly regret if my arrival there gave rise to new dissensions."—*Reuter.*

Two Nazi Officers Caught at Dockside

Stowaway Plan

By Daily Mail Reporter

TWO German Army officers, escaped prisoners, were recaptured in Liverpool Docks yesterday as they were about to smuggle aboard a vessel leaving the country.

They belonged to a party of 13 officers who escaped from a prison camp 85 miles away at Teddesley, near Penkridge, Staffordshire, on Monday night.

All but one of the men, a Luftwaffe lieutenant, have now been recaptured Squads of armed police Service men, and civilians were last night scouring the Midlands countryside for this thirteenth man.

The astuteness of a policeman led to the recapture of the two Germans in Liverpool Docks.

Noticing a movement behind some packages, he suspected pilferers Going to the spot he found the two Germans, who gave themselves up.

'Bad Nazis'

They are believed to have stolen a lift to Liverpool under the tarpaulin of a slow-moving lorry.

The 13 Germans—ten Army officers, two Luftwaffe lieutenants, and a merchant seaman—officially described as "typical bad Nazi types," made their break under cover of mist just after midnight, cutting through the barbed wire surrounding the camp after patrolling guards had passed.

After nearly 24 hours of freedom two were recaptured in the Wolverhampton area and two others in Walsall.

Six others were caught at Derby yesterday. Four of them were in a car, stolen at Burton-on-Trent, which had run out of petrol.

The missing Luftwaffe lieutenant, Heinrich Okrent, is aged 28, 5ft. 6in. tall, and stockily built, has dark hair, and was wearing blue-grey uniform with, possibly, chocolate-coloured trousers.

Another Break

While police were searching for him yesterday came news of yet another break—from Lodge Moor Camp, Sheffield, early yesterday—of seven German rankers.

Last night six were still at large. The seventh was found lying injured outside the camp barricade.

Meanwhile, hunger and cold are likely to complete the work of the military and civilian police parties seeking the eight Italian Fascists still at liberty after the mass escape of 97 prisoners from Doonfoot Camp, Ayr, last Friday night.

PM PROMISES STATEMENT

BOAC Allegations

A statement dealing with allegations made by Mr. Austen Hopkinson, M.P., against the administration of the British Overseas Airways Corporation will be made in the House of Commons after the Christmas recess.

Mr. Churchill, announcing this yesterday, said the matter would receive the direct attention of the Government.

A motion asking that a Select Committee be set up to investigate Mr. Hopkinson's allegations was tabled in the House last night by Mr. Moelwyn Hughes, K.C.

'Bevin Summons' for 127 Strikers

The Ministry of Labour is taking proceedings against the 127 boiler-makers at Vickers-Armstrong's naval yard on the Tyne who refused to resume work yesterday. The cases will be heard, it is expected, on Boxing Day.

Telegrams were sent by Mr. Bevin to these men on Monday, instructing them to return to work yesterday. Yesterday the men offered to work on a time basis, but refused to return on piece rates as ordered.

'Korda and I to Part,' says Merle

HOLLYWOOD, Wednesday.—Merle Oberon (Lady Korda) is to start divorce proceedings against Sir Alexander Korda, the film producer, it was announced in Hollywood to-day. They were married in June 1939.

"The parting is amicable," said Miss Oberon. "We have seen each other only a few times in the past two years."—*B.U.P.*

BARONESS DEFIED RIBBENTROP IN LONDON

'Gestapo Threatened Me in Their Embassy

ENGAGEMENT DRAMA

By Daily Mail Reporter

MRS. WALTER SCOTT-ELLIOT, former Austrian Baroness Maria Alice von Groeller, told me last night how she was the victim, before the war, of Gestapo threats in this country.

The story of the Baroness and her husband, Captain Walter Scott-Elliot, a former Coldstream Guards officer and Scottish land-owner, was told by Viscount St. Davids, without mentioning their names, in the House of Lords yesterday.

Lord St. Davids said that when the Baroness, who was at that time employed at the German Embassy, announced her engagement, she was "hauled in front of the Ambassador."

Then, he said, she was threatened that, unless she broke off her engagement, she would either be murdered or drugged, and her body smuggled out of the country in the diplomatic bag.

I saw Mrs. Scott-Elliot, an attractive woman of 34, while she was travelling to her husband's home at Arkleton, Dumfriesshire, last night.

"It is true," she said, "that I was called before the Ambassador, von Ribbentrop, at the time of my engagement, but the story of what took place is not quite as Lord St. Davids has told it.

'Taken Back'

"Von Ribbentrop told me that unless the engagement was broken off reprisals would take place against my family in Austria, especially against my brother, who was then 26 and of military age. What has happened to him I do not know.

"Eventually, he said that I would be taken back to Germany in some way or other."

Her husband, the baroness added, made arrangements to ensure that no attempt was made to kidnap her.

Mrs. Scott-Elliot said she came to England in 1929 to go to school and had not returned to Austria

BACK PAGE—Col. THREE

MRS. SCOTT-ELLIOT Ribbentrop threatened reprisals.

Capt. WALTER SCOTT-ELLIOT Prevented kidnapping attempt.

Our Rations May Be Cut

To Save Shipping

Daily Mail Special Corresponder

NEW YORK, Wednesday.

BRITAIN'S rations may be cut to enable vital U.S. cargoes to reach and rehabilitate Europe.

The offer has been made by Britain's Minister of State, Richard Law, now conferring with State Secretary Stettinius in Washington on the shipping space crisis.

Mr. Law has offered to cut down on Britain's imports in foodstuffs to relieve the pressure, it was disclosed in Washington to-day.

The suggestion, offered primarily as an illustration of the vital need for sending food, clothing, and machinery into such countries as Holland and Belgium, may result in the cancellation of Britain's shipments of eggs from Canada. Fruits may be definitely ruled off the British shipping lists for a further six months.

It is believed certain that if the United States is to agree to release more shipping for rehabilitation work, Britain must take a cut in foodstuffs, at least for the next six months.

The New Shipping Crisis.—BACK Page.

FINNS TO PAY £75,000,000

Finland will deliver £75,000,000 worth of goods to Russia to pay for losses caused by the Finns on Russian territory during the war, according to Moscow radio.—B.U.P.

BATTLE ON LEYTE NEARING END

Gen. MacArthur's H.Q., Leyte, Wednesday.—The Japanese Yamashita defence line has been destroyed and the battle for Leyte Island is rapidly nearing its end, according to to-day's communiqué.—Reuter.

Careless Talk: Grave New Warning

By Daily Mail Reporter

A NEW and graver warning against careless talk will shortly be issued by the security authorities. The step has been made imperative by a great increase in careless talk in Britain and on the Continent following the liberation of France, Belgium, and the Balkans.

M.I.5, whose function it is to track down spies, is overwhelmed with work. The Germans left behind many agents in the liberated countries.

Up to D-Day secrets were carefully kept. The Continent was a closed book. Now Service men are passing backwards and forwards across the Channel continuously, and a limited form of travel has been opened up for civilians.

Many Service men are returning to civilian life, and are revealing information to their families and friends which is causing anxiety.

Already, in a number of instances, valuable military information has been revealed in this country by returning Service men.

But the security authorities are more concerned about the secrets revealed inadvertently by travellers who are given facilities to see military dispositions.

They are also concerned about the opening of hotels in the south coast areas previously banned to all travellers.

Careful 'Vetting'

And they may insist that ex-Service men and women who are being taken on by the Civil Service after demobilisation should be carefully vetted before they are given jobs of high responsibility.

London might easily become a maze of espionage and counter-espionage activities, it is feared. In addition to our own Intelligence system, no fewer than eight Allied Governments are based here, each with its own staff of agents.

The work of these agents has become complicated by the extension of their activities from the purely military to the political field.

The authorities have been forced to increase their staffs with men who have particular knowledge of the many complications in European countries.

ELAS MEN ARE QUITTING ATTICA

WITHIN a few hours of General Scobie's warning that the all-out assault on E.L.A.S. strongholds will begin at 9 a.m. to-day, E.L.A.S. loud-speakers began yesterday to announce that the guerillas "will soon" withdraw from Attica.

Only "reserve troops," it was said, "will surrender their arms"—a suggestion that General Scobie's terms for peace are to be accepted

General Scobie's warning said that any insurgent guns in Athens or the Piræus still firing at nine this morning will be attacked by all the forces at his disposal.

These, he warned include land artillery, Naval guns rockets and bombs.

The bombardment will go on until the guns are destroyed, and leaflets were showered on Athens warning civilians to keep clear of the gun sites.

The political situation in Athens remains unchanged, and a statement on the position of King George of Greece over the Regency question is still awaited.

John Rallis, quisling Premier who escaped from custody when the Averoff Prison was stormed by E.L.A.S., was rearrested in Athens yesterday.

After 48 hours' liberty he asked the police to take him into custody—presumably because he feared an attempt on his life by E.L.A.S.—*Daily Mail Correspondent, Reuter, and B.U.P.*

Women Storm R.A.F. H.Q.: BACK Page.

Daily Mail

LATE WAR NEWS

NO. 15,177 ONE PENNY FOR KING AND EMPIRE SATURDAY, DECEMBER 23, 1944

RUNDSTEDT'S PANZER THRUST IS 30 MILES FROM SEDAN

Berlin Claims Meuse Reached and Battling Round Liége

GERMAN spearheads were last night reported within 20 miles of the Meuse and more than 40 miles into Belgium. These forces, presumably, are the units which Berlin says are across the River Ourthe west of St. Vith. They are within striking distance of Namur, Allied bastion on the west bank of the Meuse.

Rundstedt's main drive now appears to be switched southward towards the Bastogne area, where considerable enemy progress is believed to have been made, says Ronald Clark, B.U.P. War Correspondent. Here a big tank battle is raging in a snowstorm south-west of St. Vith, with panzers milling all round the rim of the salient on the U.S. First Army front. Heavy casualties have occurred among the German armour.

After seven days of fierce fighting there are indications only from the northern side of the gap, in the Malmédy sector, that the drive has lost some of its momentum. More than 200 panzers are reported destroyed in this area.

At the southern end of the offensive the Germans have cut right through Luxemburg past Wiltz, by-passed Bastogne, and reached a point little more than 30 miles from Sedan, SHAEF announced last night.

Captain Sertorius, Berlin military commentator, claimed last night that British reinforcements had been thrown in from Field-Marshal Montgomery's grouping. "Powerless to put a frontal stop to our surge," he said, "the Allies are pressing against the northern flank."

Earlier, Berlin said Montgomery had talked with Eisenhower and other Army leaders at an undisclosed place on the front.

Berlin claimed last night that German troops were fighting in the southern suburbs of Liége and that other forces had reached the Meuse. But the Germans admitted that Patton's Third Army attack on the southern flank had slowed down the advance against the First Army

2 a.m. Map

THIS map, showing the latest positions, will help you follow developments until the Daily Mail is published again next Wednesday.

Clifford Cables: Worse Before It's Better

From **ALEXANDER CLIFFORD,** Daily Mail Special Correspondent

WESTERN FRONT, Friday.

THE great sprawling battle of the Ardennes grows in intensity. Even now there is no possibility at all of tracing its outline. And as often as not the capture or loss of any particular village has a meaning you could never guess from the map.

The size and untidiness of what is happening makes all generalisation dangerous. But some things are emerging clearly.

One is that the force of the German drive is not yet spent. Another is that the Germans may have more reserves up their sleeves. So, the climax has not yet been reached.

We must, at all costs, avoid the blind and wishful thinking of 1940. We must admit that this armoured offensive which Rundstedt has suddenly produced out of the hat is one of really great strength and really good quality.

It is almost certainly as big a punch as Germany can possibly pack to-day. But it is still a very big punch.

MORE ADVANCES

Therefore, it is virtually certain that things must get worse before they can get better. As they lunge around from the edges of their salients the Germans will gain more ground. And we cannot rely on their making any mistakes.

It is still true that this is a chance for us. The Germans are fighting us to-day without benefit of minefields, fortifications, and defensive rivers. Obviously, it is easier to defeat an army in the field than in a Siegfried Line.

But, at the same time, the Germans have the initiative. They have concentrated their forces and chosen the time and place. They have hand-picked the advantages for themselves. We cannot possibly meet them on equal terms from the first minute.

We have to have time and space to bring our counter-measures into effect. That has been going on for the past week. It is still going on to-day.

The big and little roads of Belgium are filled with military traffic. Tanks and guns and every type of lorry are threading their way to the place appointed for them in what looks like chaos, but is, in fact, an intricately arranged plan.

The traffic is moving with admirable speed and smoothness—I checked that on miles of greasy highways to-day. And it gives an impression of immense strength.

Of course, we have immense strength. We could not have got

BACK PAGE—Col. THREE

HALL SAYS:

Spitfires in the Fight Again

From **JOHN HALL**

U.S. FIRST ARMY, Friday.

OVERALL picture of this battle improves hourly, though it is still too early to be over-optimistic. To-day the weather let up a little and we were able to use our air arm.

Sunshine dispelled mist late this afternoon, and I watched six R.A.F. Spitfires racing into the thick of the battle at tree-top height. I heard their cannon spitting a few moments after they had shot overhead.

With any luck at all we may be able to throw in heavy air support to-morrow, and if that happens I foresee reassuring news for Christmas.

If I could tell you the full story of the Allied co-operation that is going on here you would be amazed. Those Spitfires I saw this afternoon were only a part of the dovetail counter-measures.

'Aim Has Failed'

Along much of the break-through area we now have solid lines. All Rundstedt's efforts to push open the shoulders have failed.

Prisoners taken to-day have been gloomy about the operation. They said frankly that it is not going anything like so well as expected.

They admit that their aim to split the American First Army has failed. "The surprise element has gone," they said. "Now we are having to pay for everything in blood."

These prisoners were still shocked at the sight of their own dead piled by the roadsides.

The clearing mist to-day has uncovered grim spectacles on this battlefield—bodies in orderly lines as if they had been shot to pieces in parade formation. The cost for us has not been light.

Fighting Mad

More and more cases have been reported of Hun "wild-cat" columns shooting American prisoners—under the pretext that the GIs defied orders, but really because they had no means of sending them back to the German lines.

The stories of these atrocities have gone round this front and have made the Americans fighting mad.

Battle incidents given to me by the men involved show the ferocity of the fighting and the slaughter we have made of Rundstedt's tanks.

In one area a break in the front disclosed between 25 and 30 Hun tanks lying crippled and finished. They had been knocked out mostly by artillery and lay twisted and

BACK PAGE—Col. EIGHT

GERMAN RADIO TELLS BELGIANS TO FLEE

A NEW enemy radio station began broadcasting to Belgians yesterday afternoon, urging them to leave their homes "before you are slain by the onrushing Germans."

This "advice" was obviously intended to complicate the Allies' task by glutting the roads with civilians.

"Leave your homes and flee," said the announcer. "Take shelter farther inland. Do not stay in your towns and villages.

"German armies are using horrifying new weapons. Not a single human being will remain alive in sectors where these weapons will be used."—*A.P.*

The blocking of roads by civilian refugees was a favourite trick of the Germans in their great Western offensive of 1940.

Göring even issued an Order of the Day instructing the Luftwaffe to do their utmost to create chaos and panic among the helpless civil population.

Daily Mail Again on Wednesday

THE next copy of *The Daily Mail* will be in its readers' hands on Wednesday, December 27.

The Daily Mail, in common with other national newspapers, will not be published on Monday (Christmas Day) or Tuesday (Boxing Day).

But this does not mean that the great organisation which produces your favourite newspaper stands still.

The Daily Mail's war correspondents will be at their posts covering the scene of the new German offensive as they cover every other battle-front in the world.

Daily Mail cameramen, too, will be out during Christmas chronicling the news of the moment at home and overseas.

Their work will be ceaseless. And the fruits of their labours will be in your hands in

WEDNESDAY'S DAILY MAIL.

Roosevelt: War's End Not Yet in Sight

From **DON IDDON,** Daily Mail Correspondent

NEW YORK, Friday.

PRESIDENT ROOSEVELT to-day declared emphatically that the end of the war against Germany is not yet in sight. Declining to comment on the German offensive, the President said there can be no change in America's war expenditure until Germany is finally defeated.

The President reminded his Press conference that he was one of the few people who had never predicted when the war would be won.

He said the best way the fighting men could be assisted on the home front was by people sticking to the jobs which maintain a steady output of needed supplies.

The President insisted that he could give no comment on the German offensive, and that any expression by him would be as one coming from a single individual.

He said he knew very little more about the status of the German offensive than was in the news dispatches from the front, which give events up to Tuesday or Wednesday.

Mr. Roosevelt had nothing to add regarding a meeting with Churchill and Stalin.

Discussing the Atlantic Charter, he authorised the following quotation: "The objectives of the Atlantic Charter are as valid as when they were announced in 1941."

U.S. Asks "Why Weren't We Warned?"—BACK Page.

Rundstedt is Firing 'V1½'

May be a Shell

FROM all accounts now heard the Germans' new secret weapon unveiled for the benefit of Rundstedt's push is likely to be classified not as V3 or V4, but V1½.

It is apparently a barrage weapon and it probably takes the form of a long-range shell.

The other secret weapons most frequently mentioned in dispatches from the Continent now are the mysterious silver balls seen floating over the lines.

Their purpose would probably be tied up with the now elaborate German anti-aircraft measures. It is worth noting, therefore, that there has been no sign, so far, of any significant increase in Allied aircraft losses.

Beer May Run Out

There is not enough beer in some parts of the country to last over the holiday.

A leading brewer said last night that many public-houses would have to close on Christmas Day and part of Boxing Day.

French Ratify Pact

PARIS, Friday. — The Franco-Soviet Pact, drawn up during General de Gaulle's visit to Moscow, was formally ratified by the French Assembly in Paris to-day.—*B.U.P.*

MAN-POWER 'JOLT' FOR NATION

250,000 More Men Called Up

BIG SERVICE TRANSFER

By **WILSON BROADBENT,** Political Correspondent

THE War Cabinet announced from No. 10, Downing-street last night that an additional 250,000 front-line troops are to be called up for training from civil life or transferred from other services immediately.

This decision is the result of continuous Ministerial consultations which have taken place since the new German offensive was launched on the Western Front. Last night's announcement said:

In order to sustain and nourish our armies in the line, H.M. Government has decided to make available in the coming months additional fighting men.

A large part will be found by a new call-up from civil life. Some will be obtained by transfer to the Army from the Navy and R.A.F.

More will be found from the Army itself by further combing-out and reclaiming of units and individuals who have hitherto been engaged in static forms of defence or in the administrative services.

The total to be provided above previous plans will amount to a quarter of a million men.

Of course, it is true to say that it would have been necessary for such a new call-up, or comb-out, in view of the plans now being made for the war against Japan as well as the demands which will be made on Britain to join with Soviet Russia and the United States in providing armies of occupation for Germany.

It is estimated in unofficial but expert quarters that the British Army of Occupation which will be required when Germany is defeated will number at least 250,000.

HURRIED ON

Obviously, however, whatever the Government may have had in mind regarding the organisation of man-power must have been hurried by recent events. And the Premier's recent forecast of heavy fighting in the near future will be recalled.

At all times the Army, particularly, has been short of men, while in the other Services there have been, in some cases, more than have been necessary.

The decision to call up more men for front-line duty, therefore, is only part of a general tightening-up of the military machine.

It means that many young men who had selected the Navy or Air Force in preference to any other Service will find themselves in the Army.

Even men who have been in the Navy or Air Force from the early

BACK PAGE—Col. SEVEN

DRY AND COLD SNAP SOON: STRAIT CLEAR

A BIG improvement in the weather in the Strait yesterday, with the wind changing to the north-east and the barometer on the rise, may indicate that a drier and colder period is coming.

In the afternoon the French coast could be clearly seen, and at night there was bright moonlight, with the temperature at 40 degrees.

CAR LAMPS WILL BE UNMASKED

Safer Roads in Brighter Light

Daily Mail Motoring Correspondent

THE battle of the dim-out has been won by the motorists. They are to receive a Christmas present of brighter lights.

Motor vehicles will be permitted to use full headlamps without masks. January 1 is the probable date of the start of this reform.

The present regulation, which was introduced early in the war, has contributed heavily to road deaths.

Motoring and even pedestrian organisations have been protesting against it.

Tests carried out by *The Daily Mail* proved that the new dim-out lighting was a greater road menace than the complete black-out because pools of light neutralised illumination from masked headlights.

It is contended that better street lighting, or more lighting on cars, is one of the possible solutions of the problem of black-out accidents.

GRACIE FIELDS' FATHER ILL

Back from America

Gracie Fields's father, Mr. Fred Stansfield, who returned from America with his wife yesterday, was taken from the boat to Walton Hospital, Liverpool, suffering from pneumonia, and was given M. and B.

Late last night he was stated to be very ill. People who knew Gracie's parents before she became famous waited anxiously for news of her father's condition.

Mr. and Mrs. Stansfield have been with Gracie in America since the early days of the war.

Sit-down Strike is Ended

The sit-down strike of 500 employees at the factory of Ariel Motors, Bournbrook, Birmingham, ended yesterday. It began last Saturday.

Mr. J. Y. Sangster, managing director, told a full staff meeting of provisions to safeguard them in the sale of the share capital to the B.S.A. Company, which had been completed. With four exceptions, the men decided to resume work after Christmas.

HG is Treated as Civilian

A Home Guard in uniform hurt while giving assistance at a bomb incident will not get the compensation he would have had before the stand down. He will be treated as a civilian.

This is the interpretation to be placed on a letter from London District H.Q. Home Guard, which says: "Any help given to police or Civil Defence Services will be civilian compensation."

Russians Launch Latvia Drive

Soviet forces have begun a great new offensive to clear the Germans from Latvia before the opening of a fresh attack on East Prussia, the Germans announced last night.

Last night's Soviet communiqué made no reference to the Latvia attack, but reported gains east of Luceme, in Czecho-Slovakia, and north and north-west of Gyongyos in Hungary.

Attempt on Terboven

Daily Mail Special Correspondent

STOCKHOLM, Friday.—An attempt has been made to blow up the train in which Reich Commissioner for Norway Terboven was travelling, it is reported from Oslo. The attempt failed.

Harry Langdon Dead

LOS ANGELES, Friday.—Harry Langdon, veteran comedian of the stage and screen, died to-day, aged 60, after an illness lasting several weeks.—*A.P.*

SHELTER THREAT IS OVER

To be Open Even if Strike Starts

By Daily Mail Reporter

THOUSANDS of homeless Londoners — men, women, and children — went to sleep happily in Tube shelters last night after Underground maintenance staffs had given a pledge that even if the threatened Christmas strike occurs the stations will not be closed.

A maintenance official at one of the shelters said last night:

"If my colleagues decide to strike on Christmas Day, we shall continue to operate facilities for the shelterers here, and that goes for all stations where shelterers may be."

The tube railmen are demanding two days' holiday for those who work on Christmas Day, but agreements between the L.P.T.B. and the two unions involved provides for only one day in lieu of Christmas Day.

Christmas travel arrangements will be chaotic if the strike begins. London busmen have already stated that they do not intend to work later than 4 p.m., the agreed finishing time, whatever the tube workers decide to do.

The Tube is the only service capable of carrying long-distance travellers between the main-line railway termini.

The unions condemned the proposed stoppage and call upon all their members to carry on.

London Transport issued a statement last night pointing out that the Christmas holiday arrangements for the staff concerned are governed by the national agreement applicable to railwaymen.

The demand for an extra day's holiday for Christmas workers cannot be considered because the labour problem is already acute.

Telegrams were sent out last night by the unions to all branches in the London area emphasising the instruction of the joint executive committees that their members on the London Underground system should report for work on Christmas Day.

Last night the men were divided on the question of strike action.

60 GERMAN TANKS SMASHED

Between 60 and 70 German tanks have been knocked out in a battle in the sector east of Malmedy, it is reported at U.S. First Army H.Q. This represents half the tank forces of a Panzer division.—Exchange.

2

TWIN GERMAN DRIVES 15 MI. FROM MEUSE

A PATRIOT
Doesn't Waste Paper—It's Too Valuable to War Effort

5¢

Journal NEW YORK American

AN AMERICAN PAPER FOR THE AMERICAN PEOPLE

Daily 5 Cents, Saturday 5 Cents in New York City; 10 Cents Elsewhere | SUNDAY, 10 Cents in New York City and 50-Mile Zone, 15 Cents Elsewhere

No. 20,800—DAILY TUESDAY, DECEMBER 26, 1944 In Two Sections—Section One

LATEST NEWS

Find TNT In Churchill Hotel

Overflow Gifts To Prolong Yule For Maimed GIs

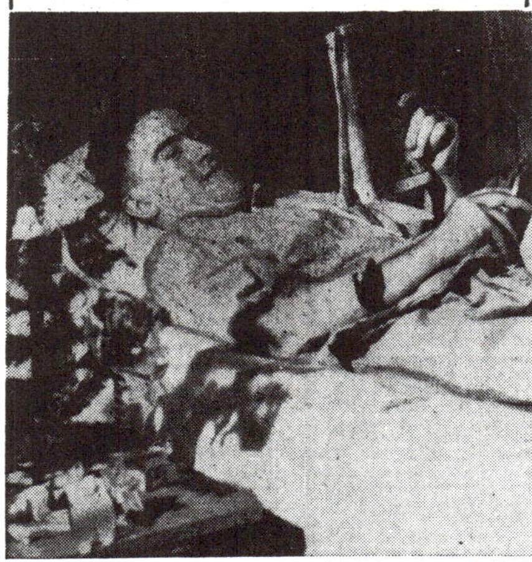

ADDED KICK . . . Pfc. Harold Cain gets a decided kick from a comic book that was among the presents he got at the Halloran Hospital through the War Wounded Christmas Fund Drive sponsored by the New York Journal-American. Overflow donations will be presented later this week to hundreds of wounded heroes now returning to this area from the fighting fronts. *(Another picture in the Pictorial Review.)* Journal-American Photo.

The promise of a real Christmas was still bright today for many hundreds of wounded and sick service men returning from the hell of European battlefronts.

For to them, at delayed Yule parties later this week, will be distributed the overflow donations of cash and gift bundles which were received too late for actual holiday use in the second N. Y. Journal-American War Wounded Christmas Fund Drive.

Altogether, between 1,500 and 2,000 bundles, and an amount of cash not yet determined, will be sent for such parties to be held at Tilton General Hospital, Fort Dix, N. J., where ambulance planes are discharged daily.

Without the largesse of a grateful New York—an open-handed generosity which made this a real Christmas once again for the hurt heroes of 17 nearby hospitals yesterday—these men would have no Christmas at all.

Assurance that every package and every cent received in the drive, no matter how late, would

Continued on Page 7, Column 6.

Butchers Shut; City Facing Meat Crisis

New York was in the grip of its worst wartime food crisis today as proprietors of 10,000 retail meat stores either shuttered their shops or began selling meat on an extremely limited basis.

Some retailers were suspending all sales, while others were following the recommendations of their leaders that they substitute a boycott of black market meat for the "holiday" voted several weeks ago.

In either case, New York's meat supplies reached a critical point and it was officially predicted that less than 10 per cent of the normal supply would be available today.

Predictions as to the number of retail stores which will remain closed varied.

WOOLLEY'S PREDICTION.

Jack Kranis, counsel for the New York City Retail Meat Dealers Committee, estimated that only 600 or 700 stores would be open.

However, Daniel P. Woolley, regional OPA administrator, predicted only 3,500 stores—about one-third of the total—would be

Continued on Page 4, Column 1.

Drop to 15° Due Today

Following a damp and dreary Christmas Day, from the standpoint of weather, sub-freezing temperatures were expected to hit the city today.

Tonight and tomorrow will be clear but increasingly cold, the local U. S. Weather Bureau predicted, wit hthe mercury down to 15 degrees in the city, and five in the suburbs.

In some parts of the State temperatures will drop below zero, according to the forecast.

Airline traffic, meanwhile, had almost ceased, with 137 flights canceled at LaGuardia Field.

Shady Racing Promoters Plan Gambling Casinos

By SYD BOEHM.

Although the above-board division of the race track industry will obey the Government's mandate to close down the tracks on Jan. 3, the racket element, more numerous and powerful than the other, already is preparing to open a vast "chain store" system of gambling casinos.

Operators of horse betting parlors in New York, Miami, New Orleans, Chicago and Los Angeles, to name a few, now are engaged in partial conversion to gambling casinos, featuring dice, chemin de fer, roulette and other games of chance.

Horse race bets will be accepted in the casinos on races run at Mexico City and Havana. Both of these tracks, due to the shutdown order in the United States, will receive hundreds of high class American thoroughbreds from Miami, New Orleans, Arcadia, Calif., and Hot Springs, Ark., where racing meets were in progress or about to commence.

In New York, according to Mayor LaGuardia, policy number betting will be stepped up to unusual proportions when many bookmakers enter the "penny ante" field.

The sweeping order by War Mobilization Director Byrnes not only closes racetracks, where some 200,000 men and women will be released from jobs, but will have a telling effect on all professional athletics.

In a letter to Maj.-Gen. Hershey, Selective Service Director, Byrnes specifically requested that the draft status of all athletes in the professional class, be reviewed.

It is difficult for the public and

Continued on Page 4, Column 2.

MADELINE DUNNIGAN
Blames Her For Plunge
Journal-American Photo.

'Robin' Employer Ends Life

By LOY WARWICK.

Death wrote a starkly tragic second chapter today in what had been the story of "Little Miss Robin Hood".

"Little Miss Robin Hood," is blonde, 22-year-old Madeline Dunnigan, of 422 First st., Brooklyn, and she came by this appellation in what the District Attorney's office described as a most original way—

She was accused of robbing her employer, the luggage firm of Gropper's Inc., at 685 Fifth ave., of $40,000, which she showered in gifts on friends and fellow-workers, but never raised her own salary as bookkeeper above $40 a week.

EMPLOYER RUINED.

So here are the last lines in this latest chapter—

"The thefts have ruined me . . . I'm going to end it all. I cannot stand it any longer."

They were penned by Oscar H. Gropper, 57, head of the firm, before he plunged to his death from his ninth floor suite at the Hotel Blackstone, 50 E. 58th st., at 1:30 a. m., while his wife, June, and

Continued on Page 5, Column 4.

Hirohito Sees War In 'Crucial Stage'

By United Press

Emperor Hirohito of Japan said today the Pacific war was entering the "crucial stage" and exhorted his 100,000,000 subjects to "intensify further their unity" and concentrate total power for "crushing the foe."

Russians Inside Budapest

MOSCOW, Dec. 26 (UP).—The Red Army stormed into Budapest from the west today after apparently completing its encirclment in a spectacular flanking sweep that doomed thousands of German and Hungarian troops to death or surrender inside the tottering capital.

A new Hungarian provisional government already was preparing to enter Budapest behind the Red Army.

German panzers, infantry and self-propelled guns counterattacked at least 25 times in the past 24 hours, but finally fell back into the city for a last-ditch stand.

81 TANKS WRECKED.

At least 81 Nazi tanks were knocked out in the breakthrough area Saturday and Sunday. Front dispatches said some Germans charged the Soviet lines drunk and singing, only to be cut down to the last man by Russian machine-gunners.

Marshal Feodor I. Tolbukhin's 3rd Ukrainian Army broke open the western flank of the Axis lines around Budapest yesterday after a swirling five-day battle that cost the Germans and Hungarians almost 20,000 men killed or captured.

A communique said the enemy was in full retreat. Thousands of Nazi and Hungarian soldiers were hemmed inside the city, however, and it seemed certain that in a matter of days at most they would have an opportunity to make good their boast to turn Budapest into another Stalingrad.

(Map on Page 2)

Athens Police Uncover Ton Of Explosive

ATHENS, Dec. 26 (UP).—Nearly a ton of dynamite was found cached in a sewer directly before the Great Britain Hotel, British and Greek government headquarters, today only a few hours before Prime Minister Churchill was to convoke a peace conference with ELAS and Greek government leaders.

British sources believed the explosives had been planted by leftwing ELAS forces in an attempt to destroy the hotel and, with it, Churchill, British Foreign Secretary Eden, Lt. Gen. Scobie, British commander in Athens, and Greek Government officials.

It was learned that the explosives had been placed in the sewer, which extends beneath the hotel, during the night some time after the arrival of Churchill and Eden in Athens had been announced.

The dynamite had been fused but not lighted. It was packed in wooden crates bearing the name of a German manufacturer and weighed approximately 1,680 pounds. Several wooden, two-man cradles for carrying the crates also were found. The cache was discovered during a routine patrol through the Athens sewers.

The explosive was Penthrite, a German type of dynamite, and was equipped with electric detonators.

(Earlier Details on Page 2).

Blood Test Chief Chaplin Defense

By JULIAN HARTT,
International News Service Staff Correspondent.

LOS ANGELES, Dec. 26.—Charlie Chaplin was expected to stake his principal hope for victory in the Joan Barry paternity suit today upon medical testimony that he could not possibly be a blood relative to Miss Barry's red-headed infant, Carol Ann.

The scientific testimony, based upon blood-comparison tests made last February, is listed as the "first defense" in Chaplin formal answer to the paternity action, launched 18 months ago by his former protegee and now entering its third calendar week in court.

The legal counter-offensive on behalf of the white-haired comedian was to be opened by his attorney, Charles E. Millikan, as soon as Joseph Scott, 77-year-old counsel for the baby, rested his case today.

Scott planned, however, to recall his star witness, the titian-haired Miss Barry, now 25, for a few further questions on re-direct examination before closing his case.

There also remained the possibility that Scott would ring down the curtain on his efforts to name Chaplin the baby's father by demanding, after Miss Barry leaves the stand, that the comedian and Carol Ann be brought into "juxtaposition" for comparison of possible physical similarities before the jury of seven women and five men.

Superior Judge Henry M. Willis already has ruled that such a request is proper. Neither defendant nor plaintiff, in their previous courtroom appearances, has yet been brought into close proximity of the other.

(Pictures on Page 3 and in Pictorial Review. Other details on Page 3).

Yank Wedge Near St. Vith Smashed

PARIS, Dec. 26 (AP).—Powerful twin German drives have squeezed out the American wedge near St. Vith and merged into a single bulge 40 miles deep that still is hammering toward the Meuse only 15 miles away, Supreme Headquarters disclosed today.

The German bulge is 35 miles wide, and by Sunday had enveloped Rochefort for the closest approach to the Meuse River.

In the heart of this bulge a surrounded American force several thousand strong fought doggedly to hold the important Belgian road hub of Bastogne after rejecting a surrender ultimatum. It is under incessant Nazi armor and infantry attacks.

Rescuers 5 Miles Away

The whole hope of this isolated force focussed to the south where Gen. Eisenhower's counterassault had beaten back up the Arlon road within five miles of Bastogne—and still was gaining ground.

The American wedge west of St. Vith had kept Field Marshal Karl con Rundstedt's drives split. A field dispatch declared Von Rundstedt apparently now was seeking a breakthrough toward Namur rather than Liege, 34 miles northeast of Namur. The Germans were more than 30 miles from Namur by Sunday.

While the huge ground battle in Belgium costly to both sides raged on, the 8th Air Force got in its fourth straight day of attacks. Thousands of German vehicles and 500 enemy planes have been knocked out by Allied fliers since the start of the counteroffensive.

Positions disclosed last night by Supreme Headquarters as of mid-day Sunday showed German advances of perhaps one to three miles in a weekend resumption of the enemy's westward thrusts. Field dispatches describing the force of the assault suggested further gains yesterday.

The general situation still was one of the Germans attempting to extend the length of their two major westward counter-offensive salients while also trying to hold off increasing American pressure on both flanks.

Although the German advances on Saturday were slight they were sufficient to indicate that a stalemate which had

Continued on Page 2, Column 3.

THE WEATHER

Partly cloudy, slightly colder.

Sun rises, 8:19 a. m.; sun sets, 5:35 p. m. High tide at Governors Island, 6:30 a. m. and 6:56 p. m.

HOURLY TEMPERATURES.

12 midnight	39	5 a. m.	38
1 a. m.	38	6 a. m.	38
2 a. m.	38	7 a. m.	37
3 a. m.	38	8 a. m.	37
4 a. m.	38	9 a. m.	37

(Complete Weather Report on Page 10)

TODAY'S INDEX

SCRIPPS-HOWARD

New York World-Telegram

Local Forecast: Today, clear, windy. Tonight, fair. Tomorrow, fair and cold.

NIGHT
LATEST NEWS
Five Cents

VOL. 77—NO. 157—IN TWO SECTIONS—SECTION ONE. NEW YORK, FRIDAY, JANUARY 5, 1945. Entered as second class matter Post Office, New York, N. Y.

2 ARMIES SLUG AHEAD, MONTGOMERY IN CHARGE

U. S., British Armor Making 'Extremely Good' Progress In Northern Wall of Bulge

By J. EDWARD MURRAY,
United Press War Correspondent.

PARIS, Jan. 5.—American and British armored divisions, fighting under the over-all command of Field Marshal Sir Bernard L. Montgomery, slugged their way through the German battle screen across the northern wall of the Ardennes today in a broadening counteroffensive that official spokesmen said was making "extremely good" progress.

Along a front of more than 40 miles covering almost the entire northern flank of the great salient Allied tanks and infantrymen were driving steadily forward against spotty Nazi resistance.

[The Associated Press said six inches and more of snow covered parts of the Belgian-Luxemburg battlefield. Visibility ranged from 50 to 300 feet. Even jeeps slid off the icy roads.]

Sparked by the driving Marshal Montgomery, spearheads of the American 1st and British 2nd armies advanced at least 1500 yards into the enemy pocket in the last 24 hours and cut the gap separating them from Lt. Gen. George S. Patton's U. S. 3rd Army in the south to 12 miles or less.

The Nazi Transocean News Agency, meanwhile, reported without Allied confirmation that German troops to the southeast had broken through the old Maginot Line fortifications on the U. S. 7th Army front and reached a point almost 20 miles south of the old German-French border in Alsace. The location of the alleged breakthrough was not disclosed.

Caught in a gigantic nutcracker between the three Allied armies—and perhaps a fourth on the basis of Berlin reports that the U. S. 9th Army also had entered the battle—the Germans still were concentrating their main forces on Gen. Patton's armor in the south.

More than 48 hours after the start of the big drive on the northern flank, the Nazis still had failed to mount a major counterattack on that front.

Germans Falling Back

Field dispatches said the Germans were falling back slowly behind a vast minefield, fighting in small groups with dug-in tanks and machine gun nests emplaced in the snow-covered ravines of the Ardennes.

Veteran tank and infantry units of the British 2nd Army swung down into the western end of the assault line between Marche and Hotton and drove an armored wedge almost a mile southeastward into the Nazi flank. [The Associated Press said the Allies had reached Waha, just south of Marche.]

A half-dozen miles to the east, an American armored column overran the Belgian hamlet of Beffe and pushed on to within about three miles northwest of La Roche, one of the four pivotal road centers inside the German pocket.

Other American units were striking squarely across the narrow waist of the salient below Grandmenil and at last reports were almost four miles south of that town, about 12 miles from a juncture with Gen. Patton's forces above Bastogne. The 1st Army spearhead was about 10 miles north of its main objective, the crossroads town of Houffalize, and the 3rd Army little more than half that distance south of the town.

Yanks Wedge Into Flank.

Between Grandmenil and Stavelot two more American wedges were ramming into the Nazi flank with increasing power after advancing four to five miles in the first two days of the offensive.

Small-scale German counterattacks in the Arbrefontaine and Bois de Tave sectors were beaten back by the Americans and late dispatches said the driving was continuing steadily.

At the same time giant Ameri-

(Continued on Page Eleven.)

3 Die in Upper Broadway Fire

Aged Women Are Victims, 30 Overcome

Servicemen Join Police and Firemen In Daring Rescues

Three aged women perished and 30 other persons, including 17 firemen, were overcome by blinding smoke early today in a spectacular three-alarm fire that raged through the top floor of a seven-story apartment building at Broadway and 96th St., where many of the 150 residents were Austrian and Jewish refugees.

While most of the occupants fled to safety down stairways and fire escapes, at least a dozen lives were saved by firemen who crawled into the seventh-floor apartments on their hands and knees under the lashing flames and the curtain of smoke.

Then, when all were removed, firemen, police and hospital attendants hastily improvised emergency hospitals in the lobby and in adjacent buildings to minister to those who had collapsed or who were nearly done in.

Servicemen Aid in Rescue.

Further aid came from at least a score of servicemen, many of whom shed their heavy winter coats and gave them to occupants who had dashed into the freezing cold in their night clothing. The temperature at the time the fire started—2:51 a. m.—was 30 degrees.

The dead are Mrs. Etta Lesser, 72, whose apartment adjoined that in which the fire started; Zalde Ash, 82, and a 75-year-old woman who could be identified only as Mrs. Bottchner. The

(Continued on Page Four.)

Wolf Trail Leads Into Wrong Lair

Frank Vorbach, 45, 213 E. 118th St., told the detectives in the Simpson St. station, the Bronx, that he had mistaken the building for the public library. Miss Conchita Olmo, 929 E. 161st St., the Bronx, told the detective that Vorbach followed her into the station, bent on prolonging amorous advances that had begun in the 42nd St. subway station.

Detective Thomas Farrell believed the 25-year-old millinery model. Vorbach was arrested, pleaded innocent to charges of disorderly conduct in Night Court last night, and was held in $500 bail to be rearraigned in Bronx Magistrate Court today.

Vorbach began annoying her, Miss Olmo told police, in the 42nd St. station and left the subway when she did, following her on the street.

Miss Olmo, in desperation, turned into the Simpson St. police station. Vorbach followed her—into the arms of Detective Farrell.

World-Telegram Index

British Take Akyab, Burma Port

Navy Rejectee Cited As 5th Army Hero

2nd Lt. Charles Shea Of Bronx Awarded Congressional Medal

Rejected three times by the navy, a 21-year-old Bronx boy was drafted by the army to become one of the war's greatest heroes, it was learned today when headquarters of the 5th Army in Italy announced he had been awarded the Congressional Medal of Honor.

The soldier, who as a staff sergeant knocked out three German machine-gun nests, killed three Germans and captured seven others, is 2nd Lt. Charles W. Shea Jr., now 23. He was commissioned in the field by Lt. Gen. Mark W. Clark for his heroic feats.

Lt. Shea's home is at 1121 Woodycrest Ave., the Bronx, where his father, Charles Sr., is building superintendent.

Promised Mother a Surprise.

His mother, Catherine, said she received a letter from Charles several weeks ago in which he said he had a big surprise for her.

"What are you going to do, get married?" she wrote back.

"No," the son wrote in a letter she received 10 days ago, "I'm going to get the Congressional Medal of Honor."

Sold Peanuts in Ball Park.

The father was pretty proud today. "He's a very ambitious boy," he said. "After school and on Saturdays and Sundays he would sell peanuts at the Polo Grounds and the Yankee Stadium. But I wish he'd come home so I could see what he looks like."

The father told proudly how Charles Jr. had been elected captain of the Nelson Arrows football and baseball team in the Highbridge section of the Bronx while he was still a schoolboy.

Award of the Medal of Honor carries a $2 monthly pay raise for Lt. Shea as long as he is in active service, plus $10 per month for life after he reaches the age of 65.

Lt. Charles W. Shea, Jr.

27 Escaped PWs Still at Large

By the Associated Press.

WASHINGTON, Jan. 5.—Twenty-seven of the 1152 Axis prisoners of war who have escaped from camps in this country are still at large, the War Department reported today.

Twenty-one are Germans and six are Italians. Fifteen Germans are fugitives from Papago Park Camp in Arizona, where 25 made a sensational Christmas Eve escape. On Jan. 1 there were 361,631 prisoners of war in 425 camps in the United States.

Fleet Captures City on Island Without Fight

Jap Garrison Flees As Attackers Pour In From Three Sides

By McQUOWN WRIGHT,
United Press War Correspondent.

WITH BRITISH FORCES AT AKYAB ISLAND, Burma, Jan. 3 (Delayed).—The largest combined operations force ever launched against the Asiatic continent seized Akyab, Burma's third largest port, without opposition today.

The Japs, who savagely repulsed smaller-scale British attempts to reach Akyab in overland thrusts through the Burma jungle from India in 1942 and 1943, evacuated the stronghold without a fight while cruisers, destroyers, transports and planes were converging on them for a mighty land, sea and air blow.

(BBC said not a shot was fired in the landing.)

Seizure of Akyab, a small island at the mouth of the Kaladan and Mayu rivers 75 miles south of the Indian Border, gave the British a harbor capable of handling ships up to 8000 tons and air bases a little more than 300 miles northwest of Rangoon.

[A Southeast Asia Command Headquarters communique said Akyab Island "is firmly in our hands," the Associated Press reported in a dispatch from Kandy, Ceylon.]

With Akyab, the British 15th Corps won control of all Arakan province west of the Kaladan

(Continued on Page Twelve.)

Gets Fourth Star

The men and women of General Cable Corp.'s Rome plant have won the coveted Army-Navy "E" award for excellence in production for the fourth time, it was announced today.

Bradley Loses Rule Of U. S. 1st and 9th

Montgomery Given Over-All Command West, North of Bulge

By the United Press.

PARIS, Jan. 5.—Field Marshal Sir Bernard L. Montgomery, commander of the British 21st Army group, has been given over-all command of the American 1st and 9th armies and is directing the assault against the Ardennes bulge from the north and west, it can be revealed today.

General of Army Dwight D. Eisenhower, supreme commander, shifted the over-command of the two armies from Lt. Gen. Omar N. Bradley, commander of the 12th Army group, to Marshal Montgomery after the German offensive disrupted communications between them and Lt. Gen. George S. Patton's 3rd Army south of the bulge.

It was also disclosed today that Marshal Montgomery has thrown units of the British 2nd Army against the Ardennes bulge.

News of the shift in command followed recent reports that Marshal Montgomery would be made deputy supreme commander under Gen. Eisenhower with jurisdiction over all ground forces on the Western Front.

There was no immediate indication whether the shift was permanent, or whether the command of the 1st and 9th Armies would revert to Gen. Bradley after the Ardennes breach has been mended and communications restored.

Gen. Bradley presumably still was commander of the 12th Army Group, though the group for the moment appeared to consist only of the 3rd Army. He decorated Gen. Patton on the battlefield only last week for the latter's leadership of the American dash across France last August.

Barring evidence to the contrary, Lt. Gen. Courtney H. Hodges and Lt. Gen. William H. Simpson retain command of the 1st and 9th Armise, respectively.

Gen. Montgomery. Gen. Bradley.

War Center Needs Told at Institute

The American War-Community Services entered the second and last day of their institute today after talks emphasized that "less articulate groups in war centers are the ones most in need of our services."

These groups, it was pointed out, are Negroes, 'teen-agers and the foreign-born. Speakers noted a growing tendency of social workers to link their programs with organized labor.

Tito's Men Cross Austrian Border

By the Associated Press.

LONDON, Jan. 5.—Yugoslav Partisan forces have crossed the Austrian border and are menacing a German arc between Klagenfurt and Graz, Marshal Tito announced today.

In a broadcast communique heard in London, Marshal Tito said the Partisans had cut the Maribor-Graz Railway line "in many places," apparently in the areas of Wildon, Leibnitz and Ehrenhausen.

Peace, It's Wonderful

By the Associated Press.

ST. JOSEPH, Jan. 5.—A wonderful spirit of love and understanding has fluttered down on St. Joe. In 37 divorce hearings scheduled, 25 plaintiffs changed their minds and asked for dismissals.

U. S. Agencies Favor Ban on Racing Wires

By the Associated Press.

WASHINGTON, Jan. 5.—Two government agencies went on record yesterday as opposing continued operation of domestic communications facilities for dissemination of racing information.

The Federal Communications Commission and the Board of War Communications also said they are opposed to the private leasing of any circuits between the United States and foreign points for the collection and distribution of racing information from outside the country.

They urged the telephone and telegraph companies to take voluntary steps to "reclaim the facilities and manpower employed exclusively or principally in the dissemination of racing information."

The companies were requested to report back within the next two weeks as to what steps were being taken.

Both agencies emphasized that their action was not intended to prevent newspapers and recognized press associations from continuing to use communication facilities for "collecting and distributing general news service, including racing information."

A Swell Recipe

By the Associated Press.

SAN FRANCISCO, Jan. 5.—Housewives who followed a recipe for "sugarless cake" given in a San Francisco newspaper know now why their product swelled to such alarming proportions. The paper said excuse it, please. It should have been 2½ teaspoons of baking powder, not 2½ cups.

Stampless Shoes? Here's How

By JOHN JENKISSON,
World-Telegram Staff Writer.

Psst! If you can keep your left foot from knowing what your right foot is up to for five minutes we'll tell you how to get shoes without coupons. Legal, too. Now stand still.

The OPA says you can buy mismates, single shoes or outmoded shoes without stamps. One buck ceiling on the mismates and old-fashioned brogans, 50 cents on the singles.

How It's Done.

On Orchard St. near Rivington St. they have mismates. They have had them for years. Business has never been so brisk. "Fifty pairs a month now we sell," says one old-timer. "Maybe there is a half size difference. What of it? Some people have very tough feet. Maybe the color is not strictly a match. So the price is low. And the shoes, they are not bad shoes at all."

How does he come by mismates? "Easy," he says. "For samples, the factory salesman takes on the road one shoe from each pair. He comes back. We buy the samples. A month later he comes back again. We buy more samples and try to get mates for the shoes we have. Sometimes we come very close. These we sell for mismates."

"And sometimes a customer can't wait for the other shoe. We sell him a single and he goes around the stores trying to match it himself. Whether he wears the single while doing this or carries it under his arm I do not know. That is his business."

Serve Self, Mates.

But for real, rockbound dilemmas you must talk to Miss Mary Schoenberg in Wynn's Bargain Center at 130 Orchard St. Miss Schoenberg's height is medium, her age possibly in the early thirties. A mass of dark hair frames her round, cheerful face.

Shoes of all kinds lie tumbled on the broad open counters which line both sides of the Center. You serve yourself. You can even try them on if you want to. Most customers do.

"That is where we have a little trouble," says Miss Schoenberg. "On this side are the 'no stamp' shoes, as you can see. Sunday is the big day here. We are open all day and the crowds are terrific. You cannot watch everybody.

Picks Two Rights.

"There is some snitching. They try on a pair and walk out, leaving us their old ones. Naturally we do not care for this but sometimes it backfires on the snitcher. It is necessary to use caution in picking mismates. We help when we are asked. The snitchers, of course, do not ask. That is where the backfiring comes in.

"Not so long ago a woman pawed over this counter for an hour. Very fussy. She left us her old shoes. She did not pay for the ones she took with her. Two days later she was back. She was sore. Claimed she had two right shoes and insisted we exchange them. That was the first good laugh we had in days."

But the OPA needn't feel to bighearted about that "no stamps for outmoded or obsolete shoes" business. They're scarce. Stick to singles and mismates—some days the hot foot, some days the cold foot, every day the itchy foot. And when you call us Old Goodie Two Shoes, smile.

London Reports Clew To Big 3 Parley Date

By the Associated Press.

LONDON, Jan. 5.—Postponement of a two-day Conservative party conference, originally scheduled to open Jan. 29, led today to renewed speculation on the possibility of an early meeting between Prime Minister Churchill, President Roosevelt and Premier Stalin.

Mr. Churchill, as well as Foreign Secretary Anthony Eden, would normally participate in the party conference.

The diplomatic correspondent of the British Press Assn. suggested that an impending meeting of "the Big Three" had been advanced and now was scheduled to take place late this month.

The Weather

(Official United States Forecast)

New York City—Today clear, windy; highest 35 degrees. Tonight fair, diminishing winds; lowest 15 to 20. Saturday fair and cold; highest 25.

New Jersey—Today colder but bright and sunny. Tonight clear and colder. Saturday fair and warmer.

TODAY'S READINGS.

	Temp.	Hum.		Temp.	Hum.
Midnight	37	..	5 a. m.	24	..
1 a. m.	37	..	6 a. m.	24	60
2 a. m.	33	..	7 a. m.	23	57
3 a. m.	30	..	8 a. m.	22	55
4 a. m.	26	..	9 a. m.	21	70
			10 a. m.	22	58

High and low a year ago, 42-37.

Nazi Photos Show How Smoothly Drive Worked—and Why It Failed

By KENNETH L. DIXON,
Associated Press Staff Writer.

WITH THE AEF ON THE BELGIAN FRONT, Jan. 3 (Delayed).—If a batch of enemy news pictures captured following a vicious fight near here is any criterion, Berlin newspapers must have been getting good pictorial coverage of the German drive into Belgium.

These are excellent pictures of a successful military operation. They were taken with the intent of showing just how well Field Marshal Karl Gerd von Rundstedt's breakthrough worked. Giving the devil his due, they show that perfectly.

Unwittingly, perhaps, they also show exactly what it was that eventually turned the tide and prevented the German panzers from reaching their objectives.

Maybe Berlin will be interested in restudying the pictures from that point of view.

The success phase naturally runs strongly through them all. There are graphic pictures of blazing American tanks, some obviously taken in the midst of intense action.

One is especially graphic, even cruelly so. It shows a Sherman tank still smoldering, its tread knocked off and the turret askew. Hanging partly out of the turret are the remains of the American tank commander. It is not a pic-

(Continued on Page Eight.)

DAILY EXPRESS

No. 13,922 | Dim-out 5.51 pm to 8.28 am | TUESDAY JANUARY 16 1945 | Moon rises 10.38 am sets 8.15 pm | One Penny

FROM ❶ The West, where Rundstedt has embarked on a hold-till-spring defence TO ❷ The East, where the offensive threatens to split German armies —

STALIN IS FORCING SWITCH

Units may already have gone East

From ALAN MOOREHEAD: Western Front, Monday

MORE than ever before, it looks as though we are going to feel the effect of the Russian attack on this front. There is already a possibility that German units are being moved to the East.

At the same time, Rundstedt has been putting his men into some really desperate fighting all along the West Wall (Siegfried Line) from Aix-la-Chapelle to Strasbourg. Villages of trifling importance are being held as though they were major objectives.

Counter-attacks have been going in upon places that could have no part in any long-range plan, nor have the German soldiers any real hope of getting anywhere. And yet the battle still goes on tonight.

BUILT UNDERGROUND

It looks as though an order has gone out from the German High Command that the West Wall resistance has got to be kept at its pitch until they find out just how far the Russians are going to advance.

With so much at stake—especially the manufacture of V2, the jet-propelled fighter and the midget submarine—it seems certain that the Germans are going to make an all-out defence to enable them to get through safely into the spring.

And then they hope to stabilise things, at least in the air and on parts of the sea.

V2, at the moment, is being fired for the most part from around The Hague. Like the jet plane, it is manufactured underground in Germany, and then sent either by train or road to the launching sites.

There is every evidence that the manufacture of V2 is increasing every week. At the moment, the only defence we have against it is a variation of the action which the Air Force call "interdiction."

That is to say, we are trying to stop V2 from ever being launched.

Days like yesterday help enormously. At last, after a week of no real air effort, the planes got up, and in vast strength. Something like 5,000 aircraft, British and American, were over Germany.

INTERDICTION

When the Germans saw them coming, they switched their fighters to the north to meet the heavies arriving from England, but the heavies went through just the same, fighting on the Battle of Britain scale.

In addition to the scores of fighters knocked down, about 60 locomotives were hit, as well as 300 or 400 lorries and railway trucks, and many bridges.

This hitting of transport is the interdiction of V2. At some point, V2 has got to emerge to the surface and offer itself as a target in the daylight as it comes westward on trucks or lorries across Germany.

So when you hear of lorries and bridges being hit, it is all part of the protection of Britain.

Since the Germans are now so far ahead of us in the manufacture of new weapons, it is their war industries above all that we are trying to blot out before the spring arrives.

With this in view the heavies descended on the German oil plants around Leipzig yesterday. The Allied fighters, now capable of going deep into Germany, had a hectic day.

12 MINUS 11

At one moment 12 German Focke-Wulf fighters were seen taking off. A few minutes later 11 of them were brought down.

All this was done in weather so harsh and bitter that it is becoming difficult to make the shortest distances, even on the ground. After a few yards your windscreen is iced over, the windscreen wiper refuses to work, and you can see nothing.

All over the place you can see trucks and jeeps and tanks skidding round in half-circles on the ice.

It was not surprising then that there was little change on the front.

As we attacked in the north in the Ardennes, the Germans attacked in the south in the Saar. Neither side got very far.

Interdiction (contd.)

Spitfire bombers attacked a V weapon railway supply line in Holland yesterday.

GONE AWAY
Into St. Hubert on horseback

THE first Allied soldier to re-enter the salient town of St. Hubert went in on horseback.

He was 25-year-old Lieutenant Ray Spreag, of Liverpool, and he had never ridden a horse before.

He was reconnoitring a mine-trapped wood in knee-deep snow when he met some civilians, who gave him the horse.

He went through a village empty of Germans, circled St. Hubert cautiously, and then rode into the town—as the Germans left.

Next day he completed 20 miles' patrolling on his horse. He named it after the regiment.

St. Hubert is named after the patron saint of hunters, the 8th century Bishop of Liege, who saw a crucifix between the horns of a stag while hunting on Good Friday.

Assault begins on Houffalize

From WILLIAM TROUGHTON

FIRST U.S. ARMY, Monday. — General Hodges' men are tonight little more than half a mile from the centre of Houffalize—the one-time central stronghold of Rundstedt's salient.

They are fighting in its outskirts in bitter cold but in the highest spirits, determined to take the town.

There is an electric feeling in the air, the feeling that always precedes the winning of a hard-won town.

Drivers of all vehicles are eager to do their utmost. Some are over-eager, and collisions through the fog and the ice on the roads are frequent.

Today I was held up half a dozen times by heavy mechanised stuff lying broadside across the road, with sweating men putting every ounce into the job of moving it from the highway.

A motto posted on every other tree says: "Keep moving, or get off the road."

TANKS ON RIDGE

Laurence Wilkinson cabled earlier:—

Our armour is on a ridge north of the seventeenth-century fortress town of Houffalize, and is ready to strike.

But it may be that the town, for which so many Americans and British and Germans have died, will in the end be taken without much of a fight.

A blizzard of snow impedes observation from the high ground where troops of General Hodges' First Army are temporarily halted.

The enemy's artillery has been silent for 36 hours now.

It seems to have been getting colder almost every day of the battle.

Woollen gloves and bare flesh freeze to the metal parts of a rifle, and a few hours without attention means certain death from freezing for the wounded.

Some German divisions have been nearly wiped out. One lost 5,000 men as prisoners.

HONGKONG BOMBED
Major blow by carrier planes

Express Staff Reporter: New York, Monday

ADMIRAL NIMITZ announced from his Pearl Harbour headquarters tonight that the first full-scale blow by carrier aircraft has been made against Hongkong, Swatow and Amoy, Japan's lifeline ports in China.

The attack was made by planes of Admiral Halsey's Third Fleet. Details are not yet available.

Swatow is about 200 miles north-east of Hongkong. Amoy is another 100 miles north-east, opposite Formosa Island, which has been the target for many recent attacks.

Halsey struck on Saturday, the day after his planes had sunk 41 Japanese ships and damaged 28 in an audacious Indo-China attack.

In these sweeps, Halsey's ships have wiped out two convoys. One was entirely sunk and all vessels in the other were either sunk, damaged or beached.

Germans lose 2 to 1
IN THE SALIENT

WASHINGTON, Monday. — Figures given tonight show that American losses in the battle of the bulge were less than half the German losses.

U.S. losses were: Killed and wounded (mostly wounded), 22,000. Missing (mostly prisoners), 18,000. **Total: 40,000.**

German losses: Killed and wounded, 50,000. Prisoners, 40,000. **Total: 90,000.**

American losses for the whole Western Front in the 23 days, December 15 to January 7, were 4,083 killed; 27,645 wounded; 20,866 missing.—Express News Service.

Allies throw in two new divisions

Messages from Supreme H.Q. say that two more divisions have gone into the attack on the north of the salient, south and west of Malmedy. Each advanced nearly a mile.

Railways to east battered

Six hundred U.S. heavies switched out of the renewed oil war yesterday to hit rail yards in Southern Germany—yards through which German reserves might be moved to meet Stalin's great attack in the east.

Forts from Italy joined in, 500 bombing communications targets in the Vienna area.

Lancasters carried on the oil war by attacking Ruhr benzol plants. The Luftwaffe, after their heavy losses of Sunday, put up little show. Three U.S. bombers were lost over South Germany.

It is announced that Allied bombers have scored three more direct hits with 1,000lb. bombs on the great Hohenzollern Bridge across the Rhine at Cologne, and drained for the third time the Mittelland Canal, link between East Germany and the Dortmund-Ems Canal (drained four times).

U.S. ace killed by A.A.

Major George E. Preddy, 25-year-old U.S. ace, who a few minutes earlier had raised his score to 32½ by downing two Me.s, was killed by A.A. fire over Liege on Christmas Day, it was announced yesterday.

Prince questioned

Prince Axel of Denmark has been questioned by the Gestapo following the discovery of arms near his house.—Brussels radio.

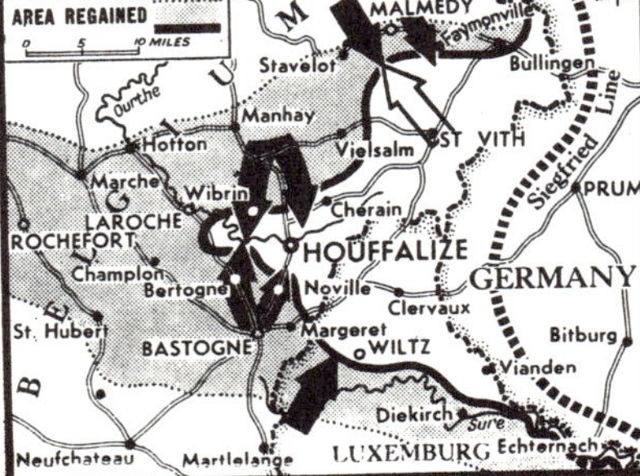

GENERAL ELECTION BUREAU
New Daily Express service

TODAY the Daily Express announces a new part of its news service—the General Election Bureau.

For two months the Bureau has been listing, checking and sorting candidates already chosen to fight the General Election.

Up to last night 746 candidates were recorded as having been adopted by all parties to contest the 640 seats that will comprise the next Parliament.

One hundred and fifteen of the 615 sitting M.P.s have announced their retirement. Many others are expected to make the same decision before long.

More than 400 new names are awaiting the approval of party headquarters.

The average age of the first batch of new candidates—as distinct from sitting M.P.s—is 40.4 years. Youngest and oldest are Liberals: the 22-year-old Captain Mark Bonham-Carter and the 78-year-old Mr Lawrence Bowman.

Among the candidates are 58 Army officers, including one brigadier. There are only four in the ranks. There are 15 Royal Air Force officers, and seven from the Royal Navy. There is one R.A.F. sergeant.

Six are barristers and solicitors, seven are farmers, four agricultural workers, three psychologists, three professors and three railway signalmen.

Only 67 women

There are two stockbrokers, two schoolmistresses, and ten journalists.

So far, contests are all set for 117 seats. Thirty-two constituencies have three candidates and three have at least four candidates.

One surprise is the shortage of women candidates. 67 out of 746 possibles.

Party H.Q.s are planning the broad outlines of their campaigns. By the end of this month it is expected that these will be the positions in each:—

CONSERVATIVE: Sixty-four present members of Parliament retiring; 125 adoptions, including eight women.

SOCIALIST: Thirty members retiring; 276 adoptions, including 24 women and 50 Service people.

LIBERAL: Two members retiring; 200 adoptions, including 18 women and 128 Service people.

COMMUNIST: Forty-two candidates, including seven women and three Service people.

COMMON WEALTH: Forty candidates, including three women and 10 Service people. They intend to fight only those seats for which they consider the Socialist Party has no chance.

Full picture

I.L.P.: Their application for affiliation to the Socialist Party has been put to the Socialists' executive. If it is turned down, as was Common Wealth's, they have 63 candidates selected, including seven women and 20 Service people.

LIBERAL NATIONAL: One of their 28 members is retiring. They have no women candidates out of their proposed 40.

NATIONAL LABOUR: No plans yet, but they expect to fight more than 20 seats, including five at present held.

The Daily Express invites constituency associations and candidates to send additional information. Every fact which will help build up a full picture of every candidate is wanted.

Address your information to the Daily Express, Fleet-street, London, and put the word "Election" in the top left-hand corner of the envelope.

Germans allowed only one suit

ZURICH, Monday.—The German surrender of clothes for the Volkssturm leaves each person with one suit or dress, one pair of shoes, one spoon, one knife and fork, one pair of sheets, and one pair of blankets. Radio sets are also being collected "for the army."—Reuter.

They fired towards the snore

BELGIUM, Monday.—A U.S. patrol heard snores in the dark. They located the sleeper, reported to their artillery, and in a few minutes German outposts were wiped out.—B.U.P.

Stanley in U.S.

WASHINGTON, Monday.—Mr. Oliver Stanley, British Secretary of State for the Colonies, arrived this afternoon by air.—Reuter.

The daily eighteen

Northern Italy had an average of 18 air raids a day in 1944.—German Overseas News Agency

Four drives West

Kielce taken—front rolling up

Express War Reporter: Stockholm, Monday

AT the end of the fourth day of the great Russian breakthrough offensive in Southern Poland, Marshal Stalin tonight announced the capture of the German stronghold of Kielce (pronounced Kel-Te, 60 miles north-east of Cracow, and 400 other places.

In those four days the Red Army has crashed 50 miles from its starting point on the Vistula through the strongest defences in the world, prepared by the Germans for many months.

Marshal Koniev's troops have fanned out from their penetration area to within 25 miles of Cracow, but their thrust is aimed at the heart of the vital German industrial centre of Silesia, only 55 miles away.

Kielce was one of the biggest German bases between the Vistula and the Reich frontier.

It is the junction of two main railways running from Germany, and its capture will cripple German attempts to switch reinforcements to threatened points.

Stalin's armies, with at least 1,500,000 fighting men, are tonight rolling up the German lines on a front of 1,000 miles, while the greatest battle of the war is taking shape in the Polish plain north-east of Cracow.

Beyond Cracow

The Germans have so far been powerless to rally their forces against Marshal Koniev and it is expected that they will fall back beyond Cracow almost to the Silesian frontier before they can make their first major challenge.

Already the German forces in Poland, estimated at about 100 divisions, are in danger of being split in two.

Koniev's strategic aims have not yet been clearly shown, but he has several possibilities open to him in addition to the direct push to Silesia.

By wheeling north and south he may trap vast German armies or force wholesale retreats.

His immediate prizes may be:—

Katowice, centre of the great steel and coal basin. This is also an important road and rail centre and may be truly called the gateway to Eastern Silesia.

Cracow itself, second largest city in Poland and centre of German government.

'Elastic defence'

The prospect of large-scale withdrawal in Poland is indicated today by German war correspondents, who say that the Wehrmacht is now resorting to "elastic defences."

Swedish correspondents in Berlin add that: "Elastic defence is an expression used by the High Command when a general retreat is imminent."

Other signs of retreat are:—

1.—A German military spokesman admitting today that "the Russians scored a considerable tactical success" which makes it impossible to judge clearly the situation on the front at least for some days.

2.—The same spokesman said that the Germans are only resisting at certain strategically important points while the main

➔ BACK PAGE, COL. THREE

SWEDEN SEES NEW V BOMBS

From E. D. MASTERMAN

STOCKHOLM, Monday.—More robot bombs, said to be of a new type, flew over Southern Sweden this afternoon.

They flew low, and it was possible to follow their course.

A Swedish official report on this new wave of bombs, which began three days ago, is expected tomorrow. Unofficial statements say the bombs are a new radio-controlled form of V2, fired for experimental purposes from a German base on Bornholm island, 30 miles from the Swedish coast.

4 a.m. LATEST

RUSSIANS WIN 116 TANKS

Moscow reports that in first 48 hours of offensive in Poland booty taken included 116 tanks, 379 guns and 1,000 lorries. Yesterday, west of Khmelnk, two German regiments were wiped out and 74 field guns and several dozen tanks and troop carriers destroyed.

Bevin may go to Greece

By GUY EDEN

PLANS are being discussed for Mr. Ernest Bevin, Minister of Labour and National Service, to visit Greece to see conditions there, and report to the Government.

Trade union leaders are expected to accompany him.

Another proposal is that a Labour attaché should be appointed to the British Embassy in Athens. Mr. W. J. Hull, of the Ministry of Labour, is expected to get the job.

Trevor Evans writes:—

Mr. Churchill, while prepared to facilitate the visit of a trade union delegation to Greece, yesterday declined a request to send a party of Socialist M.P.s.

He told a delegation of Socialists—Mr. Harold Laski, Mr. Jim Griffiths, M.P., and Mr. Aneurin Bevan, M.P., who were introduced by Mr. Arthur Greenwood—that he could not agree to a one-party visit. He hopes it will be possible for an all-party delegation of M.P.s to go to Greece within the next two months.

Transport House is prepared to provide a strong union delegation, and the deputation accepted Mr. Churchill's suggestion.

New move by Peter

Express Political Correspondent

Mr. Anthony Eden, the Foreign Secretary, yesterday discussed with M. Subasic, Yugoslav Prime Minister, King Peter's refusal to agree to the proposed Regency.

Yugoslav politicians in London said last night that the king might make another move with the object of ending the deadlock.

New steps taken to aid Europe

WASHINGTON, Monday.—Interim measures for rebuilding European economy have been agreed during the visit of Mr. Richard Law, British Minister of State, to Washington, and begin on a small scale at once, it is announced today. Ships are already loading supplies.—Express News Service.

Australia rations wheat today

MELBOURNE, Monday. — Wheat rationing in Australia is to be announced tomorrow. Drought has reduced stocks to danger point. Shortage of shipping may mean a cut in tobacco.—A.P.

They're there

The British Parliamentary Mission of 10 has arrived in Moscow.—Moscow radio.

KONIEV USED MONTY TACTICS

Germans massed in wrong place

From ALARIC JACOB: Moscow, Monday

WHEN "Monty" gets the full report on Marshal Koniev's breakthrough, as he soon will, I think he will be delighted with it, for some of Koniev's deception schemes revealed today are extraordinarily like the ones we saw at Alamein.

The Sandomierz bridgehead was not very large, and the Germans knew what was coming, but they seem to have been completely deceived as to just where the big punch was to be laid on.

For weeks beforehand the troops crossed the Vistula at night and were hidden in underground assembly points in the woods.

Tank tracks were built, named and numbered like the "Sun," the "Moon" and "Top hat" tracks at Alamein, and each tank unit had a code name and number corresponding with the track up which it was to move on the morning of battle.

Hundreds of dummy guns were massed in the wrong places. These flashed and smoked just like the real thing.

Dummy tanks

Hundreds of dummy tanks trundled about at night while monster gramophones broadcast the sound of a great tank formation rumbling forward.

Noisy "Stalinet" tractors burbled about in misleading locations, with the result that the Germans massed their reserves in the wrong places.

Today a heavy weight of men and armour is across the River Nida from a point where it joins the Vistula to an area north of where the Nida is crossed by the main road and railway linking Kielce with Cracow.

Snow fell during the night in the break-through area, but not sufficiently to impede operations.

Against orders

Captured Colonel S. Tressner, of the German 575th Regiment, admits that his men fell back against orders. They are continuing to retreat but, with the first shock over, are now going so with sufficient deliberation to mine and booby-trap extensively.

German demolition squads are active in the villages. On one cottage table, even a piece of bacon temptingly exposed had a booby-trap under the plate.

Sacks of flour are mined. Pillows are liable to explode, and there are bicycles which blow up if you touch them.

Wells have been poisoned, and the famous "Sitzkrieg specials," which the Germans first used at Kharkov and which, inserted in upholstery, explode when you sit down, have cropped up again.

Moscow quotes Opinion

Moscow radio last night quoted several times from yesterday's Daily Express leader hailing the Russian offensive.

On Cologne radio, William Joyce, "Lord Haw-Haw," said: "It is characteristic of a paper like the Daily Express to eulogise the Russians."

City's lights cut by explosions

Nearly all south Glasgow was blacked out for two hours last night after two explosions at a power station. Nobody was injured, but two men on the roof of the power station had to be rescued by the N.F.S. Public-houses were lit by candles.

Freezing

Straits: Clear, freezing.

1,000 Nazis sail away in liner

Express Staff Reporter

LIVERPOOL, Monday. — The Arundel Castle, 19,000-ton peace-time liner, left Liverpool today for Lisbon with more than 1,000 German repatriates.

They are being exchanged for an equal number of British prisoners in Germany who are expected home next month.

Many of the Germans were carried aboard on stretchers and others went up the gangways on crutches. Army Medical Corps men are travelling with them.

Motor canteens served them tea, snacks and cigarettes on the quayside.

Most of them were in the early 20s and were captured in the North African campaign. They wore Afrika Korps caps.

There were 12 women in the party and one German naval officer who stood apart from the soldiers and did not speak to them.

The Arundel Castle is also carrying Red Cross letters and parcels for British prisoners in Germany.

German radio today said: "About 5,000 German wounded from Britain and the U.S. will be brought home in two stages, as against 2,500 U.S. and British wounded from Germany."

The lights change

Allied planes are being fitted with identification lights that can be changed at will in flight. The identity colour is changed several times a day to foil tricks by German intruder planes.

FLYING TWINS WIN THEIR SECOND D.F.C.s TOGETHER

ALLEN and Eric Sherlock, 28-year-old twins, from Ontario, have each won a bar to the D.F.C.

They enlisted in the Canadian Air Force in 1942 and each won a D.F.C. in April 1944.

Before they joined up they worked together in their fruit and grocery business. They trained together, joined the same squadron (R.C.A.F. No. 427), and now both pilot Halifaxes.

The Air Ministry citation describes Allen as "a fine pilot and an enthusiastic and resourceful captain, cool and fearless"; and Eric as "a cool and skilful pilot, able to make instant decisions in an emergency."

They have just had leave in Canada—together, of course.

Footnote.—In the same list of awards a D.F.C. goes to Acting Squadron-Leader Charles Sherring, of London, "who at 41 courageously attacks any target."

Daily Mail
NO. 15,198 ONE PENNY * * * FOR KING AND EMPIRE FRIDAY, JANUARY 19, 1945
N.A.A.F.I. FREE ISSUE Distributed by ARMY WELFARE SERVICES

RED ARMY ENTER GERMANY

Nazis Hurl in Volkssturm and Police

FIRST picture of the new "Stalin" tank, playing a big part in the great Russian drive. The Germans say it weighs 50 tons, has a 5in. gun and heavy armour. It fords rivers with ease.

HOUSE-TO-HOUSE SILESIA BATTLE

From Daily Mail Special Correspondent

STOCKHOLM, Thursday.

KONIEV'S tanks, driving west from the Czestochowa area, have smashed through to the German border and were to-night engaged in bitter fighting with German battle groups flung into the line in a desperate endeavour to stem the advance while a defence is organised farther back.

This break-through was disclosed by a German News Agency report which said that battle groups and infantry had been rushed to towns and villages along the Upper Silesian border to break the impetus of the Soviet onrush.

These army units have been reinforced by every man capable of firing a rifle. The Volkssturm (Home Guard) has been rushed into the line; police have been collected from town and village to reinforce the defence.

One German version of the battle to-night said: "Upper Silesia will defend itself to the last. Men of the Volkssturm—miners, peasants, shopkeepers—are going through bitter fighting. They are fighting from this home front line . . . 500,000 men are assailing us."

As the fighting raged from hamlet to hamlet, from house to house, along the border, Koniev's men farther north, and the armies of Zhukov and Rokossovsky swept on to success after success.

To **Koniev's** men fell the great communication centre of Piotrkow, 23 miles from Lodz.

to **Zhukov** went Lowicz, 48 miles west of Warsaw on the road to Kutno, and Skierniewice, 30 miles from Lodz;

to **Rokossovsky** went 1,000 towns and hamlets, including such large towns as Modlin and Zakroczym and Przasnysz.

German admissions took Rokossovsky even farther west, and spoke of fighting in the Mlawa region, which means that the Red Army is within a dozen miles of East Prussia's southern frontier.

Rokossovsky, according to Berlin, flung 20 fresh infantry divisions into the battle to secure these successes.

ENCIRCLED

Behind the spearheads of these assaults the German defence is in many sectors dissolving into chaos.

Units have been encircled and cut off; others have been split and split again.

Commanders can be heard frantically sending out radio calls for aid that their superiors cannot send.

The background to the battle was filled in to-night by Colonel von Oldberg, military correspondent of the German Overseas News Agency, in these ominous words:

"Places far to the west have been reached by Russian spearheads to-day. Behind them, no longer in a continuous line, German forces ringed in by attackers are fighting their way back to the west.

"The German High Command is faced with the difficult task of finding a strategic solution at this moment. Only if reserves can be brought up will the High Command be in a position to determine where and when to meet the onrush."

35-MILE THRUST

For home consumption the Germans are announcing that the Russians will "find things very different" on the Reich borders.

Reserves were being rushed into the line, particularly in the south; counter-attacks were smashing at the flank of the Silesian wedge; below Czestochowa "a new barrier line is taking shape."

This line is said to run south to Cracow, into which Berlin admits the Russians have penetrated.

Moscow has not yet confirmed Lublin's report that Cracow has fallen, and it is probable that heavy fighting is in progress either in or around the city.

Below Cracow the Germans report that a Red Army attack from the Jaslo area—so far unannounced by Moscow—is "pressing towards Nowy Sacz," which represents an advance of about 35 miles by men of General Petrov's army on Koniev's left flank.

This attack they claim to be "under control," but admit that the front will have to be "levelled out to conform with the line farther north."

Lublin Poles Now Rule Warsaw

The Polish Provisional Government has taken over the administration of Warsaw, according to a statement last night by M. Osubka-Morawska, Premier of the Provisional Government, quoted by Lublin Radio.

Soviet Blow Was Timed With Allies

Washington, Thursday.

MR. HENRY STIMSON, Secretary of War, commenting on the Russian offensives, said today: "They reflect the constancy of the Russian effort, in co-operation with that the U.S., Britain, and the other Allies, to bring about the complete defeat of Germany.

"A powerful Russian offensive through Poland, aimed directly at the heart of Germany, is being linked with heavy pressure by Allied forces in France, Belgium, and Holland.

"The new Russian offensive comes at a time when American and British troops in the Ardennes have driven back the enemy with losses that must weaken his stand in the west."

Shops are 'Rationing' Potatoes

Unofficial Move During Shortage

POTATO rationing has been unofficially introduced in many areas of Britain and will remain in force until the present shortage ends.

This follows a recommendation by the Retail Fruit Trade Federation to greengrocers, who in the worst areas of shortage have already been supplying regular customers only.

In some cases, little more than 3lb. a head is being sold a week. The normal potato consumption is about 6lb.

In Liverpool, one of the worst areas, potato supplies available in the shops were at one time only 15 per cent. of normal. Many shops had no potatoes at all.

Since last week-end 761 tons have been sent to Liverpool, and a further 400 tons were expected from Northern Ireland last night. Long-keeping stocks have also been released.

'Shop-crawling'

Manchester, Newcastle on Tyne, and Brighton, all areas of more than average shortage, have begun unofficial rationing.

"People are actually shop-crawling for potatoes," one Brighton greengrocer told me. "I have never seen such a shortage here since the last war.

"There are so many women in Brighton who have nothing else to do but go on a shop-crawl. I overheard one woman the other day say that she had managed to collect 36lb. of lemons by queueing and hadn't an idea what to do with them."

Rationing has not been introduced in some areas where stocks can be drawn on. But the situation in London and the densely populated industrial areas may not improve at once.

Bad weather and the lack of labour and transport are blamed for the shortage. A small part of the main potato crop, which has been a normal one, is still in the ground, although there are hopes that it may be lifted soon.

Reprieve for Big Factory

On Merseyside

MR. DALTON, President of the Board of Trade, stated yesterday that negotiations are in progress for letting the Rootes Securities factory, at Speke, Liverpool, where thousands of workers have been given notice that they are to be discharged as redundant.

Mr. Dalton told a deputation from Liverpool City Council that he was determined that a high and continuous level of employment would be maintained at the factory.

Several firms have applied for the factory, and as soon as the Board made a decision the name of the firm would be announced.

HALF V2's FAIL TO LEAVE

Says Dutch Report

Half the V2's fired from the vicinity of the Hague fall on Dutch soil, most on the Hague itself, according to a 21-years-old Dutchman who has crossed the German lines into liberated Holland.

The Dutchman, quoted by a Dutch war correspondent, said that the rockets were brought up in lorries and fired from mobile platforms firmly secured to the ground.

They were shot from mortars carefully aimed from a car fitted with special devices. When 150ft. up the rocket's own propulsion system started to work. The launching lorries could be moved.—*Reuter.*

New Motor Fuel That Costs Nothing

TWO local authorities in the London area, Middlesex County Council and Croydon Corporation, are between them operating more than 100 motor vehicles on a fuel which costs practically nothing.

The vehicles are private cars, dust-carts, 4-ton lorries, and even vehicles with a laden weight of 11 tons. They are all running on methane—sludge gas.

Although experts had long been exploring the possibilities of methane as a motor fuel, no large-scale use was made of it in this country until Major W. H. Morgan, the Middlesex County engineer, was faced with the problem of burning sludge gas at the Mogden sewage works, Twickenham, during the black-out.

Sludge gas arises from the destruction of sewage waste and is 70 per cent. methane.

Major Morgan decided to collect the methane, and he told me yesterday that besides running vehicles on it it was used in heating the buildings and for the pumping and operation plant.

Croydon Corporation operates a fleet of 50 heavy lorries on methane. Mr. C. E. Boast, the borough engineer, says it has proved "most satisfactory."

The vehicles run three or four times longer on methane before decarbonising than when petrol is used.

Local authorities in all parts of the country are experimenting with this war-time fuel. Before long the Man in the Street may be able to buy methane in liquid form at 3d. a gallon or less.

While the gas itself costs nothing, an elaborate compressor plant is needed to liquefy it.

80-MPH GALE IN STRAIT

Ship Calls for Doctor

Mountainous seas, lashed by an 80-m.p.h. south-westerly gale, swept through the Strait of Dover last night. There was also heavy rain at times.

Waves crashed over the piers at south-east coast towns. Visibility was down to a few yards.

Dr. James Hall, the S O S sea surgeon, went out in the Walmer lifeboat to a steamer which had sent out a call for medical aid.

More Italy Ships Leave Spain

From Daily Mail Correspondent

MADRID, Thursday.—Three Italian landing barges and one trawler left Barcelona to-day to join the cruiser and four destroyers which were released by Spain on Sunday, despite German protests.

The nine vessels were manned exclusively by their original crews of 1,300 men, while less than a score declared themselves in favour of Mussolini's German-dominated Government.—*A.P.*

Capetown Beats Back Huge Fire

From Daily Mail Correspondent

CAPETOWN, Thursday.—The greatest fire ever to sweep the face of Table Mountain, roared down towards Capetown this morning and was only beaten back after it had penetrated the residential areas of the city.

Five thousand volunteers answered urgent radio calls for fire-beaters to tackle the solid five-mile blaze, advancing one mile every ten minutes. The fires are now under control, but not yet out.

Sir R. Campbell for Whitehall

Sir Ronald Ian Campbell, British Minister at Washington, has been appointed an Assistant Under-Secretary of State in the Foreign Office.

He will be succeeded by Mr. John Balfour, at present Minister in Moscow, states the Foreign Office.

Monty Bans Ice Cream

From Daily Mail Correspondent

BRUSSELS, Thursday.—A general Order of the Day from 21st Army Group H.Q. forbids all troops to buy ice-cream, owing to the danger of this product carrying typhoid germs.

P M FLAYS OPPONENTS IN ONE OF WAR'S BEST SPEECHES

Only Extremists to Press Greece Division

EDEN TO END DEBATE

By **WILSON BROADBENT,** Political Correspondent

EXTREMISTS in the Labour Party, and a few Independents who have persistently criticised the Government's policy in Greece, are expected to force a division in the House of Commons to-day, when the debate on Foreign Policy and the war situation, opened by the Prime Minister, is brought to a close.

Not more than a handful of M.P.s are likely to vote against the Government unless there is some unforeseen development.

Mr. Churchill's exposition of the Government's policy, his exposure of happenings in Greece, and his denunciation of his critics was numbered among his most powerful orations by commentators in the Lobby last night.

They declared that they had not heard him make a more dynamic and dramatic speech in this wartime Parliament.

Supporters of the Government were overjoyed at the vigour Mr. Churchill displayed.

It remains to be seen what the Opposition can offer in reply, and particular attention will be focused on the speech of Mr. Aneurin Bevan, the brilliant, but fiercely critical Welsh debater, who so frequently has crossed swords with the Prime Minister.

Grave Warning

Mr Anthony Eden will wind up the debate for the Government this afternoon.

Apart from Greece, Mr. Churchill's speech was one of the most comprehensive and confident he has ever made, embracing as it did a fervent and eloquent appeal for national unity in this, the final stage of the war in Europe.

His warning to Germany to seek peace by unconditional surrender led to an elaboration of the conditions which will be demanded of her in defeat.

Equally, his assertion of the principles underlying the purpose and determination of Britain's war, where the glory and responsibility, was conveyed in a passage which reached a degree of nobility of phrase which caused even those members most used to Churchillian oratory to pause and then to applaud excitedly.

Report of speech begins in Page TWO.

Our Tanks Smashing Roer Line

Monty Widening His Attack

BRITISH tanks have smashed through Rundstedt's defences in the 15-miles bridgehead west of the Roer river, the German News Agency admitted last night.

Three British divisions are attacking, the agency added, and German motorised forces are in action.

No confirmation has yet come from the Allied side. But Field-Marshal Montgomery's H.Q. reported a widening of the attack on the Roer salient from the Dutch "corridor" between Germany and Belgium.

After an all-night barrage by massed guns, British troops swarmed forward in a new attack north-east of Sittard. They advanced more than a mile towards the German town of Hongen.

On a ten-miles front between Sittard and Echt, Dempsey's men cleared a number of Dutch villages, after advances of up to two miles, and are edging into Germany.

St. Vith—One Mile

Stretches of the road from Sittard to Roermond, northern shoulder of the salient, are in British hands.

Sertorius, Berlin military commentator, said last night: "It remains to be seen whether this attack means more than meets the eye or whether it is just an attempt to pin down German forces."

American **First Army** troops compressing Rundstedt's salient in Belgium and Luxemburg are reported within a mile of St. Vith, one of the last bastions held by the Germans.

To the south-west they have pushed a mile beyond Cherain, where the salient is being crushed in at its most westerly point.

[illegible], Patton has flung two Third **Army** divisions over the River Sure near Diekirch. They have advanced up to two miles on a seven-miles front.

PANZERS HELD

From **COURTENAY EDWARDS,** Daily Mail Special Correspondent

SUSTEREN (Holland), Thursday.

MARKS in the trampled snow between the shattered shops and wrecked houses of this Dutch town bear witness to-day to the fierceness of the fighting yesterday before Susteren was cleared of the Germans.

British infantry have never fought more bravely than they did here when, armed only with Piats, Bren guns and rifles, they held at bay a whole "fleet" of German tanks.

I have borrowed the word "fleet" from an English officer who took part in the battle of Susteren. "They came charging through the streets just like warships going into action," he said.

"There were five or six small panzers forming a kind of protective screen round a King Tiger—just like destroyers circling round a battleship. I have never before seen the Hun use tactics quite like these."

Against this German armour our lightly armed troops held out until British tanks arrived. They sniped at the tank crews from upstairs windows and fired their Piats at the panzers from shop doorways.

One Piat crew knocked a tank right out.

Rattled by this unexpected opposition from a handful of infantrymen, the Germans lined up captured British troops and made them walk in front of the tanks as they rumbled along the main street.

Taking careful aim, our men kept firing. The tanks stopped. From out of one turret popped the head of an officer, who shouted in English: "If you shoot any more of my

BACK PAGE—Col. SIX

SEA-AIR LEADERS

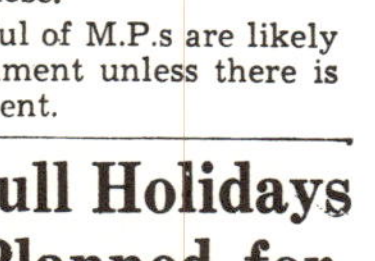

Vice-Admiral Burrough Takes on Ramsey's job.

Major-General Gale Commands the 'Airborne'

New Invasion Names are Announced

Burrough to Lead Naval Forces

By Daily Mail Reporter

TWO new names came into the Allied Command in the west last night, when the appointments were announced of:

Vice-Admiral Sir Harold M. **Burrough** to be Allied Naval Commander, Expeditionary Forces, in succession to Admiral Sir Bertram Ramsay, killed on January 2 in a Paris air crash, and of

Maj.-General Richard Nelson **Gale,** to succeed Lt.-General F. A. M. Browning as Deputy Commander of the First Allied Airborne Army.

Admiral Burrough, who is 56, has been Flag Officer Commanding Gibraltar since September 1943.

He commanded one of the three main naval forces in the North Africa landings and was awarded his second D.S.O. He gained the first in command of the naval forces in the Vaagso raid in 1941. He was knighted for his command of the escort of a great Malta convoy.

Admiral Burrough led the first combined operation in this war of British and Soviet Navies—a joint raid on enemy shipping in the Arctic port of Vardo.

He is married and has two sons and three daughters.

The Spearhead

Maj.-General Gale raised and trained the British Airborne Division which afterwards became the spearhead of the Allies' invasion.

At the outbreak of war, General Gale became G.S.O. II of a planning staff which did brilliant work in moving the British Expeditionary Force to France.

Later he became Director of Air at the War Office—a guide, philosopher and friend to all the rapidly increasing airborne forces in Britain.

It was General Gale's audacious and brilliantly executed plan which enabled the division, within a few hours of jumping into Normandy, to report that all the tasks allotted by higher command had been accomplished.

After the initial airborne assault, General Gale and his men fought in Normandy for some months.

His Beret

His D.S.O. was won during the battle of the Breville Gap, soon after the invasion began. He was also awarded the American Legion of Merit.

"His presence," says the citation, "still wearing his beret, combined with the utmost calmness and coolness, suggesting more an exercise than the middle of a very bloody battle, had such an amazing effect on the troops that wounded and attackers alike cheered and attacked with such élan as nothing could resist."

Both General Gale and General Browning are 48. General Browning was appointed Chief of Staff to Admiral Lord Louis Mountbatten, Supreme Commander South-East Asia, in November.

The Admiralty also announced last night that Rear-Admiral V. A. C. Crutchley, V.C., has been appointed Flag Officer, Gibraltar and Mediterranean Approaches, and Rear-Admiral J. H. Edelsten has been given a sea-going appointment.

Rear-Admiral Crutchley won his V.C. as a lieutenant in the Vindictive at Ostend in 1918.

Shelter Statement

Mr. Morrison, Home Secretary, told Mr. Chater (Lab., Bethnal Green), in the House of Commons yesterday that he hoped to make a statement to-day on the Bethnal Green shelter case.

Full Holidays Planned for This Year

NORMAL holidays, of peace-time duration, are in prospect this year for thousands of war workers. Industry, which has drawn up 1945 labour schedules assuming holidays will be on the same basis as last year, is expected to be recommended to follow the lead of the Civil Service, which has just been notified that holiday leave has been extended.

Personnel of Government Departments will get 24-days holiday, in addition to the usual Bank Holidays, compared with 18 days during 1944, and 16 in 1943.

Ministry of Labour officials said yesterday that they regarded the extension of Civil Service holidays as a first step towards a probable relaxation of Mr. Bevin's war-time regulations governing the number of "man-hours" which must be worked.

"If the regulations are relaxed," they said, "the result will automatically be that employers will be able to grant longer holidays."

'BRITISH ATTACK GAINS MOMENTUM'

German High Command reported late last night: "The British attack in the Roer salient is gaining momentum."

'BUILD OWN HOMES,' GERMANS TOLD

Dr. Robert Ley, German Labour Front leader, said last night: "Bombed-out people must not look for help to the authorities. They must build their temporary homes themselves."—Reuter.

'Big 3 Chief Has Spoken'

"Herr Churchill has spoken again," said a German commentator on Berlin radio last night. "We must not overlook that, whatever we think of him, he is the very mouthpiece of the 'Big Three.'"

[Mr. Churchill's call to the German people to surrender was plugged at Germany last night by Allied stations, while neutrals made the speech headline news.]

SUNDAY NEWS

Copr 1945 by News Syndicate Co. Inc. NEW YORK'S PICTURE NEWSPAPER Trade Mark Reg. U. S. Pat. Off.

5 CENTS PAY NO MORE

Vol. 24. No. 38 New York, Sunday, January 21, 1945★ Main Section, 76 Pages

(Acme Telefoto)

F.D.R. Vows Lasting Peace.

With the sound of the guns of World War II not yet stilled in their ears, wounded veterans hear President Roosevelt vow a lasting peace, in his inaugural address from the south portico of the White House. The smallest crowd in recent history witnessed the ceremonies, the second time that the Presidential oath of office has been administered at the White House.

Story on Page 2, other pictures in center fold

The Evening News

NO. 19,655 LONDON, SATURDAY, JANUARY 27, 1945 ONE PENNY

ZHUKOV'S TANKS 95 MILES FROM BERLIN, BRANDENBURG FRONTIER REACHED

"Advancing Russians Checked On The Obra," Say Nazis

BOMBERS SMASH BRESLAU: EAST PRUSSIA BLOCKADED

HITLER'S High Command announced this afternoon that Marshal Zhukov's tanks have reached the Obra River, west of Poznan, and at two points only 95 miles from Berlin.

Here is what the German communique says: "Between Lissa and the Netze river advancing enemy formations were checked in front of our positions on the Obra river. At Poznan, Schneidemuehl and north-west of Bromberg fighting continues."

Earlier the German Overseas News Agency had reported: "Zhukov's troops have reached the old Polish-German border, both north-west and south-west of Poznan."

It stated that one spearhead had been checked on the River Obra, a tributary of the Warthe, which crosses the border at a point only 95 miles from the city boundary of Berlin.

Previous German reports said the Russians had reached the frontier town of Bentschen, on the main Poznan—Berlin railway. This column would be about 12 miles south of the force which has reached the Obra.

So far there is no official news from Moscow of this latest development.

But the Associated Press correspondent in Moscow, in a message this afternoon, says:

The Germans threw armoured reserves into the sagging front north-west and south-west of Poznan to-day, seeking to cut off Marshal Zhukov's spearheads, which are now barely 100 miles from Berlin.

NETZE CROSSED

Red Fleet in Action

The enemy is endeavouring at all costs to stabilise this perilous sector, where further Soviet gains might shatter the defensive capability of the Reich.

Another Russian column has crossed the Netze river east of the important German road and rail centre of Schneidemuehl at a point about 115 miles north-east of Berlin, said Colonel Ernst von Hammer, military correspondent of the German News Agency.

Moscow also reported to-day that the Red Air Force and Red Fleet had gone into action.

The Soviet Mosquito Fleet, submarines and bombers are busy day and night blockading East Prussia, said an N.B.C. correspondent in a broadcast from Moscow.

An A.P. front-line cable said that Breslau is being reduced block by block by heavy Russian bombing.

"It is falling the way a fortress falls," said the correspondent.

Although the Russians have still made no claim to have crossed the great river barrier, the Oder, Berlin reported to-day that the river had been forded along a 130-mile front.

WHOLE DIVISIONS

Some Thrown Back

The Germans admitted that "numbers of complete Red Army infantry divisions and many tanks" were across the Oder.

As usual, the Germans claimed that some Russian units were thrown back.

Red Army infantry and armour were also reported this afternoon to be menacing Koenigsberg, Danzig, Breslau and Poznan.

Here are the latest positions:

KOENIGSBERG: Cherniakovsky's men reached a point nine miles from the city after smashing through Loetzen and Tapiau, two fortress towns.

DANZIG.—Marshal Rokossovsky's men are 20 miles from the great Baltic port.

Paris radio said to-day that Russian spearheads had reached Danzig.

BRESLAU.—Marshal Koniev's troops are across the River Oder north and south of the city. The Germans manning the Breslau defence system have been forced back. Koniev's men are ready to storm the city.

The German communique also reported deep breaches by the Russians south of the Vistula, and in the Upper Silesian industrial zone street fighting in Elbing, the town five miles from the Baltic coast.

A map showing changes in Europe since the end of January, 1944, is on the BACK PAGE.

SECRET PEP TALK ON REPAIRS

MR. DUNCAN SANDYS MEETS DELEGATES

MANY building contractors who arrived at Caxton Hall to-day for a secret meeting on bomb damage repairs were turned away at the door.

One of those refused admission was Mr. A. Mortimer, president of the Bath Master Builders' Association, who is a group leader in charge of 140 men in Lewisham.

He caught the 4.15 a.m. train from Bath and arrived at the hall without even having had breakfast.

The meeting, organised by the National Federation of Shop Stewards, was due to start at 10 o'clock, but at 10.30 delegates were still arriving, and the proceedings were held up.

Only stewards carrying invitations were admitted.

Pep Talk

Mr. Duncan Sandys, Minister of Works, gave a "pep talk" on first-aid repairs.

One delegate said: "We expect there will be a lot of dirty linen to be washed in the meeting, so we should be paid dirty money."

It was stated later that the builders were under the misapprehension that private contractors had been invited to the meeting, which, however, was for shop stewards only.

TRAINS UP TO SIX HOURS LATE

DELAYS FROM SCOTLAND

"Evening News" Reporter

MAIN-LINE trains were arriving at London termini to-day up to as much as six hours late.

The night Scottish expresses arrived at Euston between three and six hours behind schedule. Trains from Manchester were two to three hours late and from Birmingham about one hour.

Although the primary cause of the hold-up is due to weather conditions, a contributory cause is the abnormal amount of sickness among their train staff owing to the severe cold.

Delays From the West

Conditions on the G.W.R. were similar, the night expresses from South Wales, Cornwall and Devon being as much as six hours late.

The Southern Railway reported one or two West of England expresses half an hour behind time, but otherwise running was practically normal at Waterloo.

L.N.E.R. Scottish expresses were delayed up to three hours.

STALAG SEARCH FAILS

"London Man" Mystery

"Evening News" Reporter

Complete search of the list of R.A.F. prisoners known to be in Stalag Luft VII at Kreuzburg, Silesia, has failed to reveal any trace of "Sergt. Paul Vermullen," a London clerk, said by Moscow radio to have been freed by the advancing Red Army.

The Air Ministry think that the other man said to have escaped is Sergt. Donald Meese (not Mace), of Sheffield, where his widowed mother lives. He was shot down over France last June.

BOTTLE NECK

We keep open house, but only to those who bring beer with them.—Husband at Tottenham to-day.

WOMEN AND CHILDREN FLEE BERLIN

25 Special Trains Run To-day

An Associated Press cable from Stockholm to-day said:

THE evacuation of women and children began in Berlin to-day, according to three authoritative sources who have arrived in Stockholm to-day from the German capital.

Twenty-five trains were placed at the disposal of the refugees, who are boarding the trains 10 miles from Berlin.

They said the lack of rolling stock and the lack of housing elsewhere in the interior of Germany is expected to make the evacuation difficult.

In Front Line

Through the Nazi censorship the Berlin correspondent of the *Aftonbladet* was allowed to report that Berliners now feel they are "in the very front area. The atmosphere has changed—Berlin is holding its breath and watching the East."

For the first time Berlin morning newspapers appeared as a single sheet. Tram and tube services were further restricted.

Large cases with official records were seen being moved in Berlin yesterday by Wehrmacht lorries from administrative buildings to unknown destinations, it was said.

There was talk in Berlin, these sources said, that the Government was preparing to transfer to Southern Germany, probably in Wurtemberg, but there was no confirmation of this.

"Peace Move" Hints

German-inspired reports that Nazi resistance would halt with the fall of Koenigsberg were circulated to-day.

From Madrid, Lisbon and Barcelona came reports that Germany was close to accepting surrender terms due to the powerful Soviet advances.

WHEN A V-BOMB HITS THEIR HOME

Workers May Be Told

"Evening News" Reporter

The Government has a number of schemes under consideration which will enable factory workers to be told quickly when their homes have been damaged by V-bombs.

Important security questions are involved in this matter, and before any scheme is approved the authorities will have to be satisfied that there will be no leakage of information which will be of help to the enemy.

V.-bomb kills P.C.—Page Three.

MORE TROOPS LAND ON LUZON—TOKIO

Key Airfield Shelled

Japanese troops on the Philippine island of Luzon are making a determined stand south-west of Bamban against the Allied drive for Manila, and are shelling Clark Field, biggest Philippine air base just captured by the Americans.

An American force of about three divisions has just been landed in the Lingayen sector of Luzon, says Tokio.

GUNS FOIL ESCAPE

20 Nazi P.O.W.s Caught

Twenty Germans recently made an unsuccessful attempt to escape from a prisoner-of-war camp in a North Midlands town. They were seen to get through the wire barrier surrounding the camp and make for the open country. Guard posts were immediately warned and Bren guns from watch towers were trained on the men.

They dashed towards a nearby aerodrome with guards in pursuit, and then, bewildered by the firing around them, surrendered.

'HIMMLER C.-IN-C.'

In Upper Rhine

A German proclamation captured by U.S. Seventh Army troops is signed by Himmler, who is styled "German C.-in-C. Upper Rhine."

The proclamation, issued on New Year's Day, urges the Germans facing Sixth Army Group troops to re-take strips of occupied Reich territory.—B.U.P.

THE POTATO FRONT

Much More Promising

The outlook in the London potato market towards the close of the week was much more promising. Arrivals were about equal to current requirements. Demand was particularly keen, and all varieties cleared steadily.

LONDON FIREWATCH

Suspension Under Review

"Evening News" Reporter

Suspension of firewatching duties throughout London, including the City is under consideration. An announcement is likely to be made soon.

No date has so far been decided upon, but as the possibility of any further blitz has become remote it is probable that London will soon be brought into line with the rest of the country.

SWITCH IN TIME

When I married, my wife referred to me lovingly as her husband, but now I am just the old man: Husband at a Middlesex court to-day.

TRAFFIC JAM after a mishap on a toboggan run near Hemel Hempstead.

Down—And Up—In The Straits

To-day's temperatures in the Straits of Dover:

	Degrees
8 a.m.	29
9 a.m.	29
10 a.m.	28
11 a.m.	27
12 noon	26
1 p.m.	26
2 p.m.	26
3 p.m.	27

He Leaves £100,000 on Trust To Secretary

"Evening News" Reporter

BRITAIN'S pioneer cinema "king," Sir William Frederick Jury, who died last August at the age of 73, started life as a messenger boy in a firework factory. His will, published to-day, shows that he left £500,738, most of it to charity.

Sir William, who was knighted for his services in organising entertainment for the Forces in the last war, left £100,000 on trust for Miss Florence May Cook for life, his furniture, and the use of his house at St. Peter's Hill, Caversham, Reading.

Miss Cook, who was Sir William's secretary for many years, told me to-day: "I have not made any plans, and I don't know what I shall do with the money."

Fund President

Sir William was a director of cinema groups and president of the Cinematograph Trade Benevolent Fund.

Apart from a bequest of £15,000 to his sister, Mrs. Minnie Vyse, and other small legacies, he left the remainder of his fortune to charity, which included: £10,000 to the Imperial Cancer Research Fund; £5,000 each to the Royal Naval Benevolent Trust, Merchant Navy Comforts' Service, and the R.A.F. Benevolent Fund; £5,000 each to Charing Cross Hospital, Guy's, King's College, Middlesex, University College, Royal Free, St. Bartholomew's, St. George's, St. Mary's, St. Thomas's, and Westminster Hospitals.

He also left £3,000 each to the Royal Hospital for Incurables, Putney, the Royal Masonic Hospital, St. Dunstan's, and Central London Throat, Nose and Ear Hospital.

SHE GETS £10,000

"For Care and Attention"

Miss Evelyn Chesshire, of Queen's-road, Tunbridge Wells, who died last October, left £10,000 of her £22,000 fortune to Miss Iris E. Williams "in appreciation of her care and attention." Miss Chesshire also left £1,000 to Ethel M. H. Evant, £50 to Helen Kennard, who nursed her, and the residue upon trust for her niece, Naomi E. Chesshire, with the remainder to the children of her brother, George H. F. J. Chesshire.

Towing Troops Is His Speciality

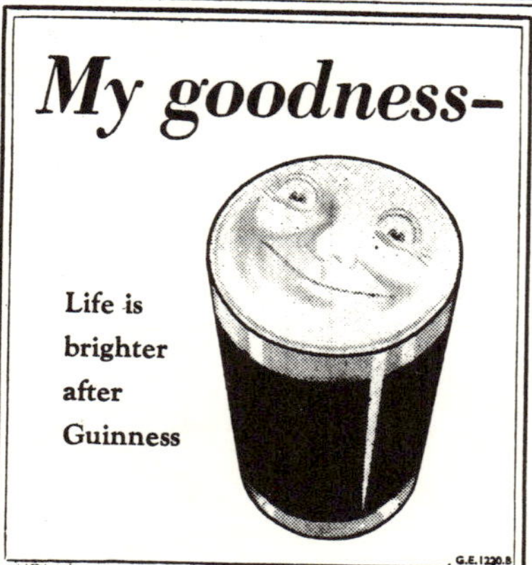

Flight-Lieutenant Philip Garrity, of Cheylesmore House, Ebury Bridge-road, London, has been awarded the D.F.C. He is one of the most experienced tow-plane navigators in the R.A.F., and helped in the airborne invasions of Sicily, Normandy and Holland.

CALLED TO THE BAR

I was reading law when a friend invited me to come out and have one.—Witness at a London court.

U.S. CLOTHES DRIVE

President Roosevelt has asked Mr. Henry Kaiser, shipbuilding magnate, to head a gigantic campaign to collect "usable used clothing for all the peoples of Europe." It will start in April.—Reuter.

Snow in the Straits To-day—And More Likely

ELECTRICITY CUT AGAIN IN SOME LONDON AREAS

Stoppage from Carlisle to S. Coast

ELECTRICITY supplies throughout the whole of England and Wales, from Carlisle to the South Coast and Land's End, were cut again to-day for about an hour between 9 and 10.

Parts of Greater London were affected by the cuts for the third time, after special appeals by the Fuel Ministry.

Areas affected included Kenton, parts of Wembley, and Hoddesdon, in Hertfordshire, served by the North Met Power Company. "Peak capacity is the trouble," said an official to-day.

In five districts of Huddersfield the switch-off lasted 35 minutes and represented a five per cent. cut in supplies. Hospitals, factories on essential work and trolleybus services were not affected.

Factories and hospitals in other areas, however, were affected.

"It is not expected that there will be further cuts to-day," said a Central Electricity Board official. "It being a Saturday the load becomes easier after midday."

Frozen Milk Came by Sleigh.—BACK PAGE.

More Londoners Home on Leave From Burma

LOOKING bronzed and fit in Britain's winter climate, another contingent of leave men from Burma and the Far East, with a sprinkling from the Mediterranean zone, landed at a Scottish port to-day.

A military band from a Scottish regiment greeted them by playing "The Brave Little Army."

The men cheered when a loud-speaker announced that "other ranks" would disembark first.

Only a few weeks ago some of these men had been sweating in a temperature of nearly 80 degrees on the road to Mandalay. The men quickly entrained for dispersal stations, where they will be fitted out with clothing more suited to British climate.

No Demonstration

The first contingents to step ashore were men from London and the Southern Counties, but practically every area in the British Isles was represented in the two ships which disembarked their khaki passengers.

There was no formality and little demonstration, but the sight of a group of N.A.A.F.I. and A.T.S. girls on the landing stage brought whoops of joy from teh men in the tender.

FOUR MEN IN A CAR

'Had Guns, Truncheon, Jemmy'

Two loaded guns, a truncheon and a jemmy were found in a car which was chased by the police, it was alleged at Uxbridge to-day when Douglas Drew, John Derek Guest and Richard Randall, all of Hayes, Middlesex, and George Cook, of South Ruislip, were charged with being concerned together in stealing the car from a Hayes cinema car park. The police said the car was driven faster and faster until P.C. Smale, in the pursuing police car, opened a door and shouted: "Stop or we shall ram you."

50 FOR TRIAL

At the Old Bailey

The trial of Frank Sanderson (28), Chequer-lane, Dagenham, who is charged with the murder of Evelyn Iris Sedgwick, 28, cafe waitress, who was found strangled in her flat at Rainham-road South, Dagenham, will take place at the next session of the Central Criminal Court, which opens on Tuesday. There are over 50 persons for trial during the session.

RELATIVELY SAFE

I went home determined to prove to my wife that I was master, but I changed my mind when I saw my mother-in-law there.—Witness at a London court.

DAY OUT FOR MUSTANGS

Despite cloud and icing conditions, Mustangs of Balkan Air Force yesterday had one of their most successful days yet when train after train was bombed and strafed on a vital stretch of railway between Novska and Brod, on the main line from Zagreb to Belgrade.

F.D.R. MAY VISIT VATICAN

President Roosevelt may visit Pope Pius—possibly during or immediately after the impending "big three" meeting, Paris radio reported to-day from Vatican City. A special protocol has been drafted providing for such a visit.

A NEW LANDING OFF BURMA COAST

FIFTH IN THE MONTH

A NEW Allied landing—the fifth in a month—has been made off the coast of Burma, says to-day's Seac communique, which reports that 15th Indian Corps troops had landed on Cheduba Island, S.W. of Ramree Island, scene of an earlier landing.

Cheduba Island, which lies off the Arakan coast, is separated from Ramree Island by a strait about five miles wide.

At the nearest point it is 35 miles from the Japanese base of Taungup, on the coast. Taungup port is protected by a number of islets just off the coast.

PRAGUE REVOLT STORY

Two hundred residents of Prague were killed by machine-guns following an insurrection in the Czecho-Slovakian capital, Brazzaville radio reported to-day.

U.S. ATTACKS NEAR JULICH

—Says Berlin

NAZI ESCAPE TRAINS BLASTED BY R.A.F.

German radio reports that the U.S. Ninth Army is attacking both sides of Julich. Allied messages so far speak only of attacks by General Simpson's forces north of Linnich.

R.A.F. Tempests flew halfway to Berlin to smash at Rundstedt's transport fleeing from the West.

Movement was reported in the region of Bremen and Niemburg.

To-day's S.H.A.E.F. communique reported that fighter-bombers destroyed a railway bridge over the Moselle, 16 miles north-east of Trier, attacked a railway yard north-east of Kaiserslautern, and road and rail transport in the Bitche and Colmar areas, bombed and strafed a convoy west of Karlsruhe, and struck at targets north-west of Haguenau.

Second T.A.F. planes attacked 31 trains, destroying 13 locomotives and damaging 18. More than 150 rail trucks were destroyed or damaged. At least one train was seen laden with troops.

Half-way between Nijmegen and Geldern enemy road transport was hit and 26 vehicles destroyed or damaged. Other reports indicate that the enemy movement out of the original bulge area has ceased.

On the British front, General Dempsey's armour and infantry swarmed across the main Roermond—Heinsberg road against weakening German resistance and entered Posterholt, six miles south of Roermond. The thrust to Posterholt marked a 1½-mile advance.

DRESS TEASE

"IT'S a pity, but they have to dress that way in case somebody suddenly switches the heat off."—By Gittins.

MISSING M.P.s

Search Goes On

Italy-based R.A.F. planes to-day continued their search for the two M.P.s, Captain R. H. Bernays and Mr. J. D. Campbell, missing on a flight from Rome to Brindisi, but so far they have not been able to trace the missing plane. Walrus float planes are co-operating in the search by combing the Adriatic for wreckage.—Reuter.

DIM-OUT 6.10 p.m. to 8.15 a.m.
Moon Rises 4.48 p.m. Sets 9.5 a.m.
Full Moon To-morrow.
Sun Sets 5.40 p.m.
Rises To-morrow 8.45 a.m.
Lighting-up Time London 6.10 p.m.

WOMEN AND CHILDREN FLEE FROM BERLIN

See This Page

Refugees arriving in Berlin from Stettin claimed that Neustettin, in West Prussia near the old Polish Corridor was being evacuated of non-essentials, says Stockholm reports. Berlin, so packed with refugees that many are continuing their journey on foot along the main roads west and south of the capital. Temperature in Berlin during past week has been six degrees below freezing point.—A.P.

NAZIS STOP COAL FOR DENMARK

German coal shipments to Denmark have been stopped "because military requirements come first," Wilhelmstrasse spokesman reported. Coal shipments to Switzerland, however, "will be continued as far as possible."

BRITAIN OWES EGYPT £300,000,000

Cairo report Egyptian newspaper "Akhbar el Yom" reports that list has been drawn up showing sums due by Britain to Egypt and that figure **exceeds £300,000,000.**

'NO WONDER HEINRICH WAS WANTED'

Heinrich Rauschmueller, for whom German radio recently put out an S O S asking him to get in touch with their Transport Ministry, is a railway repair expert, Luxembourg radio reported to-day.

"No wonde his services are so urgently required," said Luxembuorg. "Now that such tremendous damage has been done to German railway traffic."

FRENCH AMBASSADOR'S PLEA FOR MUTUAL UNDERSTANDING

M. Rene Massigli, French Ambassador, addressing school teachers from Lancashire and Cheshire at Liverpool University to-day, said that intellectual relations between Britain and France must not be confined to classical sphere.

They must pool into common ownership all their dreams, experiments, setbacks and achievements. On both sides of Channel it was essential that we should unite our efforts. No lasting collaboration and true friendship could exist without mutual understanding.

They wanted educators of British youth to possess a better knowledge of the new France.

News Chronicle

No 30,799 WEDNESDAY, JANUARY 31, 1945 ONE PENNY

LATE LONDON EDITION

HITLER: WE FIGHT, NO MATTER WHERE, TILL VICTORY

Every fit man must stake his life, even the sick must work

"WHOEVER STABS US IN THE BACK WILL DIE"

HITLER, broadcasting to the German nation from his headquarters last night, said it was now more than ever necessary to strengthen their solemn determination to fight on, no matter where and no matter under what circumstances, until final victory crowned their efforts.

"I expect every fit German to stake his life and body in battle. I expect the sick and infirm to work to the last ounce of their strength."

And Hitler uttered this warning: "Whoever stabs us in the back will die an ignominious death."

In the East a gruesome fate was exterminating men in tens and hundreds of thousands, but despite all setbacks, and all grim trials the Germans would ward it off and master it.

HIS 12 YEARS OF POWER

His speech, which lasted 21 minutes, was the shortest he has made on the anniversary of his coming into power.

He began with a review of the position in Germany during the 12 years since he became Chancellor of the Reich, when Germany had almost seven million unemployed and another seven millions working reduced hours.

Since January, 1933, only six years of peace had been granted to Germany, but in that time the German body politic had been put on a sound military basis, not in the first place by equipping it with material war-making power, but by imbuing it with the spiritual will of resistance and self-assertiveness.

He continued:

Today in the East a gruesome fate is exterminating men in their tens and hundreds of thousands, in villages and hamlets, in the country and in the cities. But by dint of the utmost exertions, and despite all setbacks, and all our grim trials, we shall ward it off and master it.

That this should even be possible is only because since 1933 the German people have undergone an inner metamorphosis.

Goose and the Fox

There is no need to argue with those fatheads who believe that an undefended Germany would, by virtue of its harmlessness, never have fallen prey to this Jewish international world conspiracy.

The defenceless goose is not spared by the fox just because she is constitutionally incapable of harbouring aggressive intentions. Nor does the wolf turn pacifist because sheep are unarmed.

Our nation's power of resistance has increased so tremendously since January 30, 1933, that it is now beyond comparison with earlier times.

By maintaining this inner strength of resistance we have the safest guarantee of final victory.

Europe today is ridden with serious disease, and the States which are suffering from this malady will either overcome it, if they mobilise their strength to resist to the full, or they will die of it.

Even he who survives such an illness can pass the crisis only by exertions which weaken him in an extreme degree.

It is, therefore, all the more our invariable principle to stop at nothing in this struggle to save our nation from the most horrible fate of all times, and to obey with unfaltering loyalty the command to preserve our nation.

Dishonourable few

The Almighty created our people. In defending their existence we defend His work. If this defence involves indescribable and unparalleled misery, suffering and pain, that only serves to enhance our love for this people.

But it also serves to imbue us with the hardness necessary to make us do our duty even at the worst moments of crisis, to do our duty not only towards honourable and eternal Germany, but also towards those dishonourable few who forswear their nationhood.

Thus, in this fateful struggle, there is only one command: He who covers himself with honour in the fight will be able to save his own life and that of his kin. He who stabs us in the back in a base and cowardly manner will inevitably die an ignominious death.

Barely a few months and weeks ago Allied statesmen quite openly outlined Germany's fate. They were subsequntly taken to task by several newspapers who urged them to show more cunning, and instead make promises, even if they had no intention of carrying them out.

"Evil spirits"

In this hour I, as an unrelenting National Socialist and fighter for my people, would like to assure these statesmen once and for all that any attempt to make an impression on Nazi Germany by using phrases of the kind used by Wilson presumes a simplicity of mind unknown in modern Germany.

It is like one sheep assuring another sheep that it would protect it against a tiger.

I repeat my prophecy of former days: not only will Great Britain be incapable of taming Bolshevism. Her own development must necessarily be more and more that of a body infected with this wasting disease.

All the small European nations who capitulated, trusting in Allied guarantees, are heading for complete extermination. This fate is so inevitable that it does not matter in the least whether it materialises a little sooner or later.

But Germany will never suffer that fate. So much is guaranteed

Continued Back Page A

Hitler—and ghost voice

News Chronicle Radio Listener

HITLER'S voice sounded at the beginning rather sepulchral, but became more normal during the rest of the speech.

Now and then there were short pauses when he turned the pages of his manuscript.

He used none of his oratorical tricks, and it seemed that the speech was made or recorded in a very large room. The words echoed as if the room had no furniture.

There were frequent interjections by a "ghost voice," which was, however, almost inaudible.

It seemed as if the ghost voice repeated two slogans. The one sounded like "Hitler is Germany's gravedigger," and the other "Hitler must go if Germany shall live."

The main object of the speech seemed to be to utter threats against weaklings and traitors.

Things we are mighty tough about—F.D.R.

WASHINGTON, Tuesday.

PRESIDENT ROOSEVELT, commending American unity in a message broadcast tonight from the White House, said: "We are a nation of free people, and free people know how to go over the top."

"The reason for this is no military secret. It is the determination of the many to work as one for the common good."

The President, whose message was read by Mrs. Roosevelt, was giving thanks for the millions contributed annually on his birthday to the National Infantile Paralysis Fund.

"Our enemies," he said, "are learning—and learning the hard way—that there are many things we are mighty tough about.

"We will never tolerate a force that destroys the life, the happiness, the free future of our children, any more than we will tolerate the continuance on earth of the brutalities and barbarities of the Nazis or of the Japanese war lords.

"We combat this evil enemy of disease at home just as unremittingly as we fight our evil enemies abroad."

New landing may outflank Manila

A new Allied landing on the west coast of Luzon, some 60 miles south of Lingayen Gulf, threatens to outflank Manila. The landing was made between San Narcisco and San Antonio, said Gen. MacArthur's communique. These two places, five miles apart, lie just north-west of Bataan.

The Japs were completely surprised. Allied troops landed without loss and drove inland.

Indian leaders silenced

Patna, India, Tuesday. — The Government of Bihar Province has issued an Order prohibiting the publication without permission of any statement or speech by any of the five Congressmen on whom internment orders were served last week-end.

12 YEARS AFTER

The latest picture of Hitler to reach London last night. It was not taken by his personal photographer Hoffmann, but is from a captured German film. Hitler, sad-faced and in sombre mood, hat in hand, is surveying the ruins of a German town, the name of which is not disclosed

40-mile columns of German refugees

THE twelfth anniversary of Hitler's rule in Germany was marked, among other things, by this description of the great exodus of German civilians from the east:

Millions of German refugees, streaming in apparently endless columns, are trekking west away from the advancing spearheads of the Red Army.

This word picture was given last night by a reporter of the German Overseas News Agency.

"This mass migration," he said, "is covering between 20 and 25 miles a day. First batches have already reached their destinations.

Horses weaken

"The refugees set out village by village and try to keep together as best they can. They vary in size from small groups comprising only a few carts to giant queues stretching for 30 or 40 miles, straggling along with many thousands of vehicles.

"Grim winter weather is making things very difficult for them. Women, children and aged persons are walking for hundreds of miles with scarcely a rest.

"Food for the horses is hard to find and the animals grow weaker every day.

"Food-stages set up by the roadside are intended to make the long road easier for the fleeing columns. Only a limited percentage of the refugees die on the way."

Another radio picture was of life in beleaguered Koenigsberg, broadcast by a German war reporter there.

"The inhabitants of the East Prussian capital," he said, "are now living in the cellars of their houses. They sleep in their clothes, they look pale-faced, their eyes are dim with overstrain.

"Defences are being manned at the fringe of the town to meet the four Russian armies and two tank corps on the move in East Prussia.

"The superiority of the enemy is overwhelming and though he has not yet succeeded in encircling Koenigsberg he may succeed."

Danzig radio broadcast this "important announcement" for the people of that area: "Men and women. Clear the snow from the highways, and particularly from the road from Dirschau to Hohenstein. This stretch must be cleared without fail. You all know what is at stake."

Another broadcast stated: "Adolf Hitler carried on the struggle for 14 years without apparent hope of success. In the end he took power. Let us remember this tonight when the call goes out for the assault against our Reich to be thrown back."

"In Berlin Now," by Denis Weaver, Page Two.

MILES 0 50 100
Koenigsberg Insterburg Gdynia EAST PRUSSIA Elbing Stolp Danzig Kolberg Marienburg Allenstein CHERNIAKHOVSKY Schwetz Bydgoszcz ROKOSSOVSKY Mlawa Stettin Stargarde Torun Schneidemuehl Woldenberg Vistula Driesen Kuestrin ZHUKOV Betsche Poznan POLAND Warsaw Berlin Frankfurt Bentschen Schwiebus Bomst Zuellichau GERMANY Oder Lodz Kottbus Guhrau Warthe Steinau KONIEV Goerlitz Breslau Dresden Oppeln Katowice CZECHOSLOVAKIA Ratibor Cracow Prague

Vast Soviet tank onslaught heads West, say Nazis

THE formidable armies of Marshal Zhukov were last night on Berlin's admission 80 miles east of the Reich capital and were still advancing.

A broadcast report by the German High Command declared: "Soviet reconnaissance thrusts between the Oder and the Netze, as well as north of the Netze, have now become merged into one vast tank-borne onslaught heading west."

A military spokesman later spoke of a Soviet force driving west beyond the Meseritz-Zuellichau line and striving to fan out between Frankfurt-on-Oder and Kuestrin—that is to say, advancing within 80 miles of Berlin.

This morning the German News Agency reported that in the area "west of Poznan, where the position has deteriorated, Soviet spearheads have achieved a deep breach."

Moscow, in its communique last night—there was no special Order from Marshal Stalin yesterday—announced the capture by Zhukov of more German towns. These included Stolzenberg, 83 miles east-north-east of Berlin; Betsche, 90 miles east; Bomst, Unruhstadt and Tirschtiegel, all on the approaches to the Zuellichau railway.

Elsewhere the communique reported steady progress, particularly in the Carpathians.

Red Army officers take out their new maps

From PAUL WINTERTON
News Chronicle Correspondent

MOSCOW, Tuesday.

THERE was a dramatic moment on the Central front west of Poznan a day or two ago when a group of Russian Staff officers took out a new set of maps and pasted them on to western margins of the old ones.

The new maps were of Pomerania and Brandenburg, and they included what is now universally referred to here as "the lair of the Fascist beast"—Berlin itself.

Some of these same officers, in the dark days when the tide of battle was going against them on the Don and in Stalingrad, had taken out these same maps and studied them and cheered themselves up in their dug-outs with the certain knowledge that one day they would be using them—or someone would—to wage war on German land.

PATIENCE IS REWARDED

Now Russian patience has been justified, for the dream has come true. There has been a great surge forward towards the German capital during the past 24 hours, and that, without any doubt, is today's story.

While Rokossovsky and Cherniakhovsky in the north, and Koniev in the south are still able to maintain their pressure and draw off vital German reserves to the defence of both flanks, the Red Army avalanche seems to be developing its full power on the crucial Central front.

Marshal Zhukov is wielding a mighty instrument. In Marshal Stalin's Order last night in honour of Zhukov's invasion of Pomerania the names of 18 infantry generals, six tank generals and seven artillery generals were mentioned.

This great army group—or part of it—has just fought a remarkable action. Coming up to the Rivers Obra and Netze after a one-day "march" on wheels of 25 miles, it came into head-on collision with German reserves

RIVER DEFENCES SHATTERED

The enemy was standing on a strong river and lake defence line, but the Russians carved their way clean through two tank and four German infantry divisions, killing 4,000 men and taking 1,000 prisoners on their way, and burst deep into Pomerania and Brandenburg.

Foremost in the tank assault which spearheaded the drive was the unit of Col.-Gen. Katukov, whose armoured brigade was first given the honour of being called a "Guards" unit after the successful counter-thrust outside Moscow in the autumn of 1941.

What is the position on the crucial Central front as the result of this drive? We know that Russian war reports have never been more cautious than in these days of brilliant victory, but even the Russians today officially put their advanced columns no more than 85 miles from Berlin.

By his push to the north-west beyond captured Woldenberg, Zhukov's men are little more than 60 miles from Stettin, at the mouth of the Oder, and it is hardly necessary to emphasise the new danger of encirclement which may soon lie ahead of the German forces in the long north-easterly salient of Pomerania.

It is not a dissimilar threat to that which will be created by Marshal Koniev to the Germans holding the long tongue of Silesia, if he can succeed in establishing and developing his bridgeheads west of the upper Oder.

Marshal Zhukov has also completely severed in many places the main railway from Berlin to Danzig, and is thereby lending useful aid to Rokossovsky's campaign in East Prussia and the border of the old Polish Corridor.

In addition to those units of the First White Russian Army which have invaded Germany, a group of some size is still investing the large German force trapped in Poznan.

The garrison of Poznan is not aware yet of the extent of the

Continued Back Page B

Czechs to recognise Lublin

By a Correspondent

Within the next few days the London Czechoslovak Government will recognise the Lublin Provisional Government of Poland.

Mr. Joseph Hejret, former Press Attaché at the Czechoslovak Legation in Warsaw, has been appointed Envoy and Minister Plenipotentiary to the Lublin Government. Mr. Hejret is editor of the London weekly "Czechoslovak," the official organ of the London Czech Government.

Into Siegfried Line, shoulder to shoulder

From NORMAN CLARK
News Chronicle War Correspondent

OUR RIVER FRONT, Tuesday.

SHOULDER to shoulder, divisions of two armies have resumed the drive into Germany.

Without a day's pause to regroup or refit, the southern flank of the U.S. First Army under Gen. Hodges and the northern wing of Gen. Patton's Third Army are pressing steadily, on a broad front, towards and into the outer defences of the Siegfried Line. [Shaef reports state that six divisions are battling on a 30-mile front.]

VON RUNDSTEDT'S FAILURE

The Third Army moved to the offensive the moment the last German soldiers had been expelled from Belgium and Northern Luxemburg, bringing to an end von Rundstedt's forced withdrawal from the Ardennes salient.

The attack into Germany has developed from the failure of the German break-out towards the Meuse.

It is the natural consequence of Mr. Churchill's promise to the Germans, in his recent review of the war, that the Western front, as well as the Eastern and Italian fronts, will "now be kept henceforward in constant flame until the climax is reached."

Further, it is proof that von Rundstedt's attempt to dislocate and delay the general advance of the armies from the west did not succeed.

Today Third Army infantry, supported by tanks and artillery, have broadened to four miles, and deepened to three-quarters of a mile, the bridgehead that they had secured across the Our

Deeper snow

Enemy attempts to counter this new lodgment inside Germany have been ineffectual so far. But the opposition is stiffening.

Advances of half a mile from Steffhausen, six miles south-east of St. Vith, to Schieback, three and a half miles farther south, have been made during a heavy snowfall that has persisted all day and is deepening the snowdrifts. The hamlet of Welchenhausen, eight and a half miles south of St. Vith, was cleared yesterday, and troops today reached a point three-quarters of a mile to the east and a mile inside Germany.

New to Third

No new ground has been broken by the Allies in this new advance into Germany, but it is new territory as far as the Third Army is concerned.

Before von Rundstedt's attack began the line that bulged another four or five miles east of the frontier was held by the U.S. First Army, by divisions that took the full weight on the narrowest of fronts of a whole panzer army on December 16.

Like the rapid re-alignment of the American divisions to hold that offensive before it reached the Meuse, the building up of United States First and Third forces to resume the march into Germany without giving the enemy an hour's respite has been an incomparable achievement.

French nearer Colmar, Back Page.

LATE NEWS

SCHACHT ARRESTED AGAIN

From Our Own Correspondent

Stockholm, Tuesday night.—The former German Finance Minister Schacht has again been arrested and is in a Berlin prison, according to a reliable source.

LONDON DIM-OUT
6.17 p.m.—8.9 a.m.
Moon rises 9.16 p.m., sets 10.43 a.m. tomorrow

Planes cut V2 lines again

THE Germans' V2 rocket lines in North and West Holland have again been attacked from the air.

Planes of the T.A.F., during 300 sorties cut the rail lines in eight places and damaged 14 locomotives and 119 waggons.

A fairly heavy German movement eastwards towards the Reich from the west coast area of Northern Holland was observed on Monday night. The columns were attacked by Mosquitoes.

Daily Mail

LATE WAR NEWS

NO. 15,219 — ONE PENNY — ★★ — FOR KING AND EMPIRE — TUESDAY, FEBRUARY 13, 1945

GERMANY'S FATE: OFFICIAL

Big Three Lay Down Framework for Peace of the World

All Reich Forces to be Disbanded | General Staff to be Broken | Arms Industry to be Eliminated | Swift Punishment for War Crimes

REICH TO MAKE GOOD ALL DAMAGE IN KIND

By WILSON BROADBENT, Diplomatic Correspondent

THE shape of the new Europe after the defeat, occupation, and all-time demilitarisation of Germany is outlined in a communiqué issued last night at the end of the Three Power Conference in the Crimean port of Yalta. It is the fullest and most dramatic declaration to emerge from any of the meetings of the leaders of the United Nations during this war.

The declaration indicates clearly that as they sat round the Conference Table, Marshal Stalin, President Roosevelt, and Mr. Churchill were so confident of an early victory over Germany that they concerned themselves mainly with the problems of the peace.

The Conference was held in the Livadia Palace at Yalta, on the southern coast of the Crimea, a district of great scenic beauty where the hillsides are covered with vineyards and thick woodlands.

It lasted eight days—twice as long as the Teheran Conference of more than a year ago. At Marshal Stalin's suggestion, it is to go down to history as the Crimea Conference.

The main points of the declaration are:

1. Nazi Germany is doomed, and the German people are warned that the cost of their defeat will be heavier if they continue to resist.

TERMS ARE READY

2. The demand for Germany's unconditional surrender is reiterated, and it is stated that the terms have been prepared, but will not be made known until the final defeat of Germany.

3. Germany is to make good "in kind to the greatest extent possible" all damage she has caused to Allied nations, this to be controlled by a commission operating in Moscow.

4. The declaration says that it is not the purpose of the Conference to destroy the people of Germany, but only when Nazis and militarism have been extirpated will there be any hope of a decent life for the Germans. To achieve this end the following programme is laid down:

All German armed forces to be disbanded.

The German General Staff to be broken up for all time and all German military equipment to be removed or destroyed.

All German industry used for military production to be eliminated or controlled.

Justice and swift punishment for all war criminals.

Nazi Party to be wiped out, and all Nazi laws, organisations, and institutions eliminated, until there is no Nazi influence remaining in Germany.

Any other measure necessary to ensure the future peace and safety of the world.

OCCUPATION ZONES

5. Each of the Three Powers will occupy separate zones of Germany under a Central Control Commission consisting of the Supreme Commanders of the Three Powers, with headquarters in Berlin. France will be invited to take a zone of occupation and participate in the work of the Control Commission.

6. The close working partnership among the three Staffs, attained at the Conference to shorten the war, will continue, as and when meetings are necessary in the future.

Other points of the Declaration include:

THE "Curzon Line," drawn after the last war, is, says the communiqué, to be Poland's eastern border, with slight modifications in Poland's favour.

YALTA, former winter playground of the Russian rich, is now a holiday and health resort.

Establishment at the earliest possible moment of an international organisation to maintain peace and security in the world, based on the foundations laid at the Dumbarton Oaks Conference.

Agreement to hold a conference of the United Nations at San Francisco on April 25 next, to prepare the Charter of such an organisation.

Declaration providing for the co-ordination of the policies of the Three Powers for the assistance of the liberated countries of Europe in their pressing political and economic problems.

Reaffirmation of the principles of the Atlantic Charter.

Agreement to set up a new and more broadly based Government in Poland, which will include leaders from inside Poland as well as outside, and the appointment of a commission in Moscow, consisting of M. Molotov, the Soviet Foreign Minister; Mr. Averell Harriman, the United States Ambassador; and Sir Archibald Clark Kerr, the British Ambassador, to consult with Polish leaders for this purpose.

Declaration that the three leaders consider that the eastern frontier of Poland should follow the Curzon Line with digressions in some regions of from five to eight kilometres in favour of Poland.

Recognition that Poland must receive substantial accessions of territory in the north and west, but agreement that the final de-

BACK PAGE—Col. SEVEN

Freed PoW: Return to be Speeded

New Pact Agreed

NEGOTIATIONS took place at the Crimea Conference for a comprehensive agreement for the care and repatriation of British Empire, U.S., and Soviet nationals liberated by the Allied Forces invading Germany.

The Agreement concluded was drawn up in two separate but identical texts, one between the British Commonwealth and the U.S.S.R., and the other between the United States and the U.S.S.R.

The Agreement between the British Commonwealth and the U.S.S.R. was signed by Mr. Eden and Molotov last Sunday.

Food Provided

Under these arrangements each ally will provide food, clothing, medical attention and other needs for the nationals of the others until transport is available for their repatriation.

In caring for British subjects and American citizens, the Soviet Government will be assisted by British and American officers. Soviet officers will assist British and American authorities in their task of caring for Soviet citizens liberated by the British and American forces.

The three Governments are pledged to ensure that all these prisoners of war and civilians are speedily repatriated.

Voluntary Work

Article 6 of the agreement reads: Ex-prisoners of war and civilians of each of the contracting parties may, until their repatriation, be employed in the management, maintenance and administration of the camp or billet in which they are situated.

"They may also be employed on a voluntary basis on other work in the vicinity of their camp in furtherance of the common war effort in accordance with agreements to be reached between the competent Soviet and British authorities. The question of payment and other conditions of labour shall be determined by agreement between these authorities

"It is understood that liberated members of respective forces will be employed in accordance with military standards and procedure and under the supervision of their own officers."

The following British prisoners of war have been liberated by the Red Army, said Lublin radio last night. They are now in Lublin in the care of the Polish authorities.

Henry Pearce, Royal Fusiliers, of Star-street, Paddington, London; **George Wallace,** Royal Northumberland Fusiliers, of London, S.E.; **Norman Cross,** of Russel Crest-walk, Welwyn Garden City, Hertfordshire; **Edward Birch,** Royal Artillery, of Brunswick-street, Manchester; Corporal **Edwin Shadwell,** 2nd Battalion Guards (?), of Queen-street, Barnsley, Yorkshire; **Samuel Thomas,** 1st Border Regiment, of Marks-lane, Main-street, Applethwaite, Cumberland; **Harry Smythed,** 1st Border Regiment, of Goldhurst-street, Oldham, Lancashire.

Paris Bandits Get £110,000 Haul

PARIS, Monday.—Twelve men yesterday held up a car containing ten Pari-Mutuel officials with a police guard on the outskirts of Paris and escaped with £110,000, the totalisator receipts from Enghien racecourse.

Ten of the men were masked and the other two wore uniforms of the American military police.—*A.P. and Reuter.*

Strait Still Warmer

Maximum temperature in the Strait of Dover yesterday was 52 deg., and by 10 p.m. it was only 1 deg. down. Except for a few hours, the day was overcast, with the barometer rising.

Full text of Big Three Declaration on Page TWO.

April 25: A 'Big 3' Mystery

Date of Peace Conference?

By Daily Mail Diplomatic Correspondent

BIGGEST talking point of the Three Power Declaration, and one which interested London diplomats last night as much as anything else, was the fact that another United Nations Conference is to start on April 25 at San Francisco.

Geneva is a long way from San Francisco.

Neither Marshal Stalin nor President Roosevelt has any love for Geneva. And they have as yet failed to nominate the new home of the proposed World Security Organisation.

But diplomats were first interested that a date should have been set for the Conference and announced.

Two Questions

Does this mean, they asked, that the Leaders at the Crimea Conference decided on all the facts before them that the war against Germany must be over by April 25?

Secondly, they wondered if the selection of San Francisco meant that President Roosevelt had persuaded Marshal Stalin to attend a conference far outside Russia for once.

At the forthcoming San Francisco conference the Charter of the new World Organisation to preserve peace is to be prepared.

This will be an important occasion, and one at which the heads of government might wish to be present.

In any case, if the war against Germany is to end before April 25, it will be necessary for the leaders to meet again to confirm the details of the Allied occupation.

Also, there is no word about Japan in the latest Three Power Declaration.

Although China was not represented at any of the meetings of the Three Powers at this Conference, as she was before the Teheran Conference, the war against Japan cannot have been overlooked.

At some time Marshal Stalin is expected to declare himself. Probably when the war against Germany has been won San Fransisco is on the way to Japan.

W. B.

'The Rhine—a French Road'

PARIS, Monday.

GENERAL DE GAULLE, addressing 20,000 Frenchmen from the balcony of the cathedral in Metz, declared: "We will make a French road of the Rhine—from one end to the other."

"French troops will gain victory on the other side of the Rhine as they have on this side," he declared. He repeatedly referred to "our Rhine."

During an informal chat with correspondents at Metz, General de Gaulle said: "What a curious peace is being prepared for us." He gave no further explanation of his remark.—*B.U.P.*

MOST human of all the pictures taken at meetings of the "Big Three," this one shows that Mr. Churchill's Cossack fur hat was the talking—and laughing—point at the Crimean Conference.

Koniev is Swinging North Towards Berlin

GREAT DOUBLE DRIVE

From Daily Mail Special Correspondent

STOCKHOLM, Monday.

MARSHAL KONIEV'S armies, fanning out from their huge bridgehead over the Oder, to-day split into two main groups and rolled north-west towards Berlin and west towards Dresden and Central Germany.

Formations attacking parallel with the Oder are reported by Berlin to have reached the area north of Sagan, little more than 100 miles from the capital.

They are nearly 50 miles beyond Liegnitz, capture of which was announced yesterday, and threaten to roll up the German front along the Oder in front of Berlin.

Formations attacking due west have captured the town of Bunzlau, on the Bober river, Stalin announced in an Order of the Day.

According to Berlin the Russians are storming the river on a front of 20 miles between Bunzlau and Sprottau, and have already won two bridgeheads.

A second Order of the Day reported the capture by General Petrov's troops of Bielsko, at the approaches to the Morava Gap through the mountains to Vienna.

Here are the main points from the Soviet communiqué:

Russian troops, resuming their attack through the Polish Corridor towards Danzig, have captured Swiecie, on the Vistula.

Operations to wipe out the German remnants in Budapest have begun. In two days 30,000 prisoners have been taken and the Royal Palace and old fortress captured.

At Torun 15,000 prisoners were taken and the Germans lost 13,000 dead. Another 3,000 prisoners have been captured on Koniev's front, bringing the total announced to-night to 48,000.

TRAP CLOSING IN SILESIA

From GEORGE MOORAD, Daily Mail Special Correspondent

Moscow, Monday.

SEALING off of the whole Silesian pocket—150 miles deep and 80 miles wide—seems imminent.

With the seizure of Liegnitz and the railways and the great Berlin to Breslau autobahn lost, the heavy enemy forces still fighting savagely in Upper and Polish Silesia have an extremely slim chance of escape.

They have remaining only a secondary road winding through Neisse, Frankenstein, and Gorlitz in the Carpathian foothills. Koniev can cut this, too, by a mere 20-miles thrust south-west from Liegnitz.

Koniev's troops are described as in the highest spirits after their surge across Central Silesia and conquest of the Oder river.

Premature thaws turned the river to spring flood, with ice packs breaking up Soviet pontoon bridges six and more times daily.

Said the Soviet commander, "That crazy river tried to stop us, but we are in flood tide, too, and it is the Nazis who are breaking up.

"See this map," pointing to the flanks right and left of Liegnitz, "everything is changing. Hour by

BACK PAGE—Col. FIVE

'Strike in West'

WASHINGTON, Monday.—The Soviet military spokesman here said to-day it must be assumed Anglo-America now "will back the Red Army's offensive with mighty blows."

So far, he added, the Allied operations had not prevented the Germans transferring a number of divisions to the East.—*A.P.*

ELAS HAS 14 DAYS TO DISARM

From DEREK PATMORE, Daily Mail Special Correspondent

ATHENS, Monday.

E.L.A.S. forces throughout Greece must disarm within 14 days under the military agreement signed to-day between E.A.M. and the Greek Government.

The minimum arms to be surrendered are: 41,500 rifles; 650 sub-machine-guns; 1,365 machine-guns; 163 mortars; 32 pieces of artillery, and 15 wireless sets.

Arms are to be handed in to E.L.A.S. guards at 37 dumps, and when the total reaches the minimum figure British troops will enter the E.L.A.S. areas to collect them on behalf of the Greek Government.

The Greek National Guard will move in with the British Army, and will be disposed about the country as the Greek Government sees fit.

At the same time a civil administration will be set up, and will organise enrolment in the National Guard area by area.

After the establishment of the National Guard in E.L.A.S. territory British troops will be considered as in reserve and not as in control.

While disarmament is in progress a British liaison officer will be stationed at E.L.A.S. headquarters at Trikkala.

At the same time a senior E.L.A.S officer will be stationed at British headquarters.

MRS. VIC OLIVER WENT WITH THE PREMIER

MR. CHURCHILL took his daughter Sarah—Mrs. Vic Oliver, wife of the comedian—to the Big Three meeting.

★

President Roosevelt was met by Mr. Churchill, Mr. Stettinius, U.S. Secretary of State, and high-ranking Americans in Malta on February 2 before the whole party went on to Yalta.

★

At the final Yalta conference, Roosevelt presented decorations to Russian and American military leaders.

★

The B.B.C. broke into its "starred programme of the week" to annouhce the Big Three statement. Then it was broadcast in full to Germany in German and Spain in Spanish.

★

Moscow radio gave the communiqué precedence on all news bulletins and played the National Anthems of Britain, Russia, and the U.S. three times.

★

Batteries of U.S. radio transmitters told the Germans the news and repeated again and again the warning that the German people would only make the cost of defeat heavier by continuing hopeless resistance.

★

Roosevelt has called on the U.S. Congress to carry out the Bretton Woods money conference agreements for world economic security.

JAPS IN MANILA ENCIRCLED

MacArthur's H.Q., Manila, Monday. — Americans of the 37th Infantry and 1st Cavalry Divisions have joined forces south of Manila. The Japanese are closely encircled and are being compressed into extinction. Fighting has been extraordinarily fierce, says General MacArthur's communiqué to-night.—Reuter.

OTTO HAPSBURG IN SWITZERLAND

Otto Hapsburg, the Austrian Pretender, arrived in Switzerland from Rome early this month, according to information reaching foreign diplomatic circles in London.—Exchange.

2

BRITISH PUSH FOR GOCH

Prum Captured

Front-line flashes from the Western Front last night gave this news of the fighting:

Montgomery.—British and Canadian troops are within four miles of the German town of Goch after clearing Cleve. They have forced the second of the three Siegfried Line Loops guarding the Northern Ruhr.

Patton.—U.S. Third Army men, ten miles in Germany, have captured the Siegfried fortress of Prum.

Siegfried Defences Breached—BACK Page.

WEDNESDAY, FEBRUARY 14, 1945

FINAL NIGHT EXTRA●

Evening Standard

37,672 DIM-OUT: 6.42 pm to 7.45 am. MOON: Sets 8.36 pm; Rises 9.58 am. ONE PENNY

THE BLASTING OF DRESDEN

1350 Forts and Liberators Over Germany To-day After Night Attack by 1400 'Planes of R.A.F. Bomber Command

KONIEV INSIDE BERLIN PROVINCE

Marshal Koniev, crossing river barriers, to-day continued his advance towards Dresden and the heart of Germany as the gap between his forces and those of Marshal Zhukov narrowed to about 15 miles.

A link-up between the two forces for an outflanking drive south of Berlin is expected soon, says Reuter.

Koniev's men are to-day storming the Queis River, half-way between Breslau and Dresden, now less than 70 miles ahead.

The Germans are said to be showing increasing alarm over the possibility of a new Oder crossing by Zhukov's forces in the sector just beyond Koniev's right wing.

A Soviet blow here would split the remaining co-ordination between the German forces on the Berlin front and those in Silesia.

In Brandenburg

Berlin to-day named Cottbus and Guben, twin bastions guarding the south-eastern approaches to the capital, as the main objectives of Koniev's northern drive.

According to the German communiqué the Russians have reached Sorau, eight miles west of Sagan, and less than 30 miles from Guben.

This means that Marshal Koniev's forces have crossed the border into Brandenburg. Sorau is five miles inside the border and under 90 miles from the Reich capital.

To-day's German communiqué also admitted that the Russians have widened their penetration area north-west of Breslau.

"In the area south-west of Breslau," it stated, "the enemy hurled freshly brought up forces into the battle. Despite the stubborn resistance of our troops who were backed by Volkssturm and alarm units, the enemy in Lower Silesia was able to gain ground to the west and north-west.

"Bunzlau was lost during bitter fighting. Many enemy attacks against the fortress of Glogau were beaten back.

"In Southern Pomerania the Russians launched vain attacks. Fighting stubbornly the defenders of Arnswalde, Schneidemuhl and Poznan held out.

Stettin Hears Guns

"In the southern part of West Prussia, the Russians continued their breakthrough attempt in the area of Konitz and Tuchel. Heavy fighting is in progress.

"Enemy attempts to push in our front on both sides of the Elbing-Koenigsberg autobahn from the west, and at Zinten from the east, failed, as did pinning-down attacks between Wormditt and Landsberg."

Massed formations of Koniev's tanks are attacking west of Breslau in tho direction of the town.

A Moscow military commentator broadcast this afternoon that Stettin can now hear the rumble of the Soviet guns.

German radio reported this afternoon that the Red Army had established another bridgehead across the Oder in the Frankfurt sector facing Berlin.

Martial Law Ends In Greece

Martial law ended in Greece to-day. The decree lifting it also annulled all sentences passed by the military courts in their trials of E.L.A.S. supporters.

To-day's Official Gazette promulgated the amnesty signed by the Government last night for all political offences committed during the events of December.

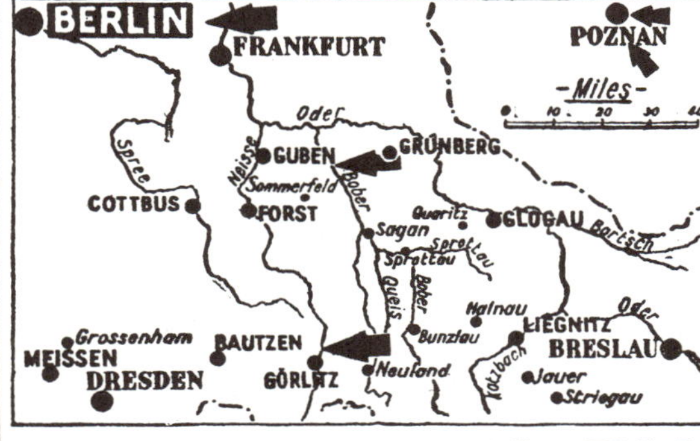

FIRES SEEN BY KONIEV'S MEN

More than 1350 Liberators and Fortresses of the U.S. Eighth Air Force to-day attacked transportation and industrial targets in Dresden, Chemnitz, and Magdeburg, and a road bridge across the Rhine at Wesel.

The bombers were escorted by more than 900 Mustangs and Thunderbolts of the same Command.

BURNING DRESDEN, POUNDED LAST NIGHT BY 800 BOMBERS OF R.A.F. BOMBER COMMAND, WAS AGAIN HIT TO-DAY BY AIRCRAFT OF THE U.S. EIGHTH AIR FORCE.

The raids were in support of Marshal Koniev's troops who are less than 70 miles away.

Russian troops may have seen the fires burning in the city last night after a double raid by our bombers. Crews of the bombers said that they could see the glow 200 miles away.

Two great blows were struck at Germany to-day. One 300-mile long stream of airplanes flew from the west, and other formations went from the south.

The Germans may be using Dresden—almost as large as Manchester—as their base against Koniev's left flank. Telephone services and other means of communication are almost as essential to the German Army as the railways and roads which meet in Dresden.

Its buildings are needed for troops and administrative services evacuated from other towns.

Dresden has large munition workshops in the old arsenal. No major attack has been made before on the town.

Six hundred more bombers struck last night at the synthetic oil plant at Bohlen, south of Leipzig, and Magdeburg.

JAPS AND PEACE

Tokyo radio, which is rigidly controlled by the Government, broadcast to-day that the Japanese Foreign Minister's policy is "not to reject any hand which offers peace."

The spokesman of the Japanese Information Bureau, Iguchi, said: "The Yalta Conference was a masterpiece of power politics.

"The only way to re-establish peace in the world is by a just policy as outlined by Foreign Minister Shigemitsu, whose principle is not to reject any hand which offers peace."—Associated Press.

10,000 Tons of Bombs on Budapest

Allied and R.A.F. bombers of the Mediterranean Allied Air Force flew more than 4500 sorties over Budapest and dropped about 10,000 tons of bombs on it between April 1 and late in 1944, says Reuter.

SUNSHINE FOR SIX HOURS

By mid-afternoon the sun had been shining in the Straits for just on six hours. The temperature at 2 p.m. was 50, and the westerly breeze had backed a little to the south-south-west.

"Last Ditch Stand In Bavaria"

The Germans are hastily preparing Bavaria for a last ditch defence, said Moscow radio to-day.

Princess Elizabeth

Princess Elizabeth, who is suffering from mumps, is "progressing normally."

MONTGOMERY ADVANCING ON THIRD SIEGFRIED BELT

Hochwald Line Is 10 Miles Ahead

Montgomery's British and Canadian tank columns are now fighting their way forward towards Rundstedt's third and final Siegfried defence belt—the Hochwald Line—guarding the west bank of the Rhine and about ten miles beyond present Allied positions, said war reports reaching Reuter to-day.

Since the offensive began six days ago Allied troops of Montgomery's command have advanced up to 10 miles into the German lines along the front of 14 miles.

Canadian troops north-east of the Reichswald Forest are extending their six-mile hold on the west bank of the Rhine.

In the Prum sector General Patton's Third Army forces are flinging back all German attempts to recapture this communications centre for roads leading to Coblenz and Cologne.

Farther south, elements of three U.S. Third Army divisions are fighting through the Siegfried defences from the Our River bridgehead between Echternach and Wallendorf.

Double Onslaught Repulses Nazis

From RONALD MONSON

WITH THE FIRST CANADIAN ARMY, Wednesday.

Flame-throwers roaring on from the south-east fringe of the Reichswald Forest belched death into the ranks of the Germans trying to prevent the British advance beyond the forest late yesterday.

Behind them came men of the North Country regiment which had carried out the final clearing up of the forest.

The enemy who survived broke and fell back before the double onslaught.

Away on the north-east of this advance other troops, moving down after mopping up near Cleve, fought their way along roads leading south-east to Udem and to Calcar.

A British motor battalion after routing out Germans from the woods just south of Cleve, dashed on down the Udem road, 2000 yards beyond Bedburg.

Hasselt Captured

Reaching the Cleve State Forest, they found it full of Germans.

The Air Force and artillery were called in and the woods were plastered from end to end.

Few of the enemy were left in fighting condition when the guns ceased and the airplanes went home.

One pocket in a copse north-

(Continued on Back Page, Col. Two)

This is How Part of the "West Wall" Looked to the British

Sergeant-major Leonard Allington, of Birmingham, and Sergeant Gordon Dudgeon, of Glasgow, inspect a captured Siegfried Line strongpoint with ten-feet thick walls, while their comrades in a Scottish artillery regiment eat a quick meal before resuming the battle.

Spitfire Up With Waaf On its Tail

Evening Standard Reporter

A Waaf flight mechanic, 35-year-old Margaret Ida Horton, of Woodmansterne-lane, Banstead, Surrey, was working on the tail of a Spitfire when the aircraft suddenly took off.

She clung on for ten minutes until the extra weight on the tail was noticed by the pilot. By then the Spitfire had gained considerable height.

Throttling back carefully the pilot landed safely with Miss Horton still clinging on.

She was severely bruised and had to be taken to hospital suffering from shock. She is now recovering.

"The matter is now subject of an inquiry," an official of the Air Ministry told me.

Parachute Padre Is War Captive

News has been received at Beaumont College, Old Windsor, that the Rev. Bernard M. Egan, who was reported missing at Arnhem, is a prisoner of war in Germany.

Rev. B. M. Egan

Fr. Egan, who was the first padre to make a parachute descent from a glider, was wounded, and is now in hospital suffering from severe injuries to his legs. He was a master at Beaumont College.

His mother, Mrs. S. A. Egan, who lives at Buntingford, Herts, told the Evening Standard to-day: "I have received five letters from my son, who is in hospital at Stalag 9. In his last letter, which I got yesterday, he told me he is now able to walk about again with the aid of two sticks

M.P. ON YALTA FLIGHT DISASTER

"Wrong Type Of 'Plane Alleged"

Mr. Granville (Ind., Eye) asked the Air Minister in Parliament to-day if he had any statement to make on the recent accident in which 15 British Service people and officials lost their lives on their way to the conference between the Prime Minister, President Roosevelt and Marshal Stalin.

Sir Archibald Sinclair replied: "I deeply regret the loss of life caused by this accident. The aircraft was a York belonging to the R.A.F. It was of standard design, and fitted with standard equipment The R.A.F. pilot and crew were highly experienced. The aircraft was obliged to come down in the sea.

"A court of inquiry are now sitting.

Mr. Granville: "There is a good deal of serious concern in the public mind as to the repetition of these accidents.

"In view of the fact that this might have happened to any of the aircraft engaged on the flight, can you give an assurance that all machines engaged in the Prime Minister's flight were given adequate mechanical supervision and inspection right throughout the journey?"

Highly Efficient

Sir Archibald.—I cannot give an assurance about right throughout the journey, but I can give an assurance that the maintenance arrangements of Transport Command are highly efficient

Earl Winterton (Con., Horsham and Worthing).—Will you look into the allegations that have been

(Continued on Back Page, Col. Five)

"Every German Will Kill, Murder, Poison"

"Every enemy, no matter when or how he penetrates into Germany, will be met by fanatical men, women and children, who know what treatment is in store for them and therefore wish to kill, murder and poison all who attempt to oppress them."

This extract from the broadcast by Paul Schmidt, the German Foreign Office spokesman, in which he declared that the Yalta declaration released Germany "from all moral scruples," was quoted by the Swedish paper Svenska Dagbladet to-day, says Reuter.

Large scale thefts of arms from Volkssturm barracks outside Berlin have sharpened German fears that a rising may be attempted once the military situation worsens, private Berlin reports to Stockholm said to-day, quoted by British United Press.

The main German long-wave radio station, Deutschlandsender, has apparently been moved from the Berlin region to a safer area.

Deutschlandsender has so far been broadcasting from Koenigswusterhausen, 15 miles south-east of Berlin. It went off the air after 1 a.m. because of approaching raiders; yet among the numerous warnings put out every few minutes by the German achtung stations there was none reporting raiders over the Berlin area.

NEWS CHRONICLE, Friday, Feb. 23, 1945

News Chronicle
No. 30,819 FRIDAY, FEBRUARY 23, 1945 ONE PENNY
LATE LONDON EDITION

SIX THOUSAND PLANES ATTACK

Grand offensive in West may be opening: Nazi general

GERMAN PEOPLE WARNED TO LOOK OUT FOR PARATROOP LANDINGS

Reich communications hit from Denmark to Italy

MORE than 6,000 planes, comprising the maximum strength available to British and American Bomber and Fighter Commands, yesterday launched the heaviest blow of the war against German communications.

Nearly all rail movement must have been brought to a halt over the greater part of Germany. Targets ranged from the Danish frontier to Italy, with spearheads almost to the Russian front. Bomb tonnage was estimated at over 3,500.

The great onslaught was still going on late last night, when Mosquitoes again hit Berlin, and German radio described a 100-mile stream of returning Allied bombers, stretching from Osnabrueck to the Zuyder Zee.

In this atmosphere of confusion and terror the German people listened to a warning from the Gauleiters of Hanover and Brandenburg provinces that paratroop landings are possible behind the Western and Eastern fronts."

The alarm would be given by the ringing for five minutes of all church bells in Germany, and local guards were told to be on the alert.

Another warning came from Gen. von Manteuffel, who said:

"The German nation is on the eve of a grand-scale Anglo-American offensive—or for that matter is already witnessing its inception.

"I call the soldiers in the East," said Manteuffel. "Listen to me.

"The soldiers on the East front may know that we mean to cover their back by our fight here in the West."

Other German military spokesmen declared that "the Allied offensive cannot be delayed much longer. The great decisive battle will be fought in the Aachen area in the near future."

The long-awaited push by the French First Army across the Rhine may be imminent, according to indications in Basle. French artillery is concentrating heavy fire on German bunker positions along the east bank of the river.

BACK WITHOUT A FLAK SCRATCH

Flying Fortresses of the 92nd Bomber Group, U.S. Eighth Air Force, back without a scratch from the raid on objectives at Wittenberge yesterday, circling an airfield in Britain before landing. Below: Maj. J. A. Smyrl, who led the group. "We fairly obliterated our targets," he said (News Chronicle pictures)

25,000 men were airborne

From a Special Air Correspondent

IN yesterday's massive assault it is estimated that upwards of 25,000 Allied airmen were airborne.

In many cases heavy bomber groups from Britain reported no enemy opposition—no flak and few fighters.

Strong fighter escorts had a field day for, in addition to shepherding their heavy charges, they played havoc at lower level all over the Reich.

Last night at Allied H.Q. and Bomber Command Intelligence officers were collecting and summing up the results of the big show. All agreed that the enemy had certainly "had it."

Not a flak hole

The experiences of three squadrons of 92nd Group give some idea of the conditions.

At a bomber station in the heart of rural England I saw the Flying Forts return in the afternoon haze. In the misty hour after dawn they had set out, each laden with 500-pounder general-purpose bombs.

They had bombed visually at midday at 12,000ft.—and all returned unscathed. Not one had a flak hole.

For the first time in history the U.S. bombing force had gone in for a lower level bombing, the attack being made at 12,000ft. instead of the usual 25,000ft.

The objective of this group was a key rail and road centre through which runs the main railway from Berlin to Hamburg.

Obliterated target

A road bridge over three converging railways makes a vital point just outside the town—this was the target.

Said Maj. James A. Smyrl, leader of the group: "We fairly obliterated our target. It was an uneventful run—no flak, no fighters and a beautiful escort. There was a haze near the ground and we made a second run before letting our bombs go. Then the target disappeared and we all came home."

The second and third squadrons on the same target reported artificial smoke clouds put up by the enemy round the bridge.

In another ship Second Lt. B. W. Lowry, navigator, who wore a picturesque trapper's fur cap for warmth, saw more of the show.

"Lovely work"

"We saw the R.A.F. at work in the distance; there were fires everywhere. One was a big magnesium blaze in a wood, as if a special factory had gone up.

"And we also had a grandstand view of lovely work by the Mustangs as they went down at a train."

First Lt. Lewis, of California, on new bombing technique: "This new low-level bombing is great—we could see much more of the target. We hit it fair and square."

Nazi torturer tries to kill himself

Johann Dell, first Nazi to be put on trial in the West for atrocities, leapt from the fourth floor of the military prison in Aachen yesterday after exclaiming to questioners, "God strike me dead if I am not telling the truth." He was Nazi mayor of Eschweiler, and was charged with committing atrocities on Russian prisoners of war.

He is not expected to live.

AIM TO PARALYSE NAZI TRANSPORT

From RONALD WALKER
News Chronicle War Correspondent

WESTERN FRONT, Thursday.

ALLIED air forces based in Britain, Holland, Belgium, France and Italy joined today in concentrating on Germany the greatest coordinated air operations in history.

Over 6,000 aircraft took part. In steady streams fighters and bombers flew into Germany with the single purpose of paralysing enemy transport and communications in a huge area of Europe.

This was the first time a record number of aircraft has been directed simultaneously on to a variety of targets scattered over such a wide area.

These air forces took part: R.A.F. 2nd Tactical, including U.S. 29th Tactical; U.S. First Tactical; U.S. 9th; U.S. 8th; R.A.F. Bomber and Fighter Commands; U.S. 15th, based in Italy.

All the aircraft involved were trying to be over their first targets and make their first attack by one o'clock.

The operations, which had taken much complicated planning in the War Room at Allied Command, introduced the third phase in the offensive against enemy transport and communications.

REICH DIVIDED INTO ZONES

This offensive began with the bombing of the main communication and transport centres—Cologne is an example—and progressed into the second phase when we began to concentrate on pounding the enemy as he attempted large scale movements on the main road and railway systems.

Today's attacks were all directed at secondary roads, railways, canals and river crossings. These the enemy has been forced to use by Phase Two.

Many weeks of photographic reconnaissance were put in, preparing the complete record of the secondary targets, which include road and rail junctions and bridges, canals, ferry crossings and rail sidings, as well as roads and rail lines.

The area of Germany, including occupied Holland, was

Continued Back Page A

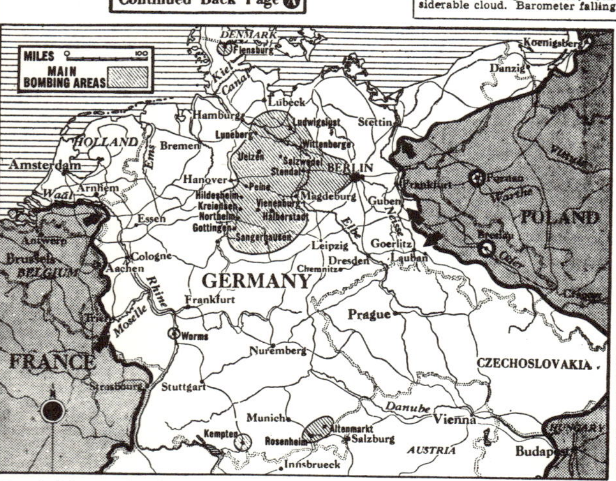

The shaded zones in this map of the Reich denote the general target areas for yesterday's great bombing assaults on German communications. The targets were in or around those towns shown in black type. They stretched from Denmark to Austria

All Denmark under curfew

A CURFEW was introduced over the whole of Denmark last night, the German News Agency announced.

It extends from 9 p.m. to 5 a.m. Restaurants and public-houses must close at 8 p.m.

Only those having a special permit will be allowed in the streets during curfew hours.

At least ten bombs exploded in Aarhus on Wednesday night, killing four people and causing the biggest fires for years, according to Stockholm reports.

Stricter counter-sabotage measures have been taken recently, and the Danes fear a new Nazi wave of terror.

The Gestapo, says the Danish Press Service, is believed to be mobilising for a blow against Denmark's underground.

Falling

Straits last night: Cool; considerable cloud. Barometer falling.

PATTON'S TROOPS CROSS THE SAAR AT TWO POINTS

From NORMAN CLARK, News Chronicle War Correspondent

MOSELLE-SAAR FRONT, Thursday Night.

IN a swirling fen fog overhanging the valley, the Third Army today forced two crossings of the Saar River. They met little opposition and pushed on.

The storming parties crossed in assault boats below Saarburg, now half-taken.

At Serrig and Tabenrodt lodgements on the east bank were achieved under the cover of fog and reinforcements were passed across.

It has been a day of swiftly-developing action, with the collapse of the whole Saar-Moselle triangle after the German lines north of Sinz were broken on Monday.

In four days Gen. Patton's tanks and infantry have won some 80 square miles of Germany, pushing 12 miles until they can now see the spires of Trier, four miles away.

Many prisoners

It is not yet a break-through—but the buckling of the triangle lines, with so heavy a toll of prisoners, has undoubtedly put the enemy in a predicament.

This crust broken, Patton's tanks moved to overwhelm and net probably most of the enemy's forces west of the Saar.

Some remnants mustered at Saarburg today to contest our advance into the eastern half of the town across the river.

The Germans fought fiercely from house to house.

World TUC Big Six may go to 'Frisco

By the Industrial Correspondent

THE World Trade Union Congress will meet again in Paris in September to give final approval to the constitution of the new International.

They will then set up a permanent organisation, with headquarters in the French capital.

Meanwhile, the interests of the world's workers will be looked after by a special World Trade Union Committee representative of the 45 organisations which attended the London Congress.

The first big job of this Committee will be to ask the United Nations' Governments to give the trade union movement a place at the San Francisco Conference which opens on April 25.

Voice at peace talks

The six leading figures at the London Congress, Citrine, Hillman, Kuznetsov, Saillant, Chu Hsueh-Fan and Toledano, will, it is expected, go to San Francisco in any event, and it is hoped that they will be invited to attend the sittings of the Conference in an "advisory and consultative" capacity.

The World Trade Union Committee, before it adjourned yesterday, demanded a voice in the peace settlement.

"Organised Labour," it was stated, "with so great a part in winning the war, cannot leave to others—however well-intentioned they may be—the sole responsibility of making the peace.

"The peace will be a good peace only if it reflects the deep resolve of the free peoples, their interests, desires and needs."

Replies have been received from leaders of the Allied Forces in the field to whom the World T.U.C. sent greetings on behalf of 60,000,000 workers.

Gen. Eisenhower writes: "With the workers and the fighting men completely devoted to the task in hand the complete defeat of the Axis is certain."

German attacks repulsed

From S. L. SOLON
News Chronicle War Correspondent

WESTERN FRONT, Thursday.

ENEMY resistance in the north is rising to a new crescendo of ferocity. With all or parts of 10 German divisions now involved there is no shortage of enemy man-power here. There appears to be more of a shortage in certain types of heavy equipment.

Scottish troops which crossed the railroad along the Goch-Udem route have been meeting fierce opposition all day. The German counter-attacks have made limited headway—in this area that may mean advances of perhaps 100 or 200 yards to another ditch or wooded patch that can be used as a new strong-point.

Pushed back

South of Hassum, three miles due west of Goch, where British troops are moving forward, other German counter-attacks have been pushed back.

In Goch itself Scottish troops have cleared all the remaining snipers and hidden Germans—adding 200 to the prisoners taken in the Goch area.

The weather continues to be mild and not as wet as our troops have learned to expect. The rivers are dropping—the Rhine, the Maas and the Roer—and they are no longer quite the same formidable barriers that they bave been for 10 gruelling weeks.

M. Bidault is to visit Mr. Eden in London

By Vernon Bartlett

THE French Foreign Minister, M. Bidault, will very shortly come to London to repay Mr. Eden's visit to Paris of last autumn and to meet other members of the British Government.

Unfortunate misunderstandings have arisen over the failure of President Roosevelt and Gen. de Gaulle to get together.

It should therefore be emphasised that the Foreign Secretary sent this invitation to M. Bidault as soon as the Crimea Conference had finished and before the British had been informed of the President's plan to see the General.

Not forgotten

In one way the unachieved meeting of these two leaders may have beneficial results.

Gen. de Gaulle has to face problems the gravity of which has admittedly been increased by Shaef's inability to release more supplies for French civilian needs.

He must, therefore, sometimes be tempted to strengthen his own position at home by diverting French discontent from his own Government to the Allies of France.

Nor has he entirely forgotten some of his less happy experiences while in exile.

Frenchmen in France, however, have also not forgotten the steady encouragement that reached them from the Anglo-Saxon countries in their most tragic moments.

And French newspaper criticism during the last few days has made it very clear that Gen. de Gaulle must not seek to increase his great and deserved popularity by encouraging his compatriots to feel that their dignity has been injured and by then defending it with resounding phrases or defiant gestures.

On the same occasion the more responsible American newspapers have gone out of their way to remind their compatriots of the inevitable sensitiveness of any people that has passed through such tragic hardships as the people of France.

Koniev reaches Neisse on 60-mile front

MARSHAL KONIEV'S forces have reached the River Neisse—an Oder tributary—on a 60-mile front, said last night's cables from Moscow.

The routine Soviet communique confirmed that the river had been reached, but beyond stating that the line of the advance extended south from Guben [65 miles south-east of Berlin], gave no indication of the extent of the front along the Neisse's east bank.

"BRIDGEHEADS AT SOME POINTS"

Berlin claimed that Soviet attempts to force the Neisse had failed, but unofficial news agency reports from Moscow said that bridgeheads had been set up at some points.

Commenting on the reaching of the river, a Moscow radio spokesman said last night: "Marshal Koniev's troops have taken from the Germans that area from which the German High Command planned to launch powerful flank attacks against the Russian armies standing along the Oder.

"This area, which is now in Russian hands, will be of utmost importance for an outflanking move on the German capital."

South of Guben, cables Paul Winterton, News Chronicle Correspondent in Moscow, Marshal Koniev's troops are within easy artillery range of Forst, on the west bank of the Neisse.

The communique reported the capture of Gross Saerchen, 54 miles from Dresden, among 60 places taken by the advancing Russians.

In Breslau suburbs

Ninety miles east of Dresden, Marshal Koniev has captured four suburbs of Breslau. A battle of annihilation is now going on in the city.

The communique indicated the fierceness of the tank fighting by announcing the destruction of 198 German panzers on all fronts on Wednesday.

And the Red Army, said Moscow radio, has a new gun in action on the Eastern front. Its most important feature is its very long range.

German losses in 40 days: Back Page

LATE NEWS

CLOSING ON GUBEN

Red Army troops captured Schenkendorf, 1½ miles south of big communications centre of Guben, said supplement to Soviet communique. In battles for Zinten, in East Prussia, 4,000 Germans were killed and 520 captured.

LONDON DIM-OUT

6.59 p.m.—7.27 a.m.

Moon rises 2.37 p.m., sets 7.7 a.m. tomorrow. Full Moon, Feb. 27.

Road rules may be stricter

Stricter rules and changed conditions for all road users after the war might include:

A more severe test for "L" drivers.

More heavily restricted speed limits and penalties for speeding.

Special cycle and pedestrian paths on new main roads.

Development of subways and bridges at busy thoroughfares.

These possibilities were hinted last night to the News Chronicle by a Ministry of War Transport official after Mr. Noel-Baker had been interrupted in Parliament when about to forecast future measures of road safety.

See Page Three.

Three-day debate on Yalta

By the Political Correspondent

THE debate on the Crimea Conference in the Commons next week will last about 22 hours spread over three days.

The War Cabinet has approved the form of the motion on which the debate is to take place.

It approves "the declaration of joint policy agreed to by the three Great Powers at the Crimea Conference and, in particular, welcomes their determination to maintain unity of action not only in achieving the final defeat of the common enemy, but, thereafter, in peace as in war."

Mr. Churchill's opening speech will probably last for two hours.

M.P. over 70 not to stand again

Rear-Admiral T. P. H. Beamish, M.P. for Lewes Division for 16 years, yesterday announced that he would not stand at the next election. He is over 70.

SUNDAY EXPRESS

FEBRUARY 25 1945 | DIM-OUT MANCHESTER 7.7 p.m. to 7.37 a.m. | Founded by LORD BEAVERBROOK | Moon rises 4.48 p.m. Sets 8.7 a.m. | TWOPENCE

Eisenhower says: 'The offensive now started will not stop'

'WE EXPECT TO DESTROY EVERY GERMAN WEST OF THE RHINE'

To meet the Russians in centre of Reich is the only way to wipe out Nazidom

SUPREME HEADQUARTERS, PARIS, Saturday.

GENERAL EISENHOWER, SUPREME ALLIED C.-IN-C., SAID TODAY THAT HIS FIRST AND NINTH ARMY OFFENSIVE ACROSS THE ROER RIVER IS "GOING AS WELL AS CAN BE EXPECTED."

In reply to a question on the extent of the attack, he replied that he hoped to destroy every German who could not get away west of the Rhine within the area of the present attack.

Germany, he said, is badly stretched out along the front. He believed Allied casualties would not be unduly heavy for the results achieved.

"Given continuation of the conditions as we see them now," he said, "and a reasonable break in the weather—and I am not asking for July Kansas weather—the attacks we are seeing now should mark the beginning of the destruction of the German forces west of the Rhine.

"I am convinced that there is only one way to defeat Germany, and that will be when the Allied armies meet the Russian armies in the centre of Germany."

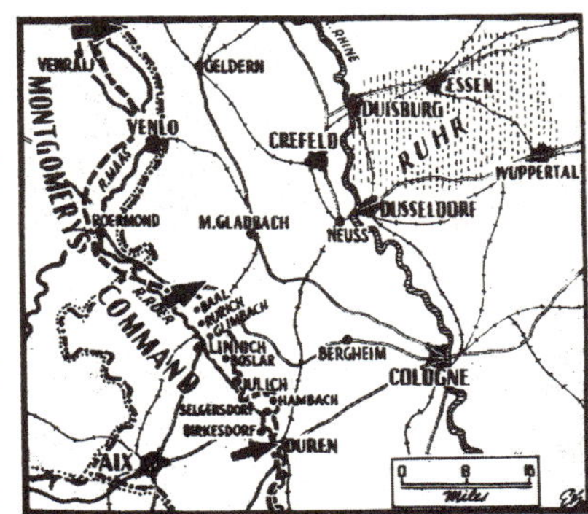

THE LAST 60 DAYS

He doubted whether there would be any formal surrender by Germany in view of the Nazi leaders' ability to keep the harassed and suffering nation together.

He said he was perfectly satisfied with the measure of liaison between the Allies and Russia, saying: "Russia has given us all information needed willingly and cheerfully."

He did not discount that the Germans would fight a guerrilla war in southern Germany, but he did not believe that once the Ruhr and Silesia were lost the Germans could maintain an organised, efficient defence for more than 60 days after their dwindling reserves of material were used up.

There was every evidence that Germany could not hold front positions in the strength they once did, and for this reason General Patton's attacks were extremely valuable in keeping the Germans from moving troops northwards, although he could not hope to achieve the decisive results of the north in terms of Germans destroyed.

General Eisenhower said that he and General de Gaulle met whenever any problem arose needing discussion—he conferred with General de Gaulle just before the First French Army operation which eliminated the Colmar pocket that had been, he said, a running sore in our side.

He disclosed that the Ninth Army had been poised for attack since February 10, and once the Ardennes threat was ended Field-Marshal Montgomery picked up the original programme by attacking in the north.

While German paper strength might seem equal to that at the time of the Normandy landing, General Eisenhower estimated that the actual effective combat strength was now far below that of last June. He pledged that there would be no let-up in aggressive fighting at any time.

Asked how formidable a barrier the Rhine would be, he replied that it would not be as formidable as the English Channel, and reminded his questioner that there had never been a successful river defence in all history.

Eisenhower has won the first round

By MONTAGUE LACEY
SUPREME HEADQUARTERS, Saturday.

GENERAL EISENHOWER, there can be no doubt, has won the first round of the new big offensive in his push to the Rhine.

With his co-ordinated attacks of the First and Ninth Armies, he not only achieved some element of surprise, but his air fleets so battered and disorganised the enemy in the Cologne plain that 19 hours elapsed before they were able to throw in any counter-attacks.

We now have a good firm front on a length of more than 15 miles over the Roer River.

It is significant that for days the German High Command has been putting out statements that the big push would come in the Cologne plain area, so they must have been ready.

THEY WERE POWERLESS

Yet in spite of their preparedness, they were powerless to stop this great American battering ram. Seen in its proper perspective, it means that our terrific Allied air fleets have won the first part of this fast developing battle and the army the second round by obtaining firm bridgeheads across the Roer.

Now we are entering on the crucial stage of the battle—perhaps the last and most important of the war.

The First and Ninth Armies are probably the best equipped forces the world has ever seen, and it is likely that we shall soon hear of new secret weapons that are being used to finally and utterly defeat the remnants of the German Army in the west.

At General Eisenhower's headquarters there is every sign of confidence as we emerge into the last momentous battle.

EVERY EFFORT WAS MADE TO GET THE

BACK PAGE, COL. SEVEN

ALLIES STORM JULICH CITADEL

ALLIED forces have fought their way into the citadel of Julich, key town barring the way to Cologne, after a great artillery barrage had pounded the strengthened defences for hours.

The capture of Julich was completed at noon with the fall of the citadel, says a Reuter cable from Field-Marshal Montgomery's H.Q.

The threat to Cologne is growing hourly as the Allies bite further into Germany and town after town falls.

Pouring across the swift-flowing Roer River Ninth Army troops have captured the German towns of Baal, Korrenzig, Broich, and Hambach in a gain of up to three and a-half miles east of the river, said a Reuter despatch yesterday.

Two miles deep

General depth of the bridgehead is now two miles. It stretches from Baal, in the north, to Hambach, in the south. Six German counter-attacks were beaten off during the night and the offensive is going well.

German resistance so far is only moderate. General Patton's Third Army troops have advanced four miles, capturing 14 German towns and villages on a 20-mile front below Prum.

First Army troops have cleared at least one-third of the town of Duren, said an A.P. message.

The Germans are thinning out their forces in occupied Holland, said Ross Munro, Reuter's correspondent with the Canadian Army in Germany.

They are pulling the troops back to the Ijssel River line runing from the Arnhem area north to the Zuider Zee.

Places of vital importance, including the rocket emplacement zone, presumably continued to be garrisoned, but there is a continuous movement of enemy troops eastwards from the main part of Holland north of the Rhine Estuary.

BERLIN SAYS: *'500,000 troops are attacking'*

BERLIN News Agency last night stated that 40 Allied divisions — nearly half a million men — are attacking on the Western Front.

Berlin expects that the offensive will spread southward "in the very near future."

The agency added:—

"An Allied offensive on a 125-mile front is about to flare up.

"Eisenhower's present offensive is his biggest yet. Soon the United States Third Army will be worked into the general scheme."

51st THERE

The agency also reported that the 51st British Infantry Division, the Highlanders, which had fought at El Alamein, in Italy, and in Normandy, was in action in the area of the road triangle Cleve-Goch-Zanten.

The German Transocean News Agency said:—

"The battle in the west is heading with giant strides towards a tremendous climax."

Alex Schmalfuss, German correspondent on the Western Front, reported that the amount of material used by the Americans in their offensive near Aix was "unparalleled in history."—Reuter and A.P.

'Open buffets till midnight'

For travellers

Captain W. G. Hall, Socialist M.P. for Colne Valley, Yorks, is to urge in Parliament that railway buffets should keep open longer to serve hungry travellers.

Most buffets open at 7.30 or eight in the morning until 10 p.m.

A Manchester manageress said last night: "The girls work long hours, but I don't think they would object to staying until midnight if the duty rota were altered."

More explosions

STOCKHOLM, Saturday.—Another series of explosions—the fifth on successive nights — last night destroyed clothing factories and several blocks of flats at Grenaa, eastern Jutland, says the Free Danish Press Service.—A.P.

8 hours' sun

There were more than eight hours' sunshine in the Straits of Dover yesterday, but a good deal of haze limited visibility. There was a cool and variable westerly breeze.

Sonia skates a million pound figure

SONJA HENIE, famour figure skater and film star who is said to earn more than any other woman in the world, has just raked in another £1,000,000 gross.

This was the yield from a 63-day tour of the ice show in which she stars. No sooner was it over than she was off to Hollywood to start a new film, "The Countess of Monte Christo."

In her recnt tour, more than 275,000 people attended 18 performances in New York alone.

Her seven ice-show tours since 196 have grossed more than £2,500,000. She has made nine films, none for less than £30,000, and she receives robust royalties from "Henie" skates, dolls, and mittens.

Sonja has a luxurious apartment in Fifth-avenue, New York, a man mansion at Beverley Hills, California, and another at Easthampton, New York.

WEAVE, YOU FOOLS, WEAVE

R.A.F. shout advice to the Luftwaffe

COMMANDER RUPERT BRABNER, Under-Secretary for Air, said at Folkestone yesterday that the R.A.F. had beaten the Germans in the air for one reason above all others—the excellence of our training. He told this story in illustration:—

On January 1 when the Germans made a great low level attack on R.A.F. forward airfields in Belgium and Holland and lost some 250 aircraft a party of R.A.F. pilots stood on a dyke bank at Antwerp and shouted to the Germans as they came over: "Weave, you fools, weave," because the inexperienced German pilots were making such a poor show.

Commander Brabner added that the Germans still had the aircraft but not the men to put in them—or if they had the men were untrained.

Koniev pouring over Neisse

THOUGH Moscow messages said there were no signs that the Red Army has opened the battle for Berlin, reports from New York and Paris last night said:—

1—Marshal Zhukov has crossed the River Oder in force.

2—Marshal Koniev, in an out-flanking move to the south, has extended his Neisse River bridgehead to within ten miles of Kottbus.

Activity on the Frankfurt-Kustrin front, which guards the road to Berlin, said Moscow, is confined to an artillery barrage which Zhukov has been pouring into the German positions from guns massed almost hub to hub for many days past.

Oder is rising

Zhukov is faced with a River Oder cutting across the battlefield which is rapidly rising and overflowing its banks.

But moves can be expected following decisive gains in the last 24 hours. With the fall of Poznan Marshal Zhukov now has cleared his main supply lines leading towards Frankfurt and Kustrin.

Once again the chief Russian pressure is being exerted on the Russian flank south of the Berlin area. Here Marshal Koniev is stepping up the pressure on the German line which runs along the River Neisse from Guben to Gorlitz.

Russian guns and tanks are moving round the fortress towns of Guben and Forst, where the Germans have thrown in more "do-or-die" detachments in their usual plan of trying to hold up the Russian advance even if only for a few days. At both towns Russian troops have broken into the eastern outskirts.

Building up

And Russian units are still moving across the Neisse and building up for the advance into the Dresden area, even though German opposition remains as grim and determined as ever in this area.

In the battle for Breslau, Koniev's tanks and storm troops are tearing the city to pieces stone by stone. Hitler has ordered the garrison to fight to the last man.

On the other hand, according to reports last night, the German garrison in the East Prussian capital of Konigsberg has pulled out and has been evacuated by sea.

Led Punjabis in mountain raid

Strongpoint captured

HOW Lieut.-Colonel Playford MacNamara led men of his 15th Punjabis a mile and a-half through the enemy lines in Italy, climbing at their head 2,500 feet, is told in the citation to the D.S.O.

One company having lost all its officers except one subadur, the colonel took charge and, says the citation, "by his presence and personal example he induced them to attack again."

After fighting all night the company cut through the wire and killed and captured all the enemy in a strongpoint. Next day Colonel MacNamara led his tired troops through three strongly wired and entrenched enemy positions and moving up and down fire-swept ground organised ammunition supply to his forward companies.

U.S. motion to raise censorship

Mr Edward R. Stettinius, U.S. Secretary of State, at the inter-American conference in Mexico City yesterday announced that the U.S. has presented a resolution asking all American republics to guarantee to their peoples "free and impartial access to information."

One of the points of the resolution was to undertake at the end of the war the earliest possible abandonment of war-time censorship.

Helping Holland

Breeders of British Friesians, the black and white cows which originally came from Holland, are to contact Dutch breeders with a view to helping to restock Holland with its native cattle.

ALL GERMANS MUST BE FANATICS, HITLER SAYS

'Only answer' to Allied blows

HITLER'S comrades of the Munich putsch went back to the Beer Cellar yesterday to hear a speech giving his "only answer" to the mounting Allied blows against the Reich.

Hitler was not there to make it himself, because "my sense of duty and work prevent me leaving headquarters even for a moment."

His speech was read for him, according to the German News Agency, to celebrate the 25th anniversary of the formation of the party's programme. It said:—

"In 1920 there was a completely paralysed nation; today there is a fanatically resisting people. Then there was a decayed order of society which had outlived itself; today there is an unshakeable people's community which is in the process of building itself.

"The danger today will not be eliminated by the righteousness of our cause, but by the force which backs it.

"Our right lies in the duty to defend our lives; it is the sacred right of self preservation.

"How difficult today's fight nas become we all well know only too well. But whatever we may lose now is insignificant compared with what we stand to lose if we do not bring this war to a victorious conclusion.

"There can only be one watchword against the Jewish Bolshevists and their western henchmen—the most fanatical determination and the last ounce of strength, which God grants a people fighting for dear life. Those who waver must, and will, perish.

'Until the end'

"But let there be no doubt—Nationalist Socialist Germany will carry on this struggle until in the end, and that will be the case this year, the historic turning point comes.

"Now power in the world will weaken our hearts.

"We have suffered so much that it only steels us to the fanatical resolve to hate our enemies a thousand times more and to regard them for what they are—destroyers of an eternal culture and annihilators of humanity.

"Out of this hate a holy will is born to oppose these destroyers of our existence with all the strength God has given us and to crush them in the end.

"If the Homeland continues to do its duty, and even does still more; if the soldier at the front takes the valiant Homeland as an example and stakes his life for his native land, then the whole world will be shattered in its assault against us.

"My own life has only the value which it possesses for the nation. I work unswervingly to re-establish and strengthen our fronts for defence and attack to create weapons of proved as wel las of novel design, to put them into action to stiffen the spirit of our resistance and, if necessary, also as in the past, to eliminate all those pests who do not want to participate in the preservation of our nationhood, or even oppose it.

'No weakness'

"I have read in the last few days in British papers that our enemies intended to destroy my Berghof (Hitler's home at Berchtesgaden).

"I am almost sorry that this has not already happened because whatever I call my own is worth no more than what belongs to my people.

"The only thing that I could not bear would be a sign of weakness among my people What makes me most happy and proud is the conviction that in its most dire distress the German people show the toughest side of their characters.

"It must be our unshakeable decision to live, every man and woman, from town or country, and to the last breath, only under the one commandment—to give our all for the liberation of our people from this emergency.

CONVOY CHARGES UNTRUE

—Says Admiralty

THE Admiralty last night described as entirely without foundation reports in the American Press concerning the conduct of British naval vessels escorting a convoy to Russia $2\frac{1}{2}$ years ago.

A further statement was promised by the Admiralty.

The allegations to which the Admiralty refer were made by a recently repatriated Baltimore seaman, Walter Sankiewicv.

'34 SHIPS SUNK'

According to his story, quoted by A.P., the British escort abandoned a Murmansk convoy in the north Atlantic in July 1943. He said that the Germans sank 34 ships, including the Carlton in which he was serving.

Sankiewicv said he understood that the British vessels departed to engage German warships in battle after being lured away by the Scharnhorst and Gneisenau.

He added that soon after the escorts left the Germans attacked with submarines and torpedo bombers. Berlin at the time claimed 36 ships sunk in the convoy.

Sankiewicv said he was picked up by a German torpedo-plane whose navigation officer showed him charts indicating the exact position of each ship in the convoy, and told him: "We worked it to come in just where the convoy was."

BIG POLITICAL TEST FOR F.D.R.

President Roosevelt is facing the greatest political test of his career, says a B.U.P. correspondent. He has to persuade doubtful Senators that the Yalta agreements are as much in U.S. interests as they are in Britain's and Russia's.

He must persuade the American people and Congress to ratify agreements with the United States' chief Allies to use Americans to keep the Germans from making war in the future.

These questions have come before the people of the United States more than once, but now a decision must be made.

U.S. airmen share town memorial

Saffron Walden (Essex) Borough Council have accepted the offer of a fighter wing of the U.S. Army Air Force to give £4,500 towards a community centre as a memorial to members of the wing killed in battle.

A hall will be built and playing fields laid out. Names of American and local men who have been killed in action will be inscribed side by side.

Chance for Forces

Men in the Forces may apply for £1,000-a-year post of Professor of Welsh History at University College of Wales, Aberystwyth.

Earl L.G. asks about village play

—BUT ANXIETY CONTINUES

By GWYN LEWIS

LLANYSTUDWY (Carnarvonshire), Saturday.—The condition of Earl Lloyd George, of Dwyfor, continues to fluctuate and give cause for anxiety that

World war news

PATTON TANKS WIPE OUT A SALIENT

General Patton's Third Army racing tanks have almost destroyed German salient north of Vianden. Germans reported completely disorganised in this sector.

Radio Page Seven

only some recovery in strength can allay.

His physicians are looking particularly for signs of improving heart action. These have been forthcoming during the past two days, but the improvement has not been at all marked and his vitality generally continues at a low ebb, except for an hour or two during the day.

It was during one of these encouraging spells this morning, after an undisturbed night, that he was able to enjoy a brief bedside chat with Alderman William Lloyd George, his 80-year-old brother, and Mr George's daughter-in-law, Mrs Dora George.

"Ll.G.," his face described to me as "painfully shrunken by illness," sat up in bed and gave his visitors a smiling welcome. He at once asked his brother: "How did the play go, Will?"

'GREAT SUCCESS'

Mr George replied: "It was a great success, David. They put up a really wonderful show. The hall was packed."

The three then talked of a performance given last night by a local dramatic society at the Criccieth village hall of a Welsh version of "Hobson's Choice," entitled for Welsh purposes, "Siopp Morgan."

Mr William Lloyd George said to me afterwards: "We just talked quietly of village affairs and local people. Historic events now taking place on the battlefields have but little interest for my brother at the moment.

"But he has enjoyed this past two days, the stimulus of half an hour's gossip. Then he falls into a doze, and it is this continually falling to sleep that worries us."

Lady Megan Lloyd George and Lady Carey Evans, the earl's daughters, called later in the day, when their father was able to leave his bed and sit in a chair for half an hour. The two had walked the mile and a-half that separates the earl's farmhouse home from his

BACK PAGE, COL. ONE

Daily Mail

NO. 15.231 ONE PENNY * * FOR KING AND EMPIRE TUESDAY, FEBRUARY 27, 1945

LATE WAR NEWS

U.S. ARMOUR BREAKS THROUGH 10 MILES FROM COLOGNE

Germans Rush to Surrender: 'No Organised Defence'

A U.S. Ninth Army staff officer, quoted by A.P., said last night: "There is no organised line left in front of us and it appears we have a breakthrough."

From WALTER FARR, Daily Mail Special Correspondent

BLATZHEIM, Near Cologne, Monday.

TO-NIGHT I am writing my dispatch only 11 miles from Cologne. Some elements of the American First Army units with which I drove into Blatzheim are probably only ten miles from the Rhineland capital—or even closer.

A tank and infantry battle is raging a few hundred yards from me on the approaches to Cologne. And, so far, we are winning it hands down.

There is no doubt that the signs of weakness we are seeing here on the Cologne plain are of the highest significance. One is almost tempted to say the battle west of the Rhine is near its climax.

What puzzles us is that the Germans have given up, almost without fighting, a whole host of key-points in front of Cologne. Altogether, since our jump-off three days ago, American troops have captured 69 towns and villages in Germany.

HARDLY A SHOT FIRED

Many of the key-points on this vital sector of the Cologne Plain are falling to us after only a few anti-tank shots or a few bursts from a machine-gun.

Just ahead of us I can see our tanks going in to complete an attack, curbing round a village. At the same moment there is a stream of German troops and civilians coming out from the other side with their hands up.

We expected fanatical resistance as we pushed into the Reich. Up to now resistance, far from fanatical, has been with certain exceptions very poor indeed.

Among the German prisoners are S.S. troops, panzer troops, and Volksgrenadiers. All types are coming in now.

As we drove with a tank unit to a village where we were mopping-up earlier to-day, Germans kept running up to our Press jeep trying to surrender to us. They say they can't make it out. To-day we've gained mile after mile without loss of men or equipment.

Among the 4,000 prisoners taken are four colonels from one division. They fought scarcely at all.

Almost all the prisoners to-day surrendered in groups.

THE NEXT 48 HOURS VITAL

From JOHN HALL, Daily Mail Special Correspondent

MONTGOMERY'S H.Q., Monday.

THE battle-tide is nearing the doorstep of the Ruhr to-night. Advances to-day brought Cologne almost within gun range and the huge industrial city of Dusseldorf and two large towns, Neuss and Munchen-Gladbach, within range of American guns.

Rundstedt, apparently, is still making up his mind, though what he has been doing behind the lines to-day has been closed to us by thick overcast.

Never do we seem to get a lucky break with the weather. Almost the only close air support we could give to-day was a short, sharp attack by medium bombers on concentrations of German artillery.

As I see the picture to-night, taking into consideration the tremendous power Montgomery has mounted both east of the Roer and in the Rhine-Maas thrust, the Germans must produce something big within the next 48 hours—or risk a catastrophe.

There are two possibilities:

1.—Rundstedt may fight on the line of the Erft Canal, adopting the favourite tactic by sitting on the escarpment east of the canal system, or

2.—He may be falling back behind the Rhine. We don't expect this, because if he did that he might as well write off the major industrial section of the Ruhr.

Whether he has abandoned hope of saving Cologne will not be known until the Americans reach the Erft, now only six miles beyond their forward patrols.

ERKELENZ IS NEARLY OURS

From NOEL MONKS, Daily Mail Special Correspondent

U.S. NINTH ARMY, Monday.

FIVE hours after beginning their assault towards Erkelenz our forward elements had effectively dealt with German arm-

BACK PAGE—Col. SEVEN

Tanks Break Through Near Bitburg

Germans Flee in Disorder

U.S. THIRD ARMY, Monday.

A SUDDEN new drive by General Patton's 4th Armoured Division near Bitburg has all the appearances of a break-through.

Patton's tanks are through a 30-miles hole in the Siegfried defences, and are within 60 miles of Coblenz.

Fall of Bitburg, hub of ten roads, is imminent. Spearheads are in its outskirts.

More than ten villages in the Bitburg area have been overrun.

Abandoned German vehicles and thousands of tons of equipment litter the highways along which the tanks sped, exploiting their penetration.

Like the Old Days

"This reminds me of the good old days when General Patton was going so fast the Germans didn't know where or when he would turn up next," one officer said.

Crack panzers were routed when the Americans took Rittersdorf, on the Nims river two miles north of Bitburg.

Sherman tanks rattled into the town after a swift dash over the river. The U.S. troops leapt from the tanks and tore into the bewildered Germans.

There was some confused small-arms fire and hand-to-hand fighting. Four German Tiger tanks rumbled into action, only to be promptly knocked out with bazookas.

Then the Germans panicked. They threw down their equipment and surrendered in masses.

One astounded German officer was shaving when a U.S. squad entered his room and captured him. —Reuter and A.P.

POLES HAVE A NEW C-in-C

No British Consent

The President of the Polish Government in London has appointed General Anders as Acting C.-in-C. of the Polish fighting forces. He will deputise for the C.-in-C., General Bor-Komorowski, now a prisoner in Germany.

In official circles in London last night it was stated that the appointment had been made without the knowledge or approval of the British Government, which took no responsibility in the matter.

General Anders recently commanded a Polish corps in Italy. He is 52

Great New Tank Push Opens

Canadians Drive for Siegfried

From COURTENAY EDWARDS, Daily Mail Special Correspondent

MAAS-RHINE FRONT, Monday Night.

FIELD-MARSHAL Montgomery to-day threw in his tanks in a big way near Calcar, at the northern tip of his 75-miles front. We are allowed to say he is using his armour in "great strength." Our tanks are heading south-east.

If they keep going in that direction they will cut through the last remaining loop of the Siegfried Line—the Hockwald "lay back." It is the first time tanks have been used on the Western Front in February on such a large scale.

This is something bigger than just a spurt in the rugged yard-by-yard slogging we have seen since the Reichswald Forest was cleared. It is a big, new attack.

It is largely a Canadian show, and infantry are going in with the tanks. The footsloggers are going forward in style—in Kangaroos and other armoured carriers.

Like Destroyers

It does you good to see them clattering to the attack with tanks milling around outside and between formations of these toughly built carriers. The tanks look like destroyers shepherding convoy merchant vessels.

They moved forward at half-past eight this morning. Four hours earlier the infantry attack had been put in, without tanks, to take the high ground south of Calcar, and to protect the left flank of the following tank thrust.

In this tank attack the infantry were completely successful. And they had, first of all, to beat off a counter-attack launched against them at half-past two this morning, just two hours before zero hour.

It took us the best part of two hours to deal with this German move, in which the enemy used tanks; but our own attack went in dead on time.

The tanks were punctual, too, and to-night some of them had reached points between two and three miles from their starting-line.

This means they are within 3,000 yards of the main Siegfried defences of the Hockwald "lay back" where Todt workers have for days been working non-stop to strengthen the maze of strong-points, anti-tank ditches, and minefields.

German opposition, mainly provided by the Sixth Paratroop Division, is strong, and is stiffening. There is no sign that events on the U.S. Ninth Army front have as yet weakened German resistance here in the slightest.

They are sending out a terrific hail of shells and mortar bombs from positions in front of the Hockwald line.

A Bold Step

Montgomery took a bold step in committing his armour on such a scale in February, despite the drying wind of the past few days.

It rained heavily here last night and many of our tanks were bogged in the mud when they left the roads to fan out across the fields. Some became sitting targets for enemy gunners.

In this new attack we have taken more than 1,000 prisoners. We are firmly established on an escarpment south of Calcar and there are patrols in the outskirts of the town.

Farther south there was bitter fighting to-day in the villages of Keppeln, on the Calcar-Udem road, and Nollen west of Keppeln.

To-day's big attack was preceded by an artillery barrage which lasted 45 minutes. And then a creeping barrage was laid down for another three-quarters of an hour, carefully arranged to move at tank speed and keep just ahead of the armour.

THE THINKERS

DESPONDENT German prisoners captured in failing to hold Montgomery's drive between Maas and Rhine.

BITTERNESS of defeat, the realisation that they have failed their Führer, utter weariness after days of constant bombardment and retreat, is shown by these Germans captured by the First Army.

RED ARMIES DRIVE FOR THE BALTIC

From Daily Mail Special Correspondent

STOCKHOLM, Monday.

MARSHALS Zhukov and Rokossovsky to-night are driving the German northern armies back against the Baltic along a front of 180 miles. It seems that Zhukov is anxious to anchor his right flank on the sea before beginning his drive for Berlin.

Three big attacks are in progress to achieve this purpose and at the same time split up and destroy the German divisions between Stettin and East Prussia.

Attack No. 1 has reached the River Ihna, two miles south of Stargard and 20 miles east of Stettin.

Attack No. 2 has made deep penetrations west of Konitz.

Attack No. 3 is being made north of Grudziadz and has carried Rokossovsky's troops to within 30 miles of Danzig.

Nearly all news of these three thrusts comes from German sources. Moscow appears to have imposed another operational black-out.

FDR APPEALS TO MOSCOW

'Work With Vatican'

From Daily Mail Correspondent

NEW YORK, Monday.—Mr. Edward J. Flynn, a personal friend of President Roosevelt, is in Moscow on a special mission for him—preparing the way for the establishment of diplomatic relations between the Vatican and Moscow.

White House sources said to-day that Mr. Roosevelt is extremely anxious to have the fullest support of the Vatican for the world security organisation.

He believes one obstacle to this is the breach between Rome and Moscow, which influences the minds of millions of Roman Catholics throughout the world against Russia.

Madras Governorship

Sir Arthur Hope, G.C.I.E., Governor of Madras, is to hold that office for a further period of six months, expiring on September 12.

PM READY FOR CRIMEA DEBATE

By WILSON BROADBENT, Diplomatic Correspondent

THE Prime Minister worked until the early hours of this morning on the speech which he will deliver when the House of Commons meets to-day to debate for three days the results of the Crimea Conference.

In the course of his speech Mr. Churchill will refer to the discussions which have taken place in the past 36 hours with M. Bidault, the French Foreign Minister, who has been the guest of Mr. Anthony Eden.

M. Bidault's talks have been purely informative. He spent Sunday night in the country with Mr. Eden and yesterday lunched with the Prime Minister. Later in the day he was received in audience by the King at Buckingham Palace.

M. Bidault will leave London for Paris to-day. He is not expected to attend the debate in the House of Commons, although an invitation was extended to him.

The debate is regarded by politicians as the most important of all the four deliberations which Parliament has had on the subject. Mr. Churchill's speech will be a comprehensive survey of the war years, the successful development of Allied strategy, and finally the resultant outline of Britain's future foreign policy.

He will defend all the Crimea decisions, and particularly the agreed plan for producing a broader based Government for Poland. It is on this issue that the Government may find a number of critics.

But in general, the Crimea decisions, as far as they are known, will be supported and approved in the vote on the confidence motion, which Mr. Churchill will move.

Berlin—Again Last Night

AFTER 100-TON SALVOS

SALVOS of 100 tons of bombs crashed down on Berlin's main stations yesterday from 11.45 until a few minutes after one o'clock in the German capital's heaviest daylight raid of the war.

More than 1,200 Flying Fortresses and Liberators, escorted by 700 fighters, made up the force which struck when the city was still suffering from its sixth successive Mosquito attack. And last night Berlin reported another raid.

This attack was said to have been made by "strong formations."

Twelve hundred and fifty tons of high-explosive bombs were dropped yesterday in daylight, and 500,000 incendiaries.

Berlin railways are vital to the German armies trying to hold back Marshal Zhukov's armies on the Eastern Front.

Nearly all supplies and troops for that front go through Berlin.

The stations bombed were the Schlesisher, which has huge repair shops and goods yards as well as a passenger station, Berlin North, a freight terminal, and the Alexanderplatz, which is a group of passenger stations.

Luftwaffe Absent

The bombs were unloaded in a city struggling with defence preparations and hundreds of thousands of refugees

German fighters did not rise to defend the capital, and bomber pilots report that flak was only moderate.

This is the second time this month the Luftwaffe has not opposed a major daylight assault.

Since the war over 60,000 tons of bombs have fallen on Berlin, or more than one ton for each 60 inhabitants.

Last night hundreds of fires were burning. Clouds of smoke billowed high up long before the last bomber pilot turned for home.

The attack was another blow in the great offensive which has been waged by the R.A.F. and the U.S. Air Forces against Germany this month, an attack in which more than 30,000 tons of bombs have been dropped on strategic targets alone.

Sixteen bombers and seven fighters are missing from the big day raid.

Attacks on Oil

Yesterday afternoon a force of R.A.F. Lancasters escorted by fighters attacked the synthetic oil plant at Dortmund.

Before the first bomb fell on Berlin yesterday an "Achtung" system had issued warnings about a stream of bombers 230 miles long heading for the capital.

Behind the Western Front, Tactical Air Force pilots reported that hundreds of square miles are now dead country as far as rail and road movement is concerned.

There is no sign of movement throughout the whole area north of the Ruhr and west of Osnabrück following the past week's air hammering.

The marshalling yards at Munster and Soest are still only three-

BACK PAGE—Col. THREE

Syria at War with Reich and Japan

BEIRUT, Monday.

SYRIA is at war with Germany and Japan. This was announced by the President, Shukri Kouatly, in the Chamber here to-day. This declaration follows conversations between the President and Allied leaders in Cairo. It may affect negotiations with the French on questions still in suspense.—*Reuter.*

Syria is the third neutral in a few days to enter the war. Turkey declared war on the Axis last Friday, and Egypt followed suit the next day.

The Egyptian Chamber of Deputies last night passed by 214 votes to 2 a motion approving Egypt's declaration of war.

SUPPLIES BY AIR FOR BRESLAU

German transport planes are trying to drop food supplies to the people of Breslau, states Moscow radio.—B.U.P.

20 DEAD IN ARMS DUMP EXPLOSION

Paris, Monday.—Twenty persons have been killed and 30 seriously injured following a munitions dump explosion in Western France, believed to have been caused by a spark from a lorry.—Reuter.

2

Brenner Hit Again

ALLIED H.Q., Italy, Monday.—Strong forces of Italy based medium bombers to-day continued their hammering of Kesselring's Brenner routes and targets in Yugoslavia. The heavies were hampered by bad weather.—*Reuter.*

THE RIGHT OF EVERY BRITON

Defence Must Be Heard

A PRISONER on trial is entitled to put his defence, no matter how absurd, to a jury, and it is for the jury and not the judge to decide when he should be stopped.

In these words yesterday, **Mr. Justice Humphreys** gave the judgment of the Court of Criminal Appeal quashing the conviction of John Canny by **Mr. Justice Macnaghten** at Winchester Assizes. He made these further points:

1. Owing to an oversight or momentary forgetfulness, Mr. Justice Macnaghten directed the jury that they could not find a verdict of unlawful wounding.

2. Owing to the judge's misreading of a medical report, he adopted the attitude throughout the trial that Canny suffered from delusions, whereas the report said he did not.

3. The result of the judge's misunderstanding was to take from the jury the right to try the man.

Fair Trial a Right

4. The judge insisted on dealing with the case as one in which the time of the jury had been wasted.

5. A man was entitled to a fair trial by a jury. The judge had no power to say the defence was no defence to put to the jury. The law said a man was entitled to take his chance of finding a stupid jury if he could get one to acquit him..

Canny, who had been convicted of wounding his wife, was discharged.

PoWs REACH ODESSA

In Next Two Days

First British prisoners freed by the Red Army—about 2,500 men—are expected at the Black Sea port of Odessa to-morrow or on Thursday on their way home.

Giving this news in Moscow yesterday, Rear-Admiral Ernest Archer, head of the British Military Mission, said 70 tons of clothing and comforts have been sent to Odessa, and another 50,000 tons accumulater in Moscow.

The War Office announced last night that 4,000 British and American sick have been removed by the Germans from Lamsdorf (Stalag 344) for an unknown destination in Germany.

Fit prisoners from Stalag 344 are on the march between Boemisch Lippa and Carlsbad. Prisoners from Stalag 8a are dividing, some going towards Kassel and some to Nuremburg. Those from Stalag 8c are moving towards Hanover and Kassel.

Warm and Sunny in the Strait

Spring-like weather in the Strait of Dover yesterday sent the temperature up to nearly 60 degrees in the early afternoon.

It was sunny for most of the day, and at 10 p.m. the temperature was still high, at 47 degrees. The barometer was rising.

The Pope Better, at Work Again

Daily Mail Special Correspondent

VATICAN CITY, Monday.—The Pope has almost recovered from his attack of influenza.

He left his apartment to-day and did a little work in his library.

Average net paid circulation for February exceeded
Daily---2,000,000
Sunday-3,700,000

DAILY NEWS

Copr. 1945 by News Syndicate Co. Inc. NEW YORK'S PICTURE NEWSPAPER Trade Mark Reg. U. S. Pat. Off.

Vol. 26. No. 220 New York, Thursday, March 8, 1945★ 48 Main + 12 Brooklyn + 8 Kings Pages 2 Cents IN CITY LIMITS | 3 CENTS Elsewhere

PATTON'S MEN REACH RHINE

Story on Page 3

Reds 29 Miles From Berlin In Oder Drive, Nazis Say

Story on Page 2

Death Shrouds Cologne Victory

In the shadow of Cologne Cathedral (background), the camera records a moment of death and victory as the Yanks sweep into the Rhine metropolis. A wounded American struggles (arrow) free from his tank which has just been blasted by an enemy shell. While one Yank runs to the rescue another dashes off to summon aid. The rest of the crew, killed in blast, are in the smoking tank. The street clock marks the hour. -A few moments later . . . (see back page).

(Official Signal Corps foto via Associated Press Wirefoto).

The Daily Sketch

SEE PAGES 4 and 5

No. 11,173 ★★ FRIDAY, MARCH 9, 1945 ONE PENNY

WE ARE OVER THE RHINE

Firm Bridgehead Against Light Resistance

'THE ALLIES CHEER YOU'

GENERAL EISENHOWER, in a message of congratulation last night to General Hodges, Commander of the U.S. First Army, said:

"The whole Allied force is delighted and cheers the U.S. First Army, whose speed and boldness won the race to establish the first bridgehead across the Rhine.

"Please tell all ranks how proud I am of them."

★ ★ ★

Courtney Hicks Hodges, tall, lean and 57, is a professional soldier.

It is said of him he is "unbeatable in the kind of command that requires deliberate method.

★ ★ ★

"G.I.s" warm to General Hodges. They know him as one of themselves . . . up from the ranks, and as the man who dubbed decorations "brag rags."

The First Army were first on to the Normandy beaches, first into Germany, and now first across the Rhine.

The three Rhine bridges at Cologne are down and partly submerged. This picture, taken from a low-flying plane, shows many of the roofless houses and vacant sites of this much-bombed city.

DEFENCES COLLAPSE LIKE A PACK OF CARDS

AMERICAN troops of General Hodges's First Army have crossed the Rhine at Remagen, between Bonn and Coblenz.

They quickly established a "firm and solid" bridgehead against light resistance and reports early this morning said it was growing hourly.

Men and materials are pouring across. Three counter-attacks have been beaten off.

Several Crossings Made—Paris Radio

To make the crossing the Americans won a dramatic race for the river with the Germans, whose defences had collapsed like a pack of cards.

Paris radio early this morning reported a second crossing between Cologne and Dusseldorf, and added that it was possible that several crossings had been made. This report was not confirmed.

How the crossing which has opened the door wide into the heart of Germany was made is vividly described in the dispatch below:

From JAMES McDOWALL

Kemsley Newspapers War Correspondent With 1st Army Troops East Of The Rhine, Thursday

THIS afternoon I stood on the east bank of the Rhine and watched First Army troops streaming rapidly across—men, guns and supply. They have been crossing and battering down light opposition on the eastern shores since ten minutes to four yesterday afternoon, when Lieut. Carl Timmerman, of West Point, Nebraska, led his infantry company from the west to the east shore after a high-speed dash through the disorganised enemy, to seize a crossing place.

We have known of the crossing since early yesterday evening, but a security black-out prevented the story being told last night. Unfortunately, no war reporters were there to watch the historic episode. Our eyes were all on Cologne, but there is some excuse, for the speed of events south of the city surprised practically everyone, including the participants in the race.

For seven hours to-day we struggled forward in streaming rain over roads sometimes 18 inches deep in liquid mud to reach the crossing. The countryside bore evidence of tough, but sporadic, fighting. Some villages were shattered, others untouched.

TURN TO BACK PAGE, COLUMN 3

British Capture Xanten, Drive On

AMERICAN First Army troops last night were quickly clearing Bonn, birthplace of Beethoven, and Bad Godesberg, where Mr. Chamberlain had his famous "Peace in our time" talks with Hitler.

First civilian resistance was met at Bonn, where the battle was more bitter than that for Cologne.

Although there were thousands of civilians in the town, the Germans poured rockets and shells into it, and many civilians were killed.

Ferries Shelled

It was announced last night that First Army infantry have captured 60,000 prisoners—equivalent to an entire German Army.

Meanwhile, the battle of the Rhine opened on the Third Army front last night as Patton's artillery shelled the ferries trying to extricate the trapped Germans, and at the same time opened up against Coblenz.

The traffic was all one-way, the Germans failing to send over a single shell.

The Fourth Armoured Division patrolled the Rhine north-west of Coblenz without meeting any resistance.

So far the Rhineland debacle has cost the Germans almost 90,000 prisoners, an uncounted number of casualties and masses of material.

Patton's troops have now captured their 200,000th prisoner.

To the north, British and Canadian troops continued to meet fanatical resistance before Xanten, but according to New York radio, they took the town and advanced beyond it.

The Wesel pocket has been reduced to less than six miles square.

Fighting in this sector is the most savage on the Western Front, and both sides have lost heavily.—Reuter, A.P. and Exchange.

3 a.m. Edition

The Daily Sketch *Headlines*

Friday, March 9

WAR

WEST: First U.S. Army make surprise crossing of the Rhine at Remagen, between Coblenz and Bonn, and secure firm bridgehead.

EAST: Zhukov consolidates ten-mile bridgehead on west bank of Oder, and reaches point 28 miles from Berlin.—Page 8.

ITALY: Vergato, guard to Bologna, threatened from three sides.

AIR: Only a few guns fire at U.S. "heavies" attacking Ruhr, once notorious "Flak Valley."—Page 8.

FAR EAST: Tanks of the "Dagger" Division are fighting in Mandalay.—Page 8

*

HOME

Conservative M.P.s propose to take action over the refusal of a war gratuity to the Women's Land Army.—Page 3.

Two hundred M.P.s support payment of the child allowance to the mother.—Page 7.

V.C. awarded to R.A.M.C. man who died in rescuing wounded commandos.—Page 3

TIMELY WORDS OF FAITH

The judgments of the Lord are true and righteous altogether. . . . In keeping of them there is great reward.

Psalm 19, 9-11.

News Chronicle

No. 30,832 — SATURDAY, MARCH 10, 1945 — ONE PENNY

LATE LONDON EDITION

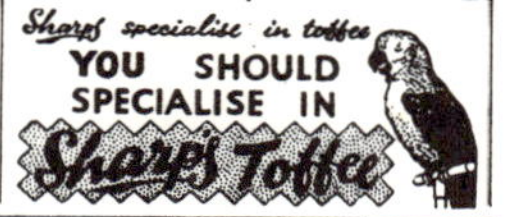

RHINE BRIDGEHEAD IS FIVE MILES DEEP

Patton links up with Hodges and closes trap round 5 Wehrmacht divisions on west bank

OUR Rhine bridgehead, now five miles deep and 10 miles wide, according to Paris dispatches, is being steadily enlarged. Tanks and infantry, pouring across into an area already packed with Allied armoured formations, are brushing aside panzer attacks against the perimeter.

Erpel, on the east bank opposite Remagen, was captured. Its inhabitants ran up white flags.

The fighting has extended beyond Erpel, according to Berlin: from Unkel, three miles north of Remagen, to Linz, two and a half miles south of Remagen.

Bonn, the German university town, has now been captured, and mopping up is in progress.

First Army H.Q. announced a link-up between the forces of Gen. Hodges and Gen. Patton's U.S. Third Army near Andernach, Rhine ferry terminus south of Remagen. This closes the trap round between five and six Wehrmacht divisions—and gives the Allies control of 100 miles of the Rhine.

Twelve towns fell to Gen. Patton downstream from the Moselle mouth. A divisional general, his staff and 3,200 troops surrendered.

Finally, far over the Rhine more than 250 big guns of the U.S. Ninth Army have begun the concerted shelling of targets in the heart of the Ruhr as far east as Essen.

This is the General who forced the Rhine

From Our Special Correspondent

WESTERN FRONT, Friday.

TROOPS, weapons and vehicles—innumerable and of every kind—are pouring down the roads to the Rhine bridgehead today.

They are moving in a way and at a speed that—it is giving no military secrets away to say it—were not intended a couple of days ago.

A great deal is being switched, and is being canalised in a new direction at a sensational pace, because of the peculiar quality of a quiet and mild-mannered man who sits at a desk with his back to a big window opening on to a balcony which he never has time to use.

Two great gifts

Lt-Gen. Courtney H. Hodges is probably the least publicised man in all the American armies. I emphasise this point because of the difficulty of trying to sketch his character.

Here is a man with no flamboyances but with two great gifts which have enabled him to lead an army with a record of success equalled by no other American general in the European theatre—the ability to move vast masses of men and equipment in the minimum of time with a profound understanding of the terrain over which they have to travel, and an instinctive comprehension of what goes on in the mind of the ordinary soldier.

Gen. Hodges

It is largely because of these qualities that Hodges has led his American First Army first out of the Normandy beach-head, first into Germany, first through the Siegfried Line, and now first across the Rhine.

There have been setbacks, but one in particular emphasises the point to keep in mind in writing of Hodges. That was during the Ardennes break-through, when in ten days he moved thousands of men and vehicles, mostly on north-south roads across supply lines which were also carrying their traffic. There was never a hitch. The Second Armoured Division caught the German spearhead at Celles and smashed it almost in sight of the Meuse.

Patience

The secret of such movement is not to yield to the temptation to get everything rolling at once, but to consider the roads and country calmly, then to move all of your men and equipment at staggered intervals.

At the lowest rating the quality of mind which works like this is expressed in infinite patience; at the highest it amounts to genius. It means that the instant a situation develops to your advantage you are able to exploit it with every atom of power at your disposal.

At his staff conferences Hodges will say little while his specialists advise. Then he announces his decisions immediately in a series of clear-cut statements which are final until a new situation develops.

Foxing the enemy

The more violently this happens the quieter becomes the atmosphere around the general. The air of a mild professor of a Middle West University intensifies. He indicates the positions on the map, issues his orders softly, succinctly, rapidly—and awaits the result.

The fashion in which he does it has foxed the Germans many times, most noticeably in the great chase across France and the Low Countries.

Hodges might have become a farmer, but listening to the tales of an old National Guard captain, and his own uncle, a veteran of the Civil War, sent him to West Point.

AND HERE THEY GO OVER THE RIVER: FIRST PICTURES

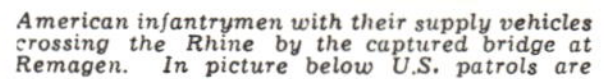

American infantrymen with their supply vehicles crossing the Rhine by the captured bridge at Remagen. In picture below U.S. patrols are guarding the bridge, which was taken in a 10-minute action without the loss of a single man

Who will get to Berlin first?

By Major PHILIP CRIBBLE
The Military Critic

THE Allies are in the straight in the race for Berlin. Will the forces of Marshal Stalin or Gen. Eisenhower be the first to reach the goal?

Fine generalship has won the First Army its deserts. To the surprise of all, the Ludendorff railway bridge over the Rhine at Remagen has been taken almost intact.

No doubt by now the bridge will have been supplemented by pontoons. Naturally there is a black-out on movements on the east bank.

There is no doubt, however, that resistance has been extremely light, and that important Allied forces are already expanding the bridgehead in preparation for a full-scale break-out.

Disorganisation

The complete disorganisation of enemy communications, both road and rail, makes enemy counter-moves to deal with this new situation extremely difficult. It is doubtful if the Germans have even tactical reserves available.

At any time, and at many points, Gen. Eisenhower may choose to make new crossings, and these threats along a 140-mile stretch of the river impose dispersion on the enemy which his exhausted and broken forces will be incapable of covering successfully.

Complete collapse is possible at any moment, but, failing this, normal precautions will impose a pause in which to build up adequate strength in the various bridgeheads before breaking out and repeating the sweeping advances in Germany that were seen in France last summer.

Within a matter of weeks Gen. Eisenhower should be knocking off the miles from the 300-odd now separating him from Berlin.

On the Eastern front Marshal Zhukov is poised in apparent readiness to open his new drive on Berlin.

Harder going

The Baltic flank is secured by Rokossovsky's successes. Here, as on the Western front, it will be impossible for the enemy to bring together the concentrations necessary to check the Russians at the several focal points through Pomerania, Brandenburg and Saxony.

The enemy's resistance on the Eastern front is still well co-ordinated, and the fighting there is likely to be much more stubborn than on the Western front east of the Rhine.

Marshal Zhukov has only 28 miles to go, but his task will not be light.

Nevertheless, if there is no exceptional interference from the weather, I favour the chances of the Russians getting there first.

Another U.S. army is on West Front

Lt.-Gen. Leonard Gerow
Commands new army

SHAEF, Friday.

THE presence on the Continent of the U.S. Fifteenth Army, commanded by Lt.-Gen. Leonard T. Gerow, was disclosed today.

The Fifteenth Army is part of Lt.-Gen. Omar Bradley's Twelfth Army Group, and this general's command is now larger than that of any other Allied commander, except possibly some of the Russian generals' commands.

It is believed that more than 1,000,000 men are now under Gen. Bradley's command.

Disclosure of the presence on the Continent of the Fifteenth Army was made during ceremonies in which Gen. Bradley and seven other generals received decorations from Gen. Alphonse Juin, Chief of Staff of the French Armed Forces.

Gen. Bradley commanded the First U.S. Army in the assault on the Continent, and Gen. Gerow the Fifth Corps at that time.

Lightning tank drive closes a Rhine ferry

From NORMAN CLARK

WITH U.S. THIRD ARMY, GERMANY, Friday.

AS two more towns on the Rhine — Andernach and Brohl—fell to swift American tank drives to the river today, and the prisoners taken in 24 hours swelled to nearly 4,000, German guns on the far bank opened fire upon our positions in the Coblenz plain.

But along a ten-mile stretch the river is under our control.

None of the river barges that have been passing up and down it in long convoys are now able to ply below Coblenz.

Bridges within range of our guns—we are on commanding ground four miles north-west of Coblenz—have been blown by the enemy, and the ferry at Andernach, nine miles north-west of Coblenz, has been suspended by our occupation of the town.

Ended now

This Rhine crossing point had been an area of frenzied evacuation activity until one of our armoured columns pounced upon it in a lightning 11-mile drive from Mayen, which has also been occupied.

The Andernach Ferry could prevent 450 troops from being captured—in the engulfing of the collapsed front west of the Rhine—on every trip it made.

From all sectors German units in retreat converged on Andernach in horse-drawn vehicles as well as lorries and on bicycles, congesting the town.

Now all that has been brought to an end by the capture and occupation of the Andernack bank.

New York rumours

New York, Friday.—Rumours were flooding New York tonight. One of them said that Hitler "intends to surrender at midnight tonight." Most of the rumours emanate from Wall Street.

REMAGEN BRIDGE WAS TAKEN IN 10 MINUTES

From STANLEY BARON
News Chronicle War Correspondent

With the U.S. First Army Across the Rhine, Friday.

A SERIES of chances for which you would have to search the whole history of war to find an equal is enabling the troops of Gen. Courtney Hodges's American First Army to build up tonight the bridgehead over the Rhine established on Wednesday afternoon by the 27th Armoured Infantry Battalion of the 9th Armoured Division.

For 24 hours there has been a security silence. Now the curtain is lifted, and here are the sensational facts.

The bridge at Remagen, south of Bonn, has been captured. The whole operation lasted exactly ten minutes.

Opposition was so little that that you can call it non-existent.

Though some of the dynamite charges which had been laid for demolition blew up while 1st-Lt. Carl Timmerman's troops making the assault were still on the bridge, there were no casualties.

Made history

By 4 p.m. the whole bridge was ours. The Rhine had been crossed and not a man lost.

To picture the whole of this incredible operation clearly I must first fill in the background, both of the previous two or three days and of the division which did the job, making history after only eight days in the line.

From the road and rail junction at Euskirchen they had driven east between the Bonn road and the line of the Ahr River flowing into the Rhine just below Remagen.

First-hand report

Their orders then were to turn south in two main columns under their respective combat commands to sweep up all the Germans retreating in a rabble from the hills and prevent them from crossing the Rhine.

They were also to take a "look-see" at the bridge at Remagen to report on its condition, since, owing to bad weather, we had had no air reconnaissance and it was believed to be destroyed.

What happened next can be put in the words of Major H. B. Mackenzie, staff officer:

"We looked on and there it was, with not a rail out of place. No one expected it to be like this. It was a gift you couldn't pass up."

And now the chain of chances began.

Perhaps the first was that the commander of the Combat Command whose troops first arrived on the scene happened to be one

Continued Back Page

Berlin gets biggest of 18 raids

BERLIN'S 228th air-raid last night was the biggest of 18 successive Mosquito attacks, in which well over 1,000 tons of bombs have been dropped, including many 4,000-pounders.

Railyards handling urgent coal and steel supplies from the Ruhr to Central Germany were heavily hit by more than 1,000 U.S. heavies yesterday.

Ten bombers and five of the 400 escort fighters are missing.

Targets were at Muenster, Osnabrueck, Rheine, Frankfurt-on-Main and Cassel—still smoking from blows by the R.A.F., whose overnight targets had also included Hamburg's U-boat assembly yards.

V 2 lines cut

By day R.A.F. Lancasters heavily bombed benzol plants near the Ruhr, while T.A.F. supported the Rhine bridgehead forces, pounding concentration points and hitting hard at Ludenscheid railyards, 20 miles from the Rhine.

Eight cuts in V 2 rail lines were made. Spitfires from Britain refuelled in France between assaults on V-targets. At one point their bombs crashed through a roof to set a large building on fire.

A thousand fighter-bombers of the Ninth provided an umbrella at Remagen. Thunderbolts hit concentrations in the Wesel bridgehead, shooting down 11 enemy planes.

More than 250 medium and light bombers attacked Ruhr Valley arms factories and other targets, destroying 14 aircraft.

Other destruction included 34 locomotives, 358 rail cars, 65 motor vehicles, nine tanks and armoured vehicles, 34 Rhine barges and 64 buildings.

From Italy Mitchells attacked four Brenner bridges; heavies struck at Graz, Austria.

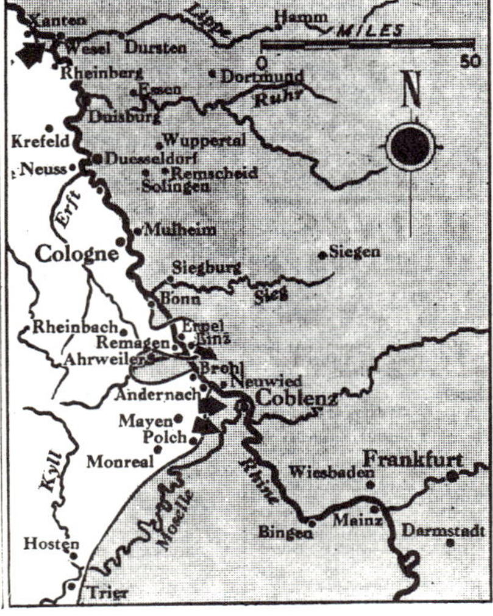

Nazi commandos raid French port

Shaef, Friday.—A small number of German commandos, presumably from the Channel Islands, raided the port of Granville, on the Normandy coast, at 1.15 this morning.

Some damage was caused, casualties were suffered on both sides, and the raiders took a small number of prisoners.

Granville is 25 miles over the bay from St. Malo and 32 from Jersey, the nearest Channel Island.

It is believed that the raid was made for propaganda purposes to take the Germans' minds off the disaster on the Rhine.

The Germans still hold valuable French ports such as St. Nazaire and Lorient.

Corvette lost

The loss of the corvette Bluebell (Lt. G. H. Walker, D.S.C., R.N.V.R.) is announced by the Admiralty.

SOVIETS FIGHT IN CENTRAL KUESTRIN

FIGHTING is going on in the centre of Kuestrin, the bastion town on the Oder guarding Berlin, according to the German commentator, von Hammer.

"The Russian offensive against Kuestrin is being carried out by considerable parts of one army, which is attacking in waves day and night. Bitter fighting is going on for every house," he said.

Moscow said that assault forces had penetrated the first anti-tank belt guarding Stettin.

German radio admitted that the Russians, continuing their attacks with strong tank forces from the Stargard area, had pierced the outer defences of Stettin.

Outflanking sweep

Meanwhile, the sweep through North-Eastern Pomerania to outflank Danzig continues.

An Order of the Day to Marshal Rokossovsky last night announced the capture of Stolp, 10 miles from the Baltic and 65 miles west of Danzig.

The routine communique added that 200 other places, including Ruegenwalde and Stolpmuende, on the coast, were taken.

'Moderate number' of U-boat victims

By the Naval Correspondent

GERMANY'S new big-scale U-boat offensive, intended to prevent the Allies from sending men and supplies to the Western front, is not meeting with great success.

The U-boats sank a "moderate" number of Allied merchant vessels last month, but the anti-submarine forces were successful in destroying more enemy submarines in the period than in January.

In disclosing these facts the monthly joint statement issued last night under the authority of the Prime Minister and the President warned that, despite the satisfactory results being achieved against the U-boats, unceasing vigilance must be maintained as any enemy with a large number of submarines always possesses a potential threat.

The new types of U-boats (apart from those fitted with the Schnorkel "breathing" tube) which the Germans are believed to possess do not appear to have gone into action yet.

LATE NEWS

4,000 GERMANS KILLED

In the storming of Stolp, 4,000 Germans were killed and 85 tanks knocked out, stated supplement to Soviet communique.

AMERICANS BREAK INTO LUZON LINE

American troops, says Gen. MacArthur's communique, have broken into the Shimbu defence line ast of Manilla, on Luzon. Substantial gains have been made near Bayanan. In the past 24 hours 137 caves have been captured and 446 entrances blown up with practically no U.S. losses.

LONDON DIM-OUT
7.25 p.m.—6.55 a.m.
Sunday 7.27 p.m.—6.53 a.m.
Moon sets 1.58 p.m., rises 6.28 a.m. tomorrow. New Moon, March 14.

300 Super-Forts fire 10 sq. miles of Tokio

From Our Own Correspondent

WASHINGTON, Friday.

TEN square miles of Tokio are afire today after the biggest raid American Army air forces have ever staged over the Japanese capital.

A fleet of 300 Super-Fortresses, bearing the greatest bomb load so far taken from bases in the Mariana Islands, carried out the raid on industrial targets, the U.S. War Department reported this afternoon.

According to a broadcast from Guam, soon after the official news was released, the huge planes all carried incendiaries and set the heart of Tokio aflame. Incendiaries were dropped in unprecedented quantities and at an unprecedented rate for 90 minutes.

Blazing cauldron

The first all-fire raid ever carried out on such a scale by Super-Fortresses left the centre of Tokio "a blazing cauldron" with flames shooting far into the sky.

The attack appears to have caught the Japs unprepared. It began at 1 a.m. (Japanese time) and shortly after the Japanese radio was heard admitting that fires were burning in the capital and indicating that the raid was still going on.

The raiding planes were officially described as the "greatest fleet of Super-Fortresses ever assembled." Well over 3,000 American pilots, radio men, bombardiers and gunners were in the air over Tokio.

[Messages from Guam said that over 1,000 tons of incendiaries were dropped in the ten-mile target area. The centre of this area is two miles from the Imperial Palace, but the outskirts are only 50 yards from the moat enclosing Hirohito's home.]

Germans have lost 53 generals in West

SHAEF, Friday.

THE Germans have lost two Field-Marshals — Rommel, who was killed, and von Kluge, who committed suicide—16 full generals and 37 other generals captured on the Western front since D-Day.

More than 4,000 German tanks have been destroyed in the same period. Excluding the Rhineland operation, 58 German divisions have been destroyed, including four paratroop divisions.

It is estimated that the Germans have run through equipment equivalent to the combat strength of 20 panzer divisions, ten having been wiped out twice over.

More than 1,000,000 Germans have been taken prisoner since D-Day.

Earl Lloyd-George

Earl Lloyd-George's condition last night was unchanged.

Pwllheli Liberal Club yesterday elected Earl Lloyd-George as president for the fifty-sixth year in succession.

BRITISH FORCES WEEKLY

Crusader

No. 145 SUNDAY, MARCH 11, 1945 Price: Two Lire

Churchill, on German soil, called for

ONE GOOD, STRONG HEAVE!

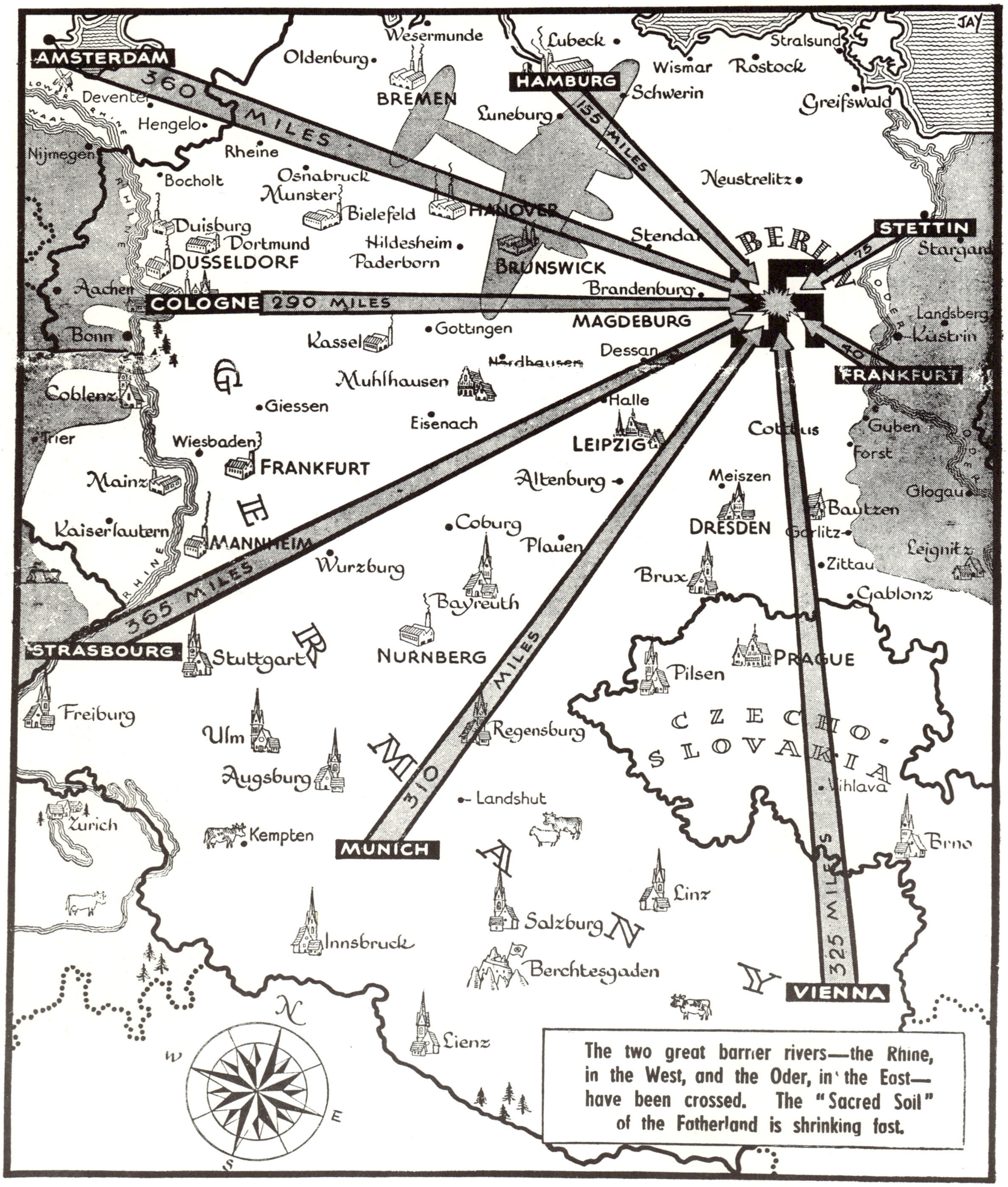

The two great barrier rivers—the Rhine, in the West, and the Oder, in the East—have been crossed. The "Sacred Soil" of the Fatherland is shrinking fast.

NEWS YOU CAN'T GET ELSEWHERE

PM Daily
FIVE CENTS
(Copyright, 1945, by The Newspaper PM, Inc.)
VOL. V — NO. 236
Tuesday, March 20, 1945
Rain
COMPLETE EDITION

Master Race!

Specimen of Hitler's Wehrmacht capture at Cologne by the 104th Division, U. S. 1st Army.
Signal Corps Photo

Nazis Race Yanks for Rhine Bridges

Pages 3-4

NAM Drives To Blow Lid Off End-of-War Profit Ceilings

Page 7

PM TELLS YOU MORE NEWS IN LESS TIME

WEDNESDAY, MARCH 28, 1945

DIM-OUT 7.56 p.m. to 6.14 a.m. Moon 7.7 p.m. to 7.29 a.m. Full Moon March 28. RADIO Page 5

LATE EXTRA

No. 17,710 ONE PENNY

No Opposition Now To Our Drive

MONTY'S TANKS 'RUNNING WILD'

Inside-Germany-Now Reports

RIBBENTROP MOVES H.Q. TO FRONTIER

AMONG many reports and rumours about "What Is Happening In The Reich?" are these:—

The entire personnel of the German Foreign Ministry, headed by Ribbentrop, has arrived in Constance, on the Swiss frontier, according to Brussels radio, which adds that Professor Sauerbruch, Hitler's personal doctor, has also arrived in Constance.

According to the Free German Press Bureau in Stockholm, Himmler has ordered the immediate evacuation of the Nazi festival city of Nuremberg.

* *

A new special police-commander—Brigade Fuehrer Erwin Kuebler—has taken over control in the Vienna area, said an official German news agency despatch to Stockholm.

* * *

Nazi Party archives are being moved to Berchtesgaden, according to Stockholm reports. Nazi Party members from Nuremberg and other German cities are flocking to join the Volkssturm, and are wearing uniform with no party badges so as to sink their identity.

KESSELRING "SACKED"

A New York "Times" despatch from Stockholm today said: "Information from a well-informed source through underground channels says that Field-Marshals Kesselring and Blaskowitz declined to succeed Rundstedt and were dismissed from the Army. Blaskowitz is said to have been placed in a concentration camp and Col.-Gen. Paul Hauser is rumoured to be the new Western front commander."

* * *

Von Bohlen, the Krupps's arms chief, is reported to have fled to Salzburg as soon as the first troops crosed the Rhine. Nazi party leaders are said to be fleeing to the Bavarian Alps and the Swis border from all parts of Germany.

* * *

From today the daily bread ration in Germany, hitherto the mainstay of the diet, is being cut to 100 grams—little more than three ounces, according to a Reuter Zurich report which adds: It is everywhere apparent that the food reserves in the Reich are now completely exhausted and that an uncontrollable food crisis—forerunner of famine—is rapidly becoming more acute.

* * *

"Iron Army discipline and court martials are not sufficient to induce a people to go on fighting without faith and conviction," said Georg Schroeder, chief correspondent of German overseas radio, in a broadcast today. After that Schroeder was cut off and the radio began sending out Morse signals.

IN THE REDOUBT

Himmler recently inspected S.S. units at Zuers Arlberg, which is now the Gestapo headquarters. Well-informed observers say that S.S. divisions are with the four panzer divisions garrisoned inside this German redoubt.

"Berlin morning papers again emphasise the growing readiness of the defence, brought on by the acuteness of the military situation in west," said the German official news agency today. "Just as it was possible to stem the onslaught on Berlin in the very last hour, this time, too, the enemy's triumph is premature.

EMMERICH REPORTED TAKEN

MONTGOMERY is still sending his troops over the Rhine at a pace which should see the whole of the Second Army across in a few days.

Paris radio today broadcast the unconfirmed report that the Germans have evacuated Emmerich. The bridgehead battle is in its last hours.

Dempsey today threatens the road centres of Borken and Bocholt. Control of Bocholt will provide a useful base for a new dash down the Munster road for the Ems River.

The towns of Brunen and Krudenberg, near Wesel, have fallen to Airborne forces.

SIMPSON NEARS ESSEN

SIMPSON'S U.S. Ninth Army are believed to be in the outskirts of Duisburg, greatest inland port in Europe.

Another column is reported to be less than seven miles from Essen.

Wehoffen has been cleared, and the Emscher Canal reached.

HODGES 60 MILES ON

HODGES'S spearheads are reported to be 60 miles east of the Rhine, and to be cracking the Dill River line.

Armoured columns are fanning out east, north and south from Limburg, and a German report today said that Wiesbaden has been taken.

Infantry, pushing south, have taken Ehrenbreitstein, opposite Coblenz.

PATTON DRIVES ON

PATTON'S Third Army, according to a radio report, are still going strong, 35 miles from Nuremberg, and little more than 150 miles from Austria.

The Germans admit that units are nearly 70 miles east of the Rhine, after reaching the River Main near Wurzburg.

Troops in Frankfort are fighting their way through the city block by block. Entry was made by a bridge which the Germans failed to destroy.

PATCH ADVANCES NINE MILES

PATCH'S U.S. Seventh Army, exploiting their bridgehead, have taken 2,500 prisoners, seized 225 square miles of enemy soil, and advanced nine miles.

French forces are also over the Rhine in this area.

British Strength Stupefies Enemy: "Every Hour Tells"

From STANLEY NASH, "Star" War Correspondent
East of the Rhine, Wednesday

MONTGOMERY'S ARMOUR IS TODAY "RUNNING WILD" MILES BEYOND BRUNEN AFTER THE BREAK-OUT FROM THE BRIDGEHEAD. OUR TANKS ARE REALLY STEAMING AHEAD NOW AND THERE IS NO OPPOSITION WORTH WORRYING ABOUT.

Every hour that passes proves conclusively that the German Army in the West is finished as a fighting unit and that the end of the war against Hitler is in sight. It may take some weeks, perhaps a little longer, to subdue the enemy remnants, but to all intents and purposes the big struggle is over.

Never have our Army leaders been more confident

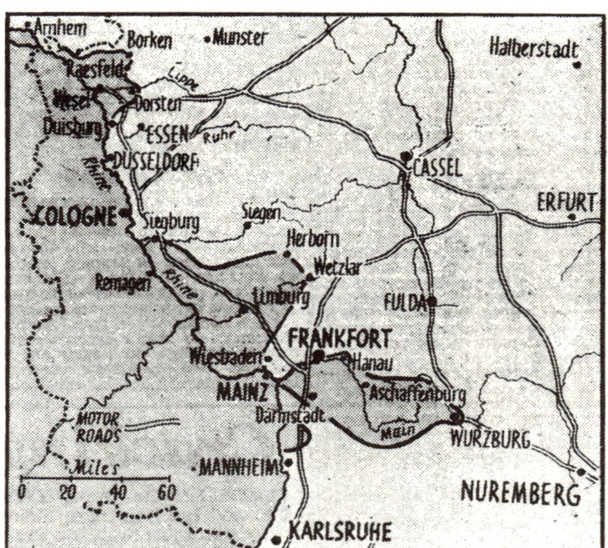

of a battle issue than they are at this time, and this issue is the defeat of Germany.

It all goes to bear out the words of the brigadier who told me, on Monday, that the Germans on his sector had "had it."

The prisoners we are taking are of different mettle from those captured in the first three days of the battle east of the Rhine. The German paratroops, who formed the greater part of the bag at first, are coming in few and far between.

In their place the Army are scooping up mixed parties of Hun soldiery in the centre of the bridgehead. They are all types, hurriedly organised into so-called fighting battalions—definitely ersatz warriors.

The amount of material flowing into Monty's bridgehead is so vast that one wonders why the enemy bother to continue the struggle. I spent hours in a jeep trying to weave a way through the convoys in the bridgehead.

In some of the narrow roads it was impossible to move west for long periods. Armour, guns and supplies of all kinds piled towards the front.

'Lambeth Bridge' On Rhine

When I did get near the Rhine again, I found notices "To Lambeth Bridge," "Westminster Bridge," and "London Bridge."

The prisoners in the bridgehead are stupefied by the sight of the masses of material we are moving over. Their faces show that they have never seen so many weapons, supplies and machinery concentrated in such a small area, even in the days of Hitler's early triumphs.

German civilians east of the river are subdued and willing to do anything they are told by the Military Government. The adults walk about with glum faces. The children show a lively interest in the passing pageant of war.

Most of the people are farmers and holdings had been particu-

CONTINUED ON BACK PAGE, Col. Three

Quins—All Girls

QUINTUPLETS—all girls—were born to Mrs. Adah Turner, wife of a Government clerk, in a Washington hospital during the night.

One was born dead and three others were described as "barely breathing" and given little chance of survival. Only the fifth seems likely to live, says Reuter.

The quins were three months premature, and averaged 1½lb., otherwise all were normal.

Mrs. Turner is 36 and is the mother of twins and eight other children.

V-Bombs Continue

During the twenty-four hours ended at dawn today, there was enemy air activity directed against Southern England. Damage and casualties have been reported.

Buy More Bonds For Victory

Jersey Observer

FINAL EDITION

WEATHER REPORT—Today: Mostly cloudy. Tonight: Cloudy; considerably cooler. Tomorrow: Cloudy; moderate temperatures.

VOL. LIV.—No. 45 | TEMPERATURE—8 A. M., 63; 9 A. M., 58; 10 A. M., 59 | FRIDAY, MARCH 30, 1945 | JERSEY CITY OFFICE 2866 Hudson Boulevard | UNION CITY OFFICE 417 36th Street | HOBOKEN OFFICE 111 Newark Street | PRICE 4 CENTS

Germans Crack Up

Enemy Surrenders By Thousands In Mass As Almost All Organized Resistance Ends

Reds 30 Miles From Vienna; Seize Danzig

Drive for Austrian Capital Along 5 Highways; At Sopron

London, March 30. — (UP) — The Red Army today was reported driving on Vienna along five highways south of the Danube and was only 30 miles from the Austrian capital at Sopron, which was reported besieged.

At Sopron the Russians were only 18 miles from the huge Austrian manufacturing and war center of Wiener Neustadt, often a target for American heavy bombers, and the rail lines linking Austria with the south.

The rail lines are also vital to the supply of the German forces still holding out in northern Yugoslavia.

The Germans were reported massing troops along the Leite River line just a few miles in advance of Soviet spearheads for a last stand to save Vienna.

One Soviet column threatened to flank Vienna from the south.

Still another column clearing the western tip of Hungary was within five miles of the Austrian border and 40 miles southeast of Vienna.

Far to the north, the great Baltic port of Danzig fell into Soviet hands the German High Command admitted.

UKRAINIAN ARMY ROLLS TO FRONTIER

Marshal Fedor I. Tolbukhin's 3rd Ukrainian Army group rolled up to the Austrian frontier on a 14-mile front yesterday and a Free Austria radio broadcast said the Soviets crossed the border at several points, liberating some villages.

The Soviets turned the German defense line based on Lake Neusiedler with the capture of the border stronghold of Koeszeg, 19 miles southwest of the 130-square-mile water barrier and 50 miles south of Vienna itself.

Koeszeg also lies 31 miles southeast of the big Messerschmitt aircraft manufacturing center of Wiener Neustadt, and 165 miles east of Adolf Hitler's mountain-top retreat at Berchtesgaden.

Another 3rd Army group column seized Kapuvar, 11 miles southeast of Lake Neusiedler, seven miles from the Austrian border and 42 miles southeast of Vienna.

More than 100 other Hungarian towns and villages were swept up in the Third Army group's advances of up to 20 miles, among them Szombathely, 54 miles east of Graz, Austria's second largest industrial center.

New Delay in Warren-Hague Writ Battle

Further legal action in the efforts of John Warren, Jersey City lawyer to have his $2,000,000 libel suit against Mayor Frank Hague of Jersey City brought to trial, was postponed yesterday for at least two weeks.

Chancellor Luther A. Campbell, at his chambers in Jersey City, reserved decision after a two-hour hearing on a motion by Warren's attorney, Theodore D. Parsons, to have the Chancery Court phase of the libel suit transferred from Hudson County to Monmouth County. Campbell gave Parsons one week to prepare a brief on his motion, and Mayor Hague's attorney, John J. Quinn, another week in which to prepare a brief in reply.

Since March 19, when Quinn obtained from Vice Chancellor Charles M. Egan, in Jersey City, Hudson County, a temporary injunction restraining Warren from proceeding with the libel suit, Warren's attorney has been seeking without success to have motions on the injunction heard before a member of Chancery Court in Long Branch or Freehold, both in Monmouth County.

Before presenting the motion today to transfer the injunction case, Parsons moved before Chancellor Champbell that the Chancellor disqualify himself to act in the matter. This would have the effect of removing it from the entire Court of Chancery. Parsons based his motion on the allegation that Campbell had prejudiced Warren's case by determining two legal questions prior to the filing of the injunction suit.

Parsons said the Chancellor had advised Hague's attorney where to file the injunction action, deciding

(See WARREN-HAGUE Page 10)

Reich Bombed in Two-Way Attacks

London, March 30—(INS)—Allied bomber formations were reported over the Reich today by the German radio.

The Nazi radio warning system also said the Italy-based Allied bombers were over Austria and that other formations were approaching Germany from the west, indicating another two-way smash against Reich targets.

British Mosquito bombers raided Berlin and other targets in northwestern Germany last night.

The German capital had been hit for 36 successive nights until inclement weather halted the Mosquito operations Wednesday night.

Reports Auto Stolen

Robert Greer, of 2801 Boulevard, Jersey City, reported to the police at 1:20 o'clock this morning that his 1935 Terraplane coach type automobile, N. J. license IH-707, was stolen from in front of 837 Bergen avenue

Treasury Balance

Washington, March 30.—(INS)—Treasury balance March 28, $15,191,713,568.47; internal revenue, $5,018,663.74; customs receipts, $29,603,113.55; receipts, $34,583,300,545; expenditures, $72,450,464,446.

"Thanks for the Paper, Keep It Coming"

All the boys like to read the news from the home community. Costs only $1 a month fully postpaid to every soldier and sailor. Costs nothing whenever there is a change of address. Forward money order or check to Subscription Department, Jersey Observer, Hoboken. Please print name and address and include your own when sending order.

Sheriff McGovern Gets Writ; Bars Fingerprinting Himself

Sheriff William J. McGovern, who has been indicted by the grand jury on a charge of failing to fingerprint other indicted Jersey City officials, cannot now take his own fingerprints even if he so wishes.

He obtained a temporary injunction from Vice Chancellor Kays, Wednesday, to stop himself from taking his own prints. The injunction is directed against Attorney General Walter D. Van Riper, State Police Superintendent Charles H. Schoeffel and "any other enforcement agent," meaning the sheriff himself.

Sheriff McGovern will have to come to court, probably on April 13, to plead to the two indictments. After he enters his plea, he would be required by law to take his own fingerprints and photograph and distribute the pictures to law enforcement agencies throughout the country.

Now his hands are tied by his own hands. Notice of the injunction was served yesterday upon Deputy Attorney Generals John Grimshaw and James R. Giuliano at the Court House.

PARIS, March 30—(UP)—German troops were reported surrendering by the thousands today as the American 1st Army cut into the enemy's rear areas 180-odd miles from Berlin, virtually enveloping the Ruhr Basin and the Nazis' last major fighting force in western Germany.

The German High Command said U. S. 3rd Army forces were 186 miles southwest of Berlin at Bad Wildungen, 19 miles southwest of Kassel. That was the closest point to Berlin reported specifically for the Americans.

The break-up of the German armies in the west appeared to have begun. The 1st Army's tank columns already had knifed 100 road miles through the rear of the enemy forces defending the Ruhr, meeting only beaten, demoralized Germans intent only on surrender.

The Allied-controlled Luxembourg radio said one of the greatest mass surrenders in history was under way all along the western front and that revolt aagainst the Nazi regime was imminent.

HODGES'S ARMY NEARS JUNCTURE

Vanguards of the 1st Army were reported in and perhaps beyond the communications center of Paderborn, gateway to the north German plain, and moving fast toward a decisive juncture with Field Marshal Sir Bernard L. Montgomery's British and American forces in the north.

At Paderborn, Lt. Gen. Courtney H. Hodges's 1st Army was less than 40 miles from a juncture with Montgomery and 59 miles southwest of Hannover, 12th city of Hitler's disintergrating Reich.

Hodges's men raced northward over more than 100 miles of twisting German roads almost without firing a shot. They reached the Paderborn area just 24 hours after the jump-off from Giessen at dawn yesterday.

The Allied-controlled Luxembourg radio said Lt. Gen. George S. Patton's American Third Army to the southeast was loose on an equally-spectacular armored drive headed for Leipzig and a possible juncture with the Red Army.

Luxembourg said Patton's men were racing into the Thuringian forest on the road to Eisenach, 155 miles southwest of Berlin and 90 miles east of Leipzig.

Both the First and Third Armies were pushing a phantom German army that melted away at their approach. Only a handful of fanatical Nazi SS Troopers opposed the First Army's triumphal sweep to Paderborn, and Patton's men were reported meeting virtually no opposition

More than 33,000 dazed German prisoners were swept up by the two American forces yesterday and United Press War Correspondent Robert Richards reported that the Nazis were falling over themselves in their rush to surrender.

PRISON CAGES ARE JAMMED

The Third Army prison cages were jammed with more than 150,000 captives rounded up in the eight-day advance beyond the Rhine, and the last major fighting force left to the enemy in western Germany was believed to comprise about 16,000 Germans reeling back before Montgomery's men in the north.

The British Second Army and units of the American Ninth Army were driving through and north of the Ruhr under a rigid security blackout. But censored field dispatches said they had hammered out gains running up to 10 miles and more in the past 24 hours, indicating they had reached an area south and perhaps southeast of Muenster where they would be 30 to 40 miles northwest of Hodges's First Army.

The import of Hodges's breakthrough and Patton's reported sweep on Eisenach was staggering. Spokesmen for the two armies said the German front had disintegrated completely in their path.

"All organized German resistance may be expected to cease very soon," reported United Press War Correspondent John McDermott from the 1st Army front.

Radio Luxembourg said tens of thousands of Nazis were laying down their arms all over the vanishing Western Front in "one of the greatest mass surrenders of all time."

"Chaos reigns and revolt against the Nazi regime is imminent," the broadcast said.

PARTIAL BLACKOUT OBSCURES MOVES

A partial security blackout obscured the location of Hodges's armored vanguards racing up behind the Ruhr into the fringe of the northern plains extending all the way back to Berlin.

Three armored task forces struck out from positions north of the captured enemy Quartermaster depot at Giessen at six a. m. yesterday and in 12 hours swept ahead 35 to 55 airline miles toward a link-up with Montgomery.

One column stabbed north and northwest to reach a point 10 miles south of Paderborn, traversing 90 miles of main highways and side roads against the feeblest opposition. Overnight they were reported to have plunged on into Paderborn, gateway to the northern plains, and on toward the Ruhr-Berlin superhighway 16 miles beyond.

Paderborn, lies 190 miles west-southwest of Berlin and the Yanks were believed to be considerable closer to the enemy capital this morning.

HODGES'S MEN ARE HALF WAY TO BERLIN

From their starting point in the Remagen bridgehead a week ago Hodges's men already had covered almost half the way to Berlin and were still going fast against little or no opposition.

In the drive on Paderborn, the big German airfield at Langeweisse, almost mid-way between Giessen and Paderborn, was captured. The Yank column met only one German fighting force en route—34 Nazi Elite Guards who tried to throw a road block across their path.

Hodges's charging tanks rode the Nazis down. Two other columns were charging northward on the east flank of the Paderborn spearhead, capturing Lelbach, 30 miles south-southeast of Paderborn and 27 miles west of Kassel, and Titmaringhausen, eight miles farther west.

Patton's 3rd Army, meanwhile, was slashing east, northeast, and southeast of Giessen at top speed against equally weak resistance.

FOURTH DIVISION FAR PAST GIESSEN

Late field dispatches, lagging hours behind Patton's racing tanks, said the Fourth Armored Division had driven 30 miles east of Giessen to capture Lauterbach and a cluster of towns in that area, including Herbstein, six miles to the south. Task forces of the Fourth Division also were riding roughshod through the non-existent German defenses 10 miles northeast to 16 miles southeast of Giessen.

The Fourth's northeastern wing was astride the Giesenach-Eisenach military highway and, according to the radio Luxembourg account, moving at top speed for Eisenach, 48 miles north-northeast of Lauterbach.

Other Third Army forces wiped out the last enemy resistance in Frankfurt, Germany's ninth city, yesterday afternoon after an unexpectedly stiff fight against a small force of Nazi Elite Guards. Wiesbaden, 15 miles to the west was cleared, and the former American internment camp at Bad Nauheim, 15 miles north of Frankfurt, was entered by units of the Sixth Armored Division.

THOUSANDS ARE ROUNDED UP

Infantrymen of the 1st and 3rd Armies were combing through the entire area overrun by their armored spearheads to round up thousands of beaten Germans by-passed in the great sweep to the north and east.

Front dispatches said the doughboys were racing ahead in trucks, armored cars, and astride the turrets of tanks, keeping pace with the flying armored spearheads.

The two armies held a continuous front of more than 125 miles, extending southeast from Paderborn to the Main River at Aschaffenburg, 25 miles southeast of Frankfurt. The 3rd Army lines jutted within 120 miles of Czechoslovakia, in the Lauterbach area, and the two armies were fewer than 250 miles from the west-bound Red armies at a number of points.

The U. S. 7th Army drew abreast of its first and 3rd Army comrades along the Main River, just south of Aschaffenburg. There the Yanks held a 12-mile bridgehead across the Main 35 miles or more beyond the Rhine and were advancing steadily eastward, against somewhat stiffer opposition.

The Germans in that sector were fighting from concrete bunkers thrown up as long ago as 1935, but they were not believed to be in sufficient strength to do more than delay the 7th Army advance.

MANNHEIM TAKEN WITHOUT A FIGHT

The big Rhine city of Mannheim on the 7th Army's southern flank, was captured without a fight yesterday. The doughboys marched in after the city's mayor had notified them by telephone that the last German troops had fled.

Mannheim was Germany's 23rd city, the largest after Cologne to be taken by the western Allies.

The 7th Army's 44th Division took over Mannheim and sent strong infantry columns seven miles southeast to enter the suburbs of Heidelburg. That famous university city appeared ready to fall, if it had not already done so.

At the northern end of the Allied battle line, the remnants of the German 1st Paratroop Army still were fighting a desperate rear guard action in and north of the Ruhr. But they were being cut up into isolated segments by the crushing weight of British and American armor thrown into a 15-mile corridor on the southwestern approaches to Muenster.

The Germans in that area already appeared to have delayed their retreat too long and they were in imminent peril of being enveloped by the north-bound U. S. 1st Army.

MONTY'S FORCES HEAD FOR MUENSTER

The security blackout permitted correspondents to say only that Montgomery's men were driving for Muenster, 227 miles west of Berlin, and had gained 10 miles from their last reported positions. That would put them 35 to 40 miles east of the Rhine and about a dozen miles from Muenster in the Duelmen-Buldern sector.

Three German bolt positions—Bocholt, Borken, and Haltern—were taken by the British, and Doersten, on the northern rim of the Ruhr, was cleared by a combined British 2nd Army and American 9th Army force.

The only major German resistance on Montgomery's front was reported along the northern flank at Emmerich, 10 miles northwest of Rees, where the Germans were being routed from cellar pillboxes by Canadian infantrymen.

The 9th Army also was making relatively slow progress through the northwestern corner of the Ruhr basin, largely because the heavily built-up factory towns had to be combed out carefully for hidden enemy nests. Duisburg was reported in American hands, and Berlin said street fighting was under way in Hamborn, Bottrop, and Gladbeck.

Flames Rage In Hoboken Warehouse

The three-story brick building on the southwest corner of 11th and Jefferson streets, Hoboken, was the well-known raging inferno this morning at press time.

The upper floors have been totally burned out, and the building was collapsing within itself.

The property is owned and occupied by the Lightfoot-Schultz Co., and is used as a warehouse for their materials for baling and packing their products.

SCENE OF OTHER FIRES

It was originally the home of the Sisal Products Company, and was the scene of many fires during the last three or four years, because of the inflammable nature of the materials used by that company.

Six engine and three truck companies were brought out on a general alarm.

Firemen are using their efforts to prevent the spread of the blaze to adjoining buildings on the east.

One of these is the Schoup-Owens, Inc., plant.

'Strong Mayor' Bill Called Dangerous

Assemblyman T. James Tumulty, Hudson County Democrat, today expressed the opinion that the so-called "strong mayor" bill to amend the Walsh Act is dangerous legislation.

Introduced by Assemblyman Joseph Solomine, Essex Republican, the bill proposed drastic revisions of commission government in Newark and Jersey City, but affects no other commission governed municipalities. It passed the Assembly over the spirited protests of Tumulty and Minority Leader Peter P. Artaserse and is now in the hands of the Senate's committee on municipalities.

Under its provisions, the mayor would have investigatory, regulatory and veto powers, and authority would be centralized in the commission. Individual commissioners would be reduced to administrative department heads.

Tumulty expressed greatest concern over the clause which would empower the mayor to remove or suspend municipal officers or employes whenever "in his opinion" they are guilty of nonfeasance, misfeasance, or malfeasance in office.

Tokyo Reports 5 Task Forces Attack Ryukyus

Round Island 25 Miles From Coast; Cebu Harbor Secured

Guam, March 30.—(UP)—Tokyo said at least five Allied task forces, including 18 battleships, were blasting away at Japan's southern approaches for the eighth straight day today in preparation for an invasion of Okinawa Island in the Ryukyus.

"The time for a decisive battle between Japan and America finally has come upon us," Tokyo quoted the newspaper Yomiuri-Hochi as saying.

Japanese estimates of the task forces which the enemy said has been hitting installations all the way from Japan proper to the Sakishimas, 600 miles to the southwest, ranged from 150 surface ships to 2,000, including transports and landing craft.

One Tokyo broadcast said "almost the entire American Pacific Fleet" was mobilized for the assault.

REPORT 25 MILES OFF COAST OF JAPAN

Though the assault was centering on Okinawa, naval and air base inland 330 miles southwest of Japan, Tokyo said one task force appeared last night and today "around" Tanega Island, only 25 miles off the coast of Japan itself.

A penetration to Tanega would be the closest approach to Japan by Allied warships of the war and would represent a ringing challenge to the remnants of the Japanese fleet to come out and fight.

(A German Transocean dispatch recorded by the United Press in London said 150 American Superfortresses raided Tokyo this morning with new type incendiary bombs and caused fires at several places.)

Four other American and British task forces were attacking islands in the Ryukus, principally Okinawa, Toky said. Estimating the number of ships at 150, the Domei Agency said they included 17 battleships, seven auxiliary aircraft carriers, 20 cruisers, 19 destroyers, 20 minesweepers and 92 landing-ship-tanks.

But the Tokyo newspaper Yomiuri Hochi said that the "enemy comes with 2,000 ships of all kinds."

Manila, March 30. — (UP) — Elements of the Americal Division secured the approaches to Cebu's big harbor in the central Philippines today with invasions of nearby Cauit and Mactan Islands.

The main city of Opon on Mactan Island, where Magellan died in the 16th Century, was seized by the assault troops while tiny Cauit, a former seaplane base just outside Cebu city's harbor, was completely occupied.

The islands were the 29th and 30th invaded by Gen. Douglas MacArthur's American forces in the Philippines.

Hague Orders Airport Site Survey Begun

Establishment of an airport in Jersey City will have the full support of Mayor Hague in connection with postwar plans under consideration by Federal authorities.

Approval of the project was expressed by the Mayor at a conference held in his office in the City Hall, yesterday afternoon, with officials of the New York Port Authority, the Jersey City Chamber of Commerce and others interested attending.

The Mayor agreed to conduct a preliminary survey looking toward establishment of an airport in Jersey City or in an adjacent municipality. No particular section of the city was mentioned as a site for the airport, and the Mayor favors a detailed study of the plan before one is selected.

At the suggestion of other conferees, the Mayor asked City Engineer James Henderson and County Engineer Frank J. Radigan to make a survey of the possibilities.

Those conferring with the Mayor included Theodore C. Wagner, president of the Jersey City Chamber of Commerce and director of the local offices of the Safeway Stores, Inc.; James J. Cullington, secretary of the Chamber of Commerce; Walter P. Hedden, director of the Department of Port Development of the Port of New York Authority; James C. Buckley, principal economist of the Department of Port Development of the Port of New York Authority, and City Comptroller Raymond M. Greer.

WANTS TO HAVE FACTS READY

It was stated that within a short time Congressional hearings will be held in Washington, D. C., relative to plans for a chain of airports throughout the country after the war.

In order to bring about a speedy development of the airport program, the federal government has under consideration the proposal to pay part of the cost with federal funds. However, present plans are in the formative stage and it is believed that out of the Congressional hear-

(See AIRPORT Page 10)

Expert Testifies Keegan Was Insane

Newark, March 30.—(UP)—Summations were made today in the murder trial of ex-Marine John J. Keegan, 24, who a defense witness said was insane when he allegedly shot his wife to death last August 1.

Dr. James B. Spradley, medical director of the New Jersey Hospital for the Insane, testified yesterday that Keegan "was suffering from dementia praecox before August 1, and as a result of difficulties he had with his wife, had a relapse at the time of the shooting.

"I say he was insane," Dr. Spradley testified.

Keegan, veteran of Guadalcanal, who was medically discharged because of battle fatigue, was charged with firing four shots into Marie Keegan, 22, while they sat in a Newark taxicab discussing their separation.

Stetson Hats, Haberdashery, Sportswear. SCHNEIDER'S, 906 Summit Ave., Union City

Index to All the Latest News

News Chronicle
No. 30,849 SATURDAY, MARCH 31, 1945 ONE PENNY
LATE LONDON EDITION

News Chronicle War Correspondents all report Victory near

S. L. SOLON — The master plan is succeeding

COLIN WILLS — Across Reich flows our quicksilver

NORMAN CLARK — Now for large-scale mopping-up

STANLEY BARON — Greatest turning movement in history

W. FORREST — Collapse finds workers leaderless

RONALD WALKER — No real life in Duisburg for six months

JAN YINDRICH — Volkssturm took first chance to go home

ANNIHILATION IS NOW AT HAND

Flood of Allied armour loose in Germany

From S. L. SOLON
News Chronicle War Correspondent

MONTGOMERY'S H.Q., Friday.

MORE than 20 armoured columns, pouring forth from the Allied armies in the greatest flood of armour yet used in this war, are loose in Ger many.

The security silence regarding the decisive advances that are being made is still on—and so is the most remarkable co-ordinated operation yet known to military history.

For the rolling armour is following a master plan from the north to the south designed to grip all of Germany and strangle what is left of the German military machine.

FIVE ARMIES DRIVE ON

Here are the latest disclosed positions of the British and American forces in Germany:

BRITISH SECOND.—Forty miles beyond the Rhine and ten miles from Muenster.

U.S. NINTH. — Fritzlar reached — 15 miles south-west of Cassel on the Frankfurt-Berlin autobahn.

U.S. FIRST. — Gen. Hodges's tanks, striking north-east, reached a point 20 miles south-west of Cassel. Paderborn, 57 miles north-east of Dortmund, was reached.

U.S. THIRD.—Gen. Patton's tanks reached a point ten miles south-west of Fulda and cleared Lauterbach, 31 miles east of Giessen.

U.S. SEVENTH.—The ancient university town of Heidelberg has been occupied.

What is happening now is not a matter of improvisation. It is a planned exploitation of the break-through that has taken place over the whole front. It is intended to bring the war to an end before the enemy will have any opportunity to regain balance and form some sort of a front.

This much can be said: the plan is succeeding and the hour of the Wehrmacht's annihilation is near.

Large German formations, behind which our armour has advanced to cut their communications, are surrendering.

German commanders are out of touch with their forces, and soldiers are discarding their arms and surrendering.

Naturally this is not happening at the same tempo throughout the front—war is not fought in such neat patterns.

Before the Third Army front the disintegration of the German Army is probably most complete, with a number of German officers urging general surrender before Patton's racing armour.

Farther north the First Army has made recorded penetrations of 90 miles.

The advance of First Army armour to a point only a few miles south of Paderborn enveloped the Ruhr in a great steel arc, cutting off all communications with German

Continued Back Page

THEY LINKED UP, RACED ON

A BRITISH sergeant gives the O.K. sign as British tanks with American troops race on from Dorsten, where men of the British Second Army and the American Ninth Army linked up

Infantry clear one town after another

From COLIN WILLS
News Chronicle War Correspondent

WITH THE SECOND ARMY, Friday.

HUNDREDS of miles of roads eastward over the green Westphalian downlands are shaking day and night with the weight of British armoured columns rolling far into Germany.

Official statements speak of advances up to 40 miles, but official statements cannot keep pace with an affair like this.

It is as though Montgomery has spilled over the Rhine a great mass of quicksilver which is running out in all directions.

Reconnaissance elements range so far from their parent units that we do not know what new and sensational locations they will get in the next report.

Following them go tank columns, with infantry mounted on tanks or travelling on Bren-carriers, track vehicles and lorries.

Artillery chases the columns, but is barely able to set up guns and carry out shoots before it is time to move on.

Infantry columns

Behind these hurrying spearheads roll solid columns of infantry divisions going in to consolidate town after town.

And back in the bridgehead and on the west Rhine every road is laden with a vast weight of reinforcements and supplies that make each incursion part of an invasion —an occupation.

These brilliant advances are not made without opposition. The Germans have no front, no solid line, but they have thrown together groups of whatever men and guns they can muster to hamper each thrust.

I passed through one village today where a few hours before a unit of the British Sixth Airborne had been challenged by 350 Germans with a number of self-propelled guns.

The airborne men, in a fierce fight, killed 110 Germans and took the rest prisoners.

And, by the time I passed, the airborne men were already many miles ahead, fighting in another town.

Wait for News

Physical obstacles cause some delay—here and there a blown bridge, here and there a small minefield.

And in several towns our own bombing has created such masses of rubble that it is impossible for tanks to pass until bulldozers are brought up to plough through, or roll ruins flat, so that tanks can roll over.

It is at present impossible to name localities reached, owing to security silence, but, when the gains from the past few days are released, it will keep you busy with a map of Germany.

It is all keeping the German High Command busy, too—and keeping them guessing.

All Reich is being mopped up

From NORMAN CLARK
News Chronicle War Correspondent

BEYOND THE MAIN, Friday.

THE war, as a military operation, is coming to an end. The pursuit is petering out into the large-scale mopping-up of engulfed pockets.

Disintegration is setting in, but it is not in an advanced stage yet. There may still be local actions.

That is the picture of this front as we see it from this sector; it is 260 miles from the nearest Russian forces.

As on previous days this week Gen. Patton's tanks have been used as a rake, the infantry as the following-up roller.

Fanning out in three columns, the Third Army tanks are in the

Low cloud, rain

Low, grey clouds and squalls of rain have followed the improved weather of the last day or two

vicinity of Treysa and Alsfeld, 29 and 40 miles respectively south of Cassel, the Grebenau 50 miles north-east of Frankfurt.

These areas have been reached after advances of 21, 15 and 7 miles respectively. One column reported meeting no resistance at all; others small arms fire.

They filed in

Another story which illustrates the completeness with which the enemy has been surprised by the swift exploitation of fast-moving situations is the case of the train which steamed into Hanau Station.

As the train pulled up to stop singing came from the compartments from troops, many of them convalescents, who had come to stop the rot. The train should have pulled into Frankfurt, but was halted by signals. The reinforcements began to detrain, thinking in the dark that this was Frankfurt.

Through the booking-office turnstile they filed — to be made prisoners.

One fortnight with Gen. Patton

With the U.S. Third Army, Friday. —Gen. Patton, in an Order to his troops tonight, disclosed that since they crossed the Moselle on March 16 they have:

Seized 6,484 square miles of enemy territory;

Captured 3,072 cities and towns; Taken 140,112 prisoners and killed or wounded 99,000 other Germans; and

Eliminated practically the entire German First and Seventh Armies.

"History records no greater achievement in such a limited time," says the Order.

This morning's war map is devoid of arrows. So swift is the Allied advance, east and west, into the Reich that exact indications of their extent are impossible

TANKS' 100 MILES IN 40 HOURS

From STANLEY BARON, News Chronicle War Correspondent

WITH THE U.S. FIRST ARMY, Friday.

TANKS of the famous 3rd Armoured Spearhead Division, commanded by Maj.-Gen. Maurice Rose, today entered Paderborn, and after one of the most dramatic switches of the war turning north from Marburg, 104 miles by road from the Rhine (65 measured by air), they have travelled more than a hundred miles in 40 hours.

At 9.35 this morning leading elements reached Paderborn, great German defence depot, and at that point, where they were 65 miles to the east of the British 7th Armoured Division, it was possible to say that the whole of the Ruhr and all the country south of it to the line of the Sieg River had been outflanked.

Analogies for the great pocket thus created are impossible. Its area is 4,000 square miles. It wipes off the map Germany's greatest industrial area. It puts the cold hands of destruction or capture over every soldier of the German Fifteenth Army and every other unit which was brushed northwards by the First Army's advance or southwards by the British Second Army and American Ninth Army as they drove into and around the Ruhr.

Unwanted planes

These two days have seen the greatest and most successful turning movement in the history of warfare, and you can leave it at that.

Air support has been cut down to the minimum. Observation planes have been able to make their reconnaissance only seldom and with difficulty.

But this does not matter. The

Continued Back Page

GERMANS CLAIM TO BE MAQUIS

From WILLIAM FORREST
News Chronicle War Correspondent

IN THE RUHR, Friday.

SOON after the opening of the Military Government office the manager of the tramways of Hamborn (three miles north of Duisburg) called to say he was anxious to get the trams running again, but had only 20 employees left.

"The others," he said, "were all Poles and Frenchmen, and they have gone."

And there were five German workers who claimed to have belonged to an underground resistance movement. They confessed that their numbers were very limited.

Was a Communist

Remembering that the Ruhr was once a Communist stronghold, we asked them how many Communists are in their movement. The question seems meaningless to them.

"Communists?" said their spokesman, as if trying to recall something from the distant past.

Then, after a pause: "Ah, yes, we have one member who used to be a Communist leader."

The collapse of Hitler's Germany finds the workers without leaders, without organisation, and, it would seem, with the memory of their former State all but obliterated by twelve years of Nazi terror.

Clocks go on an hour on Monday

Double Summer Time comes into force next Monday morning, at 1 a.m. Greenwich mean time. The clock is at present one hour in advance of Greenwich mean time, and from Monday until Sunday, July 15, it will be two hours ahead.

All clocks and watches should be put forward one hour tomorrow night. Employers are asked specially to remind their workers to do this.

Nazis start plans to win the peace

WASHINGTON officially disclosed last night details of a Nazi plan to perpetuate the doctrines of the Hitler regime.

A State Department announcement said that the U.S. Government has photographic copies of German documents "clearly indicating" these plans, some of which have already been put into operation.

Others are ready for launching on a wide scale immediately hostilities end in Europe.

Guard for mayors

The disclosure dealt with German plans for rebuilding economic, financial, propaganda and military control.

Nazi Party members, German industrialists and militarists "are planning for the renewals of prewar cartel agreements," the statement added.

Following the murder of the Burgomaster of Aachen, every mayor in Allied occupied towns behind the U.S. lines has been placed under continual guard.

V-Day "within week"

With British Second Army, Germany, Friday.—There is a firm belief at this H.Q. tonight that though the Germans will never accept unconditional surrender, V-Day could conceivably be declared within a week and almost certainly within the next month.

Biggest raid on U-boats

IN the U.S. 8th Air Force's greatest attack on naval installations, five U-boat building yards were among yesterday's targets at Wilhelmshaven, Hamburg, Bremen and Farge.

Six jet Me.s were shot down and five grounded planes destroyed by some of the 900 Mustangs which escorted 1,400 heavies. Nine bombers and three fighters are missing.

Spitfires pinpointed many targets in the rocket zone.

Mosquitoes bombed Berlin last night for the 38th time in 39 nights.

Starlit Straits

Long sunny periods; at night starlit sky and rising barometer.

LATE NEWS

RELIEF SUPPLIES FOR EUROPE

Washington, Friday.—Over 400,000 tons of Unrra supplies will be delivered to the liberated areas of Europe by the end of June, L. B. Pearson, Canadian Ambassador to the United States and chairman of Unrra's Supply Committee, said in Washington today.

LONDON DIM-OUT

Tonight	Tomorrow
8.0—6.7 a.m.	8.2—7.5 a.m.

Moon rises, 10.26 p.m.; sets, 8.24 a.m. tomorrow. New Moon, April 12

DANZIG (AND 45 U-BOATS) TAKEN: AUSTRIA INVADED

STORMING through the rest of Danzig Marshal Rokossovsky's troops yesterday completed the capture of the city—where the war began 5½ years ago—and seized 45 U-boats.

Ten thousand prisoners were taken and the booty included 140 tanks and self-propelled guns, 358 field guns, 84 planes, 15 armoured trains, 360 railway engines, over 6,000 trucks and 151 ships.

More than 39,000 Germans were killed.

The Order of the Day announcing its capture used the Polish name of Gdansk. The Polish national flag now flies over the city for the first time since 1772.

In the South Marshal Tolbukhin's troops crossed the frontier into Austria, north of Koeszeg, the Soviet communique stated last night.

A cable from Moscow said that heavy fighting was going on in the frontier zone on the direct approaches to Wiener Neustadt and that Tolbukhin was massing his troops for a break-through south of Vienna.

Meanwhile Marshal Malinovsky's armies, which are operating on both sides of the Danube, launched an offensive in Southern Slovakia on a 40-mile front and drove on for 31 miles towards the Bratislava Gap.

The new gains, announced in another Order of the Day, began with the forcing of the Rivers Hron and Nitra and the breaking of the defences on the western banks.

As the troops drove forward they captured the Slovakian side of the twin Danube town of Komarno (the Hungarian half of which fell on Wednesday) and four others, all of which were described as "powerful defence strong-points in the Bratislava direction."

More gains in Hungary by Marshal Tolbukhin's men were announced in a third Order of the Day. Keszthely, at the western end of Lake Balaton, and Zalaegerszeg, halfway to the frontier, were captured.

ALL LIFE WAS DRAINED FROM DUISBURG

From RONALD WALKER
News Chronicle War Correspondent

DUISBURG, Friday.

DUISBURG is a dead city, but it has not been killed in the way Cologne has been killed.

Duisburg has had some 25,000 tons of Bomber Command's high explosive and incendiary bombs dropped on it, but the city has ceased to live more because of the bombs that have fallen farther east than because of those within the city limits.

It is badly damaged, but only, say, about one-third as badly damaged as Cologne.

Many of its factories are still fairly intact and there are plenty of houses without a pane of glass broken—a Ruhr phenomenon. With its satellite towns and suburbs, such as Ruhrort, Hamborn and Rheinhausen, the great industrial complex sector which constituted the administrative area of Duisburg made a scattered and difficult target, with many comparatively large open spaces.

Duisburg has not been battered to extinction. It has had the life drained out of it.

You wonder how the civilians existed in a city which has had no water, light or drainage for six months.

In Duisburg today is seen what is really meant by the phrase "isolating the Ruhr."

The Daily Sketch

No. 11,192 ★★ MONDAY, APRIL 2, 1945 ONE PENNY

Sensational Break-out By Second Army: Ruhr Sealed Off In New Link-up: German Ports Are Now Wide Open

BRITISH 100 MILES BEYOND THE RHINE

50,000 In Ruhr Trap

GREAT news poured in from the Western Front all yesterday as General Eisenhower partially lifted the security "black-out."

The most sensational break-out of the whole Rhine campaign took place on Field-Marshal Montgomery's front.

General Dempsey's British Second Army troops thrust to a point 100 miles east of the Rhine, and this morning were still roaring on.

First News Of Ninth Army Reports 75-Mile Advance

The Ruhr was sealed off with the linking-up of the First and Ninth U.S. Armies at Lippstadt, 17 miles west-south-west of Paderborn, which has also been captured.

Inside this tremendous pocket, 4,800 square miles, 50,000 Germans are trapped and face annihilation or surrender.

This was the first news of the Ninth Army, whose movements have been cloaked by security silence.

It was the most spectacular of the Allied gains, and the disclosure indicates that General Simpson's tanks smashed nearly 75 miles eastwards in less than a week.

British Tank Vanguards Have By-passed Munster

Reports from the 21st Army Group said that all approaches to the great ports of North-Western Germany now appear to be wide open.

From Holland, where the V2 sites are situated, the Germans are fleeing as the Tactical Air Force strafe massed transport, and Canadian troops advance towards the Dutch-German frontier.

Berlin reports gave some indication of the extent of Montgomery's drive.

One said that tank vanguards had reached Munster, the big communications centre on the road from Hanover to Berlin, and that other tanks were operating 17 miles to the south-east.

Cassel where the Germans put up a "do-or-die" duel with the Americans has fallen German radio said this morning.

Patton Is 100 Miles From The Czech Frontier

Across the "waist" of Germany, General Patton's tanks are speeding ahead. Spearheads were last reported to be nearing Eisenach, 100 miles from the Czech frontier and 165 miles from Berlin.

Pilots operating in the Third Army area yesterday saw large concentrations of German troops and equipment headed east over all the roads in a triangle formed by Hersfeld and Erfurt, both on the road to Weimar, as its base, with its tip at Nordhausen, 57 miles north-east of Cassel on the Cassel-Leipzig road.

In the Fulda region, where armoured elements had crossed the river, our pilots destroyed 57 motor transports, five tanks, five self-propelled guns, and five armoured vehicles.

General Patch's Seventh Army have reached the Main opposite Wurtzburg after a 25-mile dash and are now more than 65 miles east of the Rhine.

A French First Army communiqué said that the Frankfurt-Karlsruhe autobahn had been crossed by French troops from their bridgehead and that about 20 places had been captured.

A link-up has been made between the Seventh Army and the French.

Luxemburg radio gave the first indication of the position of the "ghost" army, the U.S. 15th. It said this army, with the 1st, 3rd and 7th were now operating along a 140-mile front between Marburg and Nuremberg.

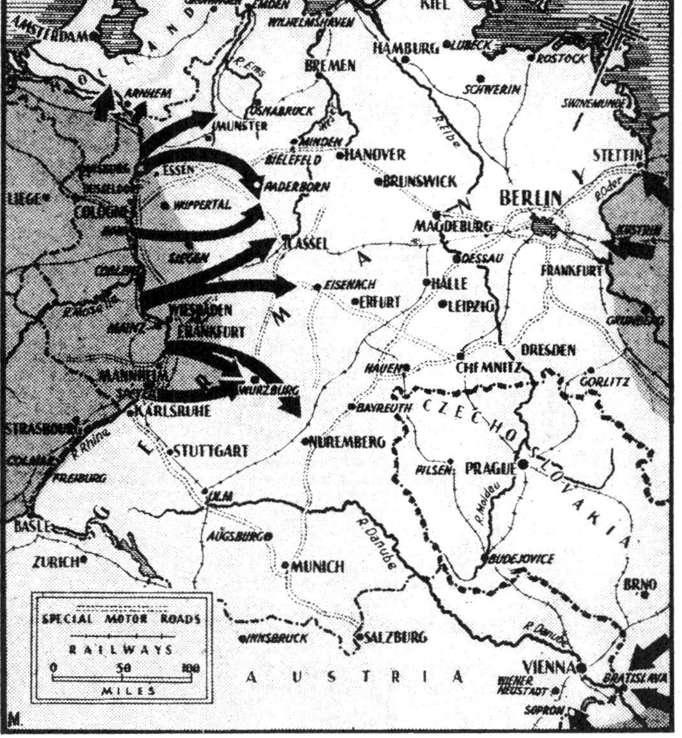

Scramble Out May End V2 Menace

From LEONARD MOSLEY, Kemsley Newspapers Correspondent with the British

ALL day long the great retreat from Holland has gone on, with German armoured fighting vehicles, lorries and high-piled, horse-drawn carts streaming back over the frontier into Germany.

Occupied Holland has been on a Nazi low-grade priority. The only units who have had all they want are those manning the V1 and V2 sites on the North Sea coast near The Hague.

Flak Cars Guard Route

Yet since 6 p.m. on Saturday, all through the night and all this morning and afternoon every road and lane leading back from the Zuyder Zee has been choc-a-bloc with enemy vehicles, and since dawn yesterday flak cars have guarded every stretch of the route.

It is not yet possible to say that the V2 sites have been evacuated. But if they have not, then it looks as if they have been left without their transport.

And the way the war was going last night it looks as if they will never get any more rockets once those they still have are shot off.

Clouds came down low yesterday and blanketed the escape routes north of Enschede. Instructions to our pilots were to "go down low and give it them."

During the night the Germans had brought up flak guns, and fire at our planes was heavy as they screamed along the lines of traffic.

Great fires burst across one road and soon spread along the whole length of a convoy.

'Stop Them' Cry

"LITTLE groups of 20 or 30 tanks are driving about as they will in Verbotenland (Germany) and nobody is arresting them," complains Dr. Ley, in an article in "Nachtausgabe," cables Cyril Marshall, "Daily Sketch" correspondent in Stockholm.

"Are there not ten million able-bodied G e r m a n s, all furnished with the world's most effective anti-tank weapon, the panzerfist (bazooka)?" he asks.

"These lawless Allied tanks cannot and must not be allowed to reach Berlin. A few thousand men such as characterised the Nazi party at the beginning could soon put an end to "the whole armoured spectre."

The Murder Gangs Are Turned Loose

Werewolf Revived By Hitler

'Daily Sketch' Listening Station

HITLER has revived the last war Werewolf organisation to carry on the fight against the Allies after the defeat of Germany.

Last night, for the first time, the organisation was named. Berlin openly called on Germans to murder Allied soldiers by any means they could. It was an open incitement to the establishment of a vast guerilla movement carried on by civilians throughout Germany.

Thus Hitler has gone back to the old organisation, formed after the last war, when an ultra-nationalist body fought the Versailles Treaty, the Weimar Republic and especially the disarmament of Germany.

'Hate Is Our Prayer'

The Werewolf broadcast said:

"The Werewolf does not recognise any considerations imposed on regular forces. All means are justified to cause the enemy harm and damage.

"Every Bolshevist, every Englishman and every American on German soil is an outlaw for the Werewolves. Wherever an opportunity arises to extinguish his life we shall grasp it gladly without respecting our own lives.

"Hate is our prayer—death our password. Woe to the enemy who wants to torture and suppress the German people. Woe to the traitors who collaborate with the enemy. They will have to face a dreadful trial."

★ ★ ★

A "DO OR DIE" order to all Germans, signed by Borman, the Nazi Party Chancellor, was broadcast on all German stations last night on Hitler's instructions. The proclamation said:

"Now the supreme hour of trial has come. The danger of renewed slavery with which our people is now being confronted demands our last and supreme effort.

"Provincial and district leaders, political leaders and heads of Party organisations have to fight in their provinces and their districts.

"They have to conquer or die. He who leaves his province without the Fuehrer's express orders, who does not fight to the last breath, is a scoundrel who will be outlawed as a deserter and treated as such."

CITY OF LIGHT

Paris turned on the lights last night for the first time since the war.

GERMAN ARMY IS LEGION OF THE LOST

From RICHARD McMILLAN, With Second Army

THE German Army is a wandering, lost legion.

Our flying columns, racing through woods along dozens of parallel roads far out beyond the main spearhead, pass bewildered German soldiers who want to surrender but can find no one to take care of them.

They are typical of all Germany. The nation is lost and leaderless.

They quake with fear as we thunder on through the maze of white flags. Then, as the columns pass and leave them unmolested they become calmer.

As they realise that they are not going to be shot, it dawns on them that one more Nazi lie has been fed to them. Our troops come as conquerors, but not in the Nazi sense.

The civilians are left alone. So they begin to pull down their white flags, smile timidly at our troops, and then get back to work.

There is no front line. You find a town with German troops in it, but it is by-passed. The Germans inside then realise it is encircled and stream out.

The Sixth (Guards) Armoured Brigade have been marching without sleep for days and nights. They are full of praise for their new companions in arms, the U.S. 17th Airborne Division, whom they took into action, the airborne men riding on the Guards' Churchill tanks.—B.U.P.

TIMELY WORDS OF FAITH

As the earth bringeth forth her bud, and as the garden causeth the things that are sown in it to spring forth; so the Lord God will cause righteousness and praise to spring forth before all the nations.

Isaiah, 61, 11.

Sunday Dispatch

144th Year. No. 7,484. 2d. APRIL 8, 1945. Radio Page 5.

A MAN TO BE WATCHED - PAGE 4

Final Hours In Bremen : Hanover By-passed—Now On To Brunswick

MONTGOMERY ON LAST LAP: 120,000 TROOPS RACING FOR BERLIN

Whole Defences Of Central Germany Crumbling

MORE than 120,000 of Field-Marshal Montgomery's men, supported by thousands of tanks and tens of thousands of other vehicles, are entering the last lap of the race eastwards 140 miles from Berlin.

British guns were last night sounding the death-knell of the great German cities of Bremen and Hanover. Monty's famous 11th Hussars, veterans of the Seventh Armoured Division—the "Desert Rats"—were this morning reported ten miles from Bremen. "Red Devils" of the Sixth Airborne Division were rapidly nearing Hanover. They were last reported at Sachsenhagen, 20 miles from the city.

Front Wide Open

A little over ten miles to the south of Hanover, American Ninth Army tanks have leapt into Schulenberg, by-passing Hanover, and are heading straight for Brunswick, only 20 miles ahead.

The German front in the north and centre is wide open, and tank spearheads of both divisions are pushing north and east against resistance varying from moderate to practically nil, cabled a *Reuter* Correspondent.

The Central German defences are crumbling as fast as did those on the Rhine, and there now seems to be little hope for the Germans west of the Elbe, 90 miles ahead.

A *B.U.P.* correspondent at Montgomery's H.Q. describes it as "the route towards the Elbe." Across the 15,000 square miles of the German plain, he says, scattered enemy columns are limping eastwards.

The 11th Hussars swept through a gap in Kesselring's tattered defences, rolling up the Weser line, and appear to be meeting virtually no mines and no opposition with the exception of an occasional suicide sniper.

The enemy is moving along roads over country as flat as East Anglia, with winds cutting in from the North Sea. Along the roads lie lonely towns and hamlets which hang out their white flags as soon as the last retreating German soldier has passed.

V-Sites Blown Up

The Germans yesterday attempted to tighten up their resistance to the Canadian thrust through North Holland while blowing up their V-sites in the line of the Canadian advance. Behind the German lines came rumbles of explosions as V-bomb sites were destroyed.

First Army troops are now also across the Weser north of Cassel, while far to the south Patton's tanks are pushing for Magdeburg, thrusting out to the north-east from their salient beyond Mulhausen.

'Stuttgart Taken'

A number of Nazi "Stud Parks," still occupied by unmarried mothers and their babies, have been found near Winterburg.

Magdeburg is some 60 miles ahead of Patton's forces and Leipzig, about the same distance away to the east, is also in the direct line of the Patton push.

German resistance is stiffening here and the enemy has even thrown in counter-attacks.

On the extreme southern end of the front, Stuttgart has been reached, according to a Brussels radio report.—*Reuter B.U.P. and A.P.*

GERMAN TANKS HELPLESS

By PAUL RENKER, Sunday Dispatch Military Analyst

WE are rapidly nearing the end of coherent military operations in Europe.

This week-end sees under way operations which are designed to cut up the German Army into individual pockets all over German territory. It is too early to say when this process will be completed, but the Germans have no means to arrest or even slow us down.

British mechanised cavalry is fanning out between the North Sea and the Ems and Weser rivers. There is no hope for the Germans to hold Bremen or Emden, and their largest naval base of Wilhelmshaven comes into immediate danger.

The Germans cannot answer our thrusts with tank counter-attacks; German tank formations no longer exist in anything larger than troop-formation—from three to ten tanks.

Hopeless Fight

The immediate spoils are the capture of the North Sea approaches and ports; the strategical consequences are even bigger:

1.—Holland may be cut off from Germany within 48 hours, and considerable German garrisons be out of the fight.

2.—Depression within the German Army will increase, as it must be known to even the lowest rank in the Wehrmacht that the fight is hopeless

3.—The Germans are being pressed back from the west into the first forefields of the larger defence of Berlin from the west.

But it is the inability of the German High Command to enforce central direction of operations and the synchronisation of any large-scale counter-measures against our swift advances which give the best sign of all.

All Germany's Gold Captured

From JOHN HALL, Sunday Dispatch Reporter in Germany

GERMANY'S entire gold reserve, millions of pounds in other currencies, and priceless art treasures from Berlin have been captured by Patton's Third Army.

The booty was found 700 yards deep in a salt mine at Merkers, 25 miles from Gotha. It was being guarded by Dr. Fritz Vieck and two other Reichsbank officials, and consisted of:

100 tons of German gold bullion;
£750,000,000 in paper marks;
£500,000 in American dollars;
£110,000 in sterling;
100,000,000 French francs;
4,000,000 Norwegian crowns;
and lesser amounts in other currencies.

The secret of the booty was given away by two women found by the military police out of doors after curfew. British prisoners of war were employed in the mine.

Owing to the door of the strong-room being jammed, the gold has not yet been seen by U.S. troops. The report of the bullion is based on Dr. Vieck's information.

RAF Clear Way For Tanks

From BARDS CONOLLY, Sunday Dispatch War Reporter

AT A FORWARD AIRFIELD OF 2ND TACTICAL AIR FORCE.

THE SPEARHEADS OF MONTGOMERY'S ARMOUR STRADDLE THE MAP OF EASTERN HOLLAND AND NORTH-WEST GERMANY IN AN UNTIDY BUT SENSATIONAL PATTERN.

In most cases the armoured columns are motoring rather than fighting, but every now and then one or other of them is halted by an isolated patch of opposition. When that happens the fighter-bombers and rocket-firing Typhoons of R.A.F. 2nd T.A.F. are called in.

In brilliant sunshine yesterday they cleared the path for our armour in more than one tough place.

The Guards Armoured Division swung along the road from Lingen to Lengerich yesterday, but there they were held up by 88mm. guns and a posse of fanatical troops.

Reddish Smoke

Typhoon pilots looked down on a line of our armour stretching three or four miles almost to the outskirts of Lengerich, but not moving on. The Typhies got the call they expected, and for the first time received an added instruction not to damage the road by bombing.

They bombed the approaches to Lengerich with the special fragmentation cluster bombs which leave no crater, and plastered the centre of the village with 500-pounders.

Lengerich was covered in a few minutes in reddish-grey smoke. The road leading to it was intact. A little later T.A.F.'s pilots watched another column of transport moving eastwards out of the village—the Huns who had escaped the bombing getting away.

Germans Blasted

Farther east, the Sixth Airborne Division, in their bridgehead across the Weser, ran into gun and mortar fire from another village. This time the Tempests were called in to do the job, and while they hammered the enemy artillery sites the airborne troops returned the compliment by silencing flak positions firing on our aircraft.

Another of our armoured columns came up against stiff opposition in Meppen, and Typhoons raced over there to blast German troops concentrations and guns with 1,000-pounders, 500-pounders, and rockets.

And in Holland, in the spots where the Canadians found the going tough, T.A.F. scored direct hits on enemy strong-points, destroyed observation posts, and silenced the guns still firing on our troops.

The opposition generally has not stiffened and at no point over the whole front is there anything like a coherent defence.

GERMANS FALLING TO PIECES

From WALTER FARR, Sunday Dispatch Reporter with General Bradley's Armoured Columns

THE Wehrmacht is falling apart. That is what a U.S. First Army Staff officer told me last night.

General Hodges' forces are pouring through the Hessian Gap, the route Napoleon took when he seized Berlin.

The Staff officer added: "We are now reaching the mopping-up stage of the war. In the Ruhr pocket are Germans with no hope of escaping. Their encirclement has left a great hole in the West Front through which we are pouring."

He said the link-up between ourselves and the Russian armies was now only a matter of time.

The German generals are refusing to serve under them. One plucked off his decorations when ordered about by a gauleiter.

The complete confusion in the ranks of the Wehrmacht is apparent from the fact that they recently planned to make their headquarters at Gotha. They were just about to move in when the Americans captured Gotha.

Stalin Said . . .

Some of General Bradley's roaming tank spearheads were last night little more than 150 miles from the Russians—and still moving rapidly eastwards.

If the Russians start pushing towards us in the area south of Berlin the historic link-up could come in about a week.

The link-up is the thing all the front-line Doughboys are talking about. It even transcends in interest the seizure of Berlin.

Some time ago, when there was a lot of talk about establishing liaison between the Russian Armies and ourselves and fixing how the entry into Berlin should be planned for the benefit of all concerned, Stalin is supposed to have said: 'Let's forget about Berlin for a moment. Let each of us get on with the business of carving up the German Armies in our particular sphere and cutting off as many big units as possible, so that the whole German Army organisation falls to pieces."

MODEL CAUGHT IN RUHR TRAP

FIELD-MARSHAL Model, former German C.-in-C. on the West Front, was reported last night to be caught in the Ruhr trap.

Dutch Massacred At 11th Hour

Canadian troops, thrusting north of Zutphen, failed by a few hours to save the lives of a number of Dutch. Overrunning what had been a concentration camp, they found the bodies of ten men, all horribly mutilated, none of whom had been dead more than 48 hours.—*Reuter.*

Bevin And The Prime Minister

MR. ERNEST BEVIN, Minister of Labour, yesterday made clear his attitude to his chief, Mr. Churchill—and also made it clear that he is going to join wholeheartedly in the election battle against the Conservative Party.

Speaking at a Labour conference at Leeds, he said: "I have profound admiration for the Premier as a national leader—unfettered. I gave him my loyalty as a national leader. But I have never given it to him as a leader of the Conservative Party.

"There is a great distinction. I want to keep that clear. I do not want to belittle any man in the Coalition, but I assure the country it is not a one-man war, nor a one-man Government.

"The Coalition has brought the country through its troubles to final victory, and credit is due to the whole team.

"It is suggested that Labour has taken a very irresponsible step in breaking up the Coalition. Let me say Labour has done nothing of the kind.

The Conservatives

"The Conservative Party is afraid to face the electors on the record of its own doings that led us into this war, and it resorts to other methods and foul suggestions.

"The Labour Party decided that, whatever the consequence, whenever the Premier dissolves Parliament we shall go to the country as an independent party.

"The Conservative Party was responsible for the government of the country for over 20 years, except for a period of two years and nine months, and it brought the country to the verge of disaster owing to its complete failure to prepare for defence or to warn the country where it was heading.

"There have been a lot of suggestions about myself. I do not know what I have done to deserve it. I have been 40 years loyal to the Labour Party, and, so far as I am concerned, I shall abide by the party decisions, whatever they might be."

HITLER HAS A NEW IDEA

FIRST indications of a general movement for even minor leaders of the Nazi Party to go underground, leaving stooges in office, as the Allied armies thrust deeper into Germany were revealed in a Hitler Order last night.

This Order laid down that burgomasters and holders of other civic posts in Germany shall not be Nazi officials.

Hitherto all the plums of office have been held almost entirely by Nazis.

The explanation given for the order was that "in these difficult times quick moves have to be made."

Actually it will mean that Nazi Party leaders in the provinces and towns will be able to escape capture, leaving behind men without the Nazi taint to deal with the Allied conquerors.

At the same time, says *A.P.*, the Nazis, who have announced their intention to carry on a last-ditch guerilla warfare, will be able to announce that civilians surrendered while the Nazis continue to resist.

According to the *B.U.P.*, people who know Germany and the Nazi outlook believe that the order is in preparation for the Nazi Party to "disappear" underground.

Make The Germans Do The Work

LADY YULE writes to the Editor of the *Sunday Dispatch*:

Sir,—Having read the most excellent article in your paper, *Sunday Dispatch*, by Mr. Clement Yorke, and having just listened to Mr Hudson's speech recorded over the radio at one o'clock on Sunday, it does make one wonder why we do not use the hundreds, if not thousands, of prisoners now in this country to do the work for which Mr. Hudson is asking for help.

These prisoners are being much better fed than our farmers, which is a disgrace, to say nothing of the civilians of this country. Why don't we make them work?

There is no harder work than land work. It looks quite easy to lift stooks up and load them on to a cart. It looks quite easy to pick up potatoes. But let anyone try it for even an hour who is not used to that sort of work and they will see how hard it is. I am not surprised at the lack of volunteers.

Most voluntary helpers on the land are quite useless. They have neither the physique nor the training for this particular job.

Again, why should civilians be called upon to give up their holidays, etc., to help feed the prisoners who have behaved so abominably to so many of our men? For a change, let them do something for us.

Yours faithfully,
ANNIE H. YULE.

Lady Yule is the widow of Sir David Yule, the Anglo-Indian merchant prince, from whom she inherited £9,000,000. She is chairman of the British National Film Company and the owner of the Rock Studios at Elstree.

Now read "The Things People Write About," in Page FOUR.

25 p.c. Of Japan's Navy Is Sunk

From DON IDDON, Sunday Dispatch New York Reporter

AN official United States Navy spokesman said last night that "25 per cent. of the major Japanese combat forces" were lost or put out of action in the great sea-and-air battle announced by Admiral Chester Nimitz, Naval C.-in-C. in the Pacific. The new losses, the spokesman said, leave the Japanese "with a Task Force that can be very easily handled by any of our major Task Forces."

The emergence of the Japanese force, the naval spokesman pointed out, was presumably an offensive action, since it was made up entirely of fast ships, although the possibility remained that it was merely an effort to escape to more tenable waters.

He added that there was the possibility that the enemy was seeking to retire to more remote positions north of the Japanese home islands, but American naval forces, he said, had been able to keep a close watch on the Japanese Fleet movements for some time.

Reuter and *B.U.P.* cables last night gave this account of the action:

The Japanese have lost their latest super battleship, the Yamato, in a great sea-and-air battle that ended only a few miles from the southern tip of Japan. Five other warships were sunk and 391 planes were shot down. The Americans lost three destroyers and seven planes.

Tokio Blitz

Just after this new shattering blow at shrinking Japanese power in the Pacific was announced, 300 fighter-escorted Super-Fortresses raided Tokio in the greatest land-based raid ever made against Japan.

News of the battle that started near Okinawa, in the Ryukyu Islands, 325 miles from Japan, was given in a dramatic communiqué from Admiral Nimitz, which said:

"During the late afternoon and evening of April 6, a large force of enemy aircraft attacked our ships and shore installations in the vicinity of Okinawa.

"Early on April 7 Navy search aircraft of Fleet Air Wing One sighted an enemy surface force which had left the Inland Sea and, passing south of Kyushu, had headed into the East China Sea.

The Chase

"A fast carrier task force, commanded by Vice-Admiral Marca Mitscher, steamed toward the enemy at high speed, and during the middle of the day brought the Japanese force under air attack.

"Our carrier aircraft, which had destroyed 245 enemy aircraft on April 6, met no air opposition over the Japanese ships, but did meet heavy anti-aircraft fire.

"At a point about 50 miles south-west of Kyushu they sank the Yamato, the light Agano class cruiser, and three destroyers.

"Three other destroyers were left burning. About three destroyers escaped from this attack.

"Our carriers lost seven aircraft in this action.

"During minor contacts on April 7 they and their aircraft shot down 30 enemy aircraft."

WRIST RADIO

By Sunday Dispatch Reporter

MR. ALFRED CLARK, who has just been elected first president of the Radio Industry Council, believes that soon we shall have radio sets that can be "worn" on the wrist.

It was Mr. Clark who worked with the "great Edison" in New York and introduced the first phonograph into England. He also invented the gramophone sound-box.

Mr. A. Clark.

He foresees great advancement in the radio world. British research and craftsmanship, he told me yesterday, are far in advance of anything else in the world market. But we need encouragement and raw materials, especially materials. The war has sapped all our supplies.

Of television he said: "It can be [illegible] all over Britain by intermediate relay stations. We already have the sites."

The Radio Industry Council has been formed by prominent firms here with an estimated working capital of £20,000,000.

Luftwaffe Lose 63

AT least 63 enemy planes, about half of which were jet-propelled, were destroyed when the Luftwaffe came up in strength to engage 1,300 Forts and Liberators with an escort of 850 fighters, which raided German targets yesterday.

The German "Achtung" radio last night reported Allied bombers again over Germany, indicating the R.A.F. was returning to action after a two-nights lull due to bad weather.

Vienna: Big Trek Out

FIGHTING in Vienna has entered its most ferocious phase, it was announced last night.

Advancing on three sides, the Red Army broke in from the south and house-to-house fighting was raging in the suburb of Moedling, only three miles from the centre of the city.

A German radio commentator said that the Germans had rushed up reserves and alarm units in an attempt to check the Russians.

Reuter stated, however, that the defenders of the city were heading for the west in great numbers.

Roads away from Vienna were said to be choked with fleeing Germans and their vehicles.

The German News Agency admitted last night that Stalin was ready to strike at the Germans on the whole stretch of the Eastern Front from the Baltic to the Carpathians.

Soviet supplementary communique this morning says Russians smashed a German offensive made with 11 tank divisions at Lake Balaton, south-west of Budapest, and during later fighting destroyed a great number of German infantry.

4,000 FREED BY TANKS

From JOHN HALL, Sunday Dispatch Reporter in Germany

THE story of a dashing American rescue column can now be told—how it was dispatched deep into enemy territory to rescue more than 4,000 Allied prisoners of war from a series of prison camps near Hammelburg.

The American Seventh Army task force raced to Hammelburg brushing aside opposition.

The prisoners, many of them British, heard the firing. Next thing tanks came smashing into the enclosures, pursued by Hun tanks.

"Get going, boys!" yelled the tank crews, and then began the battle. The prisoners scattered.

Now all the series of camps are liberated and all the men safe.

GREEK CABINET RESIGNS

GENERAL PLASTIRAS, the Greek Prime Minister, has tendered the resignation of his Cabinet to Archbishop Damaskinos, the Greek Regent, Paris radio reported last night.

LAW CASE OVER RAID SHELTER

THE question of a tenant's liability to remove his air-raid shelter on giving up possession of the house will shortly come before the High Court for decision.

A landlord is claiming damages from a former tenant who has refused to restore the lawn to its pre-war condition.

Cold In Strait

A cold north-easterly wind was blowing in the Strait of Dover last night, but the sky was clear and starlit and the barometer high.

THE DIM-OUT TO-NIGHT
London and South Coast 9.14 p.m. to 6.49 a.m.

Sun sets 8.44 p.m. Rises (Mon.) 7.19 a.m. Moon sets 3.07 p.m. Rises (Mon.) 6.31 a.m.

CHELSEA WIN CUP

Princess Elizabeth at the match. It is the first picture of her in A.T.S. uniform.

THE King and Queen, Princess Elizabeth, and Lord Wavell (Viceroy of India) were among the 90,000 people who saw Chelsea beat Millwall 2—0 in the South Cup Final at Wembley Stadium yesterday.

Five thousand Service men and women on leave watched the match as the guests of *The Daily Mail*.

Many American soldiers were there, seeing a big Soccer match for the first time, and a United States Army band played for 20 minutes before the match started.

Another Cup Final novelty was a physical fitness display on the pitch at half-time by 250 16-years-old boys drawn from the Army Cadet Force in the London district.

There was no score in the first half. Two minutes after half-time McDonald (outside left) scored for Chelsea, and three minutes later Wardle (who had been moved at half-time from outside right to inside right) got their second goal.

MORE BOMBS ON HONGKONG

Heavy bombers attacked Kowloon Dock at Hongkong, setting fire to shore installations and hitting ships and Kaitak aerodrome, said General MacArthur's communiqué this morning.—B.U.P.

GÖRING TRIES TO SELL LOOT

Himmler and Göring have agents abroad trying to sell works of art and other looted valuables to finance Nazi activities or to build up funds for their own escape, Mr. J. C. Holmes, U.S. Assistant Secretary of State in Washington, broadcast this morning.

Daily Mail

NO. 15,266 ONE PENNY ** FOR KING AND EMPIRE TUESDAY, APRIL 10, 1945

Desert Rats have entered the birthplace-land of the SS: Clifford says: 'This is something more like resistance'

BREMEN FIGHTS TO END

Boy killers of 8 meet us with hand grenades

From **ALEXANDER CLIFFORD**, Daily Mail Special Correspondent

OUTSIDE BREMEN, Monday Night.

THE Germans are really going to try to defend Bremen. Its great submarine and shipbuilding yards are less than five miles from our guns. All to-day the Seventh Armoured Division has been strengthening its grip on the southern approaches to the city.

But now something that can almost be called organised resistance is cropping up. It is only serious resistance in comparison with what has gone before.

In itself it is very small. But it does amount to an attempt to hold the city.

The German parachute divisions are still fighting down to the south-west, embattled against the left wing of the Eighth Army.

Their communications depend entirely on Bremen. Now we are all up their flank and threatening their rear.

SCRAPED UP

And they have sent for anything that can be scraped up to hold the flank and the rear. A dozen or so German self-propelled guns are roaming the flank, which is represented by the road from Bremen to Bassum.

Odd training battalions and replacement regiments have been collected to hold the approaches to Bremen itself.

S.S. men of the Horst Wessel outfit and Flemish Nazis of the Langemarck Division are reported to be preparing for action.

The Germans are quite resigned to losing Bremen in the end. They have already blown up three of the city's bridges.

They have left only one bridge for the retreat of their parachutists. Their great point is to keep a way open for the good divisions to get out.

In the last resort they will still have the ferries at the mouth of the Weser. But they want to delay it as long as possible because the parachutists are still fighting.

BRIDGES DOWN

Delay—that seems to be the only command given the Germans now. They are taking no chances about the bridges over the Weser.

They are blowing them up in good time, all the way along. It cannot ever delay us much and it cannot affect the war. It seems to be done in a spirit of spiteful national suicide.

They fight well enough, some of these odd units that the Germans are producing—especially the officers' training units and the S.S. replacement regiments.

They are very young and well-trained and unscrupulous men—the pick of Germany's fanatics.

And some of them have fought with a bravery that compels admiration. In the town of Bassum last night they had the local Hitler Youth fighting with them.

BOY KILLERS

Hard-eyed little boys of eight or ten were wielding machine pistols and hand-grenades. This really did happen here—the first genuine case in Germany that I have heard of.

This area is, as a matter of fact, something of a breeding ground for the S.S. It produces for some inscrutable reason just the right type of youth.

In Bassum for once Hitler's dream of even the children fighting really came true.

This is a great submarine area too. There is hardly a farm round here which has not got bits of submarines parked out in its cellars and barns.

The Germans scattered them around to avoid the bombing. We have even captured an entire German submarine crew who were, apparently, on leave in the neighbourhood.

The spirit of these bunches of young fanatics whom we are now occasionally meeting is perfectly illustrated in a statement by a lieutenant of the 742nd Jager Regiment.

He was, as a matter of fact, captured in Italy, but what he said sums up the contemporary Nazi view.

He declared, "whatever stretches of Germany you occupy you will never defeat the German nation. As long as there is a German alive he will fight you.

"In the occupied parts we shall fight a guerilla nerve war against you. No Allied soldier will ever feel safe on German soil.

"We shall entrench ourselves in the impenetrable mountains and forests of Southern Germany and Austria and hold whatever can be held in Italy.

"And in Germany, though outwardly we may smile and bend under the Allied yoke, we shall resort relentlessly to ambushes and tricks of partisan warfare, until every inch of sacred German soil is freed from the hated invader."

And so on. He may of course be right. But that isn't the way it has looked to us in Germany so far.

HMS Lapwing lost

The Admiralty announce that H.M. Sloop Lapwing (Commdr. E. C. Hulton, R.N.) has been lost.

It was built in 10 days

HERE it is—our first permanent railway bridge over the Rhine. Planned in England 15 months ago, to be built within a time limit of 14 days, it was completed in only ten. It was ready for traffic on Sunday.

BRAND new, beside the smashed German structure, you see the new Allied rail bridge that spans the Rhine. The steel for the girders came from Luxemburg, the wood for the piles was taken from forests in captured German territory. The Allies now have nine more bridges than the Germans ever possesssed. This great achievement of engineering was carried out in four weeks.

RUHR BURNS FROM END TO END

Clerk surrenders Krupps works

ESSEN, Monday Night.

AS the flames from giant fires consumed the Ruhr from end to end to-day the huge Krupps armament works in Essen was taken over by the Ninth Army. It was surrendered by a tall, bespectacled clerk.

At least, he handed over what the R.A.F. had left of it.

The most pulverised spot in all bomb-battered Germany has not turned a wheel since the night of March 1, when R.A.F. bombers gave it the *coup de grâce*.

Said the tired-looking clerk when he surrendered the factory to Simpson's men: "What a relief to know those awful nights and days of bombs have come to an end.

"I think about 2,000 people were killed in the last raid. After that Krupp had no lights and the Essen railroad was destroyed."

To-night the Ruhr—once the pride of Hitler's war-machine—is glowing like a colossal torch.

100,000 trapped

In ruin and flames the great industrial basin is coming down over the heads of the German troops trapped inside it.

There may be 30,000 combat troops still inside the Ruhr pocket and 70,000 more second-class troops of various categories.

Over and over again the Germans are flinging in desperate eleventh-hour efforts to hammer a way out of the trap of steel and flame.

As the Germans try to break out—particularly at the north-eastern and south-eastern corners and around bomb-shattered Hamm—Allied guns are blasting down the remaining centres of resistance.

Even farmhouses are being pulverised and reduced to rubble where the Germans try to use them as strong-points. Tanks, mortars, and

BACK PAGE—Col. TWO

Three traps close on German army

Emden menaced

MONTGOMERY'S H.Q., Monday.

KESSELRING'S Northern Front, from the Hague to Bremen, is being broken into three pockets closing in on the North Sea and the Zuider Zee—carry out a great enveloping operation.

This is how the three pockets are being formed:

1. Canadian units, after meeting paratroops dropped in Northern Holland, pushed on to Meppel, ten miles from the Zuider Zee.

2. Canadian tanks, thrusting north along the east bank of the Ems from Meppen, are barely 30 miles from the great naval arsenal of Emden.

3. The Seventh Armoured Division, by its push to Bremen, has cut off the Germans between the Ems and the Weser.

Across the Weser British Second Army troops have linked with U.S. Ninth Army men four miles from Hanover. Other British units are almost in Hanover's outskirts.

South-east of Hanover, Ninth Army tanks are less than 20 miles from Brunswick.

Clearing up the Ruhr, Ninth Army infantry have smashed into Essen and found Krupps badly damaged.—*Reuter and B.U.P.*

New style V-ramp

EXPERTS probe a queer type V-ramp, captured near Zutphen.

Big V-bomb haul

MUSEUM OF SECRETS

Alexander Clifford tells below how a British regiment captured a huge mass of German secret weapons, including V2s, on their way to the Hague, and fantastic apparatus for handling the rockets.

STEYERBERG GERMANY, Monday.

THIS tiny country railway station is a museum of V-weapons. The Inns of Court armoured cars captured the place in time to check whole train-loads of V1s and V2s that were on their way to England via Holland.

I counted 51 V1s packed in one train. There was a fantastically complicated crane affair for lifting V2s around. There was what looked like a launching apparatus for V2s. There was a train which had contained V2s.

The only things that weren't there were the V2s themselves. The Nazis got them away by the skin of their teeth.

The V2s had been on their way to The Hague when suddenly the train found its way blocked by our advance. The Nazis had to choose from among this huge mass of secret weapons what they would save.

They rushed up their special cranes. These are miracles of intricate machinery, with a powerful car engine attached to the side to move certain parts.

There are cylinders of gas underneath, and two metal semi-circular cradles on top hold the rockets and collapsible steel derricks and a dozen other mysterious parts.

Launching machine

These cranes hauled the V2s out of the train. Each rocket takes up a truck and a half, so that the train is composed of a group of three trucks, each holding two V2s.

They lie empty now, except for certain vast cylinders which may be the explosives for launching.

The Germans hoisted the rockets on to transporters and rushed them away. A farmer who watched told me they looked more like the bodies of aeroplanes than anything else. They were not painted.

The Nazis only just made it. One crane apparatus was shot through the tyres and couldn't be got away.

And they had to leave behind an apparatus on wheels involving a large horizontal metal circle with enormously strong steel "feet" below to support it. I don't see what it could have been except a launching machine.

There still remained a complete trainload of V1s. They were packed three in a truck with their wings folded alongside them. The Germans flung petrol over the train and set fire to it.

The front part of the train got alight and exploded, but I counted 51 V1s not destroyed.

The train had a remarkable ack-ack car on it, with a little wooden hut for the men to live in and a shelter of 8in. concrete for them to take refuge in.

SUNNY BUT COLD

It was sunny yesterday in the Strait of Dover, but a cold north-east wind kept the temperature down to 50deg. At 10 p.m. the barometer dropped slightly and the temperature was down to 41deg.

V-cargo goes to Norway

25-ft. Missiles

A MYSTERY cargo which has arrived in Norway may be V2s which the Germans intend to launch against Britain.

A report, received by Norwegian authorities in London yesterday, states that the cargo comprised weapons about 25ft. long. They were taken by rail to Sorlandbeg, in South-East Norway.

It is possible the weapons are midget submarines or storm boats, of which there are already many in Norwegian waters. If they are V2s they may be used against Northern England or Scotland, says the report.

London police to seek more pay

An increase in pay is to be sought by members of the Metropolitan and City Police. Application will probably be made to the Home Secretary soon for leave to submit their case to an arbitration tribunal.

It is believed that an increase of £1 10s. a week will be asked for, bringing the rate of pay of a first-class constable to £8 a week. A demand for extra holidays is also likely.

'SPEECHES CRISIS' IS GROWING

PM may vow his Cabinet to silence

By **WILSON BROADBENT**, Daily Mail Political Correspondent

AFTER the hefty, all-out attack on the Socialists delivered by Mr. Brendan Bracken, Minister of Information, in London yesterday in reply to Mr. Ernest Bevin's attack on Mr. Churchill, the Prime Minister is in a dilemma.

He has to decide quicky, before the vociferous members of his Cabinet get completely out of hand, whether to impose a vow of silence on all Ministers serving under him, or to allow their political divergences to have full play.

It is not an easy decision to make, for there has not been a comparable political situation in this country in modern times.

All the main political parties are involved in the same Government — their leaders have to sit round the same Cabinet table every day—yet all, or most of them, now show that they wish to resume party warfare.

It is thus a problem of how best to unwind decently the delicate strands of political co-operation, which have survived the stresses of the war, without causing a lot of damage to the national interest in the process

BEVIN THERE

Mr. Churchill returned to London late yesterday afternoon, after spending the week-end in the country.

He arrived in time to preside over a meeting of the Cabinet, which was attended by all senior Ministers in the Government as well as the representatives of the Dominions who are in London for the imperial policy discussions preliminary to the San Francisco Conference.

Mr. Ernest Bevin arrived in Downing-street smiling, and was followed shortly afterwards by Mr. Brendan Bracken, who had just previously delivered his attack on the Minister of Labour and National Service

They sat round the Cabinet table for over two hours and then separated. But clearly this unusual situation, which has its dramatic side, cannot be allowed to continue.

If Mr. Churchill permits Cabinet Ministers freely to criticise each other in the country, the Government will soon cease to function effectively.

This was the sober view held in Whitehall yesterday, where the week-end developments were the main topic of discussion.

Mr. Churchill's advisers in the Conservative Party are all in favour of the vow of silence until the present Government is broken up and Mr. Churchill has formed the new "caretaker" Government.

'UNDIGNIFIED'

They do not believe that it is dignified for members of the same Government to attack each other in the way that Mr. Bevin and Mr. Bracken have done.

They think that it must have a bad effect in this country as well as abroad

For instance, Mr. Bracken's political broadside was not received with any enthusiasm by the Conservative Party managers. They believe that he acted too impulsively.

They would have preferred to have ignored Mr. Bevin's criticism of the Conservative Party and left his attack on the Prime Minister to be answered by Mr. Churchill at the right time.

Their attitude to Mr. Bevin's speech was one of sorrow more than anger.

Equally, the Labour Party managers were not too happy about Mr. Bevin's speech.

While they liked its vigorous tone and the way in which he aligned himself with the official policy of the Party, they thought that it was too premature. They blame Mr. Bevin's honesty and lack of political judgment for his error in this respect.

Quite clearly Mr. Bevin made this speech without prior consultation with the Labour Party organisers

More than ever it assumes the character of a personal speech to clear up a situation about which Mr. Bevin has such strong feelings.

In dealing with such matters Mr. Bevin, in the words of one of his own party, is always certain to use the bludgeon. The fact that his speech called forth an immediate rejoinder from Mr. Bracken indicates the sensitiveness of politicians now that the war in Europe is ending.

At the same time Mr. Bracken's personal relations with Mr. Churchill must not be overlooked. His loyalty to the Prime Minister has always been one of the most remarkable features of politics in the past 15 years.

It is not known, however, whether Mr. Bracken consulted Mr. Churchill before making his speech attacking Mr. Bevin.

It is generally assumed that he did, but Mr. Churchill may not have realised what publicity the speech was to receive.

In many respects Mr. Bracken appeared to be putting forward the Conservative Party policy, and as such the party managers felt that it was untimely.

But the fighting in Europe is not over, and the Prime Minister was being urged last night to request

BACK PAGE—Col. EIGHT

MR. Arthur Greenwood, Deputy Leader of the Labour Party, said at Southwark last night: "A general election is coming pretty soon now. Mr. Brendan Bracken has put it rather earlier. I did not want it as soon as that. The fight is on."

Speech in BACK Page.

Fewer ships sunk, U-boat losses high

Russians helped us

Daily Mail Naval Correspondent

THOUGH the Germans increased their U-boat effort in March, they sank fewer Allied ships than in February. And the U-boat losses were "severe."

This was announced last night in the monthly joint statement on U-boat warfare issued under the authority of Mr. Churchill and President Roosevelt.

The last statement, covering February, said that shipping losses in that month were "moderate."

The capture of 45 submarines by the Russians at Danzig has materially assisted the Allied cause by helping to cut off the evil at its source, said last night's communiqué.

New types delayed

"The bombing and minelaying policy of the Allies has undoubtedly delayed the introduction of the new type U-boats," added the statement.

It would thus appear that the "Schnorkel" breathing device has been at least partly choked in the remaining U-boat bases in France, Holland, and Norway.

With the Allied advance on Rotterdam, Wilhelmshaven, and Hamburg, all our anti-submarine forces will soon be able to concentrate on the coasts of Norway.

Late yesterday afternoon R.A.F. Lancasters, escorted by Spitfires and Mustangs, dropped 10-ton and 5½-ton bombs on the U-boat shelters at Hamburg.

Junker city gives in

KÖNIGSBERG COLLAPSE

KONIGSBERG, Hitler's East Prussia fortress, fell to the Red Army last night after a siege lasting six weeks.

The commander, General Lasch, his Staff, and the remnants of the garrison laid down their arms at 9.30 p.m., after the Russians, storming through the city, had already captured 27,000 of its defenders in the day's fighting.

The tally of 27,000 was reached at 8 p.m., and Moscow did not disclose last night how many more were made captive by the surrender.

Moscow greeted the fall of Königsberg with the salute reserved for the fall of capitals—24 salvos of 324 guns. Capture of the fortress port releases a huge army for operations farther west—90 generals were cited in the victory order.

Berlin reported last night that Field-Marshal Schoerner, newly appointed C.-in-C. on the Eastern front, has opened a counter-offensive against Koniev's positions in Upper Silesia. The attack began at dawn yesterday from south of Ratibor, and is presumably aimed to cripple the left flank of the Russian Oder attack, and also to keep the Russians from the Czecho-Slovak industrial regions.

Meanwhile, the battle for Vienna is fast nearing its end.

The Germans last night admitted that the Red Army, "far superior" in strength to the defenders, had broken through to the Ringstrasse, the road circling the inner city.

Fighting was in progress in the museums and other buildings around this street.

Field-Marshal Schoerner and Field-Marshal Model were named by Moscow yesterday among those "wanted" for atrocities committed by the Germans in Latvia.

A special commission which investigated the atrocities said that more than 327,000 prisoners of war and 250,000 civilians were tortured to death in prison camps.

LATEST

VIENNA CENTRE CAPTURED

Soviet communiqué announces: Centre of Vienna has been captured, including the Town Hall, Parliament Buildings, and Opera House.

DESTROYED 83 PLANES ON ROADS

At least 83 enemy planes, most of them parked on or along German highways south of Munich, were destroyed yesterday by strafing Mustangs of the U.S. Eighth Air Force. Pilots estimated that from 100 to 120 planes of all descriptions were concentrated along the highway.

Daily Mirror

APL 11

No. 12,888 ONE PENNY

Registered at G.P.O. as a Newspaper.

ALLIES CAPTURE HANOVER, MONTY RACES FOR HAMBURG

ALLIED TROOPS have captured Hanover. Bremen is being tightly ringed and now Montgomery's tanks and infantry are going hell for leather to Hamburg.

Correspondents were date-lining messages from Hanover, Germany's twelfth city, last night, after a fantastic battle by the U.S. Ninth Army, had given us the city within a few hours.

Thousands of civilians crowded into the streets to watch the fighting even while tanks were exchanging shots.

There were posters all over the place calling them to arms, but they remained spectators.

A soldier grumbled: "It makes you feel silly, crouching around trying to get in a shot at a sniper while civilians pedal past on bikes and women and children tag along, just watching."

As the first tanks rolled into Hanover another tank division raced round the city in a twenty-three-mile advance to cut the motor road linking Hanover and Brunswick at a point midway between the two, 120 miles from the German capital.

At the same time Montgomery's Eleventh British Armoured Division, in a spectacular dash, north of Hanover, not only completed the city's encirclement, but cut the motor road leading to Hamburg.

Tank Country

The Sixth Airborne Division captured Fuhrberg, twelve miles north-east of Hanover, half-way point from Wesel to Berlin.

Last night Montgomery's might was pouring through a twenty-mile gap in the German lines, with Hamburg only sixty miles away, across rolling tank country.

They were building up their bridgehead across the Weser twenty miles above Bremen and closing in encirclement on the port, which was being bitterly defended.

In the narrowing Ruhr pocket, some attempts are now being made by the Germans to evacuate troops by plane during the night.

But 36,566 prisoners have already been taken.

285 of Rib's staff seized

Two hundred and eighty-five members of the German Foreign Ministry staff were seized at Mulhausen, cables Associated Press.

American tanks advanced so swiftly that the staff did not have time to flee. The captured did not include Foreign Minister von Ribbentrop or any other Ministry top figure, however.

Members of the Foreign Ministry staff who handled administrative matters for Ribbentrop were found cowering in rooms, basements, garages and the homes of friends.

Many members of the Railroad Ministry were captured ten miles away.

U.S. may get to the Elbe in few hours

SOUTH of Montgomery's dash towards the Elbe, the U.S. First Army is also pounding towards the river at a speed which may get them there in a matter of hours.

A correspondent cabled last night: Today one of our flying columns raced forty miles to Nordhausen, only fifty-three miles from the River Elbe, less than 120 miles from the Red Army on the other side of the river, and 115 miles from Berlin.

Six of these daring columns are tonight speeding across Germany north and south of Nordhausen. Some are meeting absolutely no resistance.

All of them started off between six and eight this morning. The twenty-five mile mark was passed by three o'clock this afternoon.

If they keep up this hectic pace, and there seems nothing to stop them, we shall be on the Elbe before noon tomorrow.

Patton Break-Through

On the First Army's right flank, General Patton's Third Army has got going again, breaking through up to fifteen miles at points on a fifty-six mile front towards Nuremberg.

Bavaria was entered at a new point. Five columns are throwing a loop round Erfurt, town of 136,000 people. They are two miles from Erfurt and three beyond Coburg.

GAVE ORPHANS THEIR PENSIONS

THREE THOUSAND ex-soldiers and bereaved families of the last war are giving their pensions to 2,777 orphans of this war.

That is one reason Sir Walter Womersley, Minister of Pensions and "foster-father" to them all, was yesterday able to say at Orpington, Kent: "I am never short of money for my 'family.'

"To each of those pensioners I send a letter which entitles them to stop payments to us and to draw their pension again at any time they like."

M.P. reveals another plane tragedy: 'Pilot ordered on risky flight'

MAKING grave charges against Transport Command, an M.P. told the Commons last night that an air crash which killed from sixteen to nineteen people was caused because the pilot was ordered to take off in dangerous night conditions after he had suggested he should leave in daylight.

The M.P., Mr. Bowles (Soc., Nuneaton) alleged that the crash had never been publicly revealed and that the order of the pilot had been either omitted from the record of the airfield inquiry, or expunged from it.

"I hope," said Mr. Bowles, "that the House will be sufficiently shocked to demand that a select committee be set up."

"Three weeks ago," he said, "a Liberator pilot who landed in the Azores received instructions from the briefing officer that he had to take off at night in the dark.

"Although he was heard to say he would rather take off in daylight," said Mr. Bowles, "I am told that he was almost ordered to take off at night. The terms of the order were, 'Unless you take off tonight you will have to give your reasons in writing.'"

The pilot took off according to orders. He was a Czech who might not have had a good knowledge of English. The control officer in the control tower saw that he was heading direct to the hills and told him to turn to the right.

"U.S. Pilots Resigned"

"My informant," Mr. Bowles said, "a man with twenty-five years' flying experience who was there at the time or very soon after, tells me that neither he nor any pilot with that flying experience under those conditions would have taken off.

"In fact, a senior officer would have refused and, as the Minister probably knows, there have been certain refusals by pilots of Transport Command to carry out instructions. Many of them, American civilians, have resigned.

"Whether the pilot understood English well enough or not is not known, but what happened was that this officer did not turn to the right, and

Continued on Back Page

CADET ROW: 2 PLATOONS DISBANDED

TROUBLE in a unit of Army Cadets at Worthing has resulted in the disbandment of two platoons.

They are Nos. 1 and 2 Platoons of A Company, Second Cadet Battalion of the Royal Sussex Regiment.

Discontent started two months ago when Home Guard officers took the place of cadet officers.

The boys were annoyed because the new officers persisted in wearing Home Guard flashes instead of the Cadet Force flash.

They protested — and the Home Guard flashes were removed.

A few weeks later there was trouble in the Drill Hall. Lights and band instruments were damaged, and the adjutant's room left in disorder.

Sequel to the trouble came on Friday when the C.O., Major Masterman paraded the company and disbanded No. 1 and 2 platoons.

A re-enlistment scheme has been started for members of the platoons—with certain boys barred.

Worthing police stated last night that they had no confirmation of a report that vehicles garaged at the drill hall had been "shot up."

OUR NEW TARGETS

Fighter and medium bombers attacked military targets in Czechoslovakia for the first time yesterday. Leipzig and Berlin were bombed last night.

SS BID TO KILL FRENCH GENERAL

AN attempt by six S.S. men to kill General Jean Lattre de Tassigny, Commander of the First French Army, in a raid on the General's headquarters in Alsace, was reported last night from Switzerland.

The Nazi raiders were said to have blown up a bridge across the Rhine, then attacked De Tassigny's headquarters.

They were overpowered by military police who captured five of the six Germans. The General was not injured.

According to the Swiss Press, German saboteurs and killers, at large in France, Belgium and even neutral countries including Sweden and Switzerland, are under the orders of the same headquarters that is organising the "Werewolves."

The notorious storm troop leader Skorzeny—who headed the S.S. detachment which snatched Mussolini from captivity in 1943—is now in France disguised as an American soldier, says "La Suisse."

It is also reported that special S.S. units have now been reorganised into so-called S.S. "flying squads" to help form the nucleus of a new post-defeat Nazi underground movement.

GERMAN attempts to slip two spies into Brazil for sabotage purposes, have resulted in a German being sentenced to twenty-five years' imprisonment and the liberation of a Dutch Guiana negro accomplice who revealed the plot.

Daily Mail

NO. 15,268 ONE PENNY ** FOR KING AND EMPIRE THURSDAY, APRIL 12, 1945

LATE WAR NEWS

Meeting with Russians may come at any moment now

64 TO BERLIN 125 TO LINK-UP

'Hell on Wheels' division are on the Elbe

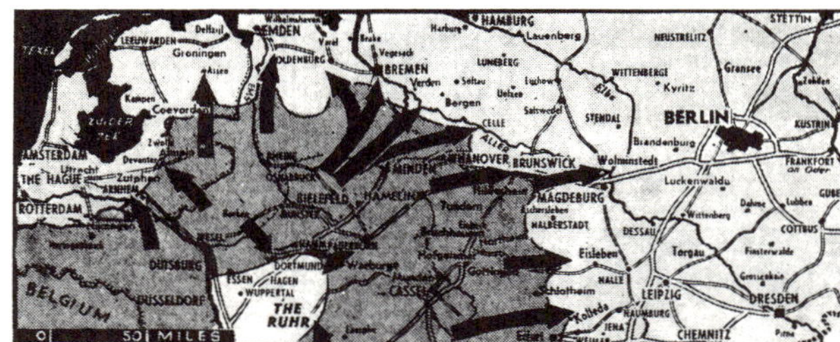

TO-DAY troops of the U.S. Ninth Army stand on the Elbe facing Berlin, only 64 miles away. Simpson's "Hell on Wheels" tanks—the famous Second Armoured Division—swept up to the river last night after tearing 55 miles across the Central German plain in less than 24 hours.

They are 125 miles from Marshal Zukhov's Russian army now poised for the final leap to Berlin from the Küstrin bridgehead on the west bank of the Oder.

Simpson's armour reached the Elbe after one of the most dramatic tank dashes of the war. When dawn broke yesterday they were in the Brunswick area. There the "Hell on Wheels" commander assembled his forces and swore to make the river by nightfall.

Then he gave the familiar order—"Let's go." The tanks raced away. Mile after mile of good, hard-surfaced roads flew past. In a few hours the factories and houses of Magdeburg appeared on the horizon.

Swinging north, the tanks smashed into Wolmirstedt. Three miles beyond lay the Elbe. Night was falling. On went the tanks, and in a short while the vow of the "Hell on Wheels" men was fulfilled.

WEHRMACHT CRUMBLING

This headlong advance to the last barrier before Berlin came as a climax to news from all fronts suggesting that the Wehrmacht is rapidly falling apart.

Kesselring's line guarding the approaches to the great North Sea ports is snapping. His "suicide" paratroops are retreating to the sea as fast as they can go. Guards tanks, and crack infantry of the British Second Army are in full pursuit.

Three vital ports are menaced—

EMDEN.—Tanks of a Polish division fighting with the Canadian First Army have driven up the Ems to within 12 miles of the city.

BREMEN.—Dempsey's Desert Rats are less than three miles from the outskirts.

HAMBURG.—British tanks, operating between the Weser and the Elbe, have captured Celle and cut the main road and railway leading south from the port.

PATTON 'BLACKED OUT'

Here are other highlights:

HOLLAND.—British and Canadian troops have begun the battle to free Western Holland and its big cities—the Hague, Rotterdam, and Amsterdam. They have stormed the River Ijsel and are pushing for Apeldoorn, home of the exiled Kaiser after the last war.

RUHR.—American airborne troops have captured Essen. Gelsenkirchen has fallen. Bochumis falling.

PATTON'S Third Army tanks are smashing forward in Central Germany under a black-out. They have captured Coburg and entered Erfurt. Coburg fell without a shot after the Americans had demanded its surrender.

HODGE'S First Army spearheads advanced 22 miles yesterday and reached Kolleda, 48 miles from Leipzig.

Essen met us with wine, song

Civilians hug the troops

U.S. NINTH ARMY, Wednesday.

AIRBORNE troops who captured Essen were met by "Welcome" signs. Civilians threw their arms around the troops and offered food, wine, and other delicacies.

Civilian revellers gathered around small fires amid the city's ruins and sang.

Jubilant crowds went to greet the troops as they crossed the Rhine-Herne Canal on pontoons. The crowd was waving white flags and carrying bottles of wine.

Opposition in the city was negligible.

When the 35th Division walked unopposed into Gelsenkirchen, Germans greeted them there too with large "Welcome" signs and other placards bearing "Thank you" in huge letters.—*A.P. and B.U.P.*

River is stormed

THE battle to free Western Holland and its great cities—the Hague, Amsterdam, and Rotterdam—has begun.

Canadian and British troops, under General Crerar, are storming across the River Ijssel from the area of Deventer, captured yesterday.

Amsterdam lies 55 miles to the west, on the Zuider Zee. Guarding it and the other big ports are about 90,000 Germans entrenched behind a network of water defences.

Crerar's powerful offensive was launched after a heavy artillery barrage.

When the noise of the guns died down the infantry surged across the Ijssel towards Appeldorn, ten miles away. Late last night the attack was reported to be "going well."

Canadians who crossed the Ijssel in assault boats have placed themselves in a position to threaten Arnhem from the rear.

Labour chiefs in Washington

WASHINGTON, Wednesday. — Mr. Ebby Edwards, chairman of the British Trades Union Congress, and Sir Walter Citrine, general secretary, have arrived in Washington.

They are here for the first meeting, expected to begin on Friday, of the administrative committee which is to carry out business between sittings of the World Labour Conferences.—*Reuter.*

Poland: Statement next week

Mr. Eden told the House of Commons yesterday that Mr Churchill proposes to make a statement next week, probably on Thursday, on the work of the Commission of Three in Moscow, and on certain other aspects of Russo-Polish relations.

He might also take the opportunity to say something about the war situation in general. A debate would follow if it was desired.

VC may oppose Bevin

A high-ranking British officer, who won the V.C. in the last war and has taken part in military missions in this war, may stand as Conservative against Mr. Ernest Bevin in Wandsworth Central at the general election, it was stated last night.

Simpson issues the big maps of Berlin

From **NOEL MONKS,** Daily Mail Special Correspondent

U.S. NINTH ARMY, Wednesday Night.

NOW the Ninth Army is rolling eastward on at least a 60-miles front. Prisoners are coming in so fast that one wonders if the word has been passed around to cease resisting.

A bigger proportion of officers is surrendering now than I've seen at any stage of the war. You can sense it on the roads that the Wehrmacht is falling apart and that the war with Germany is drawing to a close.

In the operations tent of one division I was with to-day there was a cheer from Staff officers as a great map marked "Berlin" was unrolled.

Maps mean much more to us these days than the capture of big cities. Our troops did not stay long enough in Hanover yesterday to wash the dust from their faces.

They pushed on right through the shattered city and out the other side.

It was sunny and hot, and I noticed many yearning eyes cast on one of the only factories left intact in the city—a lager brewery. But there was no stopping.

There is tremendous excitement throughout the entire army, as every man feels now that "this is really it."

100 girls of WLA strike

By Daily Mail Reporter

Nearly 100 Land Girls at the Essex War Agricultural Committee's farm at Claytye, near Upminster, went on strike yesterday as a protest against the decision not to grant them a war gratuity.

Some of the girls cycled to other farms in the district where W.L.A. girls are working and the number of strikers was quickly increased.

In the afternoon the girls, who are aged from 18 to about 22, were addressed at the farm by the county secretary, Mrs Strickland, but she failed to induce the girls to return to work.

It is expected that to-day they will be joined by 50 or 60 other land girls from the Billericay district.

Tolbukhin 42 miles beyond Vienna

Russians race for link-up

MARSHAL Tolbukhin has unleashed his tanks in a great drive towards Linz, on the "invasion road" to Southern Germany.

This was disclosed by Berlin last night, with the news that the Red Army was already 42 miles west of Vienna and half-way along the road to Linz.

Tolbukhin's men were described as attacking "on a broad front" towards the Wachan, the stretch of the Danube between Krems and Melk.

From the distances given by the Germans it would appear that the important road centre of St. Polten had been overrun.

Moscow has so far not confirmed this onslaught, although Moscow correspondents were allowed to report yesterday that Tolbukhin was building up for a drive towards Munich and Nuremberg and the U.S. armies approaching from the West, 260 miles away.

Vienna gun duel

Behind this thrust the Russian "mopping-up" teams are steadily crushing German resistance in Vienna, and have cleared still more of the small area now in enemy hands.

The Germans, who lost 2,300 men captured yesterday, are fighting back desperately from their foothold along the Danube. Both sides have heavy artillery in action.

North of the doomed city Marshal Malinovsky has sent out a wedge to complete the encirclement of the capital, and has also broken into the Czech province of Moravia.

Still farther north, the Russians have advanced 20 miles more into the Carpathians, and have captured Vrutky.

A new battle is apparently looming up on the centre of the Russian front.

Field-Marshal Schoerner, Hitler's new Commander-in-Chief in the East yesterday warned his armies that Koniev was massing tanks in the area of Güben and Forst, 60 miles south-east of Berlin.

Said Schoerner's Order of the Day: "In spite of events in the West, strong mobile reserves of the best German divisions are ample to meet the coming onslaught by two Russian tank armies."

Japs ask U.S. for news of ship

The Japanese Government has asked the U.S. Government for any information about the Japanese ship Awamaru, reported missing after delivering supplies to Allied prisoners held in Southern Asia.

Tokio radio, reporting this, states the inquiries were made through the Swiss Government.—*A.P.*

THE WARMEST DAY

It was the warmest day of the year yesterday in the Strait of Dover. The temperature reached 69deg., but the barometer was falling, and there was some rain at night.

'Free the war news'

Eisenhower order

SHAEF, Wednesday.

GENERAL EISENHOWER is trying to get the war news to the public—and the troops—as quickly as possible, and has told his censors to keep up the "freest possible flow of news."

In an interview General Eisenhower said:

"The fighting men of America and Britain and their comrades in our armies have been reared on the ideals of a free Press and free speech.

"These are the two great principles we are fighting to preserve. They are among the basic rights of mankind.

"'Public opinion wins wars, especially in democracies, and public opinion must be honestly and fearlessly informed."

☆

In an effort to give news to the fighting men, he said:

"The soldier likes to read about his unit and about his local commander. Correspondents should be encouraged rather than discouraged to mention the identity of units actually in the line when these have obviously been previously identified by the enemy.

"As a rule it would appear that after a unit has been in the line for 48 hours there is little need pretending that the enemy is ignorant of its presence."

Summing up, the Allied Supreme Commander said:

"The freest possible flow of news is the best way to keep the public informed and working in support of the war effort."—B.U.P.

3 questions of the day

Three questions of the day — with answers by Wilson Broadbent, Daily Mail Diplomatic Correspondent, based on the latest information available in London last night.

1: Where will peace talks be held?

VIENNA may be chosen as the most suitable capital for the Peace Conference—if the city is not too badly damaged, and if all-round agreement is reached.

The Peace Conference will be held when all campaigns have ended in Europe and the Far East.

There is general belief in Whitehall that the war against Japan will be over this year, and therefore preliminary discussions are taking place on the scope and objects of the Peace Conference.

Such a conference would be the natural outcome of the forthcoming San Francisco talks, where the charter of the new world security organisation is to be drafted.

2: When will V-day be announced?

V-DAY will be proclaimed in Britain when the Battle of Germany is ended, but the Government are not contemplating any elaborate celebrations.

Even when organised resistance has been smashed in Germany, it is conceivable that there will still be fighting in Italy, where the Germans have dug themselves in effectively. It will also be necessary to round up Germans in the French ports, the Channel Islands Norway and the Balkans.

In these circumstances V-Day will be more of a Thanksgiving Day, with no large-scale State celebration. It is not the Government's intention, however, to restrict private celebrations. After six years of life under the constant threat of enemy action, people will want to "let go."

3: What has become of Herr Hitler?

NEWS has reached London, from what is described as a reliable source, that Hitler is a sick and disillusioned man. It is said that the days of his power are ended, and that Himmler has superseded him.

According to one first-hand source, three things have happened:

The Nazi Party in many parts of Germany is now in process of disintegration;

The German people are less frightened of the Gestapo than they were; and

The Germans now have one earnest desire, which is to see the end of the war.

Goebbels is still a good propagandist and such stories must be treated with reserve. Yet there are people who claim to know that Himmler has seized power—for what purpose and with what object is not clear.

There have been indications that Himmler was not a do-or-die Nazi, that in certain circumstances he might try to negotiate peace

If that is one of his tricks at this moment, he is not likely to obtain a hearing from the Allies They will ignore him, as the Russians did when he put peace proposals before them more than a year ago

One story out of Germany says that Hitler looked so ill that the mark of death is upon him. Another version of events is that the Nazis, or what is left of them, will fight to the bitter end, and that Hitler "will almost certainly commit suicide."

Unless Hitler is very ill, it is difficult to imagine him subordinate to Himmler or anybody else.

AIR ACE DIES IN CRASH

Planes collide

One of the R.A.F.'s most skilful aces, Group Captain Gordon Learmouth Raphael, D.S.O., D.F.C., was killed in a crash over Woodchurch, near Ashford, Kent, yesterday. He was 30.

His Spitfire collided with another machine. Both planes were wrecked

Raphael, a Canadian from Ontario, won the D.F.C. as a bomber pilot. He received the D.S.O. in 1943 as a fighter pilot.

End of a navy: Germany's Scheer capsized and sunk by RAF

HERE is what is left of Germany's effective surface Navy—the Admiral Scheer, lying bottom-up in the inner dockyard basin at Kiel, after 600 R.A.F planes had attacked the port on Monday night. A rain of bombs capsized the ship, which is now reported sunk.

BEFORE the death-blow: The Admiral Scheer in dock prior to the great R.A.F. attack. She was a sister ship of the scuttled Graf Spee and the Lutzow (formerly Deutschland). Built in 1933, she was 600ft. long, carried six 11in. guns as chief armament, and had a speed of 26 knots.—Story in BACK Page.

These are still the Germans—1

15 British prisoners lined up and shot

From **ALEXANDER CLIFFORD,** Daily Mail Special Correspondent

OUTSIDE RETHEM, Wednesday.

IN the village of Rethem British soldiers have been taken prisoner, stood up against a blazing wall, and machine-gunned to death.

Horror has come back into the campaign Suddenly we are up against the sort of Germans who will stick at nothing.

And this is so authentic that there is no reasonable doubt.

This is the simple terrible signed statement of Private Parry, who saw it all happen:

"On the morning of April 11 [yesterday] we were attacking a village called Rethem. We were slowly pushing our way into the village against heavy concentrated small-arms fire.

"The major who was leading the party made for a large house When they had occupied the house the Germans opened up on it with a

BACK PAGE—Col. FOUR

These are still the Germans—2

'Hitler brute' betrayed in own town

From **WALTER FARR,** Daily Mail Special Correspondent

WITH HODGES' SPEARHEAD, Wednesday.

WE have captured a "Little Hitler," one of Germany's Kreisleiters (district leader).

As General Hodges' men entered the town he went into hiding and put on the uniform of a German engineer private, but he was given away by the enraged townsfolk.

They dashed to the prison cage and shouted, "He's not a soldier. He's a thug and brute. He has tortured, murdered, and raped. Let us get at him."

An American-born girl of German parents helped to track him down.

The kreisleiter told me in the prison cage, "It's not true. I did not brutalise anyone. I did not order anyone to be tortured. Some were tortured, but it was the Gestapo."

DISABLED TO GO ON LAND

Training on farms

A scheme for training disabled people for the land is announced by the Ministry of Agriculture to-day as the first instalment of the scheme to train "demobbed" men and women.

Arrangements for agricultural and horticultural training have been made in consultation with the National Farmers' Union, the National Union of Agricultural Workers, and the Transport and General Workers' Union.

Applicants without previous experience, passed by County War Agricultural Committees, will be placed on selected farms, market gardens, or similar establishments for up to 12 months' practical training with standard maintenance and dependant allowances.

THE KING AT No. 10

The King dined with the Prime Minister at No. 10, Downing-street last night

LATEST

FORTNIGHT TO GO, SAYS CANADA PM

Ottawa, Wednesday. — The Prime Minister, Mr. Mackenzie King, told Parliament to-day he would be greatly surprised if the European war was not officially declared to have ended before the start of the San Francisco conference (April 25). —A.P.

SUB. SINKS SWEDISH BOAT

Stockholm, Wednesday.—An unidentified submarine has shelled and sunk a Swedish fishing boat off Karlskrona, killing the skipper, say reports in Stockholm.—B.U.P.

2

BLA HAVE BOX OF SECRETS

The Jerrican

Millions of Jerricans, which contain petrol, oil, or water, and which are thrown from trucks or dropped from planes, made possible our armoured sweeps through France and Belgium and into Holland.

These steel boxes, made in Britain from sheet metal sent from America, are picked up by the advancing armoured spearheads and can be used many times.

Jerricans were first used by the Germans in North Africa. Thousands of women in Britain were taught how to handle great presses before the boxes could be made.

CHURCHES' MILLION FOR RELIGION IN EUROPE

CHURCH collections on V-Day will go towards a £1,000,000 fund to rebuild Christianity in Europe.

It will help to rebuild damaged churches, erect temporary churches in ruined areas, train ordinants, restart youth organisations, and provide Bibles and theological literature

The fund has the backing of the Church of England and the Free Churches.

Part of the fund will go to Pastor Martin Niemoller, head of the German Confessional Church, who has spent seven years in a concentration camp after defying Hitler.

The Bishop of Fulham Dr B S Batty whose diocese includes Western and Central Europe, said at a London service yesterday that when Pastor Niemoller was released he would be a greater religious leader than any Germany had ever had.

"It is our duty to see that every opportunity is given to him," the bishop said.

Daily Mirror APL 13

Friday, April 13, 1945
No. 12,890 ONE PENNY
Registered at G.P.O. as a Newspaper.

END IN A FEW DAYS, U.S. TOLD: BRIDGEHEAD IS 6 MILES LONG OVER ELBE

Paratroops drop near Berlin, say reports

A HIGH American General Staff Officer told the U.S. Senate Military Committee last night that the end of organised fighting in Germany will probably come within a few days.

As he spoke, Ninth Army troops who had crossed the Elbe fanned out across the Prussian Plain towards the outer defences of Berlin.

A midnight message disclosed that they hold a bridgehead six miles long and there was an unconfirmed report from French sources that paratroops have been dropped at Brandenburg, twenty miles from the capital.

INFANTRY WELL UP

It is not merely tanks which have come to the edge of this flat, treeless country across which Berlin lies. The infantry have kept pace with them to a great extent.

"A West Front in the former meaning of the word has ceased to exist," admitted Max Krull, chief military correspondent of the German News Agency. He pointed out that the danger is now that the Allies and the Russians, only 100 miles apart, will slice Germany in two.

But he maintained that before starting a big two-front drive on Berlin, the Allies would try to carve up the Nazi forces south of the capital.

GREAT LEAP BY PATTON

His fears were becoming reality last night as Patton's tanks leapt forward on a dash as spectacular as that which carried the Ninth Army to the Elbe.

They covered forty-five miles and crossed the Saale River on a stretch of thirty miles, and forged on under a news black-out. Infantry also reached the Saale and planes blitzed everything in the path of the advance.

U.S. First Army tanks also reached the Saale at a point only twenty-three miles from Leipzig.

A second big armoured punch by Patton was carried to within forty miles of the Czech frontier.

Weimar, a third of it smashed to the ground, sent an envoy on a bicycle to surrender and was occupied.

Bayreuth is threatened. The U.S. Seventh Army have captured Schweinfurt and Heilbronn and the French have taken Baden Baden.

BRITISH FRONT IS ON THE MOVE AGAIN

The British front in North Germany is on the move again.

Commandos, using knives, daggers and bayonets, yesterday extended their bridgehead over the River Aller towards Hamburg.

Thirteen miles away Celle, former gas warfare centre of the German Army, was captured by storm by Monty's crack 15th Scottish Division, which seized intact a bridge across the river.

Many gas and chemical warfare instructors were taken prisoners.

ROOSEVELT DIES ON EVE OF ALLIED TRIUMPHS

President Roosevelt—died in his sleep.

PRESIDENT ROOSEVELT died suddenly from a cerebral hemorrhage in his sleep at West Springs, Georgia, yesterday afternoon.

A White House statement said: "Vice President Truman has been notified. He was called to the White House and informed by Mrs. Roosevelt."

The White House announcement added that a Cabinet Meeting has been called.

"The four Roosevelt boys in the Services have been sent a message by their mother, which said that the President slept away yesterday afternoon."

"He did his job to the end, as he would want to," the statement continued.

The interment will be at Hyde Park (the President's New York estate) on Sunday.

Senator Harry Truman, the Vice President, Missouri County judge, and one-time Kansas City haberdasher, moves up to the highest office in the land, as a result of the President's death.

At Capitol Hill, Vice-President Truman's aides disclosed that he had left for the White House only a few minutes be-

Continued on Back Page

Sunday Pictorial

April 15, 1945
No. 1,570
TWOPENCE

It Will Be Over in Thirty Days!

HOW LONG NOW?

1 WEEK?

POLITICAL Correspondents in London last night were hinting that Mr. Churchill will announce the end of the war in Europe when he makes his statement to the House of Commons on Thursday.

It is accepted that in any case the announcement of V-Day cannot be delayed more than another month, since the link-up of the Allies and the fall of Berlin are expected hourly, and after that little fighting beyond mopping-up is anticipated.

2 WEEKS?

AT SHAEF Headquarters in Paris the view is that Mr. Churchill will postpone his victory announcement for a fortnight if only because the nominal occupation of Berlin cannot be completed in a few days. Further argument is that the V-Day declaration must wait until all danger of heavy fighting is past—and that means the capture of Bremen and Hamburg at least.

The military view is that no celebrations should take place while there is still a threat of serious casualties, and there are indications that quite a number of strong pockets of resistance remain.

One military expert considers that even after Berlin has fallen, there will still be 100,000 Germans left who will be able and willing to fight.

3 WEEKS?

PERSONAL view of Field-Marshal Montgomery is said to be that it will take another three weeks

It is known that the British military leaders are anxious to capture Amsterdam, the biggest city in Holland, before V-Day is declared, and this is not regarded as an easy expedition. Further, it is felt that Denmark should at least be given its token freedom—by cutting off the country from Germany—before the rest of Europe is asked to celebrate.

In every quarter, however, the message was: "It can't last more than a month now."

● ***And last night we were only a two hours' tank drive from Berlin.*** SEE BACK PAGE

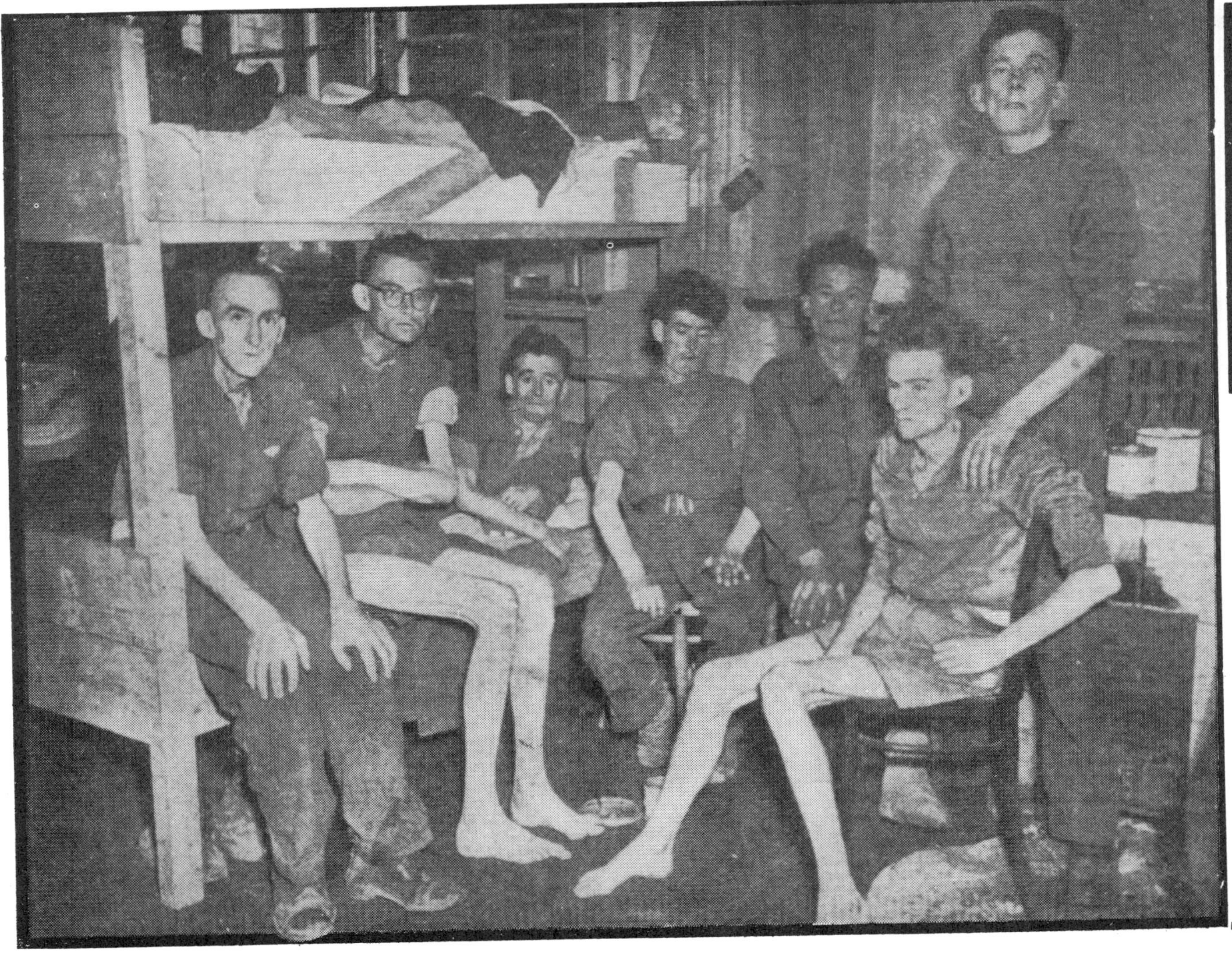

Starved In a German Prison

These are British soldiers and this is how they looked after four years in a German prison camp. They were freed at Gettingen by the Americans, and as the picture shows they were almost too weak and emaciated to smile.

Broken through lack of food, they had been sent to prison hospital. There a pretence was made at giving them treatment when all they needed were three meals a day.

Daily Mirror

APL 16

Monday, April 16, 1945
No. 12,892 ONE PENNY
Registered at G.P.O. as a Newspaper.

MONTY REACHES NORTH SEA, FIGHTING IS BITTER

Von Papen, prisoner

Captain Franz von Papen,—a picture taken as he was captured at his family home at Stockhausen, in the Ruhr. He is sixty-seven, much greyer, much less sleek, but he still sports the Tyrolean hat he has insisted on wearing for "informal" occasions for years. His capture, by U.S. troops, was a very informal affair. "Where's Hitler?" they asked. "I don't know," replied Papen the diplomat.

He decided he'd be safer with us

By Your Political Correspondent

VON PAPEN, former German Chancellor, a very crooked diplomat, and first of the Nazi leaders to be made prisoner, is likely to be brought to England in the next few days.

I understand that it has been decided, despite the fact that he holds a military rank, to treat him as a political prisoner.

Von Papen was captured in the Ruhr pocket, and the Americans are stated to be convinced that he remained in the pocket deliberately rather than return to Hitler's headquarters.

There is, in fact, definite evidence to this effect already available. He could have got out of the Ruhr by air at any time in the past week.

Himmler and Von Papen are bitter enemies, and the one-time Chancellor probably felt that he would be safer as an Allied prisoner.

All yesterday messages were passing between London and Washington on what to do with Papen.

Measures taken with him will set a precedent for the treatment of other Nazi leaders.

The position is complicated by the fact that as far as is known Papen is not on the list of major war criminals, as during most of the war he has held diplomatic status.

The Russians, however, who had much experience of Papen while he was in Ankara, hold other views, and are watching the position closely. Marshal Stalin will be consulted before any final decision is come to.

London diplomatic circles would not be surprised if the Russians ultimately ask that Papen be handed to them.

SON OF EX-KAISER (NAZI WORKER) IS CAPTURED

PRINCE August Wilhelm (57-year-old younger son of the ex-Kaiser) and 96-year-old Field-Marshal von Mackensen, a German C.-in-C. in the last war, were reported last night to have been captured by Allied troops in Germany.

The Prince at one time took part in Nazi activities and was a member of the Reichstag.

The Prince was captured in a castle near Kronberg, the residence of his aunt, Countess Margarethe of Hesse.

After interrogation he was handed over to the American military authorities.

● *The U.S. First Army has just taken its 500,000th prisoner since D-Day.*

The 500,000th was seventeen-year-old Private Stolz. All he had to say was: "I want to go home."

GERMANY was last night practically cut in two, with no communication between north and south except by precarious routes through Western Czechslovakia.

In addition, Canadians, by reaching the North Sea at two points north-west of Groningen, in Holland, have cut the German armies in the north in two.

In the south the Germans admit that Americans who by-passed Leipzig have fought their way into part of the great industrial city of Chemnitz, eighty miles from Prague, forty miles from Dresden and 100 miles from the Red Army line on the River Neisse.

But the Germans now seem to have completed their organisation to fight the last battles of the war in pockets in the north and south, with Berlin as an isolated fortress. Yesterday they rallied for last ditch battles.

On the Elbe the Allies suffered their first setback since crossing the Rhine when their bridgehead near Magdeburg was lost.

A bridge was smashed by bombardment, vehicles were swept into the water and a small - scale Dunkirk was necessary to rescue three battalions cut off on the German side of the river.

The second bridgehead, however, was extended, and along 150 miles of river the Allies are massing for the kill.

Field-Marshal Montgomery's British and Canadians met the hardest resistance at almost all points on their fronts, and there were fierce counter-attacks supported by S.S. troops.

Field-Marshal von Busch, from the Eastern front, who has taken command of the German northern armies, is showing determination to hold out at all costs the "Valhalla" defence lines, protecting the ports.

Arnhem has been cleared but there is heavy fighting at Allied canal bridgeheads in Groningen. Apeldoorn Troops of the Gross Deutschland Brigade, once Hitler's bodyguard are trying to stem the advance on Hamburg.

Commandos charged to the sound of a horn

From GEORGE McCARTHY

OVER THE ALLER, Sunday

A COMMANDO bayonet charge in daylight through a thick wood pitted with enemy entrenchments cleared a bridgehead through which the Eleventh Armoured Division crashed their way beyond the River Aller.

Night and day the Commando brigade had fought their way over the stream and into the thickly-wooded country beyond.

They had dug themselves in under heavy enemy fire and at 11 o'clock in the morning No. 6 Commando was given the order to clear the wood on the right.

They fixed bayonets and went in at full speed as, high above the din of battle, ranged the notes of a hunting horn.

It was the call to charge, and as it sounded through the trees, the noise of nearby fighting died away as though friend and foe knew this action would decide the battle.

And in that short silence a

Continued on Back Page

F.D.R. IS BURIED IN GARDEN

From John Sampson

NEW YORK, Sunday.

A WISH that Franklin Delano Roosevelt voiced only a few months ago—"All that is within me cries out to go back to my home on Hudson River"—was fulfilled today.

He was buried in the flower-covered lawn of his Hyde Park (New York) home as his family, friends, the nations' leaders and representatives of Allied countries watched in mournful silence.

A detail of grey clad cadets from neighbouring West Point fired the traditional three volleys of shots over the grave. Little Fala, President's Scottie, rolling in the warm grass a few yards away began to bark. Someone quieted him.

Then through the still pine-scented air a bugler sounded taps

The President's body was brought in a special train from Washington. All through the night, thousands of men, women and children poured from their homes and stood on embankments, bridges and other vantage points to watch the slow-moving funeral train

Some waited for hours in the drizzling rain. The train paused briefly at Baltimore and New York

There the flag - draped coffin was removed by men in uniform and borne up the steep, winding road to the wooded Roosevelt estate, where the late President played as a boy.

People lining the route wept

COOLER

Cloudy and cooler tonight and Tuesday. Low tonight, 40. High tomorrow, 48. Sunrise, 6:09; sunset, 7:33. (Chart on page 22.)

6 p.m.	42	2 a.m.	46	8 a.m.	58	Noon	*65
8 p.m.	43	4 a.m.	48	9 a.m.	64		
10 p.m.	44	6 a.m.	51	10 a.m.	68	*Unofficial.	
Midnight	45	7 a.m.	54	11 a.m.	65		

CHICAGO DAILY NEWS

FINAL Edition

70TH YEAR—90. MONDAY, APRIL 16, 1945—TWENTY-SIX PAGES. Telephone DEArborn 1111. FOUR CENTS

Truman's First Message to Congress

CARRY ON TO VICTORY

Bag 218,000 Nazis in 72 Hours

Yanks, Russ Push on Berlin

3d Army Drives To Hof, 7 Mi. of Czech Border

BULLETINS.

WITH AMERICAN 1ST ARMY — (UP) — The American 1st, 3d and 9th armies have taken more than 218,000 German prisoners in the last 72 hours in a mass roundup that at many points has lost all resemblance to war.

WITH U.S. 9TH ARMY EAST OF THE ELBE— (UP) — U.S. 9th Army troops beat off a heavy German counter-attack against their Elbe River bridgehead near Barby today after a three-hour battle.

PARIS—(AP)—The 3d Army drove within seven miles of Czechoslovakia today against the enemy's Western Front which already has been split into two commands.

Germans in the eastern segment of the severed Ruhr death pocket surrendered this morning to the American 1st Army of Lt.Gen. Hodges. Hundreds gave up without a struggle, about 3,000 joining the 143,349 previously captured in the great industrial sector.

* * *

THE GERMANS pulled troops from Berlin and tanks from the Russian front to counter the peril to their capital, 45 miles from nearest 9th Army troops. They erased one 9th Army bridgehead over the Elbe at Magdeburg, but Lt.Gen. Simpson's men deepened a second crossing to four miles within 53 miles of the capital on the open Brandenburg plain.

Germany was all but split in two by Lt.Gen. Patton's 3d Army which captured Hof (pop. 43,000), a road center eight miles from the Czech border and 76 miles from the Skoda munitions works in Pilsen.

The 1st Army tightened its siege of Leipzig, cleared the northern third of Halle and was within two miles of Dessau.

Farther south, the American 7th Army beat with five divisions to within eight miles of the Nazi citadel of Nuernberg (431,000) and

(Continued on page 4, column 3.)

Soviets Pierce Last Defenses Before Capital

BULLETIN.

LONDON — (AP) — Adolf Hitler in an order of the day to German soldiers on the Eastern Front declared tonight: "For the last time the Jewish-Bolshevist arch enemy has launched his massed attack. He is trying to destroy Germany and to wipe out our people."

LONDON — (UP) — The Red Army attacked on a 110-mile front east of Berlin today in a general offensive to capture the devastated Nazi capital and link up with Allied armies in the west.

In the first few hours of the long-expected assault, the Nazis conceded, the Russians penetrated the last-ditch Nazi defense line between Kuestrin and Frankfurt due east of Berlin and seized a new bridgehead across the Oder midway between the capital and Stettin.

The Soviet high command did not confirm the offensive immediately, but the Germans—usually first to announce such major Soviet drives—left no doubt that the supreme push from the east had begun.

* * *

MARSHAL ZHUKOV'S 1st White Russian Army threw the main weight of its all-out offensive against the German line from Wriezen, 23 miles northeast of Berlin, to Fuerstenberg, 42 miles southeast, at 3:15 a.m. under cover of a terrific air and artillery bombardment.

"Grim fighting" developed on Berlin's frontal defenses, Nazi accounts said, and Soviet forces wedged into the line in at least one point.

Farther north, a German military spokesman said, Soviet troops stormed across the lower Oder River and seized a bridgehead on the west bank near Schwedt, some 45 miles northeast of Berlin and 30 miles south of the Baltic port of Stettin.

Still other Soviet troops, possibly from Marshal Konev's 1st Ukrainian Army, went over to the

(Continued on page 4, column 1.)

Harass Japs

SAN FRANCISCO—(AP)—Guerrillas as well as American planes are harassing Japs on Hainan Island off the south China coast, the Jap Domei News Agency admitted today.

RUSSIANS DRIVE FOR BERLIN ON 110-MILE FRONT

Attacking on a 110-mile front east of Berlin the Russians have won at least one new bridgehead over the Oder near Schwedt. U.S. 9th Army forces, compelled to give up one Elbe River bridgehead near Madgeburg, are widening their second crossing near Barby. Canadian forces in the north have reached the North Sea, sealing off Holland.

[Associated Press Wirephoto.]

Leaps to Death With Husband As Witness

Mrs. John E. Winder, 47, of 7906 Bosworth av., awakened her husband today and said, "I want to show you something."

When he followed her to a window in their sixth floor apartment she leaped without warning to her death.

"It happened so fast I didn't have a chance to stop her," Winder told Sgt. Rudolph Josephson of the Rogers Park police.

* * *

MRS. WINDER, a candy store store manager in Glenmore, had been in ill health recently, her husband said.

Winder, a mechanic for the D O. James Manufacturing Co., 1140 Monroe st., said he noticed his wife was upset last night, but had no indication of a suicidal intent. The couple had been married 27 years.

Envoys Confer

MOSCOW—(AP)—Maj.Gen. Patrick J. Hurley, U.S. ambassador to China, conferred today with W. Averell Harriman, U.S. ambassador to Russia.

Mrs. Roosevelt Begins Big Task of Moving

BY EDITH GAYLORD.

WASHINGTON—(AP)—Mrs. Franklin D. Roosevelt today wasted no time in organizing the task of removing from the White House the Roosevelts' 12-year accumulation of belongings.

However worn from the shock and strain of her husband's death, Mrs. Roosevelt showed herself still possessed of her famous energy to get things done.

* * *

AWARE THAT President Truman and his family are entitled to move into the executive mansion as soon as possible, Mrs. Roosevelt left Hyde Park yesterday within an hour of burial services for her husband. She returned to Washington on the special train that also brought the Trumans.

If Mrs. Truman wishes it, as she undoubtedly will, Mrs. Roosevelt will see her to advise her on the numerous duties of the First Lady.

* * *

ASIDE FROM the thousands of ordinary family items to be removed from the White House, Mrs. Roosevelt will give special attention to the personal belongings of the late President.

There are his hundreds of valuable marine prints and ship models, his celebrated stamp collection, his thousands of books and the mementos of his presidency.

Most of these probably will be placed in the library on the Roosevelt's Hyde Park estate Mr. Roosevelt bequeathed to the government after the lifetime of his family.

* * *

MAKING the return trip with Mrs. Roosevelt was her daughter, Anna, who, with her husband, Lt.Col. John Boettiger, hurried in to find out how their 5-year-old son, Johnny, is faring. The youngster is seriously ill in a hospital.

In New York City Col. James Roosevelt, eldest of the four sons, boarded the Washington-bound train. It was the earliest moment he could reach his mother's side after a flight from Manila.

* * *

HE AND HIS three brothers have been on military duty overseas. Brig.Gen. Elliott Roosevelt, the second son, flew in from England in time to attend services in the White House Saturday and at Hyde Park yesterday.

Franklin Jr. and John were unable to return from their ships, somewhere in the Pacific.

Thousands Pour Into London to Be In on V-E Day

LONDON — (AP) — Thousands of visitors are pouring into London and jamming hotels, hopeful of being here for the celebration that will take place when V-E Day is proclaimed.

The police announced plans for concentrating hundreds of officers in central London, but the Bobbies have been instructed to allow the celebrators "considerable latitude."

A gigantic aerial parade is expected as part of the V-E day show, and Sabbath strollers got a preview yesterday as more than 1,000 U.S .8th Air Force Liberators flew low over London on their return from the attack on Germans pocketed in the Bordeaux area.

Last night R.A.F. planes engaged in exercises over the capital flashed "V's" to civilians and soldiers in the streets below. Held in the strong glare of searchlights, the planes switched their navigation lights on and off for the "V" signal.

Meet President Harry S. Truman

Turn to page 6 for the first of a series depicting President Truman as his home state of Missouri knows him.

Also on the inside:

Allies Open Knockout Push in Italy

BY RICHARD MOWRER.

Daily News Foreign Service.

WITH THE U.S. 5TH ARMY—A general offensive is on in Italy. One week after the 8th Army's attack against the forces of Gen. von Vietinghof, the 5th Army has struck hard in the mountains south of Bologna.

If, as it seems, the last Nazi resistance centers in the Alps, this major Allied effort on the Italian Front may be regarded as having a twofold purpose:

1. To cave in the breadbasket of Hitler's last defense position in mountainous central Europe—the rich plains of north Italy.

2. To destroy enemy forces in Italy.

(The Associated Press said the 5th Army has seized Mount Pigna and Mount Sette Croci and that the British are driving toward the Argenta Gap, which opens onto the flatlands leading to Ferrara and the Po River. Polish troops were closing in at a point 12 miles east of Bologna.)

* * *

HITHERTO the purpose of the Italian Front, as voiced by Allied leaders, has been to pin down German divisions which otherwise might have been transferred to the Eastern and Western Fronts.

This purpose has been achieved, Allied military sources say, because the Germans have not withdrawn from north Italy despite their disaster in the west.

The reason they haven't withdrawn is believed to be simply that they can't.

* * *

NOW the Allies are out to give the knockout punch. The Germans are well entrenched in tough terrain. Our men have to advance through mined territory.

The Germans, however, have lost a big ally in the weather, which for months had been bad enough to nullify our advantage in the air. Moreover, the Italian partisans are turning out to be more than mere hindrance to the enemy and propaganda for the Allies.

Pledges to Aid 'Common Man'

'We Shall Not Fail,' President Tells His Former Teammates

Text of the President's message is on page 9.

WASHINGTON—(AP)—President Truman promised today that the grand strategy of the war will remain "unchanged and unhampered" by his accession to the Presidency.

Making his first address to a joint session of Congress, the new President declared that this nation, along with its Allies, must shoulder the "grave responsibility' 'of making secure future peace.

To accomplish this objective, Mr. Truman said, the United States must join in punishing those guilty for bringing on the war.

"Lasting peace can never be secured if we permit our dangerous opponents to plot future wars with impunity at any mountain retreat—however distant," the President said, in apparent allusion to reports that Hitler may attempt to seek a refuge in the Bavarian Mountains of Germany.

Speaking only one day after the burial of Franklin D. Roosevelt, President Truman paid high tribute to his predecessor.

"Tragic fate has thrust upon us grave responsibilities," he said. "We must carry on.

* * *

"OUR DEVOTED leader never looked backward. He looked forward and moved forward. That is what he would want us to do.

"That is what America will do."

Mr. Truman went to the Capitol after two early morning conferences on international affairs. The first was with Secretary of State Stettinius; the second with British Foreign Secretary Anthony Eden, and Lord Halifax, the British ambassador.

* * *

LONG before the President arrived at the Capitol, police and secret service men placed a careful guard about the building.

Only holders of special cards of admission were allowed in the House gallery.

Speaking from the rostrum where he heard President Roosevelt on March 1 describe the accomplishments of the Yalta conference, Mr. Truman said that American policy remains "unconditional surrender."

Declaring that the nation is "deeply conscious" that much hard fighting remains, the President said:

"Having to pay such a heavy price to make complete victory certain, America will never become a party to any plan for partial victory. . . . We will not traffic with the breakers of the peace on the terms of the peace."

* * *

NOTING that within an hour after he took office last Thursday he had announced that the San Francisco United Nations Conference would proceed on schedule, Mr. Truman said the

(Continued on page 4, column 3.)

Truman Confers With Eden

WASHINGTON—(UP)—President Truman conferred for 20 minutes today with Anthony Eden, British foreign minister, who delivered several verbal messages from Prime Minister Churchill.

Also present were Secretary of State Stettinius and the British ambassador, Lord Halifax. Stettinius met with Mr. Truman earlier—shortly after the President arrived, in the executive office at the early hour of 8:15 a.m. —then returned to join the conference with Eden and the ambassador.

* * *

EDEN, who flew from England to attend the late President Roosevelt's funeral, told reporters as he left Mr. Truman's office:

"I was very pleased to have the privilege of calling on the President and very grateful that he found time to see me on this day when he has his first important speech to deliver.

"Naturally I brought him some messages from the Prime Minister telling him how gratified we are about the very close relations that exist between us in all our affairs."

* * *

IT WAS the new President's first full-dress foray into the field of foreign affairs—a field which will occupy much of his time in coming months.

Andrew J. Higgins, New Orleans shipbuilder, has been asked by the President to make himself available as an adviser from time to time, it was learned.

Higgins frequently was called into consultation by the White House during President Roosevelt's tenure.

Higgins met with Mr. Truman on Saturday but he declined to discuss his conversation with the President.

"I was invited over to see the new President," he said. "I found him well-possessed, confident and unperturbed. That is all I can say."

Woman Takes Poison

Mrs. Icel Deal, 56, owner of a rooming house at 3024 Harrison st., who told doctors she was "sick of being sick," died last night in County Hospital after swallowing poison. Mrs. Deal, a divorcee, was found by her son, James Deal, a printer, of the same address.

POLE LEADS NAZIS A CHASE

One of the War's Great Spy Stories

BY GEORGE WELLER.

Daily News Foreign Service.

ATHENS—Three scenes are almost enough to tell the story of Giorek Ivanoff, a Polish athlete who turned himself into a master spy.

Scene 1: The British submarine Thetis breaks the surface of the Aegean Sea on a windy, starless night off Laurion, near Athens. Three men are rowed ashore dressed as peasants.

They are two Greek Army officers, Magopoulos and Kondopoulos —soon to die before Nazi firing squads—and a dark-haired, 29-year-old Pole, Ivanoff.

Ivanoff has their money, three American $1,000 bills, which were placed inside sliced chocolate bars by British military intelligence at Cairo.

* * *

SCENE II: Three Nazi seaplanes, just taken off from the hydroplane base at Phaleron, are circling for height in formation, with hundreds of Greeks watching them.

Each of the planes, within a matter of seconds, puffs into flame and explodes into fragments.

The smoking particles fill the air, falling. Gaping Greeks and incredulous Germans watch the sight.

* * *

SCENE III: The Nazis are having another execution at the rifle range behind Kaisariani, the workers' settlement. This time it is not an execution of hostages, but authentic spies, three of them.

They are led out, one by one. The first man, tied to his stake, falls. At that moment the second, Ivanoff, whirls on the Nazi who is covering him, smashes down his handcuffs on the guard's revolver, and runs for the high wall.

He is up and over its 10 feet, but his heel is caught by a volley from a tommygun. He falls into a crowd of Greeks

(Continued on page 4, column 1.)

News Chronicle

No. 30,865 THURSDAY, APRIL 19, 1945 * * * ONE PENNY

MONTY MOVING ON HAMBURG

Belsen: The full, terrible story

From COLIN WILLS
News Chronicle War Correspondent

In Belsen Prison Camp, Tuesday (delayed).

I SPENT yesterday, last night and today here. The worst horrors I described in yesterday's dispatch are far exceeded by what I have seen since.

I got here immediately after the place had been overrun by the British 11th Armoured Division. Only a small detachment of British troops had then arrived, and it was awaiting reinforcements to take over the administration of this vast area and its 60,000 inhabitants from hundreds of Hungarian guards, with a considerable force of the Wehrmacht and between 50 and 100 S.S. men.

When I returned from sending yesterday's dispatch there were more dead lying where they had fallen from starvation.

MORE WERE DYING

Other prisoners, feeble though they were, were lifting the dead into blankets and carrying them away.

The bodies were terribly light, yet the carrying of them taxed the strength of the others.

Dozens more were lying on earth banks against walls, obviously dying. British medical units were driving up scarred roads through smoking villages where the battle had just passed and pockets of the enemy still held out in the woods, and they had not yet got here.

Neither had a food convoy nor a water convoy—perhaps more important still.

In the meantime soldiers had given out what water and tea they could.

One man, unable to stand up, sprawled on his belly across a pile of rubbish, cup to lips. He looked like a yellow stick wrapped in grey rag.

A man who had been there only one week told me he had nothing whatever to eat on three or four days, he could not remember which.

On the other days he had ¼ litre (nearly ½ pint) of turnip soup, and one day a thin slice of bread with a teaspoonful of sour milk cheese. I am weak already after a week," he said, "and my legs and arms are shrunken, for we have had to work on that diet."

"How about those who have been here many months?"

Ate grass

"Well, look around. Can you see a blade of grass? You won't find one. They have eaten all the grass."

An elderly Jew was shuffling slowly from one group of soldiers to another talking, even smiling. His head was like a little ivory skull whereon his moustache and spectacles looked gigantic.

As for the rest of him, it was just a hanging rag of striped cloth. It was as though the head were being paraded on a pole.

Like chicken pens

I passed down more than a mile of wire enclosures like huge chicken pens. Every one was crowded with people, men and women. Almost all wore the same blue-white stripes dirtied to greyness.

Some women had skirts, many pyjamas like men, a few had civilian clothes and many had bright coloured kerchiefs round their heads—a ghastly note of gaiety when you looked beneath and saw huge eyes and transparent skin stretched taut over the bones.

Many lay or sat inert. Those who could move moved. They were filled with restless, feverish excitement.

They had broken down the gates of their cages and wandered from one dusty yard to another.

To them this was marvellous freedom.

Kissed hand

Most heartrending of all was that as one passed skeleton hands would wave, skull-like faces and faces ravaged with skin disease would smile, and feeble voices call greetings.

Two women came up to me, sallow, haggard, with burning eyes—Hungarian Jewesses, looking old as time yet probably quite young as years are reckoned in the outside world.

They asked for food. I had none. I could only give them cigarettes.

They smiled delightedly and then suddenly burst into wild hysterical weeping.

One of them turned away crying in German: "Jews, Jews, Jews. All because we are Jews."

The other suddenly seized my hand and kissed it again and again

Continued Back Page A

INDISPUTABLE PROOF

By the Editor

Here, and in pictures on the back page today, the eyes of British men and women may behold for the first time some of the more revolting features of Nazi guilt. These are official pictures and the News Chronicle has decided to print them, because it is right that the world should see at close quarters indisputable proof of Germany's crimes against the human race.

Other pictures, still more horrible in detail than these, have been circulated by the military authorities, but the selection here published tell their own story plainly enough. Many times reports of Nazi cruelty and torture have seemed almost too monstrous to be true; but here is evidence that none can question and it is proper that decent citizens should look it in the face.

It is welcome news that the Allied commanders on the spot are compelling the neighbouring German population to visit the scenes of this abomination and carry out the task of burying the dead and tending the human wreckage that still survives. Every German in the Reich should be forced to see the handiwork of his fellow-countrymen: careful records should be kept, films made and exhibitions arranged at which attendance should be compulsory.

MAKING THEM SEE THE EVIDENCE
German men and women from Weimar are made to stand in a yard at Buchenwald concentration camp. In front of them is a lorry, piled high with the bodies of prisoners, which was found at the camp

Patton's patrols cross Czech border

THE Germans are "scorching" towns in the way of the armoured thrusts which are this morning threatening Hamburg from points which are only 17 and 18 miles to the south and south-east.

Dispatches from 21st Army Group H.Q. state that only patches of resistance lie ahead of Field-Marshal Montgomery's 7th and 11th Armoured Divisions, advancing over a wide area of the Lueneburg plain.

The Desert Rats (the 7th Armoured Division) have thrust forward four miles to capture Kampen, 10 miles south of the Bremen-Hamburg motor road, while an eight-mile thrust took the 11th into the outskirts of Lueneburg, eight miles from the Elbe south-east of Hamburg.

The front in the south saw the other best gain of the day.

Gen. Patton's forces crossed the border of Czechoslovakia and thrust patrols two miles inside to a point near Gottmansgrun, six miles north of Asch, in the extreme eastern tip of Bohemia.

The invasion point is ten miles east of the German village of Hof—and less than 100 miles from Prague.

[Seventeen miles to the south-east of Asch is Eger, where Henlein founded the Sudeten German Party—Hitler's spearhead in his seizure of Czechoslovakia.]

As soon as the border was crossed a sign was ceremoniously stuck into the ground.

It read: "You are now entering Czechoslovakia by courtesy of the Third Battalion 358th Infantry."

Somebody added a postscript: "Now you may fraternise, by courtesy of the same outfit."

Here is a summary of the latest position on other fronts:

Holland.—The Canadians reached the Zuyder Zee 20 miles east of Amsterdam at the village of Nulde.

New floods

The Germans have released new floods along the old Dutch Grebbe defence line, opening the flood-gates north of Amersfoort to inundate the northern borderland.

The Germans are believed to have 100,000 men in Holland to man the three water defence lines of "Fortress Holland," the inner one being in the outskirt of Amsterdam.

Canadian forces north-west of Arnhem have linked up with the forces which captured Apeldoorn.

Magdeburg.—Street fighting continues in the ruins of the city, according to Berlin.

North of the city only 90 miles separates Gen. Simpson's Ninth U.S. Army and Gen. Zhukov's Red Army troops on the Oder.

Nuremberg has been entered at four points by the U.S. Seventh Army. The city is almost encircled and its defenders, numbering 5,000 to 10,000 have heavy artillery in action.

Stuttgart area.—Further south, troops of the French First Army have encircled and are smashing up a group of 2,400 Germans south of Stuttgart.

Others, in a rapid advance into Wurtemberg province, have captured three communications centres, said the French radio.

LATE NEWS

EIGHTH TAKE ARGENTA

Rome, Wednesday.—Argenta, only remaining centre of German resistance in area west of the Comacchio Lagoon, has been taken by Eighth Army troops, it is announced in Rome.

LONDON DIM-OUT
9.32 p.m.—6.25 a.m.
Moon rises, 12.22 p.m.; sets, 4.48 a.m. tomorrow. Full Moon, April 27

1,000 heavies hit Heligoland

A MASS attack by nearly 1,000 R.A.F. heavy bombers was made yesterday on the naval base of Heligoland, which guards the approach to North-West Germany and Southern Denmark.

Canadians shared in the operation, wrecking the airfield on the neighbouring Island of Dune.

It was the first time the R.A.F. had raided the Heligoland group for 16 months.

The Americans, meanwhile, sent out 750 heavies to bomb railway marshalling yards and transformer stations in Czechoslovakia and Southern Germany.

Poland: three Powers to confer in U.S.

By VERNON BARTLETT

NEGOTIATIONS over the future of Poland will now be transferred from the U.S.S.R. to the U.S.A.

Mr. Eden and Mr. Molotov will, of course, be able to collaborate with Mr. Stettinius, the U.S. Secretary of State, in explaining to the new President the complications of Eastern Europe.

But it is now known that Sir Archibald Clark-Kerr and Mr. Harriman, British and American Ambassadors in Moscow, will also be in Washington.

These two diplomats, with Mr. Molotov, are the members of the commission instructed by the Yalta Conference to invite prominent Poles to meet and to form a Polish National Government.

In time for S.F.

It should thus be possible for the Russians to report to the commission on the negotiations they are believed to have held with Mr. Witos and other Polish leaders from inside Poland.

The commission might approve the names recommended in these Russo-Polish discussions and invite a few Poles from London or elsewhere. A National Polish Government could thus come into existence, still in time to be represented at the San Francisco conference—a subject on which Mr. Stettinius has just received a further Note from Marshal Stalin.

Five Canadian ministers resign

OTTAWA, Wednesday.

MR. MACKENZIE KING, the Canadian Prime Minister, today announced the resignation of five Cabinet Ministers.

He also announced the appointment of seven new members to the Cabinet.

Koniev, through Neisse line, is 70 miles from Patton's tanks

MARSHAL KONIEV'S right-wing troops, breaking through the Neisse River defences, have advanced 15 miles beyond the river, said Berlin last night.

The military spokesman admitted that the Soviet troops just north of the Saxony border had advanced to north-east of Spremberg, 40 miles north-east of Dresden.

This would place Koniev only 70 miles from Gen. Patton's spearheads east of Leipzig.

Koniev's southern wing troops appear to have invaded the Sudetenland, cause of the Munich crisis in 1938. The Berlin spokesman said the Soviet forces were advancing on the Troppau - Hultschin railway, which is in Czech territory near Moravska Ostrava.

"Conveyer belt"

Moscow maintained its security silence, but the Soviet censorship allowed front-line correspondents to speak of successes "in the Berlin direction."

According to German reports nine Soviet armies have been thrown into a concentric offensive on Berlin, and fighting east of the capital has risen to an "incredible pitch."

The Soviet armies were attacking under a permanent air umbrella with "fresh Soviet troops coming forward as though on a conveyer belt."

It was admitted that the Russians had advanced more than halfway from the Oder to the capital.

400 tanks go in

Another German broadcaster spoke of battles raging in the area of Kuestrin, with the Soviets throwing in as many as 400 tanks to support huge forces of infantry.

Berlin reported also: "A third big Russian battle has developed during the last few hours south of Stettin, where Russian regiments made several thrusts in the areas of Schwedt, Fiddichow and Greifenhagen."

This refers to a 17-mile stretch of the Oder extending southwards from a point 12 miles south of Stettin.

Marshal Malinovsky's troops, only nine miles from Brno, the Czech arms centre, were forging ahead against stiff resistance.

Reuter and B.U.P.

New President's first fight

WASHINGTON, Wednesday.

IN Congress today President Truman encountered his first pitched battle, when Republican Representatives launched a full-dress attack on the Government's efforts to gain sweeping new authority for tariff reductions.

The fight occurred at a public hearing opened by the Ways and Means Committee. The Republicans objected to the reading of a statement written by the Secretary of State, Mr. Stettinius, declaring that the new tariff proposals, if they became law, "would give the rest of the world a symbol of tangible proof that we mean what we say about joining with other nations in working towards a more prosperous and more secure world."

Gauleiter of Styria killed

The Gauleiter of Styria, Danziger, has been killed while leading a detachment of Hitler Youth against the Russians, German radio reported last night.

Only one pocket left at Bordeaux

Shaef, Wednesday.—The German pocket north of the Gironde River has been wiped out. The garrison surrendered after being encircled and bombed. Another 700 prisoners were taken, making a total of 6,700 for the whole operation.

South of the estuary the remaining defenders of the approaches to Bordeaux are crowded behind an anti-tank ditch in an area six miles by three.

Chaplin to ask for third trial

Hollywood, Wednesday. — Mr. Charles Chaplin will appeal against the verdict in the paternity suit brought against him by Joan Barry, declaring him to be the father of her 18-month-old baby, Carol Ann. The appeal will take the form of a motion for a third trial.

MAGDEBURG RUINS ARE ALMOST WON

From WILLIAM FORREST
News Chronicle War Correspondent

WITH THE NINTH ARMY, Wednesday.

IN Magdeburg the fight is almost finished. It has been tougher than we expected.

When the last wave of our bombers had passed over the burning city yesterday, the combined armour and infantry attack was launched.

But whatever else our bombing had obliterated, it had failed to extinguish the fanaticism of the defenders.

Against our infantry coming in from the north, suicide squads of Hitler Youth fought for their Fuehrer as they had never fought before. Against the tanks coming in from the south, every sort of gun from flak to panzerfaust was brought into play.

Backs to the Elbe

Bitter fighting raged round the city outskirts till nightfall. This morning, when the assault was resumed, resistance was lighter, and by this afternoon the young, fire-eating Nazi general who commands the garrison had been driven with the remnants of his force into the centre of the city.

Here, with their backs to the Elbe—and all the bridges blown—they were making their last stand.

Women wept

Along the main street leading out of Magdeburg to the west came groups of prisoners. German women standing at the doors of their ruined houses wept as they watched them go by.

On either side flames rose to the smoke-blackened sky from a score of unchecked fires. One more German city had been wiped off the map.

Mopping up Nuremberg Stadium

From JAN YINDRICH
News Chronicle War Correspondent

OUTSIDE NUREMBERG, Wednesday.

THE U.S. Seventh Army has broken through the outer perimeter of Nuremberg's defences and is now attacking the second ring.

Third Division troops have penetrated the second ring at one point. The 46th "Thunderbird" Division smashed through the outer perimeter and has also reached the second ring. It is at present mopping up snipers in the famous Nazi Party sports stadium, where the annual rally was held.

Almost encircled

The Nazi Stadium covers a vast area. It includes three stadiums, a zon and a Congress Holl, where the Nazi hierarchy harangued its youthful followers.

The town is almost encircled by three divisions—the third being the 42nd Infantry "Rainbow" Division, which captured one of three airfields near the town of Furth, which itself is north-east of, and linked to, Nuremberg.

Enemy seamen told: Save your ships

A BROADCAST to German merchant seamen from the Allied Supreme Command last night warned them that the time is drawing near when the North Sea ports of Germany will work under Allied control.

Every available German ship will be required to bring in supplies and to maintain essential traffic between coastal ports and with neighbouring countries, the message stated. In German waters alone there will be work for every ship that can be used.

Organise now

"The fanatics whose power has been broken from the Rhine to the Elbe will try to create starvation and chaos by ordering ships to be scuttled, by sending ships and crews into Norwegian ports, and by recruiting seamen for Volkssturm. By organising now you can frustrate that plan and protect yourselves and your ships."

As Allied troops occupy each port, masters and seamen will cease to be regarded as members of the Wehrmacht. Wages, conditions of service and social insurance benefits will be maintained.

Goebbels today

Goebbels is to speak on the radio today—the eve of Hitler's birthday, the German official news agency announced last night.

Archduke Otto now in Belgium

From Our Own Correspondent

Brussels, Wednesday.—From a reliable source I learn that Archduke Otto of Habsburg [who styles himself Emperor of Austria and King of Hungary] arrived in Belgium some days ago.

Otto's pre-war residence was at the castle of Steenockerzeel, near Brussels, but he did not return there, the estate being occupied by the military.

He is said to have come from Portugal, travelling under the name of the Duke of Bar, and he has already established contact with influential Roman Catholic quarters here.

Trial of Gen. Dentz opens

Paris, Wednesday.—The trial of Gen. Henri Dentz, Vichy High Commissioner of Syria, on charges of intelligence with the enemy, which under French law amounts to high treason, opened today.

The General attempted to excuse his action when, as Governor of Paris, he declared the capital an open city.

Dutch Haw-Haw is captured

Max Blokzijl, known as the Dutch Haw-Haw, has been arrested by Netherlands Forces of the Interior. Also caught was Lemhoff, local leader of the Dutch Nazis, who is accused of having shot many Dutchmen and tortured others.

72 degrees

The shade temperature reached 72 degrees in the Straits of Dover yesterday. At night the barometer was rising.

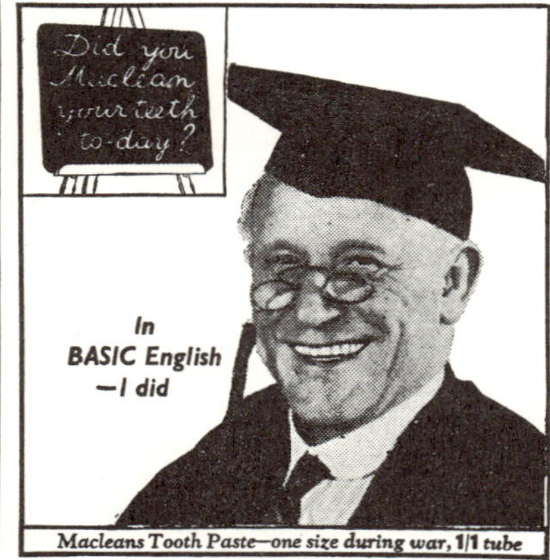

And in this message Colin Wills reports on

THE KIND OF WOMEN WHO STAFFED CONCENTRATION CAMPS

BELSEN (Hanover), Wednesday.

SHE was a stocky young woman, with a large pasty face, pale eyes and fair hair—an embodiment of the mediocre and the nondescript.

She might have brought you a cup of extra cheap coffee or you might have seen her sitting in the dingy outer office of some one-man business, with a typewriter in front of her and a novelette open in the drawer.

Yet as she stood there in the sunshine yesterday, scores of eyes watched her covertly with loathing and fear.

S.S. armband

This pallid nonentity was an evil power. That power rested in what she wore—grey tunic and shirt, white armband, and polished jackboots.

The jackboots were particularly significant, but it was the armband that interested me.

I went up to her and asked: "What are you?" She replied sullenly, "A member of the staff of Belsen concentration camp."

I touched the white armband. "What is this?" "A staff member's armlet."

"Why does it say S.S.?" "It was issued by the S.S."

"The S.S. do not issue such armbands to anybody but S.S., do they?" I demanded. No answer.

"You are S.S., aren't you?"

A long silence, while she gazed at the ground. Then, sullenly, "Yes."

"What did you do here?"

Her head jerked up and her eyes met mine for the first time, full of fear. "I don't understand," she said.

"What work did you do?" I asked. "Oh," she said, with relief, "I just worked in the office."

But that was not what the women told me—the women prisoners of Belsen camp; the gaunt hags of 20 and the walking cadavers of 50 and those unbelievable oddities in that desolate scene—the women who were still plump because they had been there only a week.

They told me how that S.S. girl and her grey-uniformed fellow-members of the women's staff had beaten them with staves and rubber truncheons, kicked them with their polished jackboots and consistently, hour by hour through the interminable days, inflicted on them every indignity and torment their cruel, twisted minds could conceive.

But their hour had come.

It was at noon, a high brilliant noon, that 24 S.S. men and 26 S.S. women were lined up on the square before the commandant's office.

The men were disarmed and searched on the spot, with British bayonets hedging them in and bristling Bren carriers ringing them.

Filmed

The women were marched into a building and searched by nurses from among the prisoners.

Then they emerged into the sunlight, with whirring movie cameras of the Army Film Unit registering close-ups of every face for history—the pasty-faced girl, a great flopping fat middle-aged woman, women whose faces showed marks of cruelty, others showing merely the callousness of animal stupidity, and half a dozen trim, alert young women, handsome in the way some Nazi young men are handsome, with hysterical magnetised vitality.

They were lined up, men and women, and told they were now prisoners. They were warned of the penalties of attempting to escape or to rebel.

They were ordered, in German, "Left turn, quick march."

And then for the first time the women prisoners looked straight into the faces of their jackbooted tormentors, their traitor sisters—for the first time they looked without fear.

Daily Mirror

APL 21

Saturday, April 21, 1945.
No. 12,897 ONE PENNY
Registered at G.P.O. as a Newspaper.

Two Russian spearheads fight within eight miles of Berlin

'LINK-UP IN FEW DAYS' WE RADIO TO SLAVE CAMPS

Diners in Corner House see two killed

By Your Special Correspondent

AS hundreds of people were eating at the Corner House, Tottenham Court-road, London, W., last night, the buzz of conversation was cracked by three revolver shots which killed a father and daughter and wounded a son at one of the tables.

Leaping to their feet, the diners saw the father fall across the table and slide to the floor with blood trickling from his mouth.

His son collapsed immediately after, and his daughter, slid off her chair and slumped on the floor.

A man standing with a smoking revolver in his hand was tackled by an Army officer and another shot went off and flew wild.

Many people panicked and women screamed and fainted in the commotion which followed the shooting.

But a young medical student fought his way through the crowd to give first aid treatment, and a woman called a priest.

The father, John Tratsart, aged fifty-seven, died in his arms. His daughter who was killed was Clair Tratsart, aged twenty-eight.

The wounded son, Hugh, aged seventeen, was taken to hospital.

Police detained another son, Jacques, aged twenty-seven.

Mr. Tratsart stayed in Norbury when he was in London on business. His home is in Northampton.

BERLIN TARGETS

Out of the 800 U.S. bombers which took part in yesterday's operations, 600 Flying Forts went to the Berlin area, attacking rail facilities to the south-west, west, north-west and north.

Blue Arrows advance with Red Army

For the first time since D-Day, SHAEF's great operational wall-map shows that blue arrows marking the Russian offensive have moved into the extreme eastern strip of the map beyond Berlin, says Associated Press.

The Russian positions are taken from the communiques of the previous day.

A SPECIAL MESSAGE FROM ALLIED SUPREME H.Q. WAS BROADCAST LAST NIGHT TO RUSSIANS AND POLES IN THE GAP BETWEEN THE RUSSIAN AND ALLIED ARMIES. IT SAID: "STAY WHERE YOU ARE. IN A FEW DAYS THE GAP WILL BE CLOSED."

"THE Russians are now approaching the boundary of Berlin." With this dramatic announcement last night the German military spokesman revealed that a second Soviet spearhead has driven closer to the capital than the motorised formations which are eight miles from the city's outskirts at Hangelsberg.

While the first force, with tanks in the lead, is fighting round the lakes of the Hangelsberg Forest, which reaches up to Berlin's eastern boundary, the second force is even nearer, battling against tank buster formations among the trees of the Sternebeck Forest.

The Germans are fighting to the last gasp, but Soviet masses—"attacking without regard for losses" — are surely and grimly overwhelming them.

Meanwhile Moscow maintained a serene official silence, though correspondents were allowed to cable that the war has "reached its last quarter of an hour," and that soon the crash of bombs on Berlin would be joined by the whistle of Russian shells.

Koniev's men are twenty-six miles from Dresden and fifty-five miles from General Patton's Americans.

Huns wanted to wear gloves to bury victims...

From DAVID WALKER

WITH THE U.S. NINTH ARMY, Friday.

AS we advance it is the same story of terrible atrocities. I came across another horror today at Gardeslegen.

Here the Huns burnt a thousand men alive, and the population have been forced to give them a decent burial, carrying the remains to a proper grave.

One or two of the Germans wanted to wear gloves, but this was forbidden, and with their bare hands they had to carry those burnt-out wrecks of humanity to a great cemetery that will for all time be a monument to German bestiality.

The 5th Division has just overrun another couple of V 2 factories, and once again we had to wade through a wide sea of misery with starving foreign labourers everywhere.

We found British Tommies, too, but, as usual, we can't give their names, though they are longing for their families to know.

Montgomery's men fight U-Boats

THE German Command has lost its grip on the great ports. A report flashed to Montgomery's headquarters last night indicated the start of a retreat.

The line the Nazis intended to hold from Bremen to Hamburg is fractured on a wide front. Only the northern exits out of Bremen are now left to the Germans.

A surprise twenty-mile thrust by tanks and infantry of the Guards Armoured Division is threatening the great German naval port of Bremerhaven at the Elbe estuary.

Submarines in the Elbe shelled British forces and our guns and planes hit back. In the battle with German warships bombers set a cruiser on fire.

The Germans in their counter-attack on the U.S. Ninth Army front have advanced their main forces three miles and their tanks fifteen miles.

NOT SO GOOD

The barometer fell all day in the Straits of Dover yesterday, and the week's brilliant spell of summery weather may not last over the week-end. Maximum temperature was 70, but by 9 p.m. the thermometer had dropped to 57.

LABOUR'S PROGRAMME FOR THE PEACE

Nationalise Bank of England, fuel, steel and transport

By Your Political Correspondent

LEADERS of the Labour Party have decided what they will do if their party is returned to power after the General Election.

They have drawn up a plan which they claim contains all that can be accomplished in the life of a single Parliament Main points are:

NATIONALISATION OF
Bank of England.
Coal mines, gas and electricity undertakings.
Inland transport (all road, rail, air and canal services).
Iron and steel industry.

Nationalisation of the land is not considered an immediate issue, but Labour "will work towards this" and as a first step local authorities will be given wider and speedier powers to acquire land.

Fair compensation is promised, but there will be a benefit for public funds from "Betterment"—that is, the increase in value of land as a result of local development.

These points are set out in a manifesto issued by the Labour Party today and which will be on sale next week, entitled "Let Us Face the Future" (price 2d.).

It explains how Labour intends to use industry in the service of the nation and in addition to the nationalisation of the three major industries and the Bank of England there is planned

Public supervision of monopolies and cartels.

(Cartoon and Editorial Comment—Page Two)

Any State help necessary to get our export trade on its feet —but on condition that the industry is efficient
Priorities in the use of raw material for essential industries, food prices to be controlled and homes for the people to come before mansions.
Rents and the prices of necessities of life to be controlled, to prevent inflation.
Better organisation of Government departments so that they will act as a spur for industry and not choke it with red tape.

Housing, says the manifesto, will be one of the earliest tests of Labour's determination to put the nation first. It may mean centralised purchasing, pooling of materials, and price control.

They will create a Ministry of Housing and Planning combining the housing powers of the Ministry of Health with the Ministry of Town and Country Planning.

In addition, Labour pledges itself to carry out the social security plans, to ensure work for all, and to see that money is no longer the passport to the best health treatment.

A Labour Government will keep and extend the new food

Continued on Back Page

Daily Mail
NO. 15,277 ONE PENNY ** FOR KING AND EMPIRE MONDAY, APRIL 23, 1945
LATE WAR NEWS

The last two miles: Berlin battles to the death with Red Army

NEARING UNTER DEN LINDEN

POZNAN — WARSAW — MINSK — KIEV — KHARKOV — ROSTOV — STALINGRAD

1,400 MILES

Link-up reported: 3-Power statement prepared

UNDER a pall of smoke from hundreds of shell-torn buildings, crack Russian assault troops were last night hacking their way to the heart of Berlin in a great scything arc from north-west to south-east. Spearheads are only two miles from Unter den Linden—Berlin's Piccadilly—according to the latest unofficial reports from Moscow.

A link-up between the American and Russian armies south of Berlin, in the Dresden area, is expected hourly. A joint Allied announcement that forward elements have met will be made, according to U.S. Ninth Army H.Q.

Walter Farr, with the U.S. First Army, cables that German reports say the Russians are only 12 miles from the First Army near Freiberg, between Dresden and Chemnitz. General Hodges' tanks are advancing to Marshal Koniev's forces under a security silence.

Observers at Supreme Allied H.Q. in Paris believe the link-up has already been made. But it has not yet been officially announced.

Patch 53 miles from Munich

When it comes it will seal off Northern Germany from the Bavarian Redoubt, now more than ever threatened by a new advance by the U.S. Seventh Army and a French drive across the Danube, through the Black Forest, to the Swiss border after the capture of Stuttgart.

French troops have reached Ludwigshafen, on the extreme western tip of Lake Constance, 40 miles from the Austrian border. They have taken Sigmaringen, to the north, and Freiberg, near the Rhine, to the north-west. Seventh Army troops have thrust through Bavaria to within 53 miles of Munich. They have captured intact a bridge over the Danube at Dillingen.

Rumours, so far unconfirmed from any other source, are reaching Stockholm that negotiations for Berlin's capitulation are going on between the Germans and the Russians.

The German-controlled Scandinavian Telegram Bureau, quoting Berlin reports, said that it was reported that Goebbels, despite his promises that he and his family would remain in the capital, had left for Mecklenburg.

Berlin's last stand is being directed by Lieut.-General Reimann, appointed military commander by Goebbels, says the German radio.

Certain quarters of Berlin are being defended by companies of boys of 12 and 14 belonging to the Hitler Youth Movement, according to a Stockholm report.

The boys receive a badge for each tank destroyed and several 12-years-old boys are said to be wearing five badges.

FIRES RAGING IN BERLIN

MOSCOW, Sunday.

ONE of the greatest concentrations of men and weapons ever assembled for the storming of a city is moving along Hitler's great broad motor-roads into Berlin.

At cross-roads, Red Army girls, wearing white gauntlets, are calmly directing streams of Soviet tanks, motorised infantry, and guns.

Stalin's troops, pushing in from the east, have crossed the Ringbahn, the suburban circular railway which runs round the city's administrative centre.

The advance is being directed along the line of the Landsberger Allee and the Frankfurter Allee in a converging movement on the heart of Berlin from points north of the Spree.

The southernmost of the two Soviet storm groups is reported to be pushing through side streets towards the Schlesischer Station near the north bank of the Spree.

PARK ABLAZE

Heavy shells are being pumped ceaselessly into Unter den Linden, the Friedrichstrasse, and the Charlottenburger Chaussee. Great fires are raging in the Tiergarten, Berlin's Hyde Park, and the hulks of great stone buildings which survived the Allied bombings.

Hundreds of the dreaded Russian rocket-firing Katushas, spreading fire and destruction, levelled the eastern outskirts of the city blasting a path for the infantrymen storming their way towards the Alexanderplatz.

The Luftwaffe is hurling its last planes into a savage attempt to delay the final march through the city. They are bombing the autobahn from Küstrin to Berlin, the great artery along which

BACK PAGE—Col. FOUR

CAPITAL PANICS AFTER BREAK-IN

Berliners cry 'Get away from Russians'

From **RALPH HEWINS,**
Daily Mail Special Correspondent

STOCKHOLM, Sunday.

UNCONTROLLABLE panic has seized the civilian population of Berlin. The cry has gone up, "Get away from the Russians," and a mad rush to escape from the city to the west has begun.

These are authentic facts telephoned direct to Stockholm by Swedish correspondents in Berlin

In the alarm and chaos which followed the Russian break-in in the north-eastern and southern outskirts yesterday the German censorship collapsed, and for the first time messages came through "in clear."

They told of desperate scrambles by thousands of people to board westbound underground trains—scrambles in which great numbers lost their lives.

Thousands more choked the roads to the west as they fought to get out of range of the Russian shells falling in the centre of the city.

Hopeless struggle

At 6.50 this morning the telephones were suddenly cut at the Berlin end and they have been "dead" ever since.

Some reports from the capital have continued to come in by way of Hamburg, where the lines are still open. They tell of a hopeless struggle by the military to regain control of the situation.

Shortly before the Berlin phones were cut the correspondent of the *Dagens Nyheter* said:

"This will probably be the last time I shall get through before the city is occupied.

"Shells are dropping near where I am telephoning. They are hitting the centre of the city. Many are falling in the Unter den Linden, the Leipzigerstrasse, and around the Brandenburger Tor."

His voice could scarcely be heard in Stockholm above the roar of the bombardment.

During an earlier call this correspondent expressed the city's surprise at the sudden deterioration of the situation.

Fight for trains

Telling the story of the crazy rush to get out of the capital, the correspondent of *Svenska Dagbladet* said:

"Crowds before the entrances to underground stations rioted when they could not get in.

"Below people were packed like sardines on the platforms, and when each train pulled in—nearly every one was already fully laden—there was a wild fight to board it.

"Wounded soldiers direct from the front were shoved mercilessly out of the way."

The correspondent of the *Stockholms Tidningen* said: "In this situation a large proportion of Berlin's inhabitants are hailing the Americans as liberators.

"Everywhere one hears Berliners asking each other: 'Why don't the Americans get going across the Elbe?' 'Why don't they advance faster to protect us from the Russians?'"

Berlin stations off the air

Daily Mail Radio Station

None of the known Berlin radio stations could be heard last night. A short-wave station was working on the overseas wavelength, but it did not announce whether the broadcast came from Berlin or another town.

Bremen—or a station which called itself Bremen radio—came on after 8 p.m. Hamburg faded out at about 8 p.m. Munich was heard at 9.20 p.m.

Hitler orders guerilla war

WESTERN FRONT, Sunday.

HITLER has told German troops, in his latest Order of the Day, to adopt Partisan warfare behind enemy lines.

The Order says: "We have got to adopt the same method which was shown and taught to us by the Russians in 1942-44.

"Our men have to infiltrate through the lines by ones or in small groups, supplied with sufficient ammunition, petrol, and other materials, and must attack only if they reach the rear areas where they can achieve complete surprise against the most sensitive points."—*Reuter and B.U.P.*

500 NAZI 'WRENS' CAPTURED

Their admiral, too

From **ALEXANDER CLIFFORD,**
Daily Mail Special Correspondent

BUXTEHUDE, Sunday.

FIVE Hundred German "Wrens" and a rear-admiral were waiting to surrender to the 11th Hussars when they drove into Buxtehude this morning.

The village lies just south of the Elbe and about 12 miles south-west of Hamburg. It is the administrative H.Q. of the enemy North Sea Command. And it surrendered almost without a shot just as an attack was being organised to take it.

I found the "Wrens" thronging the big dining hall of their ultra-modern barracks. Only the N.C.O.s wore uniform—a grey rather nondescript uniform, usually with baggy ski-ing trousers. The rest were dressed just as they pleased.

A sour-faced Oberführerin told me sharply that they were all engaged on secretarial duties. She said they were in the service of the Navy, but since they were unarmed they expected to be treated the same as the Red Cross.

She broke off and briskly detailed a patrol of girls to go to the other end of the room and collect some potatoes that were being boiled for them.

The "Wrens" crowded chattering to the windows to watch our armoured cars, but they fell silent when they saw Admiral Siegfried Engel being driven in one.

He was the commander of the

BACK PAGE—Col. SIX

Million acres flooded

WITH FIRST CANADIAN ARMY IN HOLLAND, Sunday.

AIR photos to-day showed for the first time the full extent of the disastrous flooding of the north-west polder of Holland.

What a week ago was a 50,000-acre belt of rich farmland is now a great black sheet of water, 16ft. deep.

Not a house, tree, or road is to be seen—except for a few dark blotches to mark their place beneath the surface.

No living thing could have sur-

2

vived this torrent which swept in from the Zuider Zee on April 18 when the Germans dynamited the great main dike.

In this polder area lived 15,000 Dutch farmers. There is nothing to indicate that the Germans gave them any warning or that there was any large-scale evacuation.

It was one of the world's most modern farming communities. It was won from the sea in 1930, and development went on for 15 years. The Germans erased it in 15 minutes.

Air photos taken a few hours after the great dike was blown up show waters foaming through the gaps and sweeping relentlessly across the polder.

The whole of West Holland lies at the mercy of the Germans. They can blow up as many dikes as they wish. Already 1,000,000 acres of farmland lie under the water they have released.—*Reuter.*

13 BERLIN SUBURBS CAPTURED

Moscow communiqué reports 13 suburbs of Berlin captured, including Weissensee, in north-east. At least 13,000 Germans taken prisoner on the Berlin front in the past five days. In the Dresden area, Finsterwalde has been captured.

Death camp stories did not tell all—MPs

Report this week

By Daily Mail Reporter

THE eight M.P.s and two peers who flew to Germany to collect their own evidence of the Nazi death camps came back to London yesterday.

They saw only Buchenwald. But they rejected reports that they were not given enough time in the camp and that the military authorities were brusque and unhelpful.

Their trip took three days, leaving one full day in Germany.

After seeing the first camp, they were to have gone to another, in which was a greater proportion of women and children.

But in Buchenwald there was so much to see, so many prisoners to be interviewed, that the visit stretched to four or five hours and the second was abandoned.

By splitting up, the party covered a lot of ground, and each member collected his share of the facts.

PAST DESCRIBING

"There has been no exaggeration—it beggars description," said Sir Henry Morris-Jones (Lib.-Nat., Denbigh) when the ten returned to London.

The one woman of the party, Mrs. Mavis Tate (Con., Frome), said: "Never have I seen so much suffering."

Mr. Tom Driberg (Ind., Maldon) told me: "The war correspondent stories have omitted much that is terrible. One feared to trust one's own eyes."

All in the party said that the military authorities did everything to help them.

They met three representatives of the U.S. Congress—Mrs. Claire Luce, Mr. Leonard W. Hall, and Mr. John C. Kunkel—and together saw the death chamber and the electric lift to Buchenwald's crematorium.

AMONG CHILDREN

Mrs. Tate spent much time among the 900 children left alive in the camp. One of those she talked with was a 14-years-old boy from Poland.

He had been there five years; had seen his brother shot and the rest of the family taken away to be gassed in Nazi vans. Since then he had worked 14 hours a day.

A written report is to be presented to Parliament, probably before the end of this week.

Earl Stanhope and Lord Addison were the House of Lords representatives, and the other M.P.s in the party were Sir Archibald Southby (Con., Epsom), Mr. Ness Edwards (Lab., Caerphilly), Mr. H. Graham White (Lib., Birkenhead, E.), Mr. S. Silverman (Lab., Nelson and Colne), and Lieut.-Colonel E. T. R. Wickham (Con., Taunton).

Footnote.—At General Eisenhower's request, a U.S. delegation of six Senators, six members of the House of Representatives, and 17 prominent publishers and editors is leaving by air soon to inspect German concentration camps. Its findings will be made known to the San Francisco Conference, says a *Reuter* message from Washington.

Dieppe VC back from Nazi camp

Canada's first V.C. of this war, Lieut.-Colonel Cecil Merritt, has arrived in England after 2½ years' captivity in Germany.

He won the V.C. for fearless leadership at Dieppe in 1942.

Buchenwald: What two Germans say

Hitler still 'good'

WEIMAR, Sunday.

AFTER a tour of the Buchenwald death camp to-day Rosalind von Schirach, tall, grey-haired sister of the notorious Baldur von Schirach, former leader of the Hitler Youth Movement and later Gauleiter of Vienna, said: "This barbarity has thrown Germany back into the Dark Ages."

But she still insists that Hitler is a "great and good" man.

Rosalind is living in a luxurious mansion with her father, Karl Baily Norris von Schirach, a theatrical producer. Their loyalty to Hitler has been unshaken by the shock they received when, with 1,000 Weimar citizens, they were shown the camp at Buchenwald.

The 70-years-old father said: "Hitler could not have known that such barbarities were being committed. I know the Führer. He came to see me in 1935, and he was so polite, kind, and cultured, and took such an interest in dramatic art and its application to society that I am convinced he is a man of great humanity.

"There is a ring round him. I have been told that Himmler has been at Buchenwald, and I believe he knew more of what was going on."—*Reuter.*

JETS NEARLY BEAT US

U.S. officer explains

WITH THE NINTH AIR FORCE, Sunday.—Germany's jet propelled planes came within a hair's breadth of giving the Germans air superiority over the Allied Air Forces, a high officer of the U.S. Ninth Air Force said to-night.

He explained: "We realised in February that unless we concentrated on knocking out jet-plane production we would lose our air superiority by July."—*B.U.P.*

WINDY IN THE STRAIT

Strait of Dover weather yesterday: Windy; maximum day temperature, 57; dusk temperature, 49; barometer steady.

U.S. MEN RADIO RED ARMY

'Hello . . hello, it's the Russians, all right'

From **WALTER FARR,** Daily Mail Special Correspondent

U.S. FIRST ARMY, Sunday Night.

AT seven o'clock this morning Private James Clark, of Philadelphia, listening-in on an armoured column radio, suddenly heard strange voices. He called a signals officer and said: "Say, Captain, I can hear a heck of a lot of rolling r's on this radio. Could that be the Russians?"

The radio was hooked up to a phone which, in turn, rang near the tent of Private John Dadovich, of Minneapolis, who is a Russian-speaking American.

Dadovich listened-in on the phone to get quick identification. "It's the Russians, all right," he shouted. "This is a Russian tank spearhead. An officer is giving orders about the closing of the gap between us."

This was the first actual radio contact between our field elements, although some Russian voices had been heard earlier.

Women's voices

Listening-in on one of our tank's radios, I heard a Russian officer say: "It's nearly finished. It's finished." Then he issued a series of coded messages.

Some of the dramatic messages guiding the approaching Red Army columns are issued by Red Army women operators. Their voices sound rich, musical, very clear—and very military.

We were able to listen-in to the Russians' last battles as they approached. Russian tank commanders shouted to their gunners over the radio: "Get guns ready. . . . Fire!"

There was a pause. Then other voices shouted "Good."

'They hear us'

From **NOEL MONKS,**
Daily Mail Special Correspondent

U.S. NINTH ARMY, Sunday.

FORWARD elements of the American 83rd Infantry Division established contact by field radio to-day with advancing Red Army columns. It happened soon after midday. For several hours at a reconnaissance command post we had been making attempts.

We could hear reports and orders of Red tank commanders, but could get no reply to our repeated calls.

Suddenly Lieut. Theo Prissjaschzun, of Kiev, our Russian liaison officer, cried excitedly "They hear us, they hear us."

For more than the hundredth time he had broadcast "Hello, hello, Red Army. This is Lieut. Prissjaschzun with American 83rd Division. Can you hear me?"

This time he had got a reply: "What do you want?"

Our situation here is peculiar. We are stopped dead within our bridgehead across the Elbe, with only the slightest enemy opposition before us and enough tanks and supplies to take us to Berlin. We are waiting as calmly as possible for the coming of the Russians.

British capture Marlene's sister

And a complete circus

WITH THE BRITISH SECOND ARMY, Sunday.

THE British Second Army's mixed bag during the past 24 hours includes:

A circus with two bears and two elephants;

Marlene Dietrich's sister;

Major von Cramm, brother of Baron Gottfried von Cramm, Davis Cup tennis player; and

Two genuine "werewolves."

The circus was overrun by troops and tanks, and the bears were wounded.

Major von Cramm, who surrendered, was formerly a Luftwaffe pilot.

The "werewolves," Hamburg youths aged 18 and 21, had been sent through the German lines for espionage and sabotage.—Reuter.

BLACK-OUT IN STREETS

May 1 to July 15

Britain's streets will again be blacked out from May 1 until July 15, though the black-out of windows ends to-day.

The new black-out will be enforced so that road lighting engineers can work on the street lamps and restore something very near pre-war lighting by the time the lights go up again.

The lights then may be up to 70 per cent. of the pre-war brightness, Mr. H. O. Davies, secretary of the Association of Lighting Engineers said yesterday.

9 OF 18 NAZI RAIDERS DOWN

By Daily Mail Reporter

THE Luftwaffe made a futile effort to raid British shipping on Saturday afternoon.

Of 18 torpedo-bombers seen flying in formation towards the Scottish coast nine were shot down in flames and the rest turned tail.

The Nazi planes were overtaken 150 miles from the coast by a large force of Coastal Command Mosquitoes returning from an attack on shipping in the Kattegat.

The Mosquitoes swooped on the enemy from dead astern and the fight—if it could be called a fight—was over in a few minutes. No R.A.F. plane was lost.

Wing-Commander C. M. Foxley, leading the Mosquitoes, said: "The engagement was over so quickly that I did not get a chance to sight one myself."

Another pilot said: "Five times I sighted an enemy plane but each time another Mosquito shot it down before I had time to draw a bead. The sea appeared full of blazing aircraft."

Weather
OCCASIONAL RAIN
(Details on Page 2)

3c in Suburbs
5c Elsewhere
in United States

Vol. 21. No. 261. C NEW YORK, TUESDAY, APRIL 24, 1945 FINAL 6 A.M. ★★★★

RUSSIANS HOLD HALF OF BERLIN

Yanks Close on Alpine Retreat

Stories on Page 3

(Sig. Corps Photo via International SOUNDphoto)

GEN. 'IKE' SEES NAZI SAVAGERY Charred bodies of prisoners, burned by Nazis in concentration camp at Gotha, Germany, are viewed by Gen. Eisenhower (third from left), and other high officers including Gen. Bradley (beside Gen. Eisenhower) and Gen. Patton (right).

A NAZI HAS WRITTEN TO ME

By The Editor

(SEE PAGE 6)

AIR FORCE NEWS

ITALY-BALKANS-N. AFRICA-EGYPT-LEVANT-IRAQ-PERSIA-E & W. AFRICA-SUDAN-ADEN-RHODESIA-MADAGASCAR-GIBRALTAR

MARRIED WAAF WILL BE FIRST OUT

(SEE PAGE 10)

No. 104 | FREE TO ALLIED AIR FORCE PERSONNEL | APRIL 24, 1945

M.P.s Fly To Germany At C in C's Call

BRITAIN ENRAGED BY NEW NAZI HORRORS

'High Authority's' New Evidence

PUBLIC opinion in Britain has never been so shocked and enraged in all the years of war as it has been over the terrible report of atrocities in German concentration camps. These hell-spots were captured by the advancing Allied troops, and following their discover, General Eisenhower immediately contacted Prime Minister Churchill, asking him to send a Parliamentary delegation to investigate.

The response was immediate, and the names of volunteers were submitted to the Speaker the same afternoon. Eight representatives of all political parties, flew to Germany at once.

The press at home has expressed its horror at the sickening evidence with grave leaders, and the evidence and pictures have been published without apology.

Some of the pictures have reached Air Force News office, including the two given on this page. We are not going to apologise for printing them either.

They are dreadful, and they will shock you. But this is a case where you should know the truth, coming as it does from unimpeachable sources.

You will share the anger of our folk at home that such things are possible in this century by a nation that called itself civilised.

1 These men are British soldiers. Four years ago they were fit, strong men, and they were taken prisoners by the Germans. This microgram picture from London shows them after their release last week at Gettingen by the advancing Allies. They were almost too weak and emaciated to smile. Broken through lack of food, they had been sent to a prison hospital. What they needed was not medicine but food.

2 These men, women, and children were Soviet citizens of the Lvov region. This picture has been released by the Russian Extraordinary State Committee just as it was discovered in the files of the Zolochev Gestapo. The committee which has been investigating German crimes in that area, declares that the Germans executed hundreds of thousands of Soviet civilians, war prisoners and slave workers. The dead bodies were heaped up like this after their murder before mass burial.

Daily Mirror

APL 28

Saturday, April 28, 1945
No. 12,903 ONE PENNY
Registered at G.P.O. as a Newspaper.

Four men in a Jeep SPLIT THE REICH, LINK WITH SOVIET

AMERICAN and Russian soldiers were slapping each other on the back, making whoopee in dumb show, toasting each other in everything from vodka and champagne to captured wines of Germany on the Elbe last night.

In Moscow 324 guns thundered a salute to the link-up which has cut Germany in two. Marshal Stalin broadcast personally his greetings to the Allies.

The radios of the world were broadcasting in many languages the announcements of Mr. Churchill, Mr. Truman and Marshal Stalin which gave the great news that the link-up had taken place near Torgau, northwest of Leipzig, on Thursday.

In the heart of Germany, Bill Robertson, of Los Angeles, Jim McDonald, from Massachusetts, Frank Huff, of Virginia, and Paul Staub, who comes from the Bronx, felt that they had caused it all.

For if Lieutenant Robertson, Corporal McDonald and Privates Huff and Staub weren't the first to meet the Red Army, at least they were the first to bring back proof, in the shape of a Soviet major, a captain, a lieutenant and a private.

Bill Robertson and a Russian private met on the sloping girders of a blown-up railway bridge.

"I didn't know what to say," Robertson confessed. "I pounded him on the back, shook his hand and said 'Hallo' in English."

Commanding the Russian platoon which met the Americans was Lieutenant Alexander Sylvashko, and he didn't know what to do, either.

"I didn't know whether to go riding with them, to drink vodka with them or to go and fight the Germans with

Continued on Back Page

★ First man to meet the Russians in the historic Torgau link-up was 2nd Lieutenant W. D. Robertson, of Los Angeles, photographed here with Lieutenant Alexander Sylvashko. ★

"GOERING SHOT"

Mussolini is arrested at lunch

MUSSOLINI has been arrested at Lake Como, said the Free Milan radio last night.

Turin patriots surprised his party at lunch at the small town of Nesso, a convenient spot for escape into Switzerland.

Mussolini's wife tried to enter Switzerland yesterday, but was turned back, says Swiss radio.

Marshal Rudolfo Graziani, C.-in-C. of the Fascist armed forces and former Minister of Defence in Mussolini's Government, has also been taken prisoner.

According to a German diplomat who has reached Switzerland from Munich, Goering has been shot.

Last Monday, said the diplomat, Goering wrote to Hitler asking him to stop the fighting to spare further shedding of German blood.

Himmler sent his own bodyguard to Goering's home. Goering then killed his wife, daughters and himself.

Another version was that the bodyguard mowed down Goering and his wife.

STILL TRYING

William (Haw-Haw) Joyce is in Hamburg. Speaking on the Hamburg radio last night he said Hitler was doing his best to stem the Russian surge westwards

A TORY SAYS IT —TORY VICTORIES WERE DISASTERS

MR. L. S. AMERY, Secretary for India, Tory M.P. who at the beginning of the war made a sensational attack on Chamberlain ("In the name of God, go!") last night made another sensational declaration—directed this time at his own party.

Addressing the annual meeting of Birmingham Unionist Association this old Diehard, now at seventy-two approaching the end of his political career, confessed:

"I REGARD THE 1924 AND 1935 CONSERVATIVE VICTORIES AS DISASTERS BOTH FOR THE PARTY AND THE NATION.

"In 1924 we won our election on the Zinovieff letter, but we threw overboard all positive economic policy and left ourselves helpless in face of the growing evil of chronic unemployment.

"In 1935 we won on a professed support of the policy of sanctions against Italy, while disavowing any intention of rearming to face the inevitable consequence of driving Mussolini into Hitler's arms."

Mr. Amery said that Tories were in no haste to end the coalition, but urgent decisions would have to be taken on many questions on which they and their Socialist colleagues found it hard to agree.

"Even the worst decision in such cases may be better than no decision, and party conflict better than procrastination," he added.

Lack of unity of purpose before the war brought us to the verge of ruin.

"We cannot afford in future to be divided on the essentials of foreign policy or on the needs of defence.

"We cannot afford to let down our industrial efficiency or to allow agriculture once more to become a derelict industry."

FRENCH: WE STAY

The French Cabinet yesterday backed up General de Gaulle in his refusal to give way to the request of the American Military Government in Germany that French troops now occupying Stuttgart should evacuate it in favour of American troops

7 Allied forces racing nearer Hitler redoubt

AS British, American and Russian troops break German resistance in North and Central Germany, seven Allied armies are closing on Hitler's "last stand" redoubt in the mountains of Austria and Bavaria.

General George Patton's Third Army, which has smashed across the Austrian frontier, is only sixty-five miles north-east of Salzburg, eastern pivot of the redoubt.

Regensburg (Ratisbon), sixty-two miles from Munich, birthplace of the Nazi Party, was cleared yesterday.

GENERALS CAUGHT

Seventh Army troops were eighty-five miles from Innsbruck — Austrian western anchor of the redoubt—while French troops were pushing on strongly 100 miles away.

At the same time two Red Armies were coming up from the east and the British and American 8th and 5th Armies raced towards the redoubt from Italy (see back page).

In North Germany, British troops mopping-up Bremen yesterday captured two generals—complete with their staffs—a vice-admiral and sixteen of his U-boats and a destroyer.

Major-General Werner Siber, commander of the Bremen garrison and base installations, surrendered to Major Victor W Beckhurst, commander of a company of the Somerset Light Infantry, and the major's batman in a five-decker pillbox

RASPBERRY

Major-General Becker, operational commander of all Bremen troops, surrendered a few hours later.

He gave the Nazi salute.

"The Brigadier gave him a raspberry, a good old-fashioned parade - ground rocket," said a British officer who saw the incident

Bremen is now clear except for the docks and U-boat pens above the river at the north-western end of the city.

LATE LONDON EDITION

No. 30,873 SATURDAY, APRIL 28, 1945 ONE PENNY

LINK-UP

Secret is out: Americans and Russians met at Torgau on Elbe at 4.20 p.m. Wednesday

THEY have linked up. These words, flashed round the world last night, announced the conclusion of two of the greatest military marches in modern history.

From the banks of the Volga the Red Army has battled 1,400 miles to the west; from the beaches of Normandy the Americans have fought 700 miles to the east, and at Torgau on the Elbe, in the heart of the Reich, they have at last met.

From London, from Moscow, from Washington the news was announced simultaneously.

At 4.20 p.m. on Wednesday patrols met; on the following afternoon the link was firmly forged.

Actually there were two points of contact—the first at Torgau; the second 25 miles to the south-east at Groba, a suburb of Riesa.

The three leaders issued messages. "This," said President Truman, "is not the hour of final victory in Europe, but the hour draws near."

"Our task and our duty are to complete the destruction of the enemy," said Marshal Stalin.

"We meet in true and victorious comradeship," declared Mr. Churchill. "Let us all march forward upon the foe."

A picture the world will never forget

The first handshakes. Across a rent in a bridge over the River Elbe at Torgau Russian soldiers and American soldiers stretch out their hands. They gripped, and the link-up was complete. More pictures on Back Page

OFFICER IN JEEP MADE CONTACT

Home-made banner waved from castle

From STANLEY BARON
News Chronicle War Correspondent

WITH KONIEV'S FIRST UKRAINIAN ARMY EAST OF THE ELBE, Thursday (delayed).

SEC.-LT. WILLIAM D. ROBERTSON, of Los Angeles and the Headquarters C.O. of the First Battalion of the 273rd Infantry, U.S. 69th Division, looks at the moment like being officially credited as the first man to shake hands with a soldier of Koniev's First Ukrainian Army, but I do not suppose we shall ever be sure.

This has been a wild day following a fantastic night, during which at least a couple of rival claims have come in from two different places.

PRISON CAMP—ONCE

All I am personally certain of is that I am here in the mess hall of a German barracks with the Elbe flowing fast about 250 yards behind, that I have just had lunch and drunk "victory and death to the Fascist invader" with the cropped-headed commander of the 173rd Regiment of the Ukrainian 58th (Honour Guard) Division, that Torgau, once the location of one of the biggest stalags in Germany, with thousands of British prisoners, is now an empty shell behind me with scarcely half a dozen Germans showing their heads and that the American front lines are 25 miles to the rear.

I came into Torgau this morning with a platoon of riflemen, the second to cross No Man's Land after Robertson's jeep, out on a lonely sortie, had made one contact at 4.20 last night. We drove into the market square—I shall go back to the journey in a minute—and found it completely empty.

For a minute we circled round. Then from under an arch walked three Russian soldiers, Lt. Ivan Feodor Kuzminski, Pte. Peter Melehen, and another. They paused and then they ran with arms outstretched, grabbing at any American's hand they could see.

Kuzminski spun round with a G. I. Joe clutching each hand. They thumped each other on the back. We all wrung hands. We all thumped. If there had been any lurking suspicion that any political decision on zones of interest would get in the way of our rapture at this meeting it was gone in a second. We were allies, we met and rejoiced, and I can think of nothing so exciting, so warm, so human as this encounter in this alien square.

Kuzminski began to make a little speech, but it was drowned in exclamations and shouts. Out came the cameras for the inevitable arm-in-arm pictures. Then we saw a couple of Russian fighter planes weaving overhead.

CASTLE WITH A HISTORY

Kuzminski pointed out the road to the river and we drove on down the street past the Rose Gasthaus, set on fire by shelling when Koniev's men arrived on the opposite bank on Tuesday, and still flaming.

There ahead was the Elbe, 100 yards wide and flowing fast, both girder bridges north and south down in the river, and the ancient castle, with a hole in its roof, rising up to

Continued Back Page A

Mussolini captured and Goering is reported shot dead

MUSSOLINI captured, Hitler reported dying in a Berlin deep shelter; Goering dead, either by his own hand or the executioners—this is the main news this morning of the enemy leaders.

Official Milan announcements disclosed that Italian guerillas seized Mussolini at Nesso, on Lake Como. He was trying to escape into Switzerland. With him were Graziani, chief of the Fascist armies, Pavolini, Fascist secretary-general, and Farinacci, the ex-Duce's lieutenant.

Mussolini, Pavolini and Farinacci now face trial by a people's court, Rome radio said this morning. What is to happen to Graziani is not stated.

The wife of Mussolini and their son Vittorio tried to get into Switzerland, but were turned back at the frontier.

Hitler, according to Stockholm diplomatic circles, is completely helpless, and probably unconscious, owing to brain hemorrhage. He is in a concrete shelter in the Bendlerstrasse.

Himmler's answer

Nazi leaders who remain are said to be planning to conceal the news of his expected death to stave off the mass capitulation that would follow.

Now Goering. The latest news of the deposed Luftwaffe leader came from a German diplomat who has reached Switzerland from Munich.

Goering, according to the diplomat, pleaded with Hitler to accept the consequences of a lost war. Himmler replied—by sending his bodyguard to Goering's home.

Ordered to execute judgment on himself, Goering shot his daughters and then himself. Another version is that Himmler's men did the shotting.

M. Paul Reynaud, French Premier at the time of the fall of France, M. Edouard Daladier, a former French Premier, and Gen. Gamelin, former French C.-in-C., who have been held by the Germans since the Occupation, have crossed into Switzerland, says Paris radio.

(Goering: By Vernon Bartlett, Back Page.)

On other fronts

HERE are the high-lights of yesterday's reports from Europe's main battle areas:

Berlin Front.—The Tempelhof aerodrome was captured yesterday. Koniev's troops took the suburbs of Neukoelln, Steglitz and Schmargendorf. Prisoners totalled 11,500.

Marshal Zhukov's troops are already 50 miles west of the centre of Berlin. An Order of the Day announced that they had captured Rathenau, at that distance from the capital; Potsdam, which is 15 miles out; and the Berlin suburb of Spandau. All were defence bases.

Another Order showed that Rokossovsky's troops have driven 25 miles west of the Oder to capture Prenzlau, Angermuende, 21 miles south of Prenzlau, also was taken.

An Order to Koniev announced the capture of Wittenburg, on the Elbe, 56 miles south-west of Berlin.

★

Bremen.—S. L. Solon, News Chronicle War Correspondent, cables: The city has been virtually cleared. Only a few snipers remain in a small area. Prisoners total over 7,000.

★

U.S. Third Army.—Regensburg, 60 miles north of Munich, and home of Messerschmitt factories, was captured by Patton's men. The 11th Armoured Division, which has advanced 135 miles in the past week, crossed into Austria on Thursday evening, cables Norman Clark, News Chronicle War Correspondent.

U.S. Seventh Army is threatening Augsburg, now six miles away. One column is 25 miles from Munich.

Italy.—Fifth Army troops entered Genoa. Italian partisans had previously captured a large part of the city. In the Po Valley resistance is weak and disorganised. Piacenza has been taken. Allied forces are across the Adige River at many points.

Put Dittmar on the air

GEN. KURT DITTMAR, most famous Wehrmacht radio spokesman, has surrendered to the Americans on the Elbe.

[Picture Page Three.]

Is there any good reason why the German people should be deprived of the privilege of hearing the good general's voice?

The Russians know well how to make good propaganda use of their star prisoners. For years they have put captured Wehrmacht generals on the air.

Bring Gen. Dittmar to the microphone to describe to the German people the Allied military might which he can now see with his own eyes, and to persuade them of the pointlessness of further resistance.

Tens of thousands of his old admirers would hear him—and maybe find his arguments as persuasive as of yore.

In Dittmar we hold a new V-weapon. Why not turn it on the enemy?

Dittmar's last war review in Reich

Gen. Dittmar, making his last analysis of the war on German soil—this time to his American captors—made these points:

The war would end in a few days: Hitler was in Berlin and would die there: the much-advertised German redoubt was mostly a myth: and the report of Goering's execution was probably true.

The war's most fantastic escape

A BRITISH artillery officer has just returned to England after one of the most fantastic escapes from Germany of the war.

Betrayed to the Germans after he had been parachuted into France, he was three times ordered by the Gestapo to be executed.

But he escaped first hanging, then shooting, and finally death by the injection of poison. The full story, as he told it to the News Chronicle, appears on Page Three.

The Big 3 tell the world

IN these official messages the news of the link-up was announced last night by the leaders of the three Great Powers:

FROM THE PRIME MINISTER

AFTER long journeys, toils and victories across the land and oceans, across so many deadly battlefields, the Armies of the great Allies have traversed Germany and have joined hands together.

Now their task will be the destruction of all remnants of German military resistance, the rooting out of the Nazi power and the subjugation of Hitler's Reich.

For these purposes ample forces are available, and we meet in true and victorious comradeship and with inflexible resolve to fulfil our purpose and our duty. Let all march forward upon the foe.

FROM MARSHAL STALIN

IN the name of the Soviet Government, I address you, commanders and men of the Red Army, and of the armies of our Allies.

The victorious armies of the Allied Powers waging a war of liberation in Europe, have routed the German troops and linked up on the territory of Germany.

Our task and our duty are to complete the destruction of the enemy, to force him to lay down his arms and surrender unconditionally.

The Red Army will fulfil to the end this task and this duty to our people and to all freedom-loving peoples.

I greet the valorous troops of our Allies who are now standing on the territory of Germany shoulder to shoulder with the Soviet troops and who are full of determination to carry out their duty to the end.

FROM PRESIDENT TRUMAN

THE Anglo-American armies under the command of Gen. Eisenhower have met the Soviet forces where they intended to meet, in the heart of Nazi Germany. The enemy has been cut in two.

This is not the hour of final victory in Europe, but the hour draws near, the hour for which all the American people, all the British peoples and all the Soviet people have toiled and prayed so long.

The union of our arms in the

Continued Back Page B

PETAIN ASKS FOR PICTURE OF DE GAULLE

PARIS, Friday.

MARSHAL PETAIN, escorted by 60 police, arrived by car at the fort of Mont Rouge, Paris, early today.

His wife, against whom no action is being taken, was given permission to remain with him.

Petain's first remark on going in was: "There is no portrait of De Gaulle. I would like one."

LATE NEWS

DECORATION FOR TIMOSHENKO

Order of Suvorov (First Class) has been conferred on Marshal Timoshenko for exemplary execution of orders of the Supreme Command in co-ordinating operations of second and third Ukrainian fronts, said Moscow radio.

THE STARS AND STRIPES
MEDITERRANEAN
Vol. 2, No. 147, Monday, April 30, 1945 ITALY EDITION * * TWO LIRE

MUSSOLINI EXECUTED

5th Enters Milan; 7th In Munich

Brazilians Take Nazi Division

(BULLETIN) WITH THE 15TH ARMY GROUP, April 29 — The 56th London Division of the British 8th Army, headed by the famous 169th Queens Brigade, has entered Venice.

The 2nd New Zealand Division has reached the the Piave River, scene of Italy's greatest victory in World War I.

WITH THE 15TH ARMY GROUP, April 29 — Organized German resistance in Italy was crumbling today under the paralyzing blows of two Allied Armies, gathering momentum for the knockout punch and there were signs that the complete disintegration of the German Armies had begun.

Dramatic developments were disclosed in tonight's communique

Milan has been entered by 5th Army troops.

Negotiations were in progress for the surrender of the Ligurian Army formerly commanded by Marshal Rodolfo Graziani, now a prisoner and under Allied military control.

The 148th German Infantry Division surrendered to the Brazilian Expeditionary Force, delivering up

(Continued on Page 8)

Himmler Statement Hints Hitler Death

SAN FRANCISCO, April 29 (UP) — The possibility that Heinrich Himmler may have killed Hitler, as cynical evidence to the Allies of his "good faith" in desiring to surrender Germany, was suggested in diplomatic quarters here today.

A high British source revealed first evidence in what was regarded in San Francisco as a desperate attempt by Himmler to save his own skin. These quarters assert that Himmler advised the Allies through Stockholm that Hitler "may not live another 24 hours."

The timing of the message was such that many believe Hitler may already be dead at the hands of his once trusted lieutenant."

Berlin 90 Percent In Russian Hands

MOSCOW, April 29 — The Red Army is now battling for a May Day victory in Berlin — 90 percent of which, according to United Press, is in Russian hands.

With less than 24 hours to go before the eve of the great Soviet holiday, Marshals Gregory Zhukov and Ivan Koniev have launched a crushing all-out assault on the center of the city where the Germans are now hemmed into an area roughly covering the oldest part of the Reich capital.

The Moabit section of Berlin, northwest of the Wilhelmstrasse, fell to the Red Army tonight, according to the Soviet communique.

The German High Command, gambling everything on the possibility of a last-minute "split" developing between the West and East Front Allies, has withdrawn its troops facing U. S. forces on the

(Continued on Page 8)

Yanks Push Into Shrine Of Nazism

SHAEF, April 29 — Munich, fourth largest city of Germany and birthplace of Nazism, was entered by troops of the 6th Army Group tonight. Entry into the great Bavarian city after a 20-mile advance from the west, was made by elements of Lt. Gen. Alexander M. Patch's U. S. 7th Army from the north and southwest.

Initial dispatches did not tell of any fighting within the city which for the past two days had been wracked by unrest and revolt.

Earlier today American armies had been reported converging on the city in an 80-mile arc extending from the northeast to the southwest, and dispatches tonight told of the liberation by the U. S. 3rd Army of 27,000 Allied prisoners of war from a camp at Moosburg on the Isar River, 27 miles northeast of Munich. A great number of those freed prisoners were reported to be American airmen.

There has been no indication yet that Allied Armies have reached the most notorious of German concentration camps at Dachau, eight miles northwest of Munich.

The situation within Munich remained uncertain following an apparent attempt yesterday by a group identifying itself as the "Free Bavarian Movement" and led by General Ritter von Epp, Hitler's 75-year-old commissioner for Bavaria, to take over the city's government.

Reuter's reported that a radio using the city's wave length had told of revolt within the city, and had called upon the advancing Allies to bomb Field Marshal Albert C. Kesselring's headquarters near Munich.

Later, Reuter's said, the south

(Continued on Page 8)

Patriots Also Kill Aides, Mistress

ROME, April 29—Benito Mussolini has been executed by Italian Patriots, Radio Milan, voice of the Committee of National Liberation of Northern Italy, said today.

The Radio said Mussolini was executed last night along with a number of his henchmen and his mistress.

Two British war correspondents, Christopher Lumby, of the London Times, and Stephen Barber, of the London News Chronicle, who went into Milan in advance of Allied troops, reported today that they had personally seen the bodies of Mussolini and 17 of his henchmen on display in the Piazza Loreto. They said that crowds of Italians swarmed to view the bodies, and revile them.

The correspondents reported that Mussolini and others, after having been captured near Lake Como, were taken to the village of Guilano di Mezzegere nearby. There they were tried and executed at 1620 hours on Saturday, April 28. Their bodies were carried in trucks to Milan for public display on the same spot where just a year ago 15 Patriots were executed.

Rome newspapers, like Il Giornale del Mattino and Libera Stampa, spread the news in bold, black headlines. Over all Rome quickly the report travelled, and crowds gathered around every newsstand and great excitement stirred the people. At a rally being held near Piazza Venezia in honor of the northern Patriots, loud cheering greeted the announcement.

Radio Milan did not give details of the executions, nor of the summary trial which must have preceded them. Italians in Rome believed Mussolini and his followers were stood against a wall and shot by a firing squad of Partisans.

Among the others mentioned as executed were Alessandro Pavolini, Carlo Scorza, Fernando Messasona, Goffredo Coppola, Nicola Bombacci and Claretta Petacci, mistress of Mussolini.

Pavolini was probably the chief Fascist among them. He was once Mussolini's propaganda minister. As one of a group of seven in the Fascist Grand Council, he used

(Continued on Page 8)

BENITO MUSSOLINI
Reviled In Death

Patriots Claim Fall Of Treviso, Turin

ROME, April 29 — Radio Milan from all indications firmly in the hands of Italian Patriots, claimed the liberation of Turin and of the province of Treviso, in northeast Italy today, Reuter's reported.

The radio announcement said that Turin had been liberated by the Partisans, and all its military barracks occupied.

General Mark W. Clark, 15th Army Group Commander, broadcast the following instructions to the Partisans:

"You must by all means prevent the Germans from carrying out the destruction of industrial plants and machinery," General Clark said. "On this task depends the future of Italy

The signal for a general rising of North Italian Partisans was given by Field Marshal Sir Harold R. L. G. Alexander, Allied commander in chief in Italy through the National Liberation Committee, the Milan Radio disclosed.

Truman To Tell When Nazis Fall

WASHINGTON, April 29 — Official confirmation of a German collapse—when and if it comes—will be proclaimed in person by President Harry S. Truman in a message over all radio networks, Stephen T. Early, presidential secretary, announced last night.

Early's announcement was made after the nation had broken out in a pandemonium of joy and exultation over a false report from San Francisco that Germany had surrendered.

Meanwhile, Secretary of State Edward R. Stettinius Jr. and Russian Commissar for Foreign Affairs V. M. Molotov met in a surprise session late yesterday to consider the contents of a note from Marshal Stalin to President Truman and Prime Minister Churchill.

The note, according to a Reuter's dispatch, recommended that the offer of Heinrich Himmler, chief of all Nazi defenses, to surrender Germany to the U. S. and Great Britain, be rejected.

That such an offer had been made was "confirmed in responsible Soviet quarters," Tass, the Soviet news agency, said it had been "authorized to state."

Reports from Washington and London that said that Himmler's offer had been turned down because only unconditional surrender to all three major powers would be acceptable.

The Soviet view, according to Reuter's, as expressed in Marshal Stalin's note was that Himmler might not have sufficient authority to make such an offer and that no surrender talks should be started before Nazi armed might is completely annihilated.

The Russians, Reuter's reported, are said to be determined that the Nazis should not have the slightest justification or the appearance of justification for a repetition of German propaganda after World War I that Germany could have fought on but agreed to give up.

The peace story which originated in San Francisco yesterday touched off celebrations which did not end until long after President Truman announced that rumors about the end of the war in Europe were groundless.

Radio networks throughout the

(Continued on Page 8)

Nazi Civilians Get Diet One-Third of GIs

SHAEF, April 29—German civilians will be allowed a diet about one-third that of American soldiers and slightly more than half the standard for liberated Europe, it was announced here today, according to Reuter's.

The majority of Germans will be allowed 1,150 calories daily as compared with the 4,000 daily of American soldiers and with the consumption of between 2,500 and 3,000 in the U. S., and the 2,000 which is the standard of the liberated countries.

Daily Mirror
MAY 1
Tuesday, May 1, 1945
No. 12,905 ONE PENNY
Registered at G.P.O. as a Newspaper.

LAST NAZI RADIO TELLS GERMANS: END IS NEAR

Biggest Nazi army outside Reich smashed

HIMMLER'S biggest fighting force outside the Reich has been torn to pieces by the Allied Fifth and Eighth Armies in North Italy.

Last night General Mark Clark, Allied C.-in-C. in Italy, announced:—

The German Armies in Italy have been virtually eliminated as a military force.

This destruction has been accomplished in the offensive which is now twenty-two days old for the Eighth Army and fifteen days old for the major part of the Fifth Army.

The twenty-five German divisions, some of the best in the German Army, have been torn to pieces and can no longer effectively resist our Armies.

Thousands of vehicles, tremendous quantities of arms and equipment, and over 120,000 prisoners have been captured and many more corraled.

The military power of Germany in Italy has practically ceased, even though scattered fighting may continue as remnants of the German Armies are mopped up.

Yesterday Fifth Army tanks, welcomed by church bells, entered Como, practically on the Swiss border.

Meanwhile, the Eighth Army has reached—if not already crossed—the River Piave, north of Venice.

It is approaching a link-up with Marshal Tito's Yugoslav

Continued on Back Page

THE only effective Nazi broadcasting station still operating in Germany—Hamburg radio—began last night to prepare the last surviving remnants of Hitler's "empire" for the acceptance of complete defeat and occupation

A commentator, Dr. Scharping, declared: "Everybody knows that this war is speeding with a great stride towards its end. This is an irrevocable fact.

"The end may come tomorrow and there will be hundreds of thousands, nay, millions of German children and German women standing at their windows, looking out into the empty streets towards the return of father and husband, but they will never come back."

Scharping said that the German nation had withstood "the onslaught of three Continents" as long as it was humanly possible, and went on: "Every German must continue to speak German, no matter in which area he lives

That area may be occupied by the British, the Americans or the Russians, for shorter or longer periods. We must have faith that the Elbe, the Rhine and the Oder will continue to remain German rivers."

But with Hitler's Reich on the brink of final collapse, this Nazi spokesman did not miss the chance to say that "the war was forced on Germany."

The Hamburg broadcast followed a day of conflicting Stockholm reports about the surrender negotiations between the Swedish Count Bernadotte and Himmler.

Count Bernadotte, stated to have met Himmler at Aabenraa, on the Danish-German frontier, on Sunday, was said in one report to be on his way back to Stockholm with new Nazi terms for surrender.

Another report, however, said that the Count had "gone south," presumably into Germany, following several telephone conversations. None of this was confirmed.

Churchill may get news during speech

From Your Political Correspondent

MR. CHURCHILL proposes to tell the world as much of the surrender negotiations as he can when he speaks in the House of Commons this afternoon.

Developments, however, are coming with such speed and the situation is so constantly changing that not until he has left Downing-street will he know exactly what he is to say.

Even during his statement there may be developments.

He has made arrangements so that last minute messages can be conveyed to him in the House.

Mussolini—the end

The battered body of Mussolini, with his bullet-head pulped by the boots and cudgels of his enraged countrymen, lies in the dust of the Piazza Loretto in Milan. Beside it is the body of his erstwhile mistress, Carletta Petacci. All evening the corpse of the Dictator lay in the town square while Italians milled around, spitting at it. In the end they lifted the bodies of the Duce and his mistress, tied wire round their ankles, and hung them head down from the rafters of a burned-out petrol station.

Count Sforza pronounced his epitaph: "He was a traitor and a professional liar," he said, "we could lose no time with such a rascal."

GERMANS PUT TO WORK IN BELGIAN PITS

HUNDREDS of German prisoners have been put to work in coal mines at Beringen, Belgium.

If the experiment is a success many thousands of Germans may be put to work to raise coal production.

The mineowners will pay the Government the same wage per prisoner as they would have paid to Belgian miners, but how much of this the prisoner will receive has not been decided.

DUTCH THANK US

The underground movement in Holland sent a message to London yesterday expressing their "profound gratitude" for the food that has been dropped by RAF crews over Holland. Another load was dropped to the Dutch people yesterday.

The Newspaper for the Allied Troops

Daily Mail

NO. 15,749. PRICE : 2 FRANCS — CONTINENTAL EDITION — TUESDAY, MAY 1, 1945

Daily Mail man rings up Count Bernadotte, who is reported to be bringing

NEW SURRENDER TERMS FROM HIMMLER

Statement by Mr. Churchill expected to-day

LEADERS of the United Nations were standing by yesterday for news that may end the war at any moment.

Count Bernadotte, nephew of the King of Sweden, has seen Himmler again and a reply is expected to be received to a demand that any unconditional surrender by Germany shall be to Britain, Russia and the United States.

Ralph Hewins, Daily Mail special correspondent in Stockholm, telephoned last night :—

In the first telephone call any Briton has had with Denmark for five years I spoke to-day with Count Bernadotte.

I had been putting calls to him all over Denmark since Saturday and was at lunch when I was told : « Copenhagen on the phone. » Seconds later I was speaking to the Count himself, and asked : « Are you bringing another offer from Himmler ? » He replied : « I am afraid I cannot answer that question till I reach Stockholm. »

Then I asked : « Can you throw any further light on the peace prospects ? » Count Bernadotte replied : « Not at this stage. »

Finally I asked : « Are you flying back to Stockholm to-day ? »

« No, but I am returning to-morrow, » was the reply.

Reuter's Stockholm correspondent sent this account of the negotiations : Himmler is believed, according to a usually reliable source here, to have given Count Bernadotte a capitulation offer addressed to Russia as well as to the British and Americans.

The report, which is without confirmation from any other source, adds that Count Bernadotte will hand over the offer to the Soviet Legation here when he returns to Stockholm.

Himmler is said to have made a new offer after Count Bernadotte had warned him that it was useless to try to split the Allies or lay down any conditions.

The Daily Mail political correspondent writes : Something like a record attendance of M.P.s and an atmosphere of considerable excitement are certain when the House of Commons meets this afternoon.

THEY ALL WANT TICKETS

M.P.s are being inundated with requests for tickets for the public galleries. Mr. Churchill when he takes his seat is likely to get a jubilant reception. His victory dreams have come true.

There will be an atmosphere of tension and expectancy throughout the sitting unless Mr. Churchill speaks when questions end at 3.15 p.m. I think it probable he will do so.

Mr. Churchill returned to London from the country yesterday. I understand that a meeting of the War Cabinet will consider the reply from Himmler as soon as it comes. It will simultaneously be considered by Washington and Moscow. If it is satisfactory the « cease fire » may sound early this week.

The return of Count Bernadotte to Stockholm was expected in Sweden early to-day, but he might transmit a message before this. The reply will probably be transmitted to London by the British Minister in Stockholm, Sir Victor Mallet.

If all three Allies consider that it goes far enough it is probable that the next step will be to have an « instrument of surrender » signed by the German chiefs, including the war chiefs.

The Allies have declared that the only surrender they will accept is that of the German High Command, and unless Himmler's reply incorporates agreement of the leading German generals it is possible that it will not be satisfactory.

The Allies intend to give no loophole for « a get-out » by the German Army. It is not to be allowed a chance of saying in future that the Gestapo chief surrendered against the desire of both Hitler and the generals.

But Himmler is regarded as the only man with sufficient control over the collapsing Nazi organisation to make a definite surrender. If his offer is accepted it will have to be followed by a formal surrender by the Army chiefs to both General Eisenhower and the heads of the Russian Army.

END OF THE « NORTHERN REDOUBT »

After this the « cease fire » would be sounded, and a simultaneous announcement made from the three victorious Allied capitals.

Mr. Churchill is believed not to have definitely decided yet what arrangements he will make to report the latest developments to Parliament. By this afternoon events may be very much clearer.

An American broadcaster on the Stockholm ràdio said: Count Bernadotte met Himmler at Aabenraa, near the Danish-German border.

In Stockholm everyone expressed the belief that to-day will be the big day, and that Allied acceptance will come before this week is over.

It is the general belief in Stockholm that all the Germans in Norway and Denmark will surrender, too.

A Reuter commentator, in a message last night said : According to official Norwegian estimates German forces in Norway still total well above 25,000, and it is reliably believed that their commanders are keenly interested in the alternative to unconditional surrender to the Allies which is provided by the possibility of crossing the Swedish frontier and laying down their arms « with military honours » to the Swedish authorities.

The view hitherto held in Norwegian quarters in London that the German Army intends to create a « Northern Redoubt » and fight irrespective of what happens in Germany would be seriously modified if Himmler himself were a signatory of unconditional surrender.

CRIMINALS GET INTO UNIFORM

SS troops in Norway have always been the potential core of prolonged and fanatical resistance, and an order of their own chief would rob them of their pretext to continue the struggle.

On the other hand the Wehrmacht troops would probably welcome internment by a neutral power as preferable to surrender to the Norwegians or any of their major Allies.

It is believed in informed Allied military quarters in London that the Swedes would be capable of dealing with a large-scale disarmament of the German forces in Norway, and might well prefer this solution to belated Swedish military intervention against the Germans in Norway for which the Norwegian Government is now openly pressing.

This would account for recent Swedish hesitation in giving a positive answer to Norway's official appeal for help.

It is perhaps significant that the number of German civilian administrators in Norway, many of whom would certainly qualify as war criminals, have recently been getting into military uniform, presumably with a view to sharing any advantages accorded to military personnel when hostilities cease.

The official Norwegian view is that nothing short of unconditional surrender to the Allies by the German troops in Norway is acceptable, and that any attempt to seek asylum in Sweden would defeat the ends of justice.

Footnote.—*A message from a correspondent with the U.S Forces in Germany last night said . Enemy opposition has been weaker in the last few hours and, in general, German local commanders are ready to discuss surrender terms as soon as American troops are in a position to attack them.*

'Frisco talks to go on if war ends

Daily Mail Correspondent
San Francisco, Monday.

THE World Security Conference will continue without interruption even if Germany surrenders within the next few days, it is learned here to-day.

Informed circles say that Mr. Eden, Mr. Molotov and M. Bidault have made preparations to return to their capitals should Germany's surrender be announced.

But they have arranged for deputies among their delegations to continue the work of the conference in their absence.

Minds unchanged

A meeting of the Foreign Ministers of Russia, Britain and the United States has been held to discuss the Polish question once more.

Mr. Eden and Mr. Stettinius again emphasised at this meeting that there was no question of their changing their minds on the subject of Polish representation.

Argentina raises a problem

Mr. Molotov is stated to have agreed at San Francisco that Argentina should be invited to the conference only on condition that an invitation should also be addressed to the Polish Provisional Government recognised by the Soviet Union.

The question was expected to come before the Steering Committee last night.

NO AIRFIELD FOR NAZIS

Spain issues denial

A DENIAL that war criminals are finding refuge in Spain was issued by the Spanish Foreign Office yesterday.

« Reports are being circulated by the foreign Press and radio that Spain, and particularly the Balearic Isles, are being used as a refuge for war criminals and that an aerodrome has been specially prepared for that purpose in the Balearics, » it was stated. « All that is totally false.

« There is no such aredrome, and no National Socialists or Fascists or any war criminals of any kind have landed thereon. »

British internees freed from camp

In the Marlag und Milag-Nord German prison camps for the Royal Navy and Merchant Navy, which were freed late on the night of April 27 by an armoured patrol of the Welsh Guards, were a number of British civilian internees who were transferred there from Giromagny, near Belfort, last September.

As no details are so far available, inquiries as to friends and relatives cannot yet be answered, states an official of the Consular section of the British Embassy in Paris.

As soon as further information is available it will be published.

Alexander for Vienna

Field-Marshal Alexander is reported in well-informed diplomatic circles to be going to Vienna, to discuss with the Soviet authorities issues arising from the formation of the Austrian provisional government, says Reuter's military correspondent.

Princess going back

Princess Marie-José of Piedmont wishes to go back to Italy, says a Berne message. She is waiting with her suite at Bourg-Saint-Pierre for the necessary permit.

BY taking out a subscription (rates in Page Two) or registering with your newsagent, you can make sure of getting your Continental « Daily Mail ». The newsprint shortage restricts supplies.

NEW PUSH FROM THE ELBE

British threaten to cut off Denmark

FIELD - MARSHAL MONTGOMERY now has two bridgeheads across the Elbe above Hamburg, Germany's biggest port.

American airborne troops under his command made a new crossing ten miles upstream from the point where the 15th Scottish Division established themselves on the east bank.

The British bridgehead is now seven miles wide and at one point ten miles deep. In spite of Luftwaffe attacks, sappers built bridges which are now carrying tanks and heavy traffic.

The new attack threatens to outflank Hamburg and finally seal off Schlesvig-Holstein and Denmark.

Across the Isar

Canadian troops have overrun a prisoner-of-war camp at Strucklingen, ten miles north-west of Friesoythe, while the Guards armoured Division has freed another at Sandrostel, due south of Bromervoerde. containing more than 10,000 French prisoners of war.

The U.S. 3rd Army, now across the Isar, southern branch of the Danube at three points, now controls a 60 mile stretch of the river from Freising, 17 miles north-east of Munich to Deggendorf where it joins the Danube.

They are rapidly squeezing the Germans into a pocket south of the river.

General Patton's left flank, moving into Austria north-east of Passau, is held up. Some German armour is assembling in that sector, presumably to protect the rear positions of the German army facing the Russians west of Vienna, about 80 miles away

Record capture

From Munich it is reported that the three U.S. divisions engaged in clearing the city were still encountering some resistance.

The total of prisoners freed at Moosburg camp, in Bavaria, has risen from 27,000 to 110,000.

The U.S. 7th Army is now practically knocking at the door of the Southern Redoubt. Patch's troops have skirted round the east side of Ammersee and captured Spatzenhausen, due north of Innsbruck. One spearhead was reported to be 20 miles from Innsbruck.

The 7th Army set up a new record for itself by capturing more than 35,000 prisoners in a day against crumbling opposition.

The French 1st Army has now crossed the Austrian frontier in the area of Bregenz. French troops also gained a foothold in the Bavarian Alps in the Iller Valley, south of Kempten.

On Lake Constance the French entered Friedrichshafen and also captured Lindau.

Yesterday the French communiqué added that in 30 days the French have captured 90.000 prisoners, including seven generals.

9th link up with Soviets

From NOEL MONKS
Daily Mail Special Correspondent
With the U.S. 9th Army, Germany, Monday.

AFTER nine days' waiting and watching the 9th Army made contact with the Russians to-day in the town of Apollensdorf, 30 miles south-east of our Elbe bridgehead.

A Russian tank column and cavalry unit and the U.S. 83rd Infantry Division met in Apollensdorf at 1.30 p.m., and Russian and American troops were soon toasting each other.

Now that the meeting has taken place the 9th Army's mission in this area is about completed.

Brussels honours British troops

From Daily Mail Correspondent
Brussels, Monday.

As soon as the military situation permits, British regiments, participating in the liberation of Brussels, are to be honoured by the Brussels population.

Colours will be presented to the Welsh, Grenadier, Coldstream, and Irish Guards, and a bronze plaquette to the Second Household Cavalry Regiment, the 21st Anti-Tank Regiment, the 55th Regiment Royal Artillery, the 153rd Field Regiment (Leicester Yeomanry), and the 10th Company, Scots Guards.

French land on isle off La Rochelle

French troops effected a landing yesterday on the island of Oléron, to the south of La Rochelle, Atlantic Coast headquarters announced last night.

In spite of enemy opposition they enlarged their beachhead and were making progress.

Warships and aircraft lent their aid to the operation.

THIS all-fronts-in-Europe map shows you the dispositions yesterday of the Allied Armies. They may well prove to vary little from the final fighting lines of the war in the West.

Germans in Italy can no longer resist us
— Gen. Clark

PRISONERS 120,000

GERMAN military power in Italy has practically ceased to exist. It was General Mark Clark himself who made this statement yesterday at his Command post somewhere in northern Italy.

« The Germans cannot any longer effectively resist the Allied Armies, » the general continued, according to Desmond Tighe, Reuter's special correspondent. « Twenty - five German divisions have been torn to pieces and prisoners total now over 120 000.

« Scattered fighting may continue as remnants of the German armies are mopped up. »

The Allied armies yesterday were sweeping towards both corners of the North Italian plain and were forcing by-passed Germans to surrender.

Trieste entered

Japanese American troops have entered the great industrial town of Turin, home of the Fiat works. They found the city under the control of Italian patriots.

In the Adriatic sector, Americans and South Africans captured Treviso, north of Venice.

Four German generals have been captured.

The British 13th Corps, after completing the occupation of Venice, pushed 20 miles to the north-east to reach the River Piave, with 50 miles to go to link up with Marshal Tito's Yugoslav forces who have broken into Trieste the great naval base in the Gulf of Venice.

In the north west, 5th Army troops secured Alessandria, half-way between Genoa and Turin, while the 8th Army occupied Chiaggia.

Air arm to aid hold on Germany

By PAUL BEWSHER
Daily Mail Special Correspondent

BRITAIN, the United States, and Russia will all keep « occupational air forces » in Europe after the final collapse of Germany.

General Carl Spaatz, chief of the American Strategical Air Forces in the West, made this statement yesterday in a review of the work of heavy day bombers which have now completed their strategical task in Europe.

« I do not know how long our occupational force will be here—maybe 100 years, » he said with a smile.

« We have enough machines available to provide all replacements needed for the immediate future. I don't think these heavy bombers will be much use as transport machines after the war, as they cannot be run very economically. »

General Spaatz told us he would welcome suggestions for dealing with pilots and air crews of heavy bombers when the war with Germany and Japan is finally over, as he did not think commercial aviation could absorb them all.

Transport must move

When he was asked if the day of heavy bombers was over now that V-weapons had been introduced, he replied: « No, it has just begun. Even if you build factories underground, you can attack transport moving material to them which cannot always travel underground. »

Referring to the Bavarian « redoubt », which he said was nothing compared with what they had attacked in the past, he made the same point, saying: « While we cannot dig into mountains or caves with our bombs, we can still attack exposed transport. »

The General said the Luftwaffe was caught off the balance by our big daylight attacks, as they did not expect to meet at the same time such heavy defensive power from heavy bombers and offensive power from long-range fighters.

Got them guessing

He paid high tribute to the groundwork of the Royal Air Force and its radio control and other devices, without which attacks could not have been successfully carried through.

The German Army very badly needed air support both on the Eastern and Western fronts, but so many aircraft had to be withdrawn to meet our bombing attacks.

When Normandy was invaded the Germans had a considerable force of fighters which could have been a big complication to us, but they were so deep inside Germany dealing with the bomber menace, that they could not be used against our forces.

Lord Templewood's plea for air control of Germany : Page 2.

LEGAL PURGE OF FASCISM

Italians to be tried

IMMEDIATE suspension of all arbitrary executions in Italy, following summary trials, was ordered yesterday by the Prefect of Milan. In future all suspects must be handed over to justice commissions for legal trial.

Execution of Mussolini and certain of his accomplices was necessary as proof of Italy's severance from the past, says a statement issued yesterday by the National Liberation Committee.

It adds that the necessary purge of the remaining Fascist elements could only be carried out at the end of the insurrectional period in strict legality.

THE NUMBER OF COPIES PRINTED OF YESTERDAY'S ISSUE WAS 48,515.

U.S. capture new camp of horrors

DACHAU, an even more sinister name than Buchenwald in the story of German concentration camps, yesterday yielded up some of its secrets to American troops who captured the place in their advance on Munich.

A correspondent at Supreme Headquarters says Dachau is reported to equal if not surpass the horrors of any other Nazi crime centre.

Fifty rail trucks were found crammed with bodies, and gas chambers, torture rooms, whipping posts and crematoria, similar to those at Buchenwald, were discovered.

32,000 freed

More than 32,000 political prisoners were freed, and a whole battalion of Americans was needed to restrain them from excesses.

At another camp north of Landsberg, the Americans discovered the bodies of over 400 Polish prisoners who had died from starvation. The retreating German had tried to burn the remains before leaving.

Buchenwald film for all world

Three newsreels taken at the German concentration camps at Buchenwald and Belsen are being flown to all parts of the world and will be shown in ordinary cinemas.

They were made by ordinary commercial film enterprises and some of the scenes were taken during the visit to the camps of British Members of Parliament.

Two Spanish journalists, Carlos Sentis and Matias Cirici Ventallo, are to visit German concentration camps and will report fully on the subject

Duce's family arrested

Donna Mussolini, widow of Benito Mussolini, and her two youngest children, have been arrested at Como, reported Swiss radio last night.

The children, Romano and Anna Maria, were taken to a convent.

Milan radio announced yesterday that the body of Mussolini was taken to the mortuary and officially identified.

WOMEN IN BERLIN DEFENCE

Germans fight back amid the ruins

SPECIALLY recruited battalions of German women are fighting in the streets of Berlin in a last desperate effort to stem the surge of the Red Army tanks and infantry towards the capital's last stand defences, said Duncan Hooper, Reuter's special correspondent in Moscow, last night.

German resistance is still considerable, and slaughter of defenders reached a new level yesterday as garrison commanders recklessly threw more and more troops into costly counter-attacks.

Victory salute

Soviet tanks and guns, heavily reinforced for the final battle, are rolling down streets three abreast towards the core of German resistance.

Some of the bitterest battles are raging in the burning ruins of Unter den Linden, now littered with the bodies of unshaven men of the Volkssturm and Grenadiers.

The Germans are being broken up into small groups, and their losses over the last 24 hours are likely to be the highest they have ever suffered.

It is generally believed in Moscow that the complete fall of Berlin will be celebrated with a tremendous victory salute to-day.

The German High Command dropped paratroops into Berlin but they were quickly mopped up by the Red Army.

Order of the Day

Greiswald, on the Baltic, 50 miles east of Rostock, has been captured, announced Marshal Stalin in an Order of the Day last-night.

The Order, which was addressed to Marshal Rokossovsky,, Commander of the 2nd White Russian Front, said: « Troops of the 2nd White Russian Front, continuing their offensive to-day, captured the towns of Greiswald, Treptow, Neu-Strelitz, Fuerstenberg and Grandste, important road junctions in north-western Pomerania and Mecklenberg.

A second Order, addressed to General Eremenko, commander of the 4th Ukrainian Front, said: « Troops of the 4th Ukrainian Front to-day carried by storm the town of Moravska Ostrava, important industrial centre and strongpoint in the German defences in Czecho-Slovakia.

« Simultaneously, troops of this Front also captured the town of Zlina, an important road junction in the western Carpathians. »

LATEST

60,000 Germans K.O. in one day

Some 20,000 Germans were killed or captured in Berlin in 24 hours and 40,000 more were taken prisoners from the big group surrounded, and now being finished off, to the south-east of the capital, said a message early to-day.

Electricity cut in Britain

Breakfast was rudely interrupted in many parts of Britain yesterday. Electricity supplies were cut off for nearly an hour in the morning, and many housewives were caught unprepared in the middle of cooking the morning meal.

Excessive use of current was the cause of the big switch-off, said officials of the supply companies.

Supply and distributing authorities were instructed by the Central Electricity Board to shed 5 per cent of their load, as there was not enough plant available to meet the big demand.

The order to cut was general throughout the country.

Extensive cuts were last made during the cold spell in January and February.

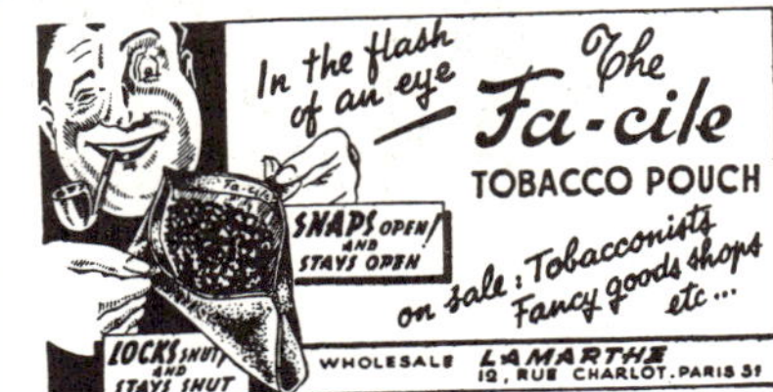

Vol. 26. No. 267 New York, Wednesday, May 2, 1945★ 56 Main + 4 Manhattan Pages 2 Cents IN CITY LIMITS | 3 CENTS Elsewhere

NAZI RADIO ANNOUNCES:

HITLER DEAD

'FELL IN COMMAND POST'

ADM. DOENITZ NAMED HEAD OF REICH, ARMY

Story on Page 3

WESTERN ITALY EDITION

UNION JACK

SPECIAL EDITION

Thursday, May 3, 1945 • • • No. 478 Two Lire

A Million Of The Enemy Lay Down Arms

FULL SURRENDER OF NAZIS IN ITALY

ALTHOUGH fighting continues in other parts of Europe, the entire enemy forces in Italy have surrendered unconditionally to the Allies under Field-Marshal Alexander. This triumphant end to the campaign was announced last evening.

Hostilities ceased at 14.00 Italian time yesterday, when nearly a million of the enemy laid down their arms in the surrender area, which includes part of Austria.

The Italian campaign, which began with Montgomery's landing at the base of the peninsula in September 1943, has thus resulted in the first mass surrender of a complete German front.

The grand climax came after the great break-through to the Po Valley by the Fifth and Eighth Armies, aided in their sweeping advance by Italian Partisans. In three weeks the German defending forces were torn to pieces. The last act is described in this special communique from AFHQ:

Enemy land, sea and air forces commanded by Col.-Gen. Heinrich von Vietinghoff-Scheel, German C-in-C S W and C-in-C Army Group "C," have surrendered unconditionally to Field-Marshal Sir Harold Alexander, Supreme Allied Commander, Mediterranean Theatre of operations.

The terms of surrender provided for the cessation of hostilities at 12 noon GMT Wednesday, May 2, 1945.

The instrument of surrender was signed on Sunday afternoon, April 29, at AFHQ Caserta, by two German plenipotentiaries and by Lt.-Gen. W. D. Morgan, Chief of Staff, AFHQ.

One German representative signed on behalf of Gen. Von Vietinghoff and the other on behalf of Ober-grupenfuehrer Karl Wolff, Supreme Commander of SS and Police and German General Plenipotentiary of the Wehrmacht in Italy.

After signing the document of unconditional surrender the two German plenipotentiaries returned by secret route to Gen. Von Vietinghoff's HQ in the High Alps to arrange surrender of the German and Italian Fascist land, air and naval forces.

Territory under Gen. Von Vietinghoff's South - Western Command includes all Northern Italy to the Isonzo River in the north-east, and the Austrian provinces of Vorarlberg, Tyrol Salzburg and portions of Carinthia and Styria.

The enemy's total forces, including combat and rear echelon troops surrendered to the Allies, are estimated to number nearly 1,000,000 men. The fighting troops include the remnants of

22 German and six Italian Fascist Divisions.

The instrument of surrender consists of six short paragraphs. Three appendices giving details appertaining to land, sea and air forces were attached to the instrument. The following terms are imposed:

1. Unconditional surrender by the German C.-in-C. South-West of all forces under his command or control on land, on sea, or in the air, to the Supreme Allied Commander Mediterranean Theatre of Operations.

2. Cessation of all hostilities on land, on sea or in the air by enemy forces at 1200 hrs. GMT, May 2, 1945.

3. The immediate immobilisation and disarmament of enemy ground, sea and air forces.

4. Obligation on the part of the German C.-in-C. South-West to carry out any further orders issued by the Supreme Allied Commander Mediterranean Theatre.

5. Disobedience of orders or failure to comply with them to be dealt with in accordance with the accepted laws and usages of war.

The instrument of surrender stipulates that it is independent of, without prejudice to, and will be superseded by any general instrument of surrender imposed by or on behalf of the United Nations and applicable to Germany and the German Armed Forces as a whole.

The instrument of surrender and appendices were written in English and German. The English version is the authentic text. The decision of the Supreme Allied Commander Mediterranean Theatre will be final if any doubt or dispute arises as to the meaning or interpretation of the surrender terms.

The signing took place in

(Continued on Page Four)

FALL OF BERLIN

Great news also came from Germany itself last night. Marshal Stalin announced the capture of Berlin and vast numbers of prisoners in a complete rout of the garrison. (See Page 4.)

Special Orders Of The Day

Special Orders of the Day were issued by the Allied commanders in Italy to mark the surrender.

From Field-Marshal Sir Harold ALEXANDER, Supreme Allied Commander, Mediterranean Theatre:

SOLDIERS, sailors and airmen of the Allied Forces in the Mediterranean Theatre:

After nearly two years of hard and arduous fighting, which started in Sicily in the summer of 1943, you stand today as the victors of the Italian campaign

You have won a victory which has ended in the complete and utter rout of the German armed forces in the Mediterranean. By clearing Italy of the last Nazi aggressor you have liberated a country of over 40,000,000 people. Today the remnants of a once proud army have laid down their arms to you—close on a million men, with all their arms, equipment and impedimenta.

You may well be proud of this great and victorious campaign which will long live in history as one of the greatest and most successful ever waged. No praise is too high for you soldiers, sailors, airmen and workers of the United Forces in Italy for your magnificent triumph.

My gratitude to you and my admiration is unbounded, and only equalled by the pride which is mine in being your Commander-in-Chief.

From Gen. Joseph T. McNARNEY, Deputy Supreme Allied Commander, Mediterranean Theatre:

THE enemy in Italy has surrendered unconditionally.

Your magnificent victories in the spring offensive left him only two alternatives, to surrender or to die.

This hour is the glorious climax to one of the greatest triumphs in the long, hard-fought war in Africa and in Europe. Your triumph will live always in the hearts and minds of our people. The attack against the enemy's so-called inner fortress began in the Mediterranean. You have come from Alamein and from Casablanca to the Alps. After the successes in North Africa you smashed the enemy in Tunisia. You drove him from Sicily. You invaded Italy, and despite ferocious resistance and incredibly difficult terrain and weather you drove him back, always back. You have destroyed the best troops he possessed. At this moment of surrender he is against the Alps, helpless under your blows to defend himself.

The victory is yours—you of the ground, sea and air forces of many nationalities who have fought hard as a single combat team The surrender today is to you.

Now, with final and complete victory in sight, let us go forward until the last foe. Japan, is crushed. Then, and not till then, will freedom-loving men and women be able to enjoy lasting peace

From Gen. Mark W. CLARK, Commanding General, 15 Army Group:

TO the soldiers of the 15 Army Group: With a full and grateful heart I hail and congratulate you in this hour of complete victory over the German enemy and join with you in thanks to Almighty God.

Yours has been a long hard fight—the longest in the war of any Allied troops fighting on the continent of Europe. You men of the Fifth and Eighth Armies have brought that fight to a successful conclusion by your recent brilliant offensive operation,

(Continued on Page Three)

THURSDAY, MAY 3, 1945

Evening Standard

37,638 MOON: Sets 10.30 am. Rises 3.23 pm LIGHTING-UP TIME: 10.26 pm. ONE PENNY

FINAL NIGHT EXTRA●

NEARLY THE END: Wehrmacht racing to surrender

DEATH OF THE GERMAN ARMY

A routed, panic-stricken rabble pour through our lines for safety

Climax is near. Ronald Monson, Evening Standard reporter with the British Army, cabled this afternoon: 'Soldiers coming into our lines believe the general surrender of the German Army has taken place. But this is unofficial.'

Montgomery has taken Hamburg without a fight. Before he marched in at 1 p.m. the Germans declared it an open city and Hamburg radio closed down. Monty has linked up with the Russians at Wismar on the Baltic. His armies are meeting no opposition.

" This," says war reporter Leslie Randall, " looks like the end. One hundred thousand Germans have surrendered "

From Baltic to Elbe the German army is choking every road in a chaotic scramble to escape the Russians and reach the British lines.

The whole army has become a disorganised rabble. Generals, S.S. chiefs, Luftwaffe, Volkssturm, with German Wrens, A.T.S. and Waafs, are streaming west over roads, fields and through woods—on foot, on cars and coaches, on bicycles—even on scooters. They are terror-stricken.

Hundreds of Germans are tearing off their uniforms and putting on civilian clothes.

Using every vessel that will float, the Germans began a wholesale evacuation by sea from Schleswig-Holstein at dawn. Behind these ports British 'planes are hammering the biggest traffic jam of the war.

More big and sensational news is forecast from Montgomery's H.Q. The end of the German army is at hand. The end of all fighting on the northern front is imminent.

THE BROKEN ARMY

'Wehrmacht is a disorganised rabble blowing like chaff into our lines before the Russian tornado'

From RICHARD McMILLAN, with British troops, Thursday.

The rout of the Wehrmacht has assumed tremendous proportions in the face of the British advance, as tens of thousands of panic-stricken Germans seek to escape the clutches of the Russians by taking refuge inside the British lines.

The scenes along the roads are beyond description. Hordes of enemy troops, in all sorts of vehicles, three abreast, struggle to get through the great traffic jam.

They are throwing off equipment, guns and ammunition to lighten the loads. Some cars are filled with high officers, privates and nurses—all jammed together. When a car breaks down there is fresh chaos.

German troops leave the convoys in thousands, rush into the woods to change into civilian clothes, and then rejoin the long stream of the broken army.

"Where can we go?" they ask British infantry. "The Russians are coming."

'Can we surrender?'

Generals limp along with N.C.O.s and all have the same question: "Can we surrender?"

British columns hourly find greater difficulty in edging through the disorganised rabble. German civilians have joined the throng, adding to the panic by rumours that "the Russians are just on our heels. Please where can we find the British lines? We want to get to safety."

German troops and civilians alike said, "Now that Berlin has fallen the war is over."

German soldiers tried to barter with the refugees

● Back Page, Col. One

HITLER NOT IN BERLIN

Russians can't find his body

MOSCOW, Thursday.—Hitler is not in Berlin. The Soviet commentator, Nikolai Tikhonov, gave this report on the front page of Pravda to-day.

"Whether he fled to the Devil's nest," said Tikhonov, "or to the other world, to the embraces of some Fascist protectorate, it's all the same. He isn't in Berlin.

"We'll find out what actually happened to him. And if he has fled we'll find him, no matter where he has found shelter."—Associated Press.

THE END OF THE GANG

Was it murder?

In spite of the story told to the Russians in Berlin that Hitler committed suicide, rumours persist that he was murdered.

Dr. Hans Fritsche, one of Goebbels's closest collaborators, told his captors in Berlin that both Hitler and Goebbels killed themselves in the capital's last hours.

But a message from Zurich passes on, with the greatest reserve, a story emanating from diplomatic sources which are still capable of maintaining contact with Germany. According to this Goering is dead, too, and all three were murdered.

Bloody accounts were settled last Friday and Saturday morning, it is said, when adherents of a group led by Doenitz or Himmler killed Hitler, Goebbels and Goering.

IS HAW HAW OURS?

William Joyce (Lord Haw-Haw) may be in our hands. He broadcast from Hamburg only two days ago.

Other captures yesterday:

Field-marshal von Sperrle, the man responsible for the London blitz, and Field-marshal Maximilian Freiherr von Weichs—by the U.S. Seventh Army.

The painter's passing

Mr. Hugh Dalton, President of the Board of Trade, addressing the Paint Research Association lunch at the Savoy to-day, said:

"If I were Mr. de Valera—thank God I am not—I would open my remarks by condoling with you on the passing of a painter.

"I think, however, you would regard it as more appropriate to drink to the future disencumbrance of this foul brute who began as a painter but who degenerated in later life and who is now in physical life degenerating further."

ANOTHER BABY KIDNAPPED

Another child was kidnapped in London last evening.

Full story on PAGE FIVE.

Midnight drinks on VE-Day

On VE-night you will be able to drink until 11.30 p.m., or even midnight—depending on where you are.

Gravesend and **Epsom** licensing magistrates announce that the hours of drinking will be extended until midnight.

Romford magistrates say they will accept applications for extensions to 11.30 p.m. for sale and midnight for drinking, while **Watford** will extend the hours to 11.30.

BATTLE HYMN OF INVASION

'How sweet the name'

The Rev. Victor A. Price, an Army padre, told the Baptist Union assembly in London to-day:

"On the eve of D-Day I held a service on board ship for the men who would be the first to break the defences of Normandy.

"I asked which hymn they would like, and instead of the usual ones they chose 'How sweet the name of Jesus sounds in a believer's ear, it soothes his troubles, heals his wounds and drives away his fear.'"

Is Prague surrender town?

Doenitz has declared Prague an open city (he used the expression "hospital city"). He has begun "negotiations for political reorganisation in the Czecho-Slovak Protectorate."

This announcement appears to foreshadow the liquidation of the German "redoubt" in Bohemia and Moravia.—Reuter.

The Evening Standard Diplomatic Correspondent writes:

There is a strong probability that it is the intention of Doenitz, in declaring Prague an open city, to set up his headquarters there in preparation for the last act in the world drama—the surrender of the German nation.

Danish fishing fleet escaping

STOCKHOLM, Thursday.—The whole of the Danish fishing fleet is leaving Denmark to escape being seized by the Germans for evacuation purposes, according to reports reaching here.

About half the fleet is said to be already in England. Other vessels have been taken to safety in Sweden.—Reuter.

Bigger bus strike

So that B.L.A. men can get home, a meeting of 200 bus men and women on strike from Old Kent-road garage to-day agreed to run the normal B.L.A. services from Victoria.

Evening Standard Reporter

Two thousand more transport workers joined the strike against London Transport's summer schedules to-day and 6750 employees are now idle.

Two trolley-bus depots—Bexley and Sutton—and four more petrol bus garages—Plumstead, Elmers End, Bromley and Old Kent-road—were closed to-day by the extension of the strike.

London Transport announce that the routes affected by the extension of the strike are:

Trolleybuses — 654 (Crystal Palace—Sutton); 696 (Woolwich—Dartford); 698 (Woolwich—Bexley Heath). Central buses—47 (Shoreditch—Farnborough); 51 (Sidcup—Farnborough); 61 (Bromley Common—Eltham); 94 (Crystal Palace — Southborough); 119 (Bromley North Station—Croydon); 138 (Bromley North Station—Hayes); 146a (Bromley North Station—Downe).

Route 12 (Harlesden — South Croydon), 126 (Beckenham Junction—Eltham), 130 (Croydon—New Addington), 194 (Forest Hill—Croydon, 227 (Penge — Chislehurst, 53A (West Hampstead—Plumstead Common), 99 (Woolwich—Erith), 21 (Moorgate—Farningham), 202 (Rotherhithe—New Cross), 243 (Peckham High-street) and also the Peckham High-street circular inter-station services.

The bus route from Dalston garage, Route 47 (Shoreditch—Farnborough) is not working, and Route 43 (Holloway Garage) is only working between Friern Barnet and Highgate instead of London Bridge.

'ISSUE SIMPLE'

All the tram-men are still out, but there has been no extension of the stoppage of trolleybuses in North London.

A spokesman for the strikers told me to-day: "The issue is very simple. We want more buses on the roads and more workers to run them.

"There will probably be a statement later in the day after meetings which are being held have passed resolutions."

A London Transport official said: "There seems to be no legitimate reason for the strike. The men have asked for more labour to cover the summer time rush hour schedule—between 6.30 and 7 p.m. Lord Ashfield, our chairman, has said that the Government will provide this labour.

" ALL BEING DONE "

"Onerous duties in connection with the spread-over system have been alleviated There is a machinery to deal with these questions, and everything possible has been, and is being, done to give the men satisfaction."

93,000 sorties over Britain

The Air Ministry stated to-day that during the war over 93,000 sorties were flown over Britain by enemy aircraft.

A SUMMER ELECTION?

By WILLIAM ALISON

The general collapse has revived speculation on the probable dates of two important events—VE-Day and the General Election.

Both depend on the unconditional surrender of the whole of the German forces, and, despite the emergence of Doenitz as the successor to Hitler, it is generally believed that the end is not far off.

So the prospects of an early General Election are strengthened almost to the extent of certainty.

All the political parties are working to be ready in June or early July.

Those M.P.s who have been forecasting an autumn election were reviewing their prophecies immediately news of the surrender in Italy became known.

NEWS CHRONICLE, Friday, May 4, 1945

News Chronicle
No. 30,878 FRIDAY, MAY 4, 1945 ONE PENNY
LATE LONDON EDITION

THE LAST HOURS

500,000 Germans yield in day British reported in Denmark Wehrmacht clashing with S.S.

THE LAST HOURS ARE AT HAND. HAMBURG HAS FALLEN; THE BRITISH AND THE RUSSIANS HAVE LINKED ON THE BALTIC FRONT. BRITISH TROOPS ARE OFFICIALLY STATED TO HAVE REACHED THE KIEL CANAL. SWEDISH MESSAGES SAY THEY ARE ACROSS THE DANISH FRONTIER.

THE WEHRMACHT RUSHES TO SURRENDER. IN 24 HOURS 500,000 GERMANS HAVE YIELDED TO THE BRITISH SECOND ARMY.

R.A.F. PLANES HAVE MASSACRED ENEMY LAND TRANSPORT NEAR LUEBECK; HAVE ATTACKED A FLEET OF 250 SHIPS MOVING TOWARDS NORWAY.

IN BERLIN THE RED ARMY IS RESTORING LIFE TO THE GERMAN CAPITAL. THE BODIES OF HITLER AND GOEBBELS HAVE NOT YET BEEN FOUND.

IN THE SOUTH THE ADVANCE GOES ON INTO THE REDOUBT. DOENITZ HAS PROCLAIMED PRAGUE AN OPEN CITY.

ALONG the North Sea-Baltic front the final words of the final chapter are being written.

There, assailed by the Russians in the east, by the British in the west, the once-powerful Wehrmacht goes down to defeat in chaos, panic and surrender.

There was big news yesterday on this front—the fall of Hamburg, of Oldenburg, the firm contact with the Red Army from Wismar on the Baltic to Wittenberge, 60 miles to the south.

OVER THE CANAL?

There was the advance to within 15 miles of Cuxhaven, the drive up the Schleswig peninsula, in which the 11th Armoured Division captured Travemuende and pushed on to the Kiel Canal.

There were the reports from Sweden that Allied guns were shelling Flensburg, on the German side of the Danish border, that the British had crossed the Kiel Canal and had reached Eckernfoerde, that the Danish frontier had been crossed, that the Wehrmacht and the S.S. were fighting in Jutland.

But all this was incidental. The great picture was that of surrender. On Wednesday, it is estimated, half a million Germans gave themselves up to the Second Army. In 24 hours at least 20 generals have surrendered.

CHAOS AND PANIC

Disorganised enemy columns fleeing west from the Russians have met other columns fleeing east from the British. Chaos, panic, surrender, but now also destruction, for the R.A.F. has joined in.

On Wednesday, in the Luebeck-Schwerin-Wismar area 1,500 transports were damaged.

At dawn yesterday the Germans tried to escape by sea, rushing from their remaining transports to their remaining ships, in an attempt to flee up both coasts of Schleswig-Holstein.

They were overtaken by the R.A.F. and in the harbours and inlets dozens of ships were sunk or damaged. On land, in the first 350 sorties yesterday 700 vehicles were destroyed.

Reports that complete German surrender is imminent are rife, but there is nothing official yet.

Doenitz, the new Fuehrer, is reported to be in Kiel, a precarious situation if the British are across the canal.

With him is his Foreign Minister von Krosigk. With the loss of Hamburg they have lost their main radio transmitter.

PRAGUE AN OPEN CITY

Doenitz has fallen back on Prague radio. Yesterday he used this station to announce:

"At the request of the German Minister of State for Bohemia and Moravia (Dr. Frank), Admiral Doenitz has declared Prague a hospital city. Negotiations for a political reorganisation in the directorative have begun.

"Any disturbance of the calm and orderly developments which could only lead to Bolshevik chaos will be suppressed by force."

The Southern Redoubt is collapsing. Patton's Third Army is seven miles from Linz. The Seventh Army is racing for Salzburg.

On all fronts the story is of collapse. The end is near.

IN THE HEART OF BERLIN

At six o'clock on the evening of May 2, 1945, the Red Flag was hoisted on the Brandenburg Gate, Berlin, and marked a new chapter in history. Three hours earlier Marshal Stalin had announced the fall of Berlin.

In the picture above, sent by wireless from Moscow, German prisoners are marching through the Gate and along the Unter den Linden to captivity.

The Brandenburg Gate was built in 1788-91 to symbolise Prussian military glory. Napoleon took the Quadriga to Paris in 1807 and the Prussians took it back in 1814.

PLANES MASSACRE NAZIS TRYING A DUNKIRK

WITH BRITISH SECOND ARMY, Thursday.

ONE of the greatest air massacres of the war has been inflicted on the Nazis in Northern Germany, some of whom are making their biggest attempt at a "Dunkirk."

Spitfires, Typhoons, Tempests and jet-propelled Meteors are playing havoc with German shipping and transport as the Germans flee from Schleswig-Holstein on both the east and west coasts.

Using everything that will float, the Germans began a wholesale evacuation by sea at dawn, while behind the ports and harbours was the biggest traffic jam of the war.

By mid-day dozens of inlets, harbours and ports on both the eastern and western coasts of Schleswig-Holstein were swarming with hundreds of ships. Trawlers, fishing smacks and tramps joined the effort to carry out a "Dunkirk."

Germans were rushing straight from transports on to the little boats and trying to put to sea in the face of Tactical Air Force attacks.

"The whole sea is dotted with craft," said one pilot.

Set on fire

A convoy of more than 50 vessels, including seven U-boats, was spotted heading north from the Kiel area this afternoon.

A 7,000-ton oil tanker in Kiel Bay and one 10,000-ton merchant ship in Luebeck Bay were left burning.

In all, dozens of ships were sunk or damaged, and more than 700 vehicles damaged in the first 350 sorties this morning.

And the massacre was still going on this afternoon.

On land, between Luebeck and Kiel, there is the greatest confusion. The prospects are that a record for destruction of vehicles will have been established by this evening.

Germans offer to free 30,000

THE Germans will consent to release 30,000 Allied prisoners from their camp at Markt Pongau, 25 miles south of Berchtesgaden, but Allied military authorities must decide how they can be got away.

Capt. Gordon Keppel, an American doctor from the camp, who has reached Switzerland, got into touch with the International Red Cross in Geneva and a high Red Cross official is expected at the frontier point of Schaanwald to obtain a full report, after which the Red Cross will negotiate with the Allies.

The prisoners include between 8,000 and 10,000 Britons, who are short of food and blankets.

A British Second Army reconnaissance formation liberated 15,000 prisoners of war in the Baltic area yesterday.

Queen Wilhelmina in Holland

Queen Wilhelmina and Princess Juliana yesterday arrived in the liberated Netherlands. The Queen will spend some time there, returning to London before again taking up permanent residence in her own country.

Searching rubble for body of Hitler

IF Hitler committed suicide in Berlin, as Fritsche, deputy of Goebbels, said when he was captured by the Soviets, then the Russians expect to find his body somewhere in the jungle of rubble that was once the centre of the great capital.

They believe that, within a few days, they will be able to tell, from the evidence they find, the whole story of what happened to Hitler.

The Russians' first tasks have been to clear the streets, deal with the fires and restore water and fuel supplies.

Food is the greatest need, even before shelter. Wherever the people find an unattended food store they attack it. The Russians have had to open several food shops already.

Like an arsenal

Last night's Soviet communique said that on Wednesday more than 134,000 German troops were taken prisoner in Berlin.

The square assigned for the surrender of weapons looks like an arsenal, so much armament is accumulated there in orderly piles.

A big square in the centre of the city is a chaos of heaped-up broken bricks, lime and concrete, from which protrude iron bars, rails and the charred tops of trees.

In the middle of this devastated area—as big as a good-sized stadium—is a gigantic crater filled with water.

Only a name

Ten-ton bombs dropped by the Allies erased several blocks of buildings and only by an enamelled board and a map is it possible to establish what it was before.

Such sights meet the Russians nearly everywhere in Berlin.

A Moscow radio commentator said last night:

"Heavy bombs hit the Reichstag. The bronze group over the Brandenburg Gate has been damaged. Hitler's Chancellery has been destroyed: bombs wrecked Goering's Air Ministry: the Gestapo building has been burnt out."

Moscow radio yesterday called on the German people to regard the fall of Berlin as a signal for the beginning of a new Germany. A member of the Free German National Committee, in a Moscow broadcast, assured his compatriots of the Soviet's good intentions.

News Chronicle Correspondent, Reuter and B.U.P.

Teschen falls

Marshal Stalin, in an Order last night, announced the capture of Teschen, in Czechoslovakia.

Hamburg rejoices as British march in

QUICK DRIVE FOR KIEL CANAL

IN surrendered Hamburg the British were witnesses of scenes of great rejoicing.

Beer halls were full. The people appeared to be very glad that Hitler is dead. Many are now freed from the oath they took to him.

The British commander ordered that the population, except the workers at the electricity and water works, must stay in their homes for the duration of the curfew he had imposed.

Responsibility for enforcing this order remains with the Hamburg police, and in the event of any disorder the occupation troops will intervene by force.

Offices and works are to close at 10 a.m. The population has been ordered to refrain from the use of electricity, and it will be impossible to broadcast announcements as power will have to be cut off.

More prisoners of war have been liberated in the Hagenau region. One camp contained 1,700 British, mostly R.A.F.

A correspondent drove past thousands of armed Germans as he was entering the city.

Germans came out to gape, lining the streets of the western suburbs. More than 20 German officers with automatics and soldiers with rifles stopped the driver, John Holbert, of Prestwich, Manchester, until they saw he belonged to the wrong army.

Another link-up

Tank spearheads of the 11th Armoured Division were last night rolling north in great strength towards the Kiel Canal and the Danish frontier. The first tanks have rumbled through Bad Segeberg, 19 miles out from Luebeck, and were last night reported a considerable distance beyond.

Another thrust by the same British division moved north of Luebeck and overran the port of Travemuende.

The 11th Armoured Division took 5,000 prisoners up to two o'clock yesterday. The 6th Airborne, tightening their grip on the Wismar sector, captured an aerodrome with the aircraft intact.

The 5th Infantry Division, mostly Yorkshiremen, continued their drive from captured Moelln and have linked up with the 11th Armoured and were in Luebeck.

Wilhelmshaven ringed

South of the British front men of the 82nd U.S. Airborne Division linked up with the Red Army near Grabow, three miles east of Ludwigslust, midway between Wittenberge and Schwerin.

Scottish vanguards moved rapidly yesterday with twin thrusts which brought them to within 12 miles from the great port of Bremerhaven.

On the other side of the Weser the doom of Wilhelmshaven and Emden appears to be sealed. The ring round Wilhelmshaven is steadily closing in after the capture of Oldenburg, whose burgomaster surrendered the town by telephone.

The "Noes" have it

The condolences of Eire with Germany on the death of Hitler, which began with a call by Mr. de Valera on the German Minister on Wednesday, were continued yesterday when Mr. McDunphy, Secretary to the President of Eire, went to express his regret.

Sweden, on the other hand, did not present condolences, while in Finland today flags will fly to celebrate the fall of Berlin.

LATE NEWS

KIEL DECLARED OPEN TOWN

German broadcast at midnight stated that Kiel and Flensburg had been declared open towns.

Moon sets, 11.34 a.m.; rises, 4.2 a.m. tomorrow. New Moon, May 11.

France will ask Spain for Laval

From Our Own Correspondent

Paris, Thursday.—The authorities here are preparing a formal demand to Spain for the extradition of Laval. Such a demand, however, might lead to a legal controversy, as the existing Treaty between France and Spain covers only cases of common law criminals.

But if Laval's extradition is asked for, and Franco declines to grant it, pressure would undoubtedly, I am told, be brought to bear by the French Government.

Laval for French gaol: by Vernon Bartlett, Back Page.

Gallup Poll shows

HOW WE SHALL SPEND V DAY

REVEALING facts on how the people of Britain plan to spend V Day are shown by the latest Gallup Poll, sent to the News Chronicle last night by the British Institute of Public Opinion.

Only 18 people in 100 are going to celebrate; 24 in 100 will rest and "do nothing," and 16 in 100 will go to church or take part in some form of thanksgiving.

Here are the answers to the question, "How do you propose to spend the first day of peace?"

	Total %
Relaxing, enjoying a well-earned rest, taking day off, doing nothing	24
Watching the celebrations	1
Celebrating, going wild, dancing in the streets	18
Like any other day, routine work	14
At home, nowhere to go	3
No celebration, since war in East will go on	2
Praying, thanksgiving	11
Going to church	5
Having a family reunion	4
Taking family to country or seaside	4
Gardening	1
Miscellaneous	2
Have not yet decided — no reply	11
	100%

Still cold

Straits last night: Cold and dull: barometer falling.

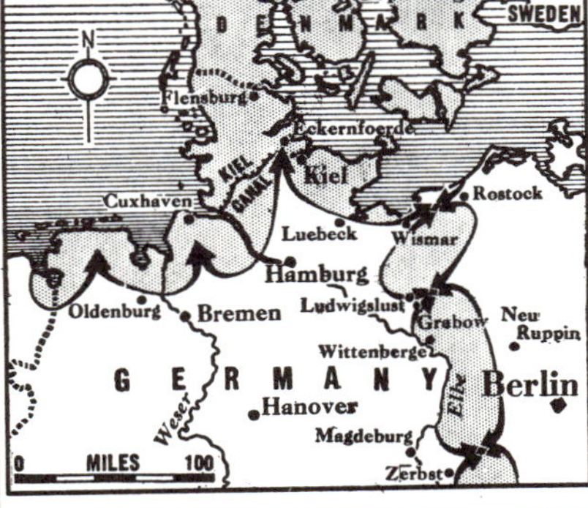

THREE NAZIS STILL SAY: FIGHT ON

WITH most of Germany's radio system out of control and defeat facing the Reich throughout Europe, confused instructions were given to the Germans yesterday from three sources.

Albert Speer, German Minister of Armaments and Production, in a broadcast to the German people over the Danish radio stated: "The direction of our lives is no longer in our hands." He admitted that the German nation was defeated.

"The devastation wrought by war on German soil can be compared only to that of the Thirty Years' War. Losses among our people through starvation and disease must not be allowed to assume the proportions of the Thirty Years' War.

"For this reason alone Grand Admiral Doenitz deems it necessary not to lay down arms. The only meaning of the struggle still being waged at this moment is our desire not to allow our German compatriots fleeing from the East to die. This last duty is incumbent on our people, who have stood up to the sufferings of this war so bravely!"

But in Western Holland Field-Marshal Blaskowitz, commanding the German forces there, issued an Order of the Day telling them to keep on fighting.

"The Fuehrer," he said, "has given his life and died a hero's death. It is now your task to keep his faith in Germany.

"Fight to defend your homes, your wives and children. He was and continues to be our Fuehrer."

And Dr. Frank, the German Minister of State for Bohemia and Moravia, issued this Order of the Day yesterday:

"For us the Fuehrer is not dead. The oath of allegiance we swore to him is from now on valid for every German to Admiral Doenitz. We will stand at his side and obey his command.

"Everyone must do his duty. Long live the nation!"

Daily Mirror

MAY 5

Saturday, May 5, 1945
No. 12,909 ONE PENNY
Registered at G.P.O. as a Newspaper.

All Hun forces in North-West Germany, Holland and Denmark give in

TRIUMPH DAY FOR MONTY'S MEN

Field-Marshal Montgomery walks out from his headquarters to meet the German delegates, coming to offer the surrender of all German forces on the British front.

ANOTHER MILLION IN GREATEST SURRENDER

AT 8 A.M. TODAY MORE THAN A MILLION GERMANS IN HOLLAND, DENMARK AND NORTH-WEST GERMANY ARE LAYING DOWN THEIR ARMS TO FIELD-MARSHAL MONTGOMERY IN THE BIGGEST MASS SURRENDER OF GERMAN FORCES SINCE THE ARMISTICE OF 1918.

THE BAG OF PRISONERS IN ITALY IS ESTIMATED AT 900,000, SO THAT IN THREE DAYS ABOUT 2,000,000 GERMANS HAVE GONE OUT OF THE WAR.

THE FIGURES FOR THE GREAT NEW SURRENDER INCLUDE 250,000 NAVAL PERSONNEL—THE SURRENDER INCLUDED ALL NAVAL SHIPS IN THE AREAS.

IT IS TRIUMPH DAY FOR FIELD-MARSHAL MONTGOMERY AND HIS MEN. THEY HAVE BEATEN THE HUN TO HIS KNEES ALONG THE WHOLE OF THEIR FRONT, AND HAVE WRITTEN "FINIS" TO THE GERMAN REICH.

And today they bring salvation to the starving millions of Holland, and freedom to the people of Denmark, crushed for five long years under the Nazi jackboot.

Amsterdam, Rotterdam, The Hague and the other cities of Holland will all be free today.

The Canadian Army, which takes over Holland, has had plans ready for over a week to rush food supplies in.

Only two major centres of German resistance now remain—in Norway and the shattered redoubt in Austria and Czechoslovakia.

In addition, the Germans still hold pockets on the west coast of France, the Channel Islands, Dunkirk, some Polish coastal territory, strips of East Prussia and Latvia, and a few pockets in the south.

That is all that is left to the enemy.

The surrender includes Heligoland and the Frisian Islands.

Negotiations had been in progress between Montgomery and the German commander in Denmark since Thursday when the British Eleventh Armoured Division broke through the enemy's north and the Second Army took half a million prisoners.

The reports from Montgomery's headquarters reveal that Admiral Doenitz was not present for the negotiations which led up to the surrender.

But Admiral Von Friedeberg, Commander-in-Chief of the German Navy, who succeeded to that position when Doenitz became "Fuehrer" led the surrender party, together with his Chief of Staff, Rear Admiral Wagner, and General Kienzl.

It was stated yesterday that they represented Doenitz and Field-Marshal

Continued on Back Page

'This is the moment,' says Monty

THE surrender was signed at a headquarters set up by Montgomery at the German Army training ground on the Luneberg Heath, south of Hamburg.

"This is the moment," was Monty's grim comment as he walked to the tent where the signing took place. He signed on behalf of the Allied Supreme Commander General Eisenhower.

The German surrender mission was headed by General-Admiral von Freideberg, C.-in-C. of the German Navy since Doenitz became Fuehrer, who with his additional rank of General was able to negotiate for the ground forces as well as the Navy.

When the mission arrived, Monty stepped out of his tent, returned their military, not Nazi, salute, and asked, as if they were vacuum cleaner salesmen, "What do you want?"

The Germans replied: "We come here to ask you to accept the surrender of three German armies which are now withdrawing in front of the Russians in the Meckleburg area."

"We are very anxious about the condition of German civilians who are fleeing as the German armies retreat in the

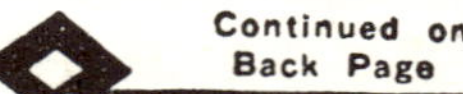

Continued on Back Page

RUNDSTEDT PRAISES MONTY

FIELD-MARSHAL VON RUNDSTEDT, recently captured former Gsrman Supreme Commander, paid striking tribute to Monty in an interview yesterday.

Monty, he said, proved himself Britain's greatest general in Libya, Tunisia, Sicily, Italy and again since D-Day.

Germany planned and wanted to invade Britain, but never really tried, because she was too weak at sea. The British fleet would have destroyed the Germans, said Rundstedt.

Rundstedt on "Why We Lost," Page 5.

Germans stupid to fight on, says Ike

THE Germans have been thoroughly whipped and failure to surrender now is due only to their stupidity or the stupidity of their leaders, said a proclamation by General Eisenhower last night.

"In the north," he says, "the remaining forces of North-Western Germany, Holland, Denmark and the Frisian Islands surrendered to Field-Marshal Montgomery.

"In the south Allied troops from General Devers's command and from Italy have joined.

"On the Czech border a panzer division gave up unconditionally to General Bradley's forces.

"On land, sea and in the air the Germans are thoroughly whipped and their only recourse is to surrender."

QUISLING'S CALL 'SAVE NORWAY'

Fuglesang, Norwegian quisling chief, in a message over Oslo radio to all quisling party members, said:

"Today it is the foremost task of our party to maintain calm and order in our country and to prevent Norway from becoming a battlefield by all means. With this end in view we are prepared to collaborate with all forces willing to do so."

No. 1,570 (B) SUNDAY, MAY 6, 1945 A KEMSLEY NEWSPAPER TWOPENCE

3 MORE GERMAN ARMIES MAKE TOTAL SURRENDER

Norway C.-in-C. Also Reported 'Ready To Capitulate'

THREE MORE GERMAN ARMIES—GROUP "G"—HAVE SURRENDERED TO U.S. GENERAL DEVERS' SIXTH U.S. ARMY GROUP, NEAR MUNICH.

This official Shaef announcement late last night added that the surrender was unconditional, and becomes effective at noon to-day.

The Scandinavian Telegraph Bureau, formerly controlled by Germans, states that General Boehme, Nazi Commander in Norway, has decided to capitulate, and an announcement was expected later last night.

An unconfirmed report stated that a British military delegation arrived by plane in Oslo yesterday, and that Terboven, Nazi Governor in Norway, has resigned.

Despite the Cease Fire on Field-Marshal Montgomery's Front at 8.0 a.m. yesterday fighting broke out in Denmark and Copenhagen,—the capital was shelled

This followed a night of street fighting when German Army troops battled alongside Danish patriots against the Nazi police.

Nazi radio tried a new trick yesterday by claiming that the German surrender is a truce "to save Europe from Bolshevism."

FULL STORY ON BACK PAGE.

SURRENDER

'SUNDAY GRAPHIC' CAMERAMAN RECORDS FIELD-MARSHAL MONTGOMERY'S GREATEST TRIUMPH AS GENERAL KINSEL SIGNS UNCONDITIONAL SURRENDER.—*See Middle Pages.*

Jersey Observer

FINAL EDITION

WEATHER REPORT—Today: Partly cloudy. Tonight: Clear. Tomorrow: Clear, becoming partly cloudy in afternoon.

VOL. LIV.—No. 77 | TEMPERATURE: 8 A. M., 49; 9 A. M., 51; 10 A. M., 54. | MONDAY, MAY 7, 1945 | JERSEY CITY OFFICE 2866 Hudson Boulevard | UNION CITY OFFICE 417 36th Street | HOBOKEN OFFICE 111 Newark Street | PRICE 4 CENTS

NAZIS QUIT!

Local Stores Closing

V-E Day Throng Fills Churches

Although there may have been some uncertainty in official circles, to the man and woman on the street, the office and the home, V-E-Day arrived this morning.

Churches filled rapidly, telephone service was disrupted and Mayors quickly issued proclamations, while retail merchants suspended business.

One of the first official acts of Mayor Thorout was to ask tavern owners not to open until late in the evening.

Without awaiting the proclamation of President Truman, retail establishments in North Hudson closed their doors this morning. A Holtnausen, in Union City, together with other merchants posted notices reading:

"Victory. Celebrate, but do not forget to buy war bonds."

Mayor Harry Thourot, Mayor Paul Cullum, of North Bergen, together with Mayor Kane of Secaucus; Mayor Meister, of Weehawken; Mayor Schnyder, of Guttenberg; all declared that V-E Day should be celebrated in accordance with plans laid prior to its announcement.

CALLS SLOW UP TELEPHONE SERVICE

Telephone service throughout Hudson County reached an all-time high this morning when telephone users were faced with unprecedented delays, varying in length to two minutes, a long time when one is used to rapid dial response.

Although the telephone company management could not estimate the number of calls which the dial equipment can take, it was said that like the human element, the dial system becomes overtaxed when everybody tries to use the telephone at once.

Telephone company officials, wilted by the upsurge of business, begged telephone users to desist.

In all proclamations of Mayors of the County, the theme was "Remember the Dead", and "Remember that the war is still to be won in the Pacific."

Mayor Frank Hague of Jersey City, in his declaration said:

"The world rejoices over the end of the European War. This news has been awaited for nearly six long years. It brings to a victorious conclusion the fight for righteousness and justice.

"In the midst of our joy and happiness, over the cessation of hostilities in that part of the world, we must pause to pray and give thanks to Almighty God for his blessings. We must pray every day.

"However, our joy is not complete. We still have to defeat the Japanese. God willing, let us hope and pray that that day is not far off. We must not, also, forget those who have made the supreme sacrifice;

(See STORES CLOSE Page 11)

STOCKS

The following prices are furnished through the courtesy of Goodbody & Co., 951 Bergen avenue Jersey City.

Stock	Price	Stock	Price
Air Reduc	47¾	Macy R H	N.S.
Alaska Juneau	NS	Martin G. L.	N.S.
Allegheny Corp	3¼	Mont Ward	61½
Al Ch & Dye	NS	Nash-Kelvin	21⅞
Am Airline	NS	Nat Cash Reg.	N.S.
Am Cab & Rad	NS	Nat Dairy Prod	N.S.
Am Can	NS	Nat Distillers	N.S.
Am Car & Fd	NS	N Y Cen RR	23⅞
Am Expt Ln	NS	No Amer Co	23⅞
AmRad&StSan	15	Ohio Oil	19⅞
Am Smelt & R	48	Pan Amer Air	24⅞
Am Tel & Tel	165½	Param Pic	31⅞
Am Tob B	75	Penn RR	37⅞
Anaconda Cop	33⅝	Pepsi-Cola	23⅞
Armour	NS	Pub Svc	N.S.
Atl Ref	34⅝	Pullman	N.S.
Bald L	NS	Radio Corp	12
B & O	17¾	Repub Steel	23⅞
Barnsdall	23⅝	Reynolds TB	NS
Bendix Avia	NS	Schenley	39⅞
Beth Steel	80½	Sears Roebuck	NS
Boeing Air	18⅞	Sinclair Oil	16⅞
Borden	NS	Socony Vac	17
Bridgept Br	NS	Sou Pac	45
Canada Dry	NS	Sperry Corp	29⅞
Carrier Corp	29¾	Stan Brds	NS
Case J I	NS	Stan Oil N J	64⅞
C & O	50½	Std Oil Sprg	11⅞
Chrysler	115½	Texas Corp	NS
Colgate-P-P	NS	United Airc	29⅞
Col G & El	5⅞	U S Rubber	59
Comml Solv	NS	U S Steel	68
Com & Sou	1	W El & Mfg	NS
Con Edison	30⅛	Willys-Over	23⅞
Cons Vultee	NS	Woolworth	NS
Curtiss-Wrt	5⅞	Western Union	NS
Deere & Co	47½	**CURB STOCK**	
Del & Hudson	49	Am Cyan B	NS
Douglas Airc	79¾	Brewst Aero	4⅞
DuPont	NS	Callite Tung	7⅞
El Auto-L	NS	Cities Service	21⅞
Gen Elec	43⅞	Creole Pet	30⅞
Gen Foods	NS	El Bd & S	13⅞
Gen Motors	70	Glen Alden	20⅞
Goodrich	61	Lake Sh M	22
Int. Nick	33⅞	Ogden Corp	5
Int Paper	26½	Pantepec	12
Int Tel	20⅞	Pioneer Gold	3⅞
Kennecott	NS	Technicolor	NS
Libby & Mc&L	NS	Unit Ci-W Str	3⅞
Lockheed	22½		
Loew's	N.S.		

All U-Boats Ordered In

Doenitz's Order Signalizes End of Sea War

London, May 7.—(UP)—Fuehrer Grand Admiral Karl Doenitz today ordered Germany's U-boat fleet, most potent weapon left the shattered Reich, to cease hostilities and return to port.

The order, revealed by the German-controlled Flensburg radio, said continuation of submarine warfare was impossible from the bases that remained in German hands in Norway and France.

Upwards of 300 German submarines probably were immobilized by the order. Between 200 and 300 were based in Norway and the remainder likely to the isolated French ports of Lorient, St. Nazaire and La Rochelle. Over 600 were sunk by the Allies during the war.

Doenitz's action ended nearly six years of what probably was the most destructive sea offensive ever waged.

Exact Allied tonnage sunk by U-Boats has not been revealed, but it probably was in eight figures. Victims ranged from tramp freighters to the British Battleship Royal Oak.

Many ships were sent to the bottom within sight of the East Coast of the United States, but an intensified air and sea patrol finally drove the raiders back to mid-Atlantic.

SUBMARINE ATTACKS HAD TWO PEAKS

The offensive reached its first peak just before the Allied invasion of North Africa and its second in the months preceding the Allied landing in Normandy.

A brief resurgence followed last winter with the introduction of a "floating lung" that enabled the U-boats to re-charge their batteries beneath the surface.

Radio Flensburg said Doenitz's order was dated last Saturday. Doenitz, first as a submarine commander in chief of the German Navy, was the master-mind behind the U-boat campaign. He sent his crews out with orders to "Kill! Kill! Kill!"

In an order of the day to U-boat crews, radio Flensburg said, Doenitz told his men that they had "fought like lions."

"Crushing superiority has compressed us into a very narrow area," he said. "Continuation of the struggle is impossible from the bases that remain."

Big Five Ponder Disposition of Pacific Islands

San Francisco, May 7.—(INS)—The Big Five have discussed specific areas "by name" which would come under the new trusteeship system, it was disclosed today.

Despite repeated official assurances that no mandated territories under the old League of Nations or captured enemy areas would be singled out by name, a reversal of this policy has come about, it was said, because of United States pressure to keep control of the North Pacific Islands seized by American armed forces.

At the same time, it was revealed, France at momentous conferences on the trusteeship issue was given oral guarantees that Indo-China—a key strategic bastion in the Pacific—would not be subordinated to joint-power rule, but would be left for France to fortify as a bastion against revived Japanese aggression.

Meanwhile, just as the United States won a salient point on keeping the Marshall, Caroline and Marianas groups—given to Japan under the Geneva league—so Great Britain has made clear that the key Mediterranean Island of Pantelleria and the Dodecanese Islands were vital to the British life-line to India.

Lord Cranbourne, in charge of trusteeship problems for the British delegation, explained that the formula of Class A, B, and C mandates under old league would be resuscitated in the new system.

However, he pointed to an overriding difference, namely, that the trustee powers would have the right to fortify their dependent areas under the conference agreement among the big five—the United States, Great Britain, China, Russia and France.

POLISH DISPUTE TO HIGHER UPS

San Francisco, May 7.—(UP)—The Polish dispute has left an ugly scar on the United Nations Conference record here and it apparently is headed today for discussion on the Truman-Churchill-Stalin level.

American and British conference officials are happy to be free of it. They are convinced that no solution of the Polish problem will be obtained here. Some of them feel that the issue never should have been raised here in the first place.

Astonishment scarcely describes the reaction here to the fact that V. M. Molotov, the poker-faced Russian Foreign Commissar, pressed for acceptance of the Communist-sponsored Polish Government in Warsaw when the Russians themselves were jailing prominent Polish Democratic leaders.

Pending further information regarding the fate of the Poles and details of the crimes of "diversionist activities against the Red Army," with which they are charged, it may be too early to say that America and Britain regard an important section of the Yalta agreement as having been scrapped. But months have elapsed now since Premier Stalin agreed with the late Presi-

(See CONFERENCE Page 11)

Mayor Hague Sees Victory By 60,000

Jersey City voters were urged yesterday by Mayor Hague to forego party affiliations in tomorrow's municipal government election and to continue the present administration in order to prevent "the planned revengeful destruction of the city by Governor Edge, former Governor Edison and the railroad interests which are sponsoring the opposition group."

In an address in which he predicted a 60,000 majority for his ticket, delivered at yesterday afternoon's windup rally of the Democratic forces at Dickinson High School, the mayor charged that "the outsiders through their Fusion stooges" seek to punish the people for supporting him in his victorious railroad tax fight.

"The full importance of this election must be realized by all of the people, regardless of politics," said the mayor, to the overflow attendance, which packed the school auditorium and the vicinity of the building.

CALLS FOR STOPPING OF "INVASION"

"It's more than just a City Commission election," he went on. "It's the opportunity for those I exposed in the railroad tax fight to get back at me and the people. It's a desperate attempt to seize control of the city government and make the people pay for their loyalty to me. While I led that fight it is a victory for the people. I'm sure the people can see through that scheme for a chance to get revenge.

"It's up to the people to decide whether or not they want this corrupt gang backing the opposition to move in on the city and gain control. I know that the people of Jersey City are not fools. Saving the city from such a spiteful group is of more importance than the election of the present officials. Past performances, including those of our opponents, have demonstrated in what direction their interests lie. The voters must corral their forces to stop such an invasion."

Besides the mayor, who was accompanied by his 17-year-old adopted daughter, Peggy Ann, other speakers were former Governor A. Harry Moore, Congressman Edward J. Hart, Congresswoman Mary T. Norton, State Senator Edward J. O'Mara, Assemblyman Peter P. Artaserse. City Commissioners Arthur

(See HAGUE Page 11)

McFeelys Win Writ to Test Indictments

Chief Justice Thomas J. Brogan, sitting at the County Court House on Saturday, granted a certiorari writ to take the misconduct in office indictment against Police Chief Edward J. McFeely and Inspector Bernard McFeely away from the Hudson criminal courts until the Supreme Court passes on the indictment.

As counsel for the two defendants, former Judge Thomas H. Brown was given leave to take testimony before Supreme Court Commissioner Edmund S. Johnson to present to the upper court reasons why he believes the charge against the McFeelys should be dismissed without a trial.

The misconduct in office indictment against the McFeelys was returned by the Hudson County Grand Jury as the result of evidence discovered accidentally when Attorney General Walter D. Van Riper's investigators raided the horse race wire rooms in the Top Hat Hotel, Union City, June 9, last.

CHARGE EVIDENCE WAS RETURNED

There the raiders found police statements and other evidence which had been taken by the Hoboken police chief and inspector as the result of a raid on a Hoboken horse race wire room in March of 1942, it was alleged.

The grand jury indicted Chief and Inspector McFeely on charges of failing properly to prosecute the defendants in the Hoboken raid. It is claimed the Hoboken police officials returned to the men they arrested

(See McFEELY Page 11)

Loose Cigarettes Banned

Washington, May 7.—(UP)—Sales of loose cigarettes of any brand will be prohibited beginning May 12, the Office of Price Administration announced today. Some dealers have been selling them for a penny each. After May 12 they must be sold by the package.

Imprisoned American Airmen Brutally Beaten by Japanese

Calcutta, May 4.—(Correct.)—(U. P.)—American airmen, liberated from the Japanese prison camp at Rangoon and revealed today row the Japanese beat and starved U. S. filers, especially B-29 crewmen, after bombing raids on Japan.

The airmen, from the first group of Americans freed in Burma, are recuperating in a hospital here. More than 400 Americans, most of them members of the air force, and approximately 600 other Allied prisoners were liberated at Rangoon.

Lieutenant Billy T. Davis (114 33 Link), Los Angeles, one of the Americans recuperating here, said the American airmen were put in a "special treatment group" on charges of indiscriminate bombing of women and children.

The men were lined up and the guards beat them with "clubs made like pick handles," Davis said. The Americans were treated worse than the other Allied prisoners, he added, and the beatings wer more severe when the Japanese guards were drunk.

"I was slapped about four times a week," Davis said. "It got so you only hoped it wouldn't hurt too bad. You forgot the humiliation."

He explained that the beatings in most cases were stopped, however, before the victim became maimed. The maltreatment was particularly severe when the Japanese suffered military reverses.

Allies Drive On Prague

Yankees, Reds Near Capital

Paris, May 7.—(INS)—U. S. 3rd Army forces, last of the western Allied battle legions still in combat, drove swiftly toward Prague today, reaching to within at least 50 miles of the Czechoslovakian capital.

Unconfirmed Prague radio reports said that American Tank Forces were only 15 miles from Prague.

Moscow, May 7.—(INS)—Two Soviet Armies stormed through Czechoslovakia today pushing the Nazis back on strife-torn Prague.

Nazi resistance along the German Baltic coast was wiped out with the Russian capture of the 324-square-mile Island of Ruegen.

Other Red Army columns delivered a terrific blow against the enemy west and northwest of Brandenburg, where they captured 17,120 Nazis and raced to the Elbe at several points.

The Soviet 4th Ukrainian Army was reported by the official Russian communique to be fighting on the approaches of Olomouc, the key rail hub, 128 miles east of Prague.

Simultaneously the 2nd Ukrainian Army fighting northeast of Bruenn, captured Kojetin, 18 miles south of Olomouc, and three other towns.

Fourth Ukrainian spearheads advanced almost 13 miles in their drive on Olomouc, scooping up more than 1,000 Nazi prisoners. Field reports indicated that Nazis were falling back on Prague, menaced from the west by the U. S. 3rd Army, along the entire reach of the Czech front.

NAZIS OFFERING STRONG RESISTANCE

Apparently the Germans in Cze-

(See PRAGUE Page 11)

Harry Little Dies; Director In Union City

Director of Public Safety Harry E. Little, of Union City, one of the best loved and most popular public officials in the county, died Saturday night in Christ Hospital, Jersey City, where he had been a patient since Tuesday.

His death, which was unexpected, resulted from coronary occlusion (a heart condition). Twenty minutes before he passed away, his wife, Hyldur (nee Johnson), had visited his bedside. When she left him he was in high spirits.

Mrs. Little had just arrived at their home, 1010 Palisade avenue, when a telephone call urged her to return to the hospital immediately. When she arrived there the commissioner had expired.

Only the commissioner's nurse was in his room when he passed away. She had been conversing with him a minute before he died, and he appeared to be all right. The nurse turned from his bedside to prepare a sedative and when she sought to administer the hypermdermic she found the commissioner dead; so sudden was his demise.

North Hudson was shocked when the news of the commissioner's death spread throughout the community. Few people knew of the seriousness of his condition; which the family kept a closely guarded secret. Even the commissioner did no know that he was seriously ill.

He was first taken ill February 24 with pneumonia, and although he responded quickly to treatment by penicilin, he developed the cardiac condition, and from the outset his attending physicians held little hope for him.

At first he showed signs of recovery, but then he suffered a newer and more severe attack and went into a decline.

Known as a worrying man—although he had a reputation for standing up under pressure—his death is believed to have been hastened by concern over his recent indictment by the Hudson County

(See HARRY LITTLE Page 11)

Doenitz Orders All Fighting Forces to Surrender to Allies

London, May 7.—(INS)—Amidst general expectancy that formal announcement of the end of hostilities in Europe will come at any moment or hour, the Flensburg Radio today broadcast disclosure that Admiral Karl Doenitz has ordered the unconditional surrender of all German fighting troops.

The announcement was made by Count Lutz Schwerin von Krosigk, German Foreign Minister.

The Flensburg Radio operates from German soil just south of the Danish frontier.

It has not yet been clarified whether or not this station is operating in concert with, and approval of, Allied military authorities.

There was no immediate confirmation of the Krosigk announcement from any authoritative source.

Reuter's military correspondent said Doenitz's order meant the end of the war in Europe—obviously a fact if German troops still in the field lay down their arms and the Allied High Command accepts the Flensburg announcement as definite and final.

He said.

"German men and women: The high command of the armed forces has today, at the order of Grand Admiral Doenitz, declared the unconditional surrender of all fighting German troops.

"As leading minister of the Reich government which the Admiral of the fleet has appointed for winding up of all military tasks, I turn at this tragic moment of our history to the German nation.

"After a heroic fight of almost six years of incomparable hardness, Germany has succumbed to the overwhelming power of her enemies.

"To continue the war would only mean senseless bloodshed and futile disintegration.

"The government, which has a feeling of responsibility for the future of its nation, was compelled to act on the collapse of all physical and material forces and to request of the enemy cessation of hostilities.

"It was the noblest task of the admiral of the fleet and of the government supporting him, after the terrible sacrifices which the war demanded, to save in the last phase of the war, the lives of a maximum number of fellow countrymen," Krosigk concluded.

"That the war was not ended immediately, simultaneously in the west and in the east, is to be explained by this reason alone.

"We end this gravest hour of the German nation and its Reich."

New York, May 7.—(INS)—The Czech patriot radio in Prague said today that Gen. Andrei A. Vlassov, renegade Russian fighting with the Nazis, had ordered all forces in the Czechoslovak capital to surrender unconditionally.

Vlassov, captured in 1942, was reported by the Nazis to have formed an army of White Russians used as occupation forces.

Shortly after 10 a. m. E. W. T., however, the German-controlled Prague radio said that German troops in Czechoslovakia did not acknowledge Doenitz's surrender announcement and would continue to fight until a free passage out of the country had been obtained.

Washington, May 7.—(INS)—The White House at 10:18 a. m., E. W. T. today declared that it had no official announcement to make on reports

(See SURRENDER Page 11)

Victory Sure, Liberation Workers Told

The Liberation candidates in the Jersey City municipal election tomorrow climaxed their campaign with a rally yesterday at which they expressed confidence in victory and at which Campaign Manager William E. Decker forecast a margin of 12,000 for the opponents of Mayor Hague.

Maintaining that the Liberation ticket would be victorious, Michael A. Fiore, speaking to more than 500 election officers and deputies at the Jewish Community Center, Belmont and Bergen avenues, warned Mayor Hague "not to burn any of the city records or documents."

He and the other candidates outlined the issues of the campaign and promised when elected to give Jersey City a businesslike administration.

ALLAN BARS POLL ASSISTANCE

Donald Allan, superintendent of elections, told the election officers that no assistance at the polls would be tolerated.

"If a person is capable of signing the registry book they have demonstrated their ability to vote with out assistance," Allan maintained.

County Tax Commissioner Carl A. Ruhlmann introduced Fiore, Paul E. Doherty, Joshua Ringle and Joseph J. Loori.

DOHERTY SEES PEOPLE "FED UP WITH HAGUE"

"We're going to win tomorrow because the people of Jersey City are fed up with Frank Hague," said Doherty.

"The election will be an honest election, and the new voting machines are silent, secret, and foolproof."

"This means," he continued, "that once the voter enters the voting booth, there is not the slightest possibility that anyone else will ever learn how he voted."

"With this new element of absolute secrecy," Doherty predicted, "no voter will have any more fear of Frank Hague. and Liberation votes will pile up to unprecedented anti-Hague heights, and of course, victory."

Doherty also said:

"Stories of Hague's desperation in this election have been reaching me anew every hour. The latest I hear is that Mr. Hague is handing out $500 to $900 to each district leader in order to force out Hague votes by hook or crook. This is one time that money won't help Mr. Hague, because most of the people who take it are going to use the secrecy of the voting machines to doublecross the 'boss' by voting for us."

Superiors Are Slammed Again By Fitzpatrick

As Patrolman George Fitzpatrick, president of the Hoboken Patrolmen's Benevolent Association, was preparing to answer departmental charges of neglect of duty and conduct unbecoming an officer, he issued another blast against departmental conditions in the form of a letter to Harry B. Gourley, president of the New Jersey State P. B. A.

Fitzpatrick is one of two First Precinct officers who will be arraigned Friday before Deputy Director of Public Safety Edward A. Mullen. The other is Patrolman Joseph Kiely, charged with neglect of duty.

He allegedly refused to take a report from two small boys who claimed they were held up by another older boys, who stole some change from them.

Charges against Fitpatrick grow out of his alleged failure to arrest two men who he says "visited his home some weeks ago with a story that Patrolman Philip Gehm, then wanted by local police on a warrant for atrocious assault and battery, was in a hospital with a severe head injury.

It is held, also, that he failed to make any report of the incident until Deputy Chief Dennis E. McFeely heard of it from other sources and questioned Fitzpatrick on it. The officer, according to the deputy chief, replied that he "was all excited and upset" and thus failed immediately to report it.

It is charged that, if the men actually went to Fitzpatrick's home with such a story, he was delinquent in his duty in not immediately arresting them for investigation, since if Gehm really was hurt it was obviously a case for police inquiry. A policeman, it is said, Fitzpatrick should have acted immediately instead of letting the pair get away.

A complaint by the father of the two small boys who were allegedly robbed of their movie money, led to the charges against Kiely. He was on traffic duty at Newark and Washington streets when the youngsters came to him with their story, it is said, and he chased them away. Kiely at first denied he was in-

(See FITZPATRICK Page 11)

Treasury Balance

Washington, May 7—(IN)—Treasury balance May 4, $10,721,990,318.70. Internal revenue, $32,362,029.81. Customs receipts, $5,369,089.35. Receipts, $38,952,834,756. Expenditures, $83,096,769,439.

No Dachau Prisoner to Reach Allies Alive, Himmler Ordered

Paris, May 7.—(UP)—Supreme Headquarters announced today that Gestapo Chief Heinrich Himmler had ordered that no prisoner at the notorious Dachau concentration camp should fall into Allied hands alive.

A SHAEF communique said the Allies had captured an order to that effect from Himmler dated April 14.

Himmler also ordered that the camp be evacuated immediately of its inmates, who numbered around 45,000.

There still are 22,000 freed prisoners at Dachau, many of them too ill to move. About 100 are dying daily from hunger, maltreatment, and typhus. Official figures given to American editors, touring German concentration camps, said that over 13,000 prisoners had died at Dachau since the beginning of the year.

Himmler's order was issued in answer to a suggestion from the camp commandant that Dachau be handed over to the Allied armies. The Gestapo chief replied:

"The handing over of the camp is not to be considered. The camp is to be evacuated immediately. No prisoners shall be allowed to fall into the hands of the enemy alive. The prisoners have behaved barbarously to the civilian population."

Index to All the Latest News

PINK EDITION

DAILY NEWS

Copr. 1945 by News Syndicate Co. Inc. NEW YORK'S PICTURE NEWSPAPER Trade Mark Reg. U. S. Pat. Off.

2¢

Vol. 26. No. 272 New York, Tuesday, May 8, 1945★ 32 Main+8 Brooklyn Pages 2 Cents IN CITY LIMITS | 3 CENTS Elsewhere

IT'S OVER IN EUROPE!

PROCLAMATION DUE AT 9 A. M.

—Stories on Pages 2 and 3

Daily Mirror (MAY 8)

Tuesday, May 8, 1945
No. 12,911 ONE PENNY
Registered at G.P.O. as a Newspaper.

VE-DAY!

PUBLIC HOLIDAY TODAY AND TOMORROW—OFFICIAL

Czechs flown from Britain to save Prague

Soon after a Czech Spitfire squadron left Britain for Czechoslovakia yesterday large formations carrying Czechoslovak ground troops also took off for home—and the battle for the liberation of Prague. The commander, before leaving, said, "This is the greatest day of my life."

IN a final burst of fiendishness, S.S. troops in Prague last night were firing the last shots of the war on helpless Czech civilians.

S.S. men went through the streets driving people out of their homes as other S.S. troops waited to mow them down with machine-guns.

So bad has been the conduct of the German troops that the Wehrmacht commander of the area broadcast a warning to his men to respect international law.

"Some breaches," he actually admitted, had occurred.

But earlier he had announced that he did not recognise what he described as the "armistice."

"German troops will continue to fight until they have secured a free passage out of the country," he added.

According to refugees who have reached Pilsen the S.S. men, knowing that they will be executed when caught, have abandoned all normal conduct.

Another Prague broadcast reached Czechoslovak circles in London yesterday. It was an S O S from the Czechs pleading for speedy Allied help and asking "send us aircraft."

It spoke of heavy fighting in the streets, said the Germans were throwing hand grenades at houses showing Czechoslovak flags and reported the bombing by German planes of broadcasting house and other public buildings.

Meanwhile Patton's famous Fourth Armoured Division is speeding towards the capital and last night was reported to be fifteen miles south of the city.

SPAIN BREAKS WITH GERMANY

Spain has severed diplomatic relations with Germany, it is officially announced in Madrid.

War winners may broadcast today

The Prime Minister will broadcast at 3 p.m. today.

It is probable that later in the afternoon General Eisenhower, Field-Marshal Montgomery and Field-Marshal Alexander will also speak over the radio to the Allied world.

At 9 p.m. the King will broadcast.

Goebbels and his family are found, poisoned

DISCOVERY has been made in Berlin of the bodies of Dr. Goebbels, his wife and their six children.

They were found by the Russians. All had taken poison and this was the cause of death.

Hitler's body has not been discovered and neither has the body of Goering.

There is now some speculation as to whether, after all, the Fuehrer and Goering may not have fled to a place of hiding.

It is pointed out, however, that their bodies may have been burned and the ashes lost in the wreckage of the burning Chancellery, or some other of Berlin's destroyed buildings.

★On top of the world In the heart of London★ an Allied soldier — he climbed the Eros statue in London's Piccadilly—gets just as high as he can to celebrate the lifting of the shadow from Europe.

Celebrations delay due to a 'technicality'

By BILL GREIG

THIS IS VE-DAY. AFTER FIVE YEARS, EIGHT MONTHS AND FOUR DAYS OF THE BLOODIEST WAR IN HISTORY BRITAIN AND HER ALLIES HAVE GAINED VICTORY IN EUROPE.

Capitulation of Germany to the Allies was announced by Doenitz yesterday—but a mere technicality in the arrangements made with Russia and America delayed the British people's celebration.

One result of the delay is that Britain's workers get two clear days' holiday—today and tomorrow. This Cabinet decision was disclosed last night.

Originally it was intended that the first day's holiday would not begin until the Prime Minister had spoken.

The announcement late last night that today will be VE-Day was the final act in a bewildering day following the German surrender.

The people thronged out into the streets all over the country. In London there were thousands in Whitehall outside Downing-street patiently waiting for the word, little aware of the drama taking place inside No 10.

There was chaos and bewilderment where there should have been celebration.

Here is the story of what happened in No. 10. When the news of the German surrender arrived the Prime Minister was ready to broadcast at 4 p.m. Hurried telephone calls were made to Marshal Stalin and President Truman so that the announcement could be made simultaneously.

Then it was that the trouble started. It was found that arrangements already made did not allow for the war ending so suddenly.

Mr. Churchill put his broad-

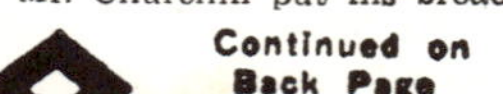
Continued on Back Page

Spend VE in camp, CO's say

"Daily Mirror" Reporter

COMMANDING officers of Army and RAF camps all over Britain told their men yesterday: "Spend VE-Day how you will, but PLEASE spend it in camp."

Thanksgiving services, concerts and later "closing time" for the canteen and sergeants' and officers' mess bars were some of the arrangements to persuade the men to stay in camp.

At an operational station near London the *Daily Mirror* was told by the Station Commander: "I have a lot of Australian air-crews here and they don't think VE day means the war is over as far as they are concerned. They've volunteered to forgo celebrations to do any odd job that comes up.

German prisoners of war have erected victory flag-poles at Catterick camp in North Yorkshire.

The Daily Sketch

SOUVENIR EDITION

No. 11,224 WEDNESDAY, MAY 9, 1945 A KEMSLEY NEWSPAPER ONE PENNY

THEY SHARED OUR ORDEALS NOW THEY REJOICE WITH US

From a balcony at Buckingham Palace the King and Queen, accompanied by Princess Elizabeth (left) and Princess Margaret (right), smile and wave at the cheering crowd, many thousands strong. (The King's broadcast is on Page 3.)

AFTER THE SURRENDER

On Monday, May 7, at 2.41 a.m., Germany surrendered unconditionally to the Allies at Rheims. Colonel-General Gustav Jodl, the new German Army Chief of Staff, signed for Germany, and General Bedell Smith for the Supreme Allied Command. In the smiling group above, taken after the signing, are (front row) Col. Zikovitch (Russia), Gen. Suslaparov (Russia), Gen. Bedell Smith (U.S.A.), Gen. Eisenhower, Air Chief Marshal Tedder (U.K.), Admiral Burrough (U.K.), Gen. Spaatz (U.S.A.), and Gen. Sevez (France).

Monty Says: 'Now Win The Peace'

"WE have won the German war. Let us now win the peace," said Field-Marshal Montgomery in a personal victory message issued last night to all ranks under his command.

"We all have a feeling of great joy and thankfulness that we have been preserved to see this day," said the message. "We must remember to give the praise and thankfulness where it is due. 'This is the Lord's doing, and it is marvellous in our eyes.'

"Let us never forget what we owe to our Russian and American Allies. This great Allied team has achieved much in war. May it achieve even more in peace.

"Without doubt, great problems lie ahead. The world will not recover quickly from the upheaval that has taken place. There is much work for each of us.

"It may be some difficult times lie ahead for our country, for each one of us personally.

"If it happens, then our discipline will pull us through. But we must

Turn to Back Page, Col. 1

TIMELY WORDS OF FAITH

Praise the Lord, all ye nations: praise him, all ye people. For his merciful kindness is great toward us. . . . Praise ye the Lord.

Psalms, 117. 1-2.

WYNFORD VAUGHAN-THOMAS is a Welshman, born in Swansea, where he was a schoolfellow of the poet Dylan Thomas. He took his degree at Exeter College, Oxford, and joined the BBC in 1936. He became one of their most distinguished war correspondents. He made the celebrated commentary from a Lancaster bomber over Berlin in 1943, and later landed on the beachhead at Anzio in Italy. He wrote the classic account of this landing, one of the most desperate episodes of the war.

His coverage of wartime events was always notable, never more so than during the Liberation of Europe, when he was in the first wave of the assault in Montgomery's crossing of the Rhine.

After the war he became a leading commentator on royal tours and took his place on all the great state occasions. He was one of the founders of HTV, the independent TV company for Wales and the West, and is a prolific author, broadcaster and TV personality.

He is married with one son, and lives overlooking the sea at Fishguard in West Wales.

JOHN FROST has been collecting historic editions of newspapers for 50 years, and his unique private library has an astonishing 25,000 editions dating back to 1640. His collection from the World War II period alone totals more than 8,000, from which 118 have been selected for *D-Day To Victory*. He saw active service during World War II in France, Belgium and Germany with the 11th Armoured Division.

He is much in demand as a lecturer on Press history, has appeared on TV and radio and also supplies period newspapers to TV and film companies.

He is married with two sons and lives in New Barnet, Hertfordshire.